CW00322368

STATISTICAL FOR BUSINES AND ECONOMICS

STATISTICAL ANALYSIS FOR BUSINESS AND ECONOMICS
Programmed for Effective Learning

THIRD EDITION

LEONARD J. KAZMIER

Arizona State University

McGRAW-HILL BOOK COMPANY

New York   St. Louis   San Francisco   Auckland
Bogotá   Düsseldorf   Johannesburg   London   Madrid
Mexico   Montreal   New Delhi   Panama   Paris
São Paulo   Singapore   Sydney   Tokyo   Toronto

STATISTICAL ANALYSIS FOR BUSINESS AND ECONOMICS

2 3 4 5 6 7 8 9 0   F G R F G R   7 8 3 2 1 0 9 8

This book was set in Univers Medium by Hemisphere Publishing Corporation.
The editor was Donald E. Chatham, Jr.; the designer was Hemisphere
Publishing Corporation; the production supervisor was Milton J. Heiberg.
The cover was designed by Edward Aho.
Fairfield Graphics was printer and binder.

Library of Congress Cataloging in Publication Data

Kazmier, Leonard J.
    Statistical analysis for business and economics.

    Includes index.
    1. Statistics—Programmed instruction. I. Title.
HA29.K353 1978   519.5'02'433   77-24765
ISBN 0-07-033439-0

To My Parents

CONTENTS

PREFACE

This book covers the methods of statistical description, inference, and decision analysis typically included in an introductory course in business and economic statistics. It is different from other books in this area in that it has been designed to enhance student comprehension by the application of instructional principles developed in research on the learning process. As such, the presentation method used in this book is intended not to replace classroom discussion and practice, but to make such participation more meaningful by helping students to identify areas in which they need further instructional guidance. Also, because of the more effective coverage of the *detail* associated with statistical analysis, relatively more classroom time can be spent in applications-oriented activity, including possibly the use of computer programs in statistical analysis and the discussion of example applications.

In terms of content, both the classical and the contemporary methods of statistical analysis are included in the chapters that comprise this book. In comparison with the second edition of this book, this third edition includes coverage of decision tree analysis, excludes coverage of game theory, and includes more exercises throughout the book. Also, descriptive measures for grouped data have been placed in a separate chapter, so that these computational methods can be omitted, and the definition (and formula) for the sample standard deviation has been changed for greater consistency with other recent texts in statistical analysis. The Instructor's Manual describes the availability of sample applications of the eight computer programs presented in Appendix A, as well as the procedure by which the FORTRAN programs for these analyses can be obtained by adopters of this book.

It is not intended that the entire text be covered in a one-semester undergraduate course. As indicated in the table below, instructors who wish to emphasize managerial decision analysis rather than economic forecasting can omit coverage of Part 7, while those wishing to give emphasis to economic forecasting and analysis can omit Part 5. For a course with no specialized emphasis, the chapters that can be omitted without any loss of continuity are Chapter 4, on descriptive measures for grouped data; Chapter 12, on the chi-square test; Chapter 14, on Bayesian inference; and Chapter 18, on index numbers. Appendix A, on application of the computer in statistical analysis, is optional in any case.

Part		Chapters
I	Introduction	1
II	Descriptive Statistics	2 to 4
III	Probability and Probability Distributions	5 to 7
IV	Sampling and Statistical Inference	8 to 12
V	Statistical Decision Analysis (optional)	13 and 14
VI	Regression and Correlation	15 and 16
VII	Economic Forecasting and Analysis (optional)	17 and 18

The structure of this book is novel in two respects. First, although every author gives attention to the appropriate sequencing of material, the development of a programmed textbook involves a frame-by-frame testing and revision with representative groups of students. Second—and this is perhaps the most visible difference—students are asked to demonstrate their developing knowledge and understanding by answering key questions and doing short sample problems as they progress through each chapter. Their own performances thus serve as feedback regarding their comprehension of the statistical concepts and techniques being presented. Students can, of course, look at the answers in the margin before attempting to answer the questions on their own and thereby nullify one of the advantages of the programmed form of presentation. The choice is theirs.

The author expresses gratitude to the following reviewers who made suggestions regarding the development of this third edition: William H. Bradley, University of Albuquerque; P. R. Huntley, University of Arkansas; and George F. Mair, Smith College. I extend special thanks to Professor Zenon S. Malinowski of the University of Connecticut, Storrs, for a particularly comprehensive and penetrating review of the second edition of this book. Appreciation is also acknowledged for the effective supervision of this project by Donald E. Chatham as the editor. Finally, I am indebted to the literary executor of the late Sir Ronald A. Fisher, F.R.S., Cambridge, and to Oliver & Boyd Ltd., Edinburgh and London, for their permission to reprint Tables III, IV, and V-A from their book *Statistical Methods for Research Workers.*

Leonard J. Kazmier

TO THE STUDENT

The format of this book is different from that of the typical textbook in that you are asked to answer key questions and to do short sample problems as you read each chapter. The answers to these questions and problems are given along the left margin of each page. Please cover these answers until you have tried to answer each question on your own, and then check your answer against the one given in the margin. By following this recommended procedure you will gain two advantages that will increase your learning effectiveness: that of having independent practice and that of being able to check on whether you understand the concepts and techniques presented in each chapter.

The development of the material in this book is relatively fast-moving and comprehensive, with little repetition as such, so you will find that you will need to pay close attention. When you experience difficulty, as indicated by an inability to answer key questions or do sample problems, put a check mark in the margin as a reminder to ask for clarification of the concept or technique during class discussion.

A review section is included at the end of each chapter. You can use this as an overall self-test after completing the chapter, as well as for later review. For reference and review purposes the symbols and formulas introduced in each chapter are listed at the end of the chapter, along with the frame numbers which identify the specific points in the chapter where the use of the symbols and formulas is described. Finally, the solutions to the first group of exercises at the end of each chapter are provided in the back of the book, and the page location of these solutions is identified in each chapter.

PART I ■
INTRODUCTION

CHAPTER 1 ■
THE USE OF STATISTICAL ANALYSIS

Statistical analysis is concerned with the overall process by which data are collected, analyzed, and interpreted. In some applications all of the relevant values can be determined, and therefore the principal objective of the analysis is interpretation. For example if the price change for each of a large number of commodities is known, then the main task may be to determine an overall index of price change that summarizes the available information. Such an analysis is called *statistical description*. On the other hand, conditions may be such that only a sample of data is obtained. For example a 100 percent inspection of manufactured parts may be too costly and a 100 percent audit of accounts may just not be feasible, given certain time limitations. In such cases the description and interpretation are subject to the risk associated with the possibility that the sample inspected is not representative of the entire group. The risk can be evaluated by the use of probability concepts, and such an analysis is called *statistical inference*. In this first chapter we discuss the distinctions between descriptive statistics and inferential statistics, consider the ways in which inductive and deductive reasoning are represented in statistical analysis, describe the kinds of numerical data that can be analyzed, and present some rules regarding the appropriate rounding of computational results.

1.1 ■ Descriptive Statistics and Inferential Statistics

Statistical analysis can be concerned with summarizing and interpreting the measured values associated with a particular set of observations, or it can be concerned with describing a larger set for which only a sample of measurements has been obtained. As indicated above, the first type of application is called "statistical description" while the second type is called "statistical inference." In recent years the techniques of statistical inference have become particularly important in the analysis of economic and business data, and hence these techniques constitute a major portion of this book.

1 When the methods of statistics are used to summarize the information that has been collected or to organize it so that comprehension of the information is made easier, then the methods are being used for the purpose of statistical [description / inference].

description

2 For example, grouping a large number of measurements and presenting the results in tables or graphs involve the use of statistical techniques for the purpose of statistical _____.

description

3 On the other hand, when we arrive at some conclusions regarding the characteristics of a larger set of variables than those actually measured, the techniques of statistical analysis are being applied for the purpose of statistical [description / inference].

inference

4 For example, on the basis of interviews conducted with 1,000 of 50,000 families residing in a metropolitan area, an economist comes to certain conclusions regarding planned consumer expenditures in that area. In this case the analytic techniques are being used for the purpose of statistical _____.

inference

5 In the following list, post a *D* for the situations in which statistical techniques are used for the purpose of description and an *I* for those in which the techniques are used for the purpose of inference.

I

_____ (a) The price movements of 50 issues of stock are analyzed to determine whether stocks in general have gone up or down during a certain period of time.

D

_____ (b) A statistical table is constructed for the purpose of presenting the passenger-miles flown by various commercial airlines in the United States.

D

_____ (c) The average of a group of test scores is computed so that each score in the group can be classified as being either above or below average.

I

_____ (d) Several manufacturing firms in a particular industry are surveyed for the purpose of estimating industrywide investment in capital equipment.

6 In statistical analysis the term "population," or "universe," is used to designate all of the elements that belong to a defined group. The term "sample" typically designates some portion of the population. In the accompanying diagram, in which the *X*'s represent individual elements, the population set is designated by the letter ___, and the sample taken from that population is designated by the letter ___.

A

B

7 The methods of statistical description can be used to describe the characteristics of either a sample or an entire population of elements, whereas the methods of inference are used only when [sample / population] data are known.

8 Or, to put it another way, the application of statistical techniques for the purpose of statistical description suggests that the characteristics of [some / all / either some or all] elements in the population have been measured.

9 On the other hand, the application of statistical techniques for the purpose of statistical inference suggests that the characteristics of [some / all / either some or all] of the elements in the population have been measured.

10 What constitutes a statistical population is entirely a matter of definition. Thus, if a statistician is interested in determining average family income in the United States, then the population of values is made up of the incomes of all families residing in _____ , whereas the income of families residing in Detroit would constitute a _____ taken from this population.

11 A statistical population need not be made up of a large number of elements, nor need it have geographic boundaries. For example, a study of the construction characteristics of all buildings, which are more than 50 stories in height would include [a great number of / relatively few] buildings in the statistical population.

12 No matter how few elements are included in a statistical population, however, a sample taken from that population [can / cannot] be larger than the population itself.

13 On the other hand, a sample taken from one population [can / cannot] contain more elements than the number included in *some other* statistical population.

14 For example, in a study of retail store sales the number of retailing establishments surveyed statewide as a sample in order to estimate statewide sales volume [can / cannot] be greater than the total number of retail stores in a particular community.

15 Furthermore the same set of measurements can be considered as a statistical population for one purpose and as a statistical sample for another purpose. When a "test of mathematical knowledge" is given to a group of college freshmen in order to come to some conclusions regarding the mathematical competence of college freshmen in general, then the scores constitute a [sample / population] ; when the scores are used only for the purpose of making course decisions for the particular students who took the test, the scores constitute a [sample / population] .

sample

population

16 When the characteristics of a population are measured, the process is called a *census*; measuring the characteristics of a sample is called *sampling*. Thus the national census carried out every 10 years in the United States includes an attempt to enumerate and describe [all / a sample] of the people in the country.

all

17 Whereas measuring the characteristics of a portion of a population describes the process of taking a sample, measuring the characteristics of an entire statistical population describes the process of taking a _____ .

census

18 Therefore the process of taking a census in order to collect, analyze, and interpret the characteristics of a population is directly related to statistical [description / inference] , and the process of sampling is always involved in statistical _____ .

description

inference

19 The characteristics, or attributes, of a population are also designated differently from the attributes of a sample. Descriptive measures of a population are called *population parameters*, but descriptive measures of a sample are called *sample statistics*. If 55 percent of a sample of registered voters who respond to a mailed questionnaire indicate favor for a particular tax proposal, this 55 percent figure is a [population parameter / sample statistic] .

sample statistic

20 Thus any descriptive measurement of a population is considered to be a [statistic / parameter] , and a descriptive measurement of a sample is a sample _____ .

parameter

statistic

21 Average family income computed for a sample of the families in a community is a sample _____ ; average family income based on a complete census of the families in the community is a population _____ .

statistic

parameter

22 At this point it might be useful to highlight the fact that the word "statistics" has at least three distinct meanings, depending on the context in which it is used. It may refer to:

(a) the procedure of statistical analysis
(b) descriptive measures of a sample
(c) the individual measurements, or elements, that make up either a sample or a population

When one becomes "an accident statistic" by being included in some count of accident frequency, the term is used in the sense of definition [a / b / c].

> c

23 According to the definitions in Frame 22, in a course of study called "Business Statistics" the term "statistics" is usually used in the sense of definition [a / b / c].

> a

24 According to the definitions in Frame 22, when such sample statistics as the proportion of a sample in favor of a proposal and the average age of those in the sample are determined, the term "statistics" is being used in the sense of definition [a / b / c].

> b

Summary

25 The two major applications of the tools of statistical analysis are directed toward the purposes of statistical _____ and statistical _____ .

> description; inference

26 The set of elements that includes all elements that belong to a group is called a "statistical _____"; a group of elements that includes a portion, but not all, of the elements that belong to the overall set is called a "statistical _____ ."

> population

> sample

27 When all the elements in a statistical population are measured, the process is referred to as "taking a _____ ." If only a portion of the elements included in a statistical population is measured, the process is called _____ .

> census

> sampling

28 A descriptive measurement of a population, such as calculation of the average value, is designated as a population _____. A similar descriptive measurement determined for a sample of values is designated as a sample _____ .

> parameter

> statistic

29 We have discussed three distinct meanings that the term "statistics" may have. See how many of these you can give below (in any order):

methods of statistical analysis	(a) _____ _____
descriptive measures of a sample	(b) _____ _____
the individual measurements in a sample or population	(c) _____ _____

1.2 ■ Inductive and Deductive Reasoning, Sampling, and Probability

Whenever the characteristics of a population, or general truths, are determined by observing the characteristics of a number of the elements that make up that population, the process of inductive reasoning, or *induction,* is involved. This has also been referred to as the process of reasoning from the *particular to the general.* On the other hand, when we begin with the characteristics of the population of elements being known, and thereby conclude what the characteristics of an element that belongs to this population must be, the process of deductive reasoning, or *deduction*, is involved. Deduction can also be viewed as the process of reasoning from the *general to the particular.* In this section we shall explore the relationship of these two categories of reasoning with the descriptive and inferential uses of statistics, the requirements associated with "good" sampling, and the role of probability theory in statistical analysis.

30 The process of reasoning from the general to the particular, by which the "general truth" must be known or given, describes [induction / deduction].

deduction

31 The process of reasoning from the particular to the general, by which individual observations serve as the basis for determining "general truths," describes [induction / deduction].

induction

32 The method of reasoning which is based on the application of a known population description or general principle is _____ .

deduction

33 For example, if it is known that the level of sales of a particular commodity invariably increases when the price is reduced, then given that the price has been reduced, we would predict a(n) [increase / decrease] in sales.

increase

34 On the other hand, when an economist attempts to discover the relationship between tax structure and the pattern of consumer spending by observing the effects of different tax policies in several specific locations, he is utilizing the reasoning process of _____ .

induction

35 Since the classical development of mathematics has been founded on beginning with basic assumed truths, or axioms, and deriving other mathematical principles based entirely on these axioms, the system is primarily [inductive / deductive].

deductive

36 The scientific method places particular emphasis on the importance of controlled and verifiable observations of particular events as a basis for discovering general truth. Because of this, the scientific method is largely [inductive / deductive].

inductive

37 The complete cycle of scientific activity includes the processes of both induction and deduction. When a scientist discovers or verifies the existence of specific principles by observing results under controlled conditions, he is reasoning from the particular to the _____ . When he is able to develop subsidiary principles, or when he applies known principles for the purpose of predicting the outcomes of specific events, he is reasoning from the _____ to the _____ .

general

general

particular

38 In using the inductive method, it is rarely the case that all the elements that belong to a particular population can be observed. Therefore conclusions arrived at by the process of induction are typically based on having observed, or measured, a _____ of elements taken from the population.

sample (or portion)

39 But because the objective of sampling is to describe not only the elements that make up the sample but also the entire population from which the elements were selected, the statistical methods that are used in conjunction with the process of induction are always those of statistical [description / inference].

inference

40 Thus the application of the methods of statistics for the purpose of inference directly represents the reasoning process of _____ .

induction

41 Because both the process of induction and the use of quantitative tools are integral parts of the scientific method, statistical inference is an extremely important branch of statistics and is today relatively more important than the application of statistical methods purely for the purpose of statistical _____ .

description

42 When a description is based on observing and/or measuring a sample of elements rather than the entire population of elements, can we ever be sure that the description is correct for all elements in the population? [Yes / No]

> No

43 Therefore the process of statistical inference invariably involves the application of probability theory, which we describe in greater detail beginning in Chapter 5, on probability. When probability theory is used in statistical inference, the risk involved in accepting a quantitative description of a population based on sample data is [eliminated / identified as to amount].

> identified as to amount

44 In statistical inference based on sample data, risk cannot be eliminated. But the amount of risk can be specifically identified by the application of _____ theory.

> probability

45 In the area of hypothesis testing, for example, the decision maker faces the choice of accepting or not accepting a particular description as being representative of a population. If he accepts the hypothesis as being true, he runs the risk that it is actually _____. On the other hand, if he adopts a conservative strategy and rejects a hypothesized description unless it is very clearly supported by sample data, he runs the risk that the description is actually _____.

> false (or untrue)

> true (or correct)

46 Frame 45 suggests that in the process of statistical inference, risk [can / cannot] be avoided, but the kind of risk that is taken [is / is not] under the decision maker's control.

> cannot
> is (since he is the one who chooses to accept or reject the hypothesis)

47 Consider now the relationship between sampling and the use of probability theory. If a number of separate samples of, say, size 50 each are taken from a population, would every sample be equally representative of the population? [Yes / No]

> No

48 Ideally, we would like to use a sampling procedure such that the representativeness of the sample would be guaranteed. Unfortunately no such procedure has been discovered or devised. Thus we can [always / sometimes / never] be sure that a particular sample is actually representative of the population from which it was sampled.

> never

49 Instead of guaranteeing that a sample is representative, the best that a "good" sampling procedure can do is to make certain that known sources of bias are not introduced in the sampling procedure. Such a sample is called a *probability sample*, which we discuss further in Chapter 8, on sampling methods and sampling distributions. In terms of the discussion above, we know that a probability sample [is / is not] necessarily representative of the population.

is not

50 Even though it does not guarantee representativeness, a probability sample has the distinct advantage that the extent to which it is likely to be representative can be stipulated by means of a specific probability statement, thus making possible the application of _____ theory for the purpose of statistical _____ .

probability

inference

51 Thus the only type of sample that makes it possible to apply statistical methods for the purpose of inference is the _____ sample.

probability

52 Since there are a number of sampling procedures that conform to the requirements of probability sampling, some of which are described in Chapter 8, the need to have a probability sample when one wishes to use statistical methods for the purpose of inference is not so restrictive as it sounds. However, if a sample includes a known source of bias, or does not conform to one of the accepted techniques of probability sampling, the methods of statistical inference [can / cannot] be legitimately used.

cannot

53 One of the requirements of a probability sample is that every element in the statistical population have a known, and usually equal, chance of being included in the sample. On this basis an investigator who chooses a sample of stock issues that, in his judgment, looks representative [does / does not] have a probability sample.

does not (The investigator is himself the source of bias in this case.)

54 A political poll taker stops a number of people at a downtown intersection to get their views. Can the methods of statistical inference be applied to this sample for the purpose of determining the political beliefs of all residents of the community? [Yes / No]

No (Only a selected, and biased, portion of the population may have occasion to walk by the particular intersection.)

Summary

55 The type of reasoning that highlights the application of *known general principles* in order to determine subsidiary principles that are consistent with these is _____ _____ .

deduction
(or deductive reasoning)

56 The type of reasoning that is dependent on observation or measurement of actual elements or events for the purpose of discovering general principles is _____ _____ .

induction
(or inductive reasoning)

57 Inductive reasoning is directly involved when the methods of statistics are applied for the purpose of statistical _____ .

inference

58 For the appropriate application of the methods of statistical inference, the statistical sample must be so chosen that it can be considered a _____ sample.

probability

1.3 ▪ Discrete and Continuous Variables

Statistical data may be either discrete or continuous. Because some of the methods of statistical analysis are specifically oriented toward one or the other of these categories of data, it is particularly important that we distinguish these two types of variables in this introductory chapter. The possible values of a *discrete* variable are usually only integers, or whole numbers, but a *continuous* variable can assume any fractional or integer value within the specified range of values. Thus discrete data are generated whenever the elements in a sample or population are *counted*, and continuous data are generated whenever the elements are *measured*.

59 The two types of variables, or data, that can be subjected to statistical analysis are termed _____ and _____ .

discrete
continuous

60 The kinds of numbers that can take on any fractional or integer value between specified limits are categorized as _____, whereas values that are usually restricted to whole-number values are called _____ .

continuous
discrete

61 The form of the data is related to whether the operation of counting or measuring has been carried out. Continuous data are generated whenever the operation of _____ is performed; discrete data are generated whenever the operation of _____ is performed.

measuring

counting

62 Thus, if we identify the number of people who use each of several brands of toothpaste, the form of the data is _____ .

discrete

63 If we determine the heights and weights of a group of college men, the form of the data is _____ .

continuous

64 In certain situations, fractional values are also discrete. For example, stock prices are generally quoted to the one-eighth of a dollar. Since other fractional values between, say, $24\frac{1}{4}$ and $24\frac{3}{8}$ cannot occur, these values can be considered discrete. However, the discrete values that we consider in this text are always integers which are associated with the process of [counting / measuring] .

counting

65 Suppose a manufacturer conducts a study to determine the average retail price being charged for his product in a particular market area. Such a value is an example of a [discrete / continuous] variable.

continuous (because various fractional values are possible)

66 In conjunction with the study in the preceding frame, suppose the manufacturer also determines the number of units sold in the area during the week in which an advertising campaign was conducted. Such a value is an example of a [discrete / continuous] variable.

discrete (since it is a count)

67 Assuming no errors in either counting or measuring, note that a "count" usually implies an "exact count." For example, if 50 units of a product are reported as being in stock, we would interpret this figure to mean that [approximately / exactly] 50 units are in stock.

exactly

68 On the other hand, a value on the continuous scale usually includes some level of approximation because there is usually the possibility that it might have been measured more accurately —i.e. with greater precision. For example, a reported weight of "48 pounds" indicated a true weight somewhere between 47.5 pounds and _____ pounds.

48.5

69 When a measurement is to be rounded, a problem which presents itself is how to round the measurement when the remainder to be rounded is exactly—500—or an even half. For example, suppose we wish to round "48.5 pounds" to whole pounds only. The usual method of rounding is to drop the remainder if the digit preceding it is an even number, and

48	

to increase the preceding digit by 1 if it is an odd number. Thus, "48.5 pounds" would be rounded to "_____ pounds" by this rule.

70 The rule given in Frame 69 is called the even-digit rule, because the last digit which is left by this system is always an even digit. By the use of this rule, rounding errors tend to be counterbalanced in the long run. Using this rule, round each of the following measurements to whole-number values.

398	
46	
5	
19	
21	

(a) 397.5
(b) 45.5
(c) 5.45
(d) 18.95
(e) 20.55

71 Using the even-digit rule, round each of the following measurements to the first place to the right of the decimal point.

21.3	
397.1	
0.0	
5.6	
5.5	

(a) 21.2505
(b) 397.05001
(c) 0.05
(d) 5.555
(e) 5.549

Review

72 (Frames 1–15) When the methods of statistics are directed toward organizing either population or sample data and making them more understandable, then they are being used for the purpose of statistical _____.

description	

When the methods are directed toward analyzing sample data in order to make decisions about a population, they are being used for the purpose of statistical _____ .

inference	

73 (Frames 16–18) When the characteristics of an entire population are measured, typically for the purpose of statistical description, this process is referred to as a _____,

census	

whereas the process of measuring the characteristics of a portion of a population is referred to as _____ .

sampling	

74 (Frames 19–21) The attributes or characteristics of a population, such as the number of elements in the population or the average of all the values, are referred to as population _____, whereas similar data for samples are referred to as sample _____ .

parameters	
statistics	

75 (Frames 22-29) The word "statistics" can be used to refer to the attributes of a sample; give two other distinct meanings that this word can have:

| individual values in a sample or population |
| methods of statistical analysis |

(a) _____

(b) _____

76 (Frames 30-41) The reasoning process of arriving at general principles or conclusions by observing particular instances, often with the associated use of statistical inference, is

| induction |

termed _____ ; the use of known general principles for the purpose of deriving other principles or making specific

| deduction |

predictions describes the process of _____ .

77 (Frames 42-46) In addition to the quantitative methods that are useful also for the purpose of statistical description, statistical inference always involves the application of

| probability |
| identifying |

_____ theory for the purpose of [eliminating / identifying] risk.

78 (Frames 47-58) A sample so chosen that every element in the population has a known, and usually equal, chance of being chosen, and which makes possible the use of the

| probability |

techniques of statistical inference, is a _____ sample.

79 (Frames 59-68) Statistical data may be either *discrete* or *continuous.* Discrete data which are generated by the opera-

| cannot |

tion of counting [can / cannot] take on fractional values. Continuous data are generated by the operation of

| measuring; can |

_____ and therefore [can / cannot] take on fractional values.

80 (Frames 69-71) In the borderline rounding situation in which the remainder associated with a measurement is exactly 5 (possibly with trailing zeros attached), we increase the value of the last significant digit by a value of 1 when that digit is an

| odd |
| even |

_____ number, but we simply drop the remainder when the last significant digit is an _____ number.

EXERCISES
(Solutions on page 587)

1.1 For each of the following four terms indicate whether the term is more closely related to working with samples or with populations by posting an *S* or *P* in front of it, and briefly give the reason for your answer.

_____ (a) statistical inference
_____ (b) parameter
_____ (c) probability theory
_____ (d) census

1.2 It has been stated that statistical inference includes an interest in statistical description, since the purpose is to describe a population of values. How, then, does statistical inference differ from statistical description? Discuss.

1.3 Particularly as contrasted to classical methods in philosophy, scientific methods have been described as being primarily inductive. What does this description imply concerning the way that scientific disciplines are developed?

1.4 What are discrete data? By what process are such data typically obtained?

1.5 For the following variables, designate a discrete variable by entering a *D* in the blank and designate a continuous variable by entering a *C* in the blank.

_____ (a) Weight of the contents of a package of cereal.
_____ (b) Diameter of a bearing.
_____ (c) Number of defective items produced.
_____ (d) Number of individuals in a geographic area who are collecting unemployment benefits.
_____ (e) The average number of customers contacted per sales representative during the past month.
_____ (f) Dollar amount of sales.

1.6 For each of the following values, identify the interval within which the true value is located.

		Limits of true value
(a)	16 ounces	_____
(b)	12.0 ounces	_____
(c)	8.45 centimeters	_____
(d)	$500 (measured to the nearest $100)	_____
(e)	$495 (measured to the nearest $1)	_____
(f)	85.875 meters	_____

1.7 Indicate how each of the following values would be rounded.

		Rounded value
(a)	5,789 (to the nearest hundred)	_____
(b)	6,501 (to the nearest thousand)	_____
(c)	130.55 (to the nearest unit)	_____
(d)	28.65 (to the nearest tenth)	_____
(e)	19.95 (to the nearest tenth)	_____
(f)	32.505 (to the nearest hundredth)	_____

1.8 When a computational result is to be rounded, such as to the first place beyond the decimal, what are the rules associated with such rounding?

ADDITIONAL EXERCISES
(Solutions are not given in back of book.)

1.9 For each of the following four terms, indicate whether the term is more closely related to working with samples or with populations by posting an *S* or *P* in front of it, and briefly give the reason for your classification.

_____ **(a)** induction
_____ **(b)** uncertainty
_____ **(c)** statistic
_____ **(d)** universe

1.10 A description of a population of values which is based on a sample inevitably includes the possibility of sampling error, since a sample is rarely exactly representative of a population. If the manager has the option of taking a "hurried" census of the data, would this solve the problem of error being included in the statistical description? Discuss.

1.11 In this chapter we have suggested that the formal development of mathematics is primarily a deductive process. Why, then, is mathematics frequently classified as a science in the popular literature and in some educational institutions?

1.12 What are continuous data? By what process are such data typically obtained?

1.13 For the following types of values, designate a discrete variable by entering a *D* in the blank and designate a continuous variable by entering a *C* in the blank.
(a) Number of units of an item held in stock: _____
(b) Ratio of current assets to current liabilities: _____
(c) Total tonnage shipped: _____
(d) Total value of inventory: _____

(e) Quantity shipped, in units: _____
(f) Volume of traffic on a toll road: _____
(g) Attendance at the company's annual meeting: _____

1.14 For each of the following values, identify the interval within which the true value is located.

	Limits of true value
(a) $32	_____
(b) $3,200 (to the nearest $100)	_____
(c) $3,200 (to the nearest $10)	_____
(d) 0.5 ounce	_____
(e) 0.50 ounce	_____
(f) 50.0 ounces	_____
(g) 155 pounds	_____
(h) 155.5 pounds	_____
(i) 150 pounds (to the nearest 10 pounds)	_____

1.15 Indicate how each of the following values would be rounded.

	Rounded value
(a) 27.27 (to the nearest tenth)	_____
(b) 27.27 (to the nearest unit)	_____
(c) 325.455 (to the nearest hundredth)	_____
(d) 325.455 (to the nearest tenth)	_____
(e) 325.455 (to the nearest unit)	_____
(f) $63.50 (to the nearest dollar)	_____
(g) $64.50 (to the nearest dollar)	_____
(h) $64.51 (to the nearest dollar)	_____

1.16 For the purpose of statistical inference a *representative* sample is to be desired. Yet, use of the techniques of inference require that a *probability* sample be obtained. Why?

PART II ■
DESCRIPTIVE STATISTICS

CHAPTER 2 ■
FREQUENCY DISTRIBUTIONS AND GRAPHIC DESCRIPTION

Frequency distributions are typically discussed early in the study of statistical methods because they provide both a method for organizing data for easier comprehension and a basis for simplifying the computation of certain sample statistics or population parameters. The use of frequency distributions in conjunction with statistical computations is included in Chapter 4. In this chapter we discuss the elements of the frequency distribution, the related construction of histograms, frequency polygons, and frequency curves, and other methods of graphic description used in presenting quantitative data.

2.1 ■ The Frequency Distribution

A frequency distribution consists of a listing of several measurement categories, or classes, with an indication of the number of observed measurements, or frequency, associated with each class. The difference between class limits and class boundaries and the determination of class intervals and midpoints are covered in this section. Unless otherwise specified, our discussion always concerns continuous, rather than discrete, data.

1 Throughout the following discussion of the grouping of data into classes the assumption is made that the data are [discrete / continuous].

continuous

2 When a number of classes of measurements is listed along with an indication of the frequency of observed measurements falling within each class, the listing is called a

frequency distribution

_____.

3 Table 2-1 lists the heights of a sample of 50 men students at a university. Since each individual measurement is separately listed in this table, the data are considered to be [grouped / ungrouped].

ungrouped

Table 2-1 ■ Heights of 50 Men Students Measured to the Nearest Inch (Ungrouped Data)

67	73	71	74	61	68	70	70	66	73
68	67	72	69	71	69	76	70	72	71
77	69	71	74	66	68	70	72	72	70
71	70	64	65	70	69	72	75	66	67
70	72	67	70	71	68	66	73	69	67

4 In contrast, data that have been entered in a frequency distribution are considered to be _____ data.

grouped

5 Table 2-2 is the frequency distribution for the measurements presented in Table 2-1. By organizing the measurements into classes, a frequency distribution makes it [easier / more difficult] to interpret a group of measurements.

Table 2-2 ■ Heights of 50 Men Students Measured to the Nearest Inch (Grouped Data)

Height	Number of students
60–62	1
63–65	2
66–68	13
69–71	20
72–74	11
75–77	3

6 However, there is a price paid for grouping data in a frequency distribution. If we refer to Table 2-1 alone, can we determine the value of each of the measurements included in this table, at least to the nearest inch? [Yes / No]

Yes

7 On the other hand, can we determine the value of each of the 50 measurements by reference to Table 2-2 alone? [Yes / No]

No

8 Although we lost some of the precision in our data through grouping, this disadvantage is offset by the fact that the interpretation of the data is made easier. Using Table 2-1, for example, it would be difficult to give an estimate of the height of most of the students, but Table 2-2 clearly indicates that the size category of ___ to ___ inches contains the greatest frequency of measurements.

69; 71

9 Thus use of a frequency distribution to organize data leads to interpretation that is [easier / more difficult] and data that are [more / less] precise.

easier

less

10 In terms of the structural properties of the classes included in a frequency distribution, each class of measurements has lower and upper limits, lower and upper boundaries, an interval, and a midpoint. Each of these values will be needed in carrying out the computations described in Chapter 4. The *class limits* are the numbers that typically serve to identify the classes in a listing of a frequency distribution. Thus, for the class whose frequency is 20 in Table 2-2, the *lower class limit* is ___ (number) and the *upper class limit* is ___ (number).

69

71

11 Similarly, for the class whose frequency is 11, 72 is the lower _____ and 74 is the _____ .

12 Are the class limits typically inclusive; i.e., would observed measurements that correspond exactly to the lower class limit or upper class limit be included in that class? (Note the values of adjoining class limits in Table 2-2.) [Yes / No]

13 Therefore what are the measured heights, to the nearest inch, that would be included in the class whose lower and upper limits are 72 and 74, respectively? ___, ___, and ___.

14 As contrasted to a class limit, a *class boundary* is the precise point that separates one class from another, rather than being a value included in one of the classes. A class boundary is typically located midway between the upper limit of a class and the lower limit of the next higher class adjoining it. Therefore the class boundary separating the class 63–65 and the class 66–68 is halfway between 65 and 66, or at the point _____ (number).

15 The precise point separating two classes is called a class _____ .

16 Of course, every class typically has a lower and an upper boundary, just as it has lower and upper limits. Using the adjoining classes 69–71 and 72–74 as an example, and first considering the class limits, we find that the values of the upper *limit* of one class and the lower *limit* of the next higher class adjoining it [are / are not] the same.

17 Still referring to the adjoining classes 69–71 and 72–74, we find that the values of the upper *boundary* of one class and the lower *boundary* of the next higher class adjoining it [are / are not] the same.

18 For the classes of Table 2-2, enter the missing lower and upper boundaries in the table below.

Class limits	Class boundaries
60–62	59.5–62.5
63–65	____-____
66–68	____-____
69–71	68.5–71.5
72–74	71.5–74.5
75–77	74.5–77.5

19 Suppose that the heights of the students had been measured to the nearest half-inch, instead of the nearest inch. Indicate the class boundaries of the two adjoining classes below.

Class limits	Class boundaries
60.0-62.5	____ - ____
63.0-65.5	____ - ____

> 59.75-62.75
> 62.75-65.75

20 If you had any difficulty in Frame 19, remember that we always consider the size of the gap between adjoining class limits, set the boundary midway in this gap, and set similar boundaries for the classes at the two ends of the distribution whose lower or upper limits do not adjoin any class. Thus the numerical value of a class boundary [does / does not] necessarily end in ".5".

> does not

21 If an obtained measurement falls precisely on a class boundary, in which class should it be placed? Though this question appears to be a troublesome one, it refers to a situation which should never occur. Consider the description given in the heading of Table 2-2. Can the measurement 65.5 be listed? [Yes / No]

> No (because measurements were to be made to the nearest inch)

22 Class boundaries are always defined more precisely than the level of measurement being used for the collection of data, and so the rounding of any fractional values would take place as part of the measurement process and *before* entry of the data into the frequency distribution. For measurement of height to the nearest inch, for example, a height of 65.5 would have been rounded as part of the original measurement process to _____ (number).

> 66 (It would have been rounded to the even integer, as explained in Section 1.3)

23 An *open-end distribution* is one in which either one or both of the classes at the two ends of the frequency distribution have no stated limits and therefore do not have associated boundaries. For the following abridged example of an open-end distribution, enter the class boundaries, indicating *none* where appropriate.

Class limits	Class boundaries
Under 30	_____
30–49	_____
50–69	_____
70+	_____

> none-29.5
> 29.5-49.5
> 49.5-69.5
> 69.5-none

24 When a definite boundary cannot be set at one or both ends of a frequency distribution, it is called an _____ distribution.

25 Having described class limits and class boundaries, let us now consider the *class interval i.* The assumption underlying this description is that a common interval size applies for all classes of a given frequency distribution. The length, or size, of the class interval is determined by subtracting the lower boundary of a class from its upper boundary. This operation can be represented by the formula $i = B_U - B_L$. For the following data,

$i =$ _____ $-$ _____ $=$ _____

Class limits	Class boundaries
15–19	14.5–19.5
20–24	19.5–24.5

26 According to the formula $i = B_U - B_L$, the size of the class interval being used in Table 2-2 is

$i =$ _____ $-$ _____ $=$ _____

27 As the name implies, the *midpoint* of a class is the point dividing the class into equal halves, on the basis of interval size. This point can be identified by adding the lower and upper limits of a class, or the lower and upper boundaries, and dividing by 2. The formulas that we can use to represent these operations are

$$\text{Midpt} = \frac{L_L + L_U}{2} \quad \text{and} \quad \text{Midpt} = \frac{B_L + B_U}{2}$$

respectively. Using either of these formulas, determine the values of the midpoints for the following data, and verify that either procedure yields the same result.

Class limits	Class boundaries	Class midpoint
15–19	14.5–19.5	___
20–24	19.5–24.5	___

28 The class midpoint is often called the *class mark*, and it is used to represent all values in the class for the purpose of certain calculations. In the table below list the class marks for the first three classes of Table 2-2.

Height	Class mark
60–62	—
63–65	—
66–68	—

61
64
67

29 The location of the class midpoint, or class mark, can be determined also by adding one-half of the interval size to the lower boundary of a class. Symbolically, this can be represented as midpt $= B_L + (\frac{1}{2})i$. Using this approach, recompute the midpoints determined in Frame 28.

$59.5 + 1.5 = 61$
$62.5 + 1.5 = 64$
$65.5 + 1.5 = 67$

1st midpt = _____ + _____ = _____
2nd midpt = _____ + _____ = _____
3rd midpt = _____ + _____ = _____

30 Now that we have described class midpoints, we can observe that the size of the class interval being used in a frequency distribution also can be determined by subtracting the midpoint of a class from that of the adjoining higher class. Symbolically, $i = \text{midpt}_{(2)} - \text{midpt}_{(1)}$. Thus, given the data below,

$22 - 17 = 5$ (which corresponds to the value determined by the general method in Frame 25)

$i =$ _____ $-$ _____ $=$ _____

Class	Class midpoint
15–19	17
20–24	22

31 Of course, the identification of the class limits, boundaries, midpoint, and interval is done for a frequency distribution that has already been constructed. In respect to the construction of a frequency distribution in the first place, there are no fixed rules concerning the appropriate number of classes to be defined or the size of the class interval to be used. It does follow, however, that for a given range of values to be grouped, the smaller the size of the class interval, the [smaller / larger] the number of classes in the frequency distribution.

larger

32 It is usually considered appropriate to construct between six and fifteen classes for a frequency distribution. However, the actual number of classes and the related size of the class interval depend on the requirements of the particular problem. In any event, we might observe that since grouping always results in some loss of precision of the data, or grouping error, the larger the size of the class interval, the [smaller / larger] is this error.

larger

33 The first step in constructing a frequency distribution is to subtract the lowest obtained measurement in the data to be grouped from the highest measurement to obtain the range R of the measurements. For the ungrouped measurements listed in Table 2-3,

49 − 16 = 33

$R =$ ___ − ___ = ___ .

Table 2-3 ▪ A Set of Ungrouped Measurements

32	26	16	44	28
40	30	31	17	30
37	32	42	31	36
49	35	21	25	40
27	25	33	34	27

34 The next step in constructing a frequency distribution is to decide on the number of classes to be used and to divide the range by this number to obtain the appropriate size of the class interval to be used. For fractional results, the interval size is typically defined at the next higher whole number (or other level of measurement involved in the particular application). If we wish to have seven classes in the frequency distribution for the data of Table 2-3, whose range of values is 33, the appropriate size of the class interval is _____ (number).

5

35 Using the class interval of 5, construct the classes to be used in conjunction with the data of Table 2-3, beginning the first class in the frequency distribution with the lower limit of 16.

Class limits

16–20	_____
21–25	_____
26–30	_____
31–35	_____
36–40	_____
41–45	_____
46–50	_____

36 For the class whose lower and upper limits are 21 and 25, respectively, the lower boundary is _____ (number), the upper boundary is _____ (number), and the class mark is ___ (number).

37 The final step in constructing a frequency distribution is to tally the number of obtained measurements falling into each of the defined classes, so that the frequency associated with each class can be determined. For the data of Table 2-3, complete the tally below and post the frequency associated with each class.

Class limits	Tally	Number of measurements, f
16–20	_____	_____
21–25	_____	_____
26–30	_____	_____
31–35	_____	_____
36–40	_____	_____
41–45	_____	_____
46–50	_____	_____

38 Since we have consistently referred to the grouping of *measurements* throughout this section we have assumed that the data being grouped are [continuous /discrete] .

39 Frequency distributions are also often constructed for discrete data as well as continuous data. In such cases, the class boundaries and perhaps midpoints are fractional values which cannot in fact occur for such data. Nevertheless, these values are required in conjunction with computational methods described in Chapter 4. Thus, for the following grouped discrete data, the lower and upper boundaries of the last class are _____ (number) and _____ (number), the midpoint of the class is _____ (number), and the class interval is _____ (number).

Number of days absent	Number of employees
0–3	3
4–7	7
8–11	2
12–15	1

2.2 ■ Histograms, Frequency Polygons, and Frequency Curves

In addition to their presentation by means of tables, the measurements included in a frequency distribution can be presented by several graphic methods. The main objective in developing graphic illustrations for the information contained in a frequency distribution is to make the interpretation of the information easier. In this section we illustrate the use of histograms, frequency polygons, and frequency curves for presenting the data contained in frequency distributions.

40 The *histogram* is one of the ways of graphically presenting a frequency distribution. Figure 2-1 is a histogram for the frequency distribution given in Table 2-2. Notice that the values listed along the horizontal axis of the histogram are class [limits / boundaries / midpoints].

boundaries

Figure 2-1 ▪ Histogram: heights of 50 men students

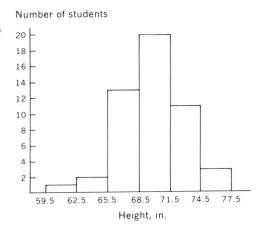

41 The values listed along the vertical axis of the graph on which the histogram is constructed indicate the _____ associated with each class.

frequencies (or number of students)

42 The width of the rectangles that make up the histogram indicates the size of the class _____.

interval

43 When all class intervals are the same, the height of each rectangle directly represents the _____ associated with each class of measurements.

frequency

44 Thus "a series of rectangles whose widths are marked off by class boundaries and whose heights are indicative of the frequency of measurements associated with each class" is a description of the graph called the _____.

histogram

45 Construct a histogram for the following frequency distribution taken from Frame 37.

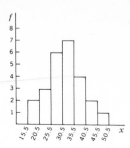

Class	f
16–20	2
21–25	3
26–30	6
31–35	7
36–40	4
41–45	2
46–50	1

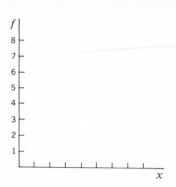

46 Another way of graphically portraying a frequency distribution is by means of a *frequency polygon*. Figure 2-2 is the frequency polygon associated with the data of Table 2-2. As is the case for the histogram, the frequency polygon identifies class frequencies along the [horizontal / vertical] axis.

vertical

Figure 2-2 ■ Frequency polygon: heights of 50 men students

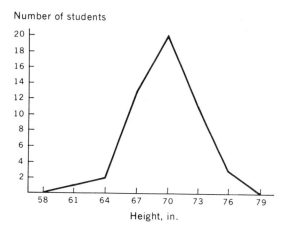

Number of students

47 Whereas the histogram identifies class boundaries along the horizontal axis, the frequency polygon identifies class _____ along the horizontal axis.

midpoints (or marks)

48 "A line graph of class frequencies plotted against class midpoints" is a description of the _____.

frequency polygon

49 Since a polygon is a many-sided *closed* figure, it is necessary to add "extra" class midpoints at the lower and upper extremes of the distribution for the adjacent non-existent classes whose frequencies are zero, so that the polygon does in fact form a closed figure with the horizontal

58; 79

50 Construct a frequency polygon for the following grouped data, for which you previously constructed a histogram.

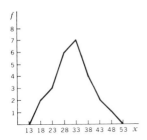

Class	f
16–20	2
21–25	3
26–30	6
31–35	7
36–40	4
41–45	2
46–50	1

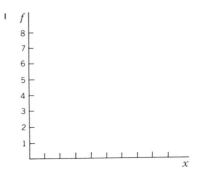

51 Since the histogram and frequency polygon are closely related, it might be useful to enter both on the same graph for purposes of comparison. Each point of the frequency polygon is located at the midpoint of the top side of each of the rectangles that make up the histogram, and these midpoints are connected to form the polygon. Accordingly, complete the construction of the frequency polygon on the graph below.

Complete the polygon by joining appropriate midpoints; the resulting figure should resemble the frequency polygon in Frame 50.

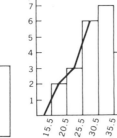

52 If the frequency polygon is smoothed, or if a curve is fitted to a frequency distribution, the obtained curve is called a *frequency curve*. Superimpose the approximate form of the frequency curve on the frequency polygon below.

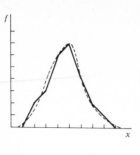

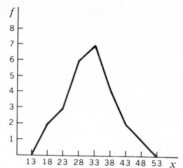

53 A curve constructed on a graph on which the horizontal axis represents various possible values of a variable and the vertical axis represents various possible frequencies, or relative frequencies, of occurrence is called a _____.

frequency curve

54 The form of a frequency curve can be described in two ways: in terms of its *departure from symmetry*, which is called "skewness," and in terms of its *degree of peakedness*, which is called "kurtosis." When we look at a frequency curve to observe whether the first half of the curve looks like the mirror image of the second half, we are giving attention to the concept of [skewness / kurtosis].

skewness

55 A distribution of measurements whose frequency curve is not symmetrical is said to be "skewed." In a skewed distribution there are extreme values at one end of the distribution that are not counterbalanced by extreme values at the other end of the distribution. Which of the following frequency curves represent distributions of measurements that are clearly skewed? (Underline the identifying letters.)

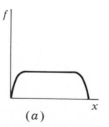

(a)

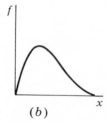

(b)

(c)

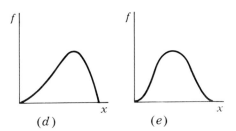

(d) (e)

b and d

56 When the few extreme values are in the direction of the higher measurements of the variable, thus forming a tail to the right, the distribution is said to be "positively skewed." In Frame 55 the frequency curve which is positively skewed is ___ (identifying letter).

b

57 On the other hand, when the tail of the distribution is in the direction of the lower values of the variable, and thus toward the origin of the graph, the distribution is said to be "negatively skewed," or skewed to the left. The frequency curve in Frame 55 which is negatively skewed is ___ (identifying letter).

d

58 Thus, of the two curves below, frequency curve *a* is _____ skewed and curve *b* is _____ skewed.

negatively; positively

(a) (b)

59 In terms of kurtosis, a frequency curve that is very flat, indicating a wide dispersion of measurements, is said to be "platykurtic"; a curve with a high peak, indicating a high concentration of measurements about some particular value, is said to be "leptokurtic"; one with an intermediate degree of dispersion and peakedness is said to be "mesokurtic." Which form of frequency curve represents a distribution in which the obtained measurements are closely clustered and vary only by small amounts from one another? [Platykurtic / Mesokurtic / Leptokurtic]

Leptokurtic	

60 Of the three curves below, the one which appears to be mesokurtic is ___ (identifying letter) and the one that appears to be platykurtic is ___ (identifying letter).

a	
c	

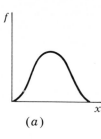 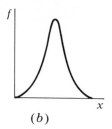 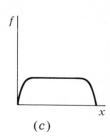

(a)   (b)   (c)

61 The three kinds of frequency curves in terms of peakedness, progressing from "flat" to "extremely peaked," are the _____ , _____ , and _____ curves.

platykurtic; mesokurtic	
leptokurtic	

62 Of course, frequency curves simultaneously vary in terms of both skewness and kurtosis. Of the curves below, the one which is both positively skewed and leptokurtic is ___ (identifying letter), and the one which is both negatively skewed and mesokurtic is ___ (identifying letter).

c	
e	

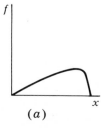 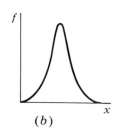 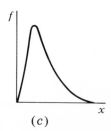

(a)   (b)   (c)

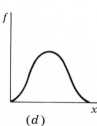 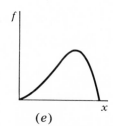

(d)   (e)

departures from symmetry	
degree of peakedness	

63 As applied to frequency curves the term "skewness" refers to _____; the term "kurtosis" refers to _____.

negatively skewed;
symmetrical; positively skewed
platykurtic; mesokurtic
leptokurtic

64 In terms of skewness a frequency curve can be _____, _____, or _____. In terms of kurtosis it can be _____, _____, or _____.

65 For the purpose of carrying out certain statistical calculations, we often need to identify the *cumulative frequency* associated with each class, as well as the frequency itself. The cumulative frequency for a class is obtained by summing the frequency for the class with the frequencies of all classes "below" it, i.e., with all classes with smaller midpoints. Accordingly, complete the cumulative-frequency (cf) column for the following data taken from Table 2-2.

Height	f	cf
60–62	1	1
63–65	2	3
66–68	13	16
69–71	20	——
72–74	11	——
75–77	3	——
Sum	50	

36
47
50

66 To provide a convenient arithmetic check on the accuracy of the cumulative frequencies, it is useful to note that, as in Frame 65, the cumulative frequency of the last (highest-valued) class is always equal to _____ _____.

the sum of all frequencies
in the distribution

67 Determine the cumulative frequencies for the following data.

	Class	f	cf
2	16–20	2	———
5	21–25	3	———
11	26–30	6	———
18	31–35	7	———
22	36–40	4	———
24	41–45	2	———
25	46–50	1	———
	Sum	25	

68 A cumulative-frequency distribution can be graphically represented by a cumulative-frequency polygon, which is also called an *ogive* (pronounced "oh-jive"). Because the frequencies associated with each class are understood to extend right up to the upper boundary of the class, these boundaries are the values posted along the horizontal axis of the ogive. For the data of Table 2-2, complete the following ogive.

Enter the cumulative frequencies for the classes whose upper boundaries are 74.5 and 77.5. The resulting diagram should resemble that of Frame 70, below.

Height	cf
60–62	1
63–65	3
66–68	16
69–71	36
72–74	47
75–77	50

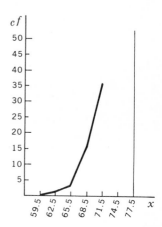

69 Thus the polygon representing the total number of frequencies, or observed measurements, up to the upper boundary of each class of a frequency distribution is called a _____ polygon, or an _____ .

cumulative-frequency; ogive

70 Just as a frequency polygon can be smoothed, or fitted with a frequency curve, so also can an ogive be smoothed, resulting in an *ogive curve.* On the graph below indicate the approximate shape of the ogive curve by superimposing it over the ogive.

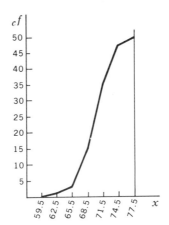

71 If the cumulative frequencies on the graph for an ogive are converted to percentages, the resulting graph is called a *percentage ogive.* Such a graph is useful because it can be used to estimate graphically the percentage of observed values below any designated value. This, then, is the *percentile point* associated with that value. For example, the percentage ogive below has been constructed from the ogive in Frame 70. As indicated by the dashed lines, we can see that the percentile point associated with the height of 70 inches is just above _____ (number).

50 (the actual percentile point is 52)

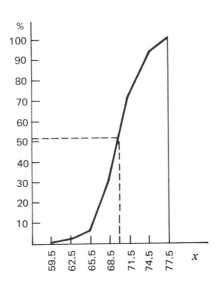

70

72 Of course, a larger percentage ogive constructed on graph paper would be required to read the percentile point with greater accuracy. But the answer to frame 71 means that 52 percent of the male students in the sample are at or below ____ inches in height.

66

73 The percentage ogive can also be used to determine the value associated with a designated percentile by reading the graph in the "other direction." Referring to the percentage ogive in Frame 71, the value which is approximately at the tenth percentile point is ____ inches. (The graphic basis for this answer is indicated below. Again, our graph is not large enough for accurate reading. The algebraic determination of percentile points is included in Section 3.3, "The Quartiles and Other Position Measures.")

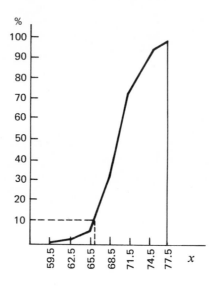

2.3 ■ Other Methods of Graphic Description

The construction of histograms, frequency polygons, frequency curves, and ogive curves is associated specifically with graphically portraying data that have been grouped in a frequency distribution. In addition to these methods, the bar chart, pictogram, line chart, and pie chart are other graphic methods that can be used whenever obtained data can be classified into a number of categories.

74 Because frequency distributions and the methods of graphic description are used for organizing statistical information that has already been collected, the methods that are considered in this chapter can be described as being primarily in the category of [statistical description / statistical inference].

75 As contrasted to the methods of graphic description that were considered in Section 2.2, the methods to be considered in this final section of the chapter can be used whenever data have been classified into categories, and therefore they are not restricted to the situation in which data have been grouped

in a _____.

76 Table 2-4 presents an analysis of the passenger car production in the United States and Canada by the four major U.S. auto companies fcr the three years 1973-1975. On the graph below, a *bar chart* has been partially constructed presenting total automobile production by year. Of the graphic methods described in the preceding section of this chapter, the bar

chart resembles a _____.

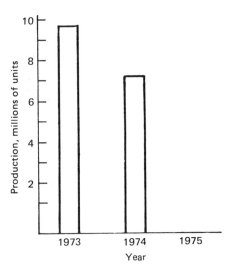

Table 2-4 ■ Car Production in the United States and Canada by the Four Major U.S. Automobile Manufacturers, 1973-1975 (In millions of units)	1973	1974	1975	Total 1973-1975
American Motors	0.36	0.35	0.32	1.03
Chrysler	1.56	1.18	0.90	3.64
Ford	2.50	2.21	1.81	6.52
General Motors	5.25	3.59	3.68	12.52
Total	9.67	7.33	6.71	23.71

Source of data: *Motor Vehicle Facts and Figures '76*, Motor Vehicle Manufacturers Association, 1976.

77 Unlike a histogram, the bar chart represents categories of data and not classes of a frequency distribution. The labels for the categories rather than class boundaries are posted along the horizontal axis; the rectangles do not touch one another, and they can be made any convenient, uniform width. With these differences in mind, complete the bar chart in Frame 76 by referring to Table 2-4 for the needed total.

The other total, which can be only approximately indicated on this small bar chart, is 6.71 million units.

78 The identification of the two axes can be interchanged, resulting in a series of horizontal bars rather than vertical bars. The partially completed bar chart below illustrates such a chart. Using the data from Table 2-4, complete this chart also.

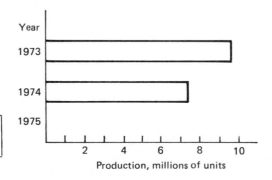

Year

Production, millions of units

The third horizontal bar should indicate 6.71 million units.

79 Thus a chart that depicts amounts against categories, with the amounts represented by a series of vertical or horizontal rectangles, is called a _____ .

bar chart

80 When associated categories of data are to be posted on the same bar chart, two methods are available. If we wish to present the two or more categories of data in a cumulative fashion, the use of a *component bar chart* is appropriate. In the partially completed chart below, notice that the component categories that make up each bar are identified. In business reports a color is often used to differentiate the components. Complete the component bar chart, using the appropriate data from Table 2-4, with G for General Motors, F for Ford, C for Chrysler, and A for American Motors.

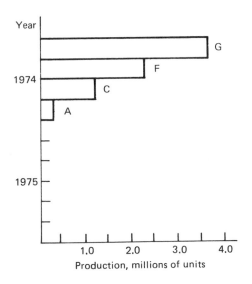

Production, millions of units

81 A bar chart in which each bar represents the cumulation of two or more identified categories of data is a _____ bar chart.

82 When we wish to highlight the comparison rather than the cumulation of the several categories of data to be included on the same bar chart, a *grouped bar chart* is useful. Accordingly, complete the construction of the grouped bar chart below, using data from Table 2-4.

Production, millions of units

83 Thus two types of bar charts can be used to identify simultaneously amounts in two or more categories: comparison of the categories is highlighted by the use of a _____ bar chart, and the cumulation of the categories is highlighted by the use of a _____ bar chart.

84 The pictogram, or picture diagram, is similar to the bar chart except that symbolic figures are used in place of the rectangles. In the pictogram below, for example, each small figure of a car represents the production of 1 million auto-mobiles. Complete this pictogram, using the data of Table 2-4.

Production of automobiles
(each figure represents 1 million automobiles)

Production for 1975 would be represented by $6\frac{2}{3}$ vehicles.

85 When small, symbolic figures are used to represent the quantities associated with each category of data, the resulting display is called a _____.

pictogram

86 Whenever the categories being tabulated represent time, as in the data of Table 2-4, they can also be graphically portrayed by means of a *line chart*. Complete the line chart below, using the data of Table 2-4.

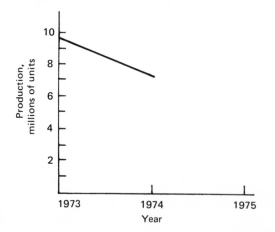

This line should be extended from the 7.33 (for 1974) to 6.71 for 1975.

87 A graph on which a series of line segments represent the relationship between time, plotted on the horizontal axis, and amounts, plotted on the vertical axis, is a _____ .

line chart

88 Finally, another widely used graphic device for indicating division of a whole into various parts is the *pie chart*. The figure below is the pie chart representing the division of total automobile manufacturing for the three-year period 1973–1975 among the major manufacturers. In the blank pie chart alongside it, complete a similar analysis for automobile production in 1975, using the data of Table 2-4.

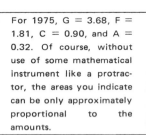

For 1975, G = 3.68, F = 1.81, C = 0.90, and A = 0.32. Of course, without use of some mathematical instrument like a protractor, the areas you indicate can be only approximately proportional to the amounts.

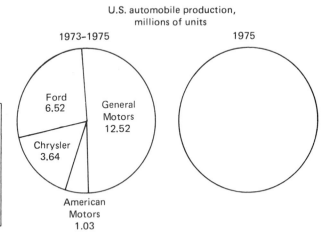

U.S. automobile production, millions of units

1973–1975

1975

Ford 6.52

General Motors 12.52

Chrysler 3.64

American Motors 1.03

89 The bar chart, pictogram, and line chart can all be used to study changes in amount or quantity over time. Can a single pie chart be used for this purpose? [Yes / No]

No (although changes could be shown by a series of pie charts)

90 As a variation of the usual pie chart, the *percentage pie chart* indicates the division of a whole into percentages. Complete the percentage pie cahrt below for the analysis of automobile production for 1975.

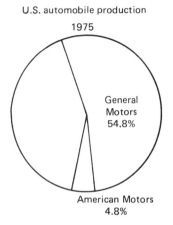

U.S. automobile production

1975

General Motors 54.8%

American Motors 4.8%

The remaining two percentages are: Ford = 27.0% and Chrysler = 13.4%.

91 (Frames 1-4) When data are categorized according to a series of classes of measurements and the associated frequency of each class is indicated, the resulting listing is called a

| frequency distribution |

_____ .

92 (Frames 5-9) In addition to its use in simplifying certain computations, the primary advantage of a frequency distribution as a descriptive tool is that it facilitates

| interpretation of data |
| precision (or accuracy) |

_____ , although the price that is paid for its use is that some _____
is lost through the process of grouping.

93 (Frames 10-17) In terms of the structural properties of the classes that make up a frequency distribution, the inclusive measurements that serve to identify a class and differentiate it

| limits |

from other classes are called class _____ , whereas the precise points that separate a class from other classes are called

| boundaries |

class _____ .

94 (Frames 18-24) Indicate the class boundaries for the following classes, which indicate that time was measured to the nearest tenth of a second.

Time, seconds	Class boundaries

| 10.95–11.95 |
| 11.95–12.95 |
| 12.95–none |

Time, seconds	Class boundaries
11.0–11.9	_____
12.0–12.9	_____
13.0 +	_____

95 (Frames 23-24) Because no upper boundary can be set for the last class of the frequency distribution given in Frame

| open-end |

94, the distribution of measurements is called an _____ distribution.

96 (Frames 25-26, 30) When the limits and boundaries of a *single* class are identified, the class interval can be

| boundary |
| boundary |

determined by subtracting the lower _____ from the upper _____ .

97 (Frames 27-29) The midpoint of a class can be determined by adding half of the interval size to the lower

| boundary |

_____ of the class.

98 (Frames 31–39) In forming a frequency distribution, the use of relatively small rather than large class intervals results in a grouping error that is relatively [small / large] and a number of classes that is relatively [small / large] .

small
large

99 (Frames 40–45) A graph on which class boundaries are located along the horizontal axis and rectangles are constructed over this axis to represent the frequency of measurements associated with each class is called a _____ .

histogram

100 (Frames 46–51) A graph on which midpoints of classes are posted along the horizontal axis, the height of the point entered on the graph above each midpoint represents class frequency, and the points are joined, thus forming a closed figure with the horizontal axis, is called a _____ .

frequency polygon

101 (Frames 52–58) In the description of frequency curves, skewness refers to departure from _____ , and kurtosis refers to degree of _____ .

symmetry
peakedness

102 (Frames 59–64) In terms of skewness a frequency curve can be described as being _____ , _____ , or _____ . In terms of kurtosis it can be _____ , _____ , or _____ .

negatively skewed
symmetrical; positively skewed
platykurtic; mesokurtic
leptokurtic

103 (Frames 65–73) The polygon that graphically represents the cumulative frequency up to the upper boundary of each class of a frequency distribution is called the "cumulative-frequency polygon," or, more popularly, the _____.

ogive

104 (Frames 74–79) A chart that can be used for any classified data and that depicts amounts by a series of vertical or horizontal rectangles is called a _____.

bar chart

105 (Frames 80–83) With reference to the two kinds of bar charts used to analyze amounts by subcategories, cumulation of the subcategories is highlighted by the _____ bar chart, and comparison of the categories is facilitated by the _____ bar chart.

component

grouped

106 (Frames 84–85) When small symbolic figures are used in place of the bars in a bar chart, the resulting display is called a _____.

pictogram

107 (Frames 86–87) A graph which portrays changes in amounts in respect to time by means of a series of line segments connecting the amounts is the _____ .

> line chart

108 (Frames 88–90) The most popular pictorial device used for indicating the sources, or parts, that make up a whole amount is the _____ .

> pie chart

Symbols Introduced in This Chapter (with Frame Numbers)

(25)	i	Class interval in a frequency distribution.
(25)	B_U	Upper boundary of a class in a frequency distribution.
(25)	B_L	Lower boundary of a class in a frequency distribution.
(27)	L_L	Lower limit of a class in a frequency distribution.
(27)	L_U	Upper limit of a class in a frequency distribution.
(27)	midpt	Midpoint of a class in a frequency distribution.
(45)	f	The class frequency, or number of observations in a particular class of a frequency distribution.
(65)	cf	The cumulative frequency associated with a class in a frequency distribution; this is the total number of observations in the frequency distribution up to, and including, the designated class.

Formulas Introduced in This Chapter (with Frame Numbers)

(25) $i = B_U - B_L$

Class interval determined by use of the upper and lower boundaries of a particular class.

(27) $\text{Midpt} = \dfrac{L_L + L_U}{2}$

or $\text{midpt} = \dfrac{B_L + B_U}{2}$

The class midpoint by use of the upper and lower limits (or boundaries) of a class.

(29) $\text{Midpt} = B_L + (\frac{1}{2})i$

The class midpoint by use of the lower boundary and the class interval value.

(30) $i = \text{midpt}_{(2)} - \text{midpt}_{(1)}$

The class interval by use of the midpoints of adjoining classes (given that the classes have equal intervals).

2.1 Given the following frequency distribution, identify the class boundaries for each class and determine the size of the class interval.

Class limits	f
3–5	1
6–8	2
9–11	2
12–14	5
15–17	4

2.2 Construct the histogram for the frequency distribution above.

2.3 Construct the frequency polygon for the frequency distribution in Exercise 2.1.

2.4 Describe the frequency curve for the data in the table above in terms of skewness.

2.5 Construct the ogive for the frequency distribution in Exercise 2.1.

2.6 Construct a percentage ogive for the frequency distribution in Exercise 2.1. Referring to this graph, (a) what is the approximate percentile point associated with a measured value of 15? (b) What is the approximate measured value at the fiftieth percentile point?

2.7 The following data report the dollar sales of three products according to region, in thousands of dollars. Construct a bar chart depicting total sales by region, using vertical bars.

Product group	Region			
	East	Midwest	West	Total
A	$ 50	$ 55	$ 70	$175
B	70	40	80	190
C	30	40	20	90
Total	$150	$135	$170	$455

2.8 Construct a component bar chart to illustrate the product breakdown of sales by region for the data in Exercise 2.7, using horizontal bars.

2.9 Construct a pie chart illustrating total sales by product for the data of Exercise 2.7.

2.10 Given the following data for sales, in $1,000s, construct a line chart illustrating total sales by year.

Product group	1975	1976	1977	1978	Total
			Year		
A	$120	$170	$160	$175	$ 625
B	160	160	180	190	690
C	10	30	60	90	190
Total	$290	$360	$400	$455	$1,505

ADDITIONAL EXERCISES

2.11 The following data are taken from the *Arizona Statistical Review*, published by the Valley National Bank (32nd ed., 1976). Assuming that age was reported to the nearest birthday (rather than the last birthday), determine the class boundaries for each class of this relative (percentage) frequency distribution.

Age Breakdown of Phoenix Area Population as Compared with the U.S. Population, 1975

Age group	Phoenix area, percent	United States, percent
Under 5	8.9	7.5
5–17	24.5	23.6
18–44	37.4	38.0
45–64	19.2	20.4
65 and over	10.0	10.5

2.12 Notice that a constant interval size is *not* used in the frequency distribution above. Identify the interval size associated with each class. Using this distribution as an example, why do you think unequal interval sizes are frequently used in statistical reports?

2.13 The table below presents the amounts of 40 personal loans in a consumer finance company. Suppose we wish to arrange the loan amounts in a frequency distribution with a total of seven classes. Assuming equal class intervals, what would be a convenient class interval for this frequency distribution?

The Amounts of 40 Personal Loans

$ 900	$1,000	$ 300	$2,000
500	550	1,100	1,000
450	950	300	2,000
1,900	600	1,600	450
1,200	750	1,500	750
1,250	1,300	1,000	850
2,500	850	1,800	600
550	350	900	3,000
1,650	1,400	500	350
1,200	700	650	1,500

2.14 Construct the frequency distribution for the data in Exercise 2.13, beginning the first class at a lower class limit of $300 and using a class interval of $400.

2.15 Prepare a histogram for the frequency distribution constructed in Exercise 2.14.

2.16 Construct a frequency polygon and frequency curve for the frequency distribution constructed in Exercise 2.14.

2.17 Describe the frequency curve constructed in Exercise 2.16 in terms of skewness.

2.18 Construct a cumulative frequency distribution for the frequency distribution constructed in Exercise 2.14 and construct an ogive for these data.

2.19 Construct the percentage ogive for the frequency distribution in Exercise 2.14. Referring to this graph, (a) what is the approximate percentile point for a loan amount of $2,000? (b) What is the approximate loan value at the thirtieth percentile point?

2.20 The data in the following table are taken from the *Survey of Current Business* published by the U.S. Department of Commerce. Construct a vertical bar chart for these data.

Construction of New One-family Structures in the United States, 1971–1976 (In thousands of units)

Year	Housing Starts
1971	1,151
1972	1,349
1973	1,132
1974	888
1975	892
1976	1,162

2.21 Construct a line chart for the housing starts for single-family structures which are reported in Exercise 2.20.

2.22 The following data are taken from the *Annual Report* of the Clark Equipment Company for 1975. Construct a line chart which indicates the income per share for the period 1966–1975.

Year	Income per share	Dividends per share
1966	$2.52	$1.00
1967	2.05	1.15
1968	2.43	1.20
1969	3.21	1.40
1970	2.92	1.40
1971	2.37	1.40
1972	3.01	1.45
1973	4.06	1.51
1974	3.68	1.60
1975	3.43	1.60

2.23 For the per-share data in Exercise 2.22, construct a component bar chart which depicts dividends per share and retained earnings per share for the 10-year period, using vertical bars.

2.24 For the per-share data in Exercise 2.22, construct a percentage pie chart depicting the percentage of income paid as dividends and the percentage retained in the firm during the three-year period 1966–1968. Construct a similar percentage pie chart for the three-year period 1973–1975. Compare the two pie charts.

An average, or "measure of central tendency," is some one value which can be used to represent a collection of observations. In this chapter, we consider the calculation and mathematical criteria associated with the arithmetic mean, median, and mode as measures of central tendency. Because quartiles, deciles, and percentiles are also of interest in descriptive statistics, these measures of relative position are also described in this chapter. In addition to measures of position, another general area of interest in descriptive statistics is the amount of dispersion, or variability, included in a set of data. In this chapter, the measures of dispersion which are described are the range, modified ranges, average deviation, standard deviation, and coefficient of variation. Throughout this chapter it is assumed that the original, observed values in the population or sample are available. In cases in which the values have been grouped in a frequency distribution and are not individually available, the computational methods presented in Chapter 4, Descriptive Measures for Grouped Data, are appropriate. In this context, the data analyzed in this chapter are considered to be *ungrouped* data.

3.1 ■ The Mean, Median, and Mode

The arithmetic mean corresponds to the popular notion of "average," and is thus the sum of all observed values divided by the number of values. The median is the middle value in a set of values arranged in order of magnitude, either lowest to highest or highest to lowest. Such an ordered set is called an *array.* The mode is that value which occurs with greatest frequency in an observed set of values. When one value occurs more frequently than any other value, the distribution of measurements is called *unimodal.* If the values at two different points are at the maximum observed frequency and about equal in occurrence, the distribution of measurements is called *bimodal.* Particularly for a small set of observations it may be that there is no repetition of observed values, in which case no mode exists as a descriptive measure for the group.

the number of measurements

1 For ungrouped data the value of the mean is determined by summing all measurements and dividing by _____ .

2 In general, sample statistics are designated by Roman letters, and population parameters are designated by Greek letters. The arithmetic mean of a sample is represented by the symbol $\overline{X}$ (read: "X bar"), whereas the mean of a population is represented by the symbol μ (read "mū"), which is a [Roman / Greek] letter.

Greek

$\overline{X}$
μ

3 Thus, in order to distinguish the sample mean from the population mean, the sample mean is represented by ___ , and the population mean is represented by ___ .

4 The statistical formula for computing a sample mean is

$$\overline{X} = \frac{\Sigma X}{n}$$

The general symbol X in the formula above denotes each of the n values that is assumed by the variable. Thus, if we have the market price for a share of stock at five different points in time, the values can be represented by the symbols X_1, X_2,

$X_3, X_4; X_5$

___ , ___ , and ___ .

5 In the statistical formula in Frame 4, n represents the total number of observations of X. In the stock-issue example of the same frame, $n = $ ___ (number).

5

6 In the statistical formula for the sample mean, Σ is the uppercase Greek letter sigma, which can be read as "sum of." In this case, then, the letter designates not a population parameter, but an arithmetic operation. ΣX would be read as

sum of X (or sigma X)

_____ .

7 Given the following values for a variable, make the appropriate substitutions in the formula and solve for the value of the sample mean: $X = 8, 6, 2$, and 4.

$\dfrac{20}{4} = 5$

$$\overline{X} = \frac{\Sigma X}{n} =$$

8 Throughout the preceding presentation we have been careful to specify that the formula is used to compute the value of a sample mean, rather than a population mean. However, when the population mean μ is being computed, the only difference in the formula is that N, which signifies number of measurements in the population, is substituted for n, which signifies the number of sample elements. Thus the formula for computing the population mean is

$\dfrac{\Sigma X}{N}$

$$\mu =$$

9 Compute the population mean for the observed values 7, 8, 5, 10, 3, carrying your answer to the first decimal place.

$$\mu =$$

$\dfrac{\Sigma X}{N} = \dfrac{33}{5} = 6.6$ (As a matter of convention, the value of the mean, median, or mode will usually be reported in this book with one additional digit beyond that included in the observed values.)

---

10 We can also take this opportunity to present some additional rules regarding the appropriate use of the summation sign. Two operations which students sometimes confuse with one another are that of summing a group of squared values, designated by ΣX^2, and that of squaring the sum of a group of values, designated by $(\Sigma X)^2$. When the formula reads ΣX^2, we square the value of each variable [before / after] summing; for the formula $(\Sigma X)^2$ we square [each variable / the sum].

---

before

the sum

---

11 Therefore, if X has the values 2, 4, and 6, then

$$\Sigma X =$$
$$\Sigma X^2 =$$
$$(\Sigma X)^2 =$$

---

2 + 4 + 6 = 12

4 + 16 + 36 = 56

12^2 = 144

---

12 Similarly, if a formula indicates that two terms following a summation sign are to be multiplied by one another or divided one by the other, the indicated arithmetic operation must be carried out *before* the summation is done. Thus the expression ΣXY indicates that summation should be carried out [before / after] the value of each X variable is multiplied by the value of the corresponding Y variable.

---

after

---

13 If we wish to sum the values of two variables first, and then multiply the sums, the correct symbolic expression for this operation is $\Sigma X \Sigma Y$ and is read as _____.

---

sum of X times sum of Y

$a\Sigma X$ (Entering the a after the summation sign would indicate that each value of X is multiplied by a before summation.)

---

14 If we wish to multiply the sum of a set of variables X by a constant a, what is the best symbolic way of representing this operation? _____

15 In fact, in Frame 14 the arithmetic result is the same whether each value or the sum is multiplied by the constant a. That is $a\Sigma X = \Sigma aX$. Demonstrate this for the values of $X = 2, 4$, and 6, and with the constant $a = 2$.

$$a\Sigma X =$$

$$\Sigma aX =$$

2(2 + 4 + 6) = 24

2(2) + 2(4) + 2(6) = 24

---

16 If we are simply summing a constant a, the arithmetic result is the same as if we had multiplied a by the number of elements (n or N). That is, $\Sigma a = na$ (or Na). For example, complete the following summation and related calculation.

$$\underline{a}$$

$$7$$
$$7$$
$$7$$
$$\underline{7}$$

28
4 X 7 = 28

$\Sigma a =$ ___

$na =$ ___ X ___ $=$ ____

17 Turning now to the calculation of the median, which is the middle value in an array, does the set of discrete values 7, 8, 5, 10, 3 constitute an array? [Yes / No] Why or why not?

No. Because they are not arranged in order of magnitude.

_____

18 Arrange the values 7, 8, 5, 10, 3 in an array and identify the value of the median. Array = _____ ;

3, 5, 7, 8, 10 (or 10, 8, 7, 5, 3)
7.0

med = ____ .

19 What is the value of the median for the numbers 5, 8, 12, 3, 9? ____ .

8.0 (Do not forget to arrange the numbers in an array before identifying the median.)

20 When there is an even number of measurements rather than an odd number of measurements, there is no one middle value. In such cases the median is assumed to be located midway between the two middle values. Accordingly, what is the value of the median for the numbers 7, 9, 2, 2, 8, 11?

7.5

____

6.0

21 What is the median for the numbers 3, 5, 6, 6, 8, 9? ____

22 Particularly when a large number of measurements is involved, it is convenient to use a position rule for locating the value representing the median of an array of measurements. When a set of measurements is arranged in order of magnitude, from X_1 to X_n, the median can be located by dividing n by 2 and adding ½. Symbolically, Med $= X_{n/2 \ + \ \frac{1}{2}}$. Using this formula, if five measurements are arranged in order of magnitude, which term represents the value of the median?

$X_{5/2\,+\,\frac{1}{2}} = X_3$ (which corresponds to the elements you identified in Frames 21 and 22)

$$\text{Med} = X_{n/2\,+\,\frac{1}{2}} =$$

23 Similarly, which sequentially numbered term represents the median when 135 measurements are arranged in order?

$X_{n/2\,+\,\frac{1}{2}} = X_{135/2\,+\,\frac{1}{2}} = X_{68}$

$$\text{Med} =$$

24 When there is an even number of measurements, the formula indicates that the median is located between two measurements. Thus, if there are 70 measurements,

$X_{70/_2\,+\,\frac{1}{2}} = X_{35\,\frac{1}{2}}$

$$\text{Med} =$$

Since terms do not have fractional sequence numbers, this sequence number indicates that the median is midway between the values of the ___ th and ___ th terms in the array.

35; 36

25 Turning now to the *mode*, which is the most frequently occurring value, what is the mode of the measurements 3, 5, 6, 9, 11, 12, 13? _____.

There is no mode

26 What is the mode for the measurements 3, 3, 3, 4, 4, 6, 7, 9, 9? ___

3.0

27 Since a single mode exists for the data of Frame 26, these measurements can be described as following a _____ distribution.

unimodal

28 On the other hand, the measurements 5, 6, 6, 6, 8, 9, 9, 9, 11, 12 can be described as following a _____ distribution.

bimodal

3.2 ■ Relationship among the Mean, Median, and Mode

In this section we consider the relationship among the mean, median, and mode from both the mathematical and the empirical point of view. First we consider the mathematical criterion, or objective, that is satisfied by each of these measures of central tendency. Then we consider how the values of the mean, median, and mode differ systematically from one another for various types of distributions of measurements.

29 The mean, median, and mode satisfy different mathematical criteria as to what constitutes the typical or average value. For a group of measurements, suppose that we wish to guess at the value of each measurement in turn. Which of the measures of central tendency, when used as the one best guess each time, would lead to the greatest number of guesses being exactly correct? (*Hint*: Consider which type of average indicates the "most frequent" measurement.) [Mean / Median / Mode]

Mode

30 Or, turning the statement about, we can say that the measure of central tendency which results in the smallest *number* of errors when it is used as the one best estimate for every measurement in the group is the [mean / median / mode].

mode

31 Symbolically, the mathematical criterion of a "good" average that is satisfied by the mode can be expressed as $N_e =$ min. That is, when the mode is used as the best estimate of the value of every measurement in a distribution of measurements, the _____ of errors is minimized.

number

32 However, we might take the *magnitude* of each error into consideration in the mathematical criterion. Suppose that e is the amount of error, and $|e|$ is the absolute value of the error without regard to its direction, or arithmetic sign. If we wish to minimize the sum of the errors that are made in estimating the value of each measurement, the mathematical criterion can be symbolically represented by [$\Sigma e^2 =$ min / $\Sigma|e| =$ min / $N_e =$ min].

$\Sigma|e| =$ min

33 The measure of central tendency that satisfies the criterion that the *sum of the absolute errors* be minimized is the median. Thus, if we take any other value in the distribution and use it as the best estimate of every measurement, the arithmetic sum of the absolute values of the errors would be [less / greater] than the sum of the errors when the median is used as the estimate.

greater

34 Symbolically, the mathematical criterion satisfied by the median can be represented by _____ = min.

$\Sigma|e|$

35 Finally, the third major criterion that can be satisfied is that the *sum of the errors squared* be minimized. This criterion is satisfied by the arithmetic mean and can be represented symbolically by ____ = min.

Σe^2

36 When it is used as the basis for estimating the value of every measurement in a distribution, the mean is that value which results in a minimum sum of the _____ .

squared errors

37 The objective of minimizing the sum of squared errors is an important one in statistical analysis, and one that we shall refer to again in later chapters. It is called the *least-squares criterion*. For measures of central tendency the least-squares criterion is satisfied by the [mean / median / mode].

mean

38 Thus there are three major mathematical criteria for determining the location of an average, and the mean, median, and mode are the three values for a collection of measurements that correspond to the requirements of each criterion. Symbolically expressed, the mode satisfies the criterion _____ .

$N_e = \min$

$\Sigma|e| = \min$

39 The median satisfies the symbolic criterion _____ .

$\Sigma e^2 = \min$

40 The mean satisfies the symbolic criterion _____ .

least-squares

41 The criterion indicating that the sum of the squared deviations should be minimized is called the _____ criterion.

Mean

42 Which measure of central tendency would have its value most affected by the addition of a few very high or very low measurements to the distribution being described? (*Hint*: It would have to be one of the two measures of central tendency whose criterion takes the magnitude of error, and not just the number of errors, into consideration.) [Mean / Median / Mode]

squared errors

43 Since the mathematical criterion satisfied by the arithmetic mean concerns not just the sum of the errors, but the sum of the _____ , it is most affected by the addition of a few measurements that are extremely high or low in relation to the general distribution of measurements.

The mode

44 On the other hand, which measure of central tendency is unaffected by the addition of a few measurements at the extreme low or high end of the distribution; i.e., which measure satisfies the mathematical criterion which does not take magnitude of error into account? _____

45 By elimination, since the mode is unaffected by extreme measurements, and since the mean is most affected, the measure of central tendency that is somewhat affected by the addition of measurements to one end of the distribution, but not to the same extent as the arithmetic mean, is the

median

_____ .

46 Let us now illustrate the nature of the effect that we have been considering. Given the following set of sample measurements, determine the values of the mean, median, and mode: $X = 3, 5, 6, 6, 7,$ and 9.

$\dfrac{36}{6} = 6.0$

$$\overline{X} = \frac{\Sigma X}{n} =$$

$X_{3.5} = 6.0$

$$\text{Med} = X_{n/2\,+\,\frac{1}{2}} =$$

6.0 (most frequent measurement)

$$\text{Mode} =$$

47 Though the example in Frame 46 does not, of course, constitute a mathematical proof, it indicates that when the distribution of measurements is symmetrical, the values of the

are equal to one another

mean, median, and mode [differ markedly / are equal to one another].

48 Now suppose we add two measurements to the distribution of six measurements given in Frame 46, and, further, let us give these relatively high values in order to observe the differential effect on the three measures of average. Given the following eight measurements, compute the values of the mean, median, and mode: $X = 3, 5, 6, 6, 7, 9, 16,$ and 20.

$\dfrac{72}{8} = 9.0$

$$\overline{X} = \frac{\Sigma X}{n} =$$

$X_{4.5} = 6.5$

$$\text{Med} = X_{n/2\,+\,\frac{1}{2}} =$$

6.0

$$\text{Mode} =$$

49 Thus, comparing the measures of central tendency for the simplified data of Frames 46 and 48, we find that the measure of average which is most affected by the addition of extreme

mean

median

mode

measurements is the _____ ; the measure which is only somewhat affected is the _____ ; the measure which is unaffected is the _____ .

50 We can also illustrate these differential effects graphically. For the following symmetrical frequency curve, indicate the relative positions of the mean, median, and mode of the distribution.

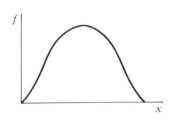

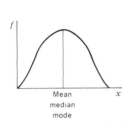

(all at the same point)

51 On the following frequency curve representing a positively skewed distribution of measurements, indicate the relative positions of the mean, median, and mode.

mode; median; mean
(from left to right)

52 Similarly, for the following negatively skewed distribution, indicate the relative positions of the mean, median, and mode.

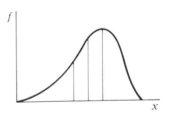

mean; median; mode
(from left to right)

53 Therefore the relationship among the values of the three principal measures of central tendency is indicative of the direction and extent of departure from symmetry of the distribution of measurements. When the values of the mean, median, and mode are all identical, the distribution is _____ . When the mean is the largest in value (and the median is larger than the mode), the distribution is

symmetrical

positively skewed

negatively skewed

_____ . When the mean is smallest in value the distribution is _____ .

54 Which measure of central tendency represents the best average depends on whether or not the distribution of measurements is skewed and on the intended use of the average. For example, given the following distribution of per-family income in a small community, which measure of central tendency would be most representative if we wish to use average family income as one basis for deciding whether or not to locate a retail outlet in the community? [Mean / Median / Mode] Why?

Median or Mode (Clearly, the mean would be misleading. Whether the median or the mode is preferable depends on the customer group to which the store will cater. If most families need to be in a particular income bracket for the store to be successful, then the mode would be the preferred measure.)

_____
_____
_____
_____
_____

Annual family income	Number of families
Under $8,000	25
$8,000–$10,999	40
$11,000–$13,999	50
$14,000–$16,999	30
$17,000–$19,999	30
$20,000–$24,999	10
$25,000–$49,999	5
$50,000–$99,999	5
$100,000+	5

55 For most descriptive purposes, the median is a better indicator of the "typical value" in a group than is the mean. The main reason is that the median is [more / less] affected by a few extremely low or extremely high values.

less

56 Even though the mean can be misleading as an indicator of what is typical, it is the most frequently used indicator when statistical analysis is directed toward inference rather than simply description. One reason for this is that in the context of statistical inference, the distributions about which we are concerned typically are symmetrical. Another reason is that the mathematical criterion satisfied by the mean—i.e., the

_____ criterion—is mathematically consistent with other statistical measures to be discussed in later chapters.

3.3 ■ The Quartiles and Other Position Measures

Quartiles, deciles, and percentiles are similar to the median in that they also subdivide a total distribution of measurements. Whereas the median divides a distribution into two halves, the quartiles divide it into four quarters, the deciles divide it into 10 tenths, and the percentile points divide it into 100 parts.

57 For the median, as for other measures of position, it is important to remember that the distribution of measurements is divided into equal portions not in terms of the number of measurement *units* on either side of the median, but in terms of the actual *frequency* of measurements on either side of the median. Thus, if the lowest possible value of a measurement is 20.0 and the highest possible value is 80.0, the median [would / would not] necessarily be located at 50.0.

58 Similarly, the quartiles divide a distribution into four quarters not in terms of the number of possible units of measurement included in each portion, but in terms of the _____ of measurements in each portion of the distribution.

59 If the one point that corresponds to the median divides the distribution into two equal halves, how many points need to be identified in order to divide a distribution into four quarters containing equal numbers of observed measurements? ___ (number)

60 Accordingly, the first, second, and third quartiles are represented by the symbols Q_1, Q_2, and Q_3, respectively. Located below the point of Q_1 are 25 percent of the measurements; 50 percent of the measurements are located below Q_2; and ___ percent of the measurements are located below Q_3.

61 Since 50 percent of the measurements are located below Q_2, to what measure of central tendency does the value of Q_2 correspond? _____

The median

62 The modification of the formula for the median in order to determine the values of the quartiles is relatively simple. For ungrouped data, where $\text{Med} = X_{n/2 + \frac{1}{2}}$,

$X_{3n/4 + \frac{1}{2}}$ (since the value of the subscript should indicate the position of the term in the array)

$$Q_1 = X_{n/4 + \frac{1}{2}} \qquad Q_2 = X_{n/2 + \frac{1}{2}} \qquad Q_3 =$$

63 For the array of values 3, 5, 6, 7, 7, 8, 9, 11, determine the values of the median and the three quartiles.

$X_{4\frac{1}{2}} = 7.0$

$X_{2\frac{1}{2}} = 5.5$

$X_{4\frac{1}{2}} = 7.0$

$X_{6\frac{1}{2}} = 8.5$

$$\text{Med} = X_{n/2 + \frac{1}{2}} =$$

$$Q_1 = X_{n/4 + \frac{1}{2}} =$$

$$Q_2 = X_{n/2 + \frac{1}{2}} =$$

$$Q_3 = X_{3n/4 + \frac{1}{2}} =$$

64 Referring to the values of the quartiles just determined, what is the percentage of measurements in the array with a value below 8.5? _____ percent.

75

65 Given the fact that deciles are the points that divide a distribution of measurements into 10 equal portions, in terms of the frequencies of the measurements, what is the formula for locating the position of the fourth decile in an array of ungrouped measurements, given that $\text{Med} = X_{n/2 + \frac{1}{2}}$?

$X_{4n/10 + \frac{1}{2}}$
(or $X_{2n/5 + \frac{1}{2}}$)

$$D_4 =$$

66 Similarly, what is the formula for determining the value at the eighty-fifth percentile point?

$X_{85n/100 + \frac{1}{2}}$

$$P_{85} =$$

3.4 ■ The Ranges

The measure of dispersion that is the easiest to compute is the range. Represented by R, it is simply the difference between the highest value and the lowest value in a collection of measurements. Because the value of the range is affected by even one extreme value, various modified ranges, such as the middle 80 percent range, are frequently computed.

67 L stands for the lowest value in a collection of measurements and H stands for the highest value. Since R is always a positive quantity, the formula that is used for computing the value of the range is $R =$ ___ − ___ .

$H - L$

68 Compute the range for the following values: 8, 10, 14, 2, 8, 12, 13.

$14 - 2 = 12$

$R = H - L =$ ___ − ___ = ___

69 The range is a crude measure of dispersion in that it is unstable. Specifically, its value depends entirely on just the two extreme measurements in the group, and thus one unusually high or low measurement affects the value of the range markedly. For example, the value that is unusually different from the others in the group of measurements given in Frame 68 is ___ (value).

2

70 If the "2" is removed from the group of measurements given in Frame 2, the resulting value of the range is _____ (value) instead of 12.

$14 - 8 = 6$

71 Because unusual and extreme values can markedly affect the value of the range, *modified ranges* are sometimes used instead. A modified range is a range for which a certain proportion of the extreme values on both ends of the array has been eliminated. For example, the "middle 90 percent range" is an example of a _____ .

modified range

72 The three modified ranges most frequently used are the middle 90 percent, middle 80 percent, and middle 50 percent. The middle 90 percent range eliminates 5 percent of the values at each end of the array, the middle 80 percent eliminates ___ percent at each end from consideration, and the middle 50 percent eliminates ___ percent at each end.

10
25

73 In order to compute a modified range, it is first necessary to solve for the appropriate percentile points. The difference between the values for the two percentile points is then the modified range. For example, in order to determine the middle

80 percent range, we first need to determine the values at the tenth percentile point and the _____ percentile point of the distribution.

74 The computation of percentile points is described in Section 3.3, and the computation of a modified range is illustrated in Exercise 3.6 at the end of this chapter. As indicated above, the three modified ranges used most frequently for descriptive purposes are the middle ____ percent, middle ____ percent, and middle ____ percent ranges.

3.5 ■ The Average Deviation

The value of the range is based on the location of the two extreme measurements in a group, whereas the value of a modified range is based on the location of the two end points after a certain percentage of the extreme values has been eliminated. Computation of the average deviation, or AD, on the other hand, takes the value of every measurement in the group into consideration. The value of AD is based on the difference, or deviation, between the arithmetic mean of a group of measurements and each of the measurements in that group.

75 Before we introduce the procedure used to compute the value of the average deviation, we first introduce the concept of a *deviation*. Unless otherwise indicated, this term always refers to the difference between a measurement and the mean of the group from which the measurement is taken. Furthermore, it is always the mean that is subtracted from the individual value, and not the other way around. Thus a positive deviation always indicates that the variable in question is [smaller / larger] than the mean, and a negative deviation always indicates that the measurement is [smaller / larger] than the mean.

76 Given the following array of population data, indicate the value of the deviation associated with each measurement.

X	$(X - \mu)$
4	_____
4	_____
6	_____
7	_____
9	_____
$\Sigma X = 30$	

77 As the name implies, the average deviation is a kind of arithmetic mean of all the deviation scores. What is the arithmetic mean of the deviation values in Frame 76?

$$\frac{0}{5} = 0$$

$$\frac{\Sigma(X - \mu)}{N} =$$

78 The sum of the deviations from the mean *always* equals zero, and therefore the average deviation is computed somewhat differently from the way that we might at first suppose. In computing the value of the mean deviation, we sum the *absolute* values of the deviations without regard to sign, rather than the signed deviation values. Thus the formulas that are used to compute the value of the average deviation for a population and for a sample are, respectively:

$$\frac{\Sigma|X - \mu|}{N}$$

Population AD =

$$\frac{\Sigma|X - \bar{X}|}{n}$$

Sample AD =

79 For the data of Frame 76, which are repeated below, complete the last column of the table and compute the value of AD, carrying your answer to the first decimal place.

	X	$X - \mu$	$|X - \mu|$
2	4	−2	_____
2	4	−2	_____
0	6	0	_____
1	7	+1	_____
3	9	+3	_____
8		$\Sigma|X - \mu| =$	

$$\frac{\Sigma|X - \mu|}{N} = \frac{8}{5} = 1.6$$

AD =

3.6 ■ The Standard Deviation

The standard deviation is the most important of the measures of dispersion because of its use in statistical inference. It is similar to the average deviation in that its computation is based upon the deviations of individual measurements from a group mean. The standard deviation of a sample is represented by the lowercase letter *s*; the standard deviation of a population of measurements is represented by the lowercase Greek letter σ (sigma). Of course, the uppercase Greek letter Σ (sigma) is used to represent the process of summation.

80 Whereas the computation of the average deviation requires the summation of the *absolute values* of the deviations, the computation of the standard deviation requires summation of the *squares* of the deviations. Therefore, the fact that deviations can be positive or negative [does / does not] present a problem in the computation of the standard deviation.

> does not (since the square of either a positive or a negative value is itself always positive)

81 For population data, the formula for the standard deviation is

$$\sigma = \sqrt{\frac{\Sigma(X - \mu)^2}{N}}$$

Thus the population standard deviation can be described as being the square root of the mean of the squared deviations. In Section 3.5 the average deviation for the following ungrouped measurements was found to be 1.6. Compute the value of the standard deviation, carrying your answer to the first place beyond the decimal.

X	$(X - \mu)$	$(X - \mu)^2$
4	−2	_____
4	−2	_____
6	0	_____
7	1	_____
9	3	_____
	$\Sigma(X - \mu)^2 =$	

> 4
> 4
> 0
> 1
> 9
> $\overline{18}$

> $\sqrt{\dfrac{18}{5}} = \sqrt{3.6} = 1.9$

$$\sigma = \sqrt{\frac{\Sigma(X - \mu)^2}{N}} =$$

82 For sample data, the formula for the sample standard deviation is

$$s = \sqrt{\frac{\Sigma(X - \bar{X})^2}{n - 1}}$$

The reason that the denominator in this formula differs from the formula for the population standard deviation and includes "−1" is that without this difference, the sample standard deviation is biased as an estimator of the population standard deviation. Because the sample standard deviation is always used to estimate the population value, the "correction factor" included in the formula above is always appropriate to improve this estimator. For the following sample data, compute the sample standard deviation.

$$\bar{X} = \frac{48}{6} = 8.0$$

$(X - \bar{X})^2$	X
9	5
1	7
0	8
0	8
1	9
_9_	11
20	

$$\sqrt{\frac{20}{6-1}} = \sqrt{4.0} = 2.0$$

$$s = \sqrt{\frac{\Sigma(X - \bar{X})^2}{n - 1}} =$$

83 The formulas that we have used thus far to compute the value of the standard deviation are referred to as *deviations formulas*. In using these formulas, the first step in the computational procedure is that every observed measurement has the value of the group _____ subtracted from it.

mean

84 The arithmetic means for the data that we have worked with in this section have all been integers (whole numbers). Is the arithmetic required in the computation of the standard deviation more involved when the mean has a fractional value? [Yes / No]
Why or why not? _____

Yes

Because the deviations would be fractional values and each of these has to be squared.

85 Because of the arithmetic difficulty typically involved in using the deviations formulas for the standard deviation, *computational formulas* have been derived to simplify the necessary calculations. For population and sample data the computational formulas are, respectively:

$$\sigma = \sqrt{\frac{\Sigma X^2 - N\mu^2}{N}}$$

$$s = \sqrt{\frac{\Sigma X^2 - n\bar{X}^2}{n-1}}$$

These formulas may appear to be more complex than the deviations formulas, but they are computationally easier to use because they do not require determination of _____ from the mean.

deviations	

86 Using the population data from Frame 81, complete the following table to obtain the needed values for using the computational formula for the standard deviation.

X	X^2
4	___
4	___
6	___
7	___
9	___
$\Sigma X = $ ___	$\Sigma X^2 = $ ___

X	X²
16	
16	
36	
49	
81	
30	198

$$\frac{30}{5} = 6.0$$

$$\mu = \frac{\Sigma X}{N} =$$

87 Now determine the value of the standard deviation for the data in Frame 86, using the computational formula.

$$\sqrt{\frac{198 - (5)(36)}{5}} = \sqrt{\frac{18}{5}} =$$
$$\sqrt{3.6} = 1.9$$

$$\sigma = \sqrt{\frac{\Sigma X^2 - N\mu^2}{N}} =$$

88 Similarly, compute the sample standard deviation for the following measurements, using the formula given in Frame 85.

X
5
7
8
8
9
11

X²
25
49
64
64
81
121
$\Sigma X = 48 \quad \Sigma X^2 = 404$

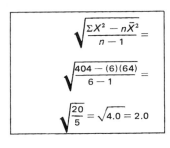

$$s = \sqrt{\frac{\Sigma X^2 - n\bar{X}^2}{n-1}} =$$

$$\sqrt{\frac{404 - (6)(64)}{6-1}} =$$

$$\sqrt{\frac{20}{5}} = \sqrt{4.0} = 2.0$$

89 We shall have to wait until Chapter 6 before we can fully illustrate the use of the standard deviation. By knowing the values of the mean and standard deviation for a set of measurements, we can often determine the percentage, or proportion, of measurements that is included within a specified distance from the mean. If we know the percentage of measurements included within a specified distance from the mean, we can also determine the percentage of measurements located outside of these limits by subtracting the known percentage from _____ (value).

100

90 For example, it is known that for a distribution of measurements whose frequency curve is both symmetrical and mesokurtic, 68 percent of the measurements are located within one standard deviation of the mean. Or, putting it another way, the interval that is defined by subtracting the value of the standard deviation from the mean and adding the value of the standard deviation to the mean includes 68 percent of the measurements for such a distribution. Thus, if the mean of a set of measurements is 100.0 and the standard deviation is 15.0, 68 percent of the measurements would be included between the values of _____ (value) and _____ (value).

85.0; 115.0 (Incidentally, these are the values of the population mean and standard deviation for many IQ tests.)

91 For a symmetrical and mesokurtic distribution, if 68 percent of the measurements are located between the limits of 100.0 ± 15.0, what percentage would be located outside of these limits? _____ percent. What percentage would be located above 115.0? _____ percent.

(100 − 68 =) 32

16 (The other 16 percent is below 85.0.)

92 The diagram below graphically illustrates the example that we have been discussing. On this frequency curve enter the percentages of measurements that would be located within the four intervals that are separated by the vertical lines on the curve, remembering that the interval $\mu \pm \sigma$ includes 68 percent of the measurements.

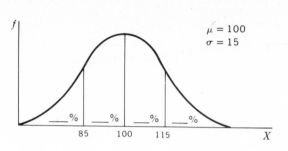

16; 34; 34; 16	

93 A frequency curve that is both symmetrical and meso-kurtic is called a *normal curve*. It is the most important type of curve from the standpoint of its use in statistical inference, and one which we consider much more fully in Chapter 7. As we have illustrated in the preceding frames, when we know that a distribution of measurements follows a normal curve, then we can designate the _____ of measurements included within a specified range of values.

percentage (or proportion, or number)

94 In discussing the nature of the standard deviation, we can also take note of a mathematical similarity to the mean. As you may recall from Section 3.2, the three principal measures of central tendency satisfy different mathematical criteria. The mathematical criterion satisfied by the mean is symbolically represented by ($N_e = \min / \Sigma_{|e|} = \min / \Sigma e^2 = \min$).

$\Sigma e^2 = \min$

95 The mathematical criterion which results in a minimum sum of the squared errors is called the _____ criterion.

least-squares

96 Now, if we substitute the term "errors" for "deviations," the measure of dispersion which uses the sum of the squared errors in its computation is the _____.

standard deviation

97 For many advanced applications in statistics, the square of the standard deviation, which is called the *variance*, is useful as a measure of dispersion. By reference to the computational formulas given in Frame 85, the computational formulas for the population and sample variance are, respectively:

$\dfrac{\Sigma X^2 - N\mu^2}{N}$ $\sigma^2 =$

$\dfrac{\Sigma X^2 - n\bar{X}^2}{n-1}$ $s^2 =$

3.7 ▪ The Coefficient of Variation

The range, modified ranges, average deviation, and standard deviation are all *absolute* measures of dispersion, in that they are expressed in terms of the particular measuring units used in collecting a set of data. On the other hand, the *coefficient of variation*, represented by the abbreviation CV, is a relative measure of dispersion. Its value is not expressed in terms of any particular unit of measurement, but as a ratio between two values. As such, it is very useful in comparing the dispersion of groups of measurements that are otherwise noncomparable.

98 For population data the coefficient of variation is defined by $CV = \sigma/\mu$, and for sample data it is defined by $CV = s/\bar{X}$. Thus, when we say that the coefficient of variation is a relative measure of dispersion, we mean that the value of the standard deviation is considered relative to the size (value) of the _____ of the distribution.

mean

99 If the sample mean of a distribution is 100.0 and the standard deviation is 15.0, the value of the coefficient of variation is

$\dfrac{15.0}{100.0} = 0.15$

$$CV = \frac{s}{\bar{X}} =$$

100 Using the coefficient of variation, we can compare the dispersion of two distributions that would otherwise be noncomparable. For example, suppose that during a particular sampled month stock issue A had a mean price of $150 with a standard deviation of $12 and stock issue B had a mean daily market price of $5 with a standard deviation of $1. In dollar terms, which stock experienced more variability in its daily market price (A / B)

A

101 Stock A certainly fluctuated more in terms of actual dollar changes, but your immediate reaction is probably that this is not the proper basis for comparison and that the dollar fluctuations relative to the average prices are more relevant. Of course, this is the basis for the coefficient of variation. Accordingly, compute the following values, using the data from Frame 100:

$\dfrac{s}{\bar{X}} = \dfrac{12.00}{150.00} = 0.08$

$$CV \text{ (stock } A) =$$

$$\frac{s}{\bar{X}} = \frac{1.00}{5.00} = 0.20$$

CV (stock B) =

$$\frac{0.20}{0.08} = 2.5$$

102 In regard to the respective average prices of stocks A and B, therefore, more variability in market price has been experienced by stock B. Relatively speaking, stock B was _____ (number) times as variable as stock A.

---

relative

103 Whereas the range, modified ranges, average deviation, and standard deviation are all absolute measures of dispersion, the coefficient of variation is a _____ measure of dispersion.

Review

104 (Frames 1-16) Below, post the formulas for computing the sample mean and the population mean.

$$\frac{\Sigma X}{n}$$

$\bar{X} =$

$$\frac{\Sigma X}{N}$$

$\mu =$

---

105 (Frames 17-24) The position rule for locating the median is symbolically represented by

$X_{n/2\ +\ \frac{1}{2}}$

Med =

---

79 and 87 (a bimodal distribution)

106 (Frames 25-28) Identify the values of the mode for the measurements 75, 79, 79, 83, 87, 87, 94. Mode = _____ .

Σe^2 ; $\Sigma |e|$

N_e

107 (Frames 29-40) In terms of the mathematical criteria satisfied by the three principal types of averages, for the mean: _____ = min; for the median: _____ = min; and for the mode: _____ = min.

---

least-squares

108 (Frames 41, 56) The mathematical criterion satisfied by the arithmetic mean is popularly referred to as the _____ criterion.

---

mode; mean

109 (Frames 42-49) The average which is least affected by extreme values on one "side" of the distribution is the _____ ; the one which is most affected is the _____ .

---

positively skewed	
negatively skewed	
symmetrical	

110 (Frames 50-53) When the mean is larger in value than the median (and the median is larger than the mode), the frequency curve representing the data can be described as being _____ ; and when the mean is smaller in value than the median, the distribution is _____ _____. When all the measures of central tendency have the same value, the distribution is _____.

median

mean

111 (Frames 54-56) In general, the measure of central tendency which best describes the "typical" value in a collection of measurements is the _____. The measure of central tendency which is most useful in the context of using probability theory for the purpose of statistical inference is the _____.

would not

112 (Frames 57, 58) Given a nonsymmetrical distribution in which the lowest-valued measurement equals 50 and the highest-valued measurement equals 100, the median of the distribution [would / would not] usually be located at 75.

113 (Frames 59-66) For measurements listed in an array, indicate below the formulas to be used for locating the position in the array of Q_3 and D_3.

$X_{3n/4 + \frac{1}{2}}$

$Q_3 =$

$X_{3n/10 + \frac{1}{2}}$

$D_3 =$

the highest observed value minus the lowest observed value

114 (Frames 67-70) The range as a measure of dispersion is equal to _____ _____ .

modified

115 (Frames 71-74) The middle 90 percent, middle 80 percent, and middle 50 percent ranges are examples of what are called _____ ranges.

absolute values (of the deviations)

116 (Frames 75-79) In the formula for AD, whether for population or sample data, it is not the values of the deviations that are averaged but the _____ _____ that are averaged.

s
σ

117 (Frames 80-82) The standard deviation of a sample is represented by the symbol __, and the standard deviation of a population is represented by the symbol __.

118 (Frames 83–88) Other than the value of n (or N), the *computational formulas* for the standard deviation require determination of the sum of the measurements and the sum of the squared measurements, whereas the *deviations formulas* require just the sum of the squared deviations. Why, then, do the deviations formulas usually involve greater arithmetic difficulty? _____

_____ .

> The deviations, which have to be squared, are usually fractional values.

119 (Frames 89–97) For a set of population measurements that is normally distributed, the interval defined by $\mu \pm$ ___ includes 68 percent of the measurements.

> σ

120 (Frames 98–103) The measure of variation that is relative rather than absolute is CV, the coefficient of _____. Its computation involves determining the ratio of the standard deviation to the _____ of the distribution of measurements.

> variation
>
> mean

Symbols Introduced in This Chapter (with Frame Numbers)

(2)	$\overline{X}$	The arithmetic mean of a sample.
(2)	μ	The arithmetic mean of a population of values.
(4)	X	A random variable.
(5)	n	The number of observations in a sample.
(6)	Σ	The uppercase Greek letter "sigma," indicating "sum of."
(8)	N	The number of elements in a designated population.
(22)	Med	Median
(60)	Q_1	First quartile.
(60)	Q_2	Second quartile.
(60)	Q_3	Third quartile.
(65)	D_4	The fourth decile.
(66)	P_{85}	85th percentile point.
(67)	L	The lowest value in a set of values.
(67)	H	The highest value in a set of values.
(67)	R	The range.
(78)	AD	Average deviation.

(81)	σ	The lowercase Greek letter "sigma," which designates the standard deviation of a population of values.
(92)	s	Standard deviation of a sample.
(97)	σ^2	Population variance.
(97)	s^2	Sample variance.
(98)	CV	Coefficient of variation.

Formulas Introduced in This Chapter (with Frame Numbers)

(4)	$\bar{X} = \dfrac{\Sigma X}{n}$	Sample mean.
(8)	$\mu = \dfrac{\Sigma X}{N}$	Population mean.
(22)	$\text{Med} = X_{n/2\,+\,\frac{1}{2}}$	Position of the median in an array.
(25)	$\text{Mode} = \text{most frequent value}$	Mode for ungrouped data.
(62)	$Q_1 = X_{n/4\,+\,1/2}$	Positions of the first, second, and third quartiles in an array.
(62)	$Q_2 = X_{n/2\,+\,1/2}$	
(62)	$Q_3 = X_{3n/4\,+\,1/2}$	
(65)	$D_4 = X_{4n/10\,+\,1/2}$	Position of the fourth decile in an array. Used to illustrate how the formula for the median can be modified to determine the value at any decile or percentile point.
(66)	$P_{85} = X_{85n/100\,+\,\frac{1}{2}}$	Position of the eighty-fifth percentile point.
(68)	$R = H - L$	Range for a set of values.
(78)	$\text{AD} = \dfrac{\Sigma\lvert X - \mu\rvert}{N}$	Average deviation for a population.
(78)	$\text{AD} = \dfrac{\Sigma\lvert X - \bar{X}\rvert}{n}$	Average deviation for a sample.
(81)	$\sigma = \sqrt{\dfrac{\Sigma(X - \mu)^2}{N}}$	Population standard deviation, deviations formula.
(82)	$s = \sqrt{\dfrac{\Sigma(X - \bar{X})^2}{n - 1}}$	Sample standard deviation, deviations formula.

(85) $\sigma = \sqrt{\dfrac{\Sigma X^2 - N\mu^2}{N}}$ Population standard deviation, computational formula.

(85) $s = \sqrt{\dfrac{\Sigma X^2 - n\bar{X}^2}{n-1}}$ Sample standard deviation, computational formula.

(97) $\sigma^2 = \dfrac{\Sigma X^2 - N\mu^2}{N}$ Population variance.

(97) $s^2 = \dfrac{\Sigma X^2 - n\bar{X}^2}{n-1}$ Sample variance.

(98) $CV = \dfrac{\sigma}{\mu}$ Coefficient of variation for a population.

(98) $CV = \dfrac{s}{\bar{X}}$ Coefficient of variation for a sample.

EXERCISES

(Solutions on pages 590–592)

3.1 For the data below, reporting employees' absences in a particular department during a three-month period, determine the values of the mean, median, and mode. The number of days absent is reported to the nearest half-day.

Employee identification number	Number of days absent
001	5.0
002	0.0
003	1.5
004	3.0
005	1.0
006	2.0
007	9.0
008	5.5
009	1.0
010	4.0
011	2.0
012	2.0

3.2 Comment upon and interpret the differences in the values of the mean, median, and mode computed in Exercise 3.1. Which of these values best represents the "typical" number of days that employees were absent?

3.3 Compute and interpret the values of Q_1, Q_2, and Q_3 for the data in Exercise 3.1.

3.4 Compute and interpret the value of D_7 for the data in Exercise 3.1.

3.5 Compute the (a) range and (b) average deviation for the data in Exercise 3.1.

3.6 Determine the middle 90 percent range for the data in Exercise 3.1.

3.7 Determine the value of the population standard deviation for the data in Exercise 3.1 by using the deviations form of the formula.

3.8 Determine the standard deviation for the data in Exercise 3.1 by using the computational formula.

3.9 Compute the value of the coefficient of variation for the data in Exercise 3.1.

3.10 Describe the similarities and the differences among the median, the quartiles, the deciles, and the percentiles as descriptive measures of position.

3.11 Throughout the remainder of this book the mean is used as the measure of central tendency. Why, then, is it considered worthwhile to discuss the computation of the median and the mode in the present chapter?

3.12 In general, which of the measures of dispersion best describes the amount of variability in a set of data?

ADDITIONAL EXERCISES

3.13 The following table reports the number of components assembled during a series of working days considered to be a statistical population. Determine the values of the mean, median, and mode for these data.

Day	Units assembled
1	8
2	7
3	7
4	6
5	8
6	7
7	9
8	7
9	6
10	6

3.14 Compute and interpret the values of Q_1 and Q_3 for the data in Exercise 3.13.

3.15 Compute and interpret the value of the eighth decile for the data in Exercise 3.13.

3.16 Determine the values of the (a) range and (b) average deviation for the data in Exercise 3.13.

3.17 Compute the population standard deviation for the data in Exercise 3.13, using the deviations form of the formula.

3.18 Determine the coefficient of variation for the data in Exercise 3.13.

3.19 The number of cars sold by each of the 10 salespeople in an automobile dealership during a particular month, arranged in ascending order, is: 2, 4, 7, 10, 10, 10, 12, 12, 14, 15. Considering the month to be the statistical population of interest, determine the (a) mean, (b) median, and (c) mode for the number of cars sold.

3.20 Which value in Exercise 3.19 best describes the "typical" sales volume per salesperson?

3.21 For the data in Exercise 3.19, determine the values at the (a) first quartile, (b) second decile, and (c) thirtieth percentile point for these sales amounts.

3.22 For the data in Exercise 3.19, determine the (a) range and (b) middle 80 percent range for these data.

3.23 Compute the average deviation for the sales data in Exercise 3.19. The mean for these values was determined to be 9.6 in Exercise 3.19.

3.24 Determine the standard deviation for the data in Exercise 3.19 by using the deviations formula and considering the group of values as constituting a statistical population.

3.25 The weights of a sample of outgoing packages in a mailroom, weighed to the nearest ounce, are found to be: 21, 18, 30, 12, 14, 17, 28, 10, 16, 25. Determine the (a) mean, (b) median, and (c) mode for these weights.

3.26 For the data in Exercise 3.25, determine the weights at the (a) third quartile, (b) third decile, and (c) 70th percentile point.

3.27 Determine the (a) range and (b) middle 50 percent range for the weights reported in Exercise 3.25.

3.28 Compute the average deviation for the sampled packages in Exercise 3.25.

3.29 Determine the (a) sample variance and (b) sample standard deviation for the data in Exercise 3.25 by use of the computational versions of the respective formulas.

3.30 The following examination scores, arranged in ascending order, were achieved by 20 students enrolled in a decision analysis course: 39, 46, 57, 65, 70, 72, 72, 75, 77, 79, 81, 81, 84, 84, 84, 87, 93, 94, 97, 97. Considering this group to be the statistical population of interest, determine the (a) mean, (b) median, and (c) mode for these scores.

3.31 Describe the distribution of test scores in Exercise 3.30 in terms of skewness.

3.32 Determine the (a) second quartile, (b) ninth decile, and (c) fiftieth percentile point for the scores in Exercise 3.30.

3.33 Determine the (a) range and (b) the middle 90 percent range for the scores in Exercise 3.30.

3.34 Compute the average deviation for the examination scores in Exercise 3.30.

3.35 Considering the examination scores in Exercise 3.30 to be a statistical population, determine the standard deviation by use of (a) the deviations formula and (b) the alternative computational formula.

CHAPTER 4 ■

DESCRIPTIVE MEASURES FOR GROUPED DATA

In this chapter we present the formulas and computational procedures for determining averages, position measures, and measures of dispersion for data that have been grouped. Because the process of grouping observed values into frequency distributions involves a loss of precision in terms of the individual measurements, descriptive measures based on grouped data are approximations of the measures that would be obtained for the original, ungrouped data. Historically, these approximations have often been used because of the reduced calculations for large data sets, but the widespread availability of computers and electronic calculators makes this reason less important. However, published data may only be available in grouped form, and in this case the methods presented in this chapter are appropriate. As in Chapter 3 for ungrouped data, the measures of central tendency which are described are the mean, median, and mode. Then the computational procedures for determining quartiles, deciles, and percentiles are presented. Finally, the measures of dispersion which are covered are the range, modified ranges, average deviation, and standard deviation.

4.1 ■ The Mean, Median, and Mode

For grouped data, the midpoint of each class is taken to represent every value in that class when computing the mean. In computing the median, the class which contains the middle value in the array is first identified, and then the position of that value within the class is determined by interpolation. For the mode, the class with the highest observed frequency is first identified, and the point of the mode is identified by reference to the observed frequencies in the two classes which adjoin the modal class.

1 When data are grouped in a frequency distribution, each class midpoint, which is represented simply by the symbol X, is taken to be representative of all measurements included in the class. The value of each class midpoint is multiplied by the frequency of measurements included in that class in order to determine the sum of the measurements included in a class. For grouped data the formula for the sample mean is thus

$$\bar{X} = \frac{\Sigma f X}{n}$$

similarly, for the population mean the formula is

$$\frac{\Sigma f X}{N} \qquad \mu =$$

2 Thus, whenever an f is included in the formula for the arithmetic mean, this indicates that the formula is to be used with [ungrouped / grouped] data.

3 Because of the placement of the summation sign in the numerator of the formula $\bar{X} = \Sigma fX/n$, summation should be carried out [before / after] multiplication of each class midpoint by its associated frequency.

4 Complete the following table as the first step toward computing the arithmetic mean for these grouped data.

Class limits	Class midpoint, X	f	fX
6–8	7	4	28
9–11	10	6	60
12–14	13	7	91
15–17	16	4	——
18–20	19	3	——
		$n = \Sigma f = 24$	$\Sigma fX =$ ——

5 Compute the sample mean for the data in Frame 4, carrying your answer to the first decimal place.

$\bar{X} =$

6 Therefore, when computing the mean for grouped data, the _____ of each class is used to approximate all of the measurements included in that class.

7 For the median, the first step in determining the value of the median is to identify the class in which the median is located. Since the median is at the middle of an array of measurements, it is useful to compute the cumulative frequency for each class in the frequency distribution so that the class containing the middle value in the distribution of measurements can be identified. The cumulative frequency for a class includes not only the number of measurements in that class but also the observed frequencies of all classes "below" that class. Accordingly, complete the cumulative-frequency (cf) column in the table below.

Class limits	f	cf
6-8	4	4
9-11	6	10
12-14	7	17
15-17	4	—
18-20	3	—
	$\Sigma f = 24$	

21

24

8 The class containing the median is the first class whose cumulative frequency cf is equal to or exceeds the sum of the frequencies divided by 2. Thus, for the data in Frame 7, we identify the median class by first determining which class is the first to have a cumulative frequency equal to or greater than ____ (number).

12 (which is 24 divided by 2)

9 For the data in Frame 7 the class containing the median is the class whose limits are ____ (number) and ____ (number).

12; 14

10 In determining the position of the median within the class containing it, two assumptions are made. The first is that the measurements included in a class are equally dispersed in it, and the second is that measurement is continuous rather than discrete. Since we are suggesting that interpolation should be used to locate the median, the alternative assumption that the midpoint of the median class represents the value of the median [is / is not] equally acceptable.

is not

11 The formula used for interpolation in determining the value of the median for the grouped data is

$$\text{Med} = B_L + \left(\frac{n/2 - cf_B}{f_c} \right) i$$

where $n = \Sigma f$. In this formula B_L is the lower boundary of the class containing the median. For the data of Table 4-1, therefore, $B_L =$ _____ (number).

11.5

Table 4-1 ■ A Frequency Distribution for Continuous Data

Class limits	Boundaries	X	f	cf
6-8	5.5-8.5	7	4	4
9-11	8.5-11.5	10	6	10
12-14	11.5-14.5	13	7	17
15-17	14.5-17.5	16	4	21
18-20	17.5-20.5	19	3	24

12 In the formula in Frame 11, cf_B is the cumulative frequency of the class before the median class. By "before" we mean the adjacent class whose midpoint has a lower value than that of the median class. For the data of Table 4-1, cf_B = ____ (number).

10

13 In the formula

$$Med = B_L + \left(\frac{n/2 - cf_B}{f_c}\right)i$$

the observed frequency in the median class is designated f_c. For the data of Table 4-1, f_c = ____ (number).

7

14 Finally, i in the formula for determining the value of the median for grouped data indicates the size of the class interval containing the median. In Table 4-1, i = ____ (number).

3

15 Determine the value of the median for the data of Table 4-1, carrying your answer to the first decimal place.

$11.5 + \left(\dfrac{12 - 10}{7}\right)3 = 12.4$

$$Med = B_L + \left(\frac{n/2 - cf_B}{f_c}\right)i =$$

16 Similarly, determine the value of the median for the data in the following frequency distribution.

Class limits	Class boundaries	X	f	cf
1-2	0.5-2.5	1.5	2	2
3-4	2.5-4.5	3.5	5	7
5-6	4.5-6.5	5.5	15	22
7-8	6.5-8.5	7.5	10	32
9-10	8.5-10.5	9.5	5	37

$4.5 + \left(\dfrac{18.5 - 7}{15}\right)2 = 6.0$

$$Med = B_L + \left(\frac{n/2 - cf_B}{f_c}\right)i =$$

17 In determining the mode for grouped data, one approach which is used is to accept the midpoint of the modal class as the best estimate. Rather than following this convention however, we determine the location of the mode by interpolation on the basis of the frequencies of measurements in the two classes adjoining the modal class. The formula used is

$$Mode = B_L + \left(\frac{d_1}{d_1 + d_2}\right)i$$

11.5	

Since B_L in this formula is the lower boundary of the class containing the mode, for the data of Table 4-1 $B_L =$ _____ (number).

18 In the formula for the mode, d_1 is the difference between the frequency in the modal class and that of the adjacent *lower* class (i.e., the adjacent class with the smaller class midpoint). For Table 4-1, $d_1 =$ _____ (number).

$7 - 6 = 1$	

19 In the formula for the mode used with grouped data, d_2 is the difference between the frequency in the modal class and that of the adjacent *higher* class. For Table 4-1, $d_2 =$ _____ (number).

$7 - 4 = 3$	

20 As in the formula for the median, i indicates the size of the _____ in which the mode is located.

class interval	

21 Calculate the value of the mode for the data of Table 4-1.

$11.5 + \left(\dfrac{1}{1+3}\right)3 = 12.25$ $\doteq 12.2$	

$$\text{Mode} = B_L + \left(\frac{d_1}{d_1 + d_2}\right)i =$$

22 Similarly, determine the value of the mode for the following frequency distribution.

Class	f
1–2	2
3–4	5
5–6	15
7–8	10
9–10	5

$$\text{Mode} = B_L + \left(\frac{d_1}{d_1 + d_2}\right)i$$

$$\text{Mode} =$$

$4.5 + \left(\dfrac{10}{10 + 5}\right)2 \doteq 5.8$	

4.2 ■ The Quartiles and Other Position Measures

Because of their conceptual similarity to the median, as indicated in Section 3.3, computation of quartiles, deciles, and percentiles is based on using variations of the basic formula for the median.

23 In order to determine the quartile values for grouped data, the general formula for the median is modified according to the position measure desired. Thus

$$Q_1 = B_L + \left(\frac{n/4 - cf_B}{f_c}\right)i \qquad Q_2 = B_L + \left(\frac{n/2 - cf_B}{f_c}\right)i$$

$$B_L + \left(\frac{3n/4 - cf_B}{f_c}\right)i$$

$Q_3 =$

24 For the data of Table 4-1, if the value of the median is 12.4, what is the value of Q_2, the second quartile?

12.4 (No additional computation is necessary, since $Q_2 = $ Med.)

$Q_2 =$

25 In computing the values of Q_1 and Q_3, we of course interpolate within the classes in which the respective quartiles are located, rather than within the class containing the median. For example, the value of Q_1 is located in the first class whose cumulative frequency (cf) equals or exceeds 25 percent of the total frequency (Σf). For the data of Table 4-1, the lower

---

8.5

boundary of the class containing the value of Q_1 is _____ .

26 Compute the value of Q_1 for the data of Table 4-1.

$$8.5 + \left(\frac{6-4}{6}\right)3 = 8.5 +$$

$$\left(\frac{2}{6}\right)3 = 9.5$$

$$Q_1 = B_L + \left(\frac{n/4 - cf_B}{f_c}\right)i =$$

27 Similarly, the value of Q_3 is located in the first class whose cumulative frequency equals or exceeds 75 percent of the total frequency. For the data of Table 4-1 the lower

---

14.5

boundary of the class containing the value of Q_3 is _____ .

28 Compute the value of Q_3 for the data of Table 4-1.

$$14.5 + \left(\frac{18-17}{4}\right)3 = 14.5 +$$

$$\frac{3}{4} = 15.25 \doteq 15.2$$

$$Q_3 = B_L + \left(\frac{3n/4 - cf_B}{f_c}\right)i =$$

29 Indicate the formula for determining the value of the fourth decile for grouped data, given that

$$\text{Med} = B_L + \left(\frac{n/2 - cf_B}{f_c}\right)i$$

$$B_L + \left(\frac{4n/10 - cf_B}{f_c}\right)i$$

$D_4 =$

30 Using the formula developed in Frame 29, above, compute the value of the fourth decile for the data of Table 4-1.

$$8.5 + \left(\frac{9.6 - 4}{6}\right)3 = 8.5 +$$
$$\left(\frac{5.6}{6}\right)3 = 11.3$$

$$D_4 = B_L + \left(\frac{4n/10 - cf_B}{f_c}\right)i =$$

4.3 ■ The Ranges

In this section we consider briefly the range and the modified ranges for grouped data.

31 For grouped data that are organized in a frequency distribution, the range is the maximum number of measurement units included in the distribution. Thus the range is equal to the difference between the upper boundary of the highest class with any frequencies in it and the lower boundary of the lowest class with any tabulated frequencies. Accordingly, the range for the data of the following frequency distribution is $R = B_U$ (highest class) $- B_L$ (lowest class)

$$20.5 - 5.5 = 15.0$$

$R =$

Class	f
6–8	3
9–11	6
12–14	7
15–17	4
18–20	2

32 Similarly, the range for the following grouped data is

$$12.5 - 3.5 = 9.0$$
(The class 13–15 has no tabulated frequencies.)

$R = \underline{\hspace{1cm}} - \underline{\hspace{1cm}} = \underline{\hspace{1cm}}$.

Class	f
4–6	10
7–9	5
10–12	3
13–15	0

upper boundary

lower boundary

33 Thus, for grouped data the range is equal to the difference between the _____ of the highest class with tabulated frequencies and the _____ of the lowest class with tabulated frequencies.

34 As is the case for ungrouped data in Section 3.4, the three modified ranges most frequently used with grouped data are the middle 90 percent, middle 80 percent, and middle 50 percent. For the middle 90 percent range, ____ percent of the values at *each* end of the distribution are eliminated from consideration.

5	

35 Computation of a modified range for grouped data is illustrated in Exercise 4.6, at the end of this chapter. As for ungrouped data, the first step in computing the middle 90 percent range, for example, is to determine the values at the _____ and _____ percentile points of the frequency distribution.

fifth; ninety-fifth	

4.4 ■ The Average Deviation

With grouped data, the value of each class midpoint is used to represent all of the measurements in the class when determining the value of the average deviation, AD, as is the case in computing the arithmetic mean for grouped data.

36 For sample data which have been grouped, the formula for the average deviations is

$$AD = \frac{\Sigma f|X - \bar{X}|}{n}$$

Similarly, for population data the formula is

$\frac{\Sigma f|X - \mu|}{N}$	

AD =

37 Using the formula $\mu = \Sigma fX/N$, determine the value of the population mean for the grouped data below.

Class	f	X	fX
1–5	2	3	—
6–10	5	8	—
11–15	2	13	—
16–20	1	18	—
	N = 10		ΣfX = —

6	
40	
26	
18	
90	

$\frac{\Sigma fx}{N} = \frac{90}{10} = 9.0$	

$\mu =$

38 Now, using the value of 9.0 that was computed as the mean of the distribution, enter the values for $|X - \mu|$ and $f|X - \mu|$ in the table below.

6	12
1	5
4	8
9	9
	34

Class	f	X	$|X - \mu|$	$f|X - \mu|$
1-5	2	3	_____	_____
6-10	5	8	_____	_____
11-15	2	13	_____	_____
16-20	1	18	_____	_____
	$N = 10$			$\Sigma f|X - \mu| =$ _____

39 Finally, compute the value of the average deviation for the grouped data in Frame 38.

$$\frac{\Sigma f|X - \mu|}{N} = \frac{34}{10} = 3.4$$

AD =

4.5 ■ The Standard Deviation

As is the case for the ungrouped data in Section 3.6, in this section we describe both the so-called deviations formulas and the computational formulas for determining the population and sample standard deviation. As before, the population and sample standard deviations are represented by the symbols σ and s, respectively. Similarly, the population and sample variances are represented by the symbols σ^2 and s^2, respectively.

40 For grouped data, the formulas for ungrouped data are modified just as the formulas for the arithmetic mean and average deviation were modified. Thus, instead of the formulas

$$\sigma = \sqrt{\frac{\Sigma(X - \mu)^2}{N}} \quad \text{and} \quad s = \sqrt{\frac{\Sigma(X - \bar{X})^2}{n - 1}} \quad \text{we used the modified}$$

formulas

$$\sqrt{\frac{\Sigma f(X - \mu)^2}{N}}$$

$$\sqrt{\frac{\Sigma f(X - \bar{X})^2}{n - 1}}$$

$\sigma =$

and $s =$

41 As in Section 3.6 for ungrouped data, the denominator in the formula for the sample standard deviation above includes a correction for biasedness based on the assumption that a sample standard deviation is called a "sample" because it is being used as a population estimator. Consider the effect of dividing by "$n - 1$" rather than by "n." Since "$n - 1$" is a smaller divisor than "n," a corrected sample standard deviation is [smaller / larger] in value as compared with an uncorrected value.

42 Therefore, if we were to overlook use of the correction factor in the formula for the sample standard deviation, we would estimate the population standard deviation as being [smaller / larger] that it actually is, in the long run.

43 For the simplified grouped data previously used for illustrating the computation of the average deviation, complete the column of information needed for computing the population standard deviation.

Class	f	X	$X - \mu$	$(X - \mu)^2$	$f(X - \mu)^2$
1-5	2	3	−6	36	———
6-10	5	8	−1	1	———
11-15	2	13	4	16	———
16-20	1	18	9	81	———
	$N = 10$				$\Sigma f(X - \mu)^2 =$

44 Complete the computation of the value of the standard deviation for the grouped data in Frame 43.

$$\sigma = \sqrt{\frac{\Sigma f(X - \mu)^2}{N}} =$$

45 Similarly, illustrate the values that have to be determined and compute the standard deviation for the following sample of grouped data, given that the mean equals 5.0.

Class	f
1-3	2
4-6	4
7-9	2
	$n = 8$

$$s =$$

46 Again, as for the ungrouped data in Section 3.6, computational formulas are available for calculating standard deviations for grouped data. The formulas for the population and standard deviation are, respectively:

$$\sigma = \sqrt{\frac{\Sigma fX^2 - N\mu^2}{N}} \quad \text{and} \quad s = \sqrt{\frac{\Sigma fX^2 - n\bar{X}^2}{n-1}}$$

These formulas usually are computationally easier to use than the formulas presented in Frame 40 because they do not require determination of _____ from the mean.

deviations

47 For the grouped population data previously used to compute the standard deviation by using the deviations formula, complete the following table in preparation for using the computational formula for the standard deviation.

		Class	f	X	X²	fX	fX²
6	18	1-5	2	3	9	___	___
40	320	6-10	5	8	64	___	___
26	338	11-15	2	13	169	___	___
18	324	16-20	1	18	324	___	___
90	1,000		N = 10			ΣfX =	ΣfX² =

48 Now compute the standard deviation for the grouped data in Frame 47, using the computational formula ($\mu = 9.0$)

$$\sqrt{\frac{1,000 - 810}{10}} = \sqrt{19.0} =$$

4.4

(which is the same as the solution using the deviations formula in Frame 44)

$$\sigma = \sqrt{\frac{\Sigma fX^2 - N\mu^2}{N}} =$$

49 Similarly, construct the necessary table and compute the standard deviation for the following sample of grouped data.

X²	fX	fX²
4	4	8
25	20	100
64	16	128
	ΣfX = 40	ΣfX² = 236

Class	f	X
1-3	2	2
4-6	4	5
7-9	2	8
	n = 8	

$$\sqrt{\frac{236 - (8)(40/8)^2}{8-1}} =$$

$$\sqrt{\frac{236 - 200}{7}} = \sqrt{5.1429} = 2.3$$

(which is the same as the answer in Frame 45)

$$s = \sqrt{\frac{\Sigma fX^2 - n\bar{X}^2}{n-1}}$$

50 Overall, we have discussed four basic varieties of the formula for the sample standard deviation. In the listing below, identify the appropriate formula by letter for each of the four types of situations involving sample data.

Deviations formula for ungrouped data: ____

$$\text{(a)} \quad s = \sqrt{\frac{\Sigma X^2 - n\bar{X}^2}{n-1}}$$

Deviations formula for grouped data: ____

$$\text{(b)} \quad s = \sqrt{\frac{\Sigma f(X-\bar{X})^2}{n-1}}$$

Computational formula for ungrouped data: ____

$$\text{(c)} \quad s = \sqrt{\frac{\Sigma f X^2 - n\bar{X}^2}{n-1}}$$

Computational formula for grouped data: ____

$$\text{(d)} \quad s = \sqrt{\frac{\Sigma(X-\bar{X})^2}{n-1}}$$

d

b

a

c

51 With reference to the list in Frame 50, the formula that is generally the easiest to use in computing the standard deviation for grouped sample data is ____ (identifying letter).

c

52 In the formulas identified in Frame 50, the particular symbol which indicates that the formula is applicable to data which have been grouped in a frequency distribution is ____.

f

Review   **53** (Frames 1–6) Below, post the formulas for computing the sample mean and the population mean for grouped data.

$\dfrac{\Sigma f X}{n}$

$$\bar{X} =$$

$\dfrac{\Sigma f X}{N}$

$$\mu =$$

54 (Frames 7–10) In determining the value of the median for grouped data, the midpoint of the class containing the median [is / is not] used as the best estimate of the value of the median.

is not

55 (Frames 11–16) In the formula

$$\text{Med} = B_L + \left(\frac{n/2 - \text{cf}_B}{f_c}\right)i$$

The lower boundary of the
class containing the median
(the first class whose cf
equals or exceeds $n/2$)

what is B_L? _____
_____
_____
_____ .

56 (Frames 17-22) In using the formula for determining
the value of the mode for grouped measurements,

$$\text{Mode} = B_L + \left(\frac{d_1}{d_1 + d_2}\right) i$$

Since d_1 and d_2 refer to the difference in frequencies between
the modal class and the adjacent lower and upper classes,
respectively, for the following data the mode would be located
near the [lower / upper] boundary of the modal class.

upper

Class boundaries	f
5.5- 8.5	1
8.5-11.5	8
11.5-14.5	6

57 (Frames 23-30) Given the formula for determining the
value of the median for grouped data,

$$\text{Med} = B_L + \left(\frac{n/2 - \text{cf}_B}{f_c}\right) i$$

Indicate the formulas for computing Q_1 and D_3.

$$B_L + \left(\frac{n/4 - \text{cf}_B}{f_c}\right) i$$

$Q_1 =$

$$B_L + \left(\frac{3n/10 - \text{cf}_B}{f_c}\right) i$$

$D_3 =$

58 (Frames 31-33) For grouped data the range is equal to

boundary

boundary

the upper _____ of the highest class with tabulated
frequencies minus the lower _____ of the lowest class
with tabulated frequencies.

59 (Frames 34-35) A modified range is one which excludes

the two ends

a certain percentage of the observations at [the center / the
two ends] of the distribution of measurements.

60 (Frames 36-39) For sample data which have been
grouped, the formula for the average deviation is

$$\frac{\Sigma f|X - \bar{X}|}{n}$$

AD =

61 (Frames 40–45) Recalling that the standard deviation for a population can be described verbally as "the square root of the mean of the squared deviations," the basic (deviations) formula for the standard deviation for grouped data is

$$\sqrt{\frac{\Sigma f(X - \mu)^2}{N}}$$

$\sigma =$

62 (Frames 46–52) Insert the denominator in the following (computational) formula for the sample standard deviation

$n - 1$

$$s = \sqrt{\frac{\Sigma f X^2 - n\bar{X}^2}{}}$$

Symbols Introduced in This Chapter (with Frame Numbers)

(1) X — In the context of a frequency distribution, the midpoint of each class.

(2) f — Observed frequency of grouped measurements in a class of a frequency distribution.

(3) ΣfX — Sum of the products of each observed class frequency multiplied by the midpoint of the class.

(4) Σf — The sum of the observed frequencies for all of the classes in a frequency distribution. $\Sigma f = n$ for a sample and $\Sigma f = N$ for a population.

(7) cf — The cumulative frequency of observed values up to and including a designated class in a frequency distribution.

(12) cf_B — The cumulative frequency of the class before a designated class; that is, it is the cumulative frequency of the adjacent class with a lower midpoint value than the designated class.

(13) f_c — Frequency of observed measurements in a designated class. Used in conjunction with identifying the position of the median and other similar measures, such as the quartiles and percentiles.

(18) d_1 — Difference between the frequency of observations in the modal class and the adjacent lower class.

(18) d_2 — Difference between the frequency of observations in the modal class and the adjacent higher class.

Formulas Introduced in this Chapter (with Frame Numbers)

(1) $\bar{X} = \dfrac{\Sigma fX}{n}$ Sample mean for data grouped in a frequency distribution.

(1) $\mu = \dfrac{\Sigma fX}{N}$ Population mean for data grouped in a frequency distribution.

(11) $\text{Med} = B_L + \left(\dfrac{n/2 - cf_B}{f_c}\right)i$ The median for grouped data.

(17) $\text{Mode} = B_L + \left(\dfrac{d_1}{d_1 + d_2}\right)i$ The mode for grouped data.

(23) $Q_1 = B_L + \left(\dfrac{n/4 - cf_B}{f_c}\right)i$ Values of the first, second, and third quartiles for grouped data.

$Q_2 = B_L + \left(\dfrac{n/2 - cf_B}{f_c}\right)i$

$Q_3 = B_L + \left(\dfrac{3n/4 - cf_B}{f_c}\right)i$

(29) $D_4 = B_L + \left(\dfrac{4n/10 - cf_B}{f_c}\right)i$ Value of the fourth decile for grouped data. Used to illustrate how the formula for the median can be modified to determine the value at any decile or percentile point.

(36) $\text{AD} = \dfrac{\Sigma f|X - \bar{X}|}{n}$ Average deviation for sample data grouped in a frequency distribution.

(36) $\text{AD} = \dfrac{\Sigma f|X - \mu|}{N}$ Average deviation for population data grouped in a frequency distribution.

(40) $\sigma = \sqrt{\dfrac{\Sigma f(X - \mu)^2}{N}}$ Population standard deviation for grouped data, deviations formula.

(40) $s = \sqrt{\dfrac{\Sigma f(X - \bar{X})^2}{n - 1}}$ Sample standard deviation for grouped data, deviations formula.

$$(46) \quad \sigma = \sqrt{\frac{\Sigma f X^2 - N\mu^2}{N}}$$

Population standard deviation for grouped data, computational formula.

$$(46) \quad s = \sqrt{\frac{\Sigma f X^2 - n\bar{X}^2}{n-1}}$$

Sample standard deviations for grouped data, computational formula.

EXERCISES

(Solutions on pages 593–595)

4.1 In an academic grading system in which A = 4.0, B= 3.0, C = 2.0, D = 1.0, and E = 0.0, a group of students has the grade-point averages reported in the following table. Compute the values of the population mean, median, and mode for this distribution of grade-point values.

Grade-point average	Number of students (f)
1.0–1.4	3
1.5–1.9	4
2.0–2.4	8
2.5–2.9	12
3.0–3.4	5
3.5–3.9	3

4.2 Comment upon and interpret the differences in the values of the mean, median, and mode in Exercise 4.1.

4.3 Compute and interpret the values of Q_1 and Q_3 for the data in Exercise 4.1.

4.4 Compute and interpret the value of the sixtieth percentile for the data in Exercise 4.1.

4.5 Compute the value of the range for the data in Exercise 4.1.

4.6 Determine the value of the middle 90 percent range for the data in Exercise 4.1.

4.7 Compute the value of the average deviation for the data in Exercise 4.1 and interpret your answer.

4.8 For the data of Exercise 4.1, compute the value of the population standard deviation, using the deviations form of the formula.

4.9 For the data of Exercise 4.1, compute the value of the population standard deviation using the computational formula. Compare your answer to that obtained in Exercise 4.8.

4.10 Briefly explain why descriptive measures calculated on the basis of grouped data are considered to be approximations.

ADDITIONAL EXERCISES

4.11 The following frequency distribution reports operating profit figures for a given month for a group of photo-processing outlets, reported to the nearest dollar. Considering this to be a statistical population, compute the average profit for the month in terms of the three measures described in the chapter.

Monthly operating profit	f
$0–$499	12
$500–$999	14
$1,000–$1,499	8
$1,500–$1,999	2

4.12 Compute the values of Q_1 and Q_3 for the data in Exercise 4.11.

4.13 Compute the value of the ninetieth percentile point for the data in Exercise 4.11.

4.14 Determine the range in operating profits for the data in Exercise 4.11.

4.15 Compute the value of the middle 80 percent range for the data in Exercise 4.11.

4.16 For the data of Exercise 4.11, compute the value of the standard deviation, using the computational formula.

4.17 The following frequency distribution reports the gross sales recorded during 32 randomly selected 10-minute periods in a discount department store. Calculate the values of the sample mean, median, and mode for these data and describe the distribution in terms of skewness.

Dollar sales level	Frequency
$40.00–$59.99	11
$60.00–$79.99	8
$80.00–$99.99	5
$100.00–$119.99	5
$120.00–$139.99	3

4.18 Compute the values of Q_1 and Q_3 for the frequency distribution in Exercise 4.17.

4.19 Determine the value of the range for the data in Exercise 4.17.

4.20 Determine the value of the middle 50 percent range for the data in Exercise 4.17.

4.21 Compute the value of the sample standard deviation for the data of Exercise 4.17, using the computational formula.

4.22 Can the value of the standard deviation computed in Exercise 4.21 be used to define the boundaries within which the middle 68 percent of the measurements in Exercise 4.17 are located? Why or why not?

4.23 Given the frequency distribution in the table below, compute the (a) mean, (b) median, and (c) mode of the loan amounts.

The Amounts of a Sample of 40 Personal Loans

Loan amount	Number of loans
$300–$699	13
$700–$1,099	11
$1,100–$1,499	6
$1,500–$1,899	5
$1,900–$2,299	3
$2,300–$2,699	1
$2,700–$3,099	1
Total	40

4.24 Describe the form of the frequency distribution of personal loan amounts in Exercise 4.23.

4.25 For the amounts of the personal loans reported in Exercise 4.23, determine the values at the (a) second quartile, (b) second decile, and (c) ninetieth percentile point.

4.26 For the amounts of personal loans reported in Exercise 4.23, determine the (a) range and (b) middle 50 percent range for the amounts of personal loans.

4.27 Compute the average deviation for the personal loan data in Exercise 4.23.

4.28 Determine the sample standard deviation for the data in Exercise 4.23 by using the computational formula.

4.29 Given the data in the table below, determine the average lifetime of the cutting tools by computing the (a) mean, (b) median, and (c) mode. Consider these to be population data.

Hours before replacement	Number of tools
0.0–24.9	2
25.0–49.9	4
50.0–74.9	12
75.0–99.9	30
100.0–124.9	18
125.0–149.9	4
Total	70

4.30 Describe the frequency distribution of the tool lifetime in Exercise 4.29 in terms of skewness.

4.31 Determine the values at the (a) third quartile, (b) seventh decile, and (c) seventy-fifth percentile for the lifetime of cutting tools, as reported in Exercise 4.29.

4.32 Compute the average deviation for the lifetime of cutting tools reported in Exercise 4.29.

4.33 Considering the data in Exercise 4.29 to be a statistical population, compute the (a) population variance and (b) population standard deviation by using the deviations formulas.

4.34 In comparison with the tool-life data analyzed in Exercises 4.29 to 4.33, the mean and standard deviation of lifetime for a second brand of tools was determined to be $\mu_2 = 61.50$ hours and $\sigma_2 = 22.30$ hours. Compute the coefficient of variation for **(a)** the first brand of tools and **(b)** the second brand of tools, and **(c)** indicate for which brand the variability of tool life is *relatively* greater.

PART III ■
PROBABILITY AND
PROBABILITY DISTRIBUTIONS

CHAPTER 5 ■ PROBABILITY

The theory of probability owes its early development to the interest of European mathematicians in games of chance during the latter part of the seventeenth century. Since then probability theory has become the basis for the development of the techniques of statistical inference that are used in all fields of basic and applied research, including economic analysis and managerial decision making. Many of the examples in this chapter refer to games of chance simply because such examples are less complex and hence serve to illustrate basic principles more clearly. In later chapters we cover specific techniques of inference and decision making as they apply to business and economic data. In this chapter we consider how probability values are determined, the range of possible values, rules for combining the probabilities of different events, and the interpretation of probability values.

5.1 ■ The Meaning of Probability

Probability values can be determined and interpreted from either an *objective* or a *subjective* point of view. In this section we discuss the objective approach, while the subjective approach is discussed in the last section of this chapter (Section 5.5). Under the objective approach, the *classical method* of determining probabilities involves a priori determination of probability values; that is, the values can be calculated before any sample trials are observed. By the *empirical method*, on the other hand, probabilities are determined on the basis of observing a sample of events. No matter which way the probabilities are determined, the objective interpretation of a probability value is that it represents the long-run relative frequency with which an event should occur in a series of observations, or trials.

1 If we place five tokens, numbered 1 through 5, in a box and then plan to withdraw one token at random from the box, the probability of the token numbered 3 being drawn is [$^1/_2$ / $^1/_3$ / $^1/_5$ / $^3/_5$].

$^1/_5$

2 In concluding that the probability of drawing token 3 is $^1/_5$, you made the assumptions and did the calculations that conform to the *classical method* of determining probabilities. One assumption that you made, which we discuss in greater detail in Section 5.3, is that the five possible events are *mutually exclusive*, that is, that on any one drawing of a token, [only one / several] of the events can occur.

only one

3 Thus, by the assumption that the events are mutually exclusive, we expect that getting both tokens 3 and 4 on one selection of tokens is [possible / impossible].

impossible

4 In addition to assuming that the events are mutually exclusive, you assumed also that the alternatives are *equally likely* to occur. For example, would you still believe that the probability of selecting token 3 is $\frac{1}{5}$ if you learned that it is half the size of the other tokens? [Yes / No]

No

5 Finally, you computed a fraction to represent the probability value in which the total number of possible events became the value of the [numerator / denominator] and the number of desired events became the value of the [numerator / denominator].

denominator

numerator

6 For example, suppose that the five tokens were numbered 1, 1, 1, 3, and 3. In this case, the probability of a 3 being selected is $[\frac{1}{2} / \frac{1}{5} / \frac{2}{5}]$.

$\frac{2}{5}$

7 The two assumptions that we made in arriving at the probability value of $\frac{2}{5}$ are that the choice of any one of the five tokens is mutually _____ and equally _____ .

exclusive; likely

8 Thus one method of determining a probability value can be stated as: "If an event can occur in N mutually exclusive and equally likely ways, then the probability of an outcome involving X is the value of the fraction $f(X)/N$, where $f(X)$ is the frequency with which X is contained in N." This is a statement of the _____ method of determining probabilities.

classical

9 When a "fair" coin is tossed, there are two mutually exclusive and equally likely events: that the face of the coin will show a head or a tail. The probability of a head is represented by the fraction $f(X)/N =$ ___ .

$\frac{1}{2}$

10 In a deck of 52 playing cards, the probability of obtaining an ace of spades on a particular drawing of one card is $f(X)/N$ = ___ .

$\frac{1}{52}$

11 The probability of drawing any spade on a particular draw of the cards is _____ .

$\frac{13}{52} = \frac{1}{4}$

12 The classical method of determining probabilities assumes a basic symmetry in the possible outcomes of an event. Thus a coin must be fair, or balanced. It is only on the basis of this assumption that an [a priori / a posteriori] calculation of probabilities is possible.

a priori

13 In many decision-making situations involving business and economic data, however, the alternative outcomes are not equally likely, nor are their respective probabilities known beforehand. This fact limits the usefulness of the _____ method of determining probabilities.

classical

14 In the classical method of determining probabilities the assumptions are made that the alternative outcomes are _____ and _____ , and the calculation of probability values is typically done [before / after] events are observed.

mutually exclusive; equally
likely; before

15 The second method of determining probability values within the objective approach is the *empirical method*, which is based on observing the events in a sample of observations, or trials. Thus, as contrasted to the classical method, the empirical method involves calculation of probability values [before / after] events are observed.

after

16 The empirical method is sometimes called the "sampling" method because the probability value is determined by observing the frequency of an event in a series of trials relative to the number of trials, or observations. Thus, if five "successes" were observed in a sample of 50 trials, the probability would be evaluated as being equal to _____ (value).

$5/_{50} = 1/_{10} = 0.10$

17 In using the empirical method of determining probabilities, as the number of observations of events is increased, the accuracy of the probability figures based on these observations is [increased / decreased].

increased

18 As the number of observations increases, the observed relative frequency of an event tends to become stable. This is often referred to as the *law of large numbers*. In Figure 5-1, for example, we have a graphic portrayal of the observed relative frequency of heads in 300 tosses of a coin. As the

| 0.50 |

number of tosses of the coin increases, the relative frequency of heads appears to stabilize at about a value of _____ .

Figure 5-1 ■ Relative frequency of heads in 300 tosses of a coin

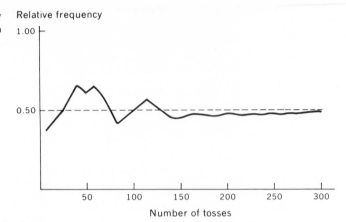

19 Notice that we stated that the relative frequency stabilized "at about" 0.50. One difficulty with the empirical method is that a probability value calculated on the basis of any finite number of observations can always be improved by making more observations. Thus probability figures based on observed relative frequency are invariably [exact / approximate].

| approximate |

20 On the other hand, unless we are willing to assume that all possible events are equally likely, the principal method available to compute objective probability values is the _____ method.

| empirical |

21 Whether the probability value is determined by the classical or the empirical method, the objective interpretation of such a value is that it represents the *long-run relative frequency* with which an event will occur. For example, if an event has a probability of 0.10, we would expect that in 100 trials it would occur about ___ (number) times.

| 10 |

22 Thus, by the objective approach probability values can be determined by either the _____ or the _____ method. Once determined the probability value is always interpreted in terms of the long-run expected relative _____ of the event in a series of observations.

| classical; empirical |

| frequency |

5.2 ■ Expressing Probability

In this section we present the standard symbol system used in elementary consideration of the topic of probability and consider the range of values that a probability figure can have.

In addition, we introduce the use of Venn diagrams for portraying the possible events associated with a single observation, or trial.

23 The symbol that we use to denote the probability of an event is P. Thus $P(A)$ denotes the probability that event ___ will occur.

A

24 Some authors prefer to use other symbols for probability instead. Thus $Pr(B)$, $p(B)$, and $pr(B)$ all refer to the probability of event B. In terms of the notation system being used in this chapter, the probability of B is represented by ____ .

$P(B)$

25 Whether the classical or the empirical method of determining probabilities is used, what is the smallest value that a probability figure can have? (Consider the lowest possible value of the expected or observed relative frequency.) _____

Zero

26 A probability of zero signifies that there is [no / some / a high] chance that the outcome in question will occur.

no

Note: Since the value of the probability figure determined by the empirical method is an approximation rather than an exact figure, a probability of zero might also indicate that the occurrence of the event is very rare, but not necessarily impossible.

27 Can the numeric value of a probability ever be negative? [Yes / No]

No (There cannot be a negative expected frequency.)

28 On the other hand, what is the maximum possible value of P (or what is the maximum possible value of the fraction representing the expected or observed relative frequency)? _____

1 (or 1.0)

Note: Again, if the empirical method has been used in calculating the value of P, a probability of 1 might indicate that a rare exception is possible, so that the event in question is virtually, but not completely, certain.

29 Therefore the lowest possible value of P, indicating very little or no chance of the event in question occurring, is _____ ; certainty or virtual certainty of an event is indicated by a probability value of ___ .

zero
1

30 Particularly in games of chance, probabilities are often expressed as odds rather than in terms of probability values as such. Thus, the odds of 3:2 (read: "3 to 2") in favor of an event suggest that for every three possible outcomes of an observation that are favorable, there are _____ that are unfavorable.

two

31 Therefore, when odds are used to designate the probability of an event, the number or proportion of possible outcomes is compared in the order of (favorable : unfavorable / unfavorable : favorable).

favorable:unfavorable

32 For example, the odds ratio for obtaining a 6 on one throw of a six-sided die would be expressed as _____.

1:5

33 Similarly, the odds ratio for obtaining a head on one toss of a fair coin, ignoring the possible on-edge outcome, would be expressed as _____.

1:1

34 Since the odds ratio involves a comparison of favorable to unfavorable possible outcomes, whereas the fraction representing probability compares the number of favorable outcomes to the total possible outcomes, given the odds, we can readily stipulate probability values, and vice versa. Given the odds favoring an event A as being $X:Y$, the probability of A is

$$P(A) = \frac{X}{X+Y}$$

For example, if the odds ratio for an event is 1:5, the probability of a favorable outcome is ____ (fraction), and the probability of an unfavorable outcome is ____.

$\frac{1}{6}$ (one favorable outcome out of the total number of six); $\frac{5}{6}$

35 Similarly, odds of 3:2 indicate that the probability of the favorable outcome is ____ and the probability of the unfavorable outcome is ____.

$\frac{3}{5}$
$\frac{2}{5}$

36 To convert a probability value to an odds ratio, we simply take the ratio of the probability of success to the probability of failure, and then adjust the ratio so that the values are integers (whole numbers). That is, $X:Y = P(A):1-P(A)$. For example, if the probability of a favorable outcome is $\frac{1}{3}$, the odds of its occurrence would be expressed as _____.

$\frac{1}{3} : \frac{2}{3} = 1:2$ (Of the total of three types of outcomes, one is favorable and two are unfavorable.)

$5/6 : 1/6 = 5:1$

37 Similarly, for a probability of $5/6$, the odds ratio for the favorable outcome is _____ .

38 The probabilities of events can be portrayed by means of a *Venn diagram.* This is a rectangular figure in which areas are allocated to each of the possible events. Thus, a rectangular figure which portrays the events which can occur in a probabilistic situation is called a _____ diagram.

Venn

39 The set of all of the possible events in a probabilistic situation is termed the *sample space*, and any single elementary event is thought of as being a *point* in that space. Thus, an enclosed sample space with one or more types of events identified in that space is also a way of describing a _____ diagram.

Venn

40 Or, turning the description about, a Venn diagram involves an enclosed _____ space with one or more types of _____ identified.

sample

events

41 A Venn diagram is used to portray all of the possible outcomes, or events, in a particular trial, or observation. However, the relative area given to an event in the diagram need not be indicative of its probability. Figure 5-2, for example, is a Venn diagram which represents $P(\underline{\quad})$ in a sample space, S.

A

Figure 5-2 Venn diagram
illustrating $P(A)$

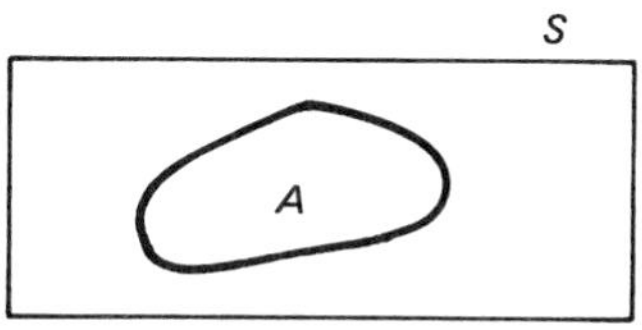

42 If $P(A)$ is the probability of event A occurring, then $P(A')$ (read "probability of not-A") is the symbol which indicates the probability of event A not occurring. Similarly, if $P(H)$ indicates the probability of obtaining a head on a single toss of a coin, then the probability of not obtaining a head on a single toss of a coin can be indicated by _____ .

$P(H')$

43 By the very nature of the two events, the probability of a successful outcome plus the probability of a nonsuccessful outcome must be equal to 1. Or, symbolically,

$P(A')$

$P(A) + \underline{\quad} = 1$

44 Figure 5-3 is a Venn diagram illustrating the principle we have just discussed. Note that the identification of A and A' involves the allocation of [all / most / none] of the sample space within the diagram.

all

Figure 5-3 Venn diagram illustrating that $P(A) + P(A') = 1$

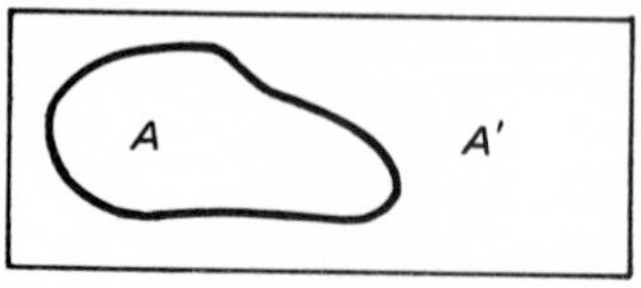

45 Another principle connected with the numeric value of probabilities is that the sum of the probabilities of all mutually exclusive and exhaustive events must be equal to 1. This implies that one of the events must occur in a given trial, or observation. Symbolically, we can represent this by the equation $\Sigma P(X) = $ ____ (value).

1

46 Thus, we can represent the total probability of outcome A either occurring or not occurring by the equation _____ _____ , and we can represent the sum of the probabilities of all mutually exclusive and exhaustive events by the equation _____ .

$P(A) + P(A') = 1$

$\Sigma P(X) = 1$

Summary

$P(X); 0$

1

47 The probability of an outcome called X is represented by _____. Its lowest possible numeric value is ____, and its highest possible numeric value is ____ .

$^4/_9$

48 When odds are used to express the probability of a favorable event, odds of 4:5 indicate a probability value of ____ (fraction).

$P(X')$

1

$\Sigma P(X)$

49 The sum of the probability of X, represented by $P(X)$, and the probability that X does not occur, represented by _____ , is equal to ____ ; the sum of all mutually exclusive and exhaustive events, represented by _____ , is also equal to 1.

5.3 ■ Mutually Exclusive and Nonexclusive Events

In a single trial, such as the drawing of a card from a deck of cards, various events are possible, some being mutually exclusive and some not. Two or more events are mutually exclusive if the occurrence of one automatically precludes the occurrence of the other. In this section we consider the rules of addition that apply in determining the probability that

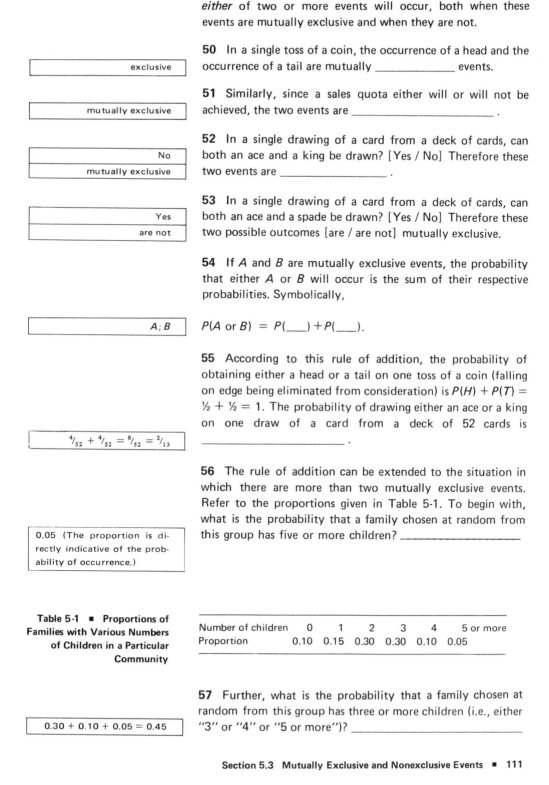

either of two or more events will occur, both when these events are mutually exclusive and when they are not.

50 In a single toss of a coin, the occurrence of a head and the occurrence of a tail are mutually _____ events.

exclusive

51 Similarly, since a sales quota either will or will not be achieved, the two events are _____ .

mutually exclusive

52 In a single drawing of a card from a deck of cards, can both an ace and a king be drawn? [Yes / No] Therefore these two events are _____ .

No

mutually exclusive

53 In a single drawing of a card from a deck of cards, can both an ace and a spade be drawn? [Yes / No] Therefore these two possible outcomes [are / are not] mutually exclusive.

Yes

are not

54 If *A* and *B* are mutually exclusive events, the probability that either *A* or *B* will occur is the sum of their respective probabilities. Symbolically,

$P(A \text{ or } B) = P(\underline{}) + P(\underline{})$.

A; B

55 According to this rule of addition, the probability of obtaining either a head or a tail on one toss of a coin (falling on edge being eliminated from consideration) is $P(H) + P(T) = \frac{1}{2} + \frac{1}{2} = 1$. The probability of drawing either an ace or a king on one draw of a card from a deck of 52 cards is _____ .

$\frac{4}{52} + \frac{4}{52} = \frac{8}{52} = \frac{2}{13}$

56 The rule of addition can be extended to the situation in which there are more than two mutually exclusive events. Refer to the proportions given in Table 5-1. To begin with, what is the probability that a family chosen at random from this group has five or more children? _____

0.05 (The proportion is directly indicative of the probability of occurrence.)

Table 5-1 ■ Proportions of Families with Various Numbers of Children in a Particular Community

Number of children	0	1	2	3	4	5 or more
Proportion		0.10	0.15	0.30	0.30	0.10	0.05

57 Further, what is the probability that a family chosen at random from this group has three or more children (i.e., either "3" or "4" or "5 or more")? _____

$0.30 + 0.10 + 0.05 = 0.45$

58 If events *A* and *B* are *not* mutually exclusive, then the probability of either *A* or *B* (or both) occurring is the probability that *A* will occur plus the probability that *B* will occur minus the probability that both *A* and *B* will occur. Symbolically,

P(A) + P(B)

$P(A \text{ or } B) = \underline{\hspace{1cm}} + \underline{\hspace{1cm}} - P(A,B)$

59 The rationale of subtracting the probability of the joint occurrence of *A* and *B* is best illustrated by the use of a Venn diagram. In which figure, 5-4*a* or 5-4*b*, are the two events represented as being mutually exclusive? (5-4*a* / 5-4*b*)

5-4*a*

Figure 5-4*a* ▪ Venn diagram for two mutually exclusive events

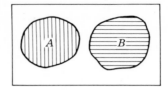

Figure 5-4*b* ▪ Venn diagram for two nonexclusive events

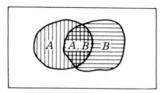

60 Now consider Figure 5-4*b*. If we were to add the probability of *A* to the probability of *B* in order to obtain the probability of either outcome *A* or outcome *B* occurring, what area in the Venn diagram would be added twice, in effect? [*A* / *B* / *A,B*]

A,B (read: "*A* and *B*")

61 Therefore the effect of subtracting the probability of the joint occurrence is to correct for the overlap in *A* and *B* when the two events are not mutually exclusive. For nonexclusive events, then, $P(A \text{ or } B) = \underline{\hspace{3cm}}$.

P(A) + P(B) − P(A,B)

62 The rule of addition for mutually exclusive events can be considered a special case of the rule for nonexclusive events. This is so since the value of $P(A,B)$ for mutually exclusive events is always equal to ___ .

zero (Note that there is no area "*A,B*" in Figure 5-4*a*.)

$^4/_{52} + {}^{13}/_{52} - {}^1/_{52} = {}^{16}/_{52} = {}^4/_{13}$

63 According to the rule of addition for nonexclusive events, what is the probability of drawing either an ace or a spade from a deck of 52 cards? _____

Summary

one

one

64 The rule of addition applies when there are several possible outcomes in a *single* trial, or observation. Thus, we gave examples involving the toss of ____ (number) coin(s) and the drawing of ____ (number) card(s) from a deck.

$P(A) + P(B)$

$P(A) + P(B) - P(A,B)$

65 When two events are mutually exclusive, the formula used to calculate the probability that either event will occur is _____ . When two possible outcomes are *not* mutually exclusive, the formula used to compute the probability that either event (or both) will occur is _____.

5.4 ■ Independent Events, Dependent Events, and Conditional Probability

When events occur in the context of two or more trials, such as in the tossing of the same coin twice in succession, the events may be independent of one another or they may be dependent. If events are independent, then the probability of a particular event occurring in a second trial is unaffected by the previous occurrence or nonoccurrence of the event. If the events are dependent, then the probability is affected by the previous outcome. In this section we consider the rules of multiplication for computing the probability of the joint occurrence of events in two or more separate trials, or observations.

66 Suppose that a fair coin is tossed twice in succession. Is the probability of obtaining a head on the second toss of the coin affected by whether or not a head was obtained on the first toss? [Yes / No]

No

67 Therefore the events associated with a coin being tossed twice in succession are [dependent / independent] events.

independent

68 The rule of multiplication states that if A and B are independent events, the probability of their joint occurrence is the product of their probabilities. The algebraic equation representing this rule is

$A ; B$

$P(A,B) = P(\underline{\quad})P(\underline{\quad})$

69 Thus the probability of obtaining two "tails" on two consecutive tosses of a coin is _____ .

$(\tfrac{1}{2})(\tfrac{1}{2}) = \tfrac{1}{4}$

70 Just as Venn diagrams are useful for portraying the possible outcomes in a single trial, *tree diagrams* are useful for portraying the events associated with multiple trials. Therefore a tree diagram is particularly useful in conjunction with applying the rule of [addition / multiplication] in computing probabilities.

> multiplication

71 Figure 5-5 presents the tree diagram for two successive tosses of a coin. The probability of any particular joint event is determined by multiplying the probability of the first event by the probability of the second event. With reference to Figure 5-5, what is the probability of obtaining a tail and then a head, in this order? _____

> $(\frac{1}{2})(\frac{1}{2}) = \frac{1}{4}$

Figure 5-5 ▪ Tree diagram for two consecutive tosses of a coin

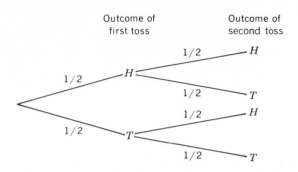

Outcome of first toss   Outcome of second toss

72 With reference to Figure 5-5, what is the probability of obtaining a head and then a tail in this order? _____

> $(\frac{1}{2})(\frac{1}{2}) = \frac{1}{4}$

73 Referring to Frames 71 and 72, therefore what is the probability of obtaining a head and a tail in *any* order on two tosses of a coin (i.e., tail and head or head and tail)?_____

> ½ (Both the *HT* and *TH* pairs of outcomes qualify; their probabilities are summed because the *HT* and *TH* sequences are mutually exclusive events.)

74 Unlike the events in games of chance, events in business and economics are seldom independent. Suppose that the probability of a corporate-tax reduction within a year has been assessed as being 0.50. Would the probability of an increase in profits during the coming year probably be affected by whether the tax reduction occurs? [Yes / No]

> Yes

75 If two events are not independent, then the concept of *conditional probability* has to be used to determine the probability of a second event. The expression $P(B|A)$ means the probability of event B occurring, given that event _____ has occurred.

> A (Note that $B|A$ is read as "B given A." It is *not* the fraction B/A.)

76 Whenever two (or more) events are dependent, the probability value which takes into account the previous occurrence of a particular event is called the _____ probability.

conditional

77 If *A* and *B* are two dependent events, the probability of their joint occurrence is the probability of *A* multiplied by the conditional probability of *B*, given that *A* has occurred. Symbolically, $P(A,B) = P(A)P(\_\_\_\_)$.

B*A*

78 For example, suppose that we have an urn with three red tokens and two black tokens. Using *R* to represent the drawing of a red token and *B* the drawing of a black token, $P(R) =$ ___ (value) and $P(B) =$ ___ (value).

$^{3}/_{5}$; $^{2}/_{5}$

79 Now, if we draw one token from the urn and do not replace it, the probabilities associated with a second drawing of a token from the urn are dependent on the outcome of the first drawing, thus exemplifying a conditional-probability situation. In the tree diagram below enter the missing probability values for the second drawing when the first token drawn and not replaced is red (*R*).

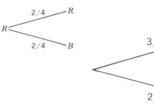
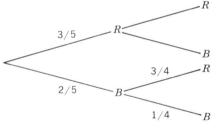

80 In the diagram of Frame 79, the conditional probability of randomly choosing a black token, given that a red token has been withdrawn, would be represented by the symbol $P(\_\_\_\_ \mid \_\_\_\_)$ and has a probability value in this case of ___ .

$(B|R)$; $^{2}/_{4}$ (or $^{1}/_{2}$)

81 Assume that a shipment of 10 motors includes one motor that is defective. Enter the probabilities associated with obtaining a nondefective (*ND*) and a defective (*D*) motor in the inspection of the first motor in this shipment on the tree diagram below.

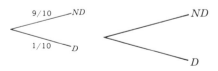

82 If we plan to inspect two motors out of the shipment, we would of course sample without replacement, since we would not want to check the same motor twice. Accordingly, enter below all the probability values for the second motor inspected, under the conditions both that the first motor inspected is nondefective and that it is defective.

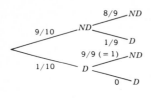 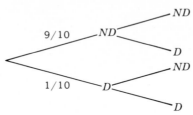

83 With reference to the tree diagram of Frame 82, what is the probability that neither of the two motors chosen at random, and without replacement, will be defective?

$(\frac{9}{10})(\frac{8}{9}) = \frac{72}{90} = \frac{4}{5}$

_____

Summary

$P(A)P(B)$

$P(A)P(B|A)$

84 Algebraically, the rule of multiplication for determining the probability of joint occurrence of two events that are independent is $P(A,B) =$ _____ ; for dependent events it is stated as $P(A,B) =$ _____ .

85 The rule of multiplication for independent events can be considered as a special case of the rule for dependent events, because when the two events are independent, then the value of $P(B|A)$ is equal to the value of $P(\underline{\quad})$.

B

86 A probability statement of the form $P(B|A)$ is called a _____ probability.

conditional

87 The diagram which is particularly useful for illustrating the possible events in two or more sequential trials or observations is called a _____ .

tree diagram

5.5 ■ Subjective Probability

Objective probabilities are based on the physical circumstances associated with an uncertain event (classical method) or are based on historical data (empirical method). Subjective probabilities, on the other hand, represent the judgment of an informed person regarding the likelihood of particular events. Two methods by which an individual's judgment can be used to determine probabilities are the *direct estimate* method and the *indifference* method. In terms of interpreting probability values, the subjective approach is that a probability value indicates the strength of belief that an event will occur in a given trial rather than representing long-run relative frequency.

88 One method of determining probabilities by the subjective approach is the *direct estimate* method. By this method a person who is in the position of having knowledge about a situation involving uncertainty is asked to estimate the probabilities of the possible events, such as product success versus product failure. For example, if a marketing manager's judgment is that the probability of a new product's success is about equal to the probability that it will fail, then the probability of success would be designated as being equal to $[^1/_3 / ^1/_2 / ^2/_3]$ and the probability of failure would be $[^1/_3 / ^1/_2 / ^2/_3]$.

½; ½

89 On the other hand, suppose that it is the manager's best judgment that product success is twice as likely as product failure. Then the probability of success is designated as being equal to $[^1/_3 / ^1/_2 / ^2/_3]$ and the probability of failure is $[^1/_3 / ^1/_2 / ^2/_3]$.

$^2/_3$; $^1/_3$

90 Thus, the subjective method by which the probability value is assessed directly by an informed individual with relevant experience is the _____ method.

direct estimate

91 The second method available for assessing probabilities by the subjective approach is the *indifference method.*[1] Several variations of this method can be used, and we describe one of these in this section. As compared with the direct estimate method, the indifference method [does not involve / also involves] the use of expert judgment to determine probabilities.

also involves (since it is also a *subjective* method)

92 If a manager finds it difficult to estimate the probability of product success by the direct method, the indifference method permits indirect determination of the probability values. For example, suppose that it is known that the gain associated with product success is $100,000 and the loss associated with product failure is $50,000. The first step in the indifference method is to ask the manager to place a money value on the overall product opportunity. That is, we ask him

[1] A general assumption underlying the use of the indifference method is that the manager is neither risk-aversive or risk-seeking, but rather, is risk-neutral in regard to his orientation toward the risk situation.

to assess such an "amount certain" as he feels has *equal value* to the opportunity involving the uncertain outcomes. Symbolically, then, the indifference method requires that the manager estimate the [left / right] side of the following equality:

left

Amount certain = expected value of risk situation

93 Suppose that after careful consideration the manager assesses the "amount certain" as being $40,000. What this means is that he feels the company should be indifferent between having the product opportunity or selling the product rights for $40,000. Thus, to be "indifferent" means that the amount certain and the risk situation should be [equal / unequal] in perceived value.

equal

94 We are now ready for the second step in the indifference method, which involves defining the algebraic equation for the general equality. Here we take advantage of the fact that the probability of product failure must equal 1.0 minus the probability of success. That is, if probability of success = P, the probability of failure = _____ .

$1 - P$

95 In statistical inference the concept of *expected* value indicates the long-run average gain (or loss) associated with a risk situation. In Frame 92 we indicated that a gain of $100,000 will occur if the product succeeds and a loss of $50,000 (gain of "−50,000") will occur if the product fails. Therefore, the expected value of the risk situation can be determined by multiplying each conditional value by the respective probability and summing the products. Enter the appropriate values in the following equation, given that "P" stands for the probability of product success.

100,000; −50,000

Expected value = (P) (_____) + $(1 - P)$ (_____)

96 We established that the "amount certain" was assessed as being $40,000 in Frame 93, and we defined the equation for the expected value in the frame above. The general equation introduced in Frame 92 was:

Amount certain = expected value of risk situation

In the space below, substitute the appropriate values and symbols in the above equality for our example.

$$40,000 = (P)(100,000) + (1 - P)(-50,000)$$

_____

97 Note that the only unknown in the above equation is P, which represents the probability of product success. Using the above equation, solve for the value of P in the space below.

$$40,000 = 100,000P - 50,000 + 50,000P$$

$$P = \frac{90,000}{150,000} = 0.60$$

_____

_____

98 Therefore, the method of indifference involves three steps. First, we ask the person making the judgment to assess an amount certain such that he would [prefer / be indifferent to] the amount certain as compared with the opportunity involving uncertainty. Then an equation is defined representing this indifference. Finally, the equation is solved for the one unknown, which is the value of the _____ .

be indifferent to

99 In terms of interpretation of probability values, by the subjective approach a probability value is interpreted as indicating the *strength of belief* that an event will occur. By contrast, when we interpret the probability value of 0.50 as indicating that an event will occur about half the time in a series of trials, such as in the repeated tossing of a fair coin, we are implicitly following the _____ approach to interpreting the probability value.

subjective probability

objective

100 However, suppose it is reported that the probability is 0.70 that a labor contract will be signed in the auto industry without a major strike. Can this situation be repeated a number of times in the given contract year, so that a series of events can be observed? [Yes / No]

No

101 The approach to interpreting probability by which the 0.70 would be indicative of strength of belief, and which is particularly suited to unique, or one-time, situations, is the _____ approach.

subjective

102 Even when a situation is not unique by nature, if we are concerned only about a single occurrence of the event, the probability figure might better be interpreted in terms of strength of _____ rather than relative frequency.

belief

103 As an example of the two different approaches to interpreting probabilities, suppose we have information which indicates that the probability of business failure in the auto-wash industry is 0.20. If this value is used for the purpose of estimating the expected frequency of business failure, the value is being interpreted by the _____ approach.

objective

104 However, if we use the probability value of 0.20 as part of the consideration in deciding on an investment in a particular car wash, then a strength-of-belief interpretation may be more meaningful, thus utilizing the _____ approach to interpreting the probability value.

subjective

Review

105 (Frames 1–14) The classical, or a priori, method of computing objective probability values is based on the assumption that the alternative outcomes are mutually _____ and _____ .

exclusive; equally likely

106 (Frames 15–20) The computation of probabilities on the basis of a sample of observations is termed the _____ method.

empirical

107 (Frames 23–29) The minimum numeric value that a probability figure can have is ___ , and its maximum possible value is ___ .

0

1

108 (Frames 30–37) If the odds expressing the probability of a favorable outcome are 3:1, the probability value for the favorable outcome is ___ (fraction). If the probability of an outcome is $\frac{1}{8}$, the odds ratio regarding its occurrence would be stated as ____ .

$\frac{3}{4}$

1:7

109 (Frames 38–41) By enclosing a sample space and identifying points within the space, any or all of the possible events in a particular situation may be portrayed by the resulting _____ diagram.

Venn

110 (Frames 42–49) The sum of the probabilities of all of the mutually exclusive and exhaustive events in a situation must be equal to a value of ___ .

1

111 (Frames 50–57) If A and B are mutually exclusive events, the probability that either A or B will occur is given by the equation $P(A \text{ or } B) =$ _____ .

$P(A) + P(B)$

$P(A) + P(B) - P(A,B)$

112 (Frames 58-65) If A and B are not mutually exclusive events, then the probability that either A or B (or both) will occur is given by the equation $P(A$ or $B) =$ _____.

$P(A)P(B)$

113 (Frames 66-74) The probability of both A and B occurring, where A and B are independent events, is represented by the equation $P(A,B) =$ _____ .

$P(A)P(B|A)$

114 (Frames 75-87) The probability of both A and B occurring, where A and B are dependent events, is represented by the equation $P(A,B) =$ _____ .

tree

115 (Frames 70-73, 79-82) The diagram which is especially useful for portraying the events associated with sequential trials, whether the events are dependent or independent, is the _____ diagram.

conditional

116 (Frames 75-77) If two events are dependent, the concept of _____ probability has to be used to determine the probability of a particular sequence of outcomes.

direct estimate

117 (Frames 88-90) The subjective method by which a probability value is assessed directly by an informed individual is the _____ method.

indifference

118 (Frames 91-98) The subjective method by which a probability value is determined indirectly, by asking the individual to designate the amount certain which has a value equal to the situation involving uncertainty and risk, is the _____ method.

objective
subjective

119 (Frames 21-22, 99-104) Interpreting a probability value as indicating the long-run relative frequency of an event is consistent with the _____ approach to probability. Interpreting a probability value as indicating the strength of belief that an event will occur in a particular observation is consistent with the _____ approach to probability.

Symbols Introduced in This Chapter (with Frame Numbers)

(23) $P(A)$ — The probability of event A.

(42) $P(A')$ — The probability that event A will not occur.

(54) P(A or B) — The probability that event *A* or event *B* (or both) will occur in a single observation.

(68) P(A,B) — The probability that event *A* and event *B* will both occur (the probability of joint occurrence).

(75) P(B|A) — The conditional probability of event *B*, given that event *A* has occurred.

Formulas Introduced in This Chapter (with Frame Numbers)

(9) $P(X) = \dfrac{f(X)}{N}$ — The probability of an event, determined by the classical, or a priori, method.

(34) $P(A) = \dfrac{X}{X+Y}$ — The probability of an event *A*, given that the odds favoring the event are $X:Y$.

(36) $X:Y = P(A):1 - P(A)$ — The odds ratio for an event *A*, given that the probability of the event is $P(A)$.

(54) $P(A \text{ or } B) = P(A) + P(B)$ — The probability of either of two mutually exclusive events *A* or *B* occurring in a single observation.

(58) $P(A \text{ or } B) = P(A) + P(B) - P(A,B)$ — The probability of either of the nonexclusive events *A* or *B* (or both) occurring in a single observation.

(68) $P(A,B) = P(A)P(B)$ — The probability of the joint occurrence of independent events *A* and *B*.

(77) $P(A,B) = P(A)P(B|A)$ — The probability of the joint occurrence of dependent events *A* and *B*.

(92) Amount certain = expected value of risk situation — General equality used to determine the subjective probability of an event in a risk situation.

(95) Expected value = (P) (monetary gain) + (1 − P) (monetary loss) — The expected (long-run) value of a risk situation, in which *P* is the probability of success and (1 − P) is the probability of failure.

Exercises
(Solutions on pages 595–596)

5.1 An inspector takes a random sample of 50 transistors manufactured during one day and finds that two are defective. What is the probability that an electronic device containing one such transistor will be inoperative because the transistor is defective? What approach and method did you use in arriving at this probability value?

5.2 A financial analyst estimates that the chances are two out of three that bond prices will decline during the coming month. Based on his assessment, what is the probability that bond prices will decline during the coming month? What approach and method did you use in arriving at this probability value?

5.3 If an adjacent tract is developed, a particular section of land will be worth $90,000 two years from now; whereas if the adjacent tract is not developed, the section will be worth $45,000. Assume that these dollar values have been corrected for taxes and finance charges and represent present values. An experienced real estate investor confides that he is willing to pay up to $60,000 for the section of land, but no more. What probability value has he implicitly assigned regarding the development of the adjacent tract of land?

5.4 For each of the following reported odds ratios, determine the equivalent probability value, and for each of the reported probability values, determine the equivalent odds ratio.
(a) A purchasing agent estimates that the odds are 2:1 that a shipment will arrive on schedule.
(b) The probability that a new component will not function properly when assembled is assessed as being $P = \frac{1}{5}$.
(c) The odds that a new product will succeed are estimated as being 3:1.
(d) The probability that the home team will win the opening game of the season is assessed as being $\frac{1}{3}$.

5.5 The following table indicates the probabilities associated with the possible demand levels for color TV sets in a particular appliance store during the next three-month period.

Number of sets	<50	50–99	100–149	150–199	≥200
Probability	0.20	0.40	0.20	0.10	0.10

(a) What is the probability that fewer than 100 sets will be demanded?
(b) What is the probability that at least 50 but not more than 199 sets will be demanded?

5.6 A personnel manager has found it useful to categorize engineering job applicants according to (1) whether they have earned a college degree in engineering, and (2) whether they have had relevant work experience. In a large number of such job applicants 70 percent have the degree whether or not they have any work experience, and 60 percent have work experience whether or not they have a degree. Fifty percent of the applicants have both the degree completed and relevant work experience. Construct a Venn diagram to portray the probabilities associated with sampling one applicant from this group, using D for degree completion and W for work experience.

5.7 For the situation described in Exercise 5.6, determine the probability that a randomly selected job applicant has either the degree completed or relevant work experience. What is the probability that the applicant has neither the degree nor work experience?

5.8 During a six-month period two-thirds of a large number of common stock issues have advanced in market price or remained unchanged while one-third have declined in price. If three common stock issues are randomly selected, construct a tree diagram illustrating the probabilities of price advances and price declines for the three stocks, using A to signify that the price of the stock has advanced or remained unchanged and D to signify a price decline. (*Hint*: This should be a three-step diagram, left to right.)

5.9 Referring to Exercise 5.8, (a) what is the probability that all three of the randomly chosen stock issues experienced a decline? (b) What is the probability that *at least* one of the stock issues declined in price? (*Hint*: Only one path in the tree diagram does *not* satisfy this requirement, and hence the probability of this particular sequence of outcomes can be substracted from 1.0 to obtain the answer.)

5.10 The probability of a general rise in consumer demand for home air-conditioning units next year is estimated to be 0.70. If this increase in demand materializes, the probability is 0.80 that the sales volume of a particular company will increase. If the rise does not occur, the probability is 0.50 that the company's sales volume will increase. Construct a tree diagram illustrating the various possible outcomes and the associated probabilities, using R and R' for a rise and no rise in general demand and I and I' for an increase and no increase in company sales, respectively.

5.11 For the situation described in Exercise 5.10, what is the probability that there will be a general rise in demand accompanied by an increase in company sales volume?

Additional Exercises **5.12** What is the probability that the sum of the dots showing on the face of two dice is seven? What approach and method did you use in arriving at this probability value?

5.13 A marketing manager in a company manufacturing office copiers indicates that he cannot estimate the probability that a new type of camera developed by the research group will be profitable. However, it is his judgment that the company should sell the patent rights to a photographic company if offered more than $100,000 but should proceed with manufacturing and marketing the camera itself if offered less than this amount. If the camera is successful, it is estimated that the present value of the profits that will be generated in the future is $300,000. If the camera is unsuccessful, the present value of the loss is $150,000. What is the probability that the camera will be successful, based on the marketing manager's estimate of the value of the patent rights?

5.14 For the situation described in Exercise 5.13, the manager of the research group estimates that the odds are 3:1 that the camera will be successful. Based on this evaluation, what is his estimate of the probability that the camera will be successful?

5.15 For each of the following reported odds ratios, determine the equivalent probability value, and for each of the reported probability values, determine the equivalent odds ratio.
(a) Probability of $P = \frac{2}{3}$ that a target delivery date will be met.
(b) Probability of $P = \frac{9}{10}$ that a new product will exceed the break-even sales level.
(c) Odds of 1:2 that a competitor will achieve a technological breakthrough.
(d) Odds of 5:1 that a new product will be profitable.

5.16 Of 1,000 assembled components, 10 have a wiring defect and 20 have a structural defect. There is good reason to assume that no component has both defects. What is the probability that a randomly chosen component will have either type of defect?

5.17 Of 100 people who participated in a consumer survey, 50 are over 30 years of age. Further, 70 of the 100 people are urban residents, rather than rural residents. Of the 70 urban residents, 40 are over 30 years old. Construct a Venn diagram illustrating the probabilities associated with sampling an individual from this survey group, in terms of being over 30 years of age and being an urban resident. Use O for over 30 and U for urban resident.

5.18 For the consumer group described in Exercise 5.17, what is the probability that a randomly chosen individual will be over 30 years old or an urban resident?

5.19 Of 500 employees, 200 participate in a company's profit-sharing plan (P), 400 have major-medical insurance coverage (M), and 200 employees participate in both programs. Construct a Venn diagram to portray the events designated P and M.

5.20 Refer to the Venn diagram prepared in Exercise 5.19.
(a) What is the probability that a randomly selected employee will be a participant in at least one of the two programs?
(b) What is the probability that a randomly selected employee will not be a participant in either program?

5.21 The probability that a new marketing approach will be successful (S) is assessed as being 0.60. The probability that the expenditure for developing the approach can be kept within the original budget (B) is 0.50. The probability that both of these objectives will be achieved is estimated at 0.30. What is the probability that at least one of these objectives will be achieved?

5.22 On the average, a sale is completed with 10 percent of potential customers that are contacted. If a salesman randomly selects two potential customers from his list and calls on them, construct the tree diagram which indicates the probabilities associated with the various sequences of outcomes, using S for sale and S' for no sale.

5.23 For the situation described in Exercise 5.22, **(a)** what is the probability that both calls will result in sales? **(b)** What is the probability that the calls will result in exactly one sale?

5.24 Three out of eight account reports prepared by a bank teller contain a procedural error. If an auditor samples two of the eight accounts, construct the tree diagram which indicates the probabilities associated with the various sequences of outcomes, using E for obtaining an account report containing the error and E' for obtaining an account report without an error.

5.25 For the sampling situation described in Exercise 5.24, **(a)** what is the probability that neither of the accounts sampled will contain a procedural error? **(b)** What is the probability that at least one of the accounts will contain a procedural error?

5.26 During a particular period, 80 percent of the common stock issues in an industry which includes just 10 companies have increased in market value. If an investor chose two of these issures randomly, what is the probability that both issues increased in market value during this period?

5.27 For the situation described in Exercise 5.26, suppose an investor chose three of these stock issues randomly. Construct a tree diagram to portray the various possible results for the sequence of three stock issues.

5.28 Referring to the tree diagram prepared in Exercise 5.27, determine each of the following probabilities.
(a) Probability that only one of the three issues increased in market value.
(b) Probability that two issues increased in market value.
(c) Probability that *at least* two issues increased in market value.

CHAPTER 6 ■
DISCRETE PROBABILITY DISTRIBUTIONS

In this chapter we begin by describing the nature of probability distributions in general and then we extend the discussions to the description of two discrete probability distributions that are frequently used in statistical inference: the binomial probability distribution and the Poisson probability distribution. The computation of probabilities is introduced by use of the tree diagram for sequential events, as described in Chapter 5. The algebraic approach to determining binomial probabilities and the use of the table of binomial probabilities are then described. For the Poisson distribution the probability values are determined by reference to a standard table of Poisson probabilities.

6.1 ■ The Nature of Probability Distributions

Probability distributions are closely related to frequency distributions. As described in Chapter 2, a frequency distribution is a listing of all possible events, or classes of measurements, with an indication of the observed frequency of each event. Similarly, a probability distribution also lists all possible events, or classes of measurements; but instead of observed frequencies, the probability associated with each event is identified.

0; 1; 2; 3

1 If three coins are tossed, the possible number of heads that can occur is ____, ____, ____, or ____.

One

2 Although there are four possible events associated with this sequence of observations, how many can actually occur on a single toss of three coins? ____ (number)

---

frequency

3 Suppose that the group of three coins is tossed 10 times, and the number of times that 0, 1, 2, and 3 heads is observed is posted in a table, as illustrated below. This tally of the observed frequency of occurrence of each event is called a _____ distribution.

Number of heads	Observed frequency
0	2
1	4
2	4
3	0

4 If we were to repeat the procedure and once again toss the three coins 10 times, would we be likely to obtain exactly the same distribution of frequencies as that reported in Frame 3? [Yes / No]

No

5 Instead of tabulating the actual frequency of occurrence of each event, we can determine and indicate the probability of each event. If we assume that the three coins are fair, would the probability of obtaining two heads, for example, change from time to time? [Yes / No]

No, since the value is based on the classical, or a priori, approach to computing probability. (See Chapter 5, Frames 1-12.)

probability

6 Whereas a listing of the *observed frequencies* of all events is called a "frequency distribution," a listing of the *probabilities* of all possible events is called a _____ distribution.

frequency

7 In terms of the definitions given in Frame 6, the following table is a [frequency / probability] distribution.

Weekly sales volume	Observed number of salesmen
Under $900	2
$900-$1,199	8
$1,200-$1,499	3
$1,500 and above	1

probability

8 In terms of the definitions given in Frame 6, the following table is a [frequency / probability] distribution.

Number of heads	Probability
0	$1/8$
1	$3/8$
2	$3/8$
3	$1/8$

events (or outcomes)

probability

9 Thus the probability distribution includes a listing of all possible _____ along with the associated _____ values.

10 Given a probability distribution, we can also develop a distribution of expected frequencies by multiplying each probability value by the total number of observations, or trials. On this basis, and by referring to Frame 8 for the probability values, complete the table below.

Number of heads	Expected frequency in 24 tosses of three coins
0	_____
1	_____
2	_____
3	_____

$\frac{1}{8} \times 24 = 3$
$\frac{3}{8} \times 24 = 9$
$\frac{3}{8} \times 24 = 9$
$\frac{1}{8} \times 24 = 3$

11 Although there are a number of probability models for developing a distribution of expected frequencies, two are extensively used in statistical inference and hence serve as the subject matter for the remainder of this chapter. These are the binomial and Poisson probability distributions. Of course, no matter what basis is used to develop a distribution of expected frequencies, the observed frequencies in any particular instance [seldom / often] exactly correspond to the long-run expected pattern.

seldom

12 Thus the expected frequencies of obtaining 0, 1, 2, and 3 heads on 24 tosses of three coins, which we determined in Frame 10, seldom *exactly* correspond to the observed frequencies in a particular case. In what way, then, is a probability distribution, or the expected frequencies derived therefrom, of any use? _____

_____

_____

Actual results tend to be close to this; in the long run this is the best estimate.

6.2 ■ The Binomial Distribution

The binomial probability distribution is actually a family of distributions all of which have certain characteristics in common. One characteristic of binomial distributions is that they are distributions of discrete data rather than continuous data. Thus a frequency distribution describing the measured voltage of a number of batteries does not lend itself to being represented by a binomial distribution, whereas a frequency distribution indicating the number of times that 0, 1, 2, and 3 batteries have been found to be defective in batches of three that are tested does lend itself to being represented by a binomial distribution. Measurement of voltage is of course on the continuous scale of measurement, as discussed in Chapter 1, whereas "number of defective batteries" represents counting rather than measuring and is thus discrete. In this section we discuss the use of tree diagrams in developing binomial distributions and then illustrate how the expansion of the binomial $(q + p)$ to various powers achieves the same result.

13 The binomial probability distribution is applicable when (1) there is a sequence of observations in which an event either occurs or does not occur in each case, (2) the events are independent, and (3) the process is stationary (the probability of the event occurring does not change from trial to trial). Illustrated below is a distribution of observed frequencies of heads on 12 tosses of three coins. If we wish to determine the probability of each outcome based on the assumption that all coins are fair, would the probability distribution that we construct be a binomial distribution? [Yes / No]

Yes

Number of heads	Observed frequency
0	2
1	5
2	4
3	1

14 Binomial distributions are so named because they can be generated by expansion of the binomial $(q + p)$ to various powers. Before we describe this procedure, we shall first illustrate how the values of the probabilities that are entered in a binomial probability distribution can be determined by the use of the familiar tree diagram. For the example in which three fair coins are tossed, complete the tree diagram below.

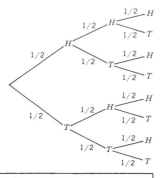

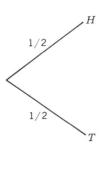

(A three-step diagram is necessary, since there is a sequence of three trials, or observations.)

15 Now, using the tree diagram, compute the probability of each possible sequence of elementary events and post each probability value in the appropriate space below. If you are experiencing any difficulty at this point, review Frames 70–83 of Chapter 5.

Probability of each sequence of elementary events

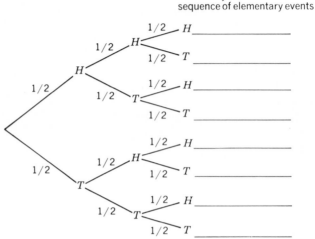

16 The diagram in Frame 15 indicates that there are eight unique sequences of events that are possible and that each has a probability of occurrence of $\frac{1}{8}$. However, if we are not concerned about maintaining the separate identity of each sequence, then some of the probabilities may be combined. For instance, if we are simply interested in the probability of obtaining one head when three coins are tossed, then it does not matter which of the three coins has fallen heads so long as it is one of them. Referring to the same tree diagram and combining probabilities where appropriate, complete the following probability distribution.

	Number of heads	*Probability*
$\frac{1}{8}$	0	___
$\frac{3}{8}$	1	___
$\frac{3}{8}$	2	___
$\frac{1}{8}$	3	___

17 The probabilities posted in the distribution in Frame 16 indicate that although there is just one sequence by which no heads or three heads can be obtained, the event which includes one head can occur in _____ (number) different ways.

three

18 Thus a probability distribution always lists all possible _____ and the value of the _____ associated with each event.

events; probability

19 In the space below, construct the tree diagram and the probability distribution for the possible number of heads when one coin is tossed.

Number of heads	Probability
___	___
___	___

0	$\frac{1}{2}$
1	$\frac{1}{2}$

20 What distinguishes the probability distribution in Frame 19 from a frequency distribution? _____

Probabilities instead of observed frequencies are reported.

21 In using tree diagrams to generate binomial probability distributions, there are two essential requirements. One is that there be two mutually exclusive elementary events at each step in the diagram, and the other is that the events in the separate steps in the diagram be independent and stationary. The latter stipulation indicates that the probability of obtaining a head, for example, [can / cannot] be different in different steps of the same tree diagram.

cannot

22 Thus the essential characteristics of a binomial distribution, from the standpoint of tree diagrams, are that at each branching in the tree diagram there be ____ (number) branches, that the probabilities in each step be [dependent on / independent of] previous outcomes, and that the probability of an elementary event be _____ from step to step.

two

independent of

constant (*or* the same)

23 The requirement that there be only two branches at each step is not necessarily as restrictive as it sounds, for problems can often be restated to conform to this requirement. For example, suppose that we are interested in the probability distribution of obtaining 0, 1, or 2 sixes when two six-sided dice are tossed. In constructing a tree diagram for this problem, how can we reduce the six branches to two branches at each step in the tree diagram? _____

_____

_____

By defining the two events at each branching as 6 and $\overline{6}$ (read: "not 6")

24 The tree diagrams for all binomial distributions contain two branches at each step and independent events whose probabilities do not change from step to step in the tree diagram. Can the values of the probabilities differ for different tree diagrams? [Yes / No] Can the number of steps in the tree diagrams representing two different binomial probability distributions be different? [Yes / No]

Yes

Yes

25 In tossing coins, we can simultaneously toss one coin, two coins, or n coins, and each situation is represented by a different tree diagram. Similarly, the probability value of the successful outcome at each step in the tree diagram might be $\frac{1}{2}$, as for a fair coin, or it might have any other value, such as a probability value of $\frac{1}{6}$ associated with a "six" being obtained on a fair die. These facts are the basis for our introductory remark that the binomial distribution [is / is not] a single distribution of probabilities and [is / is not] an entire family of related distributions.

is not

is

26 In terms of the tree diagram that can be used to determine the probability values to be entered in a binomial probability distribution, what three attributes do all such tree diagrams have in common? _____

_____

Two branches at each step, independent events, and constant probability values.

27 The two ways in which tree diagrams representing binomial distributions can vary are _____

_____

_____

_____

In the value of the probability associated with the successful outcome and the number of steps in the diagram

steps

28 When a tree diagram is used, the number of observations or trials (such as number of coins tossed, or number of manufactured components sampled for inspection) is represented by the number of _____ in the diagram.

1

29 If there is a sequence of three observations, then four types of outcomes are possible in terms of the number of "successes." For example, if a coin is tossed three times, the number of "heads" that might be observed is 0, 1, 2, or 3. Thus we can state the general rule that when there are n events in a sequence, there are $n +$ ___ (number) categories of outcomes for the overall sequence.

0; 5

6 (0 through 5 possible
defectives)

30 If five motors are sampled for the purpose of detailed inspection, the number in which some defect is found can vary from ___ (number) motors to ___ (number) motors. In this case, then, there are ____ (number) categories of outcomes.

1

31 Put another way, the number of categories of outcomes is ___ (number) greater than the number of independent events or steps represented in the tree diagram.

32 As another example of the use of a tree diagram to develop a binomial probability distribution, suppose that 10 percent of the components produced in a given manufacturing department have a particular defect. If two components are sampled, construct the tree diagram that can be used to determine the probability of 0, 1, or 2 components being defective and present the associated probability distribution in tabular form. In the tree diagram, use D to indicate a defective component and ND to indicate a nondefective component.

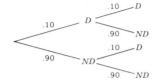

**Binomial Probability Distribution
for Number of Defective Motors**

Number defective	Probability
0	0.81
1	0.18
2	0.01

33 Using the data in Frame 32, construct the distribution of expected frequencies for the number of defective components when 100 batches of two components each are sampled.

	Number defective	Expected frequencies in 100 samples of two each
81	0	___
18	1	___
1	2	___

34 Or, using the probability distribution for a somewhat different purpose, suppose that we sample one batch of two components and find that both components are defective. Given the assumption that 10 percent of the components are defective, is this outcome possible? [Yes / No] Is this event likely to occur very often? [Yes / No] Given this observed outcome, might it be useful to consider the possibility that the overall percentage of defective components is actually greater than 10 percent? [Yes / No]

Yes

No (probability of only 0.01)

Yes (since the probability of obtaining two defective components would be greater in such a case)

35 We could continue with other examples that would require the construction of tree diagrams with different numbers of steps and different probability values. Each change along either of these lines [would / would not] change the probability distribution thereby developed. All of the distributions developed, however, could be described as being _____ probability distributions.

would

binomial

6.3 ■ Determining Binomial Probabilities Algebraically

We have used the tree diagram to introduce the binomial distribution because of your familiarity with tree diagrams from Chapter 5. Most books discuss binomial distributions from the algebraic point of view, for this is the basis for the term "binomial distribution." In the binomial $(q + p)$, p indicates the probability of "success" in a single trial and q stands for the probability of "failure."

36 If a single coin is tossed and the event "head" is designated success, then in the binomial $(q + p)$, $q =$ ___ (value) and $p =$ ___ (value).

½ (or 0.5)
½ (or 0.5)

37 Of course, the specific values of p and q can vary from problem to problem, but their sum is always 1.0, as is true also of the branches coming from one point in a tree diagram. The number of trials, or observations, in the sequence is indicated by the exponent of the binomial. Thus $(q + p)^1$, or simply $(q + p)$, is the binomial expansion for developing a probability distribution when one coin is tossed. When three coins are tossed, the binomial term to be expanded is $(q + p)$ ——. (Write in the exponent of the binomial.)

3

38 Now, for the relatively simple example involving the tossing of three coins, let us expand the binomial in terms of the appropriate power, arithmetically solve for the value of each term in the expansion, and see what this gives us. We present a technique for expanding binomial terms in Frames 47 to 55, but as you may recall from your study of algebra,

$$(q + p)^3 = q^3 + 3q^2 p + 3qp^2 + p^3$$

Now, if we substitute the values ½ for q and ½ for p, we get

$$(½)^3 + 3(½)^2 (½) + 3(½)(½)^2 + (½)^3 = \_\_\_ + \_\_\_ + \_\_\_ + \_\_\_$$

$\frac{1}{8} + \frac{3}{8} + \frac{3}{8} + \frac{1}{8}$

39 Refer to Frame 16, where we used a tree diagram to generate the binomial probability distribution for the number of heads when three coins are tossed. To what do the values in Frame 38 correspond? _____

To the probability of obtain-
ing 0, 1, 2, and 3 heads,
respectively.

40 Similarly, let us use the method of binomial expansion to determine the probability distribution for the number of defective components obtained when batches of two components are sampled and historical data indicate that 10 percent of the components have some defect. If p is defined as the probability of obtaining a defective component in a single inspection, then $q =$ _____ (number) and $p =$ _____ (number).

0.90 (or $\frac{9}{10}$); 0.10 (or $\frac{1}{10}$)

2

41 For the sampling of two components $(q + p)^n = (q + p)$ ——. (Fill in the exponent.)

42 Given that $q = 0.90$ and $p = 0.10$, and that $(q + p)^2 = q^2 + 2qp + p^2$, the values of the three terms of this expansion, corresponding to the probability of obtaining 0, 1, and 2 defective components, are _____ (number), _____ (number), and _____ (number).

0.81; 0.18
0.01

43 But when we obtain the three probability values in Frame 42, how do we know that the 0.81 is the probability of no defective components being obtained rather than the probability of both components being defective, for example? The *exponents* in the binomial expansion indicate this. Thus the first term in the binomial expansion, q^2, can be interpreted as indicating the probability of no defective components and two nondefective components; $2qp$ indicates the probability of obtaining one nondefective and one defective component, and p^2 indicates the probability of obtaining ___ (number) nondefective components and ___ (number) defective components.

0

2 (Since there is no *q* in this term, its exponent is understood to be 0.)

44 For the problem in which we tossed three coins (Frame 38), the appropriate binomial expansion is $q^3 + 3q^2p + 3qp^2 + p^3$. On the basis we have just introduced, and given that $p =$ probability of heads and $q =$ probability of tails, the first term of this expansion indicates the probability of obtaining ___ (number) head(s) and the second term indicates the probability of obtaining ___ (number) head(s).

0

1

45 Thus the exponents included in each term of the binomial expansion are useful in interpreting the meaning of the term. Now, what about the *coefficient* of each term (e.g., the 3 in $3q^2p$)? Compare the binomial expansion below with the related tree diagram. Given that the arithmetic solution of the term $3q^2p$ indicates the probability of obtaining one head and two tails, what additional information does the coefficient 3 provide about this outcome? _____

_____

_____

That there are three ways of obtaining one head and two tails (i.e., *H, T, T; T, H, T;* and *T, T, H*).

$$q^3 + 3q^2p + 3qp^2 + p^3$$

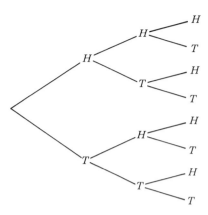

46 Thus binomial probability distributions can be developed algebraically by binomial expansions or diagrammatically by tree diagrams, and, given one type of solution, we can construct the other. For example, given the binomial expansion $q^4 + 4q^3p + 6q^2p^2 + 4qp^3 + p^4$, by noting the sum of the exponents in any one term, we can directly tell that the related tree diagram has _____ (number) steps.

four

47 The question that we have not yet discussed is: "How do you determine the exponents and coefficients for each term of a binomial expansion?" To begin with, for $(q + p)^n$ we can observe that there are always $[n - 1 / n / n + 1]$ terms in the expansion (refer to the expansion to the fourth power in Frame 46 if necessary).

$n + 1$

48 Let us first address ourselves to determining the values of the *exponents* for each term of the binomial expansion. In the expansion of $(q + p)^n$ you may have observed that the first term of the expansion is always q^n (it can also be thought of as $q^n p^0$, which equals q^n, since any value raised to the zero power equals 1). Then in the succeeding terms of the expansion the exponent of q is progressively [increased / decreased] by 1 and the exponent of p is progressively [increased / decreased] by 1 until the final term of the binomial expansion is p^n.

decreased
increased

49 Omitting all coefficients, indicate the appropriate exponents of q and p in each term of the following expansion.

$q^5 + q^4p + q^3p^2 + q^2p^3 +$
$qp^4 + p^5$

$(q + p)^5 = $ ___ + ___ + ___ + ___ + ___ + ___

50 Referring to the expansion in Frame 49 if necessary, we can also observe that for the expansion of $(q + p)^n$ the sum of the exponents of q and p in any one term of the expansion always equals $[n - 1 \,/\, n \,/\, n + 1]$.

> n

51 As contrasted to determining the values of the exponents, we can determine the values of the coefficient for each term by solving for the number of combinations. Rather than using the algebraic basis for such a solution, which is illustrated in Frame 54, we use a table of coefficients instead. Refer to Table B-2 in the Appendix. For the general binomial term $(q + p)^n$, this table can be used to determine the coefficients for $n = 1$ through $n = $ ____ (number).

> 10

52 Each line of the table corresponds to a given value of n in $(q + p)^n$, and each column corresponds to one term of the expansion. Instead of being identified as "first term," "second term," etc., the terms are more specifically identified according to the values of the exponents of ____ .

> p

53 Using Table B-2, enter the values of the coefficients in the following expansion.

> $1; 5; 10; 10; 5$
>
> 1

$(q + p)^5 = $ ___$q^5 + $ ___$q^4 p + $ ___$q^3 p^2 + $ ___$q^2 p^3 + $ ___$qp^4 + $ ___p^5

54 Similarly, expand the binomial $(q + p)^4$, using both the rules for exponents that we have presented and Table B-2 to determine the value of the coefficient for each term.

> $q^4 + 4q^3 p + 6q^2 p^2 + 4qp^3 + p^4$

$(q + p)^4 = $ _____

Note: The algebraic basis for calculating a coefficient is to determine $_nC_X$ (the number of combinations on n items taken X at a time), where n is as defined above (sample size) and X is the exponent of p in the binomial term of interest (number of "successes"). For example, for the second term in the solution above, the coefficient is

$$_nC_X = \frac{n!}{X!(n - X)!} = \frac{4!}{1!(4 - 1)!} = \frac{4 \times 3 \times 2 \times 1}{(1)(3 \times 2 \times 1)} = 4$$

which corresponds to the value given in Table B-2. In using this combinatorial formula, note that $0! = 1$.

55 $(q + p)^3 =$ _____

56 Using the expansion in Frame 55, if batches of three motors are being inspected and the assumption is made that 10 percent of the motors being received have some defect, construct the probability distribution for the number of defective motors that are obtained.

Number of defective motors	Probability
—	—
—	—
—	—
—	—

57 Since a probability distribution includes an exhaustive listing of all possible outcomes, along with related probability values, we would expect the sum of the probabilities to equal 1.0. Is this true for the data of Frame 56? [Yes / No]

58 A binomial probability distribution, or a distribution of expected frequencies based on a binomial expansion, can be presented graphically as well as in tabular form. For example, the probability of obtaining 0, 1, 2, and 3 heads on the repeated tossing of three fair coins is graphically represented on the _____ chart below.

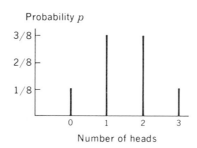

Probability p

Number of heads

59 In this section we have illustrated the fact that for certain kinds of events the probability of each possible outcome, and hence the expected frequency of that outcome, can be determined by the expansion of the _____ equation.

60 The binomial expansion applies to situations in which the probability distribution is for [continuous /discrete] data, the several elementary events which are included in the sequence (such as batches of four items being inspected) are [dependent / independent], and the probability value associated with an event [does / does not] change from trial to trial.

> discrete

> independent

> does not

61 The calculation of probabilities that is accomplished by appropriate binomial expansion can be accomplished also by the construction and use of a _____ diagram. In either case there are two ways in which binomial distributions can differ from one another. One is in the number of _____ in the sequence of events being investigated, and the other way is in the value of the _____ associated with the elementary events.

> tree

> events

> probability

62 At this stage in our discussion of statistical inference and probability theory, we cannot yet fully illustrate the practical applications of binomial probability distributions. As a brief indication of one type of use, suppose that the quality standard in a production process allows a maximum of 1 percent defective items. For batches of five items that are inspected, the actual frequency distribution has significantly more defective items than the expected distribution of frequencies which is based on a binomial distribution. What would we be likely to conclude? _____
_____
_____
_____
_____
_____

> That there are more than 1 percent defective items in the overall process. (The basis for deciding when a difference constitutes a significant departure is a key factor in such decision-making situations, and it is a factor that we consider in Chapter 10.)

6.4 ■ Determining Binomial Probabilities by Means of Tables

As indicated in the two preceding sections of this chapter, binomial probabilities can be determined by constructing relatively cumbersome tree diagrams or by expanding the binomial $(q + p)$ to the appropriate power. In this section we describe an easier method of determining such probability values for applications purposes, by using a table of binomial probabilities.

63 By either of the approaches to determining binomial probabilities which have been presented, there are two values that determine the overall distribution of probabilities: (1) the number of trials, represented by the symbol ____ ; and (2) the probability value associated with "success" in each trial represented by the symbol ____ .

n

p

64 Further, the probability value associated with any multiple, or compound event, such as the probability of three successes given $n = 5$ and $p = 0.30$, has to take into consideration the number of designated successes in the event being described. Because the "number of successes" is a variable in the context of the binomial distribution, we represent this value by the symbol "*X*." Thus, the three factors that determine the specific binomial probability value associated with a multiple event are represented by the symbols ____ , ____ , and ____ .

n

p; X

65 Or, put another way, whereas the overall binomial probability distribution is determined by the two parameters represented by the symbols ___ and ___ , the probability associated with any particular outcome included in that distribution is determined by identifying the value of ___ .

n; p

X

66 Because the binomial probability distribution is generally used in conjunction with small sample sizes only, tables of binomial probability values have been prepared for general use. Table B-3 in the Appendix is such a table. Note that this particular table can be used with sample sizes up to $n =$ ___ and with probability values up to $p =$ _____ .

30

0.50

67 For example, given that $n = 5$ and $p = 0.30$, the probability of obtaining $X = 3$ successes can be read directly from Table B-3 as being equal to 0.1323. Similarly, the probability of obtaining exactly two successes, given that $n = 5$ and $p = 0.30$, is _____ .

0.3087

68 Since the probability of obtaining X successes is in fact conditional on the values of n and p, the required probability value is described by using the conditional ("given that") notation introduced in Frame 75 of Chapter 5. Thus, the probability of obtaining three successes, given $n = 5$ and $p = 0.30$, is written $P(X = 3 \mid n = 5, p = 0.30)$. Similarly, the

$$P(X = 5 \mid n = 8, p = 0.40)$$

probability of obtaining exactly five successes, given a sample of eight items and the probability of success for each item being 0.40, can be written _____ .

0.1023

0.5000

69 As further practice in using the table, we can determine that $P(X = 5 \mid n = 30, p = 0.10) =$ _____ and $P(X = 1 \mid n = 2, p = 0.50) =$ _____ .

70 Note, however, that each of the probabilities designated above is for a particular number of successes. What if we want to determine the probability of two *or more* heads in four tosses of a fair coin? In this case, we simply use the rule of addition and add the probabilities associated with obtaining two *or* three *or* four successes: $P(X \geqslant 2 \mid n = 4, p = 0.50) = 0.3750 + 0.2500 + 0.0625 = 0.6875$. Similarly, the probability of obtaining three or more successes, given $n = 5$ and $p = 0.30$, is $P($_____$) =$ _____

$$(X \geqslant 3 \mid n = 5, p = 0.30) = 0.1323 + 0.0284 + 0.0024 = 0.1631$$

.

71 For an inequality of the "less than" type the same reasoning applies, but with the opposite end of the binomial listing of probabilities being accumulated. Thus, the probability of one or *fewer* successes, given $n = 5$ and $p = 0.30$, is

$$(X \leqslant 1 \mid n = 5, p = 0.30) = 0.1681 + 0.3602 = 0.5283$$

$P($_____$) =$ _____ .

72 Finally, we noted previously that the values of p in Table B-3 extend only to $p = 0.50$. This limitation is typical for such tables. How, then, do we determine binomial probabilities for situations in which $p > 0.50$, such as $P(X = 3 \mid n = 5, p = 0.80)$? In this case we transform the problem by looking at the number of failures rather than the number of successes which defines the event. That is, given that $n = 5$, then if the defined number of successes is $X = 3$, the associated number of failures in five trials must equal $X' =$ ___ . Further, if the probability of "success" in each trial is $p = 0.80$, the probability of failure must be $q =$ ____ .

2

0.20

2

5; 0.20

73 Therefore, $P(X = 3 \mid n = 5, p = 0.80) = P(X' =$ ___ $\mid n =$ ___ , $q =$ _____$)$. Further, the probability associated with the last expression can be obtained from Table B-3 and has a value of _____ .

0.2048

74 If the above reasoning and associated conversion aren't entirely clear to you, consider the following question. Isn't the probability of obtaining "two failures in five trials" exactly the same as the probability of obtaining "three successes in five trials"? In one case the event is described in terms of the number of successes while in the other case it is described in terms of the number of failures, but the identical event is described in either case. Similarly, indicate the transformed expression and the appropriate probability value for $P(X = 7 \mid n = 10, p = 0.70)$. _____

$P(X' = 3 \mid n = 10, q = 0.30) =$
    0.2668

75 If $p > 0.50$ and the specified outcome is defined in terms of an inequality, the conversion is a bit more involved, and from our standpoint it will be best to construct a table listing the equivalent outcomes of X and X' as an aid. The listing below is such a table for $n = 5$. For example, the first line of this table indicates that zero successes in five trials" is directly equivalent to "___ failures in five trials."

    5

$n = 5$

X	X'
0	5
1	4
2	3
3	2
4	1
5	0

76 Referring to the table above, we can also determine that "four or more successes" is directly equivalent to "one or fewer failures." Thus, for example, $P(X \geqslant 4 \mid n = 5, p = 0.80)$ $= P(X' \leqslant 1 \mid n = 5, q = 0.20) = 0.3277 + 0.4096 = 0.7373.$ Similarly, $P(X \leqslant 2 \mid n = 5, p = 0.80) =$ _____
_____ .

$P(X' \geqslant 3 \mid n = 5, q = 0.20) =$
$0.0512 + 0.0064 + 0.0003 =$
    0.0579

77 In the space below, construct a table similar to the one above for $n = 8$, and determine $P(X \geq 6 \mid n = 8, p = 0.60)$.

	$n = 8$
X	X'
0	8
1	7
2	6
3	5
4	4
5	3
6	2
7	1
8	0

$P(X \geq 6 \mid n = 8, p = 0.60) =$
$P(X' \leq 2 \mid n = 8, q = 0.40) =$
$\qquad 0.0168 + 0.0896 +$
$\qquad\quad 0.2090 = 0.3154$
(Note that we simply reverse the inequality when we use X' and q in place of X and p.)

6.5 ■ The Poisson Distribution

The binomial distribution is applicable in situations in which we wish to know the probability of observing a certain number of events given a specified number of trials. An example is determining the probability of observing various numbers of defective items, given that a specified number of items is inspected. By contrast, there are a number of situations in which the number of trials cannot be specified. This is the case when the events occur in a continuum of time or space rather than on a "per-trial" basis. Examples are the probability of a certain number of calls arriving at a switchboard during a given period of time and the probability of observing a certain number of defects on a roll of sheet steel.

78 It is not our purpose to be concerned with the mathematical formula that underlies the Poisson distribution, but rather to indicate the kinds of situations in which the Poisson distribution can be applied. Because the binomial and Poisson distributions are both concerned with the count of the number

	of events rather than the measurement of fractional values, both distributions are [discrete / continuous] probability distributions.
discrete	

79 Whereas the binomial distribution is concerned with the number of events in a given number of trials, the Poisson distribution applies when the number of [events / trials] cannot be specified and is represented by a continuum, such as a period of time.

trials

80 The idea underlying the Poisson distribution is that there is a fixed probability that an event will occur within any particular portion of the continuum, and that the events are independent. In this respect, the process underlying the Poisson distribution [is / is not] similar to the process underlying the binomial distribution.

is (since the binomial also assumes fixed probabilities and independent events)

81 However, the Poisson distribution differs from the binomial in that neither n nor p can be specified. For example, consider a 30-minute time interval at a switchboard. Since "30 minutes" is an interval and not a specified number of trials, the value of n [can / cannot] be specified.

cannot

82 The solution to this problem is to determine the mean number of calls that have been received at the switchboard in similar 30-minute periods and to use this mean expectation as the basis for determining the probabilities associated with the various possible events. In this switchboard example, the "various possible events" refers to the various number of _____ that might be received.

calls

83 As a matter of statistical convention, the mean of a Poisson process is designated by the symbol λ, which is the Greek lowercase lambda. Thus, for the binomial distribution when X, the number of successes, has been specified, the values of two parameters are required to determine the probability value: ____ and ____. For the Poisson distribution, only one parameter is required, and that is ____.

$n; p$
λ (lambda)

84 The computation of Poisson probabilities is even more tedious than that of binomial probabilities. For this reason, a table of Poisson probabilities is generally used. Such a table is included as Table B-4 in the Appendix. Note that this particular table can be used with λ values up to $\lambda =$ _____ .

10.0

85 The use of the Poisson table is very similar to the use of the binomial table. For example, the probability of observing $X = 3$ events given that $\lambda = 4.0$ is 0.1954. Similarly, the probability of observing $X = 6$ events given that $\lambda = 3.0$ is _____ .

> 0.0504

86 As is the case for binomial probabilities, conditional expressions are used to represent Poisson probabilities. Thus, the last probability in Frame 85 is represented by $P(X = 6|\lambda = 3.0)$. Similarly, the probability of observing $X = 5$ events given that $\lambda = 5.0$ is represented by _____ and has the value _____ .

> $P(X = 5|\lambda = 5.0)$
>
> 0.1755

87 As an applications example, if an average of 1.2 machine breakdowns per hour has been experienced in a factory with many similar machines, what is the probability that exactly three maintenance calls will be required in a particular hour? The probability is represented by _____ and has the value _____ .

> $P(X = 3|\lambda = 1.2)$
>
> 0.0867

88 Given that $\lambda = 1.2$ (from Frame 87), complete the probability distribution below for the various number of breakdowns that can occur by reference to Appendix Table B-4.

Number of breakdowns	Probability
0	0.3012
1	0.3614
2	0.2169
3	_____
4	_____
5	_____
6	_____
7	_____
8	_____

> 0.0867
> 0.0260
> 0.0062
> 0.0012
> 0.0002
> 0.0000

89 Of course, in applications such as the foregoing we would most likely have an interest in the probability that "three or more" maintenance calls will be required rather than just "exactly three." As was true for the binomial probabilities, the total probability associated with an inequality can be determined by use of the rule of [addition / multiplication].

> addition

90 Referring to the probability distribution in Frame **88**, the probability that three or more machine maintenance calls will be required, given that $\lambda = 1.2$, is $P(X \geqslant 3 | \lambda = 1.2) = 0.0867 + 0.0260 + 0.0062 + 0.0012 + 0.0002 = 0.1203$. Similarly, the probability that five or more maintenance calls will be required, given that an average of 1.0 call is generally required, is represented by _____ and equals _____ .

> $P(X \geqslant 5 | \lambda = 1.0)$
> $0.0031 + 0.0005 + 0.0001 =$
> 0.0037

91 For "less than" inequalities, probability values at the opposite end of the listing are accumulated. For example, the probability that one or fewer calls will be required, given that $\lambda = 1.0$, is represented by _____ and equals _____ .

> $P(X \leqslant 1 | \lambda = 1.0)$
> $0.3679 + 0.3679 = 0.7358$

92 Frequently, the mean associated with a Poisson process is not identified as such, but sufficient data are given to determine the mean for the continuum unit. For example, if one ship arrives at a particular dock every fifth day, on the average, the probability that more than one ship will arrive on a given day is represented by the expression _____ .

> $P(X \geqslant 2 | \lambda = 0.2)$

93 In the above frame, since the variable is discrete, "more than one" is the same as "two or more." Also, note that the value of lambda is always in respect to a stated continuum (length of time, in the above example). Given that one ship arrives every five days, on the average, the probability that two or more ships will arrive during a particular *two*-day period is represented by the expression _____ .

> $P(X \geqslant 2 | \lambda = 0.4)$

94 (Frames 1-12) A probability distribution involves a listing of all possible _____ with the associated _____ value for each.

> **Review**
> events; probability

95 (Frame 13) Binomial probability distributions can be used only in conjunction with data that are [discrete / continuous].

> discrete

96 (Frames 14-15) Given that 20 percent of the prospective customers who are contacted actually make a purchase, construct the tree diagram illustrating the probability values that apply when a group of three prospects are contacted, using S for "sale" and NS for "no sale."

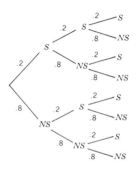

97 (Frames 16–20) Using the tree diagram of Frame 96, construct the probability distribution for the possible number of sales that can be completed when three prospects are contacted.

Number of sales	Probability
—	———
—	———
—	———
—	———

0	0.512
1	0.384
2	0.096
3	0.008

98 (Frames 21–27) In which of the following ways can the tree diagrams for *different* binomial distributions differ?

Yes
No (There are always two.)

No
Yes

(a) Number of steps [Yes / No]
(b) Number of branches at each choice point [Yes / No]
(c) Change in the value of p (or q) within a given tree diagram [Yes / No]
(d) Different values of p in different tree diagrams [Yes / No]

99 (Frames 28–35) The number of events, n, in a sequence of events is indicated by the number of _____ in the tree diagram, and the number of categories of events for the entire sequence is equal to $[n - 1 / n / n + 1]$.

steps

$n + 1$

100 (Frames 36–42, 46–53) We can develop a binomial distribution algebraically by expanding the binomial $(q + p)$ to various powers. For the example in which three sales prospects are contacted (Frames 96–97), indicate the terms of the binomial expansion.

$(q + p)^n =$ _____

$(q + p)^3 = q^3 + 3q^2 p + 3qp^2 + p^3$

101 (Frames 43–45) The exponents of the terms of the binomial expansion are useful for indicating the meaning of the probability value that each term represents. For the data of Frame 100, if $p = 0.2$, indicate the probability that two out of the three sales prospects make purchases and one does not.

$P =$ _____

$3qp^2 = 3(0.8)(0.2)^2 = 0.096$

102 (Frames 54–62) Construct the probability distribution for the data of Frames 100–101 and portray the results graphically by means of a vertical bar chart.

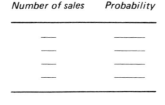

Number of sales   Probability

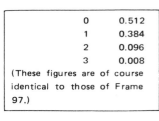

0	0.512
1	0.384
2	0.096
3	0.008

(These figures are of course identical to those of Frame 97.)

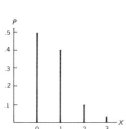

Number of sales (X)

103 (Frames 63-69) In using the table of binomial probabilities, the probability of observing exactly two successes in 10 trials, given that the probability of success in each trial is 0.40, is designated by the mathematical expression _____ _____.

$P(X = 2 | n = 10, p = 0.40)$

104 (Frames 70, 71) Suppose that we are interested in the probability of observing two *or fewer* successes, given that $n = 10$ and $p = 0.40$. How can this be done by use of the binomial table included with this chapter? _____ _____ _____.

By determining the probabilities of 0, 1, and 2 successes and adding these values.

105 (Frames 72-77) When $p > 0.50$, the problem has to be transformed before the binomial table can be used. For example, $P(X = 3 | n = 5, p = 0.70) = $ _____.
Similarly, $P(X \geqslant 3 | n = 5, p = 0.70) = $ _____ _____.

$P(X' = 2 | n = 5, q = 0.30)$

$P(X' \leqslant 2 | n = 5, q = 0.30)$

106 (Frames 78-83) For a binomial situation, the probability associated with observing a designated number of successes is dependent on the values of ___ and ___, which determine the appropriate binomial probability distribution. For a Poisson distribution the probability of observing a designated number of events is dependent on the value of the one parameter _____.

$n; p$

λ (lambda)

107 (Frames 84–93) Given that an average of 30 customers arrives at a checkout stand during each hour, the probability that more than 10 customers will arrive for service during a 10-minute interval is designated by the mathematical expression _____.

$P(X > 10 | \lambda = 5.0)$ or
$P(X \geqslant 11 | \lambda = 5.0)$

Symbols Introduced in This Chapter (with Frame Numbers)

(36) p — The proportion (probability) of "success" in a binomial sampling situation.

(36) q — The proportion (probability) of "failure" in a binomial sampling situation.

(69) $P(X | n, p)$ — The probability of X successes in a binomial sampling situation, given n observations and p, the probability of success in a single observation.

(83) λ — The lowercase Greek letter lambda, which designates the mean of a Poisson process.

(86) $P(X | \lambda)$ — The probability of observing X events in a Poisson sampling situation, given the mean of the Poisson process.

Formulas Introduced in This Chapter (with Frame Numbers)

(36) $(q + p)^n$ — The binomial expansion used to determine binomial probabilities by the algebraic approach.

(54) $_nC_X = \dfrac{n!}{X!(n - X)!}$ — The number of combinations of n items taken X at a time, used to determine the coefficient of a term in the binomial expansion.

EXERCISES
(Solutions on pages 596–598)

6.1 If 40 percent of a company's employees are in favor of a proposed new incentive-pay system, develop the probability distribution for the number of employees out of a sample of two employees who would be in favor of the incentive system by the use of a tree diagram, assuming that the total number of employees is very large. Use F for a favorable reaction and F' for an unfavorable reaction.

6.2 Develop the probability distribution for the situation described in Exercise 6.1 by expansion of the binomial $(q + p)$.

6.3 Determine the probability distribution for the situation described in Exercise 6.1 by reference to the table of binomial probabilities.

6.4 Given that 70 percent of the television viewers tuned in to a certain program also watch the sponsor's commercial, suppose that a sample of three independently chosen viewers are interviewed regarding the commercial. Develop the probability distribution for the number who actually saw the commercial by the use of a tree diagram, designating those who watched the commercial by a W and those who did not watch it by W'.

6.5 Develop the probability distribution for the situation described in Exercise 6.4 by the use of the algebraic method.

6.6 Determine the probability distribution for the situation described in Exercise 6.4 by the use of the table of binomial probabilities.

6.7 Determine the following probabilities by use of the table of binomial probabilities.

(a) $P(X = 5 | n = 10, p = 0.20)$
(b) $P(X \leqslant 3 | n = 15, p = 0.10)$
(c) $P(X > 15 | n = 20, p = 0.30)$
(d) $P(X = 7 | n = 15, p = 0.70)$
(e) $P(X \geqslant 8 | n = 10, p = 0.80)$

6.8 If 60 percent of the employees in a large firm are in favor of union representation, what is the probability that fewer than half of a random sample of 20 employees will be in favor of such representation?

6.9 Determine the following probabilities by use of the table of Poisson probabilities.

(a) $P(X = 5 | \lambda = 5.0)$
(b) $P(X \geqslant 7 | \lambda = 4.0)$
(c) $P(X > 5 | \lambda = 2.5)$
(d) $P(X = 7 | n = 15, p = 0.70)$
(e) $P(X \geqslant 8 | n = 10, p = 0.80)$

6.10 If an average of 40 service calls are required during a typical eight-hour shift in a manufacturing plant, (a) what is the probability that more than 10 service calls will be required during a particular hour? (b) What is the probability that no service calls will be required during a particular hour?

6.11 On the average, a sale is completed with 10 percent of the potential customers who are contacted. Develop the probability distribution of the number of sales that are completed, given that a sample of four customers are called upon, by constructing a tree diagram. Use S for a completed sale and S' for no sale.

6.12 Develop the probability distribution for the situation described in Exercise 6.11 by expansion of the binomial $(q + p)$.

6.13 Determine the probability distribution for the situation described in Exercise 6.11 by reference to the table of binomial probabilities.

6.14 Because of economic conditions, 30 percent of the accounts receivable in a large company are overdue. If an accountant takes a random sample of four accounts, determine the following probabilities by constructing a tree diagram. Use O for overdue and O' for not overdue.
(a) None of the sample accounts is overdue.
(b) Exactly two of the sample accounts are overdue.
(c) At least three of the sample accounts are overdue.

6.15 Determine the probabilities in Exercise 6.14 by use of the algebraic method.

6.16 Determine the probabilities in Exercise 6.14 by reference to the table of binomial probabilities.

6.17 Given that the probability is 0.05 that an individual milling machine is inoperative, construct a vertical bar chart illustrating the probability of various numbers of milling machines being inoperative at a randomly selected point in time. There are eight milling machines in all.

6.18 For the situation in Exercise 6.17 suppose that the production schedule is disrupted if fewer than eight milling machines are operating. What minimum number of milling machines should be installed so that the probability is at least 0.90 that eight machines will be operative at any particular point in time?

6.19 Determine the following probabilities by the use of the table of binomial probabilities.

(a) $P(X = 0 | n = 8, p = 0.30)$
(b) $P(X = 4 | n = 10, p = 0.60)$
(c) $P(X \leqslant 5 | n = 5, p = 0.50)$
(d) $P(X < 3 | n = 6, p = 0.40)$
(e) $P(X \geqslant 7 | n = 10, p = 0.90)$

6.20 The nature of a process is such that when it is in control only 5 percent defectives are produced, while when it is out of control 20 percent defectives are produced. A random sample of 10 items includes two defective items. Determine the probability of obtaining this sample result given that the process is in control and given that it is out of control. Based on the sample result, is it more likely that the process is in control or that it is out of control?

6.21 During a six-month period 60 percent of the common stocks listed on the New York Stock Exchange increased in market value and 40 percent decreased in market value or were unchanged. Of the 10 stocks that were "highly recommended" by a stock advisory service, eight increased in market value during this period. What is the probability that at least eight of 10 randomly selected stock issues would have increased in value during this period?

6.22 Determine the following probabilities by the use of the table of Poisson probabilities.

(a) $P(X = 0 | \lambda = 1.0)$
(b) $P(X = 5 | \lambda = 2.0)$
(c) $P(X \geqslant 5 | \lambda = 1.5)$
(d) $P(X > 8 | \lambda = 4.0)$
(e) $P(X < 2 | \lambda = 5.0)$

6.23 On the average, six people per hour use a self-service banking facility during the prime shopping hours in a department store.

(a) What is the probability that exactly six people will use the facility during a randomly selected hour?

(b) What is the probability that fewer than five people will use the facility during a randomly selected hour?

(c) What is the probability that no one will use the facility during a 10-minute interval?

(d) What is the probability that no one will use the facility during a 5-minute interval?

6.24 Suppose that the manuscript for a textbook has a total of 50 errors or mistypes included in its 500 pages, and that the errors are distributed randomly throughout the text.

(a) What is the probability that a chapter of 30 pages has two or more errors?

(b) What is the probability that a chapter of 50 pages has two or more errors?

(c) What is the probability that a randomly selected page has no error?

6.25 On the average, 10 trucks per day arrive at a loading dock and require a half-day to either load or unload. The arrival times are randomly distributed throughout the day. If seven loading spaces are available, (a) what is the probability that this will not be sufficient to handle the trucks arriving at the dock during the first half of the working day, assuming that all docks are available at the beginning of each day? (b) What is the probability if an additional loading space is constructed?

CHAPTER 7 ■
THE NORMAL PROBABILITY DISTRIBUTION

Whereas the preceding chapter was concerned with *discrete* probability distributions, the normal probability distribution is the most important *continuous* probability distribution in terms of its use in statistical analysis. In this chapter we first describe the general nature of continuous probability distributions as contrasted with discrete distributions. Afterward the specific characteristics of the normal probability distribution and the method of determining normal probabilities by the use of a standard table are described. Finally, we define the circumstances under which normal probabilities can be used as approximations of binomial and Poisson probabilities, and the circumstances under which Poisson probabilities can be used as approximations of binomial probabilities.

7.1 ■ Continuous Probability Distributions

The binomial and Poisson probability distributions described in the preceding chapter are discrete probability distributions in that the outcomes of the variable X were observed counts and could have only integer values. In contrast, whenever the value of X is based on measurement along a continuous scale, the probability distribution of the possible values of X is described as being a continuous probability distribution. Of course, measurement along a continuous scale means that any fractional value can occur.

discrete

1 The binomial and Poisson distributions described in the preceding chapter are examples of _____ probability distributions, whereas the normal distribution is an example of a _____ probability distribution.

continuous

fractional

2 As indicated in section 1.3, a continuous variable is distinguished from a discrete variable in that a continuous variable can have any [fractional / whole-number] value.

3 For discrete outcomes, it is possible to construct a probability table that lists all of the possible outcomes and associated probabilities. Considering the nature of continuous values, is it possible to construct a table which lists the probability of every possible outcome for a continuous variable? [Yes / No]

No

4 Rather than listing all of the possible outcomes, or events, a probability table can be constructed which lists all of the *classes* of outcomes that are possible. As was the case for the frequency distributions discussed in Chapter 2, each class is identified or defined in terms of the lower and upper _____ that differentiate that class from the other classes.

limits (or boundaries)

5 Of course, whereas a frequency distribution indicates the *frequency* of occurrence for each class of outcomes, a probability distribution indicates the *probability* associated with each class. Table 7-1 is an example of a probability distribution for a continuous variable. In this case, the possible outcomes have been grouped into classes whose interval size is _____ .

10.0

Table 7-1 ▪ Probability distribution for a continuous variable

Class boundaries	P
20.5–30.5	0.07
30.5–40.5	0.20
40.5–50.5	0.30
50.5–60.5	0.20
60.5–70.5	0.10
70.5–80.5	0.08
80.5–90.5	0.05

6 One difficulty associated with a tabular probability distribution for a continuous variable is that probabilities can easily be determined only for the particular classes used in the table. For example, the probability that a randomly chosen value will be "between 65.0 and 70.0" [can / cannot] easily be determined by reference to Table 7-1.

cannot (straight-line interpolation is *not* appropriate)

7 Because of such difficulties probability distributions for continuous variables are frequently presented in the form of probability curves, rather than as tables. Figure 7-1 is an example of such a curve. As was the case for the frequency curves described in Chapter 2, the characteristics of a probability curve can be described in terms of its skewness and kurtosis. In this case the curve can be described as being [positively / negatively] skewed.

positively (See Frames 55–58 of Chapter 2 for a review.)

Figure 7-1 ▪ A probability curve for a continuous variable

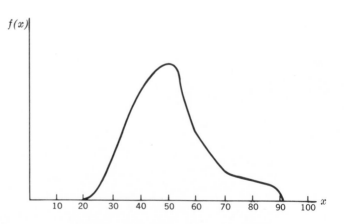

8 In Figure 7-1 note that the vertical axis is *not* labeled *"P"* (for "probability"). Rather, the *"f(X)"* stands for "function of *X*." What this means is that the probability that the variable *"X"* will be equal to, say, 35.0 [can / cannot] be determined by simply looking at the height of the curve for the value of *X*.

cannot

9 Rather, for probability curves for a continuous variable the probability of an outcome is determined by identifying the *proportion of area* of the curve that is associated with the possible outcome. For example, suppose that the proportion of the area of the curve to the left of 35.0 in Figure 7-1 is 0.15. Then the probability that a randomly sampled value of *X* will be equal to or less than 35.0 is _____ .

0.15

10 In the next section, on the normal probability distribution, we shall illustrate the determination of probabilities for a continuous variable in greater detail. Notice, however, that for a continuous variable a probability value can be determined only if a range (or interval) of possible values of *X* is identified. For example, "equal to or less than 35.0" is a range of possible values extending from negative infinity up to 35.0. Similarly, we could determine the probability that the variable *X* has a value between 40.0 and 60.0 by determining the proportion of the curve area between _____ and _____ .

40.0; 60.0

7.2 ■ The Normal Distribution

Just as was true for the binomial distribution, the normal probability distribution is actually a family of distributions with certain common characteristics. In this section we define the common characteristics of all normal probability distributions and illustrate how probabilities based on the normal probability curve can be determined.

11 You may recall that in Chapter 3, while describing dispersion, we had a brief introduction to the characteristics of the normal distribution. At that point we said that a normal distribution is one that is both symmetrical and mesokurtic. This means that the frequency curve for a normally distributed set of measurements [is / is not] skewed, [is / is not] peaked, and [is / is not] flat.

is not; is not
is not (See Chapter 3, Frames 91–93)

12 Binomial distributions vary from one another in terms of the values of *n* and *p* in the binomial $(q + p)^n$. Normal distributions vary from one another in terms of the mean and

many

standard deviation. Thus [many / few / only one] distribution(s) of measurements can be correctly described as being normally distributed.

13 The frequency curves for all distributions of measurements that approximate the normal distribution are similar in appearance; they are often described as bell-shaped, as illustrated in the diagram below. In terms of skewness and kurtosis, all frequency curves that approximate the normal probability distribution can be described as being

symmetrical; mesokurtic _____ and _____ .

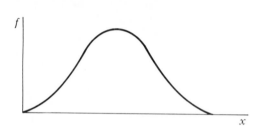

14 But you might ask: "What is the special importance of the normal probability distribution in statistical analysis?" There are two distinct answers to this question, and the one that is more important statistically cannot be adequately explained until after we discuss sampling in Chapter 8. The first reason is that many measured outcomes in nature, particularly those that are affected by a great number of causative factors, actually do yield distributions of measurements that are approximately normally distributed. In the area of personal characteristics, examples are measurements of height, physical abilities, and abilities in verbal and quantitative skills. The general observation is that near the arithmetic mean of such

many

distributions of measurements there are relatively [few / many] observed measurements, whereas for values that are increasingly smaller or larger than the mean the observed

small

number of measurements tends to be relatively [small / large].

15 For example, given that the mean score on a test of verbal skills is 100 with a standard deviation of 15, we would

fewer

expect [fewer / more] scores between 115 and 130 than between 100 and 115.

16 The second reason why the normal probability distribution is useful is that collections of sample statistics, such as sample means, tend to be normally distributed *even though* the population from which the samples were taken is not itself normally distributed. Thus, if the amount of personal debt is not normally distributed, a distribution of the average a-mounts of personal debt reported by groups of 30 respond-ents [will / will not] tend to be normally distributed.

will (We develop this con-cept in Chapter 8.)

17 Since variables that are continuous can take on any fractional value, it is not meaningful to try to specify the probability that one particular value, representing an infinitely small point along the horizontal axis of a probability curve, will occur. Rather, we specify the probability that an observed measurement will fall between two defined boundaries. To determine this probability, we begin with the assumption that the entire area under the normal probability curve is equal to a value of 1.0. Given the fact that a normal curve is symmetrical, what is the probability that a measurement chosen at random from a normally distributed set of measurements will be greater than the mean in value? $P =$ _____ .

0.50 (since half the measure-ments are on either side of the mean)

18 You may wonder why the probability value in Frame 17 is not a little less than 0.50, since the mean itself is not included in the interval. But in the continuous probability distribution we are using, any particular point, including the point at which the mean itself is located, is assumed to take up *none* of the area under the normal curve. Thus the two problems—viz., the probability that a score will be larger than the mean and the probability that a score will be equal to the mean or larger—[are / are not] considered to be identical problems for practical purposes.

are

19 If we are given the information that a proportion of 0.34 of the measurements in a normal distribution is included in the interval from the mean to the value that is one standard deviation above the mean (for the scores in Frame 15 from 100 to 115), what proportion of measurements is included in the interval from one standard deviation below the mean to one standard deviation above the mean (scores of 85 to 115) _____ .

0.68 (since the probability curve is symmetrical)

20 The illustration below summarizes the information which we have just presented. On the basis of the illustration, what is the probability that a measurement chosen at random will be larger than $(\mu + 1.0\sigma)$ (larger than a score of 115 in frame 15)? $P =$ _____

$0.50 - 0.34 = 0.16$

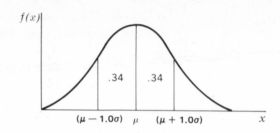

$$f(x)$$

.34 | .34

$(\mu - 1.0\sigma)$ μ $(\mu + 1.0\sigma)$ x

21 The examples in Frames 19 and 20 are virtually identical to those used in introducing the concept of the normal curve in Chapter 4. The important difference is that we are now concerned with proportions of area under the curve and with probability, instead of with percentages of measurements. Put another way, instead of using the normal distribution with a particular observed distribution of frequencies, we are using it as a _____ distribution.

---

probability

---

22 The examples in Frames 19 and 20 are based on the given information that the proportion of measurements included between μ and $(\mu + 1.0\sigma)$ for a normal distribution is 0.34. But what about other intervals under the normal curve? The table of areas under the normal curve gives proportions for various intervals that begin at the mean and extend to some point specified in terms of units of the standard deviation. Thus, given a mean of 100 and a standard deviation of 15 for a test, if we want to determine the probability of a randomly chosen score being between 100 and 130, we would want to use the table to find the proportion of area included between the point μ and the point $(\mu + \underline{\hspace{1cm}} \sigma)$.

2.0 (since 130 is two standard deviations from the mean in the positive direction)

---

23 Since we have to work with deviations in terms of standard deviation units in order to use the table we now introduce, it is convenient to use a standard formula to accomplish this transformation of measurements and to give this transformed measurement a special symbol. The measure that expresses the deviation from the mean in terms of the standard deviation is z, and it is determined by $z = (X - \mu)/\sigma$. Use this formula to determine the value of z for the score of 130 in the problem in Frame 22.

$$\frac{130 - 100}{15} = +2.0$$

$$z = \frac{X - \mu}{\sigma} =$$

24 Refer to Table B-1, "Areas under the Normal Curve." This table reports the proportions of the normal-curve area included between the mean and various values of _____.

---

z

---

25 Because there is no deviation from the mean at μ itself, in Table B-1 we note that at the mean the value of z is $z =$ ____ .

0

26 Given a mean of 50 and a standard deviation of 10 for a set of measurements that is normally distributed, suppose we wish to determine the probability that a randomly chosen measurement will be between 50 and 55. Since $\mu = 50$, that value corresponds to $z = 0$, which is the lower boundary of the interval represented in Table B-1. Therefore, the first computational step is to transform 55 into a z value.

$\dfrac{55 - 50}{10} = +0.5$

$$z = \frac{X - \mu}{\sigma} =$$

27 The next step is to utilize Table B-1 to determine the proportion of the area under the normal curve included between the mean and a z value of $+0.50$. Referring to the table, we find that the proportion equals _____ .

0.1915

28 Therefore, given a normal distribution with a mean of 50 and a standard deviation of 10, the probability that a measurement between the values of 50 and 55 will occur is _____ . The probability that a value larger than 55 will occur is _____ . The probability that a value smaller than 50 will occur is _____ .

0.1915
$0.5000 - 0.1915 = 0.3085$
0.5000 (the entire lower half of the probability curve)

29 Consider the elements of the formula $z = (X - \mu)/\sigma$. A negative value of z signifies that the interval for which a proportion (or probability) is desired is located (below / above) the mean.

below

30 Table B-1, however, reports areas only for positive deviations from the mean. In Frame 28 we found that the probability of obtaining a measurement between 50 and 55, given that the mean is 50 and the standard deviation is 10, is 0.1915. What would you expect to be the probability of obtaining a measurement between 45 and 50, in this case? $P =$ _____ .

0.1915

31 Since the normal curve is symmetrical, the proportions included on one side of the mean are equivalent to those on the other side. Therefore, when measuring areas between the mean and values of z, whether the z value is positive or negative [does / does not] affect the applicability of the table of areas under the normal curve.

does not

32 If a transformed measurement yields a positive *z* value, it is [smaller / larger] than the mean of the distribution. If a transformed measurement yields a negative *z* value, it is [smaller / larger] than the mean of the distribution.

> larger

> smaller

33 Given a normal distribution with a mean of 50 and a standard deviation of 10, what is the probability that a value between 50 and 70 will occur by chance?

> $$\frac{70-50}{10} = +2.0$$

$$z = \frac{X-\mu}{\sigma} =$$

> 0.4772 (from Table B-1)

$P =$

34 For the same distribution, what is the probability that a measurement with a value between 35 and 50 will be obtained by chance?

> $$\frac{35-50}{10} = -1.5$$

$$z = \frac{X-\mu}{\sigma} =$$

> 0.4332

$P =$

35 So far we have always had the interval begin or end at the mean. Since this is the basis upon which Table B-1 is constructed, beginning the interval at the mean makes for the easiest type of problem. If the interval does not begin at the mean, then we have to do some subtracting or adding of areas in order to arrive at the appropriate probability value. For the example we have been discussing, in which the mean is 50, suppose we want to determine the probability that a measurement falls between 60 and 70. Indicate the area of the curve in which we are interested by shading it in on the curve below.

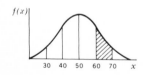
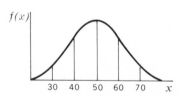

36 The proportion of the curve in Frame 35 in the shaded area cannot be directly determined by using Table B-1 because all intervals in this table begin with the mean as the lower boundary (or the mean as the upper boundary, if the z value for the other boundary is negative). However, suppose we determine the proportion between μ and 60 and the proportion between μ and 70. We can then determine the proportion of area included between 60 and 70 by subtracting the proportion included between μ and ___ from the proportion included between μ and ___ .

	60
	70

37 Refer to Table B-1 and complete the following, given that $\mu = 50$, $\sigma = 10$, and $z = (X - \mu)/\sigma$.

2.0	0.4772
1.0	−0.3413
	0.1359

Area μ to 70 = area μ to $(\mu +$ ___ $\sigma) =$ _____
−Area μ to 60 = −area μ to $(\mu +$ ___ $\sigma) = -$ _____ (subtract)
Area 60 to 70 = _____ (remainder)

38 For a distribution of measurements whose mean is 50 and standard deviation is 10, what is the probability that a randomly chosen measurement will be between 55 and 60? To aid you in setting up the problem, shade in the area under consideration on the diagram below and then determine the area by reference to Table B-1.

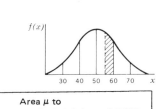

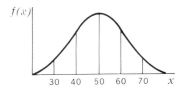

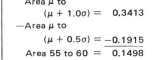

Area μ to
$(\mu + 1.0\sigma) =$ 0.3413
−Area μ to
$(\mu + 0.5\sigma) =$ −0.1915
Area 55 to 60 = 0.1498

39 For a distribution whose mean is 50 and standard deviation is 10, what is the probability that a measurement chosen at random will be larger than 65, $P(X > 65)$?

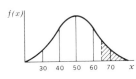

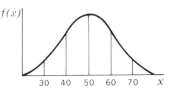

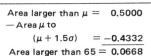

Area larger than μ = 0.5000
− Area μ to
$(\mu + 1.5\sigma)$ = −0.4332
Area larger than 65 = 0.0668

40 For a distribution of measurements whose mean is 50 and standard deviation is 10, what is the probability that a measurement chosen at random will be between the values of 35 and 45, $P(35 \leqslant X \leqslant 45)$?

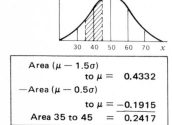

Area ($\mu - 1.5\sigma$)	
to $\mu =$	0.4332
$-$Area ($\mu - 0.5\sigma$)	
to $\mu =$	$-$0.1915
Area 35 to 45 =	0.2417

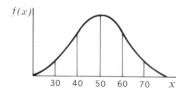

41 Now let us introduce a problem requiring addition, instead of subtraction, of areas taken from Table B-1. For the same distribution for which $\mu = 50$ and $\sigma = 10$, what is the probability that a measurement chosen at random will be between 35 and 65, $P(35 \leqslant X \leqslant 65)$?

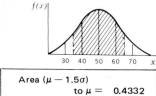

Area ($\mu - 1.5\sigma$)	
to $\mu =$	0.4332
$+$Area μ to	
($\mu + 1.5\sigma$) =	$+$0.4332
Area 35 to 65 =	0.8664

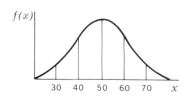

42 With $\mu = 50$ and $\sigma = 10$, what is the probability that a measurement chosen at random will be between 40 and 70, $P(40 \leqslant X \leqslant 70)$?

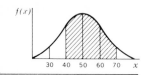

Area ($\mu - 1.0\sigma$)	
to $\mu =$	0.3413
$+$Area μ to	
($\mu + 2.0\sigma$) =	$+$0.4772
Area 40 to 70 =	0.8185

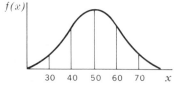

43 When the normal probability distribution is used in statistical inference, we are frequently interested in the probability that a randomly chosen measurement will have either an extremely high or an extremely low value relative to the assumed mean of the distribution. Graphically, this means that we are interested in the proportions of the area included in the two tails of the distribution. For example, if we are interested in the probability that a randomly chosen measurement will be smaller than 30 *or* larger than 70, shade in the areas on the curve below for which we need to determine proportions of area.

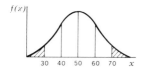 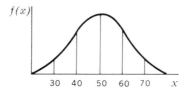

44 In using Table B-1 for the problem in Frame 43, we determine the proportion in each of the tails by subtraction, as we have done in Frames 36 to 40, and then we sum the two proportions in order to determine the probability of an extremely high *or* low value. Carry out these calculations below, using the data from Frame 43, above, and given that μ = 50 and σ = 10.

$$\begin{aligned}0.5000 - 0.4772 &= 0.0228\\+0.5000 - 0.4772 &= +0.0228\\&\ \ 0.0456\end{aligned}$$

Proportion less than 30 = _____ − _____ = _____
+Proportion greater than 70 = _____ − _____ = _____
$P(X < 30) + P(X > 70) =$ _____

45 The practical applications of the normal probability distribution can be demonstrated only after we discuss statistical inference in some detail. As indicated in Frame 44, however, one application of some importance is that by using the normal distribution we can often specify the

| probability |

_____ that the value of a particular measurement will be extremely low or extremely high relative to the value of the mean.

46 Aside from its more important uses in statistical inference, the normal distribution is widely used in interpreting the relative meanings of measurements or scores that are normally distributed, and, as it happens, many performance test scores are so distributed. Thus in interpreting the meaning of any measurement taken from a set of measurements that is nor-

| mean |
| standard deviation |

mally distributed, we need just two statistical values: the ____ of the distribution and the _____ of the distribution.

7.3 ■ Normal Approximation of Binomial and Poisson Probabilities

In Chapter 6 we presented the binomial and Poisson probability distributions and illustrated the use of the probability tables associated with these distributions. As we emphasized at that time, both of these distributions are concerned with determining probability values for outcomes that are discrete rather than continuous. On the other hand, the normal probability distribution is appropriate for analyses involving continuous variables. However, as the sample size becomes large, the probabilities that can be determined by reference to the binomial or Poisson distributions can in fact be approximated quite well by the use of the normal probability distribution. In this section we indicate why such an approximation is justified and how this substitution simplifies statistical calculations, and we define the specific requirements to be satisfied before the normal probability distribution can be used to approximate binomial and Poisson probabilities.

47 If normal curve probabilities are to be used in place of binomial probabilities, then this implies that the graphic representation of the curve should be a close fit to the bar chart which is constructed to represent the areas in respect to the binomial probabilities. Figure 7-2 presents the area bar charts for binomial probabilities based on $n = 5, n = 10$, and $n = 30$, with $p = 0.50$ in each case. In this figure, note that the normal approximation is the best fit for the sample size $n =$ _____ .

30

Figure 7-2 ■ Bar charts for binomial probabilities for $n = 5$, $n = 10$, and $n = 30$, given $p = 0.50$

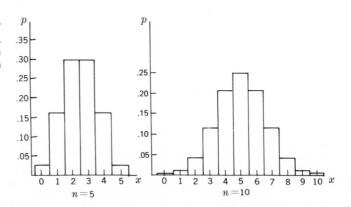

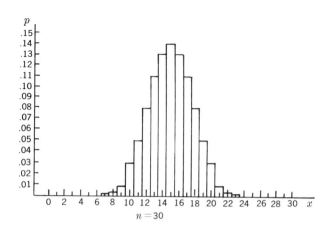

p

$n = 30$

48 Let us verify this observation by reference to some specific values. Suppose that we are interested in the probability that five heads will occur in five tosses of a fair coin. The probability value based on the normal approximation, to be discussed later in this section, is 0.1250. On the other hand the appropriate probability value based on the binomial distribution is _____ .

0.0312

49 Thus, for the outcome and sample size of Frame 48, the normal probability value is a very poor approximation of the correct binomial value. Suppose, now, that we are interested in the probability that 20 or more heads will be obtained in 30 tosses of a fair coin (we did not specify "all 30 heads" because the probability is less than 0.0001, and is not reported in binomial probability tables). The probability of obtaining 20 or more heads by the normal approximation is 0.0505, whereas the actual binomial probability is 0.0494. If these two values are rounded to two places, as is typically done with probability values, the value is _____ in both cases.

0.05

50 Therefore, by these examples we have demonstrated that the normal probabilities may be good approximations of binomial probabilities for relatively [small / large] sample sizes.

large

51 One thing you may have noticed is that we chose to use $p = 0.50$ in the above example, and that all of the binomial distributions were symmetrical in form. Suppose we had used $p = 0.20$ instead. Would all of the distributions still be symmetrical in form? [Yes / No]

No (continued in next frame)

52 With $p = 0.20$, we would generally expect the binomial distributions to be positively skewed. Figure 7-3 presents the area bar charts for binomial probabilities based on $n = 5$, $n = 10$, and $n = 30$, with $p = 0.20$ in each case. In this figure, note that the skewness appears to be relatively minor for $n =$ ____.

30

Figure 7-3 ■ Bar charts for binomial probabilities for $n = 5$, $n = 10$, and $n = 30$, given $p = 0.20$

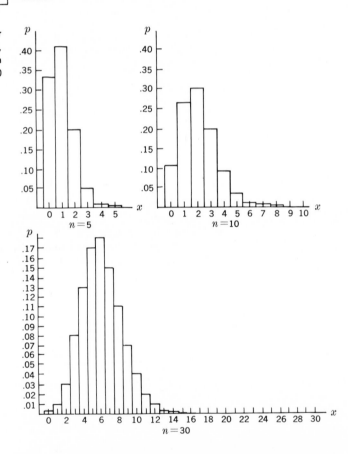

53 To present evidence for this observation by a numerical example, suppose the probability is 0.20 that a part is defective. What is the probability that 10 or more parts out of a randomly chosen group of 30 parts will be defective? By the normal approximation the probability is 0.0548, whereas the

good (but not as good as for
$p = 0.50$)

actual binomial probability is 0.0611. Thus, in this instance the normal approximation is fairly [good / poor].

54 Although the above examples indicate that the binomial probability distribution approaches normality as sample size is increased, when p is very small or very large in value then a relatively larger sample size is required for us to use the normal approximation. For the applications in this book we consider the normal probabilities to be acceptable approximations of binomial probabilities whenever $n \geqslant 30$, $np \geqslant 5$, and $nq \geqslant 5$. Therefore, if $p = 0.40$, then the minimum sample size required

30 (since n has to be *at least* 30 in any case)

is $n =$ _____ .

55 On the other hand, if $p = 0.10$, then the minimum sample size required for the use of the normal approximation is $n =$

50 (so that $np = 5$)

_____ .

56 If $p = 0.90$, the minimum sample size required for the use

50 (because $q = 0.10$ in this case)

of the normal approximation is $n =$ _____ .

57 Since the normal probabilities are *approximations* of the binomial probabilities, why should we have any interest in using such approximations? The main reason for such interest is that certain types of problems in statistical inference for discrete data are more easily handled by use of the normal distribution, as will be illustrated in Chapter 9, on estimating population values. Another reason is that tables for binomial probabilities are frequently not available for larger values of n.

binomial

For smaller values of n (less than 30), however, the [binomial / normal] probabilities should always be used.

58 Having established the requirements associated with using normal approximations of binomial probabilities, we now illustrate the computational procedure that is used. Recall that whereas any binomial distribution is determined by the size of the sample, n, and the value of p (or q, its complement), any normal distribution is defined by the value of its *mean* and

standard deviation

_____ .

59 Therefore, in order to use a normal probability distribution as a substitute for a binomial probability distribution, we need to determine the mean and standard deviation to be used. These values can be calculated by the following formulas, where the subscript "b" indicates that the distribution is binomial:

$$\mu_b = np$$

$$\sigma_b = \sqrt{npq}$$

Therefore, given a sample of $n = 30$ with $p = 0.50$, the mean of the probability distribution is equal to _____ and the standard deviation is equal to $\sqrt{(\underline{\quad})(\underline{\quad})(\underline{\quad})}$.

$$\boxed{\begin{array}{l} (30)(0.50) = 15.0 \\ \sqrt{(30)(0.50)(0.50)} = 2.74 \end{array}}$$

60 Now, suppose we wish to calculate the probability of obtaining 20 or more heads in 30 tosses of a fair coin. In order to use the normal approximation we need to interpret "20 or more" as if continuous values were being represented. That is, the class of outcomes called "20 or more" has a lower boundary which equals [19.0 / 19.5 / 20.0].

$$\boxed{\begin{array}{l} \text{19.5 (since this is the point} \\ \text{separating "19" from "20")} \end{array}}$$

61 The use of "19.5" in place of the nominal value of "20" is called a "correction for continuity," and is required because the reported count has to be a whole number. Therefore, the probability to be determined is represented by the shaded area on the diagram below. Using the standard deviation of 2.74, calculate the z value for 19.5 and determine the probability that $X \geqslant 19.5$ based on the normal approximation.

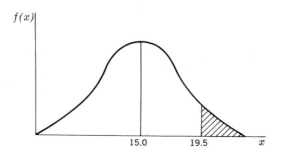

$$\boxed{\dfrac{19.5 - 15.0}{2.74} = \dfrac{4.5}{2.74} = 1.64}$$
$$z = \dfrac{X - \mu_b}{\sigma_b} =$$

$$\boxed{0.5000 - 0.4495 = 0.0505}$$
$$P =$$

62 Similarly, suppose we want to use the normal approximation to determine the probability that 10 or more parts out of a group of 30 parts will be defective, given that $p = 0.20$. First, determine the values of the mean and standard deviation for this approximation.

$$\boxed{(30)(0.20) = 6.0}$$
$$\mu = np =$$

$\sqrt{(30)(0.20)(0.80)} = 2.19$

$\sigma_b = \sqrt{npq} =$

63 Now, determine the probability that 10 or more parts are defective.

$\dfrac{9.5 - 6.0}{2.19} = \dfrac{3.5}{2.19} = +1.60$

$z = \dfrac{X - \mu_b}{\sigma_b} =$

$0.500 - 0.4452 = 0.0548$

$P =$

64 For the problem above, what is the probability that *more than* 10 parts are defective?

$\dfrac{10.5 - 6.0}{2.19} = \dfrac{4.5}{2.19} = +2.06$

$z =$

$0.5000 - 0.4803 = 0.0197$

$P =$

65 Using the information contained in the preceding two frames, what is the probability that there will be "exactly 10" defective parts by the normal approximation?

$0.0548 - 0.0197 = 0.0351$ (the probability of 10 or more minus the probability of 11 or more, which is the proportion of area between 9.5 and 10.5)

$P =$

0.0355
good

66 Based on the binomial table, $P(X = 10 \mid n = 30, p = 0.20)$ = _____ . Therefore, the normal approximation in the preceding frame is relatively [good / poor].

67 Having discussed the normal approximation of binomial probabilities, let us now consider the normal approximation of Poisson probabilities. Whereas the values of n and p determine a binomial probability distribution, a Poisson probability distribution is based on the value of its mean, represented by the symbol _____.

λ (lambda)

68 Similar to the binomial distribution, the Poisson distribution approaches the characteristics of a normal distribution as the value of λ is increased. For the purposes of this text, we shall consider the normal approximation to be acceptable when $\lambda \geqslant 10.0$. Therefore, suppose that we wish to determine the probability that 15 or more maintenance calls will be required on a particular day, given that the daily average has been 8.5 maintenance calls. Can the normal approximation be used in this case? [Yes / No]

69 On the other hand, suppose we wish to determine $P(X \geqslant 15 \mid \lambda = 10.0)$ by the normal approximation. Our first step is to calculate the mean and standard deviation for the Poisson distribution. Do this now by using the following formulas, where the subscript "Pois" indicates that the distribution is Poisson:

10.0

$$\mu_{\text{Pois}} = \lambda =$$

$\sqrt{10.0} = 3.16$

$$\sigma_{\text{Pois}} = \sqrt{\lambda} =$$

70 Now in order to determine the probability of "15 or more" maintenance calls, we need to apply the same type of correction for continuity as was applied for the normal approximation of the binomial. That is, we should in this case determine the normal curve area to the right of $X =$ _____ .

14.5

71 Finally, calculate the z value for 14.5 and determine the probability that $X \geqslant 14.5$ based on the normal approximation.

$\dfrac{14.5 - 10.0}{3.16} = \dfrac{4.5}{3.16} = +1.42$

$$z = \frac{X - \mu_{\text{Pois}}}{\sigma_{\text{Pois}}} =$$

$0.5000 - 0.4222 = 0.0778$

$$P =$$

72 Based on the Poisson table, $P(X \geqslant 15 \mid \lambda = 10.0) = 0.0835$. Therefore, the normal approximation of the Poisson probability value is in this instance relatively [good / poor].

good (e.g., both values would be rounded to 0.08)

73 For our purposes, then, we consider the normal probability distribution to be a good approximation of the binomial distribution whenever $n \geqslant$ ____ and both $np \geqslant$ ____ and $nq \geqslant$ ____ .

30

5; 5

74 Similarly, we consider the normal probability distribution to be a good approximation of the Poisson distribution whenever $\lambda \geqslant$ ____ .

10

7.4 ■ Poisson Approximation of Binomial Probabilities

As indicated in the preceding section, the normal probability distribution is considered to be a good approximation of the binomial distribution when $n \geqslant 30$, $np \geqslant 5$, and $nq \geqslant 5$. Thus, even when the sample size is relatively large ($n \geqslant 30$), the normal approximation cannot be used if p (or q) is small. Because binomial probabilities for larger sample sizes are tedious to compute, this lack of a good fit because of the skewness of the binomial distribution is unfortunate. However, given a large sample size and small value of p (or q), the Poisson distribution is a good approximation of the binomial distribution.

75 In the introduction above we have indicated that a large sample is required in order to substitute normal probabilities for binomial probabilities, and also in order to substitute Poisson probabilities for binomial probabilities. Note that by a "large sample" we mean that $n \geqslant$ ____ .

30

76 You may not have thought of a sample of size 30 as being particularly large. However, in the context of statistical analysis this is the most general definition of a large sample. In the following chapter, on sampling methods and sampling distributions, we consider further the statistical advantage of a large sample. But throughout this text "large sample" means $n \geqslant$ ____ and "small sample" means $n <$ ____ .

30; 30

77 The rule we follow in using Poisson probabilities as approximations for binomial probabilities is that $n \geqslant 30$ and $np < 5$ (or $nq < 5$, but this point is considered in Frame 82, below). Recalling the rule for substituting normal probabilities for binomial probabilities, this means that when $n \geqslant 30$, the binomial probabilities need [always / sometimes / never] be used.

never

78 Or more to the point, given that $n \geqslant 30$, then when $np \geqslant 5$ and $nq \geqslant 5$, the _____ distribution can be used to approximate binomial probabilities; while when $np < 5$ or $nq < 5$, the _____ distribution can be used to approximate binomial probabilities. Such use of normal probabilities and Poisson probabilities as approximations for binomial probabilities minimizes the need for extensive tables of binomial probabilities.

normal

Poisson

Section 7.4 Poisson Approximation of Binomial Probabilities ■ 175

79 When the Poisson probability distribution is used to approximate binomial probabilities, $\lambda = np$. This is so because np indicates the average number of events for the designated number of trials, or observations. Consider the rule for using the Poisson approximation, as given in Frame 77. In such approximation, the value of λ will always be less than the numeric value _____ (given that $p < q$).

5.0 (since $np < 5$)

80 As a numerical example, suppose that the proportion of parts defective is $p = 0.02$. Given that a random sample of $n = 30$ is taken, what is the probability that two *or more* parts will be defective? The appropriate binomial probability is 0.1205. The Poisson approximation in this case is based on $\lambda =$ _____ .

(30)(0.02) = 0.6

81 Continuing with the above example, $P(X \geqslant 2 | \lambda = 0.6) =$ _____ and thus the approximation is relatively [good / poor].

0.0988 + 0.0198 + 0.0030 + 0.0004 = 0.1220; good

82 Now, suppose that p is large but that $nq < 5$. In this case it is necessary to designate the results in terms of the outcome associated with the probability q. For example, suppose that the probability is 0.90 that a delivery will be made "on time." For a random sample of 30 deliveries the average number that we would expect to be on time (np) is _____ and the average number expected to be late (nq) is _____ .

(30)(0.90) = 27.0
(30)(0.10) = 3.0

83 Continuing with the example above, suppose we wish to determine the probability that 28 or more shipments will be on time by the appropriate Poisson approximation. In order to do this, we need to designate the results in respect to the number of late deliveries, because this is the outcome associated with the low probability. Therefore $\lambda = nq =$ _____ , and we then determine the probability that the number of late deliveries is equal to or fewer than _____ .

3.0

2 (since 28 or more "on time" = 2 or fewer "late")

84 In summary, then, Poisson probabilities can be used as approximations for binomial probabilities whenever $n \geqslant$ ___ and $np <$ ___ or $nq <$ ___ .

30

5; 5

Review

classes of outcomes only

85 (Frames 1–6) When a probability table is constructed for a continuous variable, the table lists [all possible outcomes / classes of outcomes only].

86 (Frames 7-10) When a probability value for a continuous variable is determined by reference to a probability curve, the probability is equal to the proportion of _____ under the curve associated with the outcome.

> area

87 Frames 11-16) The characteristics of the normal probability distribution, which is used in conjunction with continuous data, are such that the associated probability curve is _____ and _____ .

> symmetrical; mesokurtic

88 (Frames 17-21) A normally distributed set of measurements can be portrayed by using the normal probability curve or by organizing the data into classes and indicating the probability associated with each class. Why are not all of the possible outcomes, and the related probabilities, listed instead?

_____

_____

_____

_____

> Since the distribution of measurements is continuous, listing of all possible fractional outcomes is impossible.

89 (Frames 22-26) In Table B-1 the areas reported are for intervals whose lower boundary is at the mean and whose upper boundary is expressed in terms of _____ values. The latter symbol represents the deviation of a measurement from the mean of a distribution expressed in units of the _____ deviation.

> z

> standard

90 (Frames 27-34) Given that the mean of a distribution of measurements is at 75 with a standard deviation of 5.0, what is the probability that a measurement will be between 75 and 85?

> 2.0; 0.4772

Area 75 to 85 = area μ to $(\mu +$ _____ $\sigma) =$ _____

91 (Frames 35-39) For the same distribution, what is the probability that a measurement will be between 85 and 90 in value?

> Area μ to
> $(\mu + 3.0\sigma) =$ 0.4986
> $-$Area μ to
> $(\mu + 2.0\sigma) =$ $-$0.4772
> Area 85 to 90 = 0.0214

92 (Frame 40) For the same distribution, what is the probability that a measurement will be between 65 and 70 in value?

> Area $(\mu - 2.0\sigma)$
> to $\mu =$ 0.4772
> $-$Area $(\mu - 1.0\sigma)$
> to $\mu =$ $-$0.3413
> Area 65 to 70 = 0.1359

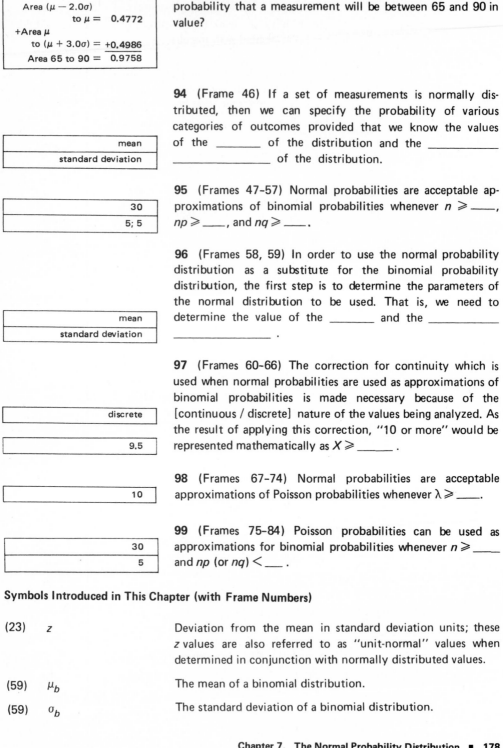

Area $(\mu - 2.0\sigma)$ to $\mu = \ \ 0.4772$ +Area μ to $(\mu + 3.0\sigma) = +0.4986$ Area 65 to 90 $= \ \ 0.9758$

93 (Frames 41-45) For the same distribution, what is the probability that a measurement will be between 65 and 90 in value?

mean
standard deviation

94 (Frame 46) If a set of measurements is normally distributed, then we can specify the probability of various categories of outcomes provided that we know the values of the _____ of the distribution and the _____ _____ of the distribution.

30
5; 5

95 (Frames 47-57) Normal probabilities are acceptable approximations of binomial probabilities whenever $n \geqslant$ ___, $np \geqslant$ ___, and $nq \geqslant$ ___.

mean
standard deviation

96 (Frames 58, 59) In order to use the normal probability distribution as a substitute for the binomial probability distribution, the first step is to determine the parameters of the normal distribution to be used. That is, we need to determine the value of the _____ and the _____ _____ .

discrete
9.5

97 (Frames 60-66) The correction for continuity which is used when normal probabilities are used as approximations of binomial probabilities is made necessary because of the [continuous / discrete] nature of the values being analyzed. As the result of applying this correction, "10 or more" would be represented mathematically as $X \geqslant$ _____ .

10

98 (Frames 67-74) Normal probabilities are acceptable approximations of Poisson probabilities whenever $\lambda \geqslant$ ___.

30
5

99 (Frames 75-84) Poisson probabilities can be used as approximations for binomial probabilities whenever $n \geqslant$ ___ and np (or nq) $<$ ___ .

Symbols Introduced in This Chapter (with Frame Numbers)

(23)	z	Deviation from the mean in standard deviation units; these z values are also referred to as "unit-normal" values when determined in conjunction with normally distributed values.
(59)	μ_b	The mean of a binomial distribution.
(59)	σ_b	The standard deviation of a binomial distribution.

(69) μ_{Pois} The mean of a Poisson distribution.

Formulas Introduced in This Chapter (with Frame Numbers)

(23) $z = \dfrac{X - \mu}{\sigma}$

Deviation from the mean in units of the standard deviation; used in conjunction with Table B-1, "Table of Areas under the Normal Curve."

(59) $\mu_b = np$

The mean of a binomial distribution.

(59) $\sigma_b = \sqrt{npq}$

The standard deviation of a binomial distribution.

(63) $z = \dfrac{X - \mu_b}{\sigma_b}$

Formula used in conjunction with the normal approximation of binomial probabilities.

(69) $\mu_{Pois} = \lambda$

The mean of a Poisson distribution.

(69) $\sigma_{Pois} = \sqrt{\lambda}$

The standard deviation of a Poisson distribution.

(71) $z = \dfrac{X - \mu_{Pois}}{\sigma_{Pois}}$

Formula used in conjunction with the normal approximation of Poisson probabilities.

EXERCISES
(Solutions on pages 598–600)

7.1 Determine each of the following probabilities by use of the table of areas under the normal curve.

(a) $P(X \leqslant 80 | \mu = 80, \sigma = 20)$
(b) $P(90 \leqslant X \leqslant 100 | \mu = 80, \sigma = 20)$
(c) $P(70 < X < 100 | \mu = 80, \sigma = 20)$
(d) $P(X < 70 | \mu = 80, \sigma = 20)$
(e) $P(X < 60 \text{ or } X > 100 | \mu = 80, \sigma = 20)$

7.2 The time required for equipment repairs carried out by company maintenance personnel follows a normal distribution with a mean of 53.0 minutes and a standard deviation of 9.0 minutes. (a) What is the probability that a randomly chosen repair job will require less than 50 minutes? (b) What is the probability that it will require more than one hour?

7.3 For the situation described in Exercise 7.2 suppose a repairman is given three randomly selected repair jobs. What is the probability that each of the jobs requires at least one hour?

7.4 The performance on a nationally standardized aptitude test in a certain professional field is reported in the form of transformed values whose mean is 500 with a standard deviation of 100. Given that the scores are approximately normally distributed, (a) about what percentage of the results are between 350 and 650? (b) Out of 10,000 test results, how many would we expect to be at a score of 700 or higher?

7.5 For the situation described in Exercise 7.4, suppose that the top 10 percent of the scores are regarded as being "distinctly superior." What is the lowest score required to be included in this category? (*Hint*: For this kind of problem you have to use Table B-1 in the reverse of the usual direction. That is, the proportion to be included in the upper tail of the distribution is known, and on this basis the *z* value is obtained from the table and is then used to solve for the unknown value of *X*.)

7.6 It is known that billing entries by new employees, before internal verification and correction, include a 5 percent error rate. (a) Given a sample of 10 billing entries completed by a new employee, what should be the probability that no errors are included? (b) What would be your interpretation of the situation if three or more errors are included in the sample of 10?

7.7 For the situation described in Exercise 7.6, suppose that a sample of 200 billing entries is inspected. (a) What is the probability that 10 or more contain an error? (b) What is the probability that 15 or more contain an error?

7.8 For the situation described in Exercises 7.6 and 7.7, suppose that the error rate is 1 percent instead of 5 percent. What is the probability that a random sample of 200 billing entries will contain four or more entires with errors?

7.9 If an average of three calls arrive at a switchboard during five-minute intervals, what is the probability that five or more calls will be received during a randomly chosen five-minute interval?

7.10 For the situation described in Exercise 7.9, what is the probability that fewer than 30 calls will be received at the switchboard during a randomly chosen hour?

7.11 Determine each of the following probabilities by use of the table of areas under the normal curve.

(a) $P(90 \leqslant X \leqslant 100 | \mu = 90, \sigma = 15)$
(b) $P(X > 110 | \mu = 90, \sigma = 15)$
(c) $P(X \leqslant 60 | \mu = 90, \sigma = 15)$
(d) $P(80 \leqslant X \leqslant 110 | \mu = 90, \sigma = 15)$
(e) $P(X < 60 \text{ or } X > 120 | \mu = 90, \sigma = 15)$

7.12 A review of a large number of investment portfolios indicates that for the preceding calendar year the average return on an investment of $10,000 was $750 with a standard deviation of $150. The above return includes capital gains as well as interest and dividend payments. (a) If the portfolio yields are approximately normally distributed, what is the probability that a portfolio selected randomly from this group has a yield of less than $500 for the year? (b) What is the probability that the yield was at least $900?

7.13 For the situation described in Exercise 7.12, three of the portfolios included in the group studied were recommended by the same advisory service. Based on chance alone, what is the probability associated with all three portfolios each yielding a return of $800 or more for the year?

7.14 The useful life of a certain brand of steel-belted radial tire has been found to follow a normal distribution with $\mu = 38,000$ miles and $\sigma = 3,000$ miles. (a) What is the probability that a randomly selected tire will have a useful life of at least 35,000 miles? (b) What is the probability that a randomly selected tire will last more than 45,000 miles?

7.15 The useful life of a certain brand of steel-belted radial tire has been found to follow a normal distribution with $\mu = 38,000$ miles and $\sigma = 3,000$ miles. A dealer orders 500 tires for resale. (a) Approximately what number of tires will last between 40,000 and 45,000 miles? (b) Approximately what number of tires will last 40,000 miles or more?

7.16 The useful life of a certain brand of steel-belted radial tire has been found to follow a normal distribution with $\mu = 38,000$ miles and $\sigma = 3,000$ miles. An individual buys four of these tires. (a) What is the probability that all four tires last at least 38,000 miles? (b) What is the probability that all four tires last at least 35,000 miles?

7.17 The amount of time required per individual at a bank teller's window has been found to be approximately normally distributed with $\mu = 130$ seconds and $\sigma = 45$ seconds. (a) What is the probability that a randomly selected individual will require less than 100 seconds to complete his transactions? (b) What is the probability that a randomly selected individual will spend between 2.0 and 3.0 minutes at the teller's window?

7.18 The amount of time required per individual at a bank teller's window is approximately normally distributed with $\mu = 130$ seconds and $\sigma = 45$ seconds. (a) Within what length of time do the 20 percent of individuals with the simplest transactions complete their business at the window? (b) At least what length of time is required for the individuals in the top 5 percent of required time?

7.19 Newsstand sales for a weekly news magazine have averaged 52,340 copies per week with a standard deviation of 2,850 copies. The distribution of sales for the weeks included in the analysis, which excluded the weeks with major national holidays, is approximately normal. What is the probability that there will be 5,000 or more unsold copies in a randomly selected week without a holiday if the publisher distributes 55,000 copies to newsstands?

7.20 For the situation described in Exercise 7.19, suppose the publisher requires that the probability that the newsstands will run out of all copies for sale be no larger than 0.05. What total number of copies should the publisher distribute?

7.21 The percentage of items that are "temporarily out of stock" is known to be 10 percent during the peak sales season in a mail-order firm. Given that an order for eight randomly selected items is placed, what is the probability that all of the items are in stock?

7.22 For the mail-order example given in Exercise 7.21, suppose that 80 randomly selected items are ordered. (a) What is the probability that all of the items are in stock? (b) What is the probability that four or fewer are "temporarily out of stock"?

7.23 For the situation described in Exercises 7.21 and 7.22, suppose that an average of 5 percent of the items are "temporarily out of stock," rather than 10 percent. For 80 randomly selected items what is the probability that two or fewer are out of stock?

7.24 During the six-hour period between the morning and afternoon peaks, an average of three cars enter an automobile service station during each 15-minute interval. What is the probability that six or more cars enter the service station in a randomly selected 15-minute interval during the six-hour period?

7.25 For the situation described in Exercise 7.24, what is the probability that 80 or more cars will enter the station for service during the entire six-hour period?

CHAPTER 8 ■

SAMPLING METHODS AND SAMPLING DISTRIBUTIONS

In Chapters 5 through 7 we have studied some of the major principles of probability and have considered some specific probability distributions. The topics of sampling methods and sampling distributions, covered in this chapter, will complete our coverage of the material that you need to know before proceeding into the principal techniques of statistical inference. From the standpoint of the sampling process itself, we consider the role of sampling in statistical inference, some general sampling problems, and methods of sampling. In the last part of the chapter we introduce and define the nature of sampling distributions, which provide the essential basis for estimating population values and testing the significance of differences between observed and expected sample values.

8.1 ■ The Role of Sampling

Whenever it is impossible, inconvenient, or expensive to measure the characteristics of every member of a population, we are obliged to estimate population values on the basis of the known characteristics of one or more samples taken from that population. Thus, through the process of statistical inference, population values, or *parameters,* can be estimated from sample values, or *statistics*. The relationship between a census and a sample was considered in Chapter 1. In computing the values of sample statistics, such as the mean and the standard deviation, it is important that we identify the population about which we are concerned and follow a sampling procedure that will permit us to generalize about that population.

1 Such measurements as the mean, median, and standard deviation can be either parameters or statistics, depending on whether a _____ or a _____ is measured.

population; sample

2 The procedure of collecting information about a population is called a _____ ; collecting information about a sample is referred to as the process of _____ .

census

sampling

3 The procedure by which the characteristics of a population are estimated on the basis of known sample values is called statistical _____ .

inference

4 Of course, not all decisions about a population need to be made on the basis of inference. For example, in the assembly of transistor radios, a final inspection to ascertain that *every* radio is operative [does / does not] involve statistical inference, whereas the selection of a *few* radios to test their endurance when subjected to physical abuse [does / does not] involve statistical inference.

does not

does

5 For any finite population, that is, a population that is made up of a known and limited number of elements, a census, or 100 percent sample, is a possibility. However, if it is expensive or inconvenient to measure every element in a population, or if the measuring process itself destroys or affects the elements, then the process of _____ needs to be used.

sampling (or statistical infer-ence)

6 An infinite population is one in which the number of elements is boundless. For example, there is no limit to the number of times a coin could be tossed to ascertain the "true" probability of the occurrence of a head. Therefore a census of an infinite population is [always / never] possible.

never

7 For the following areas of information about specified populations, indicate an *s* for those best determined by sampling and statistical inference and indicate a *c* for those best determined by a census:

s (since this is presumably destructive testing)

____ **(a)** resistance of light bulbs to high voltage

c (since we are concerned about every individual pa-tient's welfare)

____ **(b)** extent of patient recovery following operative pro-cedures

c

____ **(c)** determining the "age" of the accounts receivable in a small company

s

____ **(d)** the preference of voters in a gubernatorial election one month before the election

8 The procedures of statistical inference that we shall study in the following chapters are of three general types:

(a) point estimation
(b) interval estimation
(c) hypothesis testing

Consider the two types of estimation listed above, using the arithmetic mean as an example. The estimation of the specific values of a population mean based on the value of a sample mean involves _____ estimation.

point

9 Refer to the three types of statistical inference listed in Frame 8. Whereas *point estimation* is involved whenever the specific value of a population mean is being estimated, specifying the *range* of values within which the mean is likely to be located involves _____ .

interval estimation

10 Try to answer without referring to the frames above. Two kinds of estimation of a parameter can be made through statistical inference: _____ estimation and _____ estimation.

point; interval

11 If the mean operating life of all television tubes, based on a sample, is estimated as 8,000 hours, _____ estimation is involved. If we are able to conclude with 95 percent confidence that the true mean operating life for all tubes is between 7,500 and 8,500 hours, _____ estimation is involved in our application of statistical inference.

point

interval

12 As contrasted to statistical estimation, *hypothesis testing* is concerned with testing the likelihood that an assumed population value is correct, based on sample evidence. As was true for point and interval estimation, hypothesis testing also concerns the application of the techniques of _____ _____ .

statistical inference

13 For our television tube example, if we begin with the assumption that the average tube life is 8,500 hours (based, perhaps, on a quality control standard), determining the probability that a sample with a mean different from this could have occurred purely by chance involves _____ _____ testing.

hypothesis

14 Thus there are three major types of uses for the methods of statistical inference as aids in decision making, and these applications will be described in further detail in Chapters 9 through 11: _____ , _____ , and _____ .

point estimation; interval estimation; hypothesis testing

15 In any use of sampling and statistical inference, it is particularly important that the *sampled population* be the same as the *target population*, which is the one about which we wish to make generalizations. For the following sampling situations, indicate an *s* when the sampled population is the same as the target population and indicate a *d* when the two populations appear to differ.

d

___ **(a)** a sample of RCA television picture tubes tested for the purpose of determining the operating life of television tubes in general

s

___ **(b)** a sample of RCA picture tubes tested to determine the operating life of RCA picture tubes in general

d

___ **(c)** a sample of RCA picture tubes tested to determine the quality of RCA products in general

d

___ **(d)** a sample of college students polled to determine the general popularity of a political candidate

d (Not all voters are listed in the telephone directory!)

___ **(e)** a sample of people chosen from a telephone directory polled to determine the general popularity of a political candidate

target

16 Thus the accuracy of any inferences made on the basis of a sample is dependent on whether or not the sampled population is the same as the _____ population.

convenience

17 In addition to being chosen from the appropriate population, the sample must be chosen in a specified way in order to permit the valid use of the methods of statistical inference. In general, there are three types of samples: *convenience samples, judgment samples,* and *probability samples.* Taking those elements which happen to be most readily available for the sample would result in obtaining a _____ sample.

judgment

18 Of the three types of samples given in Frame 17, the one in which the selection of sampled elements is based on the experience and personal choice of the selector is the _____ sample.

probability

19 Finally, in contrast to the choice of items for the sample on the basis of convenience or personal choice, if the procedure followed results in every element in the population having a known, and usually equal, chance of being chosen for inclusion in the sample, the result is a _____ sample.

20 Because the choice of elements for a probability sample is usually based on a random selection, this type of sample is also called a "random sample." Indicate the types of samples described below by posting a *c* for a convenience sample, a *j* for a judgment sample, and a *p* for a probability sample.

	j

___ **(a)** A public opinion pollster stops at several locations in a town and talks to people who appear to be representative of the town's residents.

	c

___ **(b)** A pollster stations himself at a busy intersection in town to obtain interviews with a sample of the town's residents.

	c

___ **(c)** Noticing a large manufacturing plant, the pollster gets the permission of the management to have a questionnaire distributed, thus getting at the views of a cross section of the town's residents rather rapidly.

	p

___ **(d)** Using a listing of all residents in the town, he places each name on a slip of paper, places all slips in a bowl, and chooses a 10 percent sample by alternately picking a name and mixing the slips until the desired sample size is achieved.

21 Of the three types of samples described in Frame 20, the one which allows the maximum amount of selector bias in determining which items are typical of those in the population

	judgment

is the _____ sample.

22 Although a judgment sample may be a good one in terms of representativeness, the difficulty with this type of sample is that the errors due to sampling cannot be measured or predicted. Are the errors associated with a convenience sample

	No

measurable and predictable? [Yes / No]

23 Only when the selection of individual elements for sample inclusion is left to some form of chance, or random, procedure can the probability of sampling errors be estimated. Therefore the methods of statistical inference can legitimately be used only when the sample taken from the target population is a

	probability

_____ sample.

24 We can be certain about the parameters of a population only if we conduct a census *and* avoid all measurement errors. However, population parameters can be estimated with a *known degree of confidence* if the sample collected is a

	probability
	convenience; judgment

_____ sample; but this cannot be done if the sample is a _____ or _____ sample.

Summary

25 A measurement of a sample, called a "sample statistic," is often used to estimate a population characteristic, or _____ , by the application of the methods of _____ .

| parameter |
| statistical inference |

26 Three major types of applications of statistical inference, which we cover in the following chapters, are _____ , _____ , and _____ .

| point estimation |
| interval estimation; hypothesis |
| testing |

27 In order to use the methods of statistical inference appropriately, it is essential that the sampled population be the same as the _____ population. Of the three types of samples that can be taken, there is no way of knowing the degree of accuracy of a _____ or _____ sample, whereas the degree of accuracy of a _____ sample can be statistically estimated.

| target |

| convenience; judgment |
| probability |

8.2 ■ Methods of Probability Sampling

In the popular literature, probability sampling is usually called "scientific sampling." A number of specific methods have been devised to ensure the attainment of a probability sample, or scientific sample, for the purpose of using the methods of statistical inference. The first of these—simple random sampling—is the most important because it illustrates the basic requirements to be satisfied in probability sampling in general and is itself often used as part of a more elaborate sampling technique. In addition to simple random sampling, we consider systematic sampling, stratified sampling, and cluster sampling in this section.

28 The essential requirement of probability sampling, which permits the valid use of the methods of statistical inference, is that every element in the population has a(n) [known / unknown] probability of being included in the sample.

| known |

29 Recall that in the last section we mentioned that a probability sample is also referred to as a "random sample." In contrast a *simple random sample* is a particular approach to obtaining a probability, or random, sample. Simple random sampling is the most direct approach to the objective of obtaining a probability sample. Assigning a number to each element in the population, posting these on individual slips of paper and placing them in a bowl, and drawing some slips out of the bowl while thoroughly mixing them is an example of _____ in its most elementary form.

| simple random sampling |

30 For a simple random sample not only each element but also each combination of elements has the same chance of being included in the sample. Put another way, a simple random sample is one chosen in such a way that all samples of a given size, representing all possible combinations of elements, have an [equal / unequal] chance of being selected.

equal

31 The procedure in simple random sampling is such as to ensure that the personal judgment of the person collecting the sample [does / does not] enter into the choice of the elements.

does not

32 For a survey being supported by the merchants of a particular shopping center, a poll taker stops 100 people along the sidewalk to get their opinions about the center. Can this be considered a simple random sample of people who shop at the center? [Yes / No] Why or why not? _____

_____

_____

No; His selection of individuals is not likely to be random, but based on their appearance.

33 Because the method of blind choice is often difficult to put into practice, *tables of random numbers* have been constructed for use in selecting the specific elements to be included in a _____ sample.

simple random

34 Table B-9 in the Appendix is an example of a table of random numbers. Such tables often run to many pages and differ in the number of digits listed in each column. But the feature that all such tables have in common is that the numbers are listed in a [sequential / random] order.

random

35 As an example of the use of such a table, assume that there are 897 elements, numbered 001 to 897, in a population, and that we wish to take a sample of 50 elements. We would enter the table at any arbitrary point and read the digits in groups of three, reading either to the right, left, downward, or upward, and choose the elements represented by those code numbers. What would we have to do about three-digit numbers greater than 897 in value? _____

_____

_____

Ignore them, since there are no elements numbered beyond 897.

36 Just as we generally ignore values that do not represent any assigned code numbers, we also ignore any code numbers that occur a second time by chance, since it is not usually considered desirable to have the same element represented more than once in a sample. For the example in which we have elements numbered from 001 to 897, enter Table B-9 and list the first five elements that would be included in your sample:

_____ , _____ , _____ , _____ , _____ .

Any choice, but remember that you usually begin arbitrarily within the table, not at the first value from the top.

number

37 In order to be referenced with a table of random numbers, every element in the target population being sampled must be identified by a _____ .

no element in the population is represented by that number; the element has already been selected for the sample

38 A number that is obtained from a table of random numbers is ignored when_____ _____ and when _____ _____ .

39 An auditor investigates the accuracy of a large number of accounts by checking 25 accounts selected by the use of a table of random numbers. The type of probability sample he has collected would be described as being a _____ sample.

simple random

40 Thus in *simple random sampling* a blind choice or a randomization procedure is used to obtain a probability sample. In *systematic sampling*, on the other hand, elements are selected from the population at a uniform interval of a listed order, time, or space. For example, if we take a 10 percent sample of telephone subscribers listed in a directory by starting at an arbitrary point in the first 10 names and choosing every tenth name thereafter, a _____ sampling procedure is involved.

systematic

41 Systematic sampling differs from simple random sampling in that each combination of elements does not have an equal chance of being selected. For example, if every tenth sequentially numbered element is being chosen for a systematic sample, the elements numbered 233 and 235 [could / could not] both be included in the sample.

could not

42 Through the use of a systematic sample, as contrasted to the simple random sample, there is also the possibility of introducing a systematic error. For example, if every fifth house is a corner house, then a survey of households directed at adequacy of street lighting will introduce a _____ bias when every fifth house is chosen for the sample.

systematic (Either all of the sampled houses would be corner houses or none of them would be corner houses.)

43 Therefore, whenever there is some kind of sequential pattern to the elements being sampled, systematic sampling [would / would not] be an appropriate method by which to obtain a probability sample.

would not

44 On the other hand, as compared with simple random sampling, systematic sampling usually requires [more / less] time for the choice of elements to be included in the sample and thus results in a [higher / lower] sampling cost.

less

lower

45 Contacting every tenth person who purchased a new car from a dealership and obtaining his evaluation of the post-sale service that he obtained is an example of _____ sampling as applied in customer relations.

systematic

46 A third sampling method, which is based on having some knowledge about the characteristics of the population and their relationship to the variable being measured, is called *stratified sampling*. For example, in a study of student attitude toward having a college football team, if we suspect that there are important differences between undergraduate and graduate students in this regard, then the use of _____ sampling would be appropriate.

stratified

47 In a study of consumer attitudes toward a new product design, classifying individuals in the target population by sex and age groups and then taking a 10 percent sample (either simple random or systematic) from each population group in order to assure proportional representation in the sample is another example of _____ sampling.

stratified

48 Although the example just cited involved a proportionate sampling from each population group, or stratum, this is not a requirement of stratified sampling. More important, the sample from each stratum should be large enough in number so that there are sufficient data for statistical analysis. For example, in estimating the value of items held in inventory, suppose that there are 1,000 items classified as "low cost" and 50 items classified as "high cost." A 10 percent sample of the "low cost" items, or 100 items, may be sufficient. A 10 percent sample of the "high cost" items, or five items, probably [would / would not] be sufficient.

would not

49 Whether the sampling is proportionate or nonproportionate, the assurance of appropriate representation of various population groups in the sample is an advantage of _____ sampling.

stratified

50 In a study of wage rates in a given state, an analyst classifies the organizations as manufacturing, retailing, and financial and chooses a sample of employees working in each category according to some random process. The sampling procedure can be described as involving _____ sampling.

stratified

51 Finally, *cluster sampling* involves the random selection of elements in *groups*, rather than as individual elements. For example, if we wish to investigate the wage rates in manufacturing firms in a certain state, the random selection of a number of *firms* and the collection of wage rates for *all* employees in those *selected* firms would exemplify _____ sampling.

cluster

52 Cluster sampling is often used as a matter of necessity rather than choice. In the preceding example, obtaining a simple or systematic random sample of all employees working in the manufacturing firms included in the target population would probably be relatively [easy / difficult] .

difficult (since this would require obtaining listing of all employees in all firms in the statistical population)

53 Note that a sampling design can incorporate more than one of the sampling methods we are describing. For example, categorizing the firms according to type and then sampling, as we did in Frame 50, involves _____ sampling. Obtaining the sample by randomly choosing entire firms, rather than individuals, involves _____ sampling.

stratified

cluster

54 The examples of cluster sampling which we have presented would also be referred to as *single-stage sampling*, since all of the elements in the selected clusters are included in the sample. When there are two or more stages in the sampling process, the cluster sampling is called *multistage sampling.* For instance, including only the employees from randomly selected departments of the randomly selected firms would be an example of _____ sampling.

multistage (or two-stage)

55 Thus, the selection of elements in groups rather than as individual elements is referred to as _____ sampling. When all of the elements in the primary groups are included in the sample, this is called _____ sampling. When the sampling process involves the selection of subgroups from within the primary sample groups, this is called _____ sampling.

cluster

single-stage

multistage

56 When the primary groups being sampled are geographical in nature, the term *area sampling* is frequently applied to the cluster-sampling method. Because political polls often involve choices of samples within counties, then election districts, then blocks, then particular homes, such sampling can be referred to as [single- / multi-] stage _____ sampling.

multi-; area

Summary

simple random

systematic; stratified

cluster

57 The four principal sampling methods for obtaining a probability sample which we have discussed are _____ _____ , _____ , _____ , and _____ sampling.

58 Using a manufacturing process as an example, subjecting every twentieth generator produced to an intensive quality inspection involves the use of _____ sampling.

systematic

59 In the same situation, choosing groups of generators, such as a half-hour's output, and subjecting every generator in the group to an intensive inspection exemplifies _____ sampling.

cluster (or single-stage)

60 When the quality control department specifies the serial numbers of the generators to be inspected by the use of a table of random numbers, _____ sampling is involved.

simple random

61 When generators of several different types are being manufactured, sampling according to the type of generator in order to assure appropriate representation of each type in the

stratified

sample involves _____ sampling.

62 In terms of the number of steps in the sampling procedure, cluster sampling can be referred to as being either

single-stage; multistage

_____ or _____ sampling. When the groups being sampled in cluster sampling are geographic in

area

nature, the method is often called _____ sampling.

63 No matter what sampling method is used in the attempt to obtain a probability sample and minimize sampling cost, it is particularly important that every element chosen for the sample actually be included in the sample. In a consumer survey involving the use of mailed questionnaires, if 30 percent of a randomly selected sample return the questionnaires and 70 percent do not, can the 30 percent respondent group be considered a random sample of the target population? [Yes / No]

No (The 30 percent who chose to reply may have done so because of the particular views they have, thus representing a biased segment of the random sample.)

64 Therefore in studies in which people are the elements of the sample, and they can choose either to participate or not to participate, repeated followup to get as high a participation by those in the sample as possible is [unnecessary / desirable /

essential

essential].

8.3 ■ Sampling Distributions

In Chapter 7 the normal probability distribution was used to interpret the meaning of a measurement when the mean and standard deviation of a group of measurements are known. Similarly, we can interpret the meaning of a particular sample statistic, such as the sample mean, if we know that the statistic is normally distributed and can calculate the mean and standard deviation for the distribution. As contrasted to a probability distribution for individual measurements, such a distribution for a statistic is called a *sampling distribution*, and it is the basis for most of the methods of statistical inference that we cover in the following chapters. A probability distribution representing the means taken from a great many samples of the same size, for example, would be called the *sampling distribution of the mean.* In this section we focus on the sampling distribution of the mean as a specific case in point and illustrate how the mean and standard deviation of this distribution can be determined without actual recourse to collecting a large number of samples and determining their respective arithmetic means. Rather, it is possible to estimate the mean and standard deviation of such a distribution of means on the basis of only a single probability sample.

65 If we were to take two, three, four, or more random samples of the same size from a population, would we expect that the numerical values of the sample statistics, such as the means, would be identical from sample to sample? [Yes / No]

No

66 Therefore it is possible to construct a probability distribution for any collection of sample statistics, such as the sample mean; this is referred to as a _____ distribution.

sampling

67 Any probability distribution, including a sampling distribution, can be described by identifying the mean and the standard deviation of the distribution. Thus a sampling distribution of means can be described by identifying the _____ of the means and the _____ of the _____ .

mean; standard deviation
means

68 A distribution of medians would be called the _____ _____ of the _____ and could be described by identifying _____ and _____ _____ for this distribution.

sampling distribution
median
mean; standard
deviation

69 Like any standard deviation, the standard deviation of a sample statistic measures the amount of variability of a distribution of values. However, unlike measurements, variability in the value of a sample statistic, such as the sample mean, represents *sampling error* in estimating the associated population parameter. Thus the standard deviation of the mean is called the *standard error of the mean*, and it indicates the amount of sampling error in estimating the population _____ on the basis of a known sample _____ .

mean; mean

70 Similarly for the sampling distribution of medians it is more appropriate to say that this distribution can be described by identifying the mean of the medians and the _____ _____ of the medians.

standard error

71 When a population of measurements is normally distributed, the sampling distributions of statistics for samples taken from that population are also normally distributed. If we wish to use a sample statistic such as the sample mean in estimation or hypothesis testing, why would we be interested in the normality of the sampling distribution? _____

_____

_____

Because this permits us to use the normal probability distribution for the purpose of statistical inference.

72 However, if the sample size is sufficiently large, then *any* population of measurements, regardless of its form, will have sampling distributions that are normally distributed. This is called the *central-limit theorem*, and it is particularly important because it permits the use of the _____ curve in interpreting sampling distributions taken from nonnormally distributed populations.

normal probability (For the sampling distribution of the mean, the sample is sufficiently large if $n \geqslant 30$.)

73 The theorem which states that the distribution of a sample statistic, such as the sample mean, will tend to follow a normal distribution as sample size is increased, regardless of the characteristics of the parent population, is called the _____ theorem.

central-limit

74 For example, compare the populations represented at the top of Figures 8-1*a* and 8-1*b*. The population in Figure 8-1*a* follows a [normal / rectangular] distribution, and the population of Figure 8-1*b* follows a _____ distribution.

rectangular

normal

Figure 8-1*a* ■ A population with a rectangular distribution of values and associated sampling distributions of the mean for $n = 2$, $n = 5$, and $n = 30$

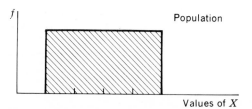

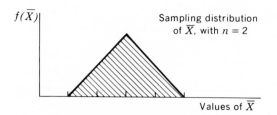

Figure 8-1a ■ A population with a rectangular distribution of values and associated sampling distributions of the mean for $n = 2, n = 5,$ and $n = 30$ (*Continued*)

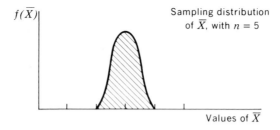

$f(\overline{X})$

Sampling distribution of $\overline{X}$, with $n = 5$

Values of $\overline{X}$

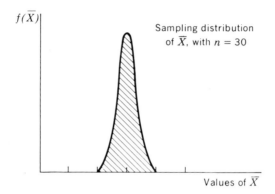

$f(\overline{X})$

Sampling distribution of $\overline{X}$, with $n = 30$

Values of $\overline{X}$

Figure 8-1b ■ A normally distributed population of values and associated sampling distributions of the mean for $n = 2, n = 5,$ and $n = 30$

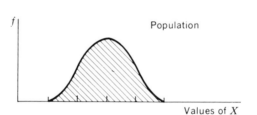

f

Population

Values of X

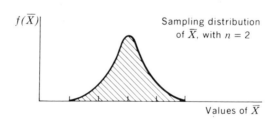

$f(\overline{X})$

Sampling distribution of $\overline{X}$, with $n = 2$

Values of $\overline{X}$

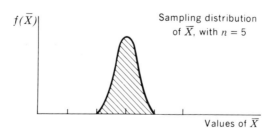

$f(\overline{X})$

Sampling distribution of $\overline{X}$, with $n = 5$

Values of $\overline{X}$

Figure 8-1*b* ▪ A normally distributed population of values and associated sampling distributions of the mean for $n = 2, n = 5,$ and $n = 30$ (*Continued*)

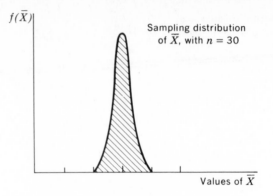

$f(\overline{X})$

Sampling distribution of $\overline{X}$, with $n = 30$

Values of $\overline{X}$

75 The three additional diagrams in each figure portray the distribution of sample means for each population under three conditions: when sample size n is equal to ___ (number), ___ (number), and _____ (number).

2; 5

30

76 As indicated by the sequence of diagrams in Figure 8-1*a*, as sample size is increased the distribution of a sample statistic becomes _____.

normal (or normally distributed; although the figures appear leptokurtic, they are in fact mesokurtic as well as symmetrical)

77 Of course, if we had to select a number of separate samples from a population in order to develop a sampling distribution, such as that for the mean, we would still face a formidable task. Fortunately, formulas for determining or estimating the characteristics of sampling distributions have been derived, making the collection of a large number of samples [necessary / unnecessary].

unnecessary

78 Refer to Figures 8-2*a* and 8-2*b*, which portray the frequency distribution of a population of test scores and the expected sampling distribution of the mean for 100 samples of 25 each (sampling with replacement of elements in the population). Comparison of these distributions indicates that the mean of a large number of sample means [does / does not] tend to be equal to the mean of the parent population.

does

Figure 8-2a ■ **Frequency distribution of aptitude test scores (N = 1,000)**

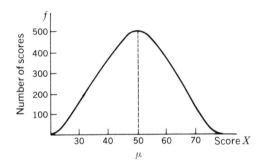

Figure 8-2b ■ **Sampling distribution of aptitude test means for 100 samples (n = 25)**

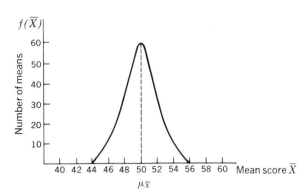

50

79 In the case of Figures 8-2a and 8-2b, $\mu_{\bar{X}} = \mu = $ _____ (number)

80 With reference to these figures, does it appear that the standard error of the mean, $\sigma_{\bar{X}}$, equals the standard deviation of the population of measurements, σ? [Yes / No]

No (Notice the difference in the width of the two distributions.)

81 Given a continuous process producing steel wire with a mean breaking strength, μ, of 300 pounds and a standard deviation, σ, of 15 pounds, the expected mean breaking strength of a large number of sample means of $n = 25$ is _____ pounds.

300

82 When sampling from a population that is infinite, or when sampling with replacement, the formula for determining the standard error of the mean, $\sigma_{\bar{X}}$, when the population standard deviation, σ, is known, is $\sigma_{\bar{X}} = \dfrac{\sigma}{\sqrt{n}}$. Therefore, for the data of Frame 81

$$\frac{15}{\sqrt{25}} = \frac{15}{5} = 3 \text{ pounds}$$

$$\sigma_{\bar{X}} = \frac{\sigma}{\sqrt{n}} =$$

83 Thus, whereas the mean of a sampling distribution of means is equal to the population mean, the standard error of the mean is always [larger / smaller] than the standard deviation of the population.

smaller (except when $n = 1$, in which case each sample is actually an individual measurement)

84 The formula $\sigma_{\bar{X}} = \sigma/\sqrt{n}$ also suggests that as the sample size n becomes larger, the standard error of the mean, $\sigma_{\bar{X}}$, becomes [larger / smaller].

smaller

85 For example, refer to the overlapping sampling distributions presented in Figure 8-3. Again, this figure indicates that as sample size is increased, the variability among sample means [increases / decreases].

decreases

Figure 8-3 ■ Distribution of a normal population and the sampling distributions of the arithmetic means for samples of size $n = 4$ and $n = 25$

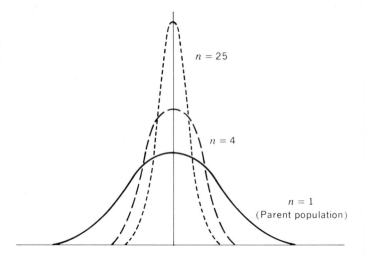

$n = 25$

$n = 4$

$n = 1$
(Parent population)

86 When sampling from a population that is finite, i.e., when there is a known value of N, and when sampling without replacement, a *finite correction factor* has to be included in the formula for the standard error of the mean, which then becomes

$$\sigma_{\bar{X}} = \frac{\sigma}{\sqrt{n}} \sqrt{\frac{N-n}{N-1}}$$

where N is the number of elements in the population and n is the number of elements in the sample. Given 65 accounts receivable with a mean age of 30 days and a standard deviation of 10 days, compute the standard error of the mean for a sample size of 16.

$$\frac{10}{\sqrt{16}} \sqrt{\frac{65-16}{65-1}} = \frac{10}{4}\sqrt{\frac{49}{64}}$$

$$= \left(\frac{10}{4}\right)\left(\frac{7}{8}\right) = 2.2$$

$$\sigma_{\bar{X}} = \frac{\sigma}{\sqrt{n}} \sqrt{\frac{N-n}{N-1}} =$$

87 With reference to the formula in Frame 86, the effect of the finite correction factor is to [increase / decrease] the value of the standard error of the mean.

decrease

88 Because the correction is negligible when the sample is only a small part of the population, the finite correction factor needs to be used only when the sample size n is more than 5 percent of the population size N. Thus, if 16 accounts are sampled from a total of 65 accounts receivable, the finite correction factor [should / need not] be used. If 16 accounts are sampled from a total of 650 accounts, the finite correction factor [should / need not] be used.

should

need not

89 In Frames 78 to 88 we have determined the mean of a large number of sample means and the standard error of this sampling distribution on the basis of knowing the mean and standard deviation of [a sample / the population].

the population

90 In most cases, however, we do not know the population parameters. Rather, we are likely to know the values of the mean and standard deviation for a single _____ .

sample

91 When we do not know the value of the population mean μ and the population standard deviation σ, then the respective sample statistics $\bar{X}$ and s are used to estimate the mean and standard error of the sampling distribution of the _____.

mean

92 Thus, when the population parameters are known, the parameters of the sampling distribution of the mean are:

$$\mu_{\bar{X}} = \mu \quad \text{and} \quad \sigma_{\bar{X}} = \frac{\sigma}{\sqrt{n}}$$

When the population parameters are not known, but the mean and standard deviation for a probability sample have been determined, the estimated parameters of the sampling distribution of the mean are:

$$\bar{X}; \frac{s}{\sqrt{n}}$$

(note the symbol for the standard error of the mean in this case)

est. $\mu_{\bar{X}} =$ _____ and $s_{\bar{X}} =$ _____

---

93 Thus there are two basic formulas for determining or estimating the standard error of the mean. In addition, each of these formulas may include the use of the finite correction factor. In total, therefore, there are _____ (number) possible formulas for computing the standard error of the mean.

four

---

94 Of the four possible formulas for computing the standard error of the mean that are listed below, which one is appropriate when sampling without replacement from a *finite population* and only the value of the *sample* standard deviation is known? [a / b / c / d]

d

(a) $\sigma_{\bar{X}} = \dfrac{\sigma}{\sqrt{n}}$

(b) $\sigma_{\bar{X}} = \dfrac{\sigma}{\sqrt{n}} \sqrt{\dfrac{N-n}{N-1}}$

(c) $s_{\bar{X}} = \dfrac{s}{\sqrt{n}}$

(d) $s_{\bar{X}} = \dfrac{s}{\sqrt{n}} \sqrt{\dfrac{N-n}{N-1}}$

---

95 In Frame 94 which formula for the standard error of the mean would be used when sampling from an *infinite population* and only the sample standard deviation is known? [a / b / c / d]

c

---

96 In Frame 94 which formula for the standard error of the mean would be used when sampling from an infinite *population* and the *population* standard deviation is known? [a / b / c / d]

a

---

97 In Frame 94 which formula for the standard error of the mean would be used when sampling from a *finite population* without replacement and the *population* standard deviation is known? [a / b / c / d]

b

98 Beginning with Chapter 9, which follows, we use the standard error of the mean in problems involving the use of statistical methods for the purpose of _____ _____ .

statistical inference (or estimation and hypothesis testing)

Review

parameters
statistics
statistical inference

99 (Frames 1-7) Population characteristics, or _____, can be estimated on the basis of knowing sample values, or _____ , by applying the methods of _____ _____ .

100 (Frames 8-10) Of the three types of statistical inference to be discussed further in later chapters, estimating the specific value of a population mean on the basis of a sample mean is an example of _____ .

point estimation

101 (Frames 9-11) Specifying a range of values within which the mean of the population is located at a known degree of confidence is an example of _____ .

interval estimation

102 (Frames 12-14) Testing the belief that an assumed population value is correct and that the difference between it and an obtained sample value is within the realm of expected chance variation involves the use of_____ .

hypothesis testing

103 (Frames 15, 16) Because we can make valid statistical inferences only about a population that has actually been sampled, it is important that the sample population be the same as the _____ population.

target

104 (Frames 17-27) Of the three types of samples that can be obtained from a target population, there is no way of describing the degree of accuracy of a _____ or _____ sample, whereas the degree of accuracy of a _____ sample can be statistically described.

convenience
judgment
probability

105 (Frames 40-45, 57, 58) Of the four principal sampling methods that we have discussed, all of which are aimed at obtaining a probability sample, the method by which every nth (fifth, tenth, etc.) element in space or time is chosen for inclusion in the sample is called _____ sampling.

systematic

106 (Frames 46-50, 61) The sampling method in which specific groups are identified within the population being sampled so that appropriate representation in the sample is assured is _____ sampling.

stratified

107 (Frames 28-39, 60) Use of a table of random numbers or some other randomizing procedure to attain a blind choice of elements to be used as part of the sample is included in _____ sampling.

simple random

108 (Frames 51-56, 59, 62-64) As the first step in the sampling process, when the procedure is such that groups of elements rather than individual elements are considered for inclusion in the sample, _____ sampling is involved. When all the elements in the selected groups are included in the sample, the procedure is called _____ sampling; when there is further selection within the selected groups, it is called _____ sampling. When the groups and subgroups represent geographic locations, the sampling procedure is often called _____ sampling.

cluster

single-stage

multistage

area

109 (Frames 65-70) A probability distribution of medians based on a designated sample size would be called the _____ distribution of the median, and it could be described by identifying the _____ and the _____ _____ of this distribution.

sampling
mean
standard error

110 (Frames 71-76) As the size of the sample is increased, any sampling distribution tends toward the normal distribution, even if the population of measurements from which it was developed was not normally distributed. This fact is important because it permits us to use the _____ distribution for the purpose of _____ .

normal probability
statistical inference

111 (Frames 77-81, 89-92) When the population mean, μ, is known, the mean of the sampling distribution of means, $\mu_{\bar{X}}$, can be specified as being equal to ____. When only a single sample mean $\bar{X}$ is known, $\mu_{\bar{X}}$ is estimated as being equal to ____.

μ

$\bar{X}$

112 (Frames 82-88, 93-98) For each of the following formulas used for computing the standard error of the mean, indicate the nature of the situation in which it would be used in terms of (a) whether σ is known; and (b) whether the population is infinite in size.

	is not	$s_{\bar{X}} = \dfrac{s}{\sqrt{n}} \sqrt{\dfrac{N-n}{N-1}}$	**(a)** σ [is / is not] known
	finite		**(b)** [infinite / finite] population

	is	$\sigma_{\bar{X}} = \dfrac{\sigma}{\sqrt{n}}$	**(a)** σ [is / is not] known
infinite (or $n \leqslant$ 5% N)			**(b)** [infinite / finite] population

	is not	$s_{\bar{X}} = \dfrac{s}{\sqrt{n}}$	**(a)** σ [is / is not] known
infinite (or $n \leqslant$ 5% N)			**(b)** [infinite / finite] population

	is	$\sigma_{\bar{X}} = \dfrac{\sigma}{\sqrt{n}}\sqrt{\dfrac{N-n}{N-1}}$	**(a)** σ [is / is not] known
	finite		**(b)** [infinite / finite] population

Symbols Introduced in This Chapter (with Frame Numbers)

(79) $\mu_{\bar{X}}$ — The mean of the sampling distribution of means.

(82) $\sigma_{\bar{X}}$ — The standard error of the mean when the population standard deviation is known.

(92) $s_{\bar{X}}$ — The estimated value of the standard error of the mean when the population standard deviation is not known.

Formulas Introduced in This Chapter (with Frame Numbers)

(79) $\mu_{\bar{X}} = \mu$ — The mean of the sampling distribution of means.

(82) $\sigma_{\bar{X}} = \dfrac{\sigma}{\sqrt{n}}$ — The standard error of the mean when the population standard deviation is known and the population is infinite in size (or $n \leqslant$ 5% N).

(86) $\sigma_{\bar{X}} = \dfrac{\sigma}{\sqrt{n}}\sqrt{\dfrac{N-n}{N-1}}$ — The standard error of the mean when the population standard deviation is known and the population is finite in size.

(92) $s_{\bar{X}} = \dfrac{s}{\sqrt{n}}$ — The standard error of the mean when the population standard deviation is not known and the population is infinite in size (or $n \leqslant$ 5% N).

(94) $s_{\bar{X}} = \dfrac{s}{\sqrt{n}}\sqrt{\dfrac{N-n}{N-1}}$ — The standard error of the mean when the population standard deviation is not known and the population is finite in size.

8.1 What is the difference between a problem situation that would be concerned with statistical estimation as contrasted with a situation in which hypothesis testing would be the appropriate statistical procedure?

8.2 Compare systematic sampling with simple random sampling. Why is systematic sampling generally the easier procedure? Under what circumstances is the use of systematic sampling questionable?

8.3 An oil company wants to ascertain the factors affecting consumer choice of gasoline service stations in a test area, and has accordingly obtained the names and addresses of all registered car owners residing in the area. Describe how this list could be used to obtain each of the four major types of probability samples that are described in this chapter.

8.4 A population consists of the four values: 3, 6, 9, and 10.

(a) Compute the population mean, μ.
(b) Compute the population standard deviation, σ.

8.5 For the population described in Exercise 8.4, suppose that simple random samples of size 2 each are taken from this population, sampling *without* replacement within each sample.

(a) List all of the possible pairs of values that can constitute a sample.
(b) For each of the pairs identified in (a), above, compute the sample mean, $\overline{X}$, and demonstrate that the mean of all possible sample means, $\mu_{\overline{X}}$, is in fact equal to the mean of the population, μ, from which the samples were taken.

8.6 For the sampling situation described in Exercises 8.4 and 8.5, (a) compute the standard error of the mean by determining the standard deviation of the sample means identified in 5(b) in respect to $\mu_{\overline{X}}$. (b) Compute the standard error of the mean by using the appropriate formula given in the chapter, and verify that the value thus computed equals the first computed value.

8.7 In a manufacturing facility involved in the manufacture of television picture tubes, suppose it is known that the average (mean) operating life of the tubes is 10,000 hours with a standard deviation of 300 hours. For samples of 36 television tubes each, what is the standard error of the sampling distribution of the mean? Interpret the meaning of the value that you have computed.

8.8 For the situation in Exercise 8.7, suppose that we have no information about the population parameters. However, for one sample of size 36 we obtain a mean operating life of 9,800 hours with a sample standard deviation of 320 hours. Estimate the value of the population mean and the value of the standard error of the mean on the basis of the sample results.

8.9 For a systematic sample of 25 stock issues taken from a listing of 257 over-the-counter issues, the market price has advanced by an average (mean) of $3 per share during a fiscal quarter, with a standard deviation of $0.50.

(a) What is the best (point) estimate of the mean price change for all 257 stock issues?
(b) For a sample of size 25, what is the estimated value of the standard error of the mean?

8.10 For Exercise 8.9, suppose the sample was taken from a very large number of over-the-counter issues. Answer the two questions included in Exercise 8.9 and indicate the implications of any differences in the numerical results.

ADDITIONAL EXERCISES

8.11 Describe the difference between the concepts of a *sampled population* and a *target population*. If there is a difference between these two populations in any particular application of statistical inference, why is it generally inappropriate simply to redefine the target population so that it is the same as the sampled population?

8.12 Distinguish among convenience, judgment, and probability samples by indicating how an auditor might use each type in investigating the accuracy of a large number of spare-parts inventory figures.

8.13 Both stratified sampling and cluster sampling involve certain groupings of the elements (members) of a population. Describe the main differences between these sampling procedures.

8.14 A population consists of just the three values 1, 3, and 8.

(a) Compute the mean, μ, and standard deviation, σ, for this population.

(b) Suppose that samples of size 2 each are taken from this population, sampling without replacement within each sample. List all of the equally likely pairs of values that can constitute a sample and compute the mean for each possible sample.

8.15 For the sampling situation described in Exercise 8.14, complete the following calculations.

(a) Demonstrate that $\mu_{\bar{X}} = \mu$.
(b) Compute the standard error of the mean by using the values of the several sample means.
(c) Compute the standard error of the mean by using the formula which does not rely on the analysis of all possible sample results.

8.16 Differentiate the meanings of the symbols σ, s, $\sigma_{\bar{X}}$, and $s_{\bar{X}}$.

8.17 It is known that the variance of the amounts included in a large number of accounts receivable is $225. If a sample of 25 accounts is taken, determine the value of the standard error of the mean to be used in conjunction with interpreting the sample results.

8.18 For the sampling situation in Exercise 8.17, suppose that there are actually 200 accounts receivable. Determine the value of the standard error of the mean and compare it with the value computed in Exercise 8.17.

8.19 A simple random sample of 50 ball bearings taken from a large number being manufactured has a mean weight of 1.5 ounces per bearing with a standard deviation of 0.1 ounce.

(a) What is the best estimate of the average per bearing weight of all bearings being manufactured?
(b) Estimate the value of the standard error of the mean.

8.20 Suppose that the 50 sampled bearings in Exercise 8.19 are taken from a particular production run that includes just 150 bearings as the total population.

(a) What is the best estimate of the average per-bearing weight for the 150 bearings?
(b) Estimate the value of the standard error of the mean and compare it with your answer in Exercise 8.19.

8.21 The mean dollar value of the sales amounts for a particular consumer product last year is known to be $\mu = \$3{,}400$ per retail outlet handling the item with a standard deviation of $\sigma = \$200$. If a large number of outlets handle the product, determine the standard error of the mean for a sample of size $n = 25$.

8.22 For the sampling situation described in Exercise 8.21, suppose only 100 retail outlets handle the product. Determine the standard error of the mean for the sample of $n = 25$ in this case, and compare your answer with the answer to Exercise 8.21.

CHAPTER 9 ■ STATISTICAL ESTIMATION

As we indicated in the preceding chapter, the three principal applications of statistical inference are directed toward the purposes of point estimation, interval estimation, and hypothesis testing. The first two of these procedures, which comprise the contents of this chapter, are both concerned with the estimation of population parameters based on known sample statistics. Throughout our discussion of these methods, the assumption will be made that the sample whose values are being used for the purpose of estimation has been selected by simple random sampling, as also discussed in the preceding chapter. Point estimates are given in the form of one number, or a particular point, whereas interval estimates identify the range of points within which a population parameter is likely to be located. Since probability values can be specified for interval estimates but not for point estimates, interval estimation is the more important of the two as a method of inference and is consequently given most of the attention in this chapter. After a brief coverage of point estimation, we consider the procedures of interval estimation as applied to the population mean, the difference between the means of two populations, and population proportions.

9.1 ■ Point Estimation

Throughout the rest of this book we differentiate estimated parameters from actual measured parameters by inserting a "cap" over the usual parameter symbol. For example, $\hat{\mu}$ (read: "mū cap") is the symbol for the estimated mean of a population. In this section we discuss several criteria used by statisticians to identify a good estimator and then present the point estimates used for the most frequently estimated population parameters: the mean, total quantity, difference between the means of two populations, standard deviation, proportion, total number in a category, and the difference between the proportions of two populations.

1 Where $\bar{X}$ and μ are the symbols used to designate the sample and population means, respectively, and p and π are used to designate the sample and population proportions, the estimated population mean is designated by the symbol ___, and the estimated population proportion is designated by the symbol ___ .

$\hat{\mu}$

$\hat{\pi}$

2 Throughout our coverage of the criteria of a good estimator, we shall use estimation of the population mean as the example. In Chapter 8 we suggested that the mean $\bar{X}$ of a randomly chosen sample is an unbiased estimator of the population mean. This factor of *unbiasedness* suggests that if

be larger than μ about as often as they are smaller than μ

we were to take a large number of random samples from a given population, the means of these samples would [all be equal to μ / be larger than μ about as often as they are smaller than μ / have no systematic relationship to the value of μ].

3 Thus the criterion of *unbiasedness* for a good estimator also suggests that the mean $\mu_{\bar{X}}$ of an infinitely large number of sample means taken from the same population, illustrated on the frequency curve below, is equal to the mean of the

population

_____ from which the samples were taken.

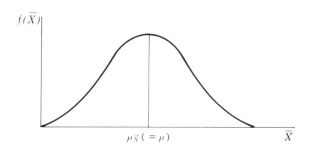

$$\mu_{\bar{X}}(=\mu)$$

4 Since the long-run average of an infinitely large number of sample means is equal to the population mean itself, we can say that $E(\bar{X})$ (read: "expected value of the sample mean") = μ. The expression $E(\bar{X}) = \mu$ is often used to represent the

unbiasedness

criterion which we have been discussing, that of _____

_____ .

5 In addition to unbiasedness, the criteria of *consistency*, *efficiency*, and *sufficiency* are used in identifying a good estimator. The criterion of consistency can be represented symbolically by $\bar{X} \to \mu$ as $n \to N$ (read "$\to$" as "approaches"). This suggests that for a consistent point estimator, as sample

comes closer and closer to the population value being estimated

size is increased, the value of the estimator generally [remains unaffected / continues to vary by the same amount / comes closer and closer to the population value being estimated].

6 The criterion of unbiasedness can be symbolized by

$\bar{X}$

$E(\_\_) = \mu$

The criterion of consistency indicates that as

$\bar{X} \to \mu$

$n \to N, \_\_ \to \_\_$

unbiasedness

consistency

7 The two criteria for point estimation which we have considered thus far are those of _____ and _____ . The criterion of *efficiency* suggests that the good estimator is one whose sampling distribution is most closely concentrated around the parameter being estimated. Put another way, that sample statistic is to be preferred as an estimator whose standard error is the [smallest / largest] in value.

smallest

8 The criterion of a good estimator that takes into consideration the relative sizes of the standard errors of alternative estimators is that of _____ .

efficiency

9 For a *symmetrically* distributed population of values, would the sample median, X_{med}, be an unbiased estimator of the population mean μ? [Yes / No] Would X_{med} be a consistent estimator of μ? [Yes / No]

Yes [since $E(X_{med}) = \mu$]

Yes (since as $n \to N$, $X_{med} \to \mu$)

10 Thus, for a symmetrically distributed population of values a sample median is both an unbiased and a consistent estimator of the population mean. For large samples it can be shown that $\sigma_{med} = 1.2533\sigma_{\overline{X}}$ (i.e., $\sigma_{med} > \sigma_{\overline{X}}$). Therefore, as compared with the sample mean, is the sample median an *efficient* estimator of the population mean? [Yes / No] Why or why not? _____ _____ _____ _____ .

No

Because its standard error is larger than that of the sample mean, which is also unbiased and consistent and would therefore be the better estimator.

11 The final criterion of a good estimator, in addition to unbiasedness, consistency, and efficiency, is that of *sufficiency*. An estimator is sufficient if it makes such use of all the available sample information that no other estimator would add any information about the [statistic / parameter] being estimated.

parameter

12 If an estimator does not make use of all available and relevant sample information, then it does not satisfy the criterion of _____ .

sufficiency

13 Of the four criteria for a good estimator, the criterion which indicates that the expected value of the estimator should be equal to the value of the parameter is that of _____ . The stipulation that the value of

unbiasedness

the estimator should approach the value of the parameter as sample size is increased concerns the criterion of _____.

consistency

14 That the standard error of an estimator should be smaller than that of other possible estimators concerns the criterion of _____ ; the requirement that an estimator should use all of the information available in a sample concerns the criterion of _____ .

efficiency

sufficiency

15 Match the list of criteria with the summary descriptions listed on the right by entering the appropriate letters:

d
a
c
b

____ unbiasedness   (a) $\overline{X} \rightarrow \mu$ as $n \rightarrow N$
____ consistency   (b) use of all available sample data
____ efficiency   (c) lowest value of standard error
____ sufficiency   (d) $E(\overline{X}) = \mu$

16 Thus the four criteria used by statisticians to define the characteristics of a good estimator are those of _____ , _____ , _____ , _____ .

unbiasedness; consistency
efficiency; and sufficiency
(in any order)

17 The criteria have not been presented with the objective that you will actually apply them in conjunction with problems presented in this book, but for the purpose of making you aware of the factors that statisticians consider in identifying good estimators. For estimating the population mean, for example, it can be shown that the sample statistic which satisfies all of the criteria discussed, and is thus the best estimator of the population mean, is the sample _____ .

mean

18 Now, it may be your reaction that statisticians are making much mathematical ado about nothing. After all, is it not obvious that the equivalent sample statistic is always the best estimator of the respective population parameter (sample mean as estimator of population mean, for example)? But let us turn an earlier example (Frames 9 and 10) around. For a symmetrically distributed population, in which the values of the mean and median coincide, would a sample mean be an *unbiased* estimator of the population median? [Yes / No] Would the sample mean be a *consistent* estimator of the population median? [Yes / No]

Yes

Yes

19 Continuing from Frame 18, given that $\sigma_{med} = 1.2533\sigma_{\overline{X}}$, which sample statistic, the mean or the median, is a more

Mean	populations? [Mean / Median]

20 Thus the equivalent sample statistic is not necessarily the best estimator of a population parameter. In addition to their use in selecting an estimator, the criteria which we have been considering are applied for the purpose of improving estimators. From Chapter 2, recall that in the formula for the population variance, $\sigma^2 = \Sigma(X - \mu)^2/N$, the divisor is N. On the other hand, in the formula for the sample variance, $s^2 = \Sigma(X - \bar{X})^2 / (n - 1)$, the divisor is $n - 1$. If the divisor were simply "n" in the latter formula, the long-run average value of such a sample variance would be somewhat smaller than the population variance, thus resulting in the estimator being

biased	[biased / unbiased] .

21 Table 9-1 presents the most frequently used estimators of population values. As indicated in Frame 20, the formula for the sample statistic which includes a correction for biasedness, thus resulting in an unbiased estimator being calculated, is the

variance (and, of course, the sample standard deviation also thus includes the correction factor)	formula for the sample _____.

Table 9-1 ■ **Frequently Used Point Estimators**

Population parameter	Estimator
Mean, μ	$\bar{X} = \dfrac{\Sigma X}{n}$
Total quantity in a population of values, $N\mu$	$N\bar{X}$
Difference between the means of two populations, $\mu_1 - \mu_2$	$\bar{X}_1 - \bar{X}_2$
Variance, σ^2	$s^2 = \dfrac{\Sigma(X - \bar{X})^2}{n - 1}$
Standard deviation, σ	$s = \sqrt{s^2}$
Proportion, π	$p = \dfrac{X}{n}$
Total number included in a category of the population, $N\pi$	Np
Difference between the proportions included in two populations, $\pi_1 - \pi_2$	$p_1 - p_2$

22 The two parameters in Table 9-1 whose meaning may not be entirely clear to you are "total quantity in a population" and "total number included in a category of the population."

Suppose that out of a population of 100 drugstores a sample of 25 stores chosen at random has an average inventory investment of $150 in a particular product (at cost). What would be the estimated average per-store inventory value for the population of 100 stores? _____

$150 (since $\hat{\mu} = \bar{X}$)

23 For the example in Frame 22, what is the *total* dollar inventory carried by the 25 sample stores? _____
What is the estimated total dollar inventory carried by all 100 stores? _____

$n\bar{X} = 25(\$150) = \$3,750$

$N\bar{X} = 100(\$150) = \$15,000$

24 Suppose that instead of being able to obtain dollar inventory figures, we can determine only whether or not each of the stores in the sample of 25 stores carries the particular product in question. If 20 of the 25 stores carry the product, the sample proportion, p, equals _____ (number). The estimated population proportion, π, equals _____ (number).

$\dfrac{20}{25} = 0.80$

0.80 (since $\hat{\pi} = p$)

25 According to the data in Frame 24, the estimated number of stores in the population of 100 stores that carry the product in question is _____ .

$Np = 100(0.80) = 80$

26 In conjunction with the criterion of consistency, we would have more confidence in the accuracy of any point estimate as sample size is [decreased / increased]. The effect of sample size on the accuracy of estimates is not easily illustrated when point estimates are involved, but this effect is readily apparent in interval estimation, considered in Section 9.2 which follows.

increased

9.2 ■ Confidence Intervals for Estimating the Population Mean

In terms of the sequence of topics in this book, we have now arrived at the first really important application of the methods of inference to problems of decision making. Specifically, we make use of the standard error of the mean and the characteristics of the normal probability distribution in order to estimate the interval of values within which a population mean or a population total is located with a known degree of confidence. Such an interval is called a *confidence interval*, and the *degree of confidence* associated with it indicates the percentage of such intervals that would include the population mean, if many such intervals based on independent sample means were computed.

27 As we have seen in Chapters 7 and 8, the proportion of the normal distribution which lies within various distances of the mean, expressed in units of the standard deviation, can be determined by reference to Table B-1, the table of areas under the normal curve. In using this table, the direction and amount of deviation of a value from the mean of a distribution are determined by using the formula $(X - \mu)/\sigma$, which is designated by the symbol ____.

z

28 There are three particular values of z that are so frequently used in problems of inference that they are worth listing separately. As indicated in Table 9-2, these are the values that serve as the boundaries for the "middle" 90, 95, and 99 percent of the distribution of measurements. Thus, just as we have previously observed that the limits defined by $\mu \pm 1.0\sigma$ include 68 percent of the measurements of a normally distributed variable, so also the limits $\mu \pm$ ____ σ include 90 percent of the measurements, $\mu \pm$ ____ σ include 95 percent of the measurements, and $\mu \pm$ ____ σ include the middle 99 percent of the measurements.

1.65
1.96
2.58

29 You should be able to verify the accuracy of the z values given in Table 9-2 by referring to Table B-1. For example, if we look up the area associated with a z value of 1.96, the proportion given in the table is ____ (number). Since this is the proportion of area included between μ and $(\mu + 1.96\sigma)$, the proportion included between $(\mu - 1.96\sigma)$ and $(\mu + 1.96\sigma)$ can be determined by multiplying the above proportion by ____ (number), resulting in a total proportion or area of ____ (number).

0.4750

2
0.9500

Table 9-2 ■ **Areas under the Normal Curve**

z, the number of standard deviation units from the mean	Area lying between $\mu - z\sigma$ and $\mu + z\sigma$
1.65	0.90
1.96	0.95
2.58	0.99

30 Given a population of values for which $\mu = 100.0$ and $\sigma = 14.0$, we can conclude that 68 percent of the measurements are included between the limits 86.0 and 114.0, which correspond to the range from $(\mu - 1\sigma)$ to $(\mu + 1\sigma)$. Similarly 90 percent of the measurements for a normally distributed variable are included between the limits ____ (number) and ____ (number), which correspond to $(\mu -$ ____ $\sigma)$ and $(\mu +$ ____ $\sigma)$.

76.9
123.1; 1.65
1.65

31 Continuing from Frame 30, we can also conclude that 95 percent of the measurements are included between 72.6 and 127.4, which correspond to $(\mu - 1.96\sigma)$ and $(\mu + 1.96\sigma)$, and that 99 percent of the measurements are included between _____ (number) and _____ (number), which corresponds to $(\mu - $ _____ $\sigma)$ and $(\mu + $ _____ $\sigma)$ on the normal probability distribution.

63.9; 136.1
2.58; 2.58

32 However, in this chapter we are concerned not with individual measurements but with sample means. Therefore we are also not concerned with the standard deviation of a population as such, but rather with the standard error of a hypothetical collection of means taken from a population. Therefore the distinction between a distribution of measurements, on the one hand, and a sampling distribution of means, on the other, is critical to an understanding of all of the remaining material in this chapter. *If you are not certain of this distinction, review Section 8.3 on sampling distributions right now!* Suppose that the sample mean of 49 randomly chosen measurements is 99.0 and it is known that the population standard deviation is 14.0. Assuming an infinite population, indicate the appropriate formula for computing the standard error for the expected distribution of sample means in respect to the population mean.

	a

(a) $\quad \sigma_{\overline{X}} = \dfrac{\sigma}{\sqrt{n}}$

(c) $\quad s_{\overline{X}} = \dfrac{s}{\sqrt{n}}$

(b) $\quad \sigma_{\overline{X}} = \dfrac{\sigma}{\sqrt{n}} \sqrt{\dfrac{N-n}{N-1}}$

(d) $\quad s_{\overline{X}} = \dfrac{s}{\sqrt{n}} \sqrt{\dfrac{N-n}{N-1}}$

33 Thus the particular formula that is used to determine the value of the standard error of the mean depends on whether or not the population standard deviation is known and whether or not the size of the population is infinite. Using the formula chosen in Frame 32, compute the standard error of the mean when $\overline{X} = 99.0$, $\sigma = 14.0$, and $n = 49$.

$\dfrac{14.0}{\sqrt{49}} = \dfrac{14.0}{7} = 2.0$

$\sigma_{\overline{X}} = \dfrac{\sigma}{\sqrt{n}} =$

34 Now, we actually do not know the value of μ, for this is the parameter whose value we wish to estimate. However, suppose the value of μ is actually 100.0. As a point estimate, is the mean of the sample data just reported a correct estimate of μ? [Yes / No]

No ($\hat{\mu}$ = 99.0, whereas μ = 100.0)

35 Rarely would a sample mean be exactly equal to μ, but the values of several sample means would tend to cluster around the value of μ, as illustrated in Figure 9-1. In the long run, what percentage of the sample means would be included within the limits designated by the dashed lines in Figure 9-1? _____ percent.

95 (Of course, this assumes that the sample means are normally distributed in respect to μ. Recall that the central-limit theorem permits this assumption given that $n \geqslant 30$, as indicated in the answer to Frame 72 in Chapter 8.)

Figure 9-1 ■ Values of several sample means in relation to the population mean

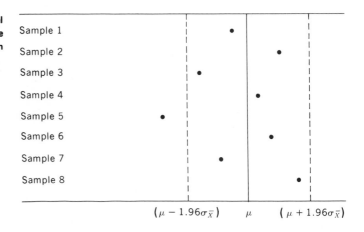

36 Given that μ = 100.0 and $\sigma_{\bar{x}}$ = 2.0 (refer to Figure 9-1 if necessary), 95 percent of a large number of sample means would lie between the values _____ (number) and _____ (number).

$\mu \pm 1.96\,\sigma_{\bar{x}}$ = 96.1
103.9

37 Compare the limits determined in Frame 36 with the

limits given in the first part of Frame 31. Why do they not correspond in value? _____
_____
_____
_____ ___
_____
_____ .

The limits in Frame 31 designate the range within which 95 percent of the *measurements* would be located, whereas the limits of Frame 36 designate the range within which 95 percent of the *sample means* would be located.

38 But of course in problems of estimation we do not know the value of the parameter, for that is what we are estimating. Furthermore we have the value of just one estimator available, that is, one sample mean. Given that $\bar{X} = 99.0$, $\sigma = 14.0$, $n = 49$, and $\sigma_{\bar{X}} = 2.0$, if we were to construct an interval as an estimate of the location of the population mean, the value that would be at the center of this interval estimate, based on our available knowledge, would be [99.0 / 100.0].

99.0

39 The value of $\bar{X}$ would be at the center of the confidence interval because this is the best (and only) estimate of μ that we have. Further, suppose that the interval is constructed by using the formula $\bar{X} \pm 1.96\ \sigma_{\bar{X}}$. For the data of Frame 38 the two limits of the confidence interval are _____ _____ (number) and _____ (number).

$99.0 \pm 1.96(2.0) =$
$99.0 \pm 3.92 = 95.1;\ 102.9$

40 The location of this confidence interval relative to the population mean is portrayed as "Sample 1" if Figure 9-2. Does this interval estimate include the point at which the population mean is in fact located? [Yes / No].

Yes

Figure 9-2 ■ Ninety-five percent confidence intervals computed about several sample means

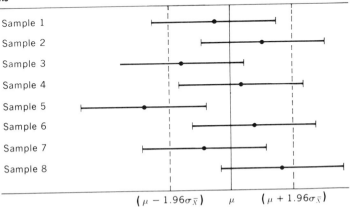

Answer column
1 (for sample 5)

41 Of the confidence intervals portrayed in Figure 9-2, how many do not include within their limits the point at which the parameter μ is actually located? ___ (number)

95

2½

2½

42 Still with reference to Figure 9-2, when using the formula $\bar{X} \pm 1.96\sigma_{\bar{X}}$ (or $\bar{X} \pm 1.96s_{\bar{X}}$) to construct the confidence interval within which the population mean is assumed to be located, what percentage of time will such intervals actually include the population mean? ____ percent. Of all such intervals that could be constructed, for what percentage of them will the value of the population mean be larger than the upper limit of the interval? ____ percent. For what percentage would the true mean be lower in value than the lower limit of the interval? ____ percent.

90

99

43 If we had used a z value of 1.65 in constructing the interval estimates for Figure 9-2, then the population mean would in the long run be included within ____ percent of these intervals; the use of 2.58 would result in the mean being included within ____ percent of the intervals.

44 Because the construction of interval estimates using appropriate standard error values and the normal probability distribution permits us to know how often such intervals will include the parameter being estimated, they are called *confidence intervals*, and the limits of a confidence interval are called *confidence limits*. Using the estimation formula $\bar{X} \pm z\sigma_{\bar{X}}$, compute the 90 percent confidence interval for estimating the population mean, given that $\bar{X} = 99.0$, $\sigma = 14.0$, $n = 49$, and $\sigma_{\bar{X}} = 2.0$.

$99.0 \pm 1.65(2.0) = 99.0 \pm$
$3.30 = 95.7$ and 102.3

Confidence limits = _____ and _____

45 Given that $\bar{X} = 99.0$, $\sigma = 14.0$, $n = 49$, and $\sigma_{\bar{X}} = 2.0$, determine the 99 percent confidence interval for estimating μ.

$99.0 \pm 2.58(2.0) = 99.0 \pm$
$5.16 = 93.8$ to 104.2

Confidence interval = _____ to _____

46 Which confidence interval, that of Frame 44 or that of Frame 45, is more likely to include the parameter being estimated? Frame [44 / 45]. Why then would the other interval ever be used; that is, what is the price paid for maximizing the confidence that the interval will include the parameter being estimated? _____

45

_____

_____

_____

The 99 percent confidence interval is wider (less precise), and thus may be less useful for decision-making purposes than the 90 or 95 percent confidence intervals.

47 Along these lines, to say that a population value, such as μ, is located between $-\infty$ (read: "minus infinity") and $+\infty$ ("plus infinity") would define the 100 percent confidence interval, but an interval this wide would have no practical value in decision making. The confidence limits that are most often used are the 95 percent limits. If a decision maker consistently uses 95 percent confidence limits in estimating population values, his interval estimates will include the population value ____ percent of the time.

48 As an example of a decision-making situation in which interval estimation of the population mean would be useful, suppose that a random sample of 49 employees taken from a total of 626 employees of a firm have an average weekly wage of $160.00 with a sample standard deviation of $10.50. Indicate the appropriate formula below for computing the standard error of the mean:

(a) $\quad \sigma_{\bar{X}} = \dfrac{\sigma}{\sqrt{n}}$

(c) $\quad s_{\bar{X}} = \dfrac{s}{\sqrt{n}}$

d (*s* rather than σ known, finite population, and $n >$ 5% *N*; see Chapter 8, Frames 94–97.)

(b) $\quad \sigma_{\bar{X}} = \dfrac{\sigma}{\sqrt{n}} \sqrt{\dfrac{N-n}{N-1}}$

(d) $\quad s_{\bar{X}} = \dfrac{s}{\sqrt{n}} \sqrt{\dfrac{N-n}{N-1}}$

49 Using formula *d* and the data in Frame 48, compute the standard error of the mean.

$$s_{\bar{X}} = \frac{10.50}{\sqrt{49}} \sqrt{\frac{626-49}{625}} =$$

$$1.50\sqrt{0.9232} = 1.50(0.96) = \$1.44$$

50 Given that $\bar{X} = \$160.00$, $s = \$10.50$, $n = 49$, $N = 626$, and $s_{\bar{X}} = \$1.44$, estimate the average weekly wage paid in the firm, using 95 percent confidence limits and carrying your answer to the second decimal place.

$$\text{Limits} = \bar{X} \pm 1.96 s_{\bar{X}} =$$

$$160.00 \pm 1.96(1.44) =$$

$$\$157.18 \text{ to } \$162.82$$

51 In Frame 50, if we had computed the 90 percent confidence limits instead of the 95 percent limits, the resulting interval would have been [narrower / wider] than the one which we obtained, whereas if we had computed the 99 percent confidence limits, the confidence interval would have been [narrower / wider].

52 In problems of the kind we have just presented, the decision maker often is as interested in estimating the total quantity, in this case the total amount of wages paid in the firm, as he is in estimating the average wage. With reference to the data in Frame 50, what is the one best (point) estimate for the total wages paid in the firm during the survey week?

$N\hat{\mu} = N\bar{X} = 626(\$160.00) = \$100, 160.00$ (from Table 9-1)

53 The general formula used to determine the confidence limits for estimating a total quantity in a population is $N\bar{X} \pm Nz\sigma_{\bar{X}}$ (or $\pm Nzs_{\bar{X}}$). The only way in which this estimation formula differs from the one used for determining confidence limits for the mean is that both terms in the formula are multiplied by _____.

N (number of elements in the population)

54 Accordingly, for the example in which $\bar{X} = \$160.00$, $s = \$10.50$, $n = 49$, $N = 626$, and $s_{\bar{X}} = \$1.44$, determine the 95 percent confidence limits for estimating the total wages paid in the company, carrying your answer to the nearest cent.

$626(160.00) \pm 626(1.96)$
$(1.44) = 100, 160.00 \pm$
$1,766.82 =$
$\$98,393.18$ and $\$101,926.82$

55 In this section we have presented the procedures for determining the confidence intervals for the population mean and the total quantity in a population. In order to make such estimates, we need to determine the value of the sample mean and the standard _____ of the mean. Finally, the confidence limits are set by utilizing the known characteristics of the _____ probability distribution.

error

normal

56 Our use of the normal probability distribution for constructing confidence intervals is based on the assumption that the sampling distribution of the mean is normally distributed. No matter what the distribution of the population itself, the central-limit theorem permits us to make the normality assumption about the sampling distribution of the mean whenever the sample size is $n \geqslant$ _____.

30

9.3 ■ Confidence Intervals for the Difference between Two Population Means

Up to now we have considered only the standard error of the mean and its use in estimation. However, *every* sample statistic has an associated standard error, and this standard error can be used in conjunction with estimating the parameter corresponding to the known statistic. Whereas we have used the estimation formula $\bar{X} \pm z\sigma_{\bar{X}}$ (or $\bar{X} \pm zs_{\bar{X}}$) for estimating the population mean, the more general formula used for defining confidence limits on the basis of using the normal probability distribution is: *point estimate* $\pm z\sigma_{stat}$, where σ_{stat} is read as "standard error of the statistic." Although we shall not describe the computation of confidence limits for such parameters as the population median, you should now be capable of making such estimates if given the appropriate point-estimate and standard-error formulas. In this section we cover estimation of the difference between the means of two populations.

57 No matter what population parameter is being estimated, the essential procedure, or formula used, is basically the same. The midpoint of the confidence interval used in estimation is always the appropriate _____ estimate of the population parameter.

58 When the normal probability distribution is used, an interval is defined with the point estimator at its midpoint by adding to it and subtracting from it a chosen value of z multiplied by the standard _____ of the statistic being used as the basis for the estimate.

59 Thus the general formula used for defining confidence limits with the normal probability distribution is _____ _____.

60 In Section 9.2, as well as in this section, we have observed that a standard error can be represented by two different symbols. For example, either $\sigma_{\bar{X}}$ or $s_{\bar{X}}$ would be read as "standard error of the mean." What is the difference between these two symbols? _____ _____ _____ _____ _____ _____ _____ _____

61 Suppose that a population whose mean is being estimated is not itself normally distributed. This would very likely be the case for the distribution of weekly wage rates, for which we estimated the average and total wages paid by a firm. Why is it still considered appropriate to use the normal probability

distribution in making these interval estimates, given a sufficient sample size? _____
_____
_____
_____
_____

62 In addition to estimating population means and total quantities, there is a frequent interest in estimating the amount of differences between the means of two populations. For example, we might be interested in estimating the difference in wage rates paid in two firms. As indicated in Table 9-1 (page 218), the point estimate used in estimating the difference between the means of two populations is _____ _____.

$$\bar{X}_1 - \bar{X}_2$$

63 As indicated by this formula, it is necessary to collect two samples, one from each of the populations in question, in order to estimate the difference between the means of the two populations. With the assumption that the standard error is computed on the basis of sample data only, the symbol that would be used to represent the standard error of the difference between two means is _____.

$$s_{\bar{X}_1 - \bar{X}_2} \ (\text{or } s_{\text{diff}})$$

64 Various forms of the computational formula for estimating the standard error of the difference between means have been developed. The formula that we shall use is not as simple as it might be, since it requires the prior computation of the standard error of each of the sample means. The formula has the advantage of brevity, however, and it also highlights the relationship between the standard error of the difference between means and the standard errors associated with the two sample means. Accordingly, the basic formula we use is[1]

$$\sigma_{\bar{X}_1 - \bar{X}_2} = \sqrt{\sigma_{\bar{X}_1}^2 + \sigma_{\bar{X}_2}^2}$$

When the standard deviations of the two populations are not known, then the standard error of the difference between

---

[1] An assumption underlying the use of the normal probability table with the standard-error formulas described in this section is that each sample is large ($n \geqslant 30$).

means is based on use of the sample standard deviations, and is:

$$s_{\bar{X}_1 - \bar{X}_2} =$$

65 In Frame 64 the value of the standard error of the difference between means can be described in words as being equal to the square root of the sum of _____

_____

_____

the squared values of the two standard errors of the mean (the sum of the variances of the two means)

66 In Section 9.2 we found that a sample of 49 employees in a particular firm had a mean wage rate of $160.00 per week with a standard error of the mean of $1.44. If a sample of 40 employees taken from another firm has a mean weekly wage of $155.00 and the standard error of the mean is $1.50, estimate the most likely difference in average weekly pay level between the two firms.

$\bar{X}_1 - \bar{X}_2 = \$160.00 -$
$\$155.00 = \$5.00$

Point estimate =

67 Using the data in Frame 66, compute the standard error of the difference between the means.

$\sqrt{s_{\bar{X}_1}^2 + s_{\bar{X}_2}^2}$
$= \sqrt{(1.44)^2 + (1.50)^2}$
$= \sqrt{2.0736 + 2.2500}$
$= \sqrt{4.3236} = \$2.08$

$$s_{\bar{X}_1 - \bar{X}_2} =$$

68 With $\bar{X}_1 = \$160.00$, $\bar{X}_2 = \$155.00$, $\bar{X}_1 - \bar{X}_2 = \$5.00$, and $s_{\bar{X}_1 - \bar{X}_2} = \$2.08$, estimate the difference in average weekly wage rates between the two firms from which these samples were taken, using 95 percent confidence limits.

$= \$5.00 \pm 1.96(2.08)$
$= \$5.00 \pm 4.08$
$= \$0.92 \text{ and } \$9.08$

Confidence limits $= (\bar{X}_1 - \bar{X}_2) \pm z s_{\bar{X}_1 - \bar{X}_2}$

69 Given the data of Frame 68, construct the 90 percent confidence interval for estimating the difference in average weekly wage between the two firms.

$$(\bar{X}_1 - \bar{X}_2) \pm zs_{\bar{X}_1 - \bar{X}_2}$$
$$= \$5.00 \pm 1.65(2.08)$$
$$= \$5.00 \pm 3.43 = \$1.57$$
$$\text{and } \$8.43$$

Confidence limits =

9.4 ■ Confidence Intervals for Proportions and Differences between Proportions

There is an important distinction between estimating a population mean and estimating a population proportion. The computation of a mean is related to the process of measurement, which involves data along a continuous scale, whereas the computation of a proportion is related to the process of counting, which involves discrete data. Because the number of "successes" which is converted into a proportion follows the binomial distribution, as explained in Chapter 6, the distribution of a proportion also follows the binomial probability distribution. But because the normal probability distribution is easier to work with than the binomial, as we indicate below, it would be convenient if the normal probability distribution could be used in conjunction with estimating population proportions. Recall that in Chapter 7 we concluded that normal probabilities are good approximations of binomial probabilities when $n > 30$, $np > 5$, and $nq > 5$. It is on the basis of this rule that the normal probability distribution is used in estimating proportions.[2]

70 Of a sample of 10 university students, four are found to be habitual smokers. Thus the proportion, p, of smokers in the sample is $X/n = {}^4/_{10} = 0.4$. What would be the one best point estimate of the value of the population proportion? (Refer to Table 9-1 if necessary.) $\hat{\pi} = $ _____ .

$p = 0.4$

71 In the preceding section on the population mean, we used the sample mean as the basis for the point estimate and we constructed the interval in respect to this point by using the _____ probability distribution. Although we would likewise begin the construction of an interval estimate for a proportion by using the sample proportion as the point estimate, the interval itself is appropriately based on the characteristics of the _____ probability distribution.

normal

binomial

[2] This rule is based on the assumption that the population proportion π is known. Because π is not known in the context of statistical estimation, the confidence intervals in this section are approximations of the correct intervals. However, these approximations are generally good for values of π between 0.10 and 0.90.

72 Based on the table of binomial probabilities (Appendix Table B-3), Table 9-3 presents the probabilities associated with the various possible outcomes when 10 students are polled regarding whether or not they smoke, given that $\pi = 0.4$. For example, this table indicates that the probability that eight of the 10 students polled will be smokers is _____ (value).

0.0106

Table 9-3 ■ Probability Distribution for Obtaining Various Numbers of Smokers in a Sample of 10 Respondents if $\pi = 0.4$

Number of smokers	Proportion of sample	Probability
0	0.0	0.0060
1	0.1	0.0403
2	0.2	0.1209
3	0.3	0.2150
4	0.4	0.2508
5	0.5	0.2007
6	0.6	0.1115
7	0.7	0.0425
8	0.8	0.0106
9	0.9	0.0016
10	1.0	0.0001

73 When we used the normal probability distribution as the basis for constructing a confidence interval, the size of the interval on each side of the point estimate was the same because the normal probability distribution is symmetrical. Would the interval estimate for the population proportion discussed above have its point estimate at the center of the interval? [Yes / No]

No (The probability distribution given in Table 9-3 is not symmetrical.)

74 Furthermore, and of even greater importance, if the point estimate of π is changed from 0.4 to some other value, the distribution of probabilities will become either more skewed or less skewed, depending on the direction of the change. This suggests that if π is to be estimated by an interval of values, the sampling distribution of the proportion for each value of π included in the interval is [the same / different].

different

75 This is a problem that was not encountered in estimating the population mean. Specifically, a change in the value of $\bar{X}$ as the estimator of μ does of course change the midpoint of the confidence interval. But such a change [does / does not] affect the size of the confidence interval and the presumed normality of the sampling distribution.

does not (The interval size as such is determined by the values of z and $\sigma_{\bar{X}}$, or $s_{\bar{X}}$, and thus is unaffected by any change in $\bar{X}$.)

76 Because the binomial distribution is different for different values of π, the use of the binomial distribution for purposes of estimation is quite complex and outside the scope of this book. Fortunately, as the sample size is increased, the binomial probability distribution approaches the normal probability distribution in its characteristics. As indicated in Section 7.3, the rule we follow to determine when it is appropriate to use the normal probability distribution as a substitute for the binomial is that n be at least 30 and np and nq each be at least equal to 5.[3] Using this rule, for the example in Frame 72, in which $n = 10$, $p = 0.4$, and $q = 0.6$, is it appropriate to use the normal distribution for the purpose of setting confidence limits? [Yes / No]

No

77 In order to use the normal distribution in estimating a population proportion, the sample size n should be at least equal to _____ (number).

30

78 Further np and nq should each be at least equal to a value of ___ (number).

5

79 For the illustration which we have been using, in which $n = 10$, $p = 0.4$, and $q = 0.6$, if we were to increase n to 65, could we then use the normal probability distribution in conjunction with defining confidence limits for the population proportion? [Yes / No] Why or why not? _____

Yes; because $n > 30$, $np > 5$, and $nq > 5$

80 If we use the general formula for estimation when the normal probability distribution serves as the basis, which always involves the definition of an interval to both sides of a point estimate, what is the specific formula to be used for determining the confidence limits for the population proportion?

$p; z$

Limits $= \_\_ \pm \_\_ s_p$

81 In the formula in Frame 80 the only symbol which we have not yet defined is s_p, which would be read as the _____ of the _____ .

standard error; proportion

[3] In the context of estimation, use of this rule results in approximate confidence intervals. (See footnote on page 230.)

82 In Section 7.3 we indicated that the standard deviation of the number of "successes" associated with a binomial distribution is:

$$\sigma_b = \sqrt{npq}$$

Note that this is the standard deviation of the *number* of successes rather than the standard deviation (standard error) of the *proportion* of successes needed for our confidence interval in Frame 80. Algebraically, the standard error of the proportion can be determined by dividing the standard deviation of the number of successes by the sample size, *n*. Thus:

$\sqrt{\dfrac{pq}{n}}$

$$\sigma_p = \frac{\sqrt{npq}}{n} = \sqrt{\frac{npq}{n^2}} = \sqrt{\phantom{\frac{npq}{n^2}}}$$

83 Since $q = (1 - p)$, the formula in the preceding frame is usually modified so that it is stated in terms of n and p only. However, note that in the context of Chapter 7, p was the known (population) probability in respect to the binomial distribution. In the context of statistical inference concerning a population proportion, the appropriate symbol for this value is π rather than p. Therefore, substituting π for p and $(1 - \pi)$ for q in the formula in the preceding frame, we have:

$\sqrt{\dfrac{\pi(1 - \pi)}{n}}$

$$\sigma_p = \sqrt{\frac{pq}{n}} = \sqrt{\phantom{\frac{pq}{n}}}$$

84 Of course, in statistical estimation concerning a proportion we do not know the value of π, because that is the population parameter being estimated. However, we do have available the point estimate p based on the probability sample. Even though p is an unbiased estimate of π, it can be shown that the standard error of the proportion based on sample data is a biased estimate and needs to include a correction. Accordingly, the formula we use for the standard error of the proportion based on *sample* data is:

$$s_p = \sqrt{\frac{p(1 - p)}{n - 1}}$$

Again, as for the standard error of the mean, when the population is finite and the sample size is more than 5 percent of the population size, then the finite correction factor needs to be included in the formula, resulting in:

$$s_p = \sqrt{\frac{p(1-p)}{n-1}} \sqrt{\frac{N-n}{N-1}}$$

Overall, then, the symbol and formula for the standard error of the proportion when π is known and the population is infinite are:

$$\sigma_p = \sqrt{\frac{\pi(1-\pi)}{n}}$$

The symbol and formula for the standard error of the proportion when π is not known and the population is infinite are:

$$s_p = \sqrt{\frac{p(1-p)}{n-1}}$$

85 Given that $p = 0.4$ and $n = 65$, compute the standard error of the proportion, using the appropriate formula taken from Frame 84 and assuming a very large population.

$$\sqrt{\frac{p(1-p)}{n-1}} = \sqrt{\frac{0.40(0.60)}{64}} =$$
$$\sqrt{\frac{0.24}{64}} = \frac{0.4899}{8} = 0.0612$$

$$s_p =$$

86 Now, referring to Table 9-2 for the appropriate z value if necessary, determine the 95 percent confidence limits for the population proportion, given that $p = 0.40$, $n = 65$, and $s_p = 0.0612$. Identify the limits to two decimal places.

$$p \pm zs_p = 0.40 \pm 1.96(0.0612)$$
$$= 0.40 \pm 0.12 = 0.28 \text{ to } 0.52$$

Interval Est. =

87 Thus, on the basis of the randomly selected sample of 65 university students, we would conclude that a proportion between _____ and _____ of the overall student group sampled are regular smokers, with a ____ percent degree of confidence that our estimate is correct.

0.28; 0.52

95

88 Any problem that requires estimation of a percentage can be handled as a problem requiring the estimation of a proportion for the purpose of setting confidence limits, and so we shall not bother to introduce any formulas for the standard error of a percentage as such. Thus, if a sample of 100 people taken from a group of 10,000 yields 65 percent who are in favor of a particular federal program, we can estimate the proportion of the population sampled who are in favor of the program and then convert the confidence limits to percentages. The first step in any event, then, is to compute the standard error of the proportion. For the data in this frame

$$\sqrt{\frac{p(1-p)}{n-1}} = \sqrt{\frac{0.65(0.35)}{99}} =$$
$$\sqrt{\frac{0.2275}{99}} = \sqrt{.002298} = 0.048$$

$s_p =$

89 Now estimate the percentage of people in the group of 10,000 who are in favor of the federal program, using 95 percent confidence limits.

$$0.65 \pm 1.96(0.048) = 0.65 \pm 0.094 = 0.556 \text{ and } 0.744$$

Limits (as proportions) =

$$55.6\% \text{ and } 74.4\%$$

Percentage limits =

90 If the limits just computed are considered too wide for the purpose of application, they can be made more precise ("tightened") for the available sample data by _____ _____.

using a lower degree of confidence in the estimation, such as 90 percent limits

91 On the other hand, if we wish to have a more precise confidence interval but are not willing to lower the degree of confidence in the accuracy of the estimate, the narrower interval can be obtained by reducing the value of the standard error, which, in turn can be achieved by [reducing / increasing] the sample size.

increasing

92 Just as the estimation of a total quantity is simply an extension of estimating the mean of a population, the estimation of the total number included in a category is an extension of estimating the population proportion. In Frame 89 we concluded that of 10,000 people a proportion between 0.556 and 0.744 are in favor of a federal program. Based on this information, the confidence limits for estimating the number of people in the group of 10,000 who are in favor of the program, at the 95 percent degree of confidence, would be _____ (number) and _____ (number).

5,560; 7,440

93 Thus, if we have established confidence limits as proportions, then we can readily establish confidence limits for the number of people (or elements) in the category being described by multiplying the proportions by _____ (symbol).

N

94 Given that the confidence interval for the population proportion is $p \pm zs_p$, the formula for estimating the total number in a category can be written as

Number = _____ ± _____

$Np \pm Nzs_p$ [or $N(p \pm zs_p)$]

95 Finally, just as we were interested in estimating the difference between the means of two populations, we might be interested in estimating the difference between the proportions of two populations. The relevant point estimate in this case is $p_1 - p_2$ and the standard error to be used is $s_{p_1 - p_2}$. Therefore the formula to be used for the confidence interval for estimating the difference between the proportions of two populations, based on the normal probability distribution, is

$\text{Diff}_{\text{prop}} = \underline{\hspace{2cm}} \pm \underline{\hspace{2cm}}$

$(p_1 - p_2) \pm zs_{p_1 - p_2}$

96 The formula for computing the standard error of the difference between proportions is constructed on the same basis as the formula for the standard error of the difference between means. Thus, where

$$s_{\overline{X}_1 - \overline{X}_2} = \sqrt{s_{\overline{X}_1}^2 + s_{\overline{X}_2}^2}$$

$$s_{p_1 - p_2} =$$

$\sqrt{s_{p_1}^2 + s_{p_2}^2}$

97 Given that a proportion of 0.45 of a random sample of people from one part of the country express approval of a particular federal program with a standard error of 0.04, and that in another part of the country a proportion of 0.55 are in favor with a standard error of 0.03, estimate the difference in the proportions of people in the two sections of the country who are in favor of the program, using 95 percent confidence limits.

$\text{Limits} = (p_1 - p_2) \pm zs_{p_1 - p_2}$

$=$

(0.55 − 0.45) ±
1.96 $\sqrt{(0.03)^2 + (0.04)^2}$
= 0.10 ± 1.96($\sqrt{0.0025}$)
= 0.10 ± 1.96(0.05)
= 0.10 ± 0.098
= 0.002 to 0.198

Review

point

interval

98 (Introduction to Chapter 9) The statistical process of estimation whereby a single, or particular, value is used to estimate a parameter is referred to as _____ estimation; the process by which the parameter is identified as being within a defined range of values at a designated degree of confidence is called _____ estimation.

$\overline{X}; \mu$
$\hat{\mu}$

99 (Frame 1) In terms of the symbols used, a sample mean is represented by ___, a population mean is represented by ___, and an estimated population mean is represented by ___.

$E(\overline{X}) = \mu$
$\overline{X} \to \mu$ as $n \to N$

100 (Frames 2-7) We have discussed four criteria used by statisticians to define the characteristics of a good estimator. Using a sample mean as an estimator of the population mean, the criterion of unbiasedness can be represented symbolically by _____, and the criterion of consistency can be represented by _____.

standard error
all available data

101 (Frames 8-16) The criterion of efficiency indicates that the value of the _____ is at a minimum; the criterion of sufficiency indicates that _____ _____ are being used in making the estimate.

small (division by "*n*" instead of "*n* − 1" would result in a smaller value)

102 (Frames 17-21) The formula for the sample standard deviation is $s = \sqrt{\Sigma(X - \overline{X})^2/n - 1}$, whereas the formula for the population standard deviation is $\sigma = \sqrt{\Sigma(X - \mu)^2/N}$. The formula for the sample standard deviation includes a correction for biasedness, and without it the sample standard deviation would tend to be too [large / small] as an estimator of the population standard deviation.

103 (Frames 22-26) In addition to estimating the mean and proportion of a population, we can also make use of sample data to estimate the total quantity in a population and the total number in a category of the population. For example, if the results associated with a random sample of 3,000 households taken from a population of 150,000 households indicate that mean gross income per household is $14,000 and that 20 percent of the households plan to purchase a new automobile during the coming year, then we would estimate

2,100,000,000
30,000

the total gross income for all 150,000 households as being
$_____ and we would estimate that the
purchase of _____ (number) automobiles is planned.

104 (Frames 27-31) For a normally distributed set of
measurements, 68 percent of the measurements are included in
the interval represented by $\mu \pm 1.0\sigma$. Similarly, 90 percent of

1.65
1.96
2.58

the measurements are included in the interval $\mu \pm$ _____σ, 95
percent are included in the interval $\mu \pm$ _____σ, and 99
percent are included in the interval $\mu \pm$ _____σ.

105 (Frames 32-37) The distinction between a standard
deviation and a standard error is that a standard deviation is a
measurement of the variability of individual measurements in
respect to a group mean, and the standard error of the mean,
as a case in point, is a measurement of the variability of

sample means
population mean

individual _____ in respect to the
_____ .

106 (Frames 38-41) Based on use of the normal probability
distribution, the general estimation formula used to define
the 95 percent confidence limits for the population mean

$\overline{X} \pm 1.96 s_{\overline{X}}$

when σ is not known is _____ .

107 (Frames 42-51) In the long run, if 90 percent confidence
intervals are used to estimate a series of different population
values, then 10 percent of these intervals will not include the
parameter being estimated. Using 95 percent confidence limits
instead of 90 percent confidence limits results in intervals

wider

which are [narrower / wider] .

108 (Frames 35-56) Use of the normal probability distribution in determining confidence limits for the mean is always
appropriate whenever $n \geqslant 30$, regardless of the distribution

central-limit

of the population values, based on the _____
theorem.

109 (Frames 52-55) The general formula used to define the
confidence limits for estimating the total quantity in a

$N\overline{X} \pm Nzs_{\overline{X}}$ [or $N(\overline{X} \pm zs_{\overline{X}})$]

population when σ is not known is_____ .

110 (Frames 57-69) When based on sample data only being known, the standard error of the difference between two means is represented by the symbol _____. Accordingly, the associated formula for determining the confidence limits for estimating the difference between the means of two populations is _____ .

$$s_{\overline{X}_1 - \overline{X}_2}$$

$$(\overline{X}_1 - \overline{X}_2) \pm z s_{\overline{X}_1 - \overline{X}_2}$$

111 (Frames 70-79) Because of the mathematical complexity connected with using the binomial distribution to construct confidence intervals for the population proportion, the normal distribution is often used as a substitute for the binomial. We consider this substitution appropriate whenever the sample size n is at least ____ (number) and np and nq are each at least equal to a value of ___ (number).

30

5

112 (Frames 79-80) When the normal probability distribution is used as a substitute for the binomial distribution, the formula used to determine the confidence limits in estimating a population proportion is _____ .

$$p \pm z s_p$$

113 (Frames 81-91) For each of the following formulas used for computing the standard error of the proportion, indicate the nature of the situation in which it would be used in terms of (a) whether π is known; and (b) whether the population is infinite or finite.

is not

infinite (or $n \leqslant 5\% \; N$)

$$s_p = \sqrt{\frac{p(1-p)}{n-1}}$$

(a) π [is / is not] known
(b) [infinite / finite] population

is not

finite

$$s_p = \sqrt{\frac{p(1-p)}{n-1}} \sqrt{\frac{N-n}{N-1}}$$

(a) π [is / is not] known
(b) [infinite / finite] population

is

infinite (or $n \leqslant 5\% \; N$)

$$\sigma_p = \sqrt{\frac{\pi(1-\pi)}{n}}$$

(a) π [is / is not] known
(b) [infinite / finite] population

is

finite

$$\sigma_p = \sqrt{\frac{\pi(1-\pi)}{n}} \sqrt{\frac{N-n}{N-1}}$$

(a) [is / is not] known
(b) [infinite / finite] population

114 (Frames 92-97) The formula used to determine the confidence interval for the total number in a category of the population, which is a variation of the formula for estimating the population proportion, is _____.

$$\boxed{Np \pm Nzs_p \; [\text{or } N(p \pm zs_p)]}$$

The formula used to determine the confidence interval for the difference between the proportions included in two different populations is _____.

$$\boxed{(p_1 - p_2) \pm zs_{p_1 - p_2}}$$

Symbols Introduced in This Chapter (with Frame Numbers)

(21)	$N\mu$	Total quantity in a population.
(21)	$N\bar{X}$	Point estimate of the total quantity in a population.
(21)	$\mu - \mu_2$	Difference between the means of two populations.
(21)	$\bar{X}_1 - \bar{X}_2$	Point estimate of the difference between the means of two populations.
(21)	π	The lowercase Greek letter pi, which designates the population proportion.
(21)	$N\pi$	Total number included in a category of the population.
(21)	Np	Point estimate of the total number in a category of the population.
(21)	$\pi_1 - \pi_2$	Difference between the proportions in two populations.
(21)	$p_1 - p_2$	Point estimate of the difference between the proportions in two populations.
(63)	$\sigma_{\bar{X}_1 - \bar{X}_2}$ or $s_{\bar{X}_1 - \bar{X}_2}$	Standard error of the difference between two means.
(84)	σ_p or s_p	Standard error of the proportion.
(96)	$s_{p_1 - p_2}$	Standard error of the difference between the proportions in two populations, based on sample data.

Formulas Introduced in This Chapter (with Frame Numbers)

(39) $\overline{X} \pm 1.96\sigma_{\overline{X}}$

The 95 percent confidence interval for estimating the population mean with the use of the normal probability distribution. In this formula, $s_{\overline{X}}$ would be used in place of $\sigma_{\overline{X}}$ when the population standard deviation is not known.

(43) $\overline{X} \pm 1.65\sigma_{\overline{X}}$

The 90 percent confidence interval for estimating the population mean.

(43) $\overline{X} \pm 2.58\sigma_{\overline{X}}$

The 99 percent confidence interval for estimating the population mean.

(53) $N\overline{X} \pm Nz\sigma_{\overline{X}}$

or $N(\overline{X} \pm z\sigma_{\overline{X}})$

Confidence interval for estimating the total quantity in a population.

(59)   Point estimate $\pm z\sigma_{stat}$ (or $\pm zs_{stat}$)

The general formula for defining the confidence interval used in estimating any population parameter by use of the normal probability distribution.

(64) $\sigma_{\overline{X}_1 - \overline{X}_2} = \sqrt{\sigma^2_{\overline{X}_1} + \sigma^2_{\overline{X}_2}}$

or $s_{\overline{X}_1 - \overline{X}_2} = \sqrt{s^2_{\overline{X}_1} + s^2_{\overline{X}_2}}$

Standard error of the difference between two means.

(68) $(\overline{X}_1 - \overline{X}_2) \pm z\sigma_{\overline{X}_1 - \overline{X}_2}$

(or $\pm zs_{\overline{X}_1 - \overline{X}_2}$)

Confidence interval for estimating the difference between the means of two populations.

(80) $p \pm zs_p$

Confidence interval for estimating a population proportion.

(83) $\sigma_p = \sqrt{\dfrac{\pi(1 - \pi)}{n}}$

Standard error of the proportion when the population proportion is known and the population is infinite in size (or $n \leqslant 5\% \, N$).

(84) $\sigma_p = \sqrt{\dfrac{\pi(1 - \pi)}{n}} \sqrt{\dfrac{N - n}{N - 1}}$

Standard error of the proportion when the population proportion is known and the population is finite in size.

$$(84) \quad s_p = \sqrt{\frac{p(1-p)}{n-1}}$$

Standard error of the proportion when the population proportion is not known and the population is infinite in size (or $n \leqslant 5\% \, N$).

$$(84) \quad s_p = \sqrt{\frac{p(1-p)}{n-1}} \sqrt{\frac{N-n}{N-1}}$$

Standard error of the proportion when the population proportion is not known and the population is finite in size.

$$(94) \quad Np \pm Nzs_p$$
$$\text{or } N(p \pm zs_p)$$

Confidence interval for estimating the total number in a designated category of a population.

$$(95) \quad (p_1 - p_2) \pm zs_{p_1 - p_2}$$

Confidence interval for estimating the difference between proportions in two populations.

$$(96) \quad s_{p_1 - p_2} = \sqrt{s_{p_1}^2 + s_{p_2}^2}$$

Standard error of the difference between the proportions in two populations, based on sample data.

EXERCISES

(Solutions on pages 603–605)

9.1 Compare the criteria of *unbiasedness* and *consistency* as factors affecting the selection of a point estimator. In addition to defining these criteria symbolically, describe them in your own words and indicate how it is possible that an estimator satisfies one of these criteria but not the other.

9.2 A marketing research analyst collects data for a random sample of 100 customers out of the 500 who purchased a particular "coupon special." The 100 people in the sample spent an average (mean) of $27.00 in the store with a standard deviation of $8.00, and 70 percent of the customers in the sample made at least one other purchase in addition to the coupon special. Based on these results identify the best single estimate for each of the following parameter values.

(a) Mean purchase amount by all 500 customers who purchased the coupon special.

(b) The standard deviation of the distribution of purchase amounts by the 500 customers.

(c) Total amount of purchases by the 500 customers.

(d) The number of customers out of the 500 who made at least one other purchase in addition to the coupon special.

9.3 In a department store an auditor finds that 49 randomly chosen charge accounts out of a total of 3,000 such accounts have a mean debit balance of $53.00 with a standard deviation of $14.00.

(a) Estimate the mean account balance of all charge accounts, using 90 percent confidence limits.
(b) Estimate the mean balance of all accounts, using 95 percent confidence limits.
(c) Estimate the mean balance of all accounts, using 99 percent confidence limits.
(d) Which one of the three estimates do you consider to be most useful? Why?

9.4 For the data of Exercise 9.3, above, estimate the total balance due for all 3,000 charge accounts:

(a) using 90 percent confidence limits
(b) using 95 percent confidence limits
(c) using 99 percent confidence limits

9.5 For two retail outlets an auditor finds that the mean charge account balance for a random sample of 50 accounts taken at one store is $45 with an associated standard error of the mean of $2, and that at the other store the mean account balance for 50 accounts is $54 with a standard error of the mean of $3. Estimate the difference between the mean account balances at the two stores, using 95 percent confidence limits.

9.6 For the data in Exercise 9.2, determine the 95 percent confidence intervals for estimating the mean purchase amount for all 500 customers and the total purchase amount for all 500 customers.

9.7 In a sample of 100 graduate business students randomly selected at several major universities offering M.B.A. programs, 60 earned their undergraduate degree in one of the social sciences. Estimate the percentage of all graduate business students in the universities surveyed who earned their undergraduate degrees in the social sciences, carrying your computation to the nearest percentage:

(a) using 90 percent confidence limits
(b) using 95 percent confidence limits
(c) using 99 percent confidence limits

9.8 For the data of Exercise 9.7, if a total of 3,000 students are enrolled in the graduate programs studied, estimate the total number who have undergraduate degrees in the social sciences, using 95 percent confidence limits.

9.9 In attempting to assess voter sentiment regarding a state bonding proposal, a legislator has a random sample of 50 people polled in each of two districts containing a large number of voters. In the first district 30 of the 50 people interviewed expressed their approval of the proposal, and in the second district 25 of the 50 people interviewed expressed approval. Estimate the difference between the percentage of people in the two districts supporting the bonding proposal, using 95 percent confidence limits.

9.10 A superintendent of schools in a small community is concerned about the proportion of voters who are likely to vote in favor of a school bonding proposal to be included in the next general election. In order to obtain a sampling of voter attitude he arranges to poll a systematic sample of 1 percent of the 6,500 registered voters in the community. Each "yes" answer in the list below indicates that the person polled is in favor of the bonding proposal, and each "no" indicates that the person is not in favor of the proposal. Determine the confidence intervals that can be used to estimate (a) the proportion of voters in favor of the proposal and (b) the total number of voters in favor of the proposal, using 95 percent confidence limits.

yes	yes	no	yes	no	yes	no
yes	yes	no	yes	yes	yes	yes
no	no	yes	no	yes	yes	yes
yes	yes	yes	no	yes	no	yes
no	yes	yes	yes	no	no	no
no	yes	no	yes	no	yes	
yes	yes	yes	yes	yes	yes	
yes	no	no	no	no	no	
no	yes	no	no	yes	no	
yes	yes	yes	yes	no	no	

ADDITIONAL EXERCISES

9.11 Discuss the criterion of *efficiency* as it applies to the selection of a point estimator. In turn, how does use of this criterion affect the interval estimate for a population parameter?

9.12 Discuss the implications of the central-limit theorem, which was first described in Chapter 8, for the process of statistical estimation.

9.13 A random sample of 50 firms taken from an industry with 1,200 firms has an average (mean) number of employees of 77.5 with a standard deviation of 20 employees.

(a) Estimate the average number of employees per firm in the entire industry, using 90 percent confidence limits.
(b) Estimate the average number of employees per firm in the entire industry, using 95 percent confidence limits.
(c) Estimate the average number of employees per firm in the entire industry, using 99 percent confidence limits.

9.14 Using the data of Exercise 9.13, estimate the total number of employees working in this industry, using 95 percent confidence limits.

9.15 Of the 50 firms described in Exercise 9.13, suppose that the employees of 20 of the firms belong to a national labor union.

(a) Estimate the percentage of all 1,200 firms whose employees belong to a national labor union, using a 90 percent confidence interval.
(b) Estimate the total number of firms whose employees belong to a national labor union, using a 90 percent confidence interval.

9.16 Referring to Exercise 9.15, in another industry made up of 1,000 firms, 30 of a sample of 50 firms are unionized. Estimate the difference between the proportion of firms whose employees are represented by a labor union in this industry and the proportion in the industry described in Exercise 9.15, using 90 percent confidence limits.

9.17 For Exercise 9.13, suppose the industry includes just 100 firms rather than 1,200 firms.

(a) Estimate the average number of employees per firm in the entire industry, using 95 percent confidence limits.
(b) Estimate the total number of employees working in this industry, using 95 percent confidence limits.

9.18 The mean diameter of a sample of $n = 100$ rods included in a shipment is 2.350 millimeters with a standard deviation of 0.050 millimeter. Estimate the mean diameter of all rods included in the shipment if the shipment contains 500 rods, using a 99 percent confidence interval.

9.19 For the shipment of rods described in Exercise 9.18, the mean weight per rod for the sample of 100 rods is 8.45 grams with a standard deviation of 0.25 gram. Estimate the total weight of the entire shipment (exclusive of packing materials), using a 99 percent confidence interval.

9.20 For a random sample of 100 households in a large metropolitan area, the number of households in which at least one adult is currently unemployed and seeking a full-time job is 12. Estimate the percentage of households in the area in which at least one adult is unemployed, using a 95 percent confidence interval.

9.21 As purchasing agent for a large company you arrange to obtain a random sample of 49 General Electric 100-watt fluorescent bulbs and to have these installed in certain work areas that include unusual (excessive) temperature conditions. Later followup indicates that the arithmetic mean of bulb life was 650 hours with a standard deviation of 50 hours.

(a) What is the best *point* estimate of mean bulb life of all General Electric 100-watt fluorescent bulbs when subjected to the excessive temperature conditions?
(b) What is the standard error of the sampling distribution of the mean? Describe what this value signifies.
(c) Determine the lower and upper limits for the 80 percent confidence interval for estimating the value of the true mean.

9.22 In reference to Exercise 9.21, for another brand of fluorescent bulbs subjected to the same extreme temperature conditions, the mean bulb life for a probability sample of 49 bulbs is 660 hours with a standard deviation of 100 hours.

(a) Determine the lower and upper limits for the 80 percent confidence interval for estimating the value of the true mean. Compare your answer with that of Exercise 9.21(c), and indicate which bulbs you would purchase, given that the prices are identical.

(b) Determine the 90 percent confidence interval for estimating the difference between the true mean life of the General Electric bulbs and that of the bulbs in this exercise.

9.23 An alumni association contacts a sample of 300 members of the class of 1970 and obtains information regarding their current income status. There were 1,000 graduates in 1970. The average annual income for the sample of 300 is $20,000 with a standard deviation of $3,500.

(a) What kind of information would you need to have about the sample and the way the information was obtained before you would proceed to use statistical estimation in conjunction with these sample data?
(b) Assuming that the requirements associated with statistical inference are satisfied, determine the 95 percent confidence interval for estimating the true mean annual income for members of the class of 1970.

9.24 For a sample of 50 firms taken from a particular industry, the mean number of employees per firm is $\bar{X}_1 = 420.4$ with $s_1 = 55.7$. There is a total of 380 firms in this industry. In a second industry, which includes 200 firms, the mean number of employees in a sample of 50 firms is $\bar{X}_2 = 392.5$ employees with $s_2 = 87.9$. Estimate the difference in the mean number of employees per firm in the two industries, using a 95 percent confidence interval.

9.25 Construct the 99 percent confidence interval for the difference between the means in Exercise 9.24.

9.26 For a sample of 30 employees in one large firm, the mean hourly wage is $\bar{X}_1 = \$7.50$ with $s_1 = \$1.00$. In a second large firm, the mean hourly wage for a sample of 40 employees is $\bar{X}_2 = \$7.05$ with $s_2 = \$1.20$. Estimate the difference between the mean hourly wage at the two firms, using a 90 percent confidence interval.

CHAPTER 10 ■
HYPOTHESIS TESTING

Both Chapter 9 and this one are concerned with statistical decision making. In Chapter 9 we described the use of the normal probability distribution in estimating population values. In the present chapter we illustrate the use of the normal and binomial probability distributions for the purpose of testing hypotheses concerning the assumed values of population parameters. Thus the new material in this chapter concerns the methodology of hypothesis testing, with use of probability distributions and standard-error formulas which are already familiar to you. Overall, in this chapter we describe the procedures concerned with testing hypotheses about the population mean, the difference between the means of two populations, the population proportion, and the difference between the proportions in two populations.

10.1 ■ Hypothesis Testing and the Null Hypothesis

The assumed value of a population parameter is tested by comparing it with the value of a point estimator based on a probability, or random, sample from the population in question. Thus, when the value of a sample mean is "very close" to the assumed value of the population mean, we would tend to accept the assumed value as being correct. On the other hand, when a sample mean is "too different" from the assumed value of the population mean, we would tend to reject the assumed population value.

1 The processes of both estimation and hypothesis testing represent methods of decision making under conditions of uncertainty, and both exemplify the use of statistics for the purpose of [description / inference].

inference

2 In the application of these two basic varieties of statistical inference, a tentative assumption regarding the value of a parameter *prior to the collection of sample data* is made in [estimation / hypothesis testing], but no such tentative assumption is made in [estimation / hypothesis testing].

hypothesis testing

estimation

3 In hypothesis testing we begin with an assumed (hypothesized) value for a population parameter, such as the population mean, collect sample data, and then determine the probability that the assumed population value is in fact correct, on the basis of the sample data. Thus, as the difference between the hypothesized value of the population mean and the observed value of the sample mean gets larger, we would be [more / less] inclined to believe that the hypothesized value is in fact the correct value.

less

4 In any hypothesis-testing situation it is useful to recognize that the accuracy of the assumed value of the population parameter, i.e., the validity of the hypothesis, cannot be tested directly. Rather, what is tested is the size of the difference between the hypothesized value of a population parameter and the observed value of a _____ .

sample statistic

5 The ideal evidence in support of a hypothesis would be the observation that the *difference* between the assumed population value and the observed sample value is equal to ____ (number).

0

6 Therefore, because the population hypothesis cannot be tested directly, the hypothesis of "no difference" is tested instead. This hypothesis is referred to as the *null hypothesis*, and it states that there is no difference between the hypothesized parameter and the actual parameter. In terms of our discussion, it is clear that the null hypothesis is involved [in every application of the methods of statistical inference / in every hypothesis-testing situation / in some, although not necessarily all, hypothesis-testing situations] .

in every hypothesis-testing situation

7 Given a manufacturing process in which the quality standard requires that the mean diameter of bearings being polished must be 0.575 inch, a sample of bearings has a mean diameter of 0.565 inch. Testing the null hypothesis in this case concerns analysis of the difference between the hypothesized population value _____ and the sample value _____ .

0.575

0.565

8 In this hypothesis-testing problem, then, the question asked is: "Is the difference between the hypothesized parameter value and the sample value (0.010) significantly different from the expected difference of ____ (value)?"

0

9 The significance of a difference between an assumed population value and an observed sample value is not based on the size of the difference alone, but on the size of the difference relative to the value of the standard error for the statistic concerned. Thus the difference of 0.010 inch referred to in Frame 8 would be evaluated relative to the value of the standard error of the _____ .

mean

10 Since we begin with the assumption that the hypothesized population value (population mean, in this case) is correct, we would expect the values of a large number of sample means to cluster symmetrically about the population value. Accordingly, on the diagram below, representing the sampling distribution of means for the problem in which the production standard requires a mean bearing diameter of 0.575 inch and the sample mean is 0.565 inch, enter the appropriate values in the two blank spaces.

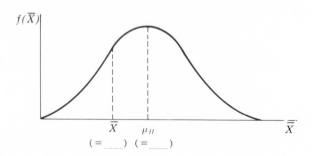

$f(\overline{X})$

$\overline{X}$ μ_{H} $\overline{\overline{X}}$
$(=\underline{\quad})$ $(=\underline{\quad})$

0.565; 0.575 (Order *is* important.)

---

11 Suppose that in Frame 10 the standard error of the mean $\sigma_{\overline{X}}$ is equal to 0.010. What is the probability that a sample mean will have a value between 0.565 and 0.585, assuming that the hypothesized population mean is correct? $P = $ _____. Accordingly, what is the probability that a sample mean will differ from the hypothesized mean by 0.010 or more, in *either* direction? $P = $ _____.

0.68
(within one standard deviation of the mean)

0.32

---

12 For another sample from the same manufacturing process, suppose that the difference between the hypothesized population mean and the sample mean is 0.020. What is the probability that a difference this large *or larger* would occur by chance? Refer to Table B-1 for needed figures.

Probability of being within these limits, in either direction, $= 2(0.4772) = 0.9544$. Probability of being outside of these limits $= 1 - 0.9544 = 0.0456$.

---

13 In the process of hypothesis testing we do not question the accuracy of the observed value of the sample statistic. Rather, we question the validity of our hypothesis regarding the value of the population parameter. Which of the two differences discussed in Frames 11 and 12, 0.010 or 0.020, would more appropriately lead to a rejection of the null hypothesis? [0.010 / 0.020]

0.020

---

14 Although the term "null hypothesis" originally was formulated to specify that there is no difference between the hypothesized parameter value and the actual parameter value, for practical purposes most books in applied statistics simply refer to the hypothesized value as the null hypothesis.

The effect is the same, because accepting the hypothesis that there is no difference between a hypothesized population mean and the actual population mean, for example, is equivalent to accepting the value of the hypothesized mean. Similarly, rejection of the null hypothesis in the case of a hypothesized population mean is equivalent to saying that the hypothesized value of the population mean is [accepted / rejected].

rejected

10.2 ■ The Level of Significance and Type I and Type II Errors

Having indicated the general basis used for accepting or rejecting a null hypothesis, our next task is to describe the specific basis for this acceptance or rejection. In relation to this decision, we run the risk of making one of two types of errors: that of rejecting a hypothesis that is in fact correct or that of accepting a hypothesis that is in fact incorrect.

15 Although there is no universal standard for accepting or rejecting a null hypothesis, one specific basis that is often used is referred to as the *5 percent level of significance.* On this basis, when the difference between the observed sample statistic and the assumed population parameter is so large that a difference of that size or larger would occur by chance with a probability of 0.05 or less when the assumed value is in fact correct, then the observed difference is considered to be significant and the null hypothesis is [accepted / rejected].

rejected

16 If the 5 percent level of significance is used as the basis for testing the hypothesis, would the null hypothesis be rejected for the data of Frame 11? [Yes / No] For the data of Frame 12? [Yes / No]

No
Yes

17 In published research in technical journals the 1 percent level of significance also is often used in hypothesis testing. Where differences which are significant at the 5 percent level often are described as being "significant," differences which are significant at the 1 percent level are described as being "very significant." Which of these two significance levels, the 5 percent or the 1 percent, would lead to more frequent rejection of correct null hypotheses when a number of hypotheses are being investigated and tested? [5 percent / 1 percent]

5 percent (since the difference required is not so large as that for the 1 percent level)

18 Figures 10-1a and 10-1b illustrate this point diagrammatically, with hypothesis testing concerning the mean as a case in point. The proportion of sample means included within the critical limits for the test at the 5 percent level is 0.95, as indicated in Figure 10-1a, and for the test at the 1 percent level the proportion within the critical limits is 0.99, as illustrated in Figure 10-1b. These diagrams are based on the assumption that the null hypothesis is in fact true. That is, that $\mu = \mu_H$ for the population. Of the two sets of limits defined in these figures, rejection of a correct null hypothesis will occur more frequently when the critical limits are set at $\mu \pm [1.96 / 2.58] \sigma_{\bar{X}}$.

1.96

Figure 10-1a ■ **Critical limits for testing a hypothesized mean at the 5 percent level of significance**

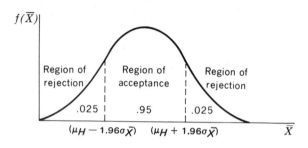

Figure 10-1b ■ **Critical limits for testing a hypothesized mean at the 1 percent level of significance**

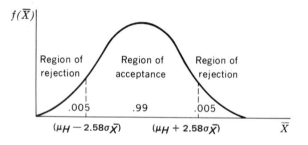

19 With reference to either Figure 10-1a or 10-1b, all of the possible values of the sample mean that are outside of the critical limits are in the region of _____ of the null hypothesis, whereas all of the values within the defined limits are in the region of _____ .

rejection

acceptance

20 In this chapter we have introduced the concept of "level of significance" to identify the probability level associated with a hypothesis-testing procedure. If a hypothesis is tested by use of the 5 percent level of significance (or, at the 0.05 level of significance), then by definition we have indicated that we shall reject the null hypothesis if the difference between the sample statistic and the assumed parameter is so large that a difference of that amount or greater would occur, on the

five	average, in _____ (number) samples out of 100 randomly chosen samples when the assumed population value is in fact correct.

21 In Chapter 9, on statistical estimation, we used the concept of the "degree of confidence." An interval estimate defined with a 95 percent degree of confidence is such that if this basis is used consistently in defining limits for population parameters, then in the long run the defined intervals will actually include the population parameters being estimated

95	_____ percent of the time and will fail to include the
5	parameters being estimated ___ percent of the time.

22 Thus the use of the concept of *degree of confidence* is always related to the application of the methods of statistical

estimation	inference for the purpose of _____ , whereas a *level of significance* is used in conjunction with the process of
hypothesis testing	_____ .

23 When the normal probability distribution is used in conjunction with *estimating* the value of a population mean, the

$\bar{X}$	value at the center of the confidence interval is $[\bar{X} / \mu_H]$. When the normal probability distribution is used in conjunction with hypothesis testing, the value at the center of
μ_H	the distribution is $[\bar{X} / \mu_H]$.

24 In the process of estimation, the confidence interval is

within	defined as being made up of those values [within / outside of] the limits $\bar{X} + z\sigma_{\bar{X}}$.

25 In hypothesis testing, the possible values of the sample mean that would lead to a rejection of the null hypothesis are

outside	those that are [within / outside] the limits $\mu_H \pm z\sigma_{\bar{X}}$.

26 When the null hypothesis is tested at the 5 percent level of significance, 5 percent of the possible values of the sample statistic are in the region of rejection when the hypothesis is in fact correct. Therefore when the 5 percent level is used in hypothesis testing, the probability of incorrectly rejecting the

0.05	null hypothesis is _____ (value).

27 Type I error is the error of incorrectly rejecting a true null hypothesis. Thus the probability of a "type I" error, or of rejecting a hypothesis that is in fact correct, is equal to the

Section 10.2 The Level of Significance and Type I and Type II Errors ■ 253

level of _____ being used in conjunction with the hypothesis-testing procedure.

28 If we decided to test a hypothesis at the 1 percent level instead of the 5 percent level, the probability of a type I error would thereby be [increased / decreased].

29 However, if the probability of a type I error is reduced by reducing the level of significance (and thus making it a more stringent test, in the sense that a larger difference is then needed to reject the null hypothesis), the type of error whose probability is then increased is that of accepting a null hypothesis that is in fact _____ .

30 Accepting a null hypothesis that is in fact false is referred to as a "type II" error. Thus, as indicated in Table 10-1, if we accept the null hypothesis, we run the risk of a type ____ error, whereas if we reject the null hypothesis, we run the risk of a type ___ error.

Table 10-1 ▪ Types of Errors and Correct Decisions in Hypothesis Testing

	Null hypothesis true	Null hypothesis false
Accept null hypothesis	Correctly accepted	Type II error
Reject null hypothesis	Type I error	Correctly rejected

31 A type I error in hypothesis testing is the one in which we incorrectly [accept / reject] a null hypothesis that is actually [true / false].

32 A type II error is the one in which we incorrectly [accept / reject] a null hypothesis that is actually [true / false].

33 The level of significance used in testing a hypothesis directly indicates the extent of risk regarding a type ___ error.

34 Determining the probability of a type II error depends on the alternative value of the parameter (since in this case the null hypothesis is in fact false). We consider the computations required to determine the probability of type II error in Section 10.4. For now, however, we can say that with sample size remaining the same, when the probability of a type I error is reduced by changing the level of significance being used, then the probability of a type II error is [increased / also reduced].

10.3 ■ Hypotheses Concerning the Population Mean

In this section we present two ways of expressing the critical limits that are used in testing a hypothesis concerning the population mean. Although the second method, in which critical limits are identified in terms of z values, is the commonly used procedure, our discussion of the first method is presented to enhance your understanding of the relationship between estimation and hypothesis testing. In hypothesis testing we may be interested in whether the actual value of the population mean is different, in either direction, from the hypothesized value of the population mean, or we may be interested only in whether the population mean is larger (or is smaller) than the hypothesized value. In the former case, when no direction is specified, the test is referred to as a *two-tailed test*, whereas the test that is specifically directed toward testing differences in one direction only is called a *one-tailed test.*

35 Throughout this section we assume that the standard error of the mean has been computed on the basis of sample data. Therefore, of those given, indicate the appropriate formula(s) which would be used to compute this standard error.

(a) $\dfrac{\sigma}{\sqrt{n}}$

(c) $\dfrac{\sigma}{\sqrt{n}} \sqrt{\dfrac{N-n}{N-1}}$

(b) $\dfrac{s}{\sqrt{n}}$

(d) $\dfrac{s}{\sqrt{n}} \sqrt{\dfrac{N-n}{N-1}}$

b and d (See Chapter 8, Frames 94–97, for a review.)

36 As a further review, of the two appropriate formulas b and d in Frame 35, above, when would formula b be used, as contrasted to formula d? _____

_____

_____

When the population is infinite in size or the sample size is less than or equal to 5 percent of the population size.

37 In testing a hypothesis concerned with the value of a population mean, first the level of significance to be used in the test is specified and then the regions of acceptance and rejection for evaluating the obtained sample mean are determined. If the 1 percent level of significance is used, indicate the percentages of sample means in each of the areas of the normal curve, below, assuming that the population hypothesis is correct.

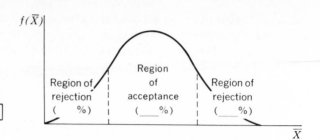

$f(\overline{X})$

Region of rejection (%)

Region of acceptance (%)

Region of rejection (%)

$\overline{X}$

0.5; 99; 0.5

38 By the first method the critical limits that separate the region of acceptance from the regions leading to rejection of the null hypothesis can be specified in a manner similar to the setting of confidence limits in the process of estimation. Thus, for testing a hypothesis at the 1 percent level, the critical limits are at $\mu_H - 2.58s_{\overline{X}}$ and $\mu_H + 2.58s_{\overline{X}}$. For testing a hypothesis at the 5 percent level, the appropriate critical limits are at _____ and _____ .

$\mu_H - 1.96s_{\overline{X}}; \mu_H + 1.96s_{\overline{X}}$

39 In contrast, the lower and upper limits of the 95 percent *confidence interval* for estimating the population mean are defined by the algebraic expressions _____ and _____ .

$\overline{X} - 1.96s_{\overline{X}}$
$\overline{X} + 1.96s_{\overline{X}}$

40 Therefore the general procedure for setting confidence limits which you learned in Chapter 9 can also be used to determine critical limits for hypothesis testing. The difference is that instead of the interval being constructed in respect to the point estimate for the population mean, it is constructed in respect to _____ _____ .

the hypothesized value of the population mean (μ_H)

41 As an example of using critical limits for testing a hypothesis about the population mean, suppose that the average (mean) value of a company's accounts receivable is claimed to be $187.50. An auditor selects a sample of 49 accounts randomly and determines that the sample mean is $175.00 and the standard deviation is $35.00. What are the critical limits for testing the validity of the claimed value of the population mean at the 5 percent level of significance? Assume that the sample is less than 5 percent of the population.

$\dfrac{35.00}{\sqrt{49}} = \dfrac{35.00}{7} = 5.00$

$s_{\overline{X}} = \dfrac{s}{\sqrt{n}} =$

187.50 ± 1.96(5.00) =
187.50 ± 9.80 =
$177.70 and $197.30

Critical limits $= \mu_H \pm 1.96 s_{\overline{X}} =$

42 For Frame 41, above, given the sample mean that was actually obtained and using the 5 percent level of significance, the null hypothesis would be [accepted / rejected].

rejected (because $175.00 is in a region of rejection; it is below $177.70)

43 For the example in Frames 41 and 42, rejection of the null hypothesis means that the claimed average accounts receivable of $187.50 [is / is not] accepted as being correct at the 5 percent level of significance.

is not

44 Is it possible that the claimed accounts receivable figure is actually correct? [Yes / No]

Yes

45 In the hypothesis-testing procedure which we have been describing, critical limits are defined in terms of the particular measurement units used (e.g., in dollars in the last example). The more popular approach to hypothesis testing, however, is to define these critical limits in terms of z values, or number of units of the standard error of the mean, and to evaluate the sample mean accordingly. The advantage of this approach is that no matter what assumed value of the population mean, or other parameter, is being tested, the same critical limits are used for a given level of significance. Thus, in terms of z units, −1.96 and +1.96 are the critical limits for tests at the _____ percent level of significance, and −2.58 and +2.58 are the critical limits for tests at the _____ percent level of significance.

5
1

46 When this approach is used, the obtained value of the sample mean has to be transformed into a z value so that it can be compared with the critical values of z. Given that

$$z = \frac{\overline{X} - \mu_H}{s_{\overline{X}}}$$

calculate the value of z for the sample mean in Frame 41, in which the hypothesized population mean was $187.50, the sample mean was $175.00 and the standard error of the mean was $5.00.

$\dfrac{175.00 - 187.50}{5.00} = \dfrac{-12.50}{5.00}$
$= -2.5$

$z =$

47 Would the obtained value of z for the sample mean result in rejecting the null hypothesis at the 5 percent level? [Yes / No] At the 1 percent level? [Yes / No]

Yes (The value is below −1.96, and is thus in a region of rejection.)

No

---

48 The normal probability curve below indicates the critical limits at the 5 percent level both in terms of original measurement units and in terms of z units for the problem we have been considering. Thus, whether the sample mean is stated as being equal to $175.00 or to −2.5 in terms of the equivalent z value, the sample mean is clearly located in the region of _____ .

---

rejection

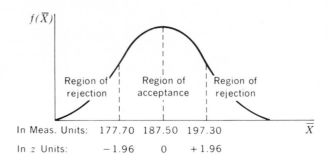

$f(\overline{X})$

Region of rejection | Region of acceptance | Region of rejection

In Meas. Units: 177.70 187.50 197.30 $\overline{X}$

In z Units: − 1.96   0   + 1.96

---

49 Rejection of the null hypothesis in Frame 48 then logically leads to acceptance of the alternative hypothesis, that is, the hypothesis that the population mean is [different from / larger than / smaller than] the hypothesized population mean.

---

different from (*not* smaller than; see Frame 50, below)

---

50 If there is an interest in testing for differences in one direction only, then this fact must be specified, along with the level of significance to be used, *before* the sample data to be used in making the test are collected. *Thus the sample data collected for the purpose of hypothesis testing* [can / cannot] *be used as the basis for deciding what hypothesis should be tested and what significance level should be employed.*

---

cannot

---

51 To employ sample data for this purpose would lead to a circularity in thinking and decision making, for data that suggest a certain hypothesis would then be used to test that hypothesis. On the other hand, would it be logically acceptable to formulate a hypothesis on the basis of one sample of

Yes (and this is a commonly
employed procedure in the
sciences)

data and test it, using a second, independently selected sample? [Yes / No]

52 Suppose that the auditor in Frame 41 is concerned only about the possibility that the average of the accounts receivable is lower than the claimed amount. This concern would be specified before the sample is drawn, and the null hypothesis that would be tested is that the actual value of the population mean is not [different from / smaller than] the claimed population average.

smaller than

53 If the auditor is interested only in the possibility that the claimed average is too high, would he need to go through the procedure of statistically testing the null hypothesis if the hypothesized mean is $187.50 (or more) and the sample mean is $175.00? [Yes / No]

Yes

54 Continuing from Frame 53, would he need to go through the procedure of statistically testing the null hypothesis if the sample mean is $200.00? [Yes / No]

No (because the sample
mean is included in the
interval of values specified
by the null hypothesis)

55 Therefore, when the null hypothesis involves an assumption of "no difference," there are two regions of rejection, and therefore such tests are called *two-tailed tests.* When the null hypothesis specifies that the population parameter is not smaller (or not larger) than the hypothesized value, there is only one region of rejection, and such tests are called _____-_____ tests.

one-tailed

56 Using a randomly chosen sample of bearings being polished by a machine, we may wish to test the null hypothesis that the true mean diameter of the bearings does not differ from the production standard, using the 5 percent level of significance. This would be a _____-tailed statistical test. On the other hand, testing the hypothesis that the bearings are not larger than the standard would involve a _____-tailed test.

two

one

57 The two figures below illustrate the differing locations of the regions of rejection for a one-tailed versus a two-tailed statistical test carried out at the 5 percent level. The one-tailed test is illustrated by Figure [a / b], and the two-tailed test is illustrated by Figure [a / b].

a

b

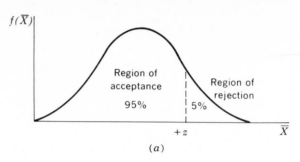

(a)

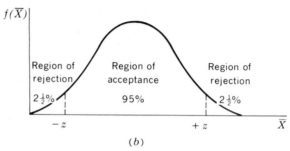

(b)

58 In Figures *a* and *b* in Frame 57, would the critical limit identified as +z have the same value, i.e., be at the same point, for the two distributions? [Yes / No] Why or why not? _____

No; Because for *a* it separates the upper 5 percent of sample means, whereas for *b* it separates the upper 2½ percent.

59 Thus the critical value or values of *z* being used to determine the significance of a difference depends on whether a one-tailed or a two-tailed test is being employed. As indicated in Table 10-2, the critical values for *z* for a two-tailed test at the 1 percent level are _____ , while the critical value of *z* for a one-tailed test at the 1 percent level is _____ .

±2.58

+2.33 (or −2.33; only one of these, depending on the direction of the test)

Table 10-2 ■ Critical Values of *z* in Hypothesis Testing

	One-tailed	Two-tailed
5%	+1.65 (or −1.65)	±1.96
1%	+2.33 (or −2.33)	±2.58

60 For a shipment of cable, suppose that the specifications call for a mean breaking strength of 2,000 pounds and a sampling of the breaking strength of a number of segments of the cable has a mean breaking strength of 1,955 pounds with an associated standard error of the mean of 25 pounds. Using the 5 percent level, test the null hypothesis that the true mean breaking strength is 2,000 pounds and interpret the result of your test, referring to Table 10-2 for the critical value(s) of z to be used.

$$\frac{1,955 - 2,000}{25} = \frac{-45}{25} = -1.8$$

$$z = \frac{\overline{X} - \mu_H}{s_{\overline{X}}} =$$

Difference not significant at the 5 percent level (critical $z = \pm 1.96$).

Interpretation: _____

_____

61 For the example in Frame 60, since we have found that the sample mean is lower in value than the hypothesized population mean, can we apply a one-tailed test instead, thus specifically determining whether the population mean might be lower in value than the hypothesized mean? [Yes / No] Why or why not? _____

No; Sample data cannot be used as the basis for deciding on the kind of test to be used with the same data.

_____

62 On the other hand, suppose that before determining the sample mean we had stipulated that we are concerned only about the possibility that the cable is weaker than called for by the specifications, but we are not concerned if it is stronger. What would then be the interpretation of the sample results in Frame 60? _____

The hypothesis that the mean strength is at least 2,000 pounds would be rejected. (z value of -1.8 is outside of critical z limit of -1.65 for a one-tailed test.)

_____

_____

_____

10.4 ■ Hypothesis Testing and Decision Making

Having established the conceptual foundation for hypothesis testing and its relationship to statistical estimation in the preceding section of this chapter, we now relate hypothesis testing to decision making. To do this we first identify the general steps followed in any application of hypothesis testing. Then we describe how the probability of a type II error can be determined when there is a specific alternative hypothesis to the null hypothesis, so that acceptance of the null hypothesis implies rejection of the specific alternative hypothesis, and rejection of the null hypothesis implies acceptance of the specific alternative hypothesis. Finally, we briefly consider the critical value used in hypothesis testing and its relationship to type I and type II errors.

63 Hypothesis testing is associated with the decision-making process in that acceptance or rejection of the null hypothesis will lead to one course of managerial action as contrasted to another course of action. For example, in the sample problem at the end of the preceding section, if we accept the hypothesis that the mean breaking strength of the cable is at least 2,000 pounds, then we would take the action of accepting and using the cable. If we reject the hypothesis, then we would _____ .

> return the cable to the manu-
> facturer (etc.)

64 Table 10-3 summarizes the general procedure of hypothesis testing using the normal distribution. Up to this point we have not specifically discussed the "alternative hypothesis" required in Step 1. In general, the alternative hypothesis includes all possible values of the parameter that are not included in the null (principal) hypothesis, and we designate the alternative hypothesis by using the subscript A, as in μ_A. Thus, if $\mu_H = 2,000$, $\mu_A \neq 2,000$; that is, the alternative hypothesis concerning the value of μ is that it is not equal to 2,000. Similarly, for a one-tailed test, if $\mu_H \geqslant 2,000$, then $\mu_A < $ _____ .

> 2,000 (discussion continued
> in Frame 65)

Table 10-3 ■ General Steps in Hypothesis Testing Using the Normal Distribution	1 State the null hypothesis and the alternative hypothesis. 2 Identify the critical z value (one-tailed test) or values (two-tailed test). 3 Compute the value of z for the obtained sample statistic. 4 Compare the value of z with the critical value(s) of z and accept or reject the null hypothesis accordingly.

65 For the one-tailed test above, if the null hypothesis is rejected, then the alternative hypothesis that the true mean is less than 2,000 must be accepted. Similarly, identify the alternative hypothesis regarding the value of the population mean for each of the following null hypotheses.

> $\mu_A \neq 30$
> $\mu_A < 1,000$
> $\mu_A > 90$

Null hypothesis	Alternative hypothesis
$\mu_H = 30$	_____
$\mu_H \geqslant 1,000$	_____
$\mu_H \leqslant 90$	_____

66 Step 2 in Table 10-3 requires that the critical z value or values be identified. Of course, this depends on the level of significance used and whether the test is one- or two-tailed. At the 5 percent level, the critical values of z associated with a test of the form $\mu_H = \mu$ are _____ and _____. The critical value for a 5 percent test of the form $\mu_H \geqslant \mu$ is ____.

67 In respect to Step 3 listed in Table 10-3, the z value that is computed in the process of hypothesis testing can be defined in general terms as:

$$z = \frac{\left(\begin{array}{l}\text{observed value}\\\text{of statistic}\end{array}\right) - \left(\begin{array}{l}\text{hypothesized value}\\\text{of parameter}\end{array}\right)}{\text{standard error of the statistic}}$$

Thus, in the preceding section of this chapter the z value computed in testing a hypothesis concerning the population mean was simply a particular application of this general formula, and it is expressed as:

$z = $ _____

68 In the following sections of this chapter we extend the application of hypothesis testing to hypotheses concerning differences between means, proportions, and differences between proportions. Suppose we want to test a hypothesis concerning the population median (med_H). Given that the standard error of the median can be represented by σ_{med}, indicate the formula for computing the z value in this case.

$z = $ _____

69 The last step in Table 10-3 concerns the acceptance or rejection of the null hypothesis, and consequent rejection or acceptance of the alternative hypothesis. As indicated in our discussion in the preceding section, if we reject the null hypothesis (and accept the alternative hypothesis), we may have done so correctly or we may have incurred a type ____ error. For a test at the 5 percent level, the probability of incorrectly rejecting a true null hypothesis is $P = $ _____.

70 Now, if the null hypothesis is *accepted*, what is the probability that we have incorrectly accepted it—i.e., what is the probability that we have incorrectly rejected a true *alternative* hypothesis? The answer is, it depends on the actual value of μ_A. Look at Figure 10-2. The top figure indicates the sampling distribution of $\overline{X}$ given that μ_H is true. Based on the values in the figure, the shaded area in the figure, which represents the region of rejection, also indicates that the probability of a type I error is $P =$ _____ .

Figure 10-2 ■ **Regions of acceptance and rejection for the null hypothesis and two specific alternative hypotheses**

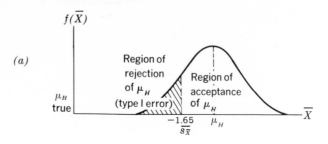

(a)

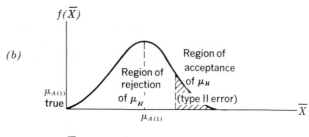

(b)

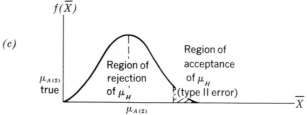

(c)

71 Still referring to Figure 10-2, the second and third figures indicate regions of acceptance and rejection for two specific alternative hypotheses, $\mu_{A(1)}$ and $\mu_{A(2)}$. Note that the critical value is "brought down" from the first figure, because it is always on the basis of the null hypothesis that critical limits are determined. For the second and third figures, the shaded areas represent the respective probabilities of incorrectly accepting the null hypothesis and thereby incurring a type ____ error. For the two specific alternative values of the parameter, $\mu_{A(1)}$ and $\mu_{A(2)}$, the probability of a type II error is greater for the alternative value that is [closer to / farther from] μ_H.

II

closer to

72 Given that the level of significance and sample size are held constant, the closer a specific value of μ_A is to μ_H, the higher the probability of a type II error. In terms of the scope of this text we do not desire an extended discussion of type

II error. But we can indicate how it can be computed for a particular value of μ_A and consider how the specific value of μ_A should be chosen. Repeating the cable problem from the preceding section, suppose that $\mu_H \geqslant 2{,}000$ and $s_{\overline{X}} = 25$. Compute the critical limit for the one-tailed test at the 5 percent level in terms of pounds of breaking strength (rather than simply in terms of the z value as such) and enter it in the figure below.

$2{,}000 - 1.65(25) =$
$2{,}000 - 41 = 1{,}959$

Critical limit $= \mu_H - 1.65 s_{\overline{X}} =$

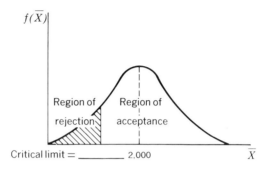

1,959

Critical limit = _____ 2,000

73 Thus, in terms of the solution above, the null hypothesis that $\mu_H \geqslant 2{,}000$ should be rejected if the sample mean $\overline{X} \leqslant 1{,}959$ pounds, for a one-tailed test at the 5 percent level. To determine the probability of a type II error associated with this decision rule, the first step is to determine the specific alternative hypothesis to be used as a point of reference. The general alternative hypothesis, of course, is $\mu_A < 2{,}000$, which includes a range of possible values of μ_A. Suppose that μ_H is in fact false and that the alternative hypothesis (μ_A) that is really correct is $\mu_A = 1{,}500$ pounds. Given that the desired mean strength was to be at 2,000 pounds strength or more, does the discrepancy between these two values appear to be important in this case? [Yes / Probably not]

Yes (assuming that we had an important reason for specifying the desired mean strength of 2,000 pounds)

Probably not (in the context of cable strength, we would assume that the specifications were not so close to our minimum needs that a 1-pound difference in strength would be important)

74 On the other hand, suppose the alternative hypothesis that is really correct is $\mu_A = 1{,}999$ pounds. Does the discrepancy appear to be important? [Yes / Probably not]

75 Therefore, an approach by which we can evaluate the probability of a type II error for a decision rule is to determine (subjectively or otherwise) *the minimum difference that is considered important.* For our cable example, suppose we decide that the difference is important if the true (alternative) average strength is 1,900 pounds or less. From Frame 72, note that we would reject μ_H and accept this alternative hypothesis only if $\bar{X} < 1,959$. Based on this decision rule, enter the specified value of μ_A and the critical sample value in the diagram below.

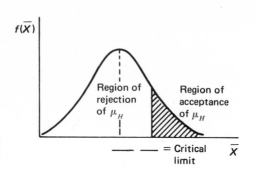

$f(\bar{X})$

Region of rejection of μ_H

Region of acceptance of μ_H

— — — = Critical limit $\bar{X}$

$\boxed{1,900; 1,959}$

76 Finally, we can determine the probability of a type II error for the example above by determining the proportion of area to the right of 1,959. The z value is:

$\boxed{\dfrac{1,959 - 1,900}{25} = \dfrac{59}{25} = +2.36}$ $z = \dfrac{1,959 - \mu_A}{s_{\bar{X}}} =$

The probability value associated with obtaining a value in the region of acceptance of the (false) null hypothesis is:

$\boxed{\begin{array}{l} 0.5000 - 0.4909 = 0.0091 \\ \doteq 0.01 \end{array}}$ $P(Z \geqslant +2.36) =$

77 In summary, beginning with Frame 72, we determined that for the one-tailed test associated with $\mu_H \geqslant 2,000$ the critical limit for accepting versus rejecting the null hypothesis at the 5 percent level is at 1,959 pounds. If the null hypothesis is in fact correct, use of this standard results in a long-run probability of a type I error of _____ (value) and a long-run probability of correctly accepting μ_H of _____ (value).

$\boxed{\begin{array}{r} 0.05 \\ 0.95 \end{array}}$

78 Continuing from Frame 77, above, we then designated that the discrepancy in mean strength is considered important if $\mu_A \leqslant 1,900$. If the true strength is in fact equal to 1,900, in

0.01	
0.99	

Frame 76 we determined that the use of the decision rule results in a long-run probability of a type II error of _____ (value). Therefore, the probability of correctly rejecting μ_H in this case is _____.

79 Table 10-4 reports the probabilities that we have determined in this sample problem. Any further development of this topic, which is beyond the scope of this book, would be concerned with two-tailed hypotheses and with "balancing" the probabilities of the two types of errors by considering the cost associated with each type of error and the relative frequency of the two states μ_H and μ_A. In general, suppose the cost associated with the two types of errors is about equal. Given that use of the critical limit of 1,959 pounds results in the probability values reported in Table 10-4, it would appear desirable to [increase / decrease] the value of the critical limit somewhat. (Refer to the figures in Frames 72 and 74.) Why?

decrease

This will reduce the probability of type I error, and will more than offset the associated increase in the probability of type II error, in terms of long-run cost.

_____

_____

_____ .

Table 10-4 ■ Probabilities of Correct Decisions and Errors for the Sample Problem

	Null hypothesis true ($\mu_H = 2,000$)	Alternative hypothesis true ($\mu_H = 1,900$)
Accept null hypothesis	0.95 (Correct action)	0.01 (Type II error)
Accept alternative hypothesis	0.05 (Type I error)	0.99 (Correct action)

10.5 ■ Hypotheses Concerning the Difference between Two Means

In this section we apply the general hypothesis-testing procedure developed in this chapter to hypotheses concerned with the difference between the means of two populations. As in the preceding chapter on statistical estimation, the relevant standard error used in this case is the standard error of the difference between two means.

80 As indicated in the preceding section, the value that is computed in the process of hypothesis testing can be defined in general terms as:

$$z = \frac{\left(\begin{array}{c}\text{observed value} \\ \text{of statistic}\end{array} - \begin{array}{c}\text{hypothesized value} \\ \text{of parameter}\end{array}\right)}{\text{standard error of the statistic}}$$

Recalling that the standard error for a difference between two means is represented by $s_{\overline{X}_1 - \overline{X}_2}$ (based on sample data), complete the formula for z that can be used for testing the assumed value of the difference between two means:

$$\boxed{\dfrac{(\overline{X}_1 - \overline{X}_2) - (\mu_1 - \mu_2)_H}{s_{\overline{X}_1 - \overline{X}_2}}}$$

$$z = \frac{() - ()_H}{s_{\overline{X}_1 - \overline{X}_2}}$$

81 In the large majority of cases in which the difference between means is tested, the hypothesis is that the two sample means came from the same population and thus that $(\mu_1 - \mu_2)_H = $ ___ (value).

$$\boxed{0}$$

82 Therefore the z value used for testing the difference between means is usually presented in a simplified form, substituting 0 for $(\mu_1 - \mu_2)_H$, as:

$$\boxed{\dfrac{\overline{X}_1 - \overline{X}_2}{s_{\overline{X}_1 - \overline{X}_2}}}$$

$$z = \frac{(\overline{X}_1 - \overline{X}_2) - (\mu_1 - \mu_2)_H}{s_{\overline{X}_1 - \overline{X}_2}} =$$

83 In Chapter 9 we estimated the "true" difference between population means with specified degrees of confidence, whereas in this chapter we are testing the assumption that there actually is no difference between the means, at a specified level of significance. Repeating the data from Chapter 9, Frame 66, if a sample of 49 employees in a particular firm has a mean wage rate of $160.00 per week with a standard error of the mean of $1.44, and a sample of 40 employees taken from another firm has a mean weekly wage rate of $155.00 and a standard error of $1.50, then

$$\boxed{\begin{array}{c}\sqrt{(1.44)^2 + (1.50)^2} = \\ \sqrt{4.3236} = \$2.08\end{array}}$$

$$s_{\overline{X}_1 - \overline{X}_2} = \sqrt{s_{\overline{X}_1}^2 + s_{\overline{X}_2}^2} =$$

84 In terms of the general steps in hypothesis testing, our hypotheses are $(\mu_1 - \mu_2)_H = 0$ and $(\mu_1 - \mu_2)_A \neq 0$. If the difference is to be tested as a two-tailed test at the 1 percent level of significance, then the critical values in terms of z are _____ and _____ .

$$\boxed{-2.58; +2.58}$$

85 Compute the value of z for the data reported in Frame 83, above, and indicate whether the null hypothesis is accepted or rejected in this case.

$z =$

Therefore the null hypothesis of no difference is [accepted / rejected].

86 Suppose, however, that before collecting the data we believed that the wages in the first firm were higher than those in the second firm. In order to determine if there is a significant difference in favor of the first firm, the null hypothesis tested is that the average wage in the first firm is *not* larger than the second firm [i.e., $(\mu_1 - \mu_2)_H \leqslant 0$]. The test then would be a _____-tailed test and the critical value of z to be used at the 1 percent level is _____ (refer to Table 10-2, if necessary), thereby resulting in the null hypothesis being [accepted / rejected] in this case.

10.6 ▪ Hypotheses Concerning the Population Proportion (Using the Binomial Distribution)

Again, as in Section 9.4, we need to distinguish between continuous and discrete data in the process of inference. In this section we illustrate the use of the binomial probability distribution for the purpose of hypothesis testing. As in Chapter 9, however, use of the normal probability distribution in place of the binomial distribution simplifies the required computations; this substitution is described and illustrated in the following section of this chapter.

87 To take a very simple situation in which the binomial distribution can be used in hypothesis testing, suppose we hypothesize that a coin is fair; i.e., $\pi_H = 0.50$ and $\pi_A \neq 0.50$. Given that we toss the coin five times and the coin lands heads all five times, can we reject the hypothesis that the coin is fair at, say, the 5 percent level of significance? In referring to Table B-3 for the binomial probabilities for the various number of heads that can occur, $p =$ _____ (value) and $n =$ _____ (value).

88 Referring to Table B-3 in the Appendix, indicate the probability of all of the possible events in the following table.

	Number of heads	P
0.0312	0	___
0.1562	1	___
0.3125	2	___
0.3125	3	___
0.1562	4	___
0.0312	5	___

89 Assume that as the alternative to the coin being fair, we had reason to believe that the coin was biased in favor of heads before the five tosses were made. Is the observed outcome in terms of number of heads significantly greater than the expected number of heads for a fair coin at the 5 percent level? [Yes / No] Why or why not? _____

_____ .

Yes; The probability of five heads occurring by chance is 0.0312, which is less than 0.05.

90 If we had not predicted the direction of bias before data collection, would the run of heads be considered significant at the 5 percent level? [Yes / No] Why or why not? _____

_____

_____ .

No; The probability of a difference this large in *either* direction is > 0.05. (Specifically, it is 0.0312 + 0.0312 = 0.0624.)

91 Similarly, suppose we begin with the null hypothesis that no more than 40 percent of the students at a particular university are habitual smokers. If we survey a random sample of 10 students, how many must be smokers in order to reject the hypothesis at the 5 percent level? To begin with, this will involve a _____-tailed test of the hypothesis.

one (Since the hypothesis specifies that no more than 40 percent are smokers, only deviations greater than 40 percent will be tested.)

92 For this problem, $\pi_H \leqslant 0.40$, $\pi_A > 0.40$, and $n = 10$. The most extreme outcome in *nonsupport* of the null hypothesis would be a sample result in which all 10 students sampled were smokers. Since this example involves the use of the same probability distribution as the example on estimation in Chapter 9, Frame 72, we can make use of a previously constructed table. According to Table 10-5, which is the same as Table 9-3, the probability of all 10 students being smokers, assuming the null hypothesis is correct, is _____ (value).

0.0001

	Number of smokers	Proportion of sample	Probability
Table 10-5 ▪ Probability Distribution for Obtaining Various Numbers of Smokers in a Sample of 10 Respondents for $\pi = 0.4$	0	0.0	0.0060
	1	0.1	0.0403
	2	0.2	0.1209
	3	0.3	0.2150
	4	0.4	0.2508
	5	0.5	0.2007
	6	0.6	0.1115
	7	0.7	0.0425
	8	0.8	0.0106
	9	0.9	0.0016
	10	1.0	0.0001

93 If eight of the 10 randomly sampled students are smokers, should the null hypothesis be rejected at the 5 percent level? [Yes / No] Why or why not? _____
_____
_____ .

Yes; Because the probability of a deviation this large or larger is < 0.05 (0.0106 + 0.0016 + 0.0001 = 0.0123).

94 On the other hand, suppose that seven of the 10 students are smokers. Would this outcome lead to the rejection of the null hypothesis, $\pi_H \leqslant 0.40$, at the 5 percent level? [Yes / No] Why or why not? _____
_____
_____
_____

No; Because the probability of a deviation this large or larger is > 0.05 (0.0425 + 0.0106 + 0.0016 + 0.0001 = 0.0548).

10.7 ▪ Hypotheses Concerning Proportions (Using the Normal Distribution)

Just as for estimation, it is more convenient computationally when the normal distribution can be used in place of the binomial in the process of hypothesis testing. As we indicated in Chapter 9, this substitution can be applied whenever the sample size n is at least 30 and np and nq are each at least equal to 5.

95 If we continue with the student-survey example of Frames 91 and 94, but increase the size of the sample from 10 to 64, then the criteria for using the normal distribution in place of the binomial [have / have not] been thereby satisfied.

have

96 As in the preceding section, $\pi_H \leqslant 0.40$ and $\pi_A > 0.40$. Since the standard error of this distribution is based on the hypothesized population proportion rather than a sample proportion, it is represented by the symbol σ_p rather than s_p. Accordingly, for the data given,

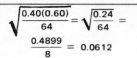

$$\sqrt{\frac{0.40(0.60)}{64}} = \sqrt{\frac{0.24}{64}} =$$

$$\frac{0.4899}{8} = 0.0612$$

(We are assuming that the sample size is less than 5 percent of the population size, and thus the finite correction factor is not necessary in the formula.)

$$\sigma_p = \sqrt{\frac{\pi_H(1 - \pi_H)}{n}} =$$

97 According to the general formula for computing a z value (Frame 67), what is the formula for z which would be computed in testing the hypothesis that no more than 40 percent of the students as a whole are habitual smokers, using p for the sample proportion and π_H for the hypothesized proportion?

$$\frac{p - \pi_H}{\sigma_p}$$

$z =$

98 Refer to Table 10-2 on page 260 if necessary. What is (are) the critical limit(s) of z to be used in evaluating the z value in Frame 96, above, at the 5 percent level of significance?

+1.65 (Sign should be included.)

Critical $z =$ _____ (value)

99 Suppose that 40 of the 64 students surveyed, or a proportion of 0.625, are habitual smokers. Calculate the value of z and indicate whether the null hypothesis is accepted or rejected, given the one-tailed test at the 5 percent level.

$$\frac{0.625 - 0.40}{0.0612} = +3.68$$

$$z = \frac{p - \pi_H}{\sigma_p} =$$

rejected (since the critical value of z is +1.65)

Therefore the null hypothesis that $\pi_H \leqslant 0.40$ is [accepted / rejected].

100 If we had not specified any direction in the null hypothesis, but had simply been testing for significance of difference in either direction, then at the 5 percent level the null hypothesis would have been [accepted / rejected].

rejected (The obtained critical ratio of +3.68 is also outside of the critical z limits of −1.96 and +1.96.)

101 Just as for sample means, we may hypothesize that an observed difference between *two* sample proportions is not significant, i.e., that they could have been obtained from the same population. In this case the formula for z can also be simplified, so that

$$\frac{p_1 - p_2}{\hat{\sigma}_{p_1 - p_2}}$$
[since $(\pi_1 - \pi_2)_H = 0$]

$$z = \frac{(p_1 - p_2) - (\pi_1 - \pi_2)_H}{\hat{\sigma}_{p_1 - p_2}} =$$

102 The symbol for the standard error in the formula above indicates that the sample proportions have been pooled. Specifically, if the null hypothesis is that there is no difference between the proportions in the two populations, then the standard error of the difference between the two proportions should not be based on the two separate estimators p_1 and p_2. Instead, the two sample proportions should be pooled so that there is a common estimator of the population proportion, as follows:

$$\hat{\pi} = \frac{n_1 p_1 + n_2 p_2}{n_1 + n_2}$$

Suppose 55 people out of a random sample of 100 people in one income group express approval of an economic policy, while 95 people out of a random sample of 200 people in another income group express such approval. As the first step in testing the null hypothesis that $\pi_1 - \pi_2 = 0$, we determine the pooled estimator of the population proportion:

$$\frac{(100)(0.55) + (200)(0.475)}{100 + 200}$$
$$= \frac{150}{300} = 0.50$$

$\hat{\pi} =$

103 Continuing from Frame 102, the standard error of the difference is based on the pooled estimate of the population proportion. To differentiate this standard error from the one defined in Chapter 9, it is represented by $\hat{\sigma}_{p_1 - p_2}$ (instead of $s_{p_1 - p_2}$) and the value for the data above is:

$$\sqrt{\frac{(0.50)(0.50)}{99} + \frac{(0.50)(0.50)}{199}}$$
$$= \sqrt{0.002525 + 0.001256}$$
$$= \sqrt{0.003782} = 0.061$$

$$\hat{\sigma}_{p_1 - p_2} = \sqrt{\frac{\hat{\pi}(1 - \hat{\pi})}{n_1 - 1} + \frac{\hat{\pi}(1 - \hat{\pi})}{n_2 - 1}} =$$

104 Continuing from Frames 102 and 103, we now test the null hypothesis that $\pi_1 - \pi_2 = 0$ at the 5 percent level of significance as follows:

$$\frac{0.55 - 0.475}{0.061} =$$

$$\frac{0.075}{0.061} = 1.23$$

$$z = \frac{p_1 - p_2}{\hat{\sigma}_{p_1 - p_2}} =$$

accepted (since the critical values of z are -1.96 and $+1.96$)

Therefore, the null hypothesis is [accepted / rejected] at the 5 percent level of significance (two-tailed test).

105 (Frames 1-9) The assumption that is in effect tested in all applications of hypothesis testing is that the difference between the hypothesized value of a population parameter and the actual value of the parameter is equal to ____ (value).

0

106 (Frames 10-14) The larger the difference between the hypothesized population parameter and a sample statistic, relative to the size of the standard error of the statistic, the [more / less] likely is it that the hypothesized value of the parameter is correct.

less

107 (Frames 15-20) When testing a null hypothesis at the 5 percent level of significance, if the assumed population parameter is in fact correct, then the probability is 0.05 that the sample statistic of a randomly selected sample will be in the region of _____ and the probability is 0.95 that the sample statistic will be in the region of _____ .

rejection
acceptance

108 (Frames 21-26) "Level of significance" is the term always used in conjunction with _____ ; "degree of confidence" is always used in conjunction with _____ .

hypothesis testing
estimation

109 (Frames 27-32) "Type I error" refers to the probability of [accepting / rejecting] a null hypothesis which is actually [true / false] ; "type II error" is the probability of [accepting / rejecting] a null hypothesis which is actually [true / false] .

rejecting
true; accepting
false

110 (Frames 33, 34) The level of significance used in testing a hypothesis is a direct indicator of the probability of type [I / II] error.

I

111 (Frames 35-44) In the first approach to setting critical limits for the purpose of hypothesis testing which we considered, the limits are defined in terms of the measurement units used. Thus, for a two-tailed test at the 5 percent level, the values of the two critical limits for testing a hypothesis concerning a population mean can be determined by solving the formula $\mu_H \pm$ _____ .

$1.96\sigma_{\bar{X}}$ (or $1.96\,s_{\bar{X}}$)

112 (Frame 45) In the more popular method of defining the critical limits, they are expressed in terms of z values, and thus the two critical limits for a two-tailed test at the 5 percent level, regardless of the parameter being tested, are simply ____ and ____ .

-1.96
$+1.96$

<table>
<tr><td>$$\frac{\bar{X} - \mu_H}{\sigma_{\bar{X}} \text{ (or } s_{\bar{X}})}$$</td></tr>
</table>

113 (Frames 46–49) When the critical limits are expressed in terms of z values, then the observed value of the sample statistic, such as the sample mean, has to be converted into units of the z scale in order to be evaluated. For the sample mean this conversion is accomplished by the formula, $z =$ _____ .

<table>
<tr><td>two</td></tr>
<tr><td>one</td></tr>
</table>

114 (Frames 50-56) When we wish to test the significance of any *difference* between a sample mean and a hypothesized population mean, the hypothesis test is described as being _____-tailed, whereas a specified interest in the sample mean being only smaller, or only larger, results in a _____-tailed test.

<table>
<tr><td>one</td></tr>
</table>

115 (Frames 57–62) As contrasted to a two-tailed test, a one-tailed statistical test includes [one / two] region(s) of rejection.

116 (Frames 63–65) Rejection of the null hypothesis always implies acceptance of an alternative hypothesis. Thus, if the null hypothesis represented by $\mu_H \geqslant 40$ is rejected, the alternative hypothesis which would be accepted is represented

<table>
<tr><td>$\mu_A < 40$</td></tr>
</table>

by _____ .

117 (Frames 66–69) When using the normal probability distribution as the basis, whether the null hypothesis is accepted or rejected depends on the comparison between a

<table>
<tr><td>z</td></tr>
</table>

computed z value and the critical ____ (value(s) based on the level of significance and type of test.

118 (Frames 70-79) The probability of type I error is represented by the proportion of area in the region of

<table>
<tr><td>null</td></tr>
</table>

rejection in respect to the _____ hypothesis. The probability of type II error depends on which specific

<table>
<tr><td>alternative</td></tr>
</table>

_____ hypothesis is used as the point of reference.

119 (Frames 80-86) In testing the null hypothesis that the means of two populations do not differ in value, the simplified formula used for computing the z value which is to be compared with the critical value(s) of z, given that only sample data are available, is:

<table>
<tr><td>$$\frac{\bar{X}_1 - \bar{X}_2}{s_{\bar{X}_1 - \bar{X}_2}}$$</td></tr>
</table>

$z =$

120 (Frames 87–94) When the hypothesis-testing situation concerns a relatively small number of independent observations for which the outcomes are dichotomized, such as in the case of "yes-no" responses, the probability distribution that should be used to determine the required probabilities is the

binomial

_____ probability distribution.

121 (Frame 95) The normal probability distribution can be used to approximate binomial probabilities if the number of observations (sample size) is at least $n =$ ___ (value) and np and nq are each at least equal to ___ (value).

30
5

122 (Frames 96–100) For testing the difference between an observed sample proportion and a hypothesized population proportion by using the normal probability distribution, the formula for calculating the z value is:

$\dfrac{p - \pi_H}{\sigma_p}$

$z =$

123 (Frames 101–104) When testing the difference between two proportions, a hypothesized population proportion is not available, but the two sample proportions are available. The z value to be compared with the critical z value(s) is obtained in this case by the formula:

$\dfrac{p_1 - p_2}{\hat{\sigma}_{p_1 - p_2}}$

$z =$

Symbols Introduced in This Chapter (with Frame Numbers)

(10)	μ_H	The hypothesized value of the population mean.
(64)	μ_A	The alternative hypothesized value of the population mean which is accepted if the null hypothesis is rejected.
(80)	$(\mu_1 - \mu_2)_H$	The hypothesized difference between the means of two populations.
(87)	π_H	The hypothesized value of the population proportion.
(87)	π_A	The alternative hypothesized value of the population proportion.
(101)	$(\pi_1 - \pi_2)_H$	The hypothesized difference between the proportions in two populations.

(102) $\hat{\pi}$

A pooled estimator of a population proportion.

(103) $\hat{\sigma}_{p_1 - p_2}$

Standard error of the difference between two proportions based on use of a pooled estimator of the population proportion.

Formulas Introduced in This Chapter (with Frame Numbers)

(25) $\mu_H \pm z\sigma_{\overline{X}}$

(or $\pm zs_{\overline{X}}$)

Critical limits for testing a hypothesized value of the mean using the original units of measurement.

(46) $z = \dfrac{\overline{X} - \mu_H}{\sigma_{\overline{X}}}$

or $\dfrac{\overline{X} - \mu_H}{s_{\overline{X}}}$

Testing a hypothesized value of the population mean by transforming the value of the sample mean into a z value. This is the procedure most frequently used.

(67) $z =$

$\dfrac{\left(\begin{matrix}\text{observed value}\\\text{of statistic}\end{matrix}\right) - \left(\begin{matrix}\text{hypothesized value}\\\text{of parameter}\end{matrix}\right)}{\text{standard error of the statistic}}$

General formula for testing the hypothesized value of any population parameter by use of the normal probability distribution.

(82) $x = \dfrac{\overline{X}_1 - \overline{X}_2}{\hat{\sigma}_{\overline{X}_1 - \overline{X}_2}}$

or $\dfrac{\overline{X}_1 - \overline{X}_2}{s_{\overline{X}_1 - \overline{X}_2}}$

Test for the significance of the difference between two means.

(96) $\sigma_p = \sqrt{\dfrac{\pi_H(1 - \pi_H)}{n}}$

Standard error of the proportion computed by the use of the hypothesized population proportion, π_H. This is the standard error value used in testing the hypothesized value of the population proportion.

(97) $z = \dfrac{p - \pi_H}{\sigma_p}$

Testing the hypothesized value of the population proportion by use of the normal probability distribution.

(102) $\hat{\pi} = \dfrac{n_1 p_1 + n_2 p_2}{n_1 + n_2}$

Pooled estimator of the population proportion based on two sample proportions.

(103) $\hat{\sigma}_{p_1 - p_2} = \sqrt{\dfrac{\hat{\pi}(1-\hat{\pi})}{n_1 - 1} + \dfrac{\hat{\pi}(1-\hat{\pi})}{n_2 - 1}}$

Standard error of the difference between two proportions based on using a pooled estimate of the population proportion.

(104) $z = \dfrac{p_1 - p_2}{\sigma_{p_1 - p_2}}$

Test for the significance of the difference between two proportions.

EXERCISES

(Solutions on pages 605–608)

10.1 Describe how statistical estimation and hypothesis testing *differ* by considering (a) the difference in the "limits" that are defined in conjunction with the two procedures; and (b) the type of problem, or application, for which each method would be used.

10.2 Discuss the concept of type I error by describing (a) how the probability of such error can be determined; (b) how the probability of such error can be reduced; and (c) why a decision maker might choose not to reduce the probability of this type of error, and might even choose to increase it.

10.3 The manufacturer of three-way light bulbs claims that the bulbs have an average life of 2,500 hours. A sample of 36 bulbs has an average (mean) life of 2,325 hours with a standard deviation of 600 hours. Carry out a hypothesis-testing procedure by identifying the null and alternative hypotheses, identifying the critical z value(s) for the test at the 5 percent level of significance, and comparing the value of z for the sample data with the critical z value(s). Designate the manufacturer's claim as the null hypothesis.

10.4 In a decision problem such as that described in Exercise 10.3, above, the purchaser would not be concerned if the manufacturer's claim is exceeded, but rather, he would be specifically concerned about the possibility that the bulbs do not live up to the claim. With this as a viewpoint, repeat the analysis for the data of Exercise 10.3.

10.5 A random sample of 64 bearings produced by a machine has a mean diameter of 0.24 inch with a standard deviation of 0.02 inch. Another batch of 64 bearings produced by the same machine the next day has a mean diameter of 0.25 inch with a standard deviation of 0.04 inch. Test the hypothesis that the machine is not out of adjustment in terms of the difference in average diameter of the bearings in the two samples, using the 5 percent level of significance.

10.6 For Exercise 10.5, above, suppose that when this type of machine goes out of adjustment, it invariably produces bearings that are smaller than those produced earlier. Giving the benefit of the doubt to the assumption that the process is in control, restate the null and alternative hypotheses for the problem presented in Exercise 10.5 and indicate the result of the test.

10.7 A salesman claims that on the average he obtains orders from at least 30 percent of his prospects. For a random sample of 10 prospects he is able to obtain just one order. Can his claim be rejected, using the 5 percent level of significance?

10.8 For the claim in Exercise 10.7, above, suppose the salesman obtains orders from 20 out of 100 randomly selected prospects.

(a) Can his claim be rejected at the 5 percent level of significance?
(b) Can his claim be rejected at the 1 percent level of significance?

10.9 The manufacturer of a new car claims that the automobile will average at least 22 miles per gallon. For 49 test runs, the car model averages 21.5 miles per gallon with a standard deviation of 2.3 miles per gallon. Can the manufacturer's claim be rejected at the 5 percent level of significance?

10.10 Referring to Exercise 10.9, above, before the highway tests were carried out, a consumer advocate claimed that the new compact car will average *no more than* 22 miles per gallon for general highway driving. Using the data of Exercise 10.9, test this claim at the 5 percent level of significance. Briefly discuss the implications regarding which hypothesis in a decision-analysis situation is taken as the principal, or null, hypothesis to be tested.

10.11 Discuss the concept of type II error by defining what it means and indicating how the probability of such an error can be determined in conjunction with a hypothesis-testing procedure.

10.12 A magazine publisher is considering the publication of a special annual issue to be offered to subscribers only. The anticipated selling price and costs are such that at least 20 percent of the 95,000 subscribers would have to purchase the special issue in order to make it economically justifiable. Therefore, the publisher has decided to prepare the annual issue only if the response to a preliminary offering to a sample of the subscribers makes it unlikely (probability less than 0.05) that the percentage of all subscribers who will buy the special issue is less than or equal to 20 percent. In other words, he conservatively assumes that the true percentage is less than or equal to 20 percent and is willing to make a positive commitment only if the sample indicates otherwise. For a random sample of 250 subscribers, 62 of the subscribers order the special issue. Determine if the publisher should prepare the annual issue.

10.13 A fertilizer manufacturer claims that the use of his product will result in a yield of at least 35 bushels of wheat per acre, on the average. Application of the fertilizer to a sample of 36 randomly selected acres results in a yield of 33 bushels per acre with a standard deviation of 5.0 bushels. Can the manufacturer's claim be rejected at the 1 percent level of significance?

10.14 Another brand of fertilizer results in an average yield of 34.0 bushels of wheat per acre on 36 randomly selected acres, with a standard deviation of 6.0 bushels.

(a) Does the average yield associated with each of the two brands of fertilizer differ significantly at the 5 percent level of significance?

(b) Suppose the first brand was predicted to be equal to or better than the second brand before sample results were known, and this prediction is the basis for the hypothesis to be tested. Can this hypothesis be rejected at the 5 percent level of significance?

10.15 For a random sample of 50 firms taken from a particular industry the mean number of employees per firm is 420.4 with a sample standard deviation of 55.7. There is a total of 380 firms in this industry. Before the data were collected, it was hypothesized that the mean number of employees per firm in this industry does not exceed 408 employees. Test this hypothesis at the 5 percent level of significance.

10.16 Suppose the analyst in Exercise 10.15 neglected to use the finite correction factor in determining the value of the standard error of the mean. What would be the result of the test, still using the 5 percent level of significance?

10.17 A random sample of 30 employees at the Secretary II level in a large organization take a standardized typing test. The sample results are $\bar{X} = 63.0$ wpm (words per minute) with $s = 5.0$ wpm. Test the null hypothesis that the secretaries in general do *not* exceed a typing speed of 60 wpm, using the 1 percent level of significance.

10.18 With reference to exercise 10.17, suppose it is considered an important difference from the hypothesized value of the mean if the average typing speed is at least at 64.0 wpm. Determine the probability of **(a)** type I error and **(b)** type II error.

10.19 For a sample of 30 employees in one large firm, the mean hourly wage is $\bar{X}_1 = \$7.50$ with $s_1 = \$1.00$. In a second large firm, the mean hourly wage for a sample of 40 employees is $\bar{X}_2 = \$7.05$ with $s_2 = \$1.20$. Test the hypothesis that there is no difference between the average wage rate being earned in the two firms, using the 5 percent level of significance.

10.20 In Exercise 10.19, suppose the null hypothesis tested was that the average wage in the second firm was equal to or greater than the average wage rate in the first firm. Can this hypothesis be rejected at the 5 percent level of significance?

10.21 The superintendent of a manufacturing department informs the plant personnel manager that he needs additional skilled operators who can assemble an average of at least three components per minute. Because several available applicants have all had prior satisfactory work experience of a similar type in the company, the personnel manager believes that they all qualify. However, he decides to obtain a 30-minute sampling of work to identify any applicant who is clearly below the required standard. For a 30-minute work sample a particular applicant assembles an average (mean) of 2.8 components per minute with a standard deviation of 0.5 component per minute. Given the viewpoint that the applicants are considered acceptable unless the work sample clearly indicates otherwise, should this applicant be placed on the job? Use the 5 percent level of significance for your test. Is there any possible (statistical) difficulty with the sampling procedure that was used to collect the data?

10.22 For the situation described in Exercise 10.21, instead of assuming that the applicants are qualified unless the sample indicates otherwise, the personnel manager cautiously begins with the assumption that the applicants are *not* qualified. A particular applicant assembles an average of 3.1 units in the 30-minute period, with a standard deviation of 0.6 unit per period. Given the viewpoint in this exercise, should this applicant be placed on the job? Use the 5 percent level of significance for your test.

10.23 A producer of a television "special" expected that 40 percent (or more) of the viewing audience would watch the show in a particular metropolitan area. A random sample of 20 households with television sets turned on yields only 6 households which are watching the show. Based on this limited sample, can the producer's hypothesis be rejected at the 10 percent level of significance?

10.24 In relation to Exercise 10.23, the sample is expanded so that 100 households with sets turned on are contacted. Of the 100 households, 30 households are tuned in to the special. Can the producer's assumption that 40 percent (or more) of the households would watch the program be rejected, using the 10 percent level of significance?

10.25 For the television special described in Exercises 10.23 and 10.24, above, it was suggested that the program might appeal differently to urban versus suburban residents, but there was a difference of opinion among the production staff regarding the direction of the difference. For a random sample of 50 urban households, 20 reported watching the show; while for a random sample of 50 suburban households, 25 reported watching the show. Can this difference be considered significant at the 5 percent level?

10.26 In many reported studies it is implied that results that are "statistically significant" are thereby important. Discuss the appropriateness of this interpretation by considering the meaning of "significant" in the context of hypothesis testing.

CHAPTER 11■

USE OF STUDENT'S t DISTRIBUTION

In our use of the normal probability distribution in problems of estimation and hypothesis testing, we have relied on the assumption that when a sampling distribution of a statistic, such as a distribution of sample means, is normally distributed, then the transformation of these values into values of z will result in a distribution that is also normal. This distribution of z values, called the "unit normal distribution," has a mean of 0 and a standard deviation of 1.0, and it is on the basis of this distribution that degrees of confidence are defined in statistical estimation and that levels of significance are determined in hypothesis testing. When the value of the standard error of the mean is computed on the basis of a known population standard deviation σ, then the standard error is designated by the symbol $\sigma_{\bar{X}}$, and the assumption that the associated z distribution is normally distributed is in fact correct, given that the population is normally distributed or that the sample is large enough so that the central-limit theorem can be used ($n \geqslant 30$ in the case of the sampling distribution of the mean). However, when the value of the standard error of the mean is computed on the basis of a *sample* standard deviation s, then the standard error is designated by the symbol $s_{\bar{X}}$ and the assumption of normality may not be correct even though the population is normally distributed. In this chapter we define the conditions under which this distribution of transformed values is not normally distributed, describe the way in which such a distribution, called a "t distribution," differs from the z distribution, and illustrate the use of such a distribution in problems of estimation and hypothesis testing. "Student's t distribution" is so named because W. S. Gosset, the British statistician who first described the distribution, published his work under the name "Student."

11.1 ■ Characteristics of the t Distribution

As indicated in the introduction above, the distribution of z used in estimation and hypothesis testing in conjunction with a normally distributed population is itself normally distributed whenever the standard error of the mean is based on the population standard deviation being known, and it is designated by the symbol $\sigma_{\bar{X}}$. This is true regardless of the sample size because the z values are computed by the formula $z = (\bar{X} - \mu)/\sigma_{\bar{X}}$, which involves subtracting a constant from every sample mean in a normally distributed set of means and dividing the result by a constant as well. However, when the value of the standard deviation of the population is not known, then the divisor is not a constant, and the resulting transformed values are not in fact normally distributed, as we illustrate in this section.

1 If a sampling distribution of the mean is normally distributed, then the z distribution into which it is converted is also normally distributed whenever the standard error of the mean is calculated on the basis of a known [sample / population] standard deviation.

> population

2 This is so because the conversion of each mean in the (hypothetical) distribution of means into a z value requires subtraction of a constant and division by a constant, thus preserving the normality of the original distribution of means. Specifically, in this case, each sample mean would be converted into a z value by applying the formula

> $\dfrac{\overline{X} - \mu}{\sigma_{\overline{X}}}$

$$z = \frac{\overline{X} - \quad}{\rule{3cm}{0.4pt}}$$

3 In the computational formula for z in Frame 2, the constant subtracted from every mean in the distribution is ____ , and the constant by which the difference is divided is ____ .

> μ
>
> $\sigma_{\overline{X}}$

4 For an infinite population, $\sigma_{\overline{X}} = \sigma/\sqrt{n}$; for a finite population, and one in which the size of the sample is more than 5 percent of the population size,

$$\sigma_{\overline{X}} = \frac{\sigma}{\sqrt{n}} \sqrt{\frac{N - n}{N - 1}}$$

Thus, when σ is known, the computed value of the standard error of the mean for a given sample size [is / is not] dependent on particular sample statistics (i.e., sample standard deviation).

> is not

5 Now let us turn our attention to the calculation of $s_{\overline{X}}$, also presuming fixed sample size. In the formula $z = (\overline{X} - \mu)/s_{\overline{X}}$ we are again subtracting a constant from every sample mean. Are we also dividing by a constant? [Yes / No]

> No (This point is explained in the following frames.)

6 Assuming an infinite population in order to simplify our discussion,

$$\frac{s}{\sqrt{n}}$$

$$s_{\overline{X}} =$$

7 Now, although n in the formula in Frame 6 is defined as a constant, the value of s will not be the same for different sample means, for there is a unique sample standard deviation associated with each sample mean. That is, each sample mean is calculated on the basis of a distribution of sample values, and each of these distributions has its own standard deviation. The direct implication of this fact is that in the formula $z = (\overline{X} - \mu)/s_{\overline{X}}$, the denominator in the fraction [does / does not] have precisely the same value for each sample mean, although all samples are of the same size.

does not

8 Subtracting a constant from every one of a normally distributed set of values and dividing the result by a constant results in a transformed set of values that is also normally distributed. Applying this principle, the values of z that will be normally distributed are those that are determined by the formula (indicate identifying letter):

a

(a) $\dfrac{\overline{X} - \mu}{\sigma_{\overline{X}}}$

(b) $\dfrac{\overline{X} - \mu}{s_{\overline{X}}}$

9 What tends to be the nature of the distribution of transformed values computed by formula b, above? It can be demonstrated mathematically that the distribution is symmetrical and platykurtic (i.e., flat), rather than symmetrical and mesokurtic, as is the normal distribution. Because the symbol z is reserved for use with the unit normal distribution, t will be used to designate such a transformed series of values that in fact [is / is not] normally distributed.

is not (See Chapter 2, Frames 54–64, for a review of the terminology used to describe the characteristics of frequency curves.)

10 Since the departure from normality is directly related to the size of the sample for which s has been calculated, there is actually a series of t distributions. The smaller the sample used, the greater the departure from normality. In other words, the smaller the sample size, the more [platykurtic / mesokurtic / leptokurtic] is the t distribution.

platykurtic

11 Or, to consider this observation from another point of view, as the sample size is increased, the associated t distribution becomes more [platykurtic / mesokurtic].

mesokurtic

12 For large sample sizes the distribution of t becomes essentially mesokurtic. Since all t distributions are symmetrical, this also suggests that with large sample sizes the distribution of t is the same as the distribution of ___ .

z (or the normal distribution)

13 What do we mean by "large sample"? In this context, any sample for which the sample size n is 30 or larger can be considered to be a large sample. For such large samples, the z distribution can be used in place of the t distribution. Because of this, the use of the t distribution has been associated with "small-sample statistics." However, this phrase can be misleading, since the z distribution also can be used with small samples ($n < 30$). Specifically, the z distribution is always the appropriate distribution for use in estimation or hypothesis testing concerning the population mean when the population is normally distributed and the value of ___ is known.

σ (or the population standard deviation)

14 Therefore would it be correct to say that the t distribution must be used whenever the sample size is small ($n < 30$)? [Yes / No] . Whenever the value of σ is not known? [Yes / No]

No; No (The z distribution can be used in its place when $n \geqslant 30$.)

15 Rather, *both* conditions must exist to make the use of the t distribution necessary in estimation or hypothesis testing concerning the value of the population mean, i.e., the conditions that the value of ___ is unknown and the sample size upon which the value of s is based is less than ___ .

σ

30

16 Further, note that the t distribution is appropriate only when the distribution of means is itself normal. Given a small sample, this means that the central-limit theorem [can / cannot] be used and therefore that use of the t distribution is appropriate only when the population being sampled approximates the _____ distribution.

cannot

normal

17 In most statistical studies the sample sizes are considerably larger than 30, and so the use of the t distribution is not required. However in certain situations involving statistical inference, such as in industrial quality control, small samples are often the rule rather than the exception. Consider the implications of the fact that the distribution of t is platykurtic. As compared with the z distribution, would the t distribution have proportionally fewer or more of the outcomes in the tails of the distribution? [Fewer / More]

More

Section 11.1 Characteristics of the t Distribution ▪ 287

18 As illustrated in the figure below, the *t* distribution has a proportionally greater area in the tails of the distribution. Therefore when interval estimates are based on the use of a *t* distribution, as contrasted to the *z* distribution, for a given degree of confidence the width of the interval will be [narrower / wider].

wider (It is necessary to go farther out from the mean to include the same proportion of area under the curve.)

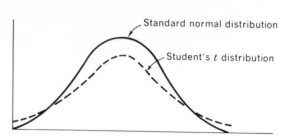

Standard normal distribution

Student's *t* distribution

19 Similarly, in hypothesis-testing applications the critical value of *t* for a given significance level, as compared with *z*, is [closer to / farther from] the center of the distribution.

farther from

20 Another way of describing the difference between the *t* and *z* distributions in hypothesis testing is to say that the required size of the difference between the hypothesized population value and the sample statistic that is necessary for rejecting the null hypothesis is greater for the [*z* / *t*] distribution.

t

21 Suppose that the *z* distribution was inadvertently used instead of the *t* distribution for setting confidence limits for estimating the population mean. For the stated degrees of confidence, the interval would be too [narrow / wide].

narrow

22 If the *z* distribution was inadvertently used instead of the *t* in a series of hypothesis-testing applications, the null hypothesis would be rejected too [seldom / often].

often

23 Thus, when the *t* distribution is used, both confidence limits and critical values differ somewhat from those determined by the use of the *z* distribution, the extent of the difference being related to the size of the _____ .

sample

24 We have stated that there is a separate *t* distribution for each possible sample size. In terms of proper statistical terminology, it is more appropriate to say that there is a separate *t* distribution associated with each of the possible

are	*degrees of freedom*. Our reference to "sample size" up to this point, however, does correctly indicate that sample size and degrees of freedom [are / are not] closely related.

25 When the *t* distribution is used in conjunction with estimating the population mean or testing its assumed value, the degrees of freedom are always equal to $n - 1$. Thus, if a sample mean is based on a sample size of 25, the degrees of freedom to be used in choosing the appropriate *t* distribution

24	are _____ (value).

26 Thus, rather than saying that there is a unique distribution of *t* associated with each possible sample size, it is more appropriate to state that there is a unique *t* distribution

degrees of freedom	associated with each of the possible _____ .

27 In contrast, are there separate distributions of *z* according

No	to sample size or degrees of freedom? [Yes / No]

28 The concept of degrees of freedom is one that we shall have further occasion to use, both in this chapter and in later ones. The concept is more easily illustrated than defined. Suppose that we have two measurements, X_1 and X_2, and that the mean of these two values, $\overline{X}$, is identified as being equal to 7.0. What are two possible values that X_1 and X_2 can have if the sample mean of 7.0 is correct?

(any two numbers whose sum is 14)	$X_1 =$ _____ and $X_2 =$ _____

29 Thus the general formula we are using in this case is

$$\frac{X_1 + X_2}{2} = 7$$

Once the value of X_1 is determined (say, $X_1 = 3$), can X_2

No (It must be 11 in this case.)	take on any one of several values? [Yes / No]

30 Thus, when there are two elements in a sample, and a sample statistic depending upon these values has been computed or specified, the number of sample elements whose

1	values can vary freely is ___ (number).

31 Similarly, we could demonstrate that if five elements make up a sample, the number of free variables, or degrees of freedom, remaining when the sample mean has been specified

4	is ___ (number).

32 In later uses of the concept of degrees of freedom, or df, the formula to determine df will vary to reflect the number of sample statistics whose values are based on the sample data. When there is one sample of n items, and the value of the sample mean has been computed for use in estimation or hypothesis testing, the appropriate formula is df = _____.

$n - 1$

33 Finally, let us look at the table we use in the remainder of this chapter. Refer to Table B-5 in the Appendix, "Areas for t Distributions." Since there is a separate distribution of t associated with each df, in this table a separate t distribution is in effect represented by each [line / column] of the table.

line

34 Notice the illustrative figure at the top of the table and compare it with the figure at the top of Table B-1, for the distribution of z. Whereas Table B-1 reports the proportion of area included between the mean of the distribution and $+z$, Table B-5 reports the proportion of the area between $+$ _____ and _____.

t; $+\infty$ (read: "plus infinity")

35 In using Table B-5, it is important to note that the values of t in a particular column are associated with a given proportion of area included in [one / both] tail(s) of the distribution.

one

36 As compared with the table for the z distribution, the table for the t distribution is quite compressed in that every line of the t table could be independently expanded into a full table of values equivalent to the table for the z distribution. The condensation of each possible table to one line of values has been achieved by presenting the t values for only selected [numbers of df / proportions of area].

proportions of area

37 We have suggested that as the degrees of freedom are increased, the t distribution approaches the z distribution in terms of its characteristics. In order to test this statement, what line of Table B-5, in terms of df, should have values that are the same as those for the z distribution? df = ___ .

∞ (infinity)

38 For example, the value of t for the 0.01 level of significance (one-tailed) with df = ∞ is equal to _____ (from Table B-5).

2.326

39 According to Table B-1, the proportion of area between the mean and $+z$ associated with a z value of $+2.33$ is _____.

0.4901

are (If the values of z presented in Table B-1 were carried to the third decimal place, there would be no difference between the diagrams.)

40 The two diagrams below illustrate the *t* and *z* values that we are comparing. Inspection of these figures indicates that the values of *t* and *z* being compared [are / are not] essentially equivalent in terms of the distribution of areas under the probability curves.

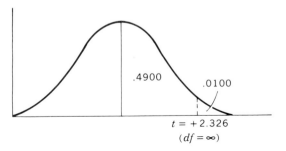

.4900   .0100

$t = +2.326$
$(df = \infty)$

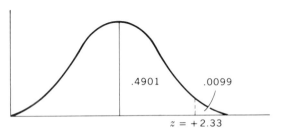

.4901   .0099

$z = +2.33$

41 Similarly, the value of *t* for the 0.025 level of significance (one-tailed) is 1.96, which is equivalent to the 0.05 level for a two-tailed test using the *z* distribution. For the 0.025 column of Table B-5, as well as for the other columns, notice that as df is reduced, the appropriate values of *t* become [smaller / larger].

larger (which is consistent with our discussion in Frames 18–23)

11.2 ■ Estimation Using the *t* Distribution

Given a normally distributed population, if the sample size is less than 30 and if the standard error is based on the sample standard deviation, rather than the population standard deviation, then we are required to use values of *t* rather than values of *z* in our estimation formulas. Except for this difference, the estimation formulas are the same as those described in Chapter 9. Thus, for example, the interval estimate for the population mean is determined by using the formula: $\overline{X} \pm ts_{\overline{X}}$. Of course, the standard error in this equation would never be designated by $\sigma_{\overline{X}}$, because a value of *z* rather than a value of *t* would then be appropriate in the estimation formula.

42 In the production of size D cells for use as flashlight batteries, the standard deviation of operating life for all batteries is $\sigma = 3.0$ hours, based on the known variability in battery ingredients. The distribution of operating life for all batteries is approximately normal. A sample of $n = 9$ batteries has a mean operating life of $\bar{X} = 20.0$ hours. Indicate the formula to be used for estimating the average life of all batteries being produced, using an estimation interval.

$\boxed{\bar{X} \pm z\sigma_{\bar{X}} \text{ (since } \sigma \text{ is known)}}$ Interval =

43 In the production of the size D cells, instead of the information given in Frame 42, suppose that the mean operating life of a sample of $n = 90$ batteries is $\bar{X} = 20.0$ hours with a sample standard deviation of $s = 3.0$ hours. The standard deviation of the population is not known in this case. Indicate the appropriate formula to be used for estimating the population mean.

$\boxed{\bar{X} \pm zs_{\bar{X}} \text{ (since } n \geqslant 30)}$ Interval =

44 In the production of size D cells, instead of the information given in Frame 42, suppose that the mean operating life of a sample of $n = 9$ batteries is $\bar{X} = 20.0$ hours with a sample standard deviation of $s = 3.0$ hours. Indicate the appropriate formula for estimating the population mean.

$\boxed{\bar{X} \pm ts_{\bar{X}} \text{ (} \sigma \text{ unknown and } n < 30)}$ Interval =

45 For the data of Frame 44 compute the value of the standard error of the mean.

$\boxed{\dfrac{s}{\sqrt{n}} = \dfrac{3.0}{3} = 1.0}$ $s_{\bar{X}} =$

46 Thus the formula for determining the confidence limits is: $20 \pm t(1.0)$. For the problem in Frame 44, what is the number of degrees of freedom to be used in looking up the value of t in Table B-5? df = _____ .

$\boxed{n - 1 = 8}$

47 In using Table B-5, we must remember that the t values posted in each column of the table are associated with a proportion of area in *one* tail of the distribution, which is indicated as the column heading. If we wish to define a 95 percent confidence interval, what proportion of the distribution would remain in each tail of the distribution, taken by itself? $p =$ _____ .

$\boxed{0.025}$

48 Therefore, in defining confidence limits by using Table B-5, the value of t to be used in constructing 95 percent confidence limits would be obtained from the column headed by [0.025 / 0.05]; the column to be used for defining 90 percent confidence limits is _____, and for defining 99 percent confidence limits it is _____.

0.025
0.05
0.005

49 Now, getting back to the estimation problem in Frame 44, define the 95 percent confidence limits for estimating the mean operating life of all size D cells being produced, given that $n = 9$, $\bar{X} = 20$ hours, $s = 3.0$ hours, and $s_{\bar{X}} = 1.0$ hour.

$\bar{X} \pm ts_{\bar{X}} = 20 \pm 2.306(1.0)$
$= 17.694$ to 22.306 hours

Interval =

50 In the solution for Frame 49 the t value was determined by looking up that value appropriate when df = ____ and the proportion of area in each tail of the distribution is _____.

8
0.025

51 If we wish to estimate a total quantity in a population instead of the population mean, how would the estimation formula that we have been using be modified?

$N\bar{X} \pm Nts_{\bar{X}}$ [or $N(\bar{X} \pm ts_{\bar{X}})$]

Total quantity =

52 Using the formula in Frame 51, estimate the total hours of useful service available from 500 batteries of the type described in Frame 49, using 95 percent confidence limits.

$500(20) \pm 500(2.306)(1.0)$
$= 10,000 \pm 1,153 = 8,847$
to $11,153$ hours

Total hours of service =

53 On the other hand, suppose we wish to estimate the difference between the means of two populations. In using the t distribution, the appropriate formula for defining the confidence limits is

$(\bar{X}_1 - \bar{X}_2); t$

Difference = _____ $\pm$ _____ $\hat{\sigma}_{\bar{X}_1 - \bar{X}_2}$

54 The meaning of $\hat{\sigma}_{\bar{X}_1 - \bar{X}_2}$ (as contrasted to $\sigma_{\bar{X}_1 - \bar{X}_2}$ and $s_{\bar{X}_1 - \bar{X}_2}$ in the preceding two chapters) is associated with the necessary assumption when using the t distribution that the standard deviations of the two populations are equal. The degrees of freedom in the two-sample case are the sum of the two sample sizes with a subtraction of one degree of freedom for each sample mean that is computed. Thus, where n_1 is the size of the first sample and n_2 is the size of the second sample, the formula for determining the degrees of freedom is

$$\boxed{n_1; n_2; 2}$$

$$df = \underline{\quad\quad} + \underline{\quad\quad} - \underline{\quad}$$

55 Suppose we wish to estimate the difference in quality between the flashlight cells being produced by two firms. A sample of 15 Foreverlast batteries has a mean operating life of 22.0 hours with a standard deviation of 6.0 hours, and a sample of 10 Yamahoho batteries has a mean operating life of 18.0 hours with a standard deviation of 3.0 hours. We compute the standard error of the difference between means by first obtaining a pooled estimate of the (common) standard deviation for the two populations. For the present example,

$$\hat{\sigma} = \sqrt{\frac{(n_1 - 1)s_1^2 + (n_2 - 1)s_2^2}{n_1 + n_2 - 2}}$$

$$\boxed{\sqrt{\frac{(14)(36) + (9)(9)}{15 + 10 - 2}} = \sqrt{\frac{585}{23}} \\ = \sqrt{25.4348} = 5.04}$$

$$\hat{\sigma} =$$

56 Using the pooled estimate of the standard deviation for the two populations, the standard error of the mean for this example is:

$$\boxed{\sqrt{\frac{25.4348}{15} + \frac{25.4348}{10}} \\ = \sqrt{4.2392} = 2.059}$$

$$\hat{\sigma}_{\bar{X}_1 - \bar{X}_2} = \sqrt{\frac{\hat{\sigma}^2}{n_1} + \frac{\hat{\sigma}^2}{n_2}} =$$

57 For the data presented in Frames 55 and 56, if we wish to estimate the difference in mean operating life between the two brands of batteries, using 90 percent confidence limits, the number of degrees of freedom to be used in conjuction with

$$\boxed{n_1 + n_2 - 2 = 25 - 2 = 23 \\ 0.05}$$

the t table is _____ , and the column heading used (proportion in each tail) is equal to _____ .

58 Estimate the difference between the mean operating life of the two brands of batteries, using 90 percent confidence limits and referring to any of the frames above for needed information. (Carry answer to two decimal places.)

$$\boxed{(\bar{X}_1 - \bar{X}_2) \pm t\hat{\sigma}_{\bar{X}_1 - \bar{X}_2} = \\ (22 - 18) \pm 1.714(2.059) \\ = 4 \pm 3.53 = 0.47 \text{ to} \\ 7.53 \text{ hours}}$$

Difference =

59 For the solution in Frame 58, what is the probability that the difference in mean operating life between the two brands of batteries is actually less than 0.47 hour?

0.05 (the proportion in the lower tail of the t distribution)

$P =$ _____

60 When we are concerned with the difference between means, note that the substitution of the z distribution for the t distribution has to follow a somewhat different evaluation from the single sample case because both samples contribute to the degrees of freedom available. Earlier in this chapter (Frame 13) we indicated that for the single sample case, sample size should be at least $n = 30$ (and so df $\geqslant 29$) in order to substitute the z distribution for the t distribution. In order to be consistent with the degrees of freedom required, therefore, in the case of the difference between means, the two samples should have a combined sample size of at least $n_1 + n_2 = $ ____ in order to use the z distribution in place of the t distribution.

31 (since df $= 29$ in this case, which is the same as when $n = 30$ for a single sample)

61 However, note again that use of the t distribution is based on the assumption that *each* population is normally distributed when the difference between means is being investigated. If the populations are *not* normally distributed, then the central-limit theorem requires that *each* sample be large, and not just that their combined size be large, in order to use the normal distribution assumption. Thus, suppose we wish to estimate the difference between means for two populations that are not normally distributed. If $n_1 = 20$ and $n_2 = 25$, df $= 43$. Can the z distribution be used in order to determine confidence limits in this case? [Yes / No] Why or why not?

_____

No; Because each sample has to be equal to 30 in order to invoke the central-limit theorem for each sampling distribution of the mean.

62 For the sampling situation described in Frame 61, above, can the t distribution be used to determine the confidence limits ?[Yes / No] Why or why not? _____

_____

_____

No; Because the t distribution is based on the assumption that the populations are normally distributed.

63 On the other hand, suppose that $n_1 = 10$, $n_2 = 15$, σ is not known, and the populations are assumed to be normal. The probability distribution that would be used to determine

t

z (as a substitute for the t; of course, the t distribution for df $= 48$ would yield more precise values)

confidence limits in this case is the ___ distribution. If each of the sample sizes is doubled, so that $n_1 = 20$ and $n_2 = 30$, the distribution that would be generally be used is the ___ distribution.

64 The normality assumption underlying the use of the t distribution is incorrectly overlooked in many instances, particularly when the user oversimplifies the role of the t distribution by considering it appropriate for any small-sample situation. Of course, the way to assure that the z distribution can be used for inferences about population means, regardless of the form of the population distribution, is to so design a research study that the sample from each population of interest is at least $n =$ ___ in size.

30

11.3 ■ Hypothesis Testing Using the t Distribution

Again, in problems involving the testing of hypotheses about the population mean or difference between means, if the sample size is less than 30 and the value of the standard error has been calculated on the basis of sample data, then the t distribution is used rather than the z, given normally distributed populations. The general formula which we introduced in Chapter 10 for computing the value of the z test statistic,

$$z = \frac{\text{(obs. value of statistic)} - \text{(hyp. value of parameter)}}{\text{standard error of the statistic}}$$

remains unchanged. But we use the t table rather than the z table in interpreting this ratio. To put it another way, the critical limits used in assessing the value of the critical ratio are defined in terms of t instead of z in this case.

65 Suppose that the production standard requires a mean battery operating life of $\mu = 22.0$ hours and the variability in ingredients is such that operating life is normally distributed and the standard deviation of operating life for all batteries being produced is $\sigma = 2.0$ hours. If a sample of $n = 9$ batteries has a mean operating life of $\bar{X} = 20.0$ hours, what are the critical z or t values with which the computed value should be compared, for a two-tailed test at the 5 percent level of significance? (Refer to any of the tables in the Appendix.)

−1.96; +1.96 (Values of z
are used in this case, since σ
is known.)

− _____ and + _____

66 Instead of the information in Frame 65, suppose that the production standard requires a mean operating life of $\mu = 22.0$ hours for the D cells and that for a sample of $n = 9$ batteries the mean operating life is $\overline{X} = 20.0$ hours with a standard deviation of $s = 3.0$ hours. Compute the value to be used in testing the population hypothesis.

$$\frac{20.0 - 22.0}{\dfrac{3.0}{\sqrt{9}}} = \frac{-2.0}{1.0} = -2.00$$

$$t = \frac{\overline{X} - \mu_H}{s_{\overline{X}}} =$$

67 Now we need to evaluate the computed t value of −2.00. In the figure below, post the critical values of t needed for significance at the 5 percent level (two-tailed) in this case. Refer to Table B-5 for these values.

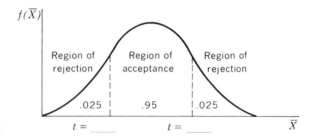

−2.306; +2.306 (df = 8)

68 Therefore the difference between the hypothesized mean and the sample mean in Frame 66 [is / is not] significant at the 5 percent level.

is not (Obtained t of −2.00 is within the region of acceptance of the null hypothesis.)

69 Suppose that we are concerned only about the possibility that the batteries are inferior to the production standard. Thus, $\mu_H \geqslant 22.0$ and $\mu_A < 22.0$. For this hypothesis, identify the general locations of the regions of acceptance and rejection of the null hypothesis on the figure below and indicate the proportion of area in each portion of the t distribution.

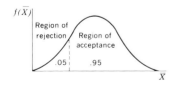

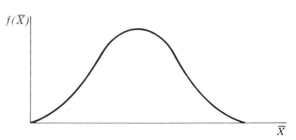

70 For testing the null hypothesis $\mu_H \geqslant 22.0$ the critical value of t for significance at the 5 percent level when $n = 9$ is ________ .

−1.860 (The sign is important.)

71 Evaluating the value of t computed in Frame 66 from the standpoint of a one-tailed test, we would conclude that at the 5 percent level the sample mean [is / is not] significantly lower than the hypothesized population mean.

is (The computed t of −2.00 is in the region of rejection.)

72 Of course, we can use the t distribution also for testing the difference between means. In Frame 55 we observed that a sample of 15 Foreverlast batteries had a mean operating life of 22.0 hours with a standard deviation of 6.0 hours and a sample of 10 Yamahoho batteries had a mean operating life of 18.0 hours with a standard deviation of 3.0 hours. In Frame 56 we found that the standard error of the difference $\hat{\sigma}_{\bar{X}_1 - \bar{X}_2} =$ ________ (value).

2.059

73 With the value identified in Frame 72, the value of t for testing the significance of the difference between the means is

$$t = \frac{\bar{X}_1 - \bar{X}_2}{\hat{\sigma}_{\bar{X}_1 - \bar{X}_2}} =$$

$$\frac{22 - 18}{2.059} = +1.94$$

74 For evaluating the t value computed in Frame 73 at the 1 percent level of significance, df = ________________, and thus the critical values of t are equal to ________ and ________.

$n_1 + n_2 - 2 = 25 - 2 = 23$

−2.807; +2.807

75 Comparing the computed t value of +1.94 with the critical t values of −2.807 and +2.807, we conclude that the null hypothesis is [accepted / rejected] at the 1 percent level of significance.

accepted (+1.94 is in the region of acceptance of the null hypothesis $\mu_1 = \mu_2$.)

76 Suppose that we anticipated the superiority of the Foreverlast batteries before seeing any of the sample results and that we wish to test this belief by giving the benefit of the doubt to the Yamahoho batteries. We formulate the null hypothesis $(\mu_F - \mu_Y)_H \leqslant 0$, with the alternative hypothesis being $(\mu_F - \mu_Y)_A > 0$. Under these conditions can we conclude that the Foreverlast batteries are superior, using the 1 percent level of significance? [Yes / No] Why or why not?
____
____
________________________________.

No; With the critical t-value of +2.500, the obtained t value of +1.94 is in the region of acceptance of the null hypothesis.

77 Just as in the use of the z distribution in hypothesis testing, we always run the risk of making an error when we either accept or reject the null hypothesis. Incorrectly accepting a false null hypothesis is termed a type ____ error; incorrectly rejecting a true null hypothesis is termed a type ____ error.

II

I (See Chapter 10, Frames 27–34, for a review of the types of errors in hypothesis testing.)

I

78 As was true for the z distribution, the level of significance used in hypothesis testing directly indicates the probability of a type ____ error associated with the critical value(s) of t.

11.4 ■ The Use of the Normal, Binomial, and t Distributions

In Chapters 9 and 10 we illustrated the appropriate use of the normal and binomial probability distributions in estimation and hypothesis testing, while in the present chapter we have given attention to the use of the t distribution. In these explanations we have also indicated the conditions under which the normal probability distribution can be used as a substitute for both the binomial and t probability distributions. In this section we briefly review the use of these three types of probability distributions in statistical inference, particularly with the view of clearly distinguishing the use of the t distribution from that of the binomial.

79 As we indicated in Chapters 9 and 10, when the binomial probability distribution is used in statistical inference, one of the characteristics of the data is that they are [discrete / continuous].

discrete

80 Thus, whenever we tabulate sample data in terms of counts, or in terms of proportions or percentages based on counts, the probability distribution most directly related to such data is the [normal / binomial].

binomial

81 However, as the size of the sample in which the counts are made is increased, the binomial distribution approaches the normal distribution in terms of its characteristics. The rule which we have followed is that the normal probability distribution can be used as a substitute for the binomial in the process of estimation or hypothesis testing whenever $n \geqslant$ ____ (number) and np and nq each are at least equal to ____ (number).

30

5

82 On the other hand, in this chapter we have observed that the t distribution is used solely in conjunction with statistical inference concerning [discrete / continuous] data.

continuous

83 Thus both the z and t distributions are basically directed toward the analysis of continuous measurements and their associated means. However, the t distribution is appropriately used in statistical inference concerning the population mean whenever the population is normally distributed and the _____ _____ of the population is unknown.

standard deviation (σ)

84 Again, under certain conditions the normal probability distribution can be used as a substitute for Student's t distribution. The general rule we use is that this substitution can be made if $n \geqslant$ _____ (value).

30

85 Thus, in statistical inference involving proportions, the two probability distributions most frequently used, depending on sample size, are the _____ and the _____ probability distributions.

binomial; normal

86 In statistical inference involving means, the two types of distributions most frequently used are the _____ and the ___ distributions.

normal; t

87 Would the t distribution ever be used in testing a hypothesis concerning the value of a population proportion? [Yes / No]

No (Either the binomial distribution or the normal distribution, as a substitute, would be used.)

Review

88 (Frames 1-4) When a set of sample means is normally distributed, we can say with assurance that the conversion of these means into values of z will result in the unit normal distribution, regardless of sample size, when the formula used for this conversion is

$$\frac{\overline{X} - \mu}{\sigma_{\overline{X}}}$$

$z =$

89 (Frames 5-8) On the other hand, when $s_{\overline{X}}$ is the divisor in the formula in Frame 88, the value of the divisor is not a constant from sample to sample, because the value of ___ will vary from sample to sample.

s (the sample standard deviation)

90 (Frame 9) The symbol z is used in conjunction with the unit normal distribution only; the distribution of values generated by the formula $(\overline{X} - \mu)/s_{\overline{X}}$ is designated as the ___ distribution.

t

91 (Frames 10, 11) As compared with the normal probability distribution, which is symmetrical and mesokurtic, Student's t distribution is symmetrical and _____ .

92 (Frames 12-14) It can be shown that the t distribution approaches the characteristics of the normal distribution as ___ increases. For purposes of practical application, we substitute the normal probability distribution for use of the t distribution whenever $n \geqslant$ _____ .

93 (Frames 15-17) On the other hand, in statistical inference concerning the population mean, the t distribution must be used whenever the population is normally distributed, ___ is unknown, and $n <$ _____ .

94 (Frames 18-23) As compared with the z distribution, a t distribution has proportionally more of its area in the [center / tails] of the distribution, thus resulting in confidence intervals that are [narrower / wider] and critical values of t in hypothesis testing that are [larger / smaller] in absolute value than those associated with use of the z distribution.

95 (Frames 24-32) In using the t table, there is a separate distribution of t for each of the possible degrees of freedom. In testing a hypothesis concerning the value of the population mean when the sample mean is based on 25 measurements, the number of degrees of freedom is _____ .

96 (Frames 33-41) The values in the t table and z table are identical when df = ___ .

97 (Frames 42-52) The formula used for specifying the confidence interval for estimating the population mean when the population is normally distributed, the standard deviation of the population of measurements is unknown, and the sample size is smaller than 30 is

Interval =

98 (Frames 53-59) Because the use of the t distribution in respect to differences between means requires the assumption that the standard deviations of the two populations are equal, the formula used to estimate the difference between two population means when t is used is:

Difference $= \overline{X}_1 - \overline{X}_2 \pm t\hat{\sigma}_{\overline{X}_1 - \overline{X}_2}$

If the two sample means are each based on an n of 15, the number of degrees of freedom used in conjunction with the t table is _____ .

$30 - 2 = 28$

---

99 (Frames 60-64) Given that the two populations are normally distributed, the probability distribution that would generally be used for estimating the difference between means when $n_1 = 20$ and $n_2 = 25$ is the _____ distribution.

---

normal

---

100 (Frames 65-71) In using the t distribution for testing a hypothesis concerning the value of the population mean, the value of t is computed by the formula

---

$$\frac{\overline{X} - \mu_H}{s_{\overline{X}}}$$

$t =$

---

101 (Frames 72-78) Similarly, we can test the difference between means by the formula

$$t = \frac{\overline{X}_1 - \overline{X}_2}{\hat{\sigma}_{\overline{X}_1 - \overline{X}_2}}$$

If $n_1 = 12$ and $n_2 = 14$ and we wish to test the null hypothesis $(\mu_1 - \mu_2)_H \leqslant 0$ at the 5 percent level of significance, then in using the t table (refer to Table B-5 if you wish), df = _____ and the heading of the column in the table to be used is [0.025 / 0.05 / 0.10].

$26 - 2 = 24$

0.05 (This is a one-tailed test; use $+t$ only, in this case.)

---

102 (Frames 79-87) Under certain conditions the normal probability distribution can be used as a substitute for both the _____ and the ___ distributions. Can the t distribution ever be used as a substitute for the binomial distribution? [Yes / No]

---

binomial; t

No

Symbols Introduced in This Chapter (with Frame Numbers)

(9) t

Refers to the t distribution, which is used in place of the unit normal distribution (z) under certain circumstances.

(32) df

Degrees of freedom.

(55) $\hat{\sigma}$

Pooled estimate of a population standard deviation.

(56) $\hat{\sigma}_{\overline{X}_1 - \overline{X}_2}$

Standard error of the difference between means when the standard deviations of the two populations are assumed to be equal.

Formulas Introduced in This Chapter (with Frame Numbers)

(32) $df = n - 1$

Degrees of freedom used in conjunction with the t distribution when testing a hypothesis concerning the population mean or when estimating the value of the population mean.

(44) $\bar{X} \pm ts_{\bar{X}}$

Confidence interval for the population mean by using the t distribution.

(51) $N\bar{X} \pm Nts_{\bar{X}}$

or $N(\bar{X} \pm ts_{\bar{X}})$

Confidence interval for the total quantity in a population determined by using the t distribution.

(53) $(\bar{X}_1 - \bar{X}_2) \pm t\hat{\sigma}_{\bar{X}_1 - \bar{X}_2}$

Confidence interval for the difference between the means of two populations determined by using the t distribution.

(54) $df = n_1 + n_2 - 2$

Degrees of freedom used in conjunction with the t distribution when testing a hypothesis concerning the difference between population means.

(55) $\hat{\sigma} = \sqrt{\dfrac{(n_1 - 1)s_1^2 + (n_2 - 1)s_2^2}{n_1 + n_2 - 2}}$

Pooled estimate of a population standard deviation based on the standard deviations of two samples.

(56) $\hat{\sigma}_{\bar{X}_1 - \bar{X}_2} = \sqrt{\dfrac{\hat{\sigma}^2}{n_1} + \dfrac{\hat{\sigma}^2}{n_2}}$

Standard error of the mean based on using a pooled estimate of the population standard deviation.

(66) $t = \dfrac{\bar{X} - \mu_H}{s_{\bar{X}}}$

Testing a hypothesized value of the population mean by use of the t distribution.

(73) $t = \dfrac{\bar{X}_1 - \bar{X}_2}{\sigma_{\bar{X}_1 - \bar{X}_2}}$

Testing the difference between means by use of the t distribution.

EXERCISES

(Solutions on pages 608–611)

11.1 Describe the situation in which it is appropriate to use the t distribution in testing a hypothesis concerning the population mean.

11.2 The t distribution is platykurtic and symmetrical, whereas the normal distribution is mesokurtic and symmetrical. Why is it, then, that the assumption that the population is normally distributed has to be made in conjunction with using the t distribution?

11.3 Each of a random sample of 10 packages of cereal has the contents, in ounces, listed in the table below.

Ounces per package

11.8	12.0
11.7	11.7
12.1	12.0
11.9	11.8
12.0	12.0

(a) Compute the mean for this sample.
(b) Compute the sample standard deviation.
(c) Compute the standard error of the mean.
(d) Assuming that the population of weights is normally distributed, estimate the average contents of cereal per package for the population from which this sample was taken, using 95 percent confidence limits.

11.4 For the data of Exercise 11.3, above, the required minimum average weight per package is 12.0 ounces. On the basis of this sample, can we reject the hypothesis that this requirement is being satisfied at the 5 percent level of significance?

11.5 A random sample of 25 employees in a small firm employing 100 people earn an average hourly wage of $4.75 with a standard deviation of 25 cents. Estimate the average hourly wage of all 100 employees to the nearest cent, using 95 percent confidence limits. The wages are assumed to be normally distributed.

11.6 For the situation described in Exercise 11.5, above, suppose that an industrial development advisor had earlier indicated that the average hourly wage paid by the firm is at least $4.85. Can his claim be rejected at the 5 percent level?

11.7 A random sample of 10 No. 303 cans of peas is taken in a canning plant, and the mean weight for the drained peas is found to be 11.0 ounces with a standard deviation of 0.30 ounce. Assuming that the weights are normally distributed, estimate the average drained weight of the peas contained in No. 303 cans, using 95 percent confidence limits.

11.8 For the data of Exercise 11.7, above, suppose that the average net weight specified per can is 11.2 ounces (drained). Assuming that we are concerned only about the alternative that the contents are underweight, rather than overweight, can we accept the null hypothesis that the average weight of drained peas for all cans being processed is at least 11.2 ounces, using the 5 percent level of significance?

11.9 In addition to the data in Exercise 11.7, 10 randomly selected cans of peas at another plant have a mean drained weight of 10.8 ounces with a standard deviation of 0.20 ounce. Estimate the amount of difference in the average weight of peas included in No. 303 cans for the two plants, using 90 percent confidence limits.

11.10 For the data of Exercise 11.9, above, test the null hypothesis that there is no difference between the mean weights packed at the two canning plants, using the 5 percent level of significance.

ADDITIONAL
EXERCISES

11.11 Describe the effects of incorrectly using the z distribution instead of the t distribution in estimating the population mean and in testing hypotheses concerning the population mean.

11.12 For practical purposes, the z distribution is used as a substitute for the t distribution when df $\geqslant 29$. Therefore, in testing a hypothesis concerning the difference between two population means, does this imply that the z distribution can *always* be used when $n_1 + n_2 \geqslant 31$? Specifically, is it necessary to assume normality of the two population distributions in this case?

11.13 An analyst in a personnel department randomly selects the records of 16 hourly employees and finds that the mean wage rate per hour is $5.50. The wage rates in the firm are assumed to be normally distributed. If the standard deviation of the wage rates is known to be $1.00, estimate the mean wage rate in the firm using an 80 percent confidence interval.

11.14 Referring to Exercise 11.13, suppose that the standard deviation of the population is not known, but that the standard deviation of the sample is $1.00. Estimate the mean wage rate in the firm using an 80 percent confidence interval.

11.15 The mean diameter of a sample of $n = 12$ cylindrical rods included in a shipment is 2.350 millimeters with a standard deviation of 0.050 millimeter. The distribution of the diameters of all of the rods included in the shipment is assumed to be approximately normal. Determine the 99 percent confidence interval for estimating the mean diameter of all of the rods included in the shipment.

11.16 For a particular consumer product, the mean dollar sales per retail outlet last year in a sample of $n_1 = 10$ stores was $\bar{X}_1 = \$3,425$ with $s_1 = \$200$. For a second product the mean dollar sales per outlet in a sample of $n_2 = 12$ stores was $\bar{X}_2 = \$3,250$ with $s_2 = \$175$. The sales amounts per outlet are assumed to be normally distributed with equal population variances for the two products. Estimate the difference between the mean level of sales per outlet last year using a 95 percent confidence interval.

11.17 From the data in Exercise 11.16, suppose the two sample sizes were $n_1 = 20$ and $n_2 = 24$. Determine the 95 percent confidence interval for the difference between the two means.

11.18 A fast-foods chain will build a new outlet in a proposed location if at least 200 cars per hour pass the location during certain prime hours. For 20 randomly sampled hours during the prime periods, the average number of cars passing the location is $\bar{X} = 208.5$ with $s = 30.0$. The statistical population is assumed to be approximately normal. The management of the chain conservatively adopted the null hypothesis that the traffic volume does *not* satisfy their requirement, i.e., $\mu_H \leqslant 200.0$. Can this hypothesis be rejected at the 5 percent level of significance?

11.19 Suppose the sample results in Exercise 11.18 are based on a sample of $n = 50$ hours. Can the null hypothesis be rejected at the 5 percent level of significance?

11.20 An automatic dispenser for soft ice cream has been set to dispense 4.00 ounces of ice cream per serving. For a sample of $n = 10$ servings, the average amount of ice cream is $\bar{X} = 4.05$ ounces with $s = 0.10$ ounce. The amounts being dispensed are assumed to be normally distributed. Basing the null hypothesis on the assumption that the process is "in control," should the dispenser be reset as a result of a test at the 5 percent level of significance?

11.21 A shipment of 100 defective machines has been received in a machine-repair department. For a random sample of 10 of the machines, the average time required to repair them is $\bar{X} = 85.0$ minutes, with $s = 15.0$ minutes. Test the null hypothesis, $\mu_H = 100.0$ minutes, using the 10 percent level of significance and based on the assumption that the distribution of repair time is approximately normal.

11.22 As reported in Exercise 11.16, for one consumer product the mean dollar sales per retail outlet last year in a sample of $n_1 = 10$ stores was $\bar{X}_1 = \$3,425$ with $s_1 = \$200$. For a second product the mean dollar sales per outlet in a sample of $n_2 = 12$ stores was $\bar{X}_2 = \$3,250$ with $s_2 = \$175$. The sales amounts per outlet are assumed to be normally distributed with equal population variances for the two products. Test the null hypothesis that there is no difference between the mean dollar sales for the two products using the 1 percent level of significance.

11.23 For the data reported in Exercise 11.22, suppose the two sample sizes were $n_1 = 20$ and $n_2 = 24$. Test the difference between the two means at the 1 percent level of significance.

11.24 A probability sample of 30 shoppers at a regional shopping center are surveyed regarding the amount of their dollar purchases at the shopping center during the immediately preceding weekly period. The average (mean) amount reported is $45.50 with a sample standard deviation of $15.80. There is good reason to believe that the dollar purchase amounts for the population of consumers are normally distributed. Using 95 percent confidence limits, estimate the population mean by the *two* methods that are acceptable in this case and compare your results.

11.25 For the situation described in Exercise 11.24, above, a shopping center representative had claimed that the average dollar purchases are at least $50 per week. Using the 5 percent level of significance, can this claim be rejected when the t distribution is used? Can the claim be rejected when the z distribution is used?

11.26 A manager is considering the purchase of several electronic calculators to be used for general computational purposes in the company offices. The price of two competitive models is comparable and the sales representative for each model claims that his model has features that will result in less time spent doing the computational work required in the offices. In order to compare the two machines the manager obtains a "loaner" from each company and determines the time required to perform a set of computational routines that are typical of the work done in the office. Of course, in carrying out the comparison the manager was careful to use several operators who are equally skilled, who do not have an established preference for one type of machine, and who had sufficient practice time to learn the use and unique features of each machine. For the first machine the mean time required for the computations was 13.5 minutes with a sample standard deviation of 3.5 minutes for 12 randomly selected employees. For the second machine the sample mean was 12.4 minutes with a standard deviation of 3.0 minutes for a second sample of 12 randomly selected employees. Determine if the difference between the sample means is statistically significant, using the 5 percent level for the test.

11.27 Two different sales incentive systems are introduced into territory A and territory B by a company's sales manager. Prior to the change the average sales level per salesman was about the same in the two regions. During the three-month comparison period the 15 salesmen in territory A have average weekly sales of $2,500 with a standard deviation of $500 and the 10 salesmen in territory B have an average sales of $2,150 with a standard deviation of $400. Assuming that the overall distribution of sales amount per salesman is normally distributed, test the null hypothesis that the average sales level associated with the two incentive systems is not in fact different, using the 5 percent level of significance.

11.28 For the situation described in Exercise 11.27, above, suppose that the incentive system used in territory B was hypothesized to be equal to or better than the other system. Can this hypothesis be rejected using the 5 percent level of significance?

11.29 The management of a company which is about to institute a new retirement plan claims that at least 70 percent of the employees favor the plan. For a random sample of 20 employees, 8 employees, or a proportion of 0.40, report that they favor the new plan. Can the management claim that a proportion of at least 0.70 favor the plan be rejected, using the 5 percent level of significance?

11.30 The promotional literature for a franchise opportunity for a gift store includes the claim that the customers of established stores spend an average of at least $10 each on purchases. A prospective investor in the franchise offering visits an established store in a nearby city and observes the purchase amounts for 20 customers at randomly selected times during the period of his visit. The average (mean) purchase amount for the sample is $8.80 with a standard deviation of $3.85. Giving the "benefit of the doubt" to the promotional claim, determine if the claim can be rejected at the 5 percent level of significance.

CHAPTER 12 ■
THE CHI-SQUARE TEST

Whenever sample data represent counts of various outcomes, the χ^2 (chi-square) test can be used to test the significance of the difference between the pattern of the obtained and the expected frequencies. Because available data can often be expressed in the form of counts, even though more precise methods of measurement were originally used, the χ^2 (pronounced "kī-square") test is versatile in its application as a hypothesis-testing procedure. In this chapter we consider some of the general assumptions underlying the use of this test, illustrate the computational procedure for one-way as well as two-way classification tables, and consider the meaning of a significant χ^2 value.

12.1 ■ Introduction

Since the χ^2 (chi-square) distribution is used in conjunction with the analysis of frequencies, it is similar to the binomial distribution in terms of some of the assumptions underlying its use. This is so because both distributions are concerned with the analysis of discrete data which represent counts, although for the binomial distribution the data are frequently analyzed in the form of proportions or percentages rather than as categorized frequencies. Although the χ^2 distribution has use in a variety of statistical procedures, the present chapter is concerned only with its use in certain types of hypothesis-testing problems (and hence this chapter is entitled "The Chi-square Test"). Whereas the binomial distribution can be used to determine if the difference between a single expected and a single obtained frequency or proportion is significant, the χ^2 distribution can be used to determine if the difference between an entire pattern of expected as contrasted to obtained frequencies is significant.

1 Like the normal, binomial, and t distributions discussed in previous chapters, the χ^2 distribution is used in conjunction with statistical inference. Unlike the distributions previously discussed, however, we shall be concerned with its use only in certain types of [estimation / hypothesis-testing] procedures.

hypothesis-testing

2 The χ^2 test is always applied to tabled data that contain frequencies, or counts, and thus the values analyzed are represented as [continuous / discrete] data.

discrete

3 As is true for any application of the methods of statistical inference, it is necessary that the sampled data which are analyzed qualify as a probability (random) sample and that

be (See Sections 8.1 and 8.2 for a review of sampling.)

the sampled and target populations [be / not be] the same.

4 As part of the requirement of probability sampling, the outcome (classification) of each event or item must not be affected by other particular outcomes. That is, each event

independent (See Section 5.4 for a review.)

must be [independent / dependent] .

5 Also, as for the binomial distribution, each observed outcome must apply to only one of the possible categories.

exclusive (See Section 5.3 for a review.)

That is, the events must be mutually _____ .

6 Thus the frequencies being tabulated for a subsequent analysis by the χ^2 test must be based upon a probability

independent

mutually exclusive (But there can be more than two categories of outcomes; this is unlike the requirement for the binomial distribution.)

sample, and they must be for events that are _____ and

_____ .

7 With a given number of categories of data, the larger the difference between observed and expected frequencies, the larger the value of χ^2. This being the case, the null hypothesis suggesting that there is no difference between the observed and the expected frequencies would be rejected when the

high

computed χ^2 is relatively [high / low] in value.

8 Thus the computed χ^2 is similar to the computed value of z or t in hypothesis testing in that critical values of χ^2 associated

can

with various significance levels [can / cannot] be specified beforehand.

9 Furthermore the critical values of χ^2 vary with the degrees of freedom associated with the data. From this standpoint the

t (And thus there are actually a number of χ^2 distributions, one associated with each degree of freedom.)

distribution of χ^2 is similar to the [z / t] distribution.

10 Table 12-1 summarizes the general steps to be completed in conjunction with using the χ^2 test. Note that the procedure

similar to (for example, see Table 10-3 on page 262)

is [similar to / different from] the procedure used when the normal distribution is used in hypothesis testing.

1 State the null hypothesis and the alternative hypothesis.
2 Identify the critical χ^2 value.
3 Compute the value of χ^2 for the sample data.
4 Compare the computed χ^2 value with the critical χ^2 value and accept or reject the null hypothesis accordingly.

expected	

11 In terms of its application, the χ^2 test can be used to test data for goodness of fit and for the independence of two classification systems, or two variables. The *goodness-of-fit test* always involves the comparison of one row (or one column) of observed frequencies with the associated [observed / expected] frequencies.

fit	

12 For example, comparing the observed pattern of unit sales with the expected unit sales for five sales territories would involve a goodness-of-_____ test.

more than one	
more than one (resulting in a two-way table)	

13 On the other hand, the null hypothesis in testing for *independence* is that there is no interaction between, say, type of product sold and sales territory. Thus the tabled observed frequencies for such a test always include [one / more than one] row and [one / more than one] column.

observed; expected (either order)	

14 We shall further consider the meaning of a significant χ^2 value in Section 12.4. Sections 12.2 and 12.3, which follow, are devoted to the computation of χ^2 values for various types of tests. No matter what the particular purpose of the test, the value of χ^2 is dependent on the relationship between _____ frequencies and _____ frequencies of tabled data.

12.2 ▪ Comparing Observed Frequencies with Expected Frequencies

To begin with, in this section we illustrate the computational procedure connected with the χ^2 (chi-square) test in the simplest situation: that in which a set of observed frequencies is analyzed to determine the probability that the set represents a chance deviation from an expected set of frequencies. For such a *goodness-of-fit test* we need to know both the observed and the expected frequencies of the various categories of outcomes, but we need not know the value of any other statistic, such as the mean or the standard deviation of measured outcomes.

15 Suppose we toss a coin 50 times and obtain 20 heads and 30 tails as the observed outcomes. Complete the table below by indicating the expected frequency of heads and tails on 50 tosses of a fair coin.

	Heads	Tails
Observed frequency, f_o	20	30
Expected frequency, f_e	___	___

25; 25

16 As observed frequencies depart more and more from expected frequencies, we are less inclined to accept the coin as being a fair coin. The null hypothesis that the population from which the sample was obtained does not differ from the fair-coin assumption can be tested by use of the ___ test.

χ^2

17 Essentially, for the null hypothesis to be accepted, the observed differences between obtained and expected frequencies must be attributable to chance (sampling) variability. The formula used to compute the value of the χ^2 test statistic is:

$$\chi^2 = \sum \frac{(f_o - f_e)^2}{f_e}$$

Thus the expected frequency for each cell of the table is subtracted from the _____ frequency and the difference is squared and divided by the expected frequency [before / after] being summed with the comparable fractions for the other categories of counts.

observed

before

18 With reference to the formula in Frame 17, can the value of χ^2 ever be negative? [Yes / No] _____

No (since the differences are squared)

19 What would a computed χ^2 value of zero indicate? _____
_____

That the observed frequencies exactly matched the expected frequencies.

20 Given the following data and formula, compute the value of χ^2, recognizing that there are two fractions that are to be summed in this case.

	Heads	Tails
f_o	20	30
f_e	25	25

$\dfrac{(20 - 25)^2}{25} + \dfrac{(30 - 25)^2}{25}$
$= \dfrac{25}{25} + \dfrac{25}{25} = 2.00$

$\chi^2 = \sum \dfrac{(f_o - f_e)^2}{f_e} = \underline{\hspace{1.5cm}} + \underline{\hspace{1.5cm}} =$

21 As was true for the t test, there is a whole family of χ^2 distributions, based on the degrees of freedom involved, and the meaning of a given χ^2 value depends on the number of degrees of freedom, or df. When the observed frequencies can all be listed along one dimension (one row or one column), there are $k - 1$ degrees of freedom, where k is the number of categories of observed frequencies. Therefore, for the χ^2 computed in Frame 20:

$$df = k - 1 = \underline{\hspace{2cm}}$$

2 − 1 = 1 (Thus, with n specified, the frequency for just *one* of the two cells can vary freely.)

22 Table B-6 in the Appendix identifies the critical χ^2 values for significance at the 5 and 1 percent levels, according to degrees of freedom. According to the table, when df = 1, the critical value of χ^2 for the difference to be considered significant at the 0.05 level is _____, and the value necessary for significance at the 0.01 level is _____ .

3.84

6.63

23 Therefore the difference between the observed and expected frequencies of Frame 20 [is / is not] significant at the 1 percent level and [is / is not] significant at the 5 percent level. At the 5 percent level, the null hypothesis that the coin is fair would be [accepted / rejected] .

is not

is not (The obtained χ^2 of 2.00 is less than either critical value.)

accepted

24 For 20 out of 60 throws of a six-sided die the value "4" has been observed on the face of the die. Complete the table below, indicating the observed frequencies as contrasted to the expected frequencies for a fair die.

	4	4'
fo	___	___
fe	___	___

20	40
10	50

25 For the data in Frame 24 calculate the value of χ^2 .

$$\chi^2 = \sum \frac{(f_o - f_e)^2}{f_e} = \underline{\hspace{1.5cm}} + \underline{\hspace{1.5cm}} =$$

$\dfrac{(20 - 10)^2}{10} + \dfrac{(40 - 50)^2}{50} =$

$\dfrac{100}{10} + \dfrac{100}{50} = 10 + 2 = 12.00$

26 Refer to Table B-6. Is the computed value of χ^2 in Frame 25 significant at the 0.01 level? [Yes / No] Explain: _____

_____

_____

Yes; with df = 1 the critical value of χ^2 for significance at this level is 6.63.

27 Since the problems in Frames 15 and 24 had just two categories of observed frequencies, they could have been approached as hypothesis-testing problems for proportions. Refer to the data of Frame 24 and use p to represent the sample proportion for the outcome "4" and q for "not 4." In this case, then $\pi_H = \frac{1}{6} = 0.17$, $p = \underline{\hspace{1cm}}$, and $q = \underline{\hspace{1cm}}$.

> 0.33
>
> 0.67

28 Since $n > 30$, $n\pi > 5$, and $n(1 - \pi) > 5$, we can use the normal distribution as an approximation of the binomial to test the null hypothesis concerning the difference between the obtained and the expected proportion (see Section 10.7 for a review), with

$$\sigma_p = \sqrt{\frac{\pi_H(1 - \pi_H)}{n}} = \sqrt{\frac{(0.17)(0.83)}{60}} \doteq 0.05$$

> $\dfrac{0.33 - 0.17}{0.05} = \dfrac{0.16}{0.05} = +3.20$

$$z = \frac{p - \pi_H}{\sigma_p} =$$

> is (Since the critical $z = \pm$ 2.58, the computed value of +3.20 is in a region of rejection.); reject

Therefore the difference [is / is not] significant at the 1 percent level and we would [accept / reject] the null hypothesis that the die is fair.

29 Thus either method of testing the null hypothesis leads to its rejection in the above example. Now turning our attention to a problem involving more than two categories of observed frequencies, suppose that a sales region has been divided into five territories, each of which was judged to have an equal sales potential. The actual sales volume for several sampled days is indicated in the chart below. Post the expected sales volume for each territory in the chart.

	Territory				
	A	B	C	D	E
Actual unit sales, fo	110	130	70	90	100
Expected unit sales, fe	___	___	___	___	___

> 100 for each space (since the null hypothesis is that overall sales are equally divided among the five territories)

30 In applying the χ^2 test to the data in Frame 29,

> $k - 1 = 5 - 1 = 4$

$df = \underline{\hspace{2cm}}$

31 Compute the value of χ^2 for the frequencies posted in Frame 29.

$$\frac{100}{100} + \frac{900}{100} + \frac{900}{100} + \frac{100}{100} +$$
$$\frac{0}{100} = \frac{2,000}{100} = 20.00$$

$$\chi^2 = \sum \frac{(f_o - f_e)^2}{f_e} =$$

32 Are the differences between observed and expected values significant at the 0.05 level? [Yes / No] Explain:_____

Yes; With df $= 4$, a χ^2 of 9.49 is needed for significance at the 0.05 level. (Note that with the comparison of five categories of frequencies, the binomial or normal probability distribution could *not* have been used for this problem.)

_____

_____

_____

12.3 ▪ Contingency Tables

All of the computational examples introduced thus far have involved the use of one-way classification tables, in that the categories of observed frequencies could all be indicated along a single row (or in a single column). When the categories of events being analyzed fall into two or more rows and two or more columns, a two-way classification table, or contingency table, is involved. As contrasted to the one-way classification table, the contingency table always concerns classification on the basis of two variables, rather than just one. In this section we describe the computational method for determining the expected frequency for each cell of a contingency table and for determining the degrees of freedom which are involved.

33 When all the classifications in a table concern a single dimension or variable, so that all categories can be listed along a single row or column, a ____-way classification table is involved in the analysis.

one

34 In contrast, a two-way classification table, or _____ table, involves analysis on the basis of two variables.

contingency

35 We use the expression $r \times k$ to represent the number of rows and number of columns, respectively, in the contingency table. Thus all one-way classification tables with one row of data can be represented as being ____ (number) $\times$ k tables.

1 (since there is always only one row)

36 Where $r \times k$ identifies the number of rows and columns in a contingency table, the simplest such two-way table has two rows and two columns. Therefore such a table can be designated as a ___ X ___ table.

37 For contingency tables the number of degrees of freedom is equal to $(r - 1)(k - 1)$. For a 2 X 2 table, therefore, the number of degrees of freedom is always equal to _____ _____ (number).

$$(2 - 1)(2 - 1) = (1)(1) = 1$$

38 Table 12-2a indicates the observed number of favorable, neutral, and unfavorable reactions to a television commercial by a random sample of men and women viewers. In terms of $r \times k$, this is a ___ X ___ table.

$$3 \times 2$$

Table 12-2a ■ Observed Reactions to a Television Commercial

	Sex		
Reaction	Men	Women	Total
Favorable	28	52	80
Neutral	20	20	40
Unfavorable	52	28	80
Total	100	100	200

39 The frequencies posted in the cells of Table 12-2a are all [observed / expected] frequencies. The degrees of freedom to be used in interpreting the value of χ^2 (chi-square) to be computed are _____ .

observed

$$(3 - 1)(2 - 1) = 2$$

40 In order to calculate the expected frequency for each cell of Table 12-2b, we make use of the marginal totals of Table 12-2a. The general formula for f_e is $f_r f_k / n$, where f_r is the sum of the frequencies posted in the row in which the cell is located, f_k is the sum of the frequencies in the column in which the cell is located, and n is the sum of all the frequencies in the table. Thus for the cell in row 1 and column 1 of Table 12-2b, the expected frequency is

$$\frac{(80)(100)}{200} = \frac{8,000}{200} = 40$$

$$f_e = \frac{f_r f_k}{n} =$$

Table 12-2b ■ Expected Reactions to a Television Commercial

	Sex		
Reaction	Men	Women	Total
Favorable	___	___	80
Neutral	___	___	40
Unfavorable	___	___	80
Total	100	100	200

41 Complete Table 12-2*b* by determining the expected frequency of each cell corresponding to the observed frequency in Table 12-2*a*.

42 Because the marginal totals in the contingency table and in the table of expected frequencies are the same, not all of the expected cell frequencies have to be computed using the formula provided above. Instead, many of the expected frequencies can be determined by subtraction from marginal totals. For example, once the expected frequency of 40 has been computed for the cell in row 1 and column 1, the expected frequency for the adjoining cell in row 1 and column 2 can be determined by subtracting ___ (number) from the marginal total of ___ (number).

43 As a matter of fact, for a 3 × 2 contingency table, once we have computed the expected frequency f_e for any two cells in different rows, the other four expected frequencies can be determined by subtraction from marginal totals. This is a direct indication that for a 3 × 2 table df = ___ (number).

44 Now, using the data in Tables 12-2*a* and 12-2*b*, calculate the value of χ^2.

$$\chi^2 = \sum \frac{(f_o - f_e)^2}{f_e} =$$

45 Refer to Table B-6 in the Appendix. Is the obtained χ^2 value of 14.40 significant at the 1 percent level? [Yes / No] Therefore, at this level of significance the null hypothesis that the television viewer's sex and the reaction to a commercial are independent (i.e., not related) is [accepted / rejected].

46 In Section 12.4, which follows, we further consider the meaning of a significant χ^2 value computed for a contingency table. For the present, and with reference to Table 12-2*a*, note that the significant χ^2 obtained in this case [does / does not] indicate that the total number of men and women repondents differed, and it [does / does not] indicate *general* favorability or unfavorability of reactions to the commercial.

47 As another computational example of the use of the χ^2 test in conjunction with a contingency table, Table 12-3*a* presents an analysis of the types of insurance policies sold by three different insurance agents during several randomly sampled time periods. The contingency table is of the dimensions ___ X ___ .

$$3 \times 3$$

Table 12-3a ▪ Types of Insurance Policies Sold by Three Agents

Type of policy	Agent			Total
	A	B	C	
A	20	12	28	60
B	10	4	4	18
C	10	24	8	42
Total	40	40	40	120

Table 12-3b ▪ Expected Sales of Insurance Policies

Type of policy	Agent			Total
	A	B	C	
A	___	___	___	60
B	___	___	___	18
C	___	___	___	42
Total	40	40	40	120

48 Calculate the expected frequencies for this contingency table and enter them in Table 12-3b.

$$f_e = \frac{f_r f_k}{n}$$

20	20	20
6	6	6
14	14	14

49 Now calculate the value of χ^2 for the data.

$$\chi^2 = \sum \frac{(f_o - f_e)^2}{f_e} =$$

$$\frac{0}{20} + \frac{-8^2}{20} + \frac{8^2}{20} + \frac{4^2}{6} + \frac{-2^2}{6}$$

$$+ \frac{-2^2}{6} + \frac{-4^2}{14} + \frac{10^2}{14} + \frac{-6^2}{14}$$

$$= \frac{128}{20} + \frac{24}{6} + \frac{152}{14} = 21.26$$

50 What is the value of df to be used in interpreting this χ^2 test statistic?

$$(r - 1)(k - 1) = (2)(2) = 4$$

df = _____ (number)

51 Is the obtained χ^2 value significant at the 5 percent level of significance? [Yes / No] Therefore at this level of significance the null hypothesis that there is no difference in the types of policies sold by the three agents is [accepted / rejected].

Yes (With df = 4, the critical value of χ^2 for the 0.05 level is 9.49.)

rejected

12.4 ■ Interpretation of the χ^2 (Chi-square) Test

The computational examples of Sections 12.2 and 12.3 have illustrated the kinds of data to which the χ^2 (chi-square) test can be applied. As a method of hypothesis testing, the χ^2 test is used for the two general types of purposes we introduced in Section 12.1, corresponding to the format of the data being analyzed. The application of the χ^2 test in a one-way classification table involves testing for *goodness of fit*, whereas its application to a contingency table involves testing for *independence* between the two variables that serve as the basis for classification in a two-way contingency table.

52 As we indicated in Section 12.1, computation of a χ^2 value for a one-way classification table always involves testing for [goodness of fit / independence of classification].

goodness of fit

53 The distribution of expected frequencies for a one-way table may follow a binomial, normal, Poisson, uniform, or any other distribution in applying the χ^2 test for the purpose of testing for _____ .

goodness of fit

54 For the previous examples of one-way tables in this chapter, the determination of expected frequencies was straightforward because the expected frequencies were all uniform in value. Refer, however, to the data of Table 12-4. Determination of the expected frequencies in this case necessitates use of the _____ distribution.

binomial

Table 12-4 ■ Number of Heads on 20 Tosses of Two Coins

	Number of heads		
	0	1	2
Observed frequency	4	8	8
Expected frequency	___	___	___

55 In order to determine the expected frequencies in Table 12-4, the probability of each of the three outcomes has to be determined by identifying the values of p and q and expanding the binomial to the appropriate power. Alternatively, we can obtain the probability values from Table B-2 in the Appendix. With $n = 2$ and $p = 0.50$, the probability values associated with obtaining 0, 1, and 2 heads on two coins are _____ , _____ , and _____ , respectively.

0.25
0.50; 0.25

56 With $n = 20$, and using the probabilities just determined in Frame 55, calculate the expected frequencies for Table 12-4 and enter them in the appropriate cells of the table.

5; 10; 5

57 Now determine the value of χ^2 based on the differences between observed and expected frequencies for the data of Table 12-4.

$$\frac{(4-5)^2}{5} + \frac{(8-10)^2}{10} +$$

$$\frac{(8-5)^2}{5} = \frac{1}{5} + \frac{4}{10} + \frac{9}{5} =$$

$$\frac{24}{10} = 2.40$$

$$\chi^2 = \sum \frac{(f_o - f_e)^2}{f_e} =$$

58 What are the degrees of freedom to be used in interpreting this χ^2 value of 2.40?

$(k-1) = (3-1) = 2$

df = _____

59 Refer to Table B-6. Is the difference significant at the 5 percent level? [Yes / No] Therefore, at this level of significance the null hypothesis that the coins are fair is [accepted / rejected].

No (With df = 2 the critical value of χ^2 for the 5 percent level is 5.99.); accepted

60 In terms of goodness of fit, therefore, the observed distribution of sample data [would / would not] be accepted as conforming to the theoretical distribution for the population, which in this case follows the _____ distribution.

would

binomial

61 In addition to testing for goodness of fit, the χ^2 test can be used also to test for independence of the two variables which are the basis for a contingency table. In this case the observed frequencies are posted in a [one-way classification table / two-way classification table].

two-way classification table

62 Any time the χ^2 test is applied to an $r \times k$ table for which r and k are greater than 1, the χ^2 test is being used as a test of [goodness of fit / the independence of two variables].

the independence of two variables

63 For example, for the contingency table presenting viewer reactions to a television commercial (Table 12-2*a* on page 317), the χ^2 test has nothing to do with considering whether men and women were appropriately represented in the sample or with the general favorability of viewer reactions. Rather, the significant χ^2 value indicates rejection of the null

independent of

hypothesis that the two classification systems are [independent of / dependent on] one another.

64 Specifically, then, the rejection of the independence assumption leads to the conclusion that there is an interaction, or relationship, between the two variables serving as the basis for classification. In Table 12-2a the reaction of the viewer can be said to be related to the _____ of the viewer.

sex

65 Similarly, the significant χ^2 value for the data of Table 12-3a (page 319) did not indicate that the individual agents differed in their total sales or that certain policies are generally more popular. Rather, it indicated that the agents differed in

the types of policies they sold.

_____ .

66 If we wish to test one of the variables of a contingency table in terms of its goodness of fit with a theoretical distribution, in addition to or instead of the test for the independence of the two variables, we can do so by applying the χ^2 test to the column or to the row totals only. For example, the following data are the marginal totals of the observed frequencies taken from Table 12-3a. Based on the null hypothesis that there is no difference in the overall popularity of the various types of policies, post the expected frequencies in the table below.

	Type of insurance policy		
	A	B	C
Actual sales, fo	60	18	42
Expected sales, fe	___	___	___

40; 40; 40 (because according to the null hypothesis, sales of the three types of policies in the population are equal)

67 Now calculate the value of χ^2 for the data in Frame 66.

$$\frac{20^2}{40} + \frac{-22^2}{40} + \frac{2^2}{40} =$$

$$\frac{888}{40} = 22.20$$

$$\chi^2 = \sum \frac{(f_o - f_e)^2}{f_e} =$$

68 With the computed value of χ^2 being 22.20, at the 5 percent level the null hypothesis that the policies do not differ in overall popularity should be [accepted / rejected].

rejected (With df = 2, the critical value of χ^2 for the 0.05 level is 5.99.)

69 Thus, whenever a one-way classification of observed frequencies is involved, the χ^2 test is directed toward testing _____ .

goodness of fit

70 Whenever observed frequencies are classified in a contingency table, the χ^2 test may be used for testing the _____ of the two variables. By applying the test to the row totals or to the column totals of a contingency table, the χ^2 test can also be used to test the goodness of _____ for either of the variables taken singly, in respect to an expected pattern of frequencies.

independence

fit

12.5 ■ Minimum Expected Frequencies and Yates' Correction for Continuity

A necessary consideration in the use of the χ^2 test is the fact that the χ^2 distributions are continuous probability distributions, while the χ^2 test statistic which is computed on the basis of counts (frequencies) is discrete. A general rule which is used to avoid serious error on this account is that the expected frequency for each category of data in a χ^2 test should be at least 5. When there is one degree of freedom, Yates' _correction for continuity_, as described below, can be applied to improve the χ^2 test statistic.

71 At the top of Table B-6 in the Appendix notice the form of the χ^2 distribution. The χ^2 test statistics which have been computed in this chapter have been considered as being essentially continuous because with relatively large cell frequencies continuity of the χ^2 distribution is approached, regardless of degrees of freedom. Thus, with large cell frequencies [few / many] fractional values of χ^2 can occur.

many

72 For the χ^2 distribution it has been determined that when expected frequencies are small, the size of χ^2 is overestimated seriously because of the fact that the counts are discrete, and not continuous, data. This occurrence, in turn, would result in [too many / too few] rejections of the null hypothesis.

too many

73 But what is a "small expected frequency"? Most statisticians suggest that an expected cell frequency of less than 5 is too small (some say 10). What can we do about it? One possible solution is to anticipate the problem and avoid it by taking a large sample size in the first place. If the sample has already been collected, another possible solution is to combine adjacent classes of data with low expected frequencies, thus [increasing / reducing] the number of categories of data being analyzed.

reducing

74 For example, in the following chart indicating the expected frequency of typographical errors in 100 business reports, the categories that might be combined are those for ___ (number) errors and ___ (number) errors.

4; 5

	Number of errors					
	0	1	2	3	4	5
Expected frequency per 100 reports, f_e	65	15	8	5	4	3

75 Even with sufficient size of the expected frequencies, the problem of the data being discrete is not eliminated. An additional improvement in the χ^2 test statistic is achieved by applying *Yates' correction for continuity*. However, this correction is appropriate only when df = 1. Therefore, could we have used it for the data of Frame 74? [Yes / No]

No (df = 6 − 1 = 5)

76 Since Yates' correction for continuity is appropriate when df = 1, it can be used with tables of two possible dimensions, in terms of $r \times k$: ___ $\times$ ___ and ___ $\times$ ___ .

1 X 2; 2 X 2 (since df = 1 for both of these tables)

77 The following formula for the χ^2 test statistic incorporates Yates' correction for continuity:

$$\chi^2 = \sum \frac{(|f_o - f_e| - 0.5)^2}{f_e}$$

In this formula $|f_o - f_e|$ means "the absolute value of the difference," without regard to arithmetic sign. The net effect of Yates' correction, then, is to reduce the size of the difference between each f_o and f_e by _____ (number) [before / after] squaring and summing.

0.5

before

78 Yates' correction for continuity is appropriate only when the degree of freedom associated with the test is df = ___ .

1

79 Now that we have introduced Yates' correction, note that we could have applied it to the illustrative problem in Frames 15-20 to improve the χ^2 test statistic. Recompute the value of χ^2 for that problem, using the formula which includes Yates' correction.

$$\frac{(4.5)^2}{25} + \frac{(4.5)^2}{25} = 1.62$$

$$\chi^2 = \sum \frac{(|f_o - f_e| - 0.5)^2}{f_e} =$$

2.00
1.62

80 Thus the effect of applying the correction for continuity in this case was to reduce the value of χ^2 from _____ (number) to _____ (number).

81 Obviously, the χ^2 distribution does not suddenly become continuous when df = 2. However, the correction which is appropriate when df > 1 is mathematically complex. In order to avoid use of an uncorrected (inflated) χ^2 value, some statisticians prefer to use Yates' correction in *all* χ^2 tests even though this correction is in fact an "overcorrection" when df > 1. Therefore, use of Yates' correction in all χ^2 tests, regardless of the degrees of freedom, would result in some computed χ^2 values being conservatively stated in that they would be somewhat [smaller / larger] than the mathematically correct value.

smaller

Review

discrete

82 (Frames 1, 2) The χ^2 test is a hypothesis-testing procedure particularly applicable for the analysis of [discrete / continuous] data.

does
does

83 (Frames 3–14) Among the characteristics of the χ^2 (chi-square) test, its use [does / does not] presume a probability sample and [does / does not] presume that the events are independent.

observed (actual); expected

84 (Frames 15, 16) Computationally, the χ^2 test is directed toward determining the significance of differences between _____ frequencies and _____ frequencies for categorized data.

expected frequency

85 (Frames 17–19) The general formula used for computing the value of the χ^2 test statistic is $\chi^2 = \Sigma[(f_o - f_e)^2 / f_e]$. Therefore, given a classification table with observed frequencies, the first thing that has to be done in carrying out the χ^2 test after the null and alternative hypotheses have been specified is to determine the _____ associated with each cell.

86 (Frames 15–19) Given that 7, 10, and 13 units of products A, B, and C, respectively, were sold during a sampled time period, complete the table below, including all of the figures needed for the computation of χ^2. Assume that an equal sales volume was expected for each of the various products.

	Product		
	A	B	C
fo	___	___	___
fe	___	___	___

87 (Frames 20-31) Compute the value of χ^2 for the data in Frame 93.

7	10	13		
10	10	10		

$$\frac{-3^2}{10} + \frac{0}{10} + \frac{3^2}{10} = \frac{18}{10} = 1.80$$

$$\chi^2 = \sum \frac{(f_o - f_e)^2}{f_e} =$$

88 (Frames 21-32) Given the computed χ^2 value of 1.80, the null hypothesis that the sampled sales could have been obtained from a population with equal sales levels for the three products is [accepted / rejected] at the 5 percent level of significance.

accepted (With df = 2, the critical value of χ^2 for the 5 percent level is 5.99.)

89 (Frames 33-39) Of 24 sampled workers who are 50 years of age or over, 4 had an industrial accident last year and 20 did not. Of 36 sampled workers under 50 years of age, 16 had industrial accidents. Construct the contingency table to represent these findings.

Observed number, f_o	Under 50	50 and over	Total
Accidents	___	___	___
No accidents	___	___	___
Total	___	___	___

16	4	20
20	20	40
36	24	60

90 (Frames 40-43) Construct a table indicating the expected frequencies for the data in Frame 89, based on the null hypothesis that there is no relationship between age category and number of accidents. The formula to be used is:

$$f_e = \frac{f_r f_k}{n}$$

(Note that only one f_e needs to be computed using the formula; the others can then be determined by subtraction from marginal totals.)

Expected number, f_e	Under 50	50 and over	Total
Accidents	___	___	___
No accidents	___	___	___
Total	___	___	___

12	8	20
24	16	40
36	24	60

91 (Frames 44-49) Compute the value of χ^2 for the data in Frame 90, using the conventional formula.

$$\frac{4^2}{12} + \frac{-4^2}{8} + \frac{-4^2}{24} + \frac{4^2}{16} = 5.00$$

(However, Yates' correction should be used; we return to this example in Frames 98-99.)

$$\chi^2 = \sum \frac{(f_o - f_e)^2}{f_e} =$$

92 (Frames 45-51) Given the computed χ^2 value of **5.00**, the null hypothesis that there is no relationship between age and number of accidents would be [accepted / rejected] at the 5 percent level of significance.

rejected (For df = 1, the critical value of χ^2 for the 0.05 level is 3.84.)

93 (Frames 52-60) When observed frequencies are posted in a one-way classification table, the χ^2 test is used for testing _____ .

goodness of fit

94 (Frames 61-65) When observed frequencies are posted in a contingency table involving classification on the basis of two variables, the χ^2 test is used for _____ _____ .

testing for the independence of two variables

95 (Frames 66-70) When the χ^2 test is applied only to the marginal row (or column) totals of a contingency table, it is being used for the purpose of testing _____ .

goodness of fit

96 (Frames 71, 72) The χ^2 distribution itself is [discrete / continuous], whereas distributions of observed frequencies are [discrete / continuous]. Consequently, the computed value of the χ^2 test statistic tends to be somewhat [underestimated / overestimated].

continuous

discrete

overestimated

97 (Frames 73, 74) Because of the discontinuity of counts, one general requirement underlying the use of the χ^2 test is that all expected cell frequencies be equal to at least ___ (value).

5

98 (Frames 75-79) Yates' correction for continuity improves the χ^2 test statistic and is the mathematically appropriate correction only when df = 1. Using the following formula for χ^2, which incorporates Yates' correction for continuity, recompute the value of χ^2 for the data in Frames 89-91.

$$\frac{3.5^2}{12} + \frac{3.5^2}{8} + \frac{3.5^2}{24} + \frac{3.5^2}{16}$$
$$= 3.83$$

$$\chi^2 = \sum \frac{(|f_o - f_e| - 0.5)^2}{f_e} =$$

---

correction for continuity
5.00; 3.83

99 (Frame 80) In this case the application of Yates' _____ led to a reduction of the value of χ^2 from _____ to _____ . In Frame 92, in which the correction for continuity was not applied, the null hypothesis that there is no relationship between age and number of accidents was rejected. With the correction, the null hypothesis would be [accepted / rejected].

accepted (the critical value of χ^2 is 3.84)

100 (Frame 81) Use of no correction factor with χ^2 tests in general results in inflated values of computed χ^2 values, particularly with a low number of degrees of freedom and expected frequencies that are not large. If Yates' correction is used when df > 1, the resulting corrected value of the χ^2 test statistic is somewhat [smaller / larger] than the mathematically correct value.

smaller

Symbols Introduced in This Chapter (with Frame Numbers)

(1) χ^2 The chi-square test statistic.

(15) f_o An observed frequency.

(15) f_e An expected frequency.

Formulas Introduced in This Chapter (with Frame Numbers)

(17) $\chi^2 = \sum \dfrac{(f_o - f_e)^2}{f_e}$ The value of the χ^2 (chi-square) test statistic.

(21) $df = k - 1$ Degrees of freedom when the χ^2 test is used to test goodness of fit.

(37) $df = (r - 1)(k - 1)$ Degrees of freedom when the χ^2 test is used to test for independence between two variables.

(40) $f_e = \dfrac{f_r f_k}{n}$ The expected frequency for the cell of a contingency table based on the assumption that no relationship exists between the two variables.

(77) $\chi^2 = \sum \dfrac{(|f_o - f_e| - 0.5)^2}{f_e}$ The formula for the χ^2 test statistic which includes Yates' correction for continuity.

12.1 Describe the use of the χ^2 (chi-square) test for the purpose of testing goodness of fit. In your discussion, justify the view that such a test is properly considered to be in the category of statistical inference.

12.2 A new promotional campaign aimed at selling central air conditioning was used in marketing area A while marketing area B used the traditional method of sales promotion during a sampled week. The table below reports unit sales during the month preceding the study and during the week in which the new promotional effort was used.

	Marketing area	
	A	B
Sales in prior month	120	180
Sales in sampled week	45	55

(a) Based on the null hypothesis that there is no difference in the effect of the new and old promotional efforts, determine the expected unit sales for the two areas during the sampled week. (*Hint*: The total unit sales of 100 during the sampled week should not simply be equally allocated to the two areas; rather, it should be allocated according to the proportion of sales in the two areas during the prior month.)

(b) Compute the value of χ^2 and indicate whether the null hypothesis is accepted or rejected at the 5 percent level of significance.

(c) Briefly discuss the implications of the result of your test in (b), above.

12.3 For Exercise 12.2, above, suppose that the two sales areas used in the study were generally about equal in sales volume during preceding periods, rather than having the indicated difference in the prior month's sales. Repeat the test and interpret your results in this case.

12.4 In order to study shifts in consumer preferences, an automobile manufacturer arranges interviews with a random sample of 50 men and 50 women who purchased a car manufactured by the company during the preceding year. The following table summarizes the responses to one of the questions concerned with the most important additional safety feature desired.

		Additional feature desired			
Respondents	Disk brakes	Collapsible steering wheel	Automatic door locks	Speed warning buzzer	Total
Men	15	25	5	5	50
Women	5	15	20	10	50
Total	20	40	25	15	100

(a) Determine the expected cell frequencies for this contingency table.
(b) Compute the value of χ^2.
(c) Is the difference between the pattern of obtained and expected frequencies significant at the 1 percent level?
(d) Interpret the meaning of the results of your test in (c), above.

12.5 For the data of Exercise 12.4, suppose it had been suggested that there is no real difference in consumer preferences for the four safety features listed. Test this assumption at the 1 percent level of significance.

12.6 In order to investigate the relationship between employment status and credit risk status, a loan company manager has a study of 100 randomly chosen accounts conducted, with the following tabulated results.

	Status at time of loan		
Present status of loan	Employed	Unemployed	Total
In default	10	8	18
Not in default	60	22	82
Total	70	30	100

(a) Compute the value of the χ^2 test statistic for these data.
(b) Given the null hypothesis that there is no relationship between employment status and credit status, what is the result of this test at the 5 percent level of significance?

12.7 In conjunction with the data presented in Exercise 12.6, above, it has been the loan company's experience that at any randomly selected point in time about 10 percent of the accounts are technically in default. Does the sample differ significantly from the historical pattern, using the 5 percent level of significance?

12.8 For Exercise 12.6, suppose the data had been as follows:

Present status of loan	Status at time of loan		
	Employed	Unemployed	Total
In default	5	13	18
Not in default	65	17	82
Total	70	30	100

(a) Determine the expected cell frequencies for this contingency table.

(b) Compute the value of χ^2, using the appropriate formula.

(c) Indicate whether the null hypothesis that there is no relationship between employment status and credit status would be accepted or rejected at the 5 percent level of significance.

12.9 Sales records for previous periods indicate that dollar sales per customer at a discount department store have averaged $18 with a standard deviation of $6. Further, the sales amounts have been normally distributed. For a random sample of 200 customers on the day following a change in pricing policy the sales amounts per customer are distributed as indicated in the table below. Using the χ^2 test, does the sample frequency distribution differ significantly from the hypothesized probability distribution, using the 5 percent level of significance? (*Hint*: Use the given mean and standard deviation to determine the proportion of sales that is expected in each class of the frequency distribution, based on the normal curve assumption. Then determine the expected frequencies based on these proportions.)

Sales amount	Number of customers
Below $9.00	15
$9.00–$11.99	15
$12.00–$14.99	35
$15.00–$17.99	50
$18.00–$20.99	40
$21.00–$23.99	25
$24.00–$26.99	15
$27.00–$29.99	5

12.10 In a college course in statistics the historical distribution of grades has been 10 percent A, 30 percent B, 40 percent C, 10 percent D, and 10 percent E. A particular class with 50 students enrolled completes the semester with 8 students earning a grade of A, 17 with B, 20 with C, 3 with D, and 2 with E. Does the distribution of this sample of grades differ significantly from the historical pattern, using the 5 percent level of significance? Interpret the result of the test.

ADDITIONAL EXERCISES **12.11** Describe the use of the χ^2 (chi-square) test for the purpose of testing for independence. In your discussion indicate the meaning of accepting and of rejecting the null hypothesis in such a test. In what sense can a test for independence be considered a type of "goodness of fit" test?

12.12 The table below presents the preferences of a consumer panel in respect to the taste of four brands of Rhine wine. Test the null hypothesis that the consumer preferences for the four brands are equal, using the 1 percent level of significance.

Consumer Panel Preferences for Four Brands of Rhine Wine

	Brand			
A	B	C	D	Total
30	20	40	10	100

12.13 Before the results reported in Exercise 12.12 were observed, it was hypothesized that brand C is preferred by as many people as the other three brands combined. Test this hypothesis at the 1 percent level of significance.

12.14 In general, 20 percent of the people stop to watch a cookingware demonstration in a department store. For a new demonstration format, only 3 of 40 people stop to watch the demonstration. Is this result significantly different from the expected number based on previous experience, using the 5 percent level of significance?

12.15 A manufacturer of automobile radiators has decided to expand his product line to include automobile air-conditioners that are not factory-installed. Four models of air-conditioners that are offered for sale by other manufacturers are the economy, standard, deluxe, and custom models. During the past three years these four models have accounted for 40 percent, 30 percent, 20 percent, and 10 percent of the market, respectively. In order to determine appropriate production levels for each model of air-conditioner, the manufacturer collects data for a random sample of 400 auto air-conditioner installations completed during the past month and finds that 190 were the economy model, 100 were the standard model, 50 were the deluxe model, and 60 were the custom model. Using these data, test the assumption that the historical distribution of sales for the four models has not changed, using the 5 percent level of significance.

12.16 An elementary school principal has for some time suspected that there is a relationship between the income level of parents and their attendance at school programs and activities, but the relationship has not been entirely clear. Accordingly, for a particular month he takes note of such attendance and classifies each family in the categories called "never," "occasionally," and "regular." Available socio-economic data also make it possible to classify each family in the "low," "middle," and "high" categories in terms of income. The classification of the 420 families is indicated in the table below. Test the null hypothesis that there is no relationship between income category and extent of program participation, using the 5 percent level of significance.

Program participation	Low	Middle	High	Total
Never	28	48	16	92
Occasional	22	65	14	101
Regular	17	74	3	94
Total	67	187	33	287

12.17 In conjunction with the data of Exercise 12.16, above, it is known that 20 percent of the families are in the "low" income category, 70 percent are in the "middle" income category, and 10 percent are in the "high" income category. Does the pattern of families included in the sample differ significantly from this expected distribution, using the 5 percent level of significance? Interpret the result of the test.

12.18 In order to put a one-year warranty into effect, the buyers of a small appliance are required to mail a postcard on which several questions relating to the purchase are asked. From a large number of these postcards, a random sample of 100 are selected for analysis. The following frequencies, based on the sample of postcards, describe the purchasers according to place of purchase and source of product knowledge.

	Place of purchase			
Source of knowledge	Department store	Discount store	Appliance store	Total
Friend	10	5	5	20
Newspaper	15	30	5	50
Magazine	5	5	20	30
Total	30	40	30	100

(a) Determine the expected cell frequencies.

(b) Compute the value of χ^2.

(c) Test the null hypothesis that there is no relationship between place of purchase and source of knowledge, using the 5 percent level of significance.

(d) Would the conclusion be different if the 1 percent level were used?

12.19 In conjunction with the data of Exercise 12.18, above, the management of the company has assumed that the appliance is sold in about equal quantities in the three types of stores. Test this hypothesis at the 5 percent level of significance.

12.20 In conjunction with the data of Exercise 12.18, the management of the company has assumed that 40 percent of the purchases are influenced by friends, 40 percent by newspaper ads, and 20 percent by magazine ads. Test this hypothesis at the 1 percent level of significance.

12.21 Before the data for Exercise 12.18 had been collected, it was suggested that newspaper ads are particularly effective for discount store buyers and magazine ads are more influential with buyers at appliance stores. Test the null hypothesis that there is no such relationship, using the 1 percent level of significance.

12.22 In order to compare the quality of rheostats shipped by two subcontractors, a sample of 80 rheostats was taken from recent shipments by each supplier and the following numbers of defects of any type were noted. The sales representative for supplier B suggests that the difference observed is only a chance difference and is not reflective of the general quality of the rheostats being supplied by his company.

		Supplier		
Inspection result		A	B	Total
Defective		4	12	16
Nondefective		76	68	144
Total		80	80	160

(a) Determine the expected cell frequencies.

(b) Test the sales representative's claim at the 5 percent level of significance.

12.23 It has been the experience of a trucking firm that the number of truck arrivals per hour at a loading terminal can be represented as a Poisson process with $\lambda = 3.0$. For 60 sampled hours during a particular month the frequency distribution of the number of arrivals per hour is reported in the table below. Using the 5 percent level, does this distribution differ significantly from the expected distribution based on the Poisson distribution with $\lambda = 3.0$? Briefly discuss the outcome of the test.

Number of truck arrivals (per hour)	f
0	0
1	4
2	10
3	14
4	12
5	12
6 or more	8
Total	60

PART V ■
STATISTICAL
DECISION ANALYSIS

CHAPTER 13 ■
DECISION
ANALYSIS

Beginning with the coverage of sampling methods and the concept of sampling distributions in Chapter 8, we have been concerned with the use of methods of statistical inference. The methods of estimation and hypothesis testing that we have described are regarded as being classical methods of statistical inference from the standpoint of the present development of statistical methods. Whereas the classical methods of inference are based on probability samples alone and are restricted to the objective approach to interpreting probability values, recent developments in statistical inference make it possible to incorporate economic consequences in the analysis, to include such sources of information as managerial judgment in the data being analyzed, and to interpret probabilities by means of the subjective as well as the objective approach, as described in Chapter 5. The developments of the past few years represent a distinct break with the relative-frequency orientation of the classical methods, and have been referred to as "Bayesian statistics" or "statistical decision theory." In this chapter we particularly concern ourselves with incorporating economic consequences in the decision process, while the next chapter, on Bayesian inference, is concerned with incorporating judgment in the decision process. Accordingly, in the present chapter we first describe the several criteria that can be used to identify the "best decision," given that economic consequences are known but the probabilities of various events are unknown. Then, we consider the appropriate basis for analysis given that both economic consequences and probabilities are known. In the final section of this chapter we describe decision tree analysis, which is applicable to decision situations involving a sequence of events and decisions.

13.1 ■ Decision Making Based upon Economic Consequences Alone

In general, statistical decision analysis is involved whenever a decision is to be made under conditions of *uncertainty.* In such a case, the economic consequence of any decision act depends on which of several possible states of nature (e.g., level of consumer demand) in fact occurs. The probability values associated with the states may or may not be known, and in this section of the chapter we assume that they are not known. When the probabilities are not known, three different criteria that can be used to identify the "best decision" are the *maximin, maximax,* and *minimax regret* criteria, and these are described in this section. Incidentally, some statisticians have used the term *decision making under risk* to refer specifically to the situations in which the probability values are known, but the term *uncertainty* is more generally used and includes the alternatives of the probability values either being known or not being known.

1 Suppose that an electronics firm has perfected a television receiver with a three-dimensional picture and now faces several alternative choices regarding the scheduling of production and related market-promotion activities for the receiver. Consumer acceptance of the product within the next 10 years is considered certain, but the timing of that acceptance is uncertain, partly because of the receiver's necessarily high price. Table 13-1 presents four decision alternatives, ranging from immediate full-scale production and promotion to limited production in five years. Similarly, the possible consumer reactions (states of nature) range from immediate acceptance to acceptance in eight years. Thus each figure in Table 13-1 represents the economic consequences associated with each possible combination of _____ and

decision act; state of nature (or production decision and consumer acceptance)

_____ .

Table 13-1 ■ Decision Acts, States, and Economic Consequences for the Television Receiver Problem (In millions of dollars)

Decision act	Consumer acceptance			
	Immediate	*2 years*	*5 years*	*8 years*
Immediate production and promotion	$80	$40	$−10	$−50
Limited production now	30	40	30	10
Limited production in 2 years	20	30	40	15
Limited production in 5 years	5	10	30	30

2 A table such as Table 13-1, which identifies possible decision acts, states, and economic consequences, is often called a *decision table.* In determining the best decision act when the probabilities of the states are unknown, a prime consideration is the decision maker's general attitude toward the possible losses and gains. For example, the manufacturer might be rather cautious, or pessimistic, and choose that decision act which *maximizes* the *minimum* value (economic consequence) that can occur. This is called the *maximin criterion.* For the decision to go into immediate production,

−50 (a loss)

10
15
5

limited production in two years (since the minimum value of 15 million dollars is greater than any other minimum value)

minimum value (and hence, at least this level of return is assured)

80

immediate production and promotion (since the other three values are 40, 40, and 30, respectively)

maximax

maximin

what is the minimum result that can occur? _____ million dollars.

3 Similarly, the minimum value possible for limited production now is _____ million dollars; for limited production in two years it is _____ million dollars; and for limited production in five years it is ___ million dollars.

4 Therefore, if we use the *maximin* criterion as the basis for the decision, the decision alternative in Table 13-1 that would be chosen is _____

_____ .

5 Hence use of the maximin criterion results in maximizing the _____ that can occur.

6 Another criterion, which might be used by a decision maker who is considerably more optimistic, is the *maximax*. As the name implies, the objective in this case is to *maximize* the *maximum* value that can occur. For the decision to begin immediate production and promotion, the maximum conditional value indicated in Table 13-1 is _____ million dollars.

7 Similarly, consider the maximum value that can occur for the other three decision acts. If the maximax criterion is used as the basis for the decision, the alternative that would be chosen is _____

_____ .

8 Thus the criterion whereby the maximum conditional value is maximized is called the _____ criterion; the criterion whereby the minimum conditional value is maximized is called the _____ criterion.

9 Finally, the third possible criterion, called *minimax regret*, looks at the decision problem from a point of view that is neither so pessimistic nor so optimistic as the maximin and maximax criteria, respectively. After the uncertain state is in fact known, to the extent that the decision act was not "perfectly matched" with that state there will be an opportunity loss, or regret, associated with the decision. As the name implies, the *minimax-regret criterion* is the one by which the decision maker minimizes the _____ that can occur, no matter what the state.

maximum regret

10 To illustrate the meaning of an opportunity loss, or regret, suppose that the 3-D television receiver wins consumer acceptance in five years. The highest value associated with this state is _____ million dollars.

40 (for the decision, limited production in two years)

11 If any decision other than limited production in two years had been chosen, there would be an opportunity loss, or regret, in terms of the difference between the value associated with the best decision act under the circumstances and the value associated with the decision that was actually made. For the state, acceptance in five years, the amount of regret associated with the decision to go into immediate production would be _____ million dollars; for limited production now it would be _____ million dollars; and for limited production in five years it would be _____ million dollars.

$40 - (-10) = 50$

$40 - 30 = 10$

$40 - 30 = 10$

12 Table 13-2 presents the opportunity losses, or regrets, associated with each possible combination of decision act and state. In terms of the minimax-regret criterion, the decision maker attempts to minimize the maximum regret that can occur. For the decision to go into immediate production and promotion, for example, the maximum regret that can occur is _____ million dollars.

80 (i.e., if the true state is acceptance in eight years, the best-matched decision for this state results in a payoff of 30 million dollars instead of a loss of 50 million dollars)

Table 13-2 ▪ Opportunity Losses, or Regrets, for the Television Receiver Problem (In millions of dollars)

Decision act	Consumer acceptance			
	Immediate	2 years	5 years	8 years
Immediate production and promotion	$ 0	$ 0	$50	$80
Limited production now	50	0	10	20
Limited production in 2 years	60	10	0	15
Limited production in 5 years	75	30	10	0

13 A table such as Table 13-2, which identifies possible decision acts, states, and conditional opportunity losses (regrets), is often called a *loss table.* Review the opportunity losses associated with each of the decision alternatives in Table 13-2. The decision act that is best from the standpoint of the minimax regret criterion is _____ _____ .

14 In this section, in which we have assumed that the probabilities associated with the several possible states are not known, we have illustrated the use of three decision criteria, called the _____ , _____ , and _____ _____ .

15 Depending on the criterion used, different decision acts might be considered best. For the case illustration involving the production of the new 3-D television receiver, for example, use of the maximin criterion would result in the decision _____ . Use of the maximax criterion would result in the decision _____ . Use of the minimax regret criterion would result in the decision _____ .

16 Thus, a decision act may be the "best act" in respect to one orientation toward possible losses and gains but not in respect to other orientations. For example, the decision act which could produce the largest gain of all (if a favorable state occurs) is the best act from the standpoint of the _____ criterion.

17 If the decision maker prefers to focus on the consequences if the "worst happens," perhaps because of his overall economic position, then he would tend to use the _____ criterion as a basis of evaluating decision alternatives.

18 The decision maker who tends to consider "missed profit" as representing a loss comparable to an experienced financial loss will want to minimize the amount of either such loss (or the combination thereof). From this standpoint, the criterion by which the alternative decisions should be evaluated is the _____ criterion.

19 The three criteria we have described can be used when the probabilities associated with the various possible states are not known. Essentially, each of the possible (conditional) economic consequences is considered equally in the analysis. But in general, is it likely to be the case that a large conditional value, for example, is as likely as other conditional results in a decision situation involving uncertainty? [Yes / No]

No

20 Thus, one difficulty with all three criteria we have described in this section is that all of the possible states are in effect given equal consideration, even though some may have a low probability of occurrence. In the next section of this chapter the decision criterion to be used when probabilities are known is described. Some decision analysts would argue that the three criteria described in the present section should never be used, because one way or another the probabilities are always available. Specifically, they suggest that if historical or sample data regarding the relative frequency of the several possible states are not available, then expert judgment should be used to estimate the probabilities. In other words, from this viewpoint it is held that if objective probabilities are not available, then _____ probabilities should always be used, rather than performing the analysis with no probability values at all.

subjective

13.2 ■ The Expected Value Criterion

When the probability of each possible state is known or can be estimated in addition to the conditional economic consequences having been identified, then the appropriate criterion to be used in determining the best decision act is the expected value criterion. The expected value for each decision act is obtained by multiplying each conditional value associated with that act by the probability of the state and summing these products, as we illustrate in this section. By this approach, the decision maker follows a strategy whereby his long-run expected gain is maximized. That is, the orientation is not so much toward consequences given that a decision will be made only once, but rather it is toward the average economic consequence which would be experienced over a series of similar decision opportunities.

21 If X represents each of the conditional values associated with a decision act and $P(X)$ represents the probability that the conditional value will occur, then the *expected value* of the decision act is equal to $\Sigma XP(X)$. That is, each conditional value is multiplied by the _____ of that value occurring [before / after] summation.

probability

before

22 Let us illustrate the computation of expected values by considering a decision situation involving just two decision alternatives. Suppose that a retailer has the opportunity to sell a portion of his slow-moving stock to a liquidator for $1,800. Since the items in question are children's toys, he is also aware that he may do better financially by keeping them in stock through the approaching Christmas shopping season and selling them at a discount. As the first step in his analysis, he prepares a table of the conditional values, or consequences, for this decision situation. Table 13-3 indicates that there are four "states" in his analysis, each of which indicates a possible percentage of the toys that would be sold (at discount) if kept in his store. The conditional values associated with the decision act "keep in stock" range from $_____ to $_____ . On the other hand, the conditional values associated with "sell now" are all equal to $_____ .

1,400
2,000
1,800 (because this is the amount the retailer would receive in this case no matter what the market demand might have been)

Table 13-3 ■ Decision Table for the Retailer Problem

	Percentage of stock that will be sold			
Decision act	70%	80%	90%	100%
Keep in stock	$1,400	$1,600	$1,800	$2,000
Sell now	1,800	1,800	1,800	1,800

23 Of course, for the data of Table 13-3 the retailer can apply one of the criteria discussed in the preceding section of this chapter, since no probability values for the states have yet been introduced. Thus, if he is somewhat cautious and uses the maximin criterion, he would choose the decision act "_____"; if he is more optimistic and uses the maximax criterion, he would choose the decision act "_____ ."

sell now (thus assuring himself of the $1,800 result)
keep in stock

24 But in order to do a more complete and realistic analysis, the retailer wishes to include the probability for each of the states. His best judgment is that the probability values for the four states identified in Table 13-3 are 0.20, 0.20, 0.40, and 0.20, respectively. With this information available, we can now determine the expected value for each decision act. Let us first consider the decision act "keep in stock." Given the general formula, EV (*expected value*) $= \Sigma XP(X)$, determine the expected value for this decision alternative by completing the calculations below:

Decision Act: Keep in Stock	Conditional value, X	Probability, P(X)	XP(X)
	$1,400	0.20	$ 280
320	1,600	0.20	_____
720	1,800	0.40	_____
400	2,000	0.20	_____
1,720		$EV = \Sigma XP(X) = \$$ _____	

25 In order to evaluate this decision act, we compare this expected value with the expected value for the other available act and choose that act whose expected value is largest. Because the act "sell now" has the conditional value of $1,800 no matter what state occurs, that conditonal value is also the expected value. Let us illustrate this in the table below:

Decision Act: Sell Now	Conditional value, X	Probability, P(X)	XP(X)
360	$1,800	0.20	$ _____
360	1,800	0.20	_____
720	1,800	0.40	_____
360	1,800	0.20	_____
1,800		$EV = \Sigma XP(X) = \$$ _____	

26 Therefore, given the conditional values and the probabilities of the states for the retailer's decision problem, the act "keep in stock" has an expected value of $_____ while the act "sell now" has an expected value of $_____ . Accordingly, the best act from the standpoint of the expected value criterion is "_____."

1,720
1,800

sell now

27 Note that the expected value of $1,720 for the act "keep in stock" is *not* one of the outcomes that can actually occur in this particular (single) decision-making situation. Rather, it is a kind of long-run _____ if the decision situation and accompanying results were to be repeated a number of times.

average

28 The decision problem in Frames 22 to 27 is relatively simple, in that only two decision alternatives are available and the expected value had to be calculated for just one of the alternatives. When the expected value criterion is applied to a situation in which there are several decision alternatives, we would carry out several independent summations represented by the symbol $\Sigma XP(X)$, one for each of the [outcomes / decision acts].

decision acts (The summation represents the expected payoff associated with a *decision*.)

29 Suppose that the revenue associated with the use of each car in a commuter train is $200 and the cost associated with the use of each car is $80. What is the conditional value associated with using five commuter cars if five are in fact needed? _____.
What is the conditional value associated with the use of five cars if only two are in fact needed? _____

$5(\$200) - 5(\$80) =$
$\$1,000 - \$400 = \$600$

$2(\$200) - 5(\$80) =$
$\$400 - \$400 = $ 0

30 Thus both revenue and cost figures have to be considered in determining the conditional values in this kind of problem. Table 13-4 presents the conditional values associated with every possible combination of decision act and state ranging from zero through five commuter cars, each value having been computed in the same way as in Frame 29. Thus Table 13-4 indicates that if two cars are provided and two cars are needed, the conditional value is _____, whereas if three cars are provided and one is needed, the conditional value is _____.

$240

$-\$40$ (a loss)

Table 13-4 ▪ **Decision Table for the Commuter Car Problem**

Number provided	Number needed					
	0	1	2	3	4	5
0	$ 0	$ 0	$ 0	$ 0	$ 0	$ 0
1	−80	120	120	120	120	120
2	−160	40	240	240	240	240
3	−240	−40	160	360	360	360
4	−320	−120	80	280	480	480
5	−400	−200	0	200	400	600

31 In terms of the expected value that we wish to maximize, as represented by $EV = \Sigma XP(X)$, all of the numbers entered in Table 13-4 represent values of [$X / P(X)$].

X

32 Table 13-5 presents the probabilities for the various states, i.e., for the number of commuter cars needed, based on a study of previous demand patterns. Thus the values in this table are to be used as values of [$X / P(X)$] in calculating the expected values.

$P(X)$

Number needed	Probability
0	0
1	0.10
2	0.20
3	0.30
4	0.30
5	0.10

33 Since all values of X and $P(X)$ are identified in Tables 13-4 and 13-5, respectively, the task now remaining is to determine the expected values associated with each of the decision alternatives of attaching zero through five commuter cars to the train. The table below illustrates the computation of the expected value associated with the decision to provide five cars for the train. Complete the calculations and determine the expected value associated with this decision.

Decision Act: Provide Five Commuter Cars

Number needed	Conditional value, X	Probability, $P(X)$	$XP(X)$
0	−$400	0	$0
1	− 200	0.10	−20
2	0	0.20	0
3	200	0.30	60
4	____	____	____
5	____	____	____
		EV $= \Sigma XP(X) = \$$____	

400*	0.30†	120
600	0.10	60
		$220

*From Table 13-4.
†From Table 13-5.

---

34 Note, again, that the expected value does not indicate an economic result which can occur on any given run of the commuter train. Rather, it indicates the average value in the long run, assuming that the probability distribution used as the basis for the decision continues to apply. Thus, given the payoff values of Table 13-4 and the probability distribution of Table 13-5, the expected (average) value associated with providing five commuter cars is _____ .

$220

35 Table 13-6 presents the expected values for all six decision alternatives, each of the values having been determined in the same way as for the decision to provide five cars in Frame 33. According to this table, the best decision act from the standpoint of the expected value criterion is to provide _____ (number) commuter cars.

three or four (Either decision results in the same expected payoff.)

Table 13-6 ■ Expected Values Associated with Providing Zero to Five Commuter Cars	Number provided	Expected payoff
	0	$ 0
	1	120
	2	220
	3	280
	4	280
	5	220

36 Note, however, that in maximizing expected value, we have not necessarily considered all variables that in fact influence long-run success. If we consistently provide four cars, in what percentage of the train runs will there be more demand for commuter cars than there are cars provided? _____ percent

10 (from Table 13-5)

37 It is conceivable that one commuter reaction to a shortage of cars might be to switch to another mode of travel, thereby changing the probability distribution associated with the possible states of demand. Thus the criterion of expected value is one possible criterion and [does / does not] substitute for managerial responsibility for evaluating the decision criteria themselves.

does not

38 As another kind of illustration indicating that the expected value criterion may not always be the appropriate one, note the data given in Table 13-7. Using these data, determine the expected values for the two decision alternatives in the table below.

	State	Decision A			Decision B		
		X	$P(X)$	$XP(X)$	X	$P(X)$	$XP(X)$
$-1,000$ $-20,000$	a	$-2,000	0.5	$____	$-40,000	0.5	$____
6,000 30,000	b	12,000	0.5	____	60,000	0.5	____
$ 5,000 $ 10,000				EV = ΣXP(X) = $____			EV = ΣXP(X) = $____

Table 13-7 ■ States, Probabilities, and Conditional Values Associated with Two Decision Alternatives	Possible states and probabilities	
	State a	State b
Decision	($p = 0.50$)	($p = 0.50$)
A	$ -2,000	$12,000
B	-40,000	60,000

39 From the standpoint of the expected value criterion, decision B is clearly superior to decision A. But why might a businessman with modest financial resources make decision A instead? _____

_____

40 Therefore, after identifying the best decision act from the standpoint of the expected value criterion, the decision maker should review the conditonal values (consequences) that could occur with that "best decision" in order to determine its continued acceptability. This kind of review should then be done with the nonpreferred acts to determine if there are any special gain opportunities that enhance the desirability of other decision acts. In realistic decision situations, therefore, managers usually have to evaluate the possible decision alternatives from the standpoint of [a single decision criterion / several decision criteria] .

| several decision criteria |

41 The need for several decision criteria is not appealing to the decision theorists who have been involved in developing the techniques of decision analysis, because in this circumstance it may be difficult for two decision analysts to agree on what is the best decision, even with the conditional values and probabilities given. Therefore, in recent years decision theorists have directed their efforts toward formulating a decision criterion that would be the appropriate one [for any decision situation / for certain types of situations only] .

| for any decision situation |

42 The approach by which decision theorists have attempted to achieve this unified objective is called *utility theory*. Discussion of utility theory is beyond the scope of this book. Generally, the approach is based on the assumption that monetary values are not necessarily appropriate measures of the true value of a consequence to the decision maker. Therefore, a generalized basis for measuring value, called *utility*, is formulated instead. From this standpoint, a conditional table of values would include conditional utilities rather than the conditional _____ values we have used in all of the examples included in this section.

| monetary (or financial, etc.) |

43 Similarly, from the standpoint of utility theory the best decision act is not necessarily the act with the highest expected monetary value, but rather it is the act with the highest expected _____ .

| utility |

44 As a final opportunity to use the criterion of expected monetary value, let us again consider the 3-D television receiver problem which was discussed in Section 13.1. Table 13-1 is repeated here for your reference. Suppose it is the management's judgment that the probabilities of the states identified in the table are 0.30, 0.40, 0.20, and 0.10, respectively. In the working table below determine the expected value for the decision act, immediate production and promotion.

Table 13-1 ■ Decision Acts, States, and Economic Consequences for the Television Receiver Problem (In millions of dollars)

Decision act	Consumer acceptance			
	Immediate	2 years	5 years	8 years
Immediate production and promotion	$80	$40	$−10	$−50
Limited production now	30	40	30	10
Limited production in 2 years	20	30	40	15
Limited production in 5 years	5	10	30	30

Decision Act: Immediate Production and Promotion

	Conditional value, X	Probability, P(X)	XP(X)
24	$ 80	0.30	$____
16	40	0.40	____
−2	−10	0.20	____
−5	−50	0.10	____
33		$EV = \Sigma XP(X) =$ $____	

45 By a similar computational routine determine the expected values for the other three decision alternatives in the working space below.

EV (Lim. prod. now) = 32
EV (Lim. prod. 2 yrs) = 27.5
EV (Lim. prod. 5 yrs) = 14.5

46 Based on the expected value criterion alone, the best decision act is "_____

immediate production and promotion

33

_____," which has the highest expected monetary value of ____ million dollars.

47 Suppose, however, that the occurrence of a large monetary loss (say, larger than 10 million dollars) would put the company in a position of serious financial jeopardy. The decision act that would probably be chosen as being the best act is "_____."

13.3 ■ Decision Tree Analysis

The analysis of decision tables is appropriate when some one decision has to be made in the context of uncertain event states. In a broader context, however, an overall decision situation may involve a sequence of decisions to be made in conjunction with several uncertain events or states. In such a circumstance, *decision tree analysis* has been found to be a useful technique whereby the overall decision situation can be portrayed and the best decision act at each point, including the initial choice point, can be identified. The criterion which serves as the basis for identifying the best acts in decision tree analysis is the expected value criterion.

48 Exhibit 13-1 presents a decision problem which will serve to illustrate the method of analysis throughout this section of the chapter. Because the example problem involves a sequential decision situation, the method of analysis which is

decision tree

useful in such a case is _____ analysis.

Exhibit 13-1 ■ A Sequential Decision Problem

A manufacturer has been presented with a proposal for a new product, and must decide whether or not to develop it. The cost of the development project is $200,000, with a probability of 0.70 that the project will be successful. If the product is successfully developed, the manufacturer must then decide as to whether to begin manufacturing the product at a high level or at a low level. If demand is high, the incremental profit given a high level of manufacturing is $700,000, and given a low level of manufacturing is $150,000. If demand is low, the incremental profit given a high level of manufacturing is $100,000, and given a low level of manufacturing is $150,000. All of these incremental profit values are *before* subtraction of the $200,000 development cost, and thus are gross figures. The probability that the market will be high is estimated as $P = 0.40$, and that it will be low as $P = 0.60$.

49 The first step in the analysis is to construct the decision tree which represents the overall decision situation. Such a tree includes *decision points* and *chance events*. In a decision tree, the sequential points at which choices of acts are required are

decision

represented as _____ points.

chance

50 In a decision tree, the sequential points at which probabilistic events will occur are represented as _____ events.

decision points
chance events

51 Whereas *tree diagrams*, introduced in Chapter 5, are used only to represent a sequence of chance events, decision trees are used to represent a sequence of _____ and _____ .

52 A decision tree is constructed from left to right, according to the time sequence in which the decisions will be made and the sequence in which the events will occur. Refer to Exhibit 13-1. We begin construction of the tree diagram for this decision problem by portraying the first decision point. In the diagram below, identify the two choices at the initial decision point for the situation described in Exhibit 13-1 by entering these on the two branches of this partial diagram.

Develop

Don't develop

(By convention, a square is used to designate a decision point.)

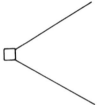

53 For the decision problem presented in Exhibit 13-1, if the product is not developed then this action terminates the decision problem, and with an economic consequence of $0, as indicated in the lower portion of the diagram below. If the decision is made to develop the product, enter the events which can then occur in the top portion of the diagram below, with respective probabilities of each event identified. (Refer to Exhibit 13-1.)

Successful development ($P = 0.70$)

Unsuccessful development ($P = 0.30$)

(By convention, a circle is used to designate a chance event.)

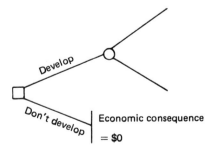

54 If development is successful, then the manufacturer has to make another decision. If the development is unsuccessful, the project will be terminated. Referring to the description in Exhibit 13-1, enter the two choices at this next decision point in the diagram below and also enter the economic consequence of terminating the project.

Manufacture high level
Manufacture low level

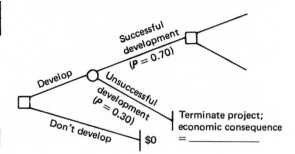

−$200,000

55 Following the choice of a manufacturing level, the final event described in Exhibit 13-1 concerns the level of demand. Indicate the two possible demand levels and their respective probabilities in our evolving decision tree, below.

High demand (P = 0.40)
Low demand (P = 0.60)

High demand (P = 0.40)
Low demand (P = 0.60)

56 To complete the decision tree for the problem in Exhibit 13-1, we now enter the economic consequences associated with each of the combinations of manufacturing level and demand level. Enter these four possible consequences in the diagram below.

$500,000

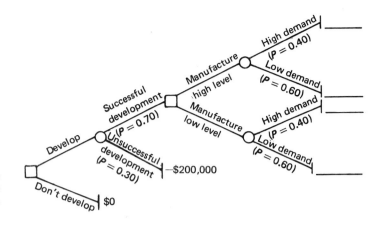

−$100,000
−$50,000

−$50,000 (*Note:* The $200,000 development cost is subtracted from each incremental profit amount given in Exhibit 13-1).

expected value

57 Now that we have completed the construction of the decision tree for the problem described in Exhibit 13-1, the second major step is to identify the best decision at each decision point. As indicated in the introduction to this section, the criterion which is used as the basis for identifying the best acts in decision tree analysis is the _____ criterion.

58 The process of determining expected values and identifying best acts requires that we work from right to left in the decision tree, as will be illustrated below. For this reason, this process of analysis is sometimes called "folding back" the decision tree. Refer to the complete decision tree in Frame 56. As the first step in folding back from right to left, we note that the decision "Manufacture high level" is followed by two possible economic consequences with associated probabilities, while the decision "Manufacture low level" is followed by two other possible economic consequences with associated probabilities. In the decision tree below, enter the expected values associated with these two decision acts.

$(0.40)(\$500,000) +$
$(0.60)(-\$100,000) =$
$\$140,000$

$(0.40)(-\$50,000) +$
$(0.60)(-\$50,000) =$
$-\$50,000$

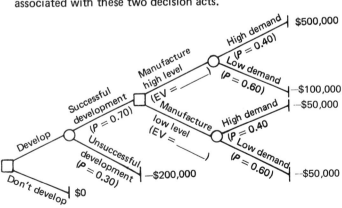

59 Referring to the expected values just calculated in Frame 58, the best decision act at this choice point is "_____ _____."

60 Referring to the diagram below, we now consider the economic consequences associated with the initial choice point in the decision tree, which will then complete the process of folding back. If we choose to develop the product, there is a probability of 0.70 of the economic result being _____ and a 0.30 probability that it will be _____ .

61 In the decision tree above, post the expected value for "Develop," compare this expected value with the value associated with "Don't develop," and identify the best decision act at this initial decision point in the decision tree.

62 Figure 13-1 presents the complete decision tree for the problem described in Exhibit 13-1, including the expected values associated with the decision choices and identification of the best acts. Referring to this figure, we see that based on the expected value criterion the best act at the initial decision point is "_____." If product development is successful, the best act at the second decision point in this sequential decision problem is "_____."

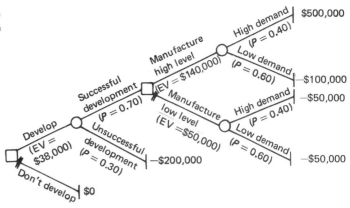

Figure 13-1 ■ Complete decision tree for the decision problem described in Exhibit 13-1

63 In completing this example, we note that decision tree analysis provides the manager with an opportunity to portray the overall decision situation in a concrete form, and thereby have an opportunity to observe decision implications that might otherwise not be obvious. For example, even though the expected value favors the decision "Develop" in Figure 13-1, what is the overall probability that this decision will result in a profit? P(Positive economic consequence) = _____ _____ .

By the rule of multiplication for the joint occurrence of two independent events, $P =$ P(Successful development) X P(High demand) = (0.70) X (0.40) = 0.28 (All other joint occurrences culminate in negative values; see Section 5.4 for a review of the rules of multiplication.)

Review

64 (Frames 1–20) When the probabilities of the states in a decision situation under uncertainty are not identified, the three decision criteria that might be used are called the _____ , _____ , and _____ criteria.

maximin; maximax; minimax regret (any order)

65 (Frames 1–8) Of the three criteria in Frame 64, above, the one that can be described as being most (and perhaps wishfully) optimistic is the _____ , and the one that is most conservative is the _____ .

maximax

maximin

66 (Frames 9–12) In decision analysis, the difference between the best conditional value for a particular state of

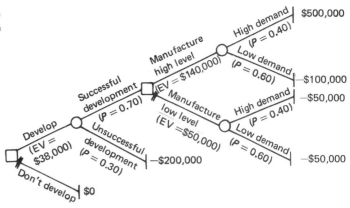

Review ■ 357

opportunity loss (or regret)	nature and the conditional value associated with an act is referred to as the _____ for that act.

67 (Frames 13-20) The decision criterion which is concerned with minimizing the largest opportunity loss that can occur as

minimax regret	the result of the decision that is made is the _____ criterion.

68 (Frames 21-26) In the decision-making situation in which both the conditional economic consequences and the probability distribution related thereto have been identified, the criterion used as the basis for choosing the decision alternative

expected value	is the _____ criterion.

69 (Frames 27-33) The *expected value* for a particular decision act is determined by multiplying each conditional

probability	value by the associated _____ value and summing the products.

70 (Frames 34-39) The *expected value* refers to the expected

as a long-run average	value of the gain or loss [in a particular event / as a long-run average].

71 (Frames 40-47) One difficulty with the criterion of maximizing expected monetary value is that [small / large]

large	conditional losses may not be given enough attention or weight. The approach by which decision theorists have
utility	attempted to eliminate such difficulties is called _____ theory.

72 (Frames 48-51) The method of analysis which is particularly appropriate when the decision situation involves a

decision tree	sequence of events and required decisions is _____ analysis.

73 (Frames 52-56) In terms of direction, a decision tree is

left; right	developed sequentially from _____ to _____ . Each
square	decision point is represented symbolically by a _____ and
circle	each chance event is represented symbolically by a _____ .

74 (Frame 57) The criterion which is used as the basis for determining the best acts in decision tree analysis is the

expected value	_____ criterion.

75 (Frames 58-63) In decision tree analysis, the best acts are identified by a process called "folding back," which, in terms

of direction, involves working from _____ to _____ in the decision tree.

| right; left |

Symbols Introduced in This Chapter (with Frame Numbers)

(24) EV   Expected value associated with a decision act.

Formulas Introduced in This Chapter (with Frame Numbers)

(24) $EV = \Sigma XP(X)$ The expected value associated with a particular decision act, given that the probabilities of the states are available.

EXERCISES
(Solutions on pages 615–619)

13.1 What is a "decision criterion"? Describe the decision criteria that are available for the decision-making situation in which the probability values associated with the states are not available.

13.2 A small retail store has the choice of ordering 0, 1, 2, or 3 stereo sets from a distributor. The markup on each set is $90 and the amount of loss on any set it does not sell is $120.

(a) Determine the best decision act from the standpoint of the maximin criterion.
(b) Determine the best decision act from the standpoint of the maximax criterion.
(c) Determine the best decision act from the standpoint of the minimax regret criterion.
(d) In this stock-ordering situation in which the probabilities associated with the states (levels of demand) are not known, which decision would you make? Why?

13.3 For the stock-ordering situation described in Exercise 13.2, above, the retailer estimates that the probabilities associated with his selling 0, 1, 2, or 3 stereo sets within the relevant period of time are 0.10, 0.40, 0.30, and 0.20, respectively. Determine the best decision act from the standpoint of maximizing the expected value associated with the decision.

13.4 The following decision table presents the conditional values (returns) associated with three different investment decisions for a two year period. Given that the probabilities associated with the states are not available, determine the best decision act from the standpoint of: (a) the maximin criterion; (b) the maximax criterion; and (c) the minimax regret criterion.

	State of economy during period		
Investment	Recession	Stable	Expansion
Savings account	$ 1,000	$ 1,000	$ 1,000
Common stock	−700	1,000	2,000
Stock options	−10,000	−5,000	12,000

13.5 For the investment decision described in Exercise 13.4, above, suppose that the investor estimates that the probability values associated with the three states are 0.20, 0.50, and 0.30, respectively. Determine the best decision act from the standpoint of maximizing the expected monetary value associated with the decision.

13.6 A major aerospace company is considering the submission of a bid for a government contract. If a bid is submitted, an expenditure of $300,000 will be required to perform the initial research and development activities which are necessary to define the operational goals to be included with the bid. The estimated profit that can be realized during the time span of the contract is $500,000, including consideration of the initial expenditure on research and development. If the contract is not awarded to the company, about half of the initial research and development cost is considered a loss, with the other half applicable to other company projects. Construct the table of conditional monetary values for this decision-making situation and identify the best decision acts ("bid" or "not bid") from the standpoint of the maximin, maximax, and minimax regret criteria.

13.7 For the situation described in Exercise 13.6, above, management estimates that there is a 40 percent chance that the company will be awarded the contract. Determine the best decision act based on taking this probability value into consideration.

13.8 Given the necessity of choosing the one best decision from several possible acts, describe the decision analysis approach used for a situation involving uncertainty. Indicate what type of information you would need to determine and how you would organize this information for the purpose of analysis.

13.9 In general, decision analysts prefer to use the expected value criterion rather than the maximin criterion as the basis for identifying the best decision act. Under what circumstances, however, might the maximin criterion be preferred?

13.10 A retailer buys a certain item for $3 per case and sells it for $5 per case. The high markup reflects the perishability of the product, since it has no value after five days. Based on experience with similar products, the retailer is confident that the demand for the item will be in the range of 9 to 12 cases, inclusive.

(a) Construct the decision table for this inventory problem, indicating the possible monetary consequences associated with ordering 9, 10, 11, or 12 cases of this perishable item.
(b) Determine the best decision act from the standpoint of the maximin criterion.
(c) Determine the best decision act from the standpoint of the maximax criterion.
(d) Determine the best decision act from the standpoint of the minimax regret criterion.

13.11 For the decision situation described in Exercise 13.10, above, suppose that the retailer further estimates that the probabilities associated with selling 9 to 12 cases of the item are 0.30, 0.40, 0.20, and 0.10, respectively. Determine the best decision from the standpoint of maximizing the expected monetary value.

13.12 An investor is presented with the opportunity of buying common stock in a newly formed electronics company in the amount of $10,000. If the company is successful, the investment will be tripled in value. Otherwise, the entire investment will be lost. Determine the best decision acts ("Invest" or "Don't invest") from the standpoint of the maximin, maximax, and minimax regret criteria.

13.13 For the investment decision described in Exercise 13.12, above, the investor estimates that there is about a 40 percent chance the company will fail. Taking this information into consideration, what is the best decision? Is this the decision *you* would make? Why or why not?

13.14 Several weeks before an annual "Water Carnival," a college fraternity must decide to order either blankets or beach umbrellas (or neither) for resale at the event. The conditional values associated with the possible decisions are dependent on the weather conditions on the day of the event and are identified in the table below. Determine the best acts from the standpoint of the maximin, maximax, and minimax regret criteria.

Item ordered	Weather	
	Cool	Hot
Blankets	$50	−$25
Beach umbrellas	−40	75
Neither	0	0

13.15 For the decision problem described in Exercise 13.14, above, one of the members of the fraternity calls the weather bureau and learns that during the past 10 years the weather has been "hot" on seven of the ten days on the date when the Water Carnival is to be held. Determine the best decision act by using this information to estimate the probabilities associated with the two states.

13.16 An investor is considering placing a deposit of $10,000 to reserve a franchise opportunity for a new residential area for one year. There are two areas of uncertainty associated with this sequential decision situation: whether or not a prime franchise competitor will decide to locate an outlet in the same area and whether or not the residential area will develop to be a moderate or large market. Overall, then, the investor must first decide whether to deposit the initial $10,000 as a down payment for the franchise. Then during the one-year period the decision of the competing franchise system will be revealed, and the investor estimates that there is a 50–50 chance that the competing franchise system will also develop an outlet. After the decision of the competing system is known, the investor must then decide whether or not to proceed with constructing the franchise outlet. If there is competition and the market is large, the net gain during the relevant period is estimated as being $15,000; if the market is moderate, there will be a net loss of $10,000. If there is no competition and the market is large, the net gain will be $30,000; if the market is moderate, there will be a net gain of $10,000. All of these net figures include consideration of the franchise deposit fee of $10,000. The investor estimates that there is about a 40 percent chance that the market will be large. Based on this information, construct the decision tree for this situation.

13.17 Referring to your decision tree in Exercise 13.16, determine the best act at the initial decision point ("Deposit" or "Don't deposit").

13.18 For the sequential decision problem in Exercises 13.16 and 13.17, determine the probability that there will be a profit if the initial deposit is made. Also consider the implications of making the initial deposit, in terms of the best acts at the next decision points in your decision tree.

CHAPTER 14 ■ BAYESIAN INFERENCE

In the preceding chapter we indicated that when both the conditional economic consequences *and* the probabilities of the states are available for a decision situation involving uncertainty, or risk, then the *expected value* criterion is used to identify the best decision act. Overall, this chapter is concerned with how the probabilities associated with the several possible states can be revised and improved based on sample data associated with the decision situation. The implication of such a revision is that the expected monetary values associated with several decision alternatives would themselves be changed by such a revision, thereby possibly resulting in a different decision act being identified as the best act. In order to develop your understanding of the basic procedure by which such revisions are accomplished, we first consider the concepts of objective, subjective, and conditional probability. After this review, the use of Bayes' theorem to revise an individual probability value is explained. In the third section of this chapter the use of Bayesian revision is extended to entire probability distributions, while the last section is concerned with how the expected value of additional information can be determined.

14.1 ■ Objective, Subjective, and Conditional Probability

In this section we review the concepts of objective, subjective, and conditional probability which were presented in Chapter 5. Several methods of determining probability values are described in that chapter. When a probability value is interpreted as indicating the long-run relative frequency of an event, the objective approach is being followed. When a probability value is interpreted as indicating the strength of belief that an event will occur, then the subjective approach is being followed. The coverage of conditional probability and dependent events in this section provides an appropriate foundation for studying Bayes' theorem in the following section.

1 When a probability value of 0.90 is interpreted as meaning that in the long run a given event will occur in 90 percent of the observations, the approach that is being followed is the [objective /subjective] approach to probability.

objective

2 Objective probability values may be determined by the *classical* method or by the *empirical* method. When we make a large number of observations and tabulate the frequency of various outcomes, the method of determining probability would be described as [classical / empirical].

empirical (See Section 5.1 for a discussion of these and related concepts.)

3 No matter which of the two methods of determining the probability values is used, the objective approach to the interpretation of probability suggests that such a value represents (Circle the best choice):

(a) $\dfrac{\text{Frequency of an event}}{\text{Total number of observations}}$

(b) $\dfrac{\text{Total number of observations}}{\text{Frequency of an event}}$

4 In contrast, the subjective interpretation of probability values is not concerned with the relative or expected frequency of an event. Rather, it is concerned with the strength of a decision maker's belief that an event will or will not occur. As such, the subjective approach is particularly suitable for decision-making situations that [occur only once / are repetitive].

5 Subjective probability values may be determined by the *direct estimate* method or by the *indifference* method. The method by which the probability value is determined algebraically based on the "amount certain" that the decision maker assesses as being the equivalent of a risk situation exemplifies the [direct estimate / indifference] method.

6 One advantage of using the subjective approach to probability is that the methods of statistical inference can then be applied to [repetitive / unique] situations.

7 However, the use of the subjective approach is not limited to unique situations or observations. Suppose a decision maker **(a)** first estimates the probability that a product will exceed break-even based on his experience with similar products, then **(b)** conducts a sampling study of actual consumer reactions, and finally **(c)** revises his original probability value according to the results of the sampling study. The final (revised) probability value would be described as being determined by the [objective approach / subjective approach / combination of the two approaches].

8 The idea of combining the two approaches to probability is discussed further in the remaining sections of this chapter. In general, however, we can observe that the methods of statistical estimation and hypothesis testing which have been discussed in the preceding chapters of this book are all based on the [objective approach / subjective approach / combination of the two approaches] to determining probability values.

objective approach

9 In Chapter 5 we considered the distinction between independent and dependent events. Independent events are those in which the probability of an event in a particular observation is unaffected by the outcomes of other observations. On the other hand, such an effect does occur in the case of dependent events. Thus the repeated tossing of a fair coin represents a series of [dependent / independent] events. The drawing of cards from a deck of cards *without replacement* represents a series of _____ events.

independent

dependent (See Section 5.4 for a review.)

10 The binomial, normal, t, and χ^2 (chi-square) distributions, which have served as the basis for the methods of statistical inference that we have studied, all are based on the requirement that the several sample observations be [dependent / independent].

independent

11 By posting the missing probability values in the simple tree diagram below, illustrate the proposition that the tossing of a fair coin twice in succession represents two independent events.

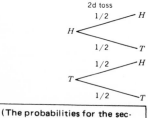

(The probabilities for the second toss are unaffected by the outcome of the first toss.)

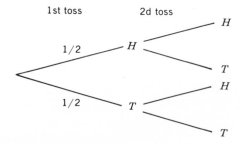

12 On the tree diagram below post the missing probability values associated with drawing a spade from a deck of 52 cards on each of two successive draws, drawing *without replace-*

ment. S signifies a spade outcome and *S'* signifies a non-spade outcome.

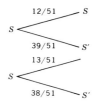

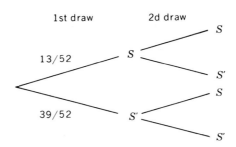

13 For independent events we can designate the probability of an outcome *B* by the symbol *P(B)*, regardless of the outcome of any other event. For dependent events the probability of outcome *B*, given that outcome *A* has occurred in a related event, is designated by the symbol _____ .

P(B|A) (read: "the probability of *B* given that *A* has occurred"; this is *not* a fraction)

14 The kind of probability value designated by the symbol *P(B|A)*, which can occur only for dependent events, is called _____ probability.

conditional

15 To extend the related concepts of dependent events and conditional probability to a managerial decision-making situation, suppose that the probability is 0.60 that our major competitor will decide to diversify his products, and if he does, the probability is 0.80 that he will build a new plant. If he decides not to diversify, the probability is 0.40 that he will build the plant. Enter the probability values for the various events in the tree diagram below, in which *D* indicates the decision to diversify and *B* indicates the decision to build a new plant.

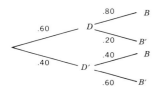

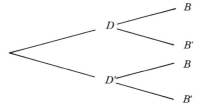

16 Since the probability of building the new plant varies with the decision of whether or not to diversify, the two decision

| dependent |

situations, or events, can be described as being _____ . Further, all of the probability values for B and B' posted in Frame 15 can be described as being _____ probability values.

| conditional |

| 0.80 |
| 0.40 |

17 In the tree diagram in Frame 15, $P(B|D) =$ _____ (value) and $P(B|D') =$ _____ (value).

18 According to the data of Frame 15, the probability that our competitor will diversify *and* build a new plant is:

| $P(D)P(B|D) = (0.60)(0.80) =$ 0.48 (See Chapter 5, Frames 80-89, for a review.) |

$P($ ____ $)P($ ____ $) =$

19 Given the values in Frame 15, even if we do not know whether our competitor has decided to diversify, we can still determine the overall probability that he will build a new plant. The decision to build can be made in either of two mutually exclusive ways: with diversification or without. Thus, using the rule of addition for this either-or situation,

| $(0.60)(0.80) + (0.40)(0.40)$ $= 0.48 + 0.16 = 0.64$ (See section 5c for a review of the rule of addition.) |

$P(B) = P(D)P(B|D) + P(D')P(B|D') =$

20 Similarly, the overall (unconditional) probability that he will *not* build, given no information regarding his decision to diversify, is:

| $P(D)P(B'|D) + P(D')P(B'|D')$ $= (0.60)(0.20) + (0.40)(0.60)$ $= 0.12 + 0.24 = 0.36$ |

21 Since the possible decisions to build or not to build are mutually exclusive as well as exhaustive, in that only one of these events can occur and there are no other possible events, the overall probabilities of building $P(B)$ and not building $P(B')$, computed in Frames 19 and 20, should add up to a value of ____ .

| 1.0 (They do: 0.64 + 0.36.) |

22 Once a decision regarding diversification is made known, however, we can modify the probabilities associated with building by direct reference to the tree diagram in Frame 15. Thus, if we learn that the decision has been made *not* to diversify, then $P(B|D') =$ _____ and $P(B'|D') =$ _____ .

| 0.40; 0.60 |

14.2 ■ Bayes' Theorem

Algebraically, Bayes' theorem represents the analysis of conditional probabilities for the purpose of "backward" inference, that is, for determining the conditional probability of a particular outcome in the earlier of two observations involving dependent events, given the outcome of the second observation. For example, given that our competitor is in fact building a new plant, we might be interested in determining the probability that he has decided to diversify. The direction of inference is thus the reverse of that considered in Section 14.1, and this leads to applications of Bayes' theorem that may not at first be obvious. The change in direction of inference permits us to take account of additional knowledge about uncertain events and to revise the probability values associated with such events on the basis of the known outcomes of related events. In this section we consider the meanings of *prior probability* and *posterior probability* as used in Bayes' theorem, introduce the computations that are associated with this theorem, and finally consider the meaning or interpretation of the posterior probabilities that are determined by use of the computational procedure.

23 Two terms used in the Bayesian revision of probability values are *prior probability* and *posterior probability*. Since the essence of Bayes' approach is that it describes a procedure by which probability values can be modified on the basis of later evidence, the probability that is associated with an event *before* there is any knowledge of associated outcomes is called

| prior |

_____ probability.

24 Thus prior probabilities are the probability values prior to sample information. On the other hand, when such a probability value is modified by our knowledge of the outcome of an associated (dependent) event, the resulting

| posterior |

modified value is called _____ probability.

25 As indicated in the introduction to this section, Bayes' theorem is used in conjunction with dependent events and conditional probabilities, but with the usual direction of inference reversed. Refer to Figure 14-1, which presents the tree diagram for the problem discussed in Section 14.1. The *prior probability* that our competitor has decided to diversify

| 0.60 |

(i.e., with no knowledge of related events) is _____ (value)

Figure 14-1 ■ Tree diagram
depicting the probabilities
associated with a competitor's
possible decisions

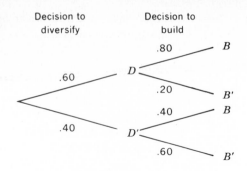

Decision to
diversify

Decision to
build

.80 — B

.60 — D

.20 — B'

.40 — B

.40 — D'

.60 — B'

26 Now suppose that we observe that he is in fact building a new plant. Does this action on his part necessarily indicate that he has decided to diversify? [Yes / No]

No (since the decision to build could also have been made along with the decision not to diversify)

27 Thus we would like to determine the probability that our competitor has decided to diversify, given that he is building the new plant. In terms of the symbol used, this posterior probability value, which takes the new information into account, can be represented by $P(\_\_\_\_\_)$.

$(D|B)$

28 Can we directly determine the value of $P(D|B)$ by reference to Figure 14-1? [Yes / No]

No [The value of $P(B|D)$ is directly indicated, but not $P(D|B)$.]

29 Rather than simply presenting Bayes' formula for computing posterior probabilities, let us illustrate its algebraic relationship to the formulas already introduced in Chapter 5. In that chapter what formula was used to determine the probability of the joint occurrence of two *dependent* events, A and B?

$P(A)P(B|A)$ (See Chapter 5, Frames 80-89.)

$P(A,B) =$

30 Conceptually, we can reverse the two events and have the second event considered first. In this case

$P(B)P(A|B)$

$P(B,A) =$

31 Referring to Frames 29 and 30, note that the conditional probabilities with which we worked in Section 14.1 are of the

$P(A|B)$

$P(B|A)$ type, whereas posterior probabilities are the conditionals designated by the symbol _____ .

32 As the next step in developing a formula for determining $P(A|B)$, we can take advantage of the fact that $P(B,A) = P(A,B)$, since "B and A" and "A and B" are alternative ways of describing the same joint occurrence of two events. Therefore, it follows that the right sides of the following two equations are also equal to one another:

$$P(B,A) = P(B)P(A|B)$$
$$P(A,B) = P(A)P(B|A)$$

Algebraically, then, we can say that:

$P(A)P(B|A)$

$$P(B)P(A|B) =$$

33 Then, solving the final equation in Frame 32 for the value of the posterior probability, we have:

$\dfrac{P(A)P(B|A)}{P(B)}$

$$P(A|B) =$$

34 The equation that you have just developed is a simple statement of Bayes' theorem. It is not necessary for you to memorize this equation for our purposes, but you should now be able to use it and interpret the resulting value. Getting back to the question originally posed in Frame 26, if we observe that our competitor is in fact building a new plant, and we wish to determine the probability that he has decided to diversify, substitute the appropriate symbols for the solution of this problem, referring to the general formula in Frame 33:

$\dfrac{P(D)P(B|D)}{P(B)}$

$$P(D|B) =$$

35 Of the required values for solving this formula, the overall probability that our competitor will build a new plant, $P(B)$, is not directly represented in the tree diagram in Figure 14-1. As we noted in Section 14.1, however, this value can be determined by adding the probabilities of the two circumstances under which the plant might be built; that is (in symbols),

$P(D')P(B|D')$

$$P(B) = P(D)P(B|D) +$$

36 Therefore for computational purposes the complete general formula used to determine the posterior probability is

$$P(A|B) = \frac{P(A)P(B|A)}{P(A)P(B|A) + P(A')P(B|A')}$$

Using this formula for the data of Figure 14-1, solve for the value of the posterior probability that our competitor has decided to diversify, given that he is building the new plant.

$$\frac{(0.60)(0.80)}{(0.60)(0.80) + (0.40)(0.40)} =$$
$$\frac{0.48}{0.48 + 0.16} = \frac{0.48}{0.64} = 0.75$$

$$P(D|B) = \frac{P(D)P(B|D)}{P(D)P(B|D) + P(D')P(B|D')} =$$

37 In Figure 14-1, before the additional information regarding building of the plant, the probability assigned to the decision to diversify was _____ (value), and in the language of Bayesian revision this value is designated as the _____ probability. With the additional information considered, the probability that our competitor has decided to diversify is now identified as _____ (value) and is designated as the _____ probability.

0.60
prior

0.75
posterior

38 Incidentally, a posterior probability may be either higher or lower in value than the associated prior probability. If our competitor had decided *not* to build the new plant, then the posterior probability assigned to his having decided to diversify would be [less than 0.60 / equal to 0.60 / greater than 0.60].

less than 0.60

39 To satisfy yourself in this regard, determine the posterior probability that our competitor has decided to diversify, given that he is *not* building a new plant, using the formula below.

$$\frac{(0.60)(0.20)}{(0.60)(0.20) + (0.40)(0.60)} =$$
$$\frac{0.12}{0.12 + 0.24} = \frac{0.12}{0.36} = 0.33$$

$$P(D|B') = \frac{P(D)P(B'|D)}{P(D)P(B'|D) + P(D')P(B'|D')} =$$

40 Thus the value of the Bayesian approach to inference is that it provides a basis for modifying probabilities based on evidence from related events. Some statisticians, however, have expressed concern about the direction and type of reasoning inherent in this approach. First, probability values are being assigned to an outcome that has, in fact, already either occurred or not occurred (although the decision maker is not in the position of knowing the outcome). Furthermore, not only has the event already taken place, but it will not take place again. According to our previous discussion, these kinds of concerns are most likely to be expressed by those who believe that statistical inference should be based only on the [objective / subjective] approach to interpreting probability values.

objective

41 If one applies a strength-of-belief interpretation to the posterior probability values, then the "backward reasoning from effect to cause" inherent in the Bayesian revision of probabilities does not present any additional difficulties other than those always encountered in the _____ approach to interpreting probability values.

subjective

14.3 ■ Prior and Posterior Probability Distributions

In Section 14.2, on Bayes' theorem, we presented the use of Bayes' formula for determining posterior probabilities. The concept of revising probabilities on the basis of associated evidence is not restricted to individual probability values, but, rather, it can be extended to an entire probability distribution. Thus, in the present section we begin with a prior probability distribution of fractions defective and revise these probabilities on the basis of observed sample results, thereby forming a posterior probability distribution. The techniques presented and illustrated in this section apply to discrete probability distributions only. Techniques associated with the revision of continuous probability distributions, such as the normal distribution, are included in more advanced texts in statistical analysis.

42 Suppose that when a manufacturing process is in control, the proportion defective is 0.01, and when it is out of control, the porportion defective is 0.10. The following table lists the number of lots associated with each state during an extended period. On the basis of this historical information, enter the probability of each state in the last column of the table.

Fraction defective	Number of lots	P
0.01	40	___
0.10	10	___
	50	

0.80
0.20

43 Now, suppose that a sample of 10 items is taken and one item is found to be defective. Since the probability of obtaining any particular sample result is conditional on the fraction defective for the overall batch, the results of a sample can be used to revise the probabilities in the table above by means of _____ formula.

44 Before proceeding with the use of Bayes' formula, enter the appropriate probabilities on the first branching in the following tree diagram.

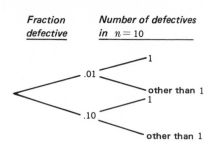

45 In order to revise the prior probability of 0.80 that the fraction defective is 0.01, we need to determine the probabilities in the second branchings of the tree diagram above. For example, we need to determine $P(X = 1 | n = 10$, fraction defective $= 0.01)$. Because the probability that a single randomly sampled item will be defective is equal to the fraction defective for the overall batch, the value for $P(X = 1 | n = 10$, fraction defective $= 0.01)$ can be obtained from the table of _____ probabilities.

46 Specifically, $P(X = 1 | n = 10, p = 0.01) = $ _____ .

47 Similarly, determine the value of the remaining three probabilities in the second branching and enter them on the tree diagram below. Note that the probability of "other than 1" can most easily be obtained by subtraction in each case.

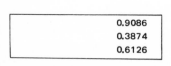
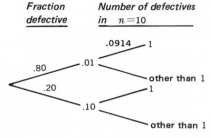

48 In the example above, note that the probability values used in conjunction with the binomial table were 0.01 and 0.10, and *not* 0.80 and 0.20. The latter values represent the probabilities associated with the two states. But given that a particular state (fraction defective) is true, the probability that one randomly chosen item will be defective is equal to the

---
fraction defective

_____ itself.

49 Beginning with the general expression for Bayes' formula below, revise the prior probability that the true fraction is 0.01, given that one item in a random sample of 10 items is found to be defective. *To simplify the required computations, round the four conditional probabilities identified in Frame 47 to 0.09, 0.91, 0.39, and 0.61, respectively.*

$$\frac{(0.80)(0.09)}{(0.80)(0.09) + (0.20)(0.39)} =$$
$$\frac{0.072}{0.072 + 0.078} = \frac{0.072}{0.150} = 0.48$$

$$P(A|B) = \frac{P(A)P(B|A)}{P(A)P(B|A) + P(A')P(B|A')} =$$

50 Either by subtraction or by using Bayes' formula again, we can also conclude that the probability that the true fraction defective is 0.10 is equal to approximately 0.52. Therefore, complete the table below, which reports the probability distribution of the fractions defective prior to collecting the sample and the distribution after taking sample results into consideration.

0.80; 0.48
0.20; 0.52

Fraction defective (state)	Prior P	Posterior P
0.01	_____	_____
0.10	_____	_____

51 The procedure we have just illustrated is of course identical to the procedure presented in Section 14.2, except that we have highlighted the fact that by revising the individual probability values we have in effect revised the entire probability distribution. Now we present an alternative approach to revising a probability distribution that is easier to use than the Bayes' formula itself, especially when there are more than two possible states in the probability distribution. As the first step, enter the conditional probabilities from Frame 47 in column 3 of the table below. Then round these values to two places to simplify the required computations.

State (1)	Prior P (2)	Conditional probability of sample result (No. def. = 1) (3)	Joint probability (Col. 2 × Col. 3) (4)
0.01	0.80	___ ≐ ___	_____
0.10	0.20	___ ≐ ___	_____

0.0914 ≐ 0.09
0.3874 ≐ 0.39

52 The first value you entered is $P(X = 1 | n = 10, p = 0.01)$ and the second is $P(X = 1 | n = 10, p = 0.10)$. Now, enter the joint probability values in column 4, above, by multiplying each prior probability value by the rounded associated conditional probability.

0.072
0.078

53 As you can verify by reference to Frame 49, these are the same joint probability values that are included in Bayes' formula, and the sum of these probability values is equal to the sum in the denominator of Frame 49. The final step in the calculation of the posterior probabilities by this tabular approach is to divide each joint probability value in column 4 by the sum of this column, and to enter this result in column 5. Do this now.

State (1)	Prior P (2)	Conditional probability of sample result (3)	Joint probability (Col. 2 × Col. 3) (4)	Posterior P (Col. 4 ÷ sum) (5)
0.01	0.80	0.09	0.072	_____
0.10	0.20	0.39	0.078	_____
			0.150	==========

0.48
0.52
1.00

54 Of course, these are the same posterior probabilities as calculated by the use of Bayes' formula. When the probability distribution has only two possible states, the tabular approach represents little, if any, advantage. However, as the number of states is increased, the required computations associated with using Bayes' formula become increasingly unwieldy, whereas the tabular approach remains basically the same. As a further and more realistic example of the tabular approach, suppose that there are four possible states, as indicated in the table below. Again, a sample of $n = 10$ has been taken and one item is found to be defective. As the first step in determining the posterior probability distribution, enter the appropriate probability values in column 3, below. Again, round these to two places in order to simplify required computations. (Of course, such rounding should not be done with regular end-of-chapter exercises and actual applications; rather, an electronic calculator should be used.)

	State (1)	Prior P (2)	Conditional probability of sample result (No. def. = 1) (3)
0.0914 ≐ 0.09	0.01	0.60	____ ≐ ____
0.3151 ≐ 0.32	0.05	0.20	____ ≐ ____
0.3874 ≐ 0.39	0.10	0.10	____ ≐ ____
0.2684 ≐ 0.27	0.20	0.10	____ ≐ ____

55 By referring to Frame 53 if necessary, enter the appropriate label for column 4 in the table above and enter the joint probabilities.

Joint probability (Col. 2 × Col. 3) (4)
0.054
0.064
0.039
0.027
0.184

56 Finally, determine the posterior probabilities and enter these in the table in Frame 53, rounding the values to two places to the right of the decimal point.

Posterior P (Col. 4 ÷ sum) (5)
0.29
0.35
0.21
0.15
1.00

57 Note that the effect of the sample result was to shift the probabilities in the direction of the sample proportion defective of 0.10. For example, the prior probability that the true proportion defective is 0.10 is _____ , whereas the posterior probability is _____ .

0.10
0.21

58 What we have illustrated, then, is the use of a tabular approach for determining a posterior probability distribution. Our examples concerned use of binomial probabilities, but the technique is not limited to such sampling situations. For example, the table below presents three possible states as being the true mean in a Poisson process. Given that one maintenance call was required on a sampled day, determine the conditional probabilities in column 3, below, and then round the values to two places.

True average of maint. calls per day, λ (1)	Prior P (2)	Conditional probability of sample result (3)	Joint probability (4)	Posterior P (5)
1.0	0.20	___ $\doteq$ ___	___	___
3.0	0.30	___ $\doteq$ ___	___	___
5.0	0.50	___ $\doteq$ ___	___	___

0.3679 $\doteq$ 0.37
0.1494 $\doteq$ 0.15
0.0337 $\doteq$ 0.03

Joint P (4)	Post. P (5)
0.074	0.55
0.045	0.34
0.015	0.11
0.134	1.00

59 Of course, the conditional probabilities above are for $P(X = 1 | \lambda = 1.0)$, $P(X = 1 | \lambda = 3.0)$, and $P(X = 1 | \lambda = 5.0)$. Now, complete the table above by calculating the joint probabilities and posterior probabilities.

60 As expected, since the sample result is most supportive of $\lambda = 1.0$, the posterior probability distribution has shifted toward this state. For example, we can note that the prior probability that $\lambda = 1.0$ is _____, whereas the posterior probability is approximately _____ .

0.20
0.55

61 Of course, in the classical approach to statistical inference only the sample information serves as the basis for estimating the parameters of a population. In the Bayesian approach, as exemplified by the examples in this section, the posterior probability distribution is based on both the _____ information and the _____ information.

prior
sample

14.4 ■ The Value of Information

In the preceding section we described how sample information is used to revise a prior probability distribution, thus resulting in a posterior probability distribution. From the standpoint of decision analysis, a particular sample result has value only if it results in a change in the decision act which is identified as being best. In this section we describe how the estimated gain associated with a particular sample result can be determined. Then we extend the analysis to describe how the expected value of perfect information can be determined—that is, the value of information that would remove all uncertainty from the decision situation.

62 The table below repeats the possible fractions defective and the prior probability distribution used as an illustration in the preceding section on prior and posterior probability distributions. Suppose that each lot is comprised of 1,000 items and that the cost of inspecting each item is 2 cents. Based on this information, enter the conditional cost of "100 percent inspection" for each fraction defective in the table below.

Fraction defective	Prior P	Cost of 100% inspection
0.01	0.60	$ _____
0.05	0.20	_____
0.10	0.10	_____
0.20	0.10	_____

20.00
20.00
20.00
20.00

(No matter which fraction defective is true, the cost of inspection is $0.02 X 1,000.)

---

63 In the absence of 100 percent inspection, the defective items become part of an assembled component and have to be replaced at a cost of 40 cents each. Suppose that the true fraction defective is 0.01. Whereas the cost of 100 percent inspection is $_____ , the cost associated with no inspection (and replacement of defective items) is $_____ .

20.00

1% Def. X 1,000 = 10
Def; 10 X $0.40 = $4.00

---

64 Therefore, if the true fraction defective is 0.01, the best decision act is [100 percent inspection / no inspection] .

no inspection

---

65 Of course, under conditions of uncertainty we do not know the true fraction defective. In the table below, enter the cost of "no inspection" for the other fractions defective that can occur, determining these costs in a manner similar to the procedure for the 0.01 fraction defective.

Fraction defective	Prior P	Cost of 100% inspection	Cost of no inspection
0.01	0.60	$20.00	$ 4.00
0.05	0.20	20.00	_____
0.10	0.10	20.00	_____
0.20	0.10	20.00	_____

20.00
40.00
80.00

---

66 Up to this point the probability distribution associated with the fractions defective has played no role in our calculations. But in order to determine the expected costs of "100 percent inspection" and "no inspection," we multiply the conditional costs by probabilities. This procedure is analogous to the computation of the expected monetary values in Chapter 13. Using the prior probability distribution, determine the expected costs in regard to inspection by completing the table below.

		Fraction def.	Prior P	Cost of 100% inspec.	Cost of no inspec.	Exp. cost of 100% inspec.	Exp. cost of no inspec.
		0.01	0.60	$20.00	$ 4.00	$12.00	$ 2.40
		0.05	0.20	20.00	20.00	4.00	4.00
2.00;	4.00	0.10	0.10	20.00	40.00	_____	_____
2.00;	8.00	0.20	0.10	20.00	80.00	_____	_____
20.00;	18.40					Exp. cost = $_____	Exp. cost = $_____

67 As contrasted to expected monetary value, the best act is the one with the *lowest* expected cost. Therefore, given the situation above, the best decision act is [100 percent inspection / no inspection], with an associated expected cost of $_____ .

no inspection

18.40

68 However, suppose we take a small random sample out of the batch of 1,000 items in order to help us regarding the "100 percent inspection" decision. Any particular sample has value to us only if it causes us to change the decision from what it was before obtaining the sample result. This makes sense intuitively, and let us illustrate this idea by continuing with the illustration from the preceding section of this chapter. Whereas we used the *prior* probability distribution as a basis of comparison for the inspection costs in the above analysis, when a sample result is available, it is then appropriate to use the _____ probability distribution.

posterior

69 The table below lists the posterior probabilities associated with each state, given that a sample of $n = 10$ included one defective item, as determined in the preceding section of this chapter, as well as the conditional costs. Incidentally, for the purpose of our illustration, we do not bother to make the minor adjustments in conditional costs based on the fact that 990 items now remain in the batch rather than 1,000. Using the posterior probabilities, complete the table below to determine the expected cost of "100 percent inspection" and "no inspection."

Fraction def.	Posterior P	Cost of 100% inspec.	Cost of no inspec.	Exp. cost of 100% inspec.	Exp. cost of no inspec.
0.01	0.29	$20.00	$ 4.00	$ 5.80	$ 1.16
0.05	0.35	20.00	20.00	7.00	7.00
0.10	0.21	20.00	40.00	_____	_____
0.20	0.15	20.00	80.00	_____	_____
				Exp. cost = $_____	Exp. cost = $_____

4.20; 8.40
3.00; 12.00
20.00 28.56

100% inspection
20.00

70 Therefore, after the results of the sample are included in our analysis, the best decision is "_____ ," with an expected cost of $_____ .

71 Now, what was the sample worth? Its estimated value is based on the difference between the expected cost associated with the decision we would have made without the sample results and the expected cost associated with the best decision, *both expected costs based on the posterior distribution.* In this case, the value of the sample was $ _____ − $ _____ = $ _____ .

28.56; 20.00
8.56

72 Again, note that only the expected costs associated with the *posterior* distribution are used. It might be tempting to think that the estimated value of the sample result should be the difference between the expected cost prior to the sample and the expected cost after the sample. But because the sample information has the general effect of revising and *updating* the prior probabilities, only the [prior / posterior] distribution should be used in estimating the value of the particular sample.

posterior

73 To illustrate this point one other way, suppose that the sample result is such that it does not change our decision. Specifically, suppose that the posterior cost associated with the best decision is lower than the prior cost of the best act, but that the same act is still the best act after the sample. The expected gain would have been achieved whether or not the sample were taken. Therefore, does the sample have any value in such a circumstance? [Yes / No]

No

74 Note that the procedure we have presented can be used to determine the estimated value of a particular sample *after* it has been taken. Procedures have also been developed to determine the expected value of a sample *before* it has been taken, but these are beyond the scope of this book. Again, a particular sample has value only if it causes the decision maker to change his decision and thereby reduce costs or improve profits as based on the [prior / posterior] expected values.

posterior

75 Even though we do not here consider the expected value of sample information prior to sampling, we can consider the expected value of perfect information (EVPI). By "perfect information" is meant such information that all uncertainty would be removed from the decision situation. In the fractions defective problem, for example, this would mean that whenever the true state is known to be 0.01, we would choose [100 percent inspection / no inspection]; and whenever the true state is known to be 0.20, we would choose [100 percent inspection / no inspection].

no inspection

100 percent inspection (based on the conditional costs in Frame 65)

76 The basic approach used to determine the expected value of perfect information (EVPI) is to determine the long-run expected (average) cost with perfect information and compare it with the expected cost under uncertainty. Referring to Frame 66, for the fractions defective problem, the expected cost of the best act under uncertainty (and without the sample information) is $ _____ .

18.40

77 Further, under conditions of uncertainty this expected cost is achieved in the long run by always choosing "no inspection." However, with perfect information would we always choose the same act when faced with the decision situation? [Yes / No]

No

78 Rather than consistently choosing the one act which is best in the long run, with perfect information we choose the act that is the best for the specific situation. Given that the probability values in the table below represent historical relative frequencies of occurrence of each state, we expect that the lots will contain only 0.01 fraction defective ___ percent of the time.

60

Fraction defective	P	Cost of 100% inspection	Cost of no inspection
0.01	0.60	$20.00	$ 4.00
0.05	0.20	20.00	20.00
0.10	0.10	20.00	40.00
0.20	0.10	20.00	80.00

79 Assume that whenever "100% inspection" and "no inspection" have the same cost, we choose "100% inspection" in order to minimize later delays in correcting defective components. Then for the situation above, in the long run we would choose "no inspection" _____ percent of the time and we would choose "100% inspection" _____ percent of the time.

<table>
<tr><td>60 (for fraction of 0.01)</td></tr>
<tr><td>40 (whenever the fraction defective is known to be 0.05 or greater)</td></tr>
</table>

80 In the table below, enter the conditional cost associated with each fraction defective, given that the best decision act is chosen.

Fraction defective	P	Best act	Conditional cost	Expected cost
0.01	0.60	No inspection	$_____	$_____
0.05	0.20	100% inspection	_____	_____
0.10	0.10	100% inspection	_____	_____
0.20	0.10	100% inspection	_____	_____
			Exp. cost = $_____	

<table>
<tr><td>4.00</td></tr>
<tr><td>20.00</td></tr>
<tr><td>20.00</td></tr>
<tr><td>20.00</td></tr>
</table>

81 Next, determine the expected cost with perfect information by multiplying each conditional cost by the relative frequency (probability) of occurrence and summing these values in the last column of the table above.

<table>
<tr><td>$2.40</td></tr>
<tr><td>4.00</td></tr>
<tr><td>2.00</td></tr>
<tr><td>2.00</td></tr>
<tr><td>$10.40</td></tr>
</table>

82 The expected cost of the best act under *uncertainty* was $18.40. Therefore, the EVPI for this problem is $_____ − $_____ = $_____ .

<table>
<tr><td>18.40</td></tr>
<tr><td>10.40; 8.00</td></tr>
</table>

83 Even though perfect information is seldom available in risk situations, the EVPI represents the upper limit of value for *any* information. For the fraction defectives problem, for example, suppose that a process has been developed that detects excess (over 0.01) defectives "most of the time," and that it costs $10 to apply the process to each batch of 1,000

No; Because the cost exceeds
EVPI, and no information
can be worth more than this
amount.

items. Should the process be used? [Yes / No] Why or why not? _____

_____

_____

14.5 ■ Expected Opportunity Loss

The expected value of perfect information serves as the upper limit for the value of any sample information. As illustrated in the preceding section, EVPI can be determined by taking the difference between the expected value with perfect information and the expected value of the best act under conditions of uncertainty. Another way of determining EVPI is to calculate the expected opportunity loss (EOL) of the best act. In the present section we illustrate the calculation of expected opportunity losses and relate these to expected monetary values and EVPI. Finally, we also describe an alternative approach to determining the expected value with perfect information. As in the previous sections our interest continues to be restricted to decision problems which involve discrete probability distributions, rather than continuous probability distributions.

84 In the preceding section we were concerned with a sample problem involving potential costs, and so the value of a particular sample or the value of perfect information was based on expected cost savings. If the decision problem involves a choice among several investment alternatives each of which has an expected gain, then the value of a particular sample or of perfect information is based on changes in expected _____ .

gain (etc.)

85 Again, a sample has value only if it leads to a change in the investment decision, while the perfect information implies that the investment choice is always suited to each circumstance. Therefore, under perfect information the same act [would / would not] be chosen at each decision opportunity.

would not

86 The following table of conditional values identifies the investment results associated with the investment of $10,000 in common stock as contrasted to a savings account, given different states of the economy during the coming year. The probabilities are subjective, in that they are based on the analyst's judgment. As the first step in determining the EVPI associated with this investment problem, identify the best investment choice by determining the expected monetary value associated with each act.

	State of economy	P	Conditional values Common stock	Conditional values Savings account	Expected values Common stock	Expected values Savings account
	Expansion	0.40	$1,000	$500	$400.00	$200.00
210.00; 150.00	Stable	0.30	700	500	_____	_____
−300.00; 150.00	Recession	0.30	−1,000	500	_____	_____
310.00; 500.00					Exp. value = $_____	Exp. value = $_____

87 Therefore, the best decision act is to place the $10,000 in a savings account, with an associated expected value (gain) of $500. As the next step in determining the EVPI, in the table below enter the best investment act for each state and the conditional value associated with each act.

State of economy	P	Best investment	Conditional values	Expected value
Expansion	0.40	_____	$_____	$_____
Stable	0.30	_____	_____	_____
Recession	0.30	_____	_____	_____
			Exp. value = $_____	

> Common stock; 1,000
> Common stock; 700
> Savings account; 500

> $400.00
> 210.00
> +150.00
> Exp. value = $760.00

88 Now, determine the expected value with perfect information, utilizing the last column in the table above.

> $260.00 (that is, $760.00 − 500.00, which then equals EVPI)

89 Therefore, investment information or advice that has the effect of removing all risk and uncertainty in this decision problem has an expected value of $ _____ .

90 We have illustrated the calculation of the EVPI for problems involving both conditional costs and conditional gains. We now present an alternative method of calculating EVPI in order to further highlight the meaning and application of certain concepts in decision analysis. Recall the concept of opportunity loss, or regret. For example, referring to the table of conditional values in Frame 86, the opportunity loss associated with "Savings account," given that the state of the economy actually turns out to be "Stable," is $_____ .

> 200 (the difference between the conditional value of $500 and the best value for that state, which is $700. See Section 13.1 to review the concept of opportunity loss, or regret.)

91 Similarly, enter the opportunity losses in the remaining cells of the following table by referring to Frame 86.

| State of economy | P | Opportunity losses | |
		Common stock	Savings account
Expansion	0.40	$ _____	$ _____
Stable	0.30	_____	200
Recession	0.30	_____	_____

92 Now we introduce the concept of *expected opportunity loss* (EOL). As implied by the concept name, the EOL for any act is determined by multiplying each of the conditional opportunity losses for that act by the associated _____ value and summing these products.

93 Whereas the expected value for an act identifies the long-run expected gain associated with the decision act, the long-run average amount by which the expected value associated with a decision act differs from the best value possible in each case is called _____ (   ).

94 Determine the EOL associated with each of the decision acts in our investment problem by completing the following table.

| State of economy | P | Cond. op. losses | | Exp. op. losses | |
		Common stock	Savings account	Common stock	Savings account
Expansion	0.40	$ 0	$500	$ 0	$200.00
Stable	0.30	0	200	_____	_____
Recession	0.30	1,500	0	_____	_____
				$ _____	$ _____

95 The best decision act is the one which has the lowest EOL associated with it. In this case, the best decision act is "_____ _____" with an EOL of $_____ .

96 As would be expected, this is the same decision act that was identified as being optimum in terms of maximizing expected value, since the act with the largest expected value should logically have the lowest expected opportunity loss. Now what does all of this have to do with the EVPI? Referring to Frame 89, note that the EVPI for this decision problem

260.00	
260.00	

equals $ _____ and the EOL of the best act (from Frame 95) equals $_____ .

97 This is more than a coincidence. *The EOL of the best act is always equal to EVPI.* This is logical, since EOL is the average amount by which the best possible value is missed, while EVPI was calculated earlier in this section by taking the difference between the expected value of the decision opportunity with perfect information and the expected value of the *best* act under conditions of [certainty / uncertainty].

uncertainty

98 Therefore, as an alternative to calculating EVPI by the type of subtraction done earlier, we can also determine EVPI by calculating the _____ of the best act.

expected opportunity loss
(EOL)

99 Further, we can also observe that the expected value associated with a decision act plus the expected opportunity loss associated with the same act should logically equal the expected value with perfect information. From Frame 88, the expected value with perfect information for this problem equals $760. From Frames 86 and 94, for the decision act "Common stock" the expected value + EOL = $_____ + $_____ = $_____ . For "Savings account" the expected value + EOL = $_____ + $_____ = $_____ .

310.00
450.00; 760.00
500.00; 260.00; 760.00

100 So there are also two methods by which expected value with perfect information can be calculated. One way is to identify the best act, given each state, and determine the expected value by multiplying the conditional values by the proportion of times each would occur and summing these products. Another way is to choose some act (usually the optimum act) and sum the expected _____ and expected _____ associated with that act.

value
opportunity loss (EOL)

Review

101 (Frames 1-8) Of the two approaches to interpreting the meaning of a probability value, the one that is particularly applicable when the value applies to a situation that is unique and will occur only once is the _____ approach. On the other hand a repetitive situation lends itself to being interpreted by the _____ approach.

subjective
objective

102 (Frames 9-11) The methods of inference heretofore discussed have required that the sample observations be

independent	[dependent / independent] and have led to the interpretation of probabilities in terms of the [objective / subjective] approach.
objective	

103 (Frames 12–22) The conditional probability that B will occur, given that A did not occur, is designated by the symbol

$P(B|A')$ _____ .

104 (Frames 23–25) In the language of Bayesian revision, the probability value that is identified before any knowledge of the outcome of a related event is called the _____

prior

probability. When the value is modified on the basis of a known outcome in a related event, the revised probability

posterior

value is called the _____ probability.

105 (Frames 26–39) Where the general symbol which is used to represent a conditional probability value is $P(B|A)$, the probability whose value is determined by use of Bayes' formula is represented by the general symbol _____ .

$P(A|B)$

106 (Frames 40, 41) The meaning of the posterior probability computed by Bayes' formula is most readily interpreted by

subjective

the [objective / subjective] approach to probability.

107 (Frames 42–50) When it is known that a batch or shipment of parts has a fraction defective at one of several specific and discrete levels, the conditional probability of obtaining a particular sample result for each fraction defective

binomial

can be determined by reference to the _____ probability distribution.

108 (Frames 51–61) In the tabular approach to determining posterior probabilities the final step in the calculation is concerned with using the column of values labeled "joint probability." In effect, each value in this column represents a

numerator

value in the [numerator / denominator] of Bayes' formula while the sum of this column represents the [numerator /

denominator

denominator] of Bayes' formula.

109 (Frames 62–68) Sample information has value [only if /

only if

whether or not] the optimum act changes as the result of the sample.

110 (Frames 69–74) The estimated value of sample information is determined by subtracting the expected cost of the act

| | identified as best after the sample, with the expected cost based on the [prior / posterior] distribution, from the expected cost of the act identified as best before the sample, with the expected cost based on the [prior / posterior] distribution. |

| posterior |
| posterior |

111 (Frames 75-83) The expected value of perfect information (EVPI) can be determined by subtracting the expected value under conditions of _____ from the expected value with _____ .

| uncertainty |
| perfect information |

112 (Frames 84-98) EVPI can also be determined by calculating the _____ of the best decision act under uncertainty.

| expected opportunity loss |
| (EOL) |

113 (Frames 99, 100) Finally, an alternative approach to determining the expected value with perfect information is to add the expected value associated with *any* decision act to the _____ associated with the same act.

| expected opportunity loss |
| (EOL) |

Symbols Introduced in This Chapter (with Frame Numbers)

(33) $P(A|B)$ A posterior (revised) probability value.

(76) EVPI   Expected value of perfect information.

(92) EOL   Expected opportunity loss.

Formulas Introduced in This Chapter (with Frame Numbers)

(19) $P(B) = P(A)P(B|A)$
$\qquad + P(A')P(B|A')$

The unconditional (overall) probability of an outcome in the second of two related events.

(33) $P(A|B) = \dfrac{P(A)P(B|A)}{P(B)}$

Bayes' formula for determining the value of the posterior (revised) probability.

(36) $P(A|B) = \dfrac{P(A)P(B|A)}{P(A)P(B|A) + P(A')P(B|A')}$

The computational version of Bayes' formula for determining the value of the posterior probability.

EXERCISES

(Solutions on pages 619-622)

14.1 Box *A* is known to contain one penny (*P*) and one dime (*D*) while box *B* contains two dimes. A box is chosen randomly and then a coin is randomly selected from the box.

(a) Construct a tree diagram to portray this situation involving sequential events.

(b) If box *A* is selected in the first step, what is the probability that a dime (*D*) will be selected in the second step?

(c) If a dime (*D*) is selected in the second step, what is the probability that it came from box *A*?

(d) If a penny (*P*) is selected in the second step, what is the probability that it came from box *A*?

14.2 If a manufacturer plans a major change in the new model of his product, the probability is 0.70 that he will begin making production-line modifications before September 1. On the other hand, if he does not plan a major change, the probability is only 0.20 that he will begin production-line modifications before September 1. In terms of the historical pattern of model changes, it is estimated that there is about a 40 percent chance that a major model change is planned for this year.

(a) Construct a tree diagram to represent the possible outcomes in this situation, which involves dependent events. In your diagram use *M* to signify a major change in the new model, *M'* for no major change, *L* for production-line modifications being made before September 1, and *L'* for the production-line changes not being made before September 1.

(b) Refer to your tree diagram. If the manufacturer has decided not to make a major model change, what is the probability that production-line modifications are *not* begun before September 1?

(c) What is the overall (unconditional) probability that production-line modifications will begin before September 1, given no information as to the type of model change being planned?

14.3 For the uncertain situation described in Exercise 14.2, above, suppose we observe that production-line modifications have in fact begun before September 1.

(a) What is the prior probability that the manufacturer has decided to make a major change in the new model?

(b) What is the posterior probability that the manufacturer has decided to make a major change in the new model?

14.4 When a particular manufacturing process is in control, it produces 1 percent defectives; whereas when it is out of control, it produces 10 percent defectives. At any randomly chosen point in time the probability is just 1 in 20 that the process is out of control. The items are produced in sets of 100 items. The cost of a "100 percent inspection" of each set, including reworking any and all defectives, is $400. In the absence of inspection it costs $200 to replace each defective item entering the assembly process. In terms of the long-run expected cost, would it be better to carry out "100 percent inspection" or to put the items into the assembly process without any inspection?

14.5 For the decision problem described in Exercise 14.4, above, determine the expected value (cost) with perfect information. Compare this value with the expected value associated with the best act and briefly indicate the reason for the difference.

14.6 Using the expected value calculated in Exercise 14.5, above, determine the EVPI for the decision situation described in Exercise 14.4 and briefly interpret the meaning of this value.

14.7 For the decision problem described in Exercise 14.4, suppose that a random sample of 10 items taken from a set of 100 items is found to include one defective item. Recompute the expected costs, taking this information into consideration, and indicate whether the remaining 90 items should be subjected to 100 percent inspection or be accepted without further inspection, given that 100 percent inspection of the 90 items would cost $360.

14.8 Estimate the value of the sample information that was obtained in Exercise 14.7, above. Determine this value only in respect to the 90 items that remain in the set after the 10 items have been sampled.

14.9 In June of a particular year an economist estimates that the probability is 0.70 that the (then) present rate of expansion in the national economy will continue for the remainder of the calendar year. Based on historical data, in a year of continued expansion steel orders in July have increased over July of the previous year in 80 percent of the cases, while in years in which the economy leveled or declined steel orders increased in 30 percent of the cases.

(a) Construct a tree diagram to represent this situation

involving uncertainty, using the symbols E for continued expansion in the national economy, E' for no further expansion, I for an increase in steel orders in July, and I' for no increase in sales orders in July.

(b) Determine the unconditional probability that steel orders will increase in July.

14.10 For the situation described in Exercise 14.9, above, at the end of July the economist learns that orders for steel declined during the month. Given this information, what is the probability that the expansion in the national economy will continue during the second half of the year?

14.11 Discuss the expected value of perfect information (EVPI) by describing how it can be determined and how such a value is interpreted.

ADDITIONAL EXERCISES

14.12 Suppose there are two urns, U_1 and U_2. U_1 contains two red tokens and one green token, while U_2 contains one red token and two green tokens.

(a) An urn is randomly selected, and then one token is randomly selected from the urn. The token is red. What is the probability that the urn selected was U_1?

(b) An urn is randomly selected, and then two tokens are randomly selected (without replacement) from the urn. The first token is red and the second token is green. What is the probability that the urn selected was U_1?

14.13 Refer to the urns described in Exercise 14.12.

(a) Suppose an urn is randomly selected, and then two tokens are randomly selected (without replacement) from the urn. Both tokens are red. What is the probability that the urn selected was U_1?

(b) Suppose an urn is randomly selected and then two tokens are randomly selected, *but with the first selected token being placed back in the urn before the second token is drawn.* Both tokens are red. What is the probability that the urn selected was U_1?

14.14 Eighty percent of the vinyl material received from Vendor A is of exceptional quality while only 50 percent of the vinyl material received from Vendor B is of exceptional quality. However, the manufacturing capacity of Vendor A is limited, and for this reason only 40 percent of the vinyl material purchased by our firm comes from Vendor *A*. The other 60 percent comes from Vendor *B*. An incoming shipment of vinyl material is inspected and it is found to be of exceptional quality. What is the probability that it came from Vendor *A*?

14.15 Gasoline is being produced at three refineries with daily production levels of 100,000, 200,000, and 300,000 gallons, respectively. The proportion of the output which is below the octane specifications for "name-brand" sale at the three refineries is 0.03, 0.05, and 0.04, respectively. A gasoline tank-truck is found to be carrying gasoline which is below the octane specifications, and therefore the gasoline is to be marketed outside of the name-brand distribution system.

(a) Determine the probability that the tank-truck came from each of the three refineries without reference to the information that the shipment is below the octane specifications.

(b) Determine the probability that the tank-truck came from each of the three refineries given the additional information that the shipment is below the octane specifications.

14.16 An investment analyst estimates that there is about a 50 percent chance of an "upturn" in the chemical industry during the first quarter of a particular year, with the possibilities of "no change" and a "downturn" being about equal. A client is considering the investment of $10,000 in a mutual fund specializing in chemical industry common stocks or else investing in corporate AAA-rated bonds yielding 8.0 percent per year. If the chemical industry experiences an upturn during the first quarter, the value of the mutual fund shares (including dividends) will increase by 15.0 percent during the next twelve months. On the other hand, if there is no change, the value will increase by 3.0 percent, and if there is a downturn, the value will *decrease* by 10.0 percent. Do not consider any commission costs in your analysis.

(a) Construct the table of conditional values (decision table) which identifies the alternative decision acts available to the investor, the possible states, the probabilities of the states, and the conditional economic consequences for this decision situation.

(b) Identify the best decision act from the standpoint of maximizing the expected value associated with the decision.

14.17 For the decision problem in Exercise 14.16, above, determine the expected value with perfect information and the EVPI.

14.18 For the decision problem in Exercise 14.16, by a somewhat simplified approach the investment analyst defines "upturn" to mean that (at least) 70 percent of the usual users of chemical products increase their order amounts, "no change" to mean that (about) 50 percent of the users increase their order amounts, and "downturn" to mean that 30 percent (or fewer) of the users increase their order amounts. He contacts a random sample of 20 users of chemical products and finds that 14 of these are increasing their order amounts over previous periods.

(a) Revise the prior probability distribution regarding the three possible states of the chemical industry, as given in Exercise 14.16, by taking this sample result into consideration.

(b) Using the posterior probability distribution, determine the best decision act and compare it with your answer in Exercise 14.16(b).

14.19 Estimate the value of the sample information that was obtained in Exercise 14.18.

14.20 Using the posterior distribution determined in Exercise 14.18, determine the expected value with perfect information and the EVPI after the sample has been taken. Compare your results with those in Exercise 14.17.

14.21 For the college fraternity decision problem described in Exercises 13.14 and 13.15, determine the EVPI by two approaches: one based on the expected value with perfect information and the other based on determining EOL values. Compare the results of your two computations.

14.22 For the fraternity decision problem described in Exercises 13.14 and 13.15, suppose that the fraternity need not commit itself to buying the blankets or beach umbrellas until three days before the event. Therefore, the members decide to add the weatherman's forecast as additional information to the historical data regarding the occurrence of "cool" versus "hot" weather on the day of the outing. In general, the weatherman has greater success predicting cool weather than hot weather. Specifically, for days that are in fact cool he has correctly forecast the weather 90 percent of the time. For days that are in fact hot he has correctly forecast the weather 70 percent of the time for a forecast made three days in advance.

(a) Construct a tree diagram, using C and H to designate the historical occurrence of cool and hot weather, respectively, and using FC and FH to designate the forecast of each type of weather condition.

(b) Refer to your tree diagram. What is the probability that the weather forecaster will be correct in his three-day forecast?

14.23 For the decision situation described in Exercise 14.22, above, suppose that the three-day point has arrived and the weatherman forecasts cool weather on the day of the outing. Taking this information into consideration, identify the best decision act (order blankets, order beach umbrellas, or order neither).

14.24 Estimate the value of the weather forecast provided in Exercise 14.23, above.

14.25 Describe how the value of a sample can be estimated, given that the sample has been collected and the particular results have been observed.

CHAPTER 15 ■
LINEAR REGRESSION ANALYSIS

When two continuous variables are related, so that a change in one variable is associated with a systematic change in the other variable, *regression analysis* can be used to derive an equation by which the value of one variable can be estimated when the value of the other variable is known. In contrast, *correlation analysis*, which will be covered in Chapter 16, is concerned with measuring and expressing the closeness of the relationship between two variables. In this chapter we consider the graphic and algebraic methods of determining the equation for a straight line, the uses of the equation for purposes of estimation, and measurement of the reliability, or accuracy, of these estimates.

The term *simple regression* indicates that the value of a variable is being estimated on the basis of a known value in one other variable only. In contrast, *multiple regression*, which is beyond the scope of this book, is concerned with estimation on the basis of known values in two or more other variables. As is indicated by the title of this chapter, all of the computational procedures that are discussed are concerned only with linear relationships rather than curvilinear relationships. This point is explained in Section 15.1.

15.1 ■ The Graphic Analysis of Simple Linear Regression

Suppose that the score on a selection test and the performance rating after six months on the job are available for each of a group of industrial trainees working in a manufacturing firm, as indicated in Table 15-1. In this section we use the scatter

Table 15-1 ■ Selection Test Scores and Performance Ratings for a Sample of Industrial Trainees

Sampled individual	Selection test score	Performance rating, 20-point scale
1	88	17
2	85	16
3	72	13
4	93	18
5	70	11
6	74	14
7	78	15
8	93	19
9	82	16
10	92	20
11	79	14
12	84	15
13	71	12
14	77	13
15	87	19
16	87	17
17	72	10
18	77	12
19	82	14
20	76	13

diagram as a graphic device for describing the relationship between selection test scores and performance ratings, and we illustrate the meaning of a regression line by reference to the scatter diagram.

1 In regression analysis we always identify at least two continuous (rather than discrete) variables such that systematic changes in the value of one variable are associated with changes in the value of the other variable. In Table 15-1, for example, the two variables being considered are _____ _____ and _____ .

| selection test score |
| performance rating |

2 The principal objective in regression analysis is that of estimating the value of one variable when the value of at least one other variable is known. For the data of Table 15-1, the values of which variable would most likely be estimated (i.e., which one would we be interested in predicting)? _____ _____ .

| performance rating |

3 In regression analysis the *independent variable* is the one used as the basis for estimating the value of another variable. For the data of Table 15-1 the independent variable is _____ _____ .

| selection test score |

4 The *dependent variable*, on the other hand, is the variable whose values are being estimated. For the data of Table 15-1 the dependent variable is _____ .

| performance rating |

5 If the net profit earned by a number of business firms is estimated on the basis of published gross-sales figures, net profit would be the _____ variable and gross sales would be the _____ variable in the regression analysis.

| dependent |
| independent |

6 *Simple regression analysis* involves estimation on the basis of known values in one other variable, whereas *multiple regression analysis* involves estimation on the basis of known values in two or more other variables. Therefore regression analysis for the data of Table 15-1 would involve [simple / multiple] regression analysis.

| simple |

7 Estimating net profit on the basis of gross sales involves [simple / multiple] regression analysis.

| simple |

8 Estimating consumer spending in a number of communities on the basis of number of people employed and the average wage level in each community involves [simple / multiple] regression analysis.

multiple

9 In regression analysis there can be just one [independent / dependent] variable, but there may be more than one [independent / dependent] variable.

dependent

independent

10 In this chapter we are concerned only with regression problems involving one independent and one dependent variable. Thus all problems presented in this chapter are concerned with _____ regression analysis.

simple

11 For simple regression analysis the values for the independent and dependent variables can be represented on a two-dimensional graph. Typically, the horizontal axis, or X axis, is used to present the values for the independent variable, and the vertical axis, or Y axis, is used for values of the _____ variable.

dependent

12 On the blank graph below enter the appropriate labels for the two axes, using the variables of Table 15-1.

Performance rating

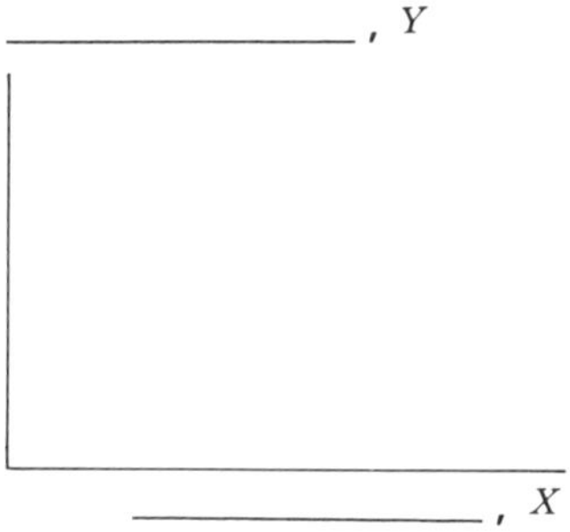

_____ , Y

_____ , X

Selection test score

X

independent

Y; dependent

13 Thus the horizontal axis, or ___ axis, always designates values of the _____ variable, and the vertical axis, or ___ axis, always designates values of the _____ variable.

14 On the graph below enter the one dot that would indicate that an individual had a test score of 85 and a performance rating of 16.

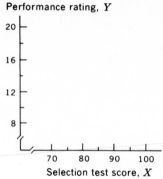

Performance rating, Y

Selection test score, X

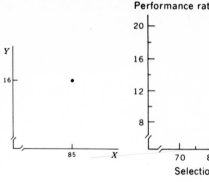

15 The value of the independent variable is represented by the position of the dot in respect to the [X / Y] axis; the associated value of the dependent variable is represented by the position of the dot relative to the [X / Y] axis.

X

Y

16 On the graph below enter the dot representing a selection test score of 75 and a performance rating of 12.

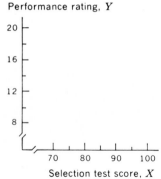

Performance rating, Y

Selection test score, X

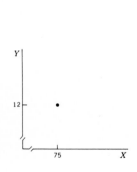

90; 16

17 What are the values of the X and Y variables indicated by the dot entered on the graph below? $X =$ _____ and $Y =$ _____

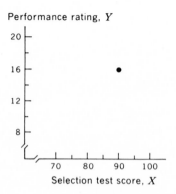

Performance rating, Y

Selection test score, X

18 Figure 15-1 is a graphic portrayal of all the pairs of values reported in Table 15-1. As indicated by the title of this figure, a graph indicating all the associated values for an independent and a dependent variable is called a _____ diagram.

scatter

Figure 15-1 ■ Scatter diagram relating selection test scores to performance ratings for a sample of industrial trainees

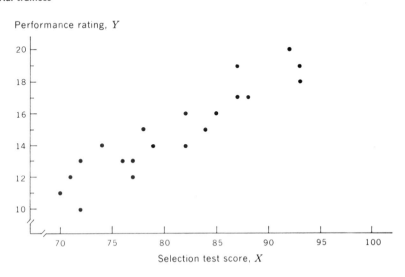

19 Because it visually portrays the relationship between the independent and dependent variables, construction of a _____ diagram is typically the first technical step in regression analysis.

scatter

20 Preceding any of the technical steps of regression analysis, of course, is the choice of variables to be analyzed and the collection of sample data. Thus regression analysis is typically applied for the purpose of statistical [description / inference].

inference (Thus the test scores and performance ratings represent a *sample* of values.)

21 Construction of the scatter diagram provides visual evidence regarding the nature of the relationship between the two variables. The relationship may be linear, that is, tending to follow a straight line, or curvilinear. The scatter diagram in

Figure 15-1, for example, portrays a relationship that appears to be essentially [linear / curvilinear].

22 In order to estimate the value of the Y variable on the basis of the X variable, we need to locate the position of the line that best represents the relationship between X and Y, as indicated by the location of the dots in the scatter diagram. This line can then be used for estimating the value of the Y variable for any given value of the ___ variable.

23 Such a line going through the dots of the scatter diagram is called a *regression line*. One method of constructing a regression line is by the freehand method, which is simply based on visual examination of the scatter diagram. On this basis, construct a best-fitting straight line through the points on Figure 15-1.

24 According to your regression line, what would be the estimated performance rating associated with a selection test score of 75? _____ (number)

25 Again it should be noted that this kind of estimating is being done in the context of statistical inference. That is, we would be interested in predicting performance level [for the 20 trainees in the sample only / for potential trainees not included in the original sample].

26 The regression line can also be determined mathematically, rather than by the freehand method. In Section 15.2 we present a statistical basis for doing this. As in this section, however, we shall continue to be concerned not with curvilinear relationships but only with those that are _____ in form.

Summary	
regression analysis	**27** The method that is used for estimating the value of one continuous variable when the value of a related continuous variable is known is called _____ .
dependent independent	**28** The variable whose value is estimated is called the _____ variable; the variable whose value is known, and which serves as the basis for estimation, is called the _____ variable.
dependent	**29** In any regression analysis, whether simple or multiple, there can be only one [independent / dependent] variable.
simple multiple	**30** When there is only one independent variable, _____ regression analysis is involved, whereas the existence of more than one independent variable results in _____ regression analysis.
X (or horizontal) Y (or vertical)	**31** In a two-dimensional scatter diagram, which is typically constructed in conjunction with simple regression analysis, the values of the independent variable are scaled along the ___ axis, and the values of the dependent variable are typically scaled along the ___ axis.
regression	**32** In order to estimate the value of the Y variable on the basis of knowing the value of the X variable, the location of the _____ line in the scatter diagram must be determined.

15.2 ■ The Least-squares Criterion in Fitting a Straight Line

Depending on the statistical standard, or criterion, that is used, a number of different straight lines could be considered the best-fitting lines for the data of a scatter diagram. In fitting a line, the most frequent basis used by statisticians is the *least-squares criterion*. By this standard the best-fitting line is the one for which the sum of all of the squared differences between the estimated and actual values of the dependent variable is minimized. Of course, the least-squares criterion also serves as the basis for determining the value of the arithmetic mean for a set of measurements, as discussed in Chapter 3. There is thus a direct tie-in between the mean, as a sample statistic, and the least-squares regression line. The regression line relating two variables can be thought of as a "mean line" in the sense that it represents the average relationship between X and Y for all possible values of these variables.

33 The general form of the equation for a regression line which we use is $Y_c = a + bX$, in which Y_c is the estimated, or computed, value of the dependent variable and X is the known value of the _____ variable.

independent

34 The two constants a and b in the regression equation

$$Y_c = a + bX$$

also have a specific meaning. a indicates the value of Y_c when $X = 0$. Therefore, for the regression equation $Y_c = 5 + 2X$, the regression line intersects the Y axis at the point where $Y = $ ____ .

5 (since $X = 0$ at this point)

35 For $Y_c = a + bX$, b indicates the slope of the regression line. The regression equation $Y_c = 5 + 2X$ indicates that for each increase of one unit in the value of X, Y_c increases by ____ units.

two

36 On the graph below enter the regression line represented by the equation $Y_c = 5 + 2X$.

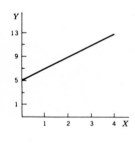
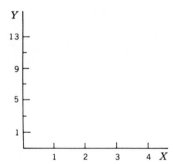

37 On the graph below enter the regression line represented by the equation $Y_c = 3 + X$.

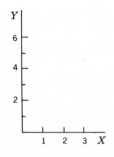

38 Thus, for $Y_c = a + bX$, Y_c is the estimated value of Y, a indicates the value of Y_c at the point where $X =$ ___ , b is the rate of change of ___ with respect to X, and X is the known value of the _____ variable.

39 If the points entered on a scatter diagram are somewhat dispersed and do not all fall precisely along a single straight line, is it possible to avoid all errors, or discrepancies, in the estimated values of Y based on a straight-line regression equation? [Yes / No]

40 For example, the regression line entered on the following graph represents the equation $Y_c = 2 + X$. However, most of the points in the scatter diagram do not lie exactly on the line, indicating that for these points the actual values of Y differ from the _____ values of ___ .

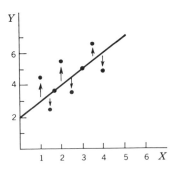

41 In the graph in Frame 40 the direction and size of the discrepancies between the estimated and actual values of the Y variable are indicated by the small _____ entered on the diagram.

42 One criterion that we could use for determining the location of the best-fitting straight line for a scatter diagram is to choose that line for which the *sum of the absolute values of the discrepancies* (errors) between estimated and actual values of the dependent variable is minimized. As in our discussion of measures of central tendency in Chapter 3, this criterion is represented by $[N_e = \min / \Sigma|e| = \min / \Sigma e^2 = \min]$.

43 The most frequently used criterion for determining the location of the regression line, however, is the least-squares criterion. This criterion is represented by $[N_e = \min / \Sigma|e| = \min / \Sigma e^2 = \min]$.

44 Thus the mathematical criterion typically used as the basis for determining the regression line is the same as the criterion underlying the computation of the [mean / median / mode] as a measure of central tendency.

45 The least-squares regression line can therefore be thought of as a kind of mean line through the points of the scatter diagram. What is minimized by the location of this line is the sum of the squared discrepancies between the _____ and _____ values of the Y variable.

estimated
actual

46 Using the equation for a straight line, $Y_c = a + bX$, we can satisfy the least-squares criterion by using the following formulas to solve for b and a:

$$b = \frac{\Sigma XY - n\overline{X}\overline{Y}}{\Sigma X^2 - n\overline{X}^2}$$

$$a = \overline{Y} - b\overline{X}$$

In the formula for finding the value of b, n refers to the number of *pairs* of measurements of the independent and dependent variables. For the simplified data of Table 15-2, for example, $n =$ ___ (number).

5

Table 15-2 ▪ **Partial Data Relating Two Variables**

Person	X	Y
A	3	9
B	2	8
C	1	5
D	3	10
E	1	8

47 As a step toward finding the value of b for the regression-line equation for the data of Table 15-2, complete the following calculations:

Person	X	Y	XY	X²
A	3	9	27	9
B	2	8	16	4
C	1	5	5	1
D	3	10	___	___
E	1	8	___	___
	$\Sigma X = 10$	$\Sigma Y = 40$	$\Sigma XY =$ ___	$\Sigma X^2 =$ ___

30	9
8	1
86	24

48 Now substitute the appropriate values from the table in Frame 47 in the following formula and solve for b:

$$\frac{86 - 5(2)(8)}{24 - 5(4)} = \frac{6}{4} = 1.5 \qquad b = \frac{\Sigma XY - n\bar{X}\bar{Y}}{\Sigma X^2 - n\bar{X}^2}$$

49 Using the figures in Frames 47 and 48, solve the formula for a:

$$8 - 1.5(2) = 5 \qquad a = \bar{Y} - b\bar{X} =$$

50 Thus, in terms of the regression-line formula, $Y_c = a + bX$, the regression line which satisfies the least-squares criterion for the data of Table 15-2 is represented by the equation

$$5 + 1.5X \qquad Y_c = \underline{\quad\quad} + \underline{\quad\quad}$$

51 On the graph below plot the scatter points for the data of Table 15-2.

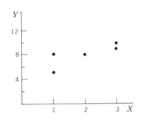

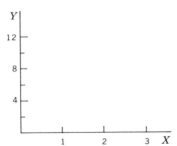

52 Now enter the regression line represented by the equation $Y_c = 5 + 1.5X$ on the graph in Frame 51.

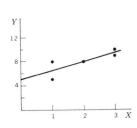

53 Whereas the locations of the scatter points in respect to the Y axis indicate actual values of the dependent variable, the regression line indicates the estimated values of the dependent variable based on the regression equation. For each of the five available values of X given in Table 15-2, compute the estimated value of the dependent variable Y_c, using the equation $Y_c = 5 + 1.5X$.

	X	Y	Y_c
9.5	3	9	___
8.0	2	8	___
6.5	1	5	___
9.5	3	10	___
6.5	1	8	___

54 In Frame 52 the fact that the scatter points did not all coincide with the location of the regression line indicated the existence of some discrepancy between actual and estimated values of the dependent variable. In the table in Frame 53 this discrepancy is indicated by the difference in values (if any) between the column labeled ___ and the column labeled ___ .

$Y; Y_c$

55 For the data included in the table in Frame 53, the sum of the errors squared can thus be computed by using the equation

$0.25 + 0 + 2.25 + 0.25 + 2.25 = 5.00$

$$\Sigma(Y - Y_c)^2 = \underline{\quad} + \underline{\quad} + \underline{\quad} + \underline{\quad} + \underline{\quad}$$
$$= \underline{\quad}$$

56 Can any other regression line result in a smaller sum of squared deviations between the estimated and actual values of the dependent variable (Y) for the data of Table 15-2? [Yes / No]

No

57 Thus, for the data of Table 15-2, the equation $Y_c = 5 + 1.5X$ and the regression line that it represents can be said to satisfy the _____ criterion.

least-squares

58 Typically, we would collect many more pairs of sample measurements of the independent and dependent variables than the five reported in Table 15-2, but the procedure for finding the regression equation would be identical to the solution just completed. As another simplified exercise, complete the following table as the first step in determining the regression equation for the data.

X	Y	X^2	XY
6	8	36	48
7	10	49	70
4	4	16	16
3	2	9	6
$\Sigma X = 20$	$\Sigma Y = 24$	$\Sigma X^2 = $ 110	$\Sigma XY = $ 140

59 Solve for b, using the usual formula:

$$\frac{140 - 4(5)(6)}{110 - 4(25)} = \frac{20}{10} = 2$$

$$b = \frac{\Sigma XY - n\overline{X}\,\overline{Y}}{\Sigma X^2 - n\overline{X}^2} =$$

60 Using the values from Frames 58 and 59, solve for a:

$6 - 2(5) = -4$

$$a = \overline{Y} - b\overline{X} =$$

61 Thus the equation for this least-squares regression line is $Y_c =$ ___ $+$ ___ . The value of -4 for a indicates that the value of the dependent variable is -4 when the value of the independent variable is equal to ___ (number).

$-4 + 2X$

0

62 On the graph below enter the regression line represented by the equation $Y_c = -4 + 2X$.

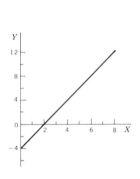
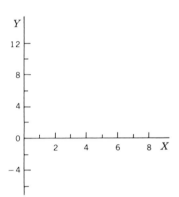

15.3 ■ Use of the Regression Equation

If we were to use the regression equation simply to estimate values of the dependent variable that are in fact already known, there would be little point to determining this equation. Typically, however, the data used as the basis for constructing the regression equation constitute a random sample from a larger population of values for which the equation is to be used. Correct use of the linear regression equation is based on the assumptions that: (1) the form of the relationship between the two variables is linear; and (2) the dependent variable is a random variable, rather than having its value designated.

63 In Section 15.1 we illustrated a scatter diagram relating selection test scores with performance ratings on the job for a group of industrial trainees. What is the possible value of a regression equation based on these data; i.e., for what purpose

to estimate (predict) the performance levels for training-program applicants, based on their test scores (etc.)

might this regression equation be used? _____

_____

_____

64 Thus the values of *a* and *b* in the regression equation, $Y_c = a + bX$, are based on analysis of a particular sample, although they are then used as the estimated values for the regression equation representing an entire population of relationships. For our purpose we need not go into a detailed consideration of this point, except to note that just as a sample mean $\overline{X}$ is used as the unbiased estimate of the population mean μ, so also are the population regression equation values of α and β estimated by the sample values ___ and ___ , respectively.

$a; b$

65 Once a regression equation is determined, we would use it as the basis for estimating the value of the _____ variable when the value of the _____ variable is known.

dependent

independent

66 There are numerous reasons why the value of a dependent variable might not be known. For example, if we are estimating the useful life of batteries on the basis of knowing the quantity of a certain ingredient, the only way to obtain the actual value of the dependent variable (battery life) would be to subject the batteries to a destructive test. Similarly, why might selection tests be used to estimate the level of job performance? _____

_____

_____

Job performance has not yet occurred; *prediction* of performance is involved.

67 Another factor that needs to be considered in the use of a regression equation is the meaning of the words "independent" and "dependent." These words are used in a statistical sense only and are not meant to imply that one variable actually causes another. In other words, the possibility of estimating or predicting the value of the dependent variable when the value of the independent variable is known [does / does not] necessarily imply causation.

does not (We discuss this point in greater detail in Frame 99, in Chapter 16, on correlation.)

68 For example, since the amounts of both personal spending *and* personal saving tend to increase as income increases, one could determine the regression equation by which the amount of personal spending could be estimated when the amount of personal saving is known (or vice versa). In this case the independent variable is so labeled simply because its value happens to be [known / unknown]. It is clear that saving does not cause spending.

known

69 If we wish to reverse our direction of prediction and estimate the value of the variable represented along the X axis, which is typically the independent variable, we need to exercise some caution. In spite of what might be an intuitive expectation, one cannot usually use the same regression line for predicting X from Y as is used for predicting ___ from ___.

Y; X

70 The reason for this is that the regression line that satisfies the least-squares criterion when the actual and estimated values of the Y variable are compared is usually not the same as the regression line that satisfies the least-squares criterion for the X variable. In the graph below, for example, the line which would be used to estimate Y when X is known is represented by the equation _____ , but the line which would be used to estimate X when Y is known is represented by the equation _____ .

$Y_c = a + bX$

$X_c = a' + b'Y$

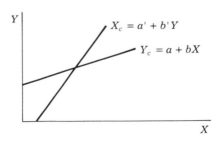

71 To illustrate the point further, the regression line represented by the equation $X_c = a' + b'Y$ on the graph below minimizes the sum of the squared deviations between the actual and estimated values of X, as indicated by the [horizontal / vertical] deviations posted on the graph, whereas the equation $Y_c = a + bX$ minimizes the [horizontal / vertical] deviations on the graph.

horizontal

vertical

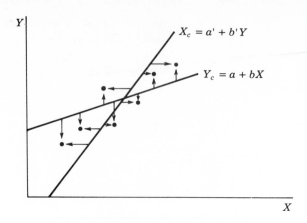

$$X_c = a' + b'Y$$

$$Y_c = a + bX$$

72 A general limitation on the reversal of the direction of prediction in regression analysis is that the variable being estimated (which is therefore considered the dependent variable) must be a *random variable*. By *random* we mean that the various values occur in the context of a sampling process and are not designated or set by the analyst. On this basis, would it be statistically permissible to estimate the selection test scores of trainees based on performance ratings on the job (and thus reverse the direction of prediction)? [Yes / No] Why or why not? _____

Yes; Because the test scores are a random variable.

73 If we have a regression analysis concerned with estimating battery life based on the quantity of a particular ingredient used in the batteries, can we statistically reverse the direction of prediction? [Yes / No] Why or why not? _____

No; The quantity of the ingredient is not a random variable. Rather than the quantity being "sampled," it is set at various values.

74 The only mathematical case in which the same regression equation (but solving for the other variable) can be used to estimate either Y from X or X from Y is when the two regression lines exactly coincide. This occurs only when every scatter point entered on the graph falls exactly along the line in question, resulting in [no / some / extensive] deviation between estimated and actual values of either variable.

no

75 In mathematics, when the value of one variable can be determined *exactly* when the other variable is known, the variables are said to have a *functional relationship*. For example, the scatter diagram below represents the functional relationship between two variables, labeled X and Y. Such precise functional relationships are unusual for business and economic data, but they do occur in the physical sciences. In this case the same regression line satisfies the least-squares criterion when predicting either Y from X or ___ from ___ .

$X; Y$

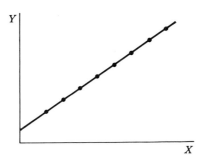

76 For data in the social sciences, business, and economics, there is invariably a degree of error involved in making predictions of one variable based on knowledge of another variable. The standard, or criterion, that is used for locating the best line to be used for making such estimates is the _____ criterion.

least-squares

77 One might ask: Just how good is a given estimate based on the use of a regression equation? The computation of the *standard error of estimate*, discussed in Section 15.4, which follows, provides us with the basis for answering this type of question. It represents the degree of scatter of the [estimated / actual] values of the dependent variable in respect to the regression line.

actual (The estimated values are represented along the regression line itself.)

15.4 ■ The Standard Error of Estimate

The standard error of estimate is a measure of the degree of scatter of the actual values of a dependent variable in respect to the regression line used for estimating that variable. As such, this measure provides us with the basis for determining just how closely the actual value of the dependent variable is likely to correspond to its estimated value. There are two different symbols for the standard error of estimate, depending on whether population or sample data serve as the basis for determining the value. Thus $\sigma_{Y.X}$ is the population standard error of estimate based on the entire population of data, and $s_{Y.X}$ is the estimate of the population standard error of estimate based on sample data. Correct use of the standard error of estimate in regression analysis is based on the following two assumptions about the population: (1) the deviations from the regression line are *normally distributed* for any given value on the line; and (2) the standard deviation (standard error) in respect to the regression line has the same value at all points along the line (*homoscedasticity*). These assumptions are in addition to the usual regression-analysis assumptions that the variables are continuous variables and are linearly related.

78 The value of the standard error of estimate is indicative of the amount of discrepancy between the estimated and actual values of the _____ variable.

> dependent (*Y*)

79 The graph below presents a visual portrayal of the relationship of the standard error of estimate to the regression line used to estimate values of the dependent variable. Thus the standard error of estimate represents the degree of scatter of the [estimated / actual] values of the dependent variable in respect to the _____ line.

> actual

> regression

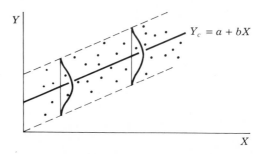

80 The formulas for $\sigma_{Y.X}$ and $s_{Y.X}$ are very similar. The first formula is used when the standard error of estimate is computed for [population / sample] data, while the latter is applicable to [population / sample] data.

> population

> sample

81 The formula for the population standard error of estimate is:

$$\sigma_{Y.X} = \sqrt{\frac{\Sigma(Y - Y_c)^2}{N}}$$

The formula for the sample standard error of estimate also requires the squaring and summing of discrepancies, the only difference being that this sum is divided by $n - 2$ rather than population size. Therefore, the formula for the sample standard error of estimate is:

$$\sqrt{\dfrac{\Sigma(Y-Y_c)^2}{n-2}}$$

$$s_{Y.X} = \sqrt{\rule{3cm}{0pt}}$$

82 When the regression equation is based on sample values, both *a* and *b* in the regression equation are sample statistics. Because of this, two degrees of freedom are lost when the standard error of estimate is based on Y_c values obtained from such a regression equation. It is for this reason that the denominator in the formula for $s_{Y.X}$ is _____ .

$$\boxed{n-2}$$

83 Because regression equations are typically used in conjunction with *sampling* and for the purpose of statistical inference, the symbol for the form of the standard error of estimate which is most frequently computed and used is [$\sigma_{Y.X}$ / $s_{Y.X}$].

$$\boxed{s_{Y.X}}$$

84 Match the appropriate formulas with the symbols below, using the code letters.

$$\boxed{b}$$

$$\boxed{a}$$

$$s_{Y.X} = \underline{\quad}$$

$$\sigma_{Y.X} = \underline{\quad}$$

(a) $= \sqrt{\dfrac{\Sigma(Y-Y_c)^2}{N}}$, where the values of Y constitute all such values in the population

(b) $= \sqrt{\dfrac{\Sigma(Y-Y_c)^2}{n-2}}$, where the values of Y are sample values

85 The following are the actual and estimated values of the dependent variable, Y, for the data presented in Table 15-2. Considering this to be a random sample taken from a large population of values, compute the missing values in the table below.

Y	Y_c	$Y-Y_c$	$(Y-Y_c)^2$
9	9.5	−0.5	0.25
8	8.0	0	0
5	6.5	_____	_____
10	9.5	_____	_____
8	6.5	_____	_____
		$\Sigma(Y-Y_c)^2 =$ _____	

−1.5	2.25
0.5	0.25
1.5	2.25
	5.00

86 For the data in Frame 85, and by the appropriate formula from Frame 84,

$$\sqrt{\frac{\Sigma(Y - Y_c)^2}{n - 2}} = \sqrt{\frac{5.00}{3}} = \sqrt{1.67} \doteq 1.3$$

$$s_{Y.X} =$$

87 Of course, both formulas in Frame 84 are based on the computation of deviation values and are therefore not as convenient to use as computational formulas that do not require determination of deviation values. Given below are the computational versions of these formulas, which we use in the end-of-chapter exercises. Since we typically wish to estimate the population standard error of estimate on the basis of a sample of data, the formula below which is most frequently used is formula [a / b].

b

(a) $\sigma_{Y.X} = \sqrt{\dfrac{\Sigma Y^2 - a\Sigma Y - b\Sigma XY}{N}}$

(b) $s_{Y.X} = \sqrt{\dfrac{\Sigma Y^2 - a\Sigma Y - b\Sigma XY}{n - 2}}$

88 The use of the standard error of estimate is similar to the use of the standard error of the mean in statistical estimation, in that we use it to define an interval for the value being estimated. However, note that in the case of the standard error of estimate the interval is for the individual value of Y_c, and not for the mean of Y_c. Therefore, the central-limit theorem does not apply in this case and it [is / is not] necessary to assume that the deviations in respect to the regression line are normally distributed.

is

89 Whereas a *confidence interval* is concerned with estimating a population parameter, the standard error of estimate is used to estimate (or predict) an *individual value* of a dependent variable. To differentiate such estimation from estimation of a parameter, the interval estimate for a value of the dependent variable is called a *prediction interval.* Thus a prediction interval is conditional on the value of the _____ variable being known.

independent

90 Given the assumption that the deviations in respect to the

z (or normal probability)

t (But the z distribution can be used as a substitute when $n \geqslant 30$.)

regression line are normally distributed, either the normal probability (z) table or the t table is used to define a prediction interval. When the population standard error of estimate is based on analysis of population data, the ___ table is used. When the value of the population standard error of estimate is based on sample data, the ___ table is appropriately used.

---

t

91 The appropriate probability table to be used in conjunction with the standard error of estimate computed in Frame 86 is the ___ table.

92 In constructing a confidence interval for the population mean on the basis of sample data, the point estimate used is $\overline{X}$ and the interval estimate is $\overline{X} \pm ts\overline{X}$. Similarly, in constructing a prediction interval for the value of Y when X is known, the appropriate point estimate Y_c and the interval estimate that incorporates the use of $s_{Y.X}$ is _____ .[1]

$Y_c \pm ts_{Y.X}$ (or $Y_c \pm zs_{Y.X}$ if $n \geqslant 30$)

93 Thus, with $n - 2 = 3$ degrees of freedom and a standard error of estimate of 1.3, within what limits would approximately 95 percent of the actual values of the dependent variable, Y, be located with respect to the expected regression line value, Y_c?

$Y_c \pm ts_{Y.X} = Y_c \pm$ $(3.182)(1.3) = Y_c \pm 4.1$

Limits =

94 Or, to put it another way, and using the data from Frame 93, the probability that an actual value of the dependent variable will differ by more than 4.1 measurement units in either direction from the estimated, or predicted, value of the dependent variable is _____ (value).

0.05

---

[1] This formula is an approximation, since it is based on the assumption that the true regression line, rather than an estimated regression line, has been determined. For a complete analysis, more comprehensive textbooks in statistics include determination of the standard error associated with estimating the intercept (α) and slope (β) of the population regression line. However, when the sample size is relatively large, the prediction interval based simply on the use of $s_{Y.X}$ as the standard error is a satisfactory approximation of the interval determined by a complete analysis.

95 What would be the principal disadvantage of using a regression equation for the purpose of estimation without computing and making use of the associated standard error of estimate? _____

We would have no way of expressing the accuracy of the estimates being made.

_____ .

96 (Frames 1-10) The term "simple regression analysis" indicates that _____ (number) independent variable(s) and _____ (number) dependent variable(s) are involved in the analysis.

Review

one

one

97 (Frames 11-14) In the graphic portrayal of the relationship between two variables, values of the independent variable are typically represented along the _____ axis and values of the dependent variable are represented along the _____ axis.

horizontal (or X)

vertical (or Y)

98 (Frames 15-21) A graph on which all the related values of the independent and the dependent variable are represented by dots entered in a coordinate system is called a _____ _____ .

scatter diagram

99 (Frames 22-32) The one best line that can be drawn through the pattern of dots entered in a scatter diagram is called the _____ line.

regression

100 (Frames 41-45) The statistical standard that is most frequently used for determining the equation, and location, of the regression line is the _____ criterion.

least-squares

101 (Frames 33-35) In the equation for the regression line $Y_c = a + bX$, a represents the value of Y_c when $X =$ ___, and b represents the rate of change of _____ with respect to ___ .

0

$Y_c; X$

102 (Frames 36-40) For the equation $Y_c = 4 + 0.5X$, enter the regression line on the graph below.

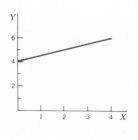

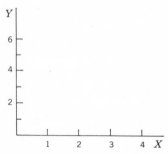

103 (Frames 41–45, 56, 57) What value is minimized by the use of the least-squares criterion for determining the equation for a regression line? _____

_____

_____

104 (Frames 46-55, 58-62) The values of a and b in the equation $Y_c = a + bX$ can be determined by solving the appropriate formulas. Given the simplified sample data and computational formulas below, determine the values of a and b and indicate the complete regression equation.

X	Y	XY	X^2
9	5	45	81
6	3	18	36
8	5	___	___
5	3	___	___
$\Sigma X = 28$	$\Sigma Y = 16$	$\Sigma XY = $___	$\Sigma X^2 = $___

$$b = \frac{\Sigma XY - n\bar{X}\bar{Y}}{\Sigma X^2 - n\bar{X}^2} =$$

$a = \bar{Y} - b\bar{X} =$

Therefore $Y_c =$

105 (Frames 63-68) Once a regression equation is deter-mined, for what purpose is it typically used? _____

_____

_____

106 (Frames 69-77) If we wish to reverse our direction of estimation, can we usually use the established regression equation for the dependent variable Y by solving it for X? [Yes / No] Why or why not? _____

_____

_____

_____

107 (Frames 78, 79) The measure which provides us with the basis for identifying the amount of expected discrepancy associated with the use of the regression equation is the standard error of _____ .

108 (Frames 80–84) There are two symbols for the standard error of estimate, depending on the type of data used in computing it. Match the appropriate deviations versions of the formulas with the symbols listed below, using the code letters.

a	

$s_{Y.X} =$ ___

$$(a) = \sqrt{\frac{\Sigma(Y - Y_c)^2}{n - 2}}$$

b	

$\sigma_{Y.X} =$ ___

$$(b) = \sqrt{\frac{\Sigma(Y - Y_c)^2}{N}}$$

109 (Frames 85, 86) The following sample data are based on the information presented and the regression equation determined in Frame 104. Using the appropriate formula from the listing in Frame 108, determine the estimated value of the population standard error of estimate.

0.4	0.16
0.2	0.04
	0.40

X	Y	Y_c	$Y - Y_c$	$(Y - Y_c)^2$
9	5	5.2	−0.2	0.04
6	3	3.4	−0.4	0.16
8	5	4.6	___	___
5	3	2.8	___	___
			$\Sigma(Y - Y_c)^2 =$ ___	

$\sqrt{\dfrac{\Sigma(Y - Y_c)^2}{n - 2}} =$ $\sqrt{0.20} = 0.447$

$s_{Y.X} =$

110 (Frames 87–89) In estimating the population mean, the interval which is defined is called a _____ interval. In estimating an individual value of a dependent variable in regression analysis, the interval which is defined is called a _____ interval.

confidence

prediction

111 (Frames 90–95) Whereas Y_c represents the point estimate of the value of the dependent variable, the prediction interval which incorporates the use of the estimated population standard error of estimate is represented by _____ ± _____ . The number of degrees of freedom used in conjunction with this estimation formula is _____ (number).

Y_c; $t s_{Y.X}$ (or $\pm z s_{Y.X}$ if $n \geqslant$ 30); $n - 2$

Symbols Introduced in This Chapter (with Frame Numbers)

(33) Y_c Estimated value of the dependent variable Y in regression and correlation analysis.

(34) a The constant in the regression equation which indicates the value of Y_c at $X = 0$.

(35) b The constant in the regression equation which indicates the slope of the regression line.

(81) $\sigma_{Y.X}$ The standard error of estimate based on population data.

(81) $s_{Y.X}$ The standard error of estimate based on sample data.

Formulas Introduced in This Chapter (with Frame Numbers)

(33) $Y_c = a + bX$

General equation for a straight line used in regression analysis.

(48) $b = \dfrac{\Sigma XY - n\overline{X}\,\overline{Y}}{\Sigma X^2 - n\overline{X}^2}$

The value of b in the equation for the straight line which satisfies the least-squares criterion.

(49) $a = \overline{Y} - b\overline{X}$

The value of a in the equation for the straight line which satisfies the least-squares criterion.

(81) $\sigma_{Y.X} = \sqrt{\dfrac{\Sigma(Y - Y_c)^2}{N}}$

The standard error of estimate for a population of values.

(81) $s_{Y.X} = \sqrt{\dfrac{\Sigma(Y - Y_c)^2}{n - 2}}$

The standard error of estimate based on sample data.

(87) $\sigma_{Y.X} = \sqrt{\dfrac{\Sigma Y^2 - a\Sigma Y - b\Sigma XY}{N}}$

Computational formula for the standard error of estimate for a population of values.

(87) $s_{Y.X} = \sqrt{\dfrac{\Sigma Y^2 - a\Sigma Y - b\Sigma XY}{n - 2}}$

Computational formula for the standard error of estimate for a sample of values.

(93) $Y_c \pm t s_{Y.X}$

(or $\pm z s_{Y.X}$)

Prediction interval for a value of the dependent variable in regression analysis.

15.1 Construct a scatter diagram for the sample data in the table below which relate the values of two variables.

X	Y
3	5
4	10
6	9
7	12

15.2 Determine the least-squares regression equation for estimating Y when X is known for the data of Exercise 15.1, above, and enter the associated regression line on the scatter diagram.

15.3 For the data of Exercise 15.1, determine the regression equation for estimating X when Y is known and enter the associated regression line on the scatter diagram. How is it possible for *both* this line and the one determined in Exercise 15.2 to satisfy the least-squares criterion? In reversing the usual direction of prediction, what statistical assumption is required in respect to the variable X?

15.4 Compute the standard error of estimate to be used in conjunction with the regression equation of Exercise 15.2, assuming that the pairs of values represent a random sample. Use the deviations version of the formula.

15.5 Using 95 percent prediction limits and utilizing the results of Exercises 15.2 and 15.4, estimate the value of the Y variable, given that $X = 6$. What statistical assumption is required in conjunction with the construction and use of such a prediction interval?

15.6 A home furnishings concern has noted that there seems to be a relationship between the volume of business and the level of housing starts six months earlier in the metropolitan areas in which the firm operates. In order to study this relationship, the firm randomly selects 12 months from the past five years and tabulates the number of housing starts and the monthly dollar volume of sales six months later (in thousands of dollars), as indicated in the table below. Indicate which of these variables would logically be considered the independent variable in a regression analysis and which would be considered the dependent variable.

Monthly housing starts	Sales volume ($1,000s)	Monthly housing starts	Sales volume ($1,000s)
450	9.5	650	13.5
150	6.0	225	8.0
200	6.2	500	13.0
600	5.5	280	8.8
250	7.5	350	9.0
300	10.0	400	12.0

15.7 Construct a scatter diagram for the data of Exercise 15.6, above.

15.8 Determine the least-squares regression equation for the data of Exercise 15.6.

15.9 Compute the standard error of estimate for the data of Exercise 15.6, using the computational version of the formula included in Frame 87.

15.10 Using the results of your computations in Exercises 15.8 and 15.9, determine the approximate 90 percent prediction interval for estimating the dollar volume of home furnishings sales in a particular month, given that new housing starts six months earlier were at 550 units.

ADDITIONAL EXERCISES

15.11 Construct a scatter diagram for the simplified data relating the values of two variables, as listed in the table below. The data are a random sample from a population.

X	Y
1	8
3	5
6	5
8	2

15.12 Algebraically determine the least-squares regression equation for estimating Y when X is known, and enter the associated regression line on the scatter diagram constructed in Exercise 15.11, above.

15.13 Note the algebraic sign of the b coefficient in your regression equation of Exercise 15.12, above, and indicate the general meaning of the algebraic sign associated with b.

15.14 Compute the standard error of estimate for the data of Exercise 15.11, using the deviations version of the formula.

15.15 Determine the approximate 90 percent prediction interval for Y given that $X = 4$.

15.16 In order to investigate the relationship between the level of advertising in local newspapers and the level of sales, the marketing manager of a company in a consumer products field has applied different amounts of advertising funds in five market areas during each of two weeks. In all, therefore, 10 different advertising amounts were used. The following table indicates the level of advertising in hundreds of dollars and the level of sales in thousands of dollars for the 10 test weeks. Construct a scatter diagram for these data.

Level of advertising ($100s)	Level of sales ($1,000s)
10.5	17.3
6.0	14.0
8.7	19.1
9.3	14.5
11.8	20.0
7.5	16.3
15.0	23.8
6.3	14.0
8.5	17.3
5.4	13.3

15.17 Determine the least-squares regression equation for the data of Exercise 15.16, above.

15.18 Compute the standard error of estimate for the data of Exercise 15.16, using the computational version of the formula.

15.19 For the population from which the sample of Exercise 15.16 was obtained, determine the approximate 95 percent prediction interval for the weekly dollar level of sales, given that $1,000 is spent on advertising in local newspapers during the week.

15.20 Determine the 95 percent prediction interval for the weekly dollar level of sales in Exercise 15.16, given that $3,000 is spent on advertising. Considering the assumptions underlying statistical inference in general and regression analysis in particular, what would you say about the interpretation and use of this prediction interval?

15.21 The table below presents sample data relating the number of hours spent by individual students outside of class on a course in statistics during a three-week period, and the score on an examination given at the end of this period. Plot these data on a scatter diagram.

Sampled student	Hours of study, X	Examination grade, Y
1	20	64
2	16	61
3	34	84
4	23	70
5	27	88
6	32	92
7	18	72
8	22	77

15.22 Referring to the data in Exercise 15.21, **(a)** determine the regression equation for predicting the examination grade given the number of hours spent on the course, and enter the regression line on the scatter diagram constructed in Exercise 15.21. **(b)** Use the regression equation to estimate the examination grade of a student who devoted 30 hours of study to the course material.

15.23 Refer to the data in Exercise 15.21 and the results in Exercise 15.22, and construct the 90 percent prediction interval for the examination score given that a student devoted 30 hours to course preparation, using the standard error of estimate as the measure of uncertainty.

15.24 The table below presents data relating the number of weeks of experience in a job involving the wiring of miniature electronic components and the number of components which were rejected during the past week for 12 randomly selected workers. Plot these sample data on a scatter diagram.

Sampled worker	Weeks of experience, X	Number of rejects, Y
1	7	26
2	9	20
3	6	28
4	14	16
5	8	23
6	12	18
7	10	24
8	4	26
9	2	38
10	11	22
11	1	32
12	8	25

15.25 Referring to the data in Exercise 15.24, **(a)** determine the regression equation for predicting the number of components rejected given the number of weeks of experience, and enter the regression line on the scatter diagram. Comment on the nature of the relationship as indicated by the regression equation. **(b)** Estimate the number of components rejected for an employee with three weeks of experience in the operation.

15.26 Refer to the data in Exercise 15.24 and the results in Exercise 15.25, and construct the approximate 95 percent prediction interval for the number of components rejected for an employee with three weeks of experience in the job.

CHAPTER 16 ■ CORRELATION

In Chapter 15 we described the use of regression analysis to derive the equation by which values of one variable can be estimated when the values of an associated variable are known. In this chapter we describe the technique of correlation, which is concerned with measuring and expressing the closeness of the relationship between two variables. After introducing the meaning of the correlation coefficient in terms of the least-squares regression line, we review the historical development of the Pearson correlation coefficient r and its computation, present the computational procedure for determining the correlation between ranked variables, and consider the use of multiple and partial correlation. Finally, we address ourselves to the interpretation of correlation values as signifying causation.

16.1 ■ The Meaning of the Correlation Coefficient

The coefficient of correlation indicates the degree of association between an independent and a dependent variable. In this section we consider the possible values that a correlation coefficient can have, relate these to the characteristics of the scatter diagram for the data being studied, and interpret its value in terms of the associated coefficient of determination, r^2.

1 The value of a correlation coefficient r can vary between -1.0 and $+1.0$. The *sign* attached to the correlation coefficient indicates the *direction* of the change in the dependent variable as the value of the independent variable is increased. Thus a positive correlation coefficient indicates that as the value of the independent variable increases, the value of the associated

| increases |

dependent variable [increases / decreases].

2 Similarly, a negative correlation coefficient indicates that as the value of the independent variable increases, the value of

| decreases |

the dependent variable [increases / decreases].

3 For example, since the expenditure on education by family units tends to go up with an increase in income level, the correlation coefficient expressing the degree of relationship

| positive |

between these two variables would have a [positive / negative] sign.

4 At a given income level, as the present level of personal debt increases, the amount of planned purchases for a subsequent period decreases. The coefficient of correlation representing this relationship would have a [positive /

| negative |

negative] sign.

5 Whereas the sign of the correlation coefficient indicates the direction of the relationship, its *absolute value* (value without regard to sign) indicates the *extent* of the relationship. As we have already indicated, the largest absolute value the correlation coefficient can have, indicating perfect correlation, is _____ (number).

1.0

6 Of the following correlation coefficients, the one that indicates the highest extent of relationship is [+.70 / −.80 / +.25].

−.80 (since the absolute value without regard to sign is the indicator of extent of relationship)

7 A perfect correlation indicates that if the value of the independent variable is known, the value of the associated dependent variable can be determined without error. Therefore the *two* values of the correlation coefficient that indicate perfect correlation between two variables are _____ (number) and _____ (number).

−1.0
+1.0

8 The *one* value of the correlation coefficient that indicates absolutely no relationship between the values of the two variables is ___ (number).

0

9 Although we do not use the scatter diagram to compute the value of the correlation coefficient, it can be used to illustrate the extent and direction of the correlation. According to the definitions of positive and negative correlation given above, the diagram below which indicates perfect negative correlation is diagram [a / b].

a

(a)   (b)

10 The value of the coefficient of correlation for the data of Figure *b* in Frame 9, above, would be _____ (number).

+1.0

11 The closer the points on a scatter diagram are clustered around the regression line used for estimating the dependent variable, the higher is the absolute value of the correlation coefficient. Of the following scatter diagrams, the one that indicates no correlation is [a / b / c]; the one that indicates moderate correlation is [a / b / c]; and the one that indicates a relatively high degree of correlation is [a / b / c].

| c |
| b |
| a |

(a) (b) (c)

12 In the diagrams in Frame 11, above, notice also that when the correlation is zero, no matter what the known value of the independent variable X, the estimated value of the dependent variable is always equal to ___ (symbol).

| $\bar{Y}$ |

13 In the regression line represented by the equation

$$Y_c = a + bX$$

b indicates the slope of the best-fitting line, as discussed in Chapter 15, on regression analysis (Frames 33–35). Therefore, whenever the correlation coefficient has a negative value, the value of b in the associated regression equation will be [positive / negative].

| negative |

14 In Chapter 15 we also considered the standard error of the estimate, which indicates the degree of scatter of the points in a scatter diagram in respect to the _____ .

| regression line |

15 As we observed, the smaller the value of the standard error of estimate, the closer will be the correspondence between the actual and estimated values of the [independent / dependent] variable.

| dependent |

16 Therefore the smaller the value of the standard error of estimate, the [smaller / larger] is the absolute value of the associated correlation coefficient.

| larger |

17 The fact that this kind of relationship exists makes it possible to define the sample correlation coefficient in terms of the standard error of estimate based on sample data, although it would generally not be computed on this basis. With r representing the correlation coefficient, for sample data it can be stated that

$$r^2 = 1.00 - \frac{s^2_{Y.X}}{s^2_Y}$$

Thus this formula indicates that when the standard error of estimate for predicting Y from X($s_{Y.X}$) is equal to zero, $r^2 =$ _____ (number).

> 1.00

18 Along these lines we can also note that if $r^2 = 1.00$, then $r =$ _____ (number) or _____ (number).

> $-1.00; +1.00$

19 s_Y in the formula in Frame 17 is the standard deviation of the Y variable. Although it is not obvious in that formula, there is a definite limit to the possible magnitude of $s_{Y.X}$. To begin with, if there is no relationship at all between the X and Y variables, then the best estimate for Y, no matter what the value of X, is $\overline{Y}$, and the standard deviation about this estimate is represented by the symbol _____.

> s_Y

20 Since $s_{Y.X} = s_Y$ when there is absolutely no relationship between the two variables, $s_{Y.X}$ can approximately never be larger than s_Y itself. Accordingly, the largest value that the fraction $s^2_{Y.X}/s^2_Y$ can have is _____ (number).

> 1.00^1

21 Since $r^2 = 1.00 - (s^2_{Y.X}/s^2_Y)$, if $s_{Y.X} = s_Y$, then $r^2 =$ ___ (number) and $r =$ ___ (number).

> 0
>
> 0

22 More significant than the arithmetic manipulations we have been presenting is the essential meaning that the formula in Frame 17 conveys. In statistical analysis, the squared value of the standard deviation is called the *variance*. Recalling that the general formula for the sample standard deviation is $s = \sqrt{\Sigma(X - \overline{X})^2/n - 1}$, the variance can be described as an estimate of the average of the squared deviations from the _____ in the population of values being sampled.

> mean

---

[1] For sample data, the maximum value of this fraction is somewhat greater than 1.00, because in the formula for $s_{Y.X}$ the divisor is $n - 2$ (see page 417), while in the formula for s the divisor is $n - 1$ (see page 66). However, for population data the maximum value of this fraction is 1.00.

23 The formula for r^2 in Frames 17 and 21 contains a ratio between two variances. Since the term "total variance" is used to refer to the largest amount of variance that we can have in estimating the value of the Y variable, the total variance is represented by the symbol $[s_Y^2 \,/\, s_{Y \cdot X}^2]$.

s_Y^2

24 Since $s_{Y \cdot X}^2$ represents the variance associated with our estimate of the Y variable which remains even after use of our knowledge regarding the value of the X variable, it is referred to as the [explained / unexplained] variance.

unexplained

25 Thus the appropriate verbal description of the formula for r^2 represented in Frame 17 is [**a** / **b**] below:

a

$$\text{(a)} \quad r^2 = 1 - \frac{\text{unexplained variance}}{\text{total variance}}$$

$$\text{(b)} \quad r^2 = 1 - \frac{\text{total variance}}{\text{unexplained variance}}$$

26 Since the fraction in the formula in Frame 25 represents the *proportion of unexplained variance* when values of the dependent variable are being estimated based on knowledge of the independent variable, then subtracting this proportion from 1.00 identifies the proportion of _____ variance.

explained

27 Thus the value of r^2 indicates the proportion of the variance in the dependent variable explained by knowledge of the _____ variable.

independent

28 Because r^2 is actually easier to interpret in general terms than is the value of the coefficient of correlation, r, itself, it has been given its own name and is referred to as the "coefficient of determination." For a correlation coefficient of .50 the associated coefficient of determination is _____ (number).

$(.50)^2 = .25$

29 For a correlation coefficient of $+.70$, the associated coefficient of _____, r^2, is .49.

determination

30 If the correlation between a test of manual dexterity and work errors is $-.40$, then knowledge of the independent variable serves to explain ___ percent of the variance in the dependent variable.

16

variance
determination

31 Whereas s signifies a sample standard deviation and r signifies a sample coefficient of correlation, s^2 signifies a sample _____ and r^2 signifies a sample coefficient of _____ .

sign
absolute value

32 The direction of relationship between two variables is indicated by the _____ of the correlation coefficient, and the extent of the relationship is indicated by its _____ _____ .

decreased
increased

33 As the degree of dispersion around the regression line of a scatter diagram is decreased, the value of the standard error of estimate is [increased / decreased] and the absolute value of the correlation coefficient is [increased / decreased] .

determination (r^2)

34 The proportion of the variance in the dependent variable that is statistically explained by knowledge of the independent variable is directly indicated by the value of the coefficient of _____ .

35 In symbols, the value of the coefficient of determination can be defined as:

$1.00 - \dfrac{s^2_{Y.X}}{s^2_Y}$

$r^2 =$

16.2 ■ Development of the Pearson Correlation Coefficient r

In this section we briefly trace the historical development of correlation analysis and the development of the computational formula for the correlation coefficient. Although a number of correlation methods now exist, the Pearson product-moment correlation coefficient r is the most important in that all of the others represent modifications of this method for specific data situations. Appropriate use of the Pearson formula requires (1) that both variables be random variables; (2) that both of the variables be on a continuous scale, that is, that they be measured rather than categorized; (3) that there be only one independent and one dependent variable; (4) that the relationship between the two variables be linear; and (5) that each variable be normally distributed for any given value of the other variable. To take care of the situations in which one or more of these requirements cannot be satisfied, alternative correlation procedures have been developed as substitutes for the Pearson r.

scatter

36 The development of the correlation coefficient is related to the work of Sir Francis Galton during the latter part of the nineteenth century. Being interested in problems of heredity, he investigated the relationship between the height of parents (fathers) and the height of their offspring (sons). To begin with, since no statistical technique was available to measure this relationship, he entered the pairs of measurements on a two-dimensional graph, thus essentially constructing a _____ diagram.

regression lines (or straight lines)

37 Figure 16-1 illustrates the type of scatter diagram that Galton constructed. Then, as is also indicated in the figure, he entered the best-fitting _____ to be used for the purpose of estimation.

Figure 16-1 ■ Scatter diagram and regression lines depicting the relationship between the height of the parent and the height of the offspring

Height of offspring, Y

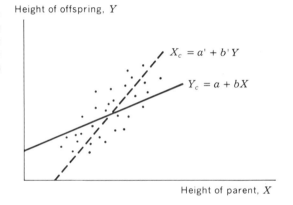

$X_c = a' + b'Y$

$Y_c = a + bX$

Height of parent, X

38 The techniques of regression analysis, discussed in Chapter 15, were not available at the time. In determining the regression line for predicting Y from X, Galton computed the mean of each column of values in the scatter diagram and connected them with the best fitting straight line by the freehand method. Similarly, to determine the regression line for predicting X from Y, he computed the mean of each [row / column] and connected these by a straight line.

row

39 Galton then solved for the values of a and b in the equation $Y_c = a + bX$ by using his graph. As indicated in Chapter 15, a is the value of Y_c on the graph when $X = $ ___ (number), and b indicates the _____ of the regression line in respect to the X axis.

0

slope (See Chapter 15, Frames 33–38.)

40 Similarly, he used the other regression line to determine

0
slope

the values of a' and b' in the equation $X_c = a' + b'Y$. In this case a' is the value of X on the regression line when $Y = $ ___ (number), and b' indicates the _____ of this regression line in respect to the Y axis.

41 Galton was apparently the first to refer to these lines as *regression lines*. He so named them because he thought they indicated that there is a regression toward the *group* mean in inherited characteristics. Specifically, he noted that short parents tended to have children [shorter / taller] than themselves and tall parents tended to have children [shorter / taller] than themselves.

taller

shorter

42 Thus Galton concluded that "nature abhors extremes" and named the best-fitting lines on the graph _____ lines.

regression

43 In passing, it should be noted that Sir Francis Galton was concerned about the "regression toward the mean" not just in regard to height, but in regard to a number of human characteristics, including intelligence. Why would a characteristic like height particularly lend itself to statistical study? _____ .

It is easily measured (etc.).

44 Refer to Figure 16-2. By using the *deviation values* $x = (X - \bar{X})$ and $y = (Y - \bar{Y})$ instead of the original measured values X and Y, he was able to simplify the regression equations. As we can conclude by reference to Figure 16-2, the use of deviation values simplifies the two regression equations because the result is that $a = $ ___ (value) and $a' = $ ___ (value).

0
0

Figure 16.2 ■ Regression lines depicting the relationship between the height of parent and the height of offspring in terms of deviation values

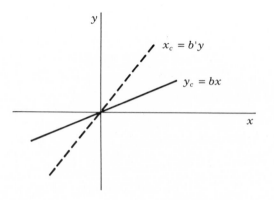

45 From Figure 16-2, the regression equation for predicting y_c when x is known is $y_c =$ ___ .

46 Galton now began to wonder whether the extent of the relationship between the two variables could not be expressed by some one number, rather than by two separate regression equation values b and b'. In order to represent the two axes of his graph in terms of a common scale, he transformed the deviation values to values on the z scale by dividing each deviation value by the associated standard deviation. Thus $z_X = x/s_X$ [where $x = (X - \bar{X})$] and $z_Y =$ _____ .

47 The regression lines for the z values of X and Y are illustrated in Figure 16-3. In this case the regression equations for predicting z_Y from z_X and z_X from z_Y are, respectively:

$z_{Y_c} =$

$z_{X_c} =$

Figure 16-3 ■ Regression lines depicting the relationship between the height of the parent and the height of the offspring in terms of z values

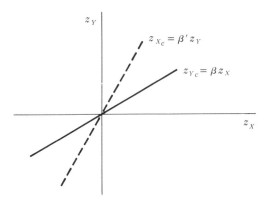

48 On the basis of these series of transformations and graphic analyses, Galton found that β almost equaled the value of β' in the equation in Frame 47, and he believed that the difference (in the second decimal place) was due entirely to graphic reading error. If true, this discovery would be significant because it would provide the basis for expressing the degree of relationship between two variables in terms of [only one / two distinct] value(s).

49 Galton turned to Karl Pearson, a mathematician and

biologist, and asked him to prove that β is equal to β' in the regression equations given in Frame 47. Pearson was in fact able to demonstrate that both β and β' are equal to $\Sigma(z_X z_Y)/n$ and are thus equal to one another. Pearson chose r as the symbol for the measure of relationship because both he and Galton referred to this value as the "regression coefficient." Since then this value has come to be referred to as the

| correlation |

_____ coefficient.

50 Specifically, the symbol r refers to the "Pearson product-moment correlation coefficient." It has been so named because the word "moment" refers to the sum of something divided by n, and in the formula $r = \Sigma(z_X z_Y)/n$ the sum of

| z values; n |

the product of each pair of _____ is divided by ___ .

51 It would be very cumbersome to have to transform every measured value of X and Y into a z value in order to compute r. Therefore the alternative computational formula normally used, which is directly equivalent to the product-moment formula and can be used with the measured values of X and Y, is

$$r = \frac{n\Sigma XY - \Sigma X \Sigma Y}{\sqrt{n\Sigma X^2 - (\Sigma x)^2}\,\sqrt{n\Sigma Y^2 - (\Sigma Y)^2}}$$

Unless a computational error has been made, the value of r determined by the use of this formula can never be less than

| −1.0; +1.0 |

−____ (number) or more than +____ (number).

Summary **52** Reviewing the material above, the early work in regression analysis which paved the way for the development of the concept of correlation was carried out by _____

| Sir Francis Galton |

_____ (name).

53 The mathematician who developed the formula for the coefficient of correlation and used the symbol r to represent it

| Karl Pearson |

was _____ (name).

54 Whereas the equation for a regression line permits us to estimate the value of a dependent variable given the value of the independent variable, the correlation coefficient expresses

| relationship |

the degree of _____ between two variables.

16.3 ■ Applications of Correlation Analysis

In this section we illustrate the computation of the Pearson r for simple linear correlation and consider the basis which is used for concluding that a given sample correlation value does or does not represent a statistically significant relationship between two variables. Use of the correlation coefficient to determine the value of the standard error of estimate to be used with the associated regression equation is also illustrated.

55 Given the data of Table 16-1, which is the same simplified example used to illustrate the computation of the least-squares regression line in Chapter 15, substitute the appropriate values in the equation below, but do not carry out any of the computations.

$$\boxed{\frac{5(86)-(10)(40)}{\sqrt{5(24)-(10)^2}\sqrt{5(334)-(40)^2}}} \qquad r = \frac{n\Sigma XY - \Sigma X\Sigma Y}{\sqrt{n\Sigma X^2 - (\Sigma X)^2}\sqrt{n\Sigma Y^2 - (\Sigma Y)^2}} =$$

$$\boxed{\left(= \frac{430-400}{\sqrt{20}\sqrt{70}} = \frac{30}{\sqrt{1,400}}\right.}$$

$$\boxed{\left. = \frac{30}{37.417} = +.80\right)}$$

Table 16-1 ■ Partial Data Relating Two Variables

Person	X	Y	XY	X^2	Y^2
A	3	9	27	9	81
B	2	8	16	4	64
C	1	5	5	1	25
D	3	10	30	9	100
E	1	8	8	1	64
	$\Sigma X = 10$	$\Sigma Y = 40$	$\Sigma XY = 86$	$\Sigma X^2 = 24$	$\Sigma Y^2 = 334$

56 For the computational result in Frame 55, since $r = +.80$, the proportion of the variance in the dependent variable Y, which is explained by knowledge of the independent variable, is _____ (number).

$\boxed{.64 \ (=r^2)}$

57 The statistic r^2, which serves as one basis for interpreting the value of the correlation coefficient, is referred to as the coefficient of _____.

$\boxed{\text{determination}}$

58 In addition to interpreting the value of the correlation coefficient in terms of the coefficient of determination, we might also ask whether the size of the sample correlation coefficient is large enough to indicate that the population correlation coefficient is in fact different from zero. Would you expect that the sample size needs to be considered in determining the significance of a correlation coefficient? [Yes / No] Why or why not? _____

_____ .

Yes; There is a greater likelihood of a chance relationship in a small sample (etc.).

59 Accordingly, Table B-7 in the Appendix indicates the various values of the sample correlation coefficient needed to conclude that it is significantly different from 0 at the .05 and .01 levels, based on sample size as reflected in the degrees of freedom. Refer to Table B-7. For the data of Table 16-1, df = _____ (number).

$n - 2 = 5 - 2 = 3$

60 Refer again to Table B-7. When df = 3, the value of r needed to conclude that the population correlation coefficient is different from 0 at the 5 percent level of significance is _____ (number).

.8783

61 Therefore the obtained r of +.80 [is / is not] significantly different from 0 at the 5 percent level. How large does the sample size have to be before a correlation coefficient of this size is significant at the 5 percent level? $n = $ ___.

is not

7 (df = 5)

62 In Chapter 15 we reported selection test scores and performance ratings for a sample of 20 industrial trainees. If we were to calculate the correlation coefficient representing the degree of association between the two variables, the minimum value of r needed to consider it as being significantly different from 0 at the .05 level is _____ (number).

.4438 (df = 18)

63 Suppose that we obtain a correlation coefficient of +.18 for a *population* of 100 pairs of measurements. Would we use Table B-7 to determine the significance of this correlation coefficient? [Yes / No] Why or why not?_____

_____ .

No; Table B-7 is used to test hypotheses about the population given *sample* data.

64 Thus when we conclude that a given sample correlation coefficient is significant at some probability level by using Table B-7, we are concluding that the population correlation coefficient is different from ___ (value).

0

65 If we wish to ascertain further whether the value of a correlation coefficient is high enough to be important for

some applied purpose, this [is also / is not] indicated by use of Table B-7.

66 In addition to its principal use in expressing the extent of relationship, the sample correlation coefficient can be used to determine the value of the standard error of estimate, $s_{Y.X}$, by a computational procedure that is simpler than the one introduced in Chapter 15. Given that $s_Y = 1.87$ for the distribution of Table 16-1, substitute the appropriate values in the following formula by referring to any of the frames above, but do not necessarily carry out the computations.

$1.87\sqrt{1-(.80)^2}\sqrt{\dfrac{4}{3}}$

$[= 1.87(.60)(1.15) = 1.29$

$\doteq 1.3]$

$$s_{Y.X} = s_Y\sqrt{1-r^2}\ \sqrt{\frac{n-1}{n-2}} =$$

67 Thus the computed value of 1.3 for $s_{Y.X}$ corresponds to the value computed in Frame 86 of Chapter 15. Notice, however, that in the present procedure for computing the standard error of estimate, the only sample statistic that we have to compute *when r has already been determined* is _____ (symbol).

s_Y (the standard deviation of the Y variable)

68 In Chapter 15 we indicated that because the typical objective is to estimate the population standard error of estimate on the basis of sample data, the computational formula listed below which is most frequently used is formula [a / b].

b

(a) $\sigma_{Y.X} = \sqrt{\dfrac{\Sigma Y^2 - a\Sigma Y - b\Sigma XY}{N}}$

(b) $s_{Y.X} = \sqrt{\dfrac{\Sigma Y^2 - a\Sigma Y - b\Sigma XY}{n-2}}$

69 However, when the value of the Pearson correlation coefficient r has already been computed, the formula for estimating the population standard error of estimate which would frequently be used because it results in a simpler computational routine is [a / b / c].

c

(a) $s_{Y.X} = \sqrt{\dfrac{\Sigma Y^2 - a\Sigma Y - b\Sigma XY}{n-2}}$

(b) $s_{Y.X} = \sqrt{\dfrac{\Sigma(Y - Y_c)^2}{n-2}}$

(c) $s_{Y.X} = s_Y\sqrt{1 - r^2}\sqrt{\dfrac{n-1}{n-2}}$

70 In addition to using the formulas presented in Frames 46 to 50 of Chapter 15 for solving for the values of a and b in $Y_c = a + bX$, these values for the regression line that satisfies the least-squares criterion can also be determined by an alternative formula that utilizes the value of r. Unlike the computation of the standard error of estimate, however, the present formula does not present any special computational advantage over the procedure presented in Chapter 15 and thus is presented here only to inform you of its existence. Using r, the least-squares regression equation for estimating Y when X is known can be defined as

$$Y_c = \left(\overline{Y} - r\,\frac{s_Y}{s_X}\,\overline{X}\right) + \left(r\,\frac{s_Y}{s_X}\right)X$$

Referring to the equation for a straight line, $Y_c = a + bX$, in the equation above,

$a =$

and $b =$

$\overline{Y} - r\dfrac{s_Y}{s_X}\overline{X}$

$r\dfrac{s_Y}{s_X}$

16.4 ■ Rank Correlation

Among the alternative correlation procedures used in place of the Pearson r under special circumstances, one of the most popular in terms of extent of use is the rank correlation. It is often referred to as "Spearman's rank correlation coefficient," in honor of the statistician who first developed the procedure in the early 1900s. As the symbol we use suggests, r_{rank} is a measure of the extent of relationship between two variables, X and Y, each of which is expressed as a series of ranks rather than measurements.

71 Like the Pearson correlation coefficient, the Spearman rank correlation coefficient ranges in possible value from -1.0 to $+1.0$. Therefore the value of r_{rank} that indicates the lowest degree of relationship between the two ranked variables is ___ (number).

0

72 Table 16-2 lists the ranks assigned by two securities analysts to 12 investment opportunities in terms of the degree of investor risk involved. The formula for the rank correlation coefficient is

$$r_{rank} = 1 - \frac{6\Sigma D^2}{n(n^2 - 1)}$$

For the data of Table 16-2, $n = $ ___ (number).

Investment	Rank by analyst 1	Rank by analyst 2
A	7	6
B	8	4
C	2	1
D	1	3
E	9	11
F	3	2
G	12	12
H	11	10
I	4	5
J	10	9
K	6	7
L	5	8

73 The only other value we need in order to determine the rank correlation coefficient is ΣD^2. Given that D equals the difference between the two ranks assigned to each investment opportunity, complete the table below and determine the value of ΣD^2.

Investment	Rank by analyst 1	Rank by analyst 2	D	D²
A	7	6	1	1
B	8	4	4	16
C	2	1	1	1
D	1	3	−2	4
E	9	11	−2	4
F	3	2	1	1
G	12	12	___	___
H	11	10	___	___
I	4	5	___	___
J	10	9	___	___
K	6	7	___	___
L	5	8	___	___
			$\Sigma D^2 =$	___

74 Refer to the completed table in Frame 73. For the data of Table 16-2:

$$1 - \frac{6(40)}{12(143)} = 1 - \frac{20}{143}$$

$$= \frac{123}{143} = +.86$$

$$r_{rank} = 1 - \frac{6\Sigma D^2}{n(n^2 - 1)} =$$

75 Spearman's r_{rank} is generally used when measurements along a continuous scale cannot be obtained but rankings can be obtained. If measured data are transformed into ranks, the value of r_{rank} will usually differ somewhat from the value of r that would have been computed. However, the r_{rank} may be "good enough" for certain purposes, or it may be used as the basis for deciding whether or not to proceed to a computation of r itself. For the data below, indicate the ranks assigned to each variable, from highest to lowest. *In case of tied observations, each of the tied observations is assigned the average of the ranks which would have been assigned if no ties had occurred.*

			5	5
			1.5	3
			4	2
			1.5	1
			3	4

	Overall performance rating		Rank	
Super-visor	Of the supervisor	Of the subordinates	Of the super-visor	Of the sub-ordinates
A	70	75	____	____
B	95	83	____	____
C	85	92	____	____
D	95	95	____	____
E	90	80	____	____

76 Using the ranks which are reproduced below, determine the value of ΣD^2.

			0	0
			−1.5	2.25
			2	4
			0.5	0.25
			−1	1
				7.50

Supervisor	Supervisor's rank	Subordinates' rank	D	D²
A	5	5	____	____
B	1.5	3	____	____
C	4	2	____	____
D	1.5	1	____	____
E	3	4	____	____
			$\Sigma D^2 =$	____

77 Finally, solve for the value of r_{rank} using the data in the table in Frame 77.

$$1 - \frac{6(7.5)}{5(24)} = 1 - \frac{45}{120}$$

$$= \frac{75}{120} = .625 = +.62$$

$$r_{rank} = 1 - \frac{6\Sigma D^2}{n(n^2 - 1)} =$$

78 The Spearman rank correlation coefficient is used whenever the pairs of values for two variables are ranked rather than measured. As compared with r, r_{rank} requires [more / less] computational effort and is [more / less] accurate.

less

less (since it is essentially a substitute for r)

16.5 ■ Multiple and Partial Correlation and the Meaning of Correlation Values

In this section we define and give examples of the coefficient of multiple correlation and the coefficient of partial correlation. However, we do not cover the associated computational procedures as such, which are beyond the scope of this book. Typically, these values are determined by the use of computer programs. In addition we consider the meaning of correlation values in general, particularly in terms of their being interpreted as indicating causation.

79 The coefficient of multiple correlation R is useful as an extension of the Pearson r whenever we wish to measure the relationship between two or more independent variables on the one hand with one dependent variable on the other. Thus the coefficient of multiple correlation always involves more than one [independent / dependent] variable.

independent

80 The symbol for the coefficient of multiple correlation R is usually written with a subscript, and in the subscript the number 1 always refers to the single dependent variable. Thus $R_{1.23}$ indicates that the coefficient is a measure of the relationship between the dependent variable and two other variables, identified by the numbers ___ and ___.

2; 3

81 Similarly, $R_{1.234}$ indicates the correlation between the dependent variable and [two / three / four] other variables, taken as a group.

three

82 Thus, if an economist wishes to ascertain the amount of relationship of the level of consumer debt with the levels of household income and interest rates taken together, the coefficient that would be appropriately computed is the coefficient of _____ correlation.

multiple

83 Similarly, the personnel manager interested in assessing the correlation of the performance ratings for a group of industrial trainees with a general ability test and a test of mechanical comprehension taken together could also make use of the coefficient of multiple correlation. The appropriate symbol and subscripts for the correlation coefficient would in this case be _____ (symbol).

$R_{1.23}$

84 Instead of measuring the relationship between a single dependent variable and a number of independent variables, the technique of *partial correlation* permits us to measure the extent of relationship between one dependent variable and one independent variable with other specified independent variables "held constant" statistically. In simple correlation, such as the correlation between general-ability test scores and performance ratings, are other independent variables, such as extent of mechanical comprehension, held constant? [Yes / No]

No (Other variables are ignored, but not controlled.)

85 The lowercase r is used as the symbol for the coefficient of partial correlation, with the subscripts indicating the two principal dependent and independent variables by listing them first and then designating the variables held constant. Thus $r_{14.23}$ indicates that the correlation reported is between variables ___ and ___ and that the variables held constant are those numbered ___ and ___ .

1; 4
2; 3

86 If we want to determine the relationship between the height of corn and the amount of rainfall, with days of sunshine held constant, the appropriate statistic to compute is the coefficient of _____ correlation.

partial

87 Where variable 1 is the level of personal debt, variable 2 is the level of household income, and variable 3 is the level of interest rates, the coefficient of partial correlation indicating the relationship between personal debt and interest rates, with income held constant, is designated by _____ (symbol).

$r_{13.2}$

88 The material presented in this section thus far may be summarized: The relationship between a single dependent variable and several independent variables taken as a group can be determined by computing a coefficient of _____ _____. The relationship between a single dependent variable and a single independent variable, with other specified independent variables held constant, can be determined by computing a coefficient of _____ _____.

multiple correlation

partial correlation

89 No matter what type of correlation coefficient is computed, whether the Pearson r, Spearman r_{rank}, coefficient of multiple correlation, or coefficient of partial correlation, interpretation of the coefficient as indicating causation should be done with caution. If a coefficient expresses the relationship between amount of rainfall and height of corn, or level of

Yes	income and level of savings, is a cause-effect relationship likely? [Yes / No]

90 If a positive correlation were found between level of expenditure and level of savings, would you consider this as an

No	indication of cause and effect? [Yes / No]

91 Thus the correlation coefficient indicates the extent of the relationship as such, but it does not necessarily indicate the existence of a cause-effect relationship between the variables. Among other reasons, two variables may have a high relationship with one another because they are effects of a common cause. For example, in Frame 91 the levels of personal expenditure and savings might both be the effects of

personal income (etc.)	the level of _____ .

92 In addition to having a common cause, two variables that are positively related may be separated by several steps in a cause-effect chain of events. For example, in the medical field it has been discovered that there is this sequence of events: warm, humid air → breeding of mosquitoes → activity of mosquitoes in an area → transportation of malaria micro-organisms → incidence of malaria. In terms of this sequence, then, would the existence of warm, humid weather in certain geographic areas be positively related to the incidence of

Yes ("Malaria" literally means "bad air.") No (though they make it possible for the causative factors to operate)	malaria? [Yes / No] Are these weather conditions the cause of malaria? [Yes / No]

93 In addition to the possibility of a common cause or being separated by several steps in a cause-effect sequence, many correlations in business and economics represent mutual cause-effect relationships. For example, investor optimism may affect stock market price changes, and stock market price

investor optimism	changes may, in turn, affect _____ .

94 A sample correlation coefficient indicating a significant degree of relationship can represent:

(a) a direct cause-effect relationship
(b) two variables influenced by a common cause
(c) two variables that are several steps removed in a cause-effect sequence
(d) two variables with a mutual cause-effect relationship within certain limits
(e) sampling error

In terms of the last possibility, if an obtained correlation coefficient is significant at the 5 percent level, the probability that the coefficient represents nothing but a chance relationship is _____ (number).

0.05 (See Section 10.2 for a discussion of the types of errors in hypothesis testing.)

95 Of the five possible meanings of a correlation coefficient reviewed in Frame 95, write the identifying letters of those that would have possible value in business decision making and economic forecasting: _____ (letters).

a, b, c, d

96 Thus, even though two variables do not enter into a direct cause-effect relationship, knowledge of a relatively stable relationship between them may nevertheless be highly useful. For example, cyclical changes in demand for a product may invariably follow similar changes for another product. Although the reason for the correlation may be unclear, its existence may be useful for the purpose of _____.

forecasting (or decision making, etc.)

97 Similarly, if a relationship is found between performance on a test of mechanical comprehension and performance ratings on a particular job, a direct cause-effect relationship is certainly not implied, because both the test score and the ratings represent evaluations of performance. Rather, both are probably effects of a common set of _____.

causes (previous education, experience, and innate ability)

98 Thus a correlation coefficient need not represent a direct cause-effect relationship in order to have practical value, for the existence of a relationship may be useful in any event. Put another way, the only correlation coefficient that cannot be useful in decision making or forecasting is one whose value represents _____.

sampling error (or an accidental correlation)

Review

direction

extent

99 (Frames 1–12) The sign of a correlation coefficient indicates the _____ of relationship between two variables; its absolute value indicates the _____ of relationship.

increased

100 (Frames 13–16) As the degree of dispersion in respect to the regression line of a scatter diagram is increased, the value of the standard error of estimate is [increased / decreased] and decreased

the absolute value of the correlation coefficient is [increased / decreased].

101 (Frames 17-25) Where $s^2_{Y.X}$ is the unexplained variance and s^2_Y is the total variance, one way to define the value of the correlation coefficient is to note that

$$\frac{s^2_{Y.X}}{s^2_Y}$$

$$r^2 = 1.00 - \frac{\qquad\qquad}{\qquad\qquad} \begin{array}{l}\text{(symbol)}\\\text{(symbol)}\end{array}$$

102 (Frames 26-35) Since the value of r^2 represents the proportion of the variance in one variable that is explained by knowledge of the other variable, it has been called the coefficient of _____.

determination

103 (Frames 36-43) In his work which led to the formulation of the coefficient of correlation, Sir Francis Galton entered pairs of values representing the heights of parents and their children on a _____ diagram, and he called the best-fitting straight lines entered on this diagram _____ lines.

scatter

regression

104 (Frames 44-48) In his attempt to transform each scale of measurement to a common base, Galton first computed the deviation values for each measured height and plotted these on a scatter diagram, and then he transformed the heights into ___ values and plotted these on the diagram.

z

105 (Frames 49-54) Karl Pearson, the mathematician, was able to prove that in the equations $z_{Y_c} = \beta z_X$ and $z_{X_c} = \beta' z_Y$, both β and β' are equal to $\Sigma z_X z_Y / n$. He then designated this by the symbol ___ and called it the _____ coefficient.

r

regression (Since then it has been called the "Pearson product-moment correlation coefficient," or simply the "correlation coefficient.")

106 (Frames 55-65) Suppose a sample of 20 pairs of measurements yields a correlation coefficient of .60. Would this indicate that the population correlation coefficient is different from zero at the 1 percent level of significance? [Yes / No] Why or why not? _____
_____.

Yes (According to Table B-7, the required coefficient is .5614.)

107 (Frames 66-70) In addition to its use as a measure of relationship, r can be used in determining the regression equation for predicting Y from X (or X from Y) and in computing the value of the associated standard of error of estimate. Of these two, the use of r is more likely to simplify the computation of the [regression equation / standard error of estimate].

standard error of estimate

108 (Frames 71–78) The Spearman rank correlation coefficient (r_{rank}) is used whenever [one / both] of the variables in the correlation analysis is (are) ranked and, as compared with the Pearson r, requires [more / less] computational effort.

both

less

109 (Frames 79–83) If we want to determine the extent of the relationship between a single dependent variable and several independent variables taken as a group, we would appropriately compute the coefficient of _____ _____.

multiple correlation

110 (Frames 84–88) If we want to determine the extent of the relationship between a single dependent variable and a single independent variable, but at the same time hold the effects due to one or more other independent variables constant, we would appropriately compute the coefficient of _____.

partial correlation

111 (Frames 89-94) In this chapter we identified five possible meanings of a sample correlation coefficient in terms of causation. Give two meanings, other than a direct cause-effect relationship, that a correlation coefficient can represent.

(See Frame 94 for the listing.)

(a) _____

(b) _____

112 (Frames 95-98) Of the five possible meanings of the sample correlation coefficient that were described, the only one that always indicates a lack of usefulness for economic forecasting or managerial decision making is the one for which the correlation represents only _____.

sampling error

Symbols Introduced in This Chapter (with Frame Numbers)

(1) r Coefficient of correlation.

(17) r^2 Coefficient of determination.

(72) r_{rank} The rank correlation coefficient.

(73) D The difference between the two ranks assigned to a particular item (in rank correlation).

(80) $R_{1.23}$ Coefficient of multiple correlation between the dependent variable, always indicated by the subscript 1, and two independent variables, indicated by 2 and 3 in this case.

(85) $r_{14.23}$ Coefficient of partial correlation between variables 1 and 4, with variables 2 and 3 statistically held constant in this case.

Formulas Introduced in This Chapter (with Frame Numbers)

(17) $r^2 = 1.00 - \dfrac{s_{Y.X}^2}{s_Y^2}$ The coefficient of determination. This formula is used to illustrate that r^2 represents the proportion of explained variance in the dependent variable, but it is seldom used for computational purposes.

(25) $r^2 = 1 - \dfrac{\text{unexplained variance}}{\text{total variance}}$ Verbalized version of the formula in Frame 17.

(50) $r = \dfrac{\Sigma z_X z_Y}{n}$ The Pearson product-moment coefficient of correlation.

(51) $r = \dfrac{n\Sigma XY - \Sigma X \Sigma Y}{\sqrt{n\Sigma X^2 - (\Sigma X)^2}\sqrt{n\Sigma Y^2 - (\Sigma Y)^2}}$ Computational formula for the Pearson coefficient of correlation.

(66) $s_{Y.X} = s_Y\sqrt{1 - r^2}\,\sqrt{\dfrac{n-1}{n-2}}$ The sample standard error of estimate based on a known value of r^2.

(70) $Y_c = \left(\overline{Y} - r\dfrac{s_Y}{s_X}\overline{X}\right) + \left(r\dfrac{s_Y}{s_X}\right)X$ The least-squares regression equation for a straight line based on using the value of the correlation coefficient.

(72) $r_{rank} = 1 - \dfrac{6\Sigma D^2}{n(n^2 - 1)}$ The rank correlation coefficient.

EXERCISES
(Solutions on pages 625–628)

16.1 For the simplified data below, which served as the basis for the first several exercises at the end of Chapter 15 on regression analysis, compute the value of the Pearson correlation coefficient. Assuming that the data represent a random sample of pairs of values from a large population, is the obtained correlation coefficient different from zero at the 5 percent level of significance?

X	Y
3	5
4	10
6	9
7	12

16.2 Transform the values in Exercise 16.1, above, into ranks and compute the rank correlation coefficient.

16.3 Determine the least-squares regression equation for estimating the value of Y when X is known by applying the formula presented in Frame 70 of this chapter. Compare the equation with the one determined in Exercise 15.2.

16.4 Compute the standard error of estimate to be used in conjunction with the equation determined in Exercise 16.3, above, by applying the formula which makes use of the value of the correlation coefficient, as presented in Frame 66 of this chapter. Compare the result with the value determined in Exercise 15.4.

16.5 The data concerning monthly housing starts and sales of home furnishings presented in Exercise 15.6 are repeated below. Compute the value of the correlation coefficient for these data and indicate whether the value is significant at the 5 percent level.

Monthly housing starts	Sales volume ($1,000s)	Monthly housing starts	Sales volume ($1,000s)
450	9.5	650	13.5
150	6.0	225	8.0
200	6.2	500	13.0
600	5.5	280	8.8
250	7.5	350	9.0
300	10.0	400	12.0

16.6 Identify the assumptions that are required in respect to the variables in Exercise 16.5 in order to use correlation analysis with the data.

16.7 Determine the value of the coefficient of determination for the data of Exercise 16.5 and interpret the value as it applies to the sample data.

16.8 How would the coefficient of determination computed in Exercise 16.7, above, be interpreted in reference to the population from which the sample was obtained?

16.9 Determine the standard error of estimate for the data in Exercise 16.5 by using the computed value of the correlation coefficient, r. Compare your answer with the result of using the computational formula in Exercise 15.9.

16.10 Describe the coefficient of multiple correlation by indicating how it represents an extension of the Pearson correlation coefficient.

ADDITIONAL EXERCISES

16.11 For the simplified data below, which are repeated from Exercise 15.11, compute the value of the Pearson correlation coefficient. Assuming that this is a sample from a large population, is the relationship significant at the 5 percent level?

X	Y
1	8
3	5
6	5
8	2

16.12 Consider the sign of the correlation coefficient determined in Exercise 16.11, above, and indicate what it means. Similarly, indicate the relationship between the sign of the correlation coefficient and the regression equation for estimating Y given X, as determined in Exercise 15.12.

16.13 Transform the values in Exercise 16.11 into ranks and compute the value of the rank correlation coefficient.

16.14 For the data of Exercise 16.11, compute the value of the standard error of estimate to be used in conjunction with estimating the value of Y when X is known by applying the formula which utilizes the value of r. Compare your answer with the answer obtained in Exercise 15.14.

16.15 The following data relating level of advertising and level of sales are here repeated from Exercise 15.16. Compute the Pearson correlation coefficient for these data and determine if the correlation value is significantly different from zero at the 5 percent level.

Level of advertising ($100s)	Level of sales ($1,000s)
10.5	17.3
6.0	14.0
8.7	19.1
9.3	14.5
11.8	20.0
7.5	16.3
15.0	23.8
6.3	14.0
8.5	17.3
5.4	13.3

16.16 Consider the nature of the variables included in Exercise 16.15. Is it statistically appropriate to compute a correlation coefficient for these data? Why or why not?

16.17 A staff manager is considering the appointment of several people to a task force which is to consider the appropriate company policy regarding product development during the next decade. He asks two of his assistants to rank the eight economic analysts employed in the department in terms of their expertise in long-range forecasting, so that he can use these rankings as a guide for assigning two of the analysts to the task force. The requested rankings are listed below. Determine the extent of agreement between the two assistants by computing the correlation coefficient for these data.

Economist	Rank by assistant 1	Rank by assistant 2
A	3	1
B	4	2
C	6	5
D	1	4
E	7	8
F	2	3
G	8	6
H	5	7

16.18 Given the correlation coefficient computed in Exercise 16.17, above, how would you go about interpreting this value? Note that since only eight economic analysts are employed in the department, these data constitute a population rather than a sample.

16.19 The data below are repeated from Exercise 15.21. Calculate the value of the Pearson correlation coefficient for these sample data, and determine whether the value is significant at the 1 percent level of significance.

Sampled student	Hours of study, X	Examination grade, Y
1	20	64
2	16	61
3	34	84
4	23	70
5	27	88
6	32	92
7	18	72
8	22	77

16.20 Compute the value of the coefficient of determination for the data in Exercise 16.20, and interpret the meaning of this value.

16.21 The data below are repeated from Exercise 15.24. Calculate coefficient of correlation for these data and determine whether the value is significantly different from zero, using the 5 percent level of significance in the test.

Sampled worker	Weeks of experience, X	Number of rejects, Y
1	7	26
2	9	20
3	6	28
4	14	16
5	8	23
6	12	18
7	10	24
8	4	26
9	2	38
10	11	22
11	1	32
12	8	25

16.22 Determine the coefficient of determination for the data in Exercise 16.21, and interpret the meaning of this value.

16.23 Interpret the meaning of each of the following correlation values.

(a) $r_{13.2} = .40$
(b) $r_{12} = -.60$

(c) $r_{rank} = .30$
(d) $R_{1.23} = .50$

16.24 The value of a correlation coefficient can be considered in terms of "significance" and in terms of the associated coefficient of determination. Discuss these two methods of interpretation and indicate how they relate to one another.

16.25 Briefly discuss the coefficient of partial correlation and indicate how it differs from the Pearson coefficient of correlation.

CHAPTER 17 ■
TIME-SERIES ANALYSIS

A time series is made up of a set of observations taken for specified, and usually equal, intervals of time. The principal approach to the analysis of time-series data is concerned with identifying the time-related factors that influence each of the periodic values in the series. Once such factors have been identified, they are used to project time-series values for future periods. Unfortunately, future events and their outcomes are not necessarily from the same population as past events and their outcomes, and hence the methods of statistical inference cannot be used in conjunction with forecasting. The result is that forecasts cannot be presented in terms of probability values based on the concept of sampling distributions. Rather, time-series analysis is a statistical procedure whose accuracy and success depend to a considerable extent on the appropriateness of the judgments made by the statistical analyst. In the sections below we present the conventional approach to identifying the components of a time series and consider the use of the trend and seasonal components in forecasting.

17.1 ■ The Components of a Time Series

As indicated in the introduction above, there is no way by which to evaluate contrasting approaches to time-series analysis in terms of the methods of statistical inference. A widely used approach to time-series analysis is that of identifying the major time-related factors that appear to influence the individual values in a time series. From this standpoint the principal components of a time series are the *trend, seasonal, cyclical,* and *irregular* components.

1 A series of measurements taken at specified times, and listed in tabular form, is called a _____ .

time series

2 Time-series data also are often portrayed graphically, as the hypothetical series of Figure 17-1. On such a graph the time periods are represented along the [horizontal / vertical] axis, and the quantities are represented along the [horizontal / vertical] axis.

horizontal

vertical

3 Of the components that affect the individual values in a time series, the most important is usually *trend*, which is defined as the long-term underlying growth movement in a time series. Thus the component of trend can be determined only if time-series data are available for a number of [weeks / months / years].

years

4 The long-term component in a time series that underlies the growth movement (or decline) in the series and is usually

Figure 17-1 ■ The component of a time series

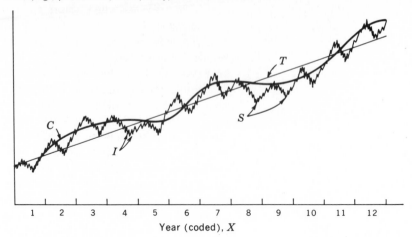

Level (e.g., production, sales, etc.), Y

Year (coded), X

<table>
<tr><td></td></tr>
</table>

trend	attributed to advances in population or technology is called _____ .
T	**5** In Figure 17-1 the data of the time series are represented by the jagged line extending toward the upper right-hand corner of the graph. The straight line which represents the trend line for the series is identified by the symbol ___ .
for a period of more than one year	**6** The *seasonal* component of the time series refers to a pattern of change which recurs regularly over time. Furthermore this movement must be completed within the duration of a year and repeat itself year after year in order to qualify as a seasonal change. It follows, therefore, that in order to identify the seasonal component in a time series, it is necessary to collect data [for one year only / for a period of more than one year] .
seasonal	**7** The increase in the sale of lawn fertilizer each spring and its decline during certain other months exemplify the _____ component in a time series.
S (There is a seasonal increase near the middle of each year and then a seasonal drop.)	**8** In Figure 17-1 the seasonal component of the time series is identified by the symbol ___ .

9 In addition to the trend and seasonal components of a time series, the *cyclical* component can be identified. Cyclical movements are similar to the seasonal, in that they also are

would not	repetitive, wavelike movements, but they differ in that the movements are of longer duration and are less predictable in duration and amplitude. Thus a cyclical movement requiring a total of four years for its completion [would / would not] be an unusual phenomenon.

10 The fairly long-term movement in a time series, not so persistent as trend, which often requires several years for its completion is the _____ component.

cyclical	

11 The business cycle is the prime example of a cyclical component that has had considerable attention devoted to it by economists. In Figure 17-1 the cyclical component is identified by the symbol ___ .

C	

12 Finally, the movements that represent quick changes that are normally of short duration and are not characterized by smooth, regular patterns make up the *irregular* component of the time series. Is it conceivable that through analysis the causes underlying irregular movements in a time series could be identified? [Yes / No]

Yes (e.g., specific government actions, price increases, or industrial disputes)

13 The day-to-day and week-to-week fluctuation in the level of lawn-fertilizer sales that is related to variations in the weather would constitute some of the short-term changes contributing to the _____ component of the time series.

irregular	

14 In Figure 17-1 the irregular component of the time series is identified by the symbol ___ .

I	

15 Thus in Frames 3 to 14 we have introduced the four components identified in conventional time-series analysis: the

trend; seasonal; cyclical
irregular

_____ , _____ , _____ , and _____ components.

16 To complete our introduction to the conventional model of time-series analysis, we need to specify how the trend (T), seasonal (S), cyclical (C), and irregular (I) components interact in their effect on specific values in the series. The most generally accepted model assumes that any given value, Y, in the time series is a *product* of the effects of components T, S, C, and I at that point in time. Thus, algebraically stated,

$T \cdot S \cdot C \cdot I$ (or: $T \times S \times C \times I$)

$Y =$ _____

17 An alternative approach to combining the components of a time series is to assume that their effects are additive rather than multiplicative, resulting in the equation $Y = \underline{\hspace{2cm}}$.

$T + S + C + I$

18 Under the additive assumption the contribution of the seasonal component, for example, remains at the same level of magnitude for a given part of the year, no matter what the overall level of time-series values. Under the multiplicative assumption, as overall time-series values increase, the absolute size of the seasonal fluctuation from period to period [remains at the same level / also increases].

also increases

19 Throughout this chapter we follow the prevalent assumption regarding the relationship among the components of the time series, that is, that they are [additive / multiplicative] in their interaction.

multiplicative

20 Much of time-series analysis consists of identifying and eliminating the effect in time-series values of each of the components in turn; this process is often referred to as the *decomposition* of the time series. The first component typically identified is that which represents the long-term, slowly moving forces affecting the time-series values, that is, the component of _____ .

trend

21 In our analysis of trend, presented in Section 17.2, which follows, it will be represented as a best-fitting line, and in this respect its calculation is similar to that for fitting a regression line. Therefore one of the methods by which the trend line can be located is by the use of the _____ criterion.

least-squares

22 After identifying the trend component of the time series, the next component we identify is that which underlies the regular and relatively short-term upward and downward movements in the series, that is, the _____ component.

seasonal

23 Finally, if the trend, T, and seasonal, S, influences on time-series values are removed or averaged out, the remaining components whose effects are thus highlighted by the process of decomposition are the _____ and _____ components.

cyclical (C)

irregular (I)

24 Because the cyclical and irregular components may follow no systematic regularity, they are often identified as the remainder, or residual, of the decomposition of a time series. Algebraically, since $Y = T \cdot S \cdot C \cdot I$, then if Y, T, and S are known, we can solve for the combined components C and I by the algebraic equation

$$\boxed{\dfrac{Y}{T \cdot S}} \qquad C \cdot I =$$

25 In the remainder of this chapter we illustrate the computational procedures that can be represented by such algebraic formulas. The basic approach of identifying and removing the effect of time-series components, which is particularly important for identification of the cyclical and irregular components, is often referred to as the

$$\boxed{\text{decomposition}} \qquad \underline{\hspace{3cm}} \text{ of a time series.}$$

17.2 ■ Trend Analysis

Because the contents of this chapter represent an introduction to the methods of time-series analysis, rather than a coverage in depth, we describe several of the techniques available for determining the location of the trend line without extended discussion of the particular circumstances under which each would be most appropriate. Again, the analyst's judgment as to which technique to use is particularly crucial because there is no way of evaluating one approach in contrast to another by the use of the methods of statistical inference. Rather, all methods and judgments have to await the test of time, assuming that they play a role in forecasting. In this section we illustrate the use of the freehand method, the method of semiaverages, the method of moving averages, and the method of least squares as approaches to identifying the trend line for the number of new automobiles registered annually in the United States from 1951 to 1970, inclusive.

26 The method of identifying the location of the trend line which is mathematically least sophisticated is the *freehand method*. By this approach the location of the line on the time-series graph is entirely dependent on the judgment (or whim) of the analyst studying the data, with no numerical calculations necessarily involved. Is it possible that a trend line so constructed might turn out to be more useful for forecasting purposes than one identified by one of the more sophisticated mathematical methods? [Yes / No]

$$\boxed{\begin{array}{l} \text{Yes (The decision to use a} \\ \text{particular mathematical} \\ \text{method is itself a judgment,} \\ \text{and one which may prove to} \\ \text{be incorrect.)} \end{array}}$$

27 Figure 17-2 portrays factory sales of domestic passenger cars in the United States between 1951 and 1975. On this graph enter a freehand trend line, either as a straight line or otherwise, and extend this line for the year 1976. Ignore your actual knowledge of automobile sales in 1976 and construct your trend line entirely on the basis of the data for the years 1951–1975. Based on your freehand trend line, the forecast of factory sales of cars for 1976 is approximately _____ million units.

28 Now let us apply some of the mathematically more sophisticated techniques to the same data. The *method of semiaverages* consists of separating the data into two parts, preferably equal in terms of the time span involved, averaging the values within the two parts, and thus establishing two points for locating the trend line. As typically used, therefore, the method of semiaverages results in trend lines that are [straight lines only / either straight or curved].

29 Table 17-1 lists the factory sales of domestic passenger cars, in millions of units, for the years 1951–1975. As indicated in the footnote of the table, the average number of

5.674

7.712

car sales for the years 1951–1962 was _____ million units, and the average number of factory car sales for the years 1963–1975 was _____ million units.

Table 17-1 ■ Factory Sales of Domestic Passenger Cars from Plants in the United States, 1951–1975, and Computation of Five-year Moving Averages (In millions of units)*

Year	Factory sales, millions of units	Five-year moving total	Five-year moving average
(1)	(2)	(3)	(4)
1951	5.090		
1952	4.154		
1953	5.954	28.216	5.643
1954	5.352	28.749	5.750
1955	7.666	30.548	6.110
1956	5.623	28.726	5.745
1957	5.953	28.848	5.770
1958	4.132	27.712	5.542
1959	5.474	27.491	5.498
1960	6.530	28.292	5.658
1961	5.402	31.604	6.321
1962	6.754	33.684	6.737
1963	7.444	36.255	7.251
1964	7.554	39.190	7.838
1965	9.101	39.506	7.901
1966	8.337	40.469	8.094
1967	7.070	40.722	8.144
1968	8.407	37.808	7.562
1969	7.807	37.593	7.519
1970	6.187	38.876	7.775
1971	8.122	39.548	7.910
1972	8.353	38.462	7.692
1973	9.079	38.348	7.670
1974	6.721		
1975	6.073		

*For the method of semiaverages, the arithmetic mean for 1951 to 1962 (12 years) is 5.674 and for 1963 to 1975 (13 years) it is 7.712.

Source of data: U.S. Department of Commerce, *Survey of Current Business.*

30 Our next step is to enter these two points on Figure 17-2 and construct the appropriate straight line. In reference to the horizontal (time) axis of Figure 17-2, each average value should be entered over the midpoint of the span of years that it represents. For example, the average of 5.674 million units for the 12-year period of 1951 through 1962 should be entered on the graph above the midpoint between the two adjoining years _____ and _____ .

1956; 1957 (For 1963–1975, the midpoint is at the year 1969.)

31 Now connect these two points on Figure 17-2, forming a straight line, and label this trend line *SA*. Based on this trend line, the projected new-car-registration figure for 1976 is approximately _____ million units.

8.8

32 As contrasted to the method of semiaverages, the *method of moving averages* typically results in the plotting of several points and therefore does not usually result in a straight trend line. Its major purpose is to accomplish a smoothing of data when there are cyclical or other irregular year-to-year variations in the values of the time series. On the basis of the data of Table 17-1 and Figure 17-2, does it appear that the method of moving averages would have any use in this case? [Yes / No]

Yes (There are certainly marked year-to-year variations.)

33 We normally choose to use an odd number of years for the computation of a moving average so that the averages will be centered at particular years rather than being between years. Accordingly, columns 3 and 4 of Table 17-1 present the five-year moving totals and five-year moving averages for the data of column 2. Thus, of the first two totals in column 3, 28.216 million units is the total for the five years from _____ through _____ , and 28.749 million units is the total for the five years from _____ through _____ .

1951
1955
1952; 1956

34 Similarly for the moving averages, 5.498 million units is the average for the years _____ through _____ , and 5.658 is the average for the years _____ through _____ .

1957; 1961
1958; 1962

35 Now plot the values given in column 4 of Table 17-1 on the graph of Figure 17-2, connect these points by a series of straight lines, and label the result *5M*. If we were to project the five-year moving average to 1971 as the basis for forecasting, the method at this point would be most similar to that of the [freehand method / method of semiaverages].

freehand method (except, of course, that moving averages rather than time-series values serve as the basis for the projection in this case)

36 One consideration regarding the method of moving averages is that the number of categories of data is reduced by its application. For example, whereas we began with 25 categories of data in Table 17-1, calculation of the five-year moving averages results in a reduction to ___ (number) categories of data.

21

37 Thus far we have considered the freehand, semiaverages, and moving-average methods of describing trend. Now we illustrate the application of the method of least squares, as described in Chapter 15, for determining the values of a and b in the equation for the straight line. In this application, Y_c is the trend value to be estimated and X is the specified year. Thus the general equation for the straight line being used in this analysis is

---

$a + bX$ (If in doubt, see Section 15.2.)

$$Y_c = \underline{\hspace{2cm}}$$

38 Table 17-2 contains the necessary worksheet data for this analysis. Solving first for b, substitute the appropriate values in the formula below, but do not necessarily carry out the arithmetic solution.

$$\frac{2{,}346.797 - 25(13.0)(6.994)}{5{,}525 - 25(169)}$$

$$= \frac{73.747}{1{,}300} = 0.057$$

$$b = \frac{\Sigma XY - n\bar{X}\bar{Y}}{\Sigma X^2 - n\bar{X}^2} =$$

Table 17-2 ■ Factory Sales of Domestic Passenger Cars from Plants in the United States, 1951–1975, and Calculations Required for Determining the Trend Line, the Resulting Expected Factory Sales, and the Cyclical Relatives

Year	Year coded, X	Factory sales, millions of units, Y	XY	X^2	Expected factory sales, Y_c	Cyclical relative $Y/Y_c \times 100$
(1)	(2)	(3)	(4)	(5)	(6)	(7)
1951	1	5.090	5.090	1	6.310	80.7
1952	2	4.154	8.308	4	6.367	65.2
1953	3	5.954	17.862	9	6.424	92.7
1954	4	5.352	21.408	16	6.481	82.6
1955	5	7.666	38.330	25	6.538	117.3
1956	6	5.623	33.738	36	6.595	85.3
1957	7	5.953	41.671	49	6.652	89.5
1958	8	4.132	33.056	64	6.709	61.6
1959	9	5.474	49.266	81	6.766	80.9
1960	10	6.530	65.300	100	6.823	95.7
1961	11	5.402	59.422	121	6.880	78.5
1962	12	6.754	81.048	144	6.937	97.4
1963	13	7.444	96.772	169	6.994	106.4

Table 17-2 ■ Factory Sales of
Domestic Passenger Cars from
Plants in the United States,
1951–1975, and Calculations
Required for Determining the
Trend Line, the Resulting
Expected Factory Sales, and
the Cyclical Relatives
(Continued)

Year	Year coded, X	Factory sales, millions of units, Y	XY	X^2	Expected factory sales, Y_c	Cyclical relative $Y/Y_c \times 100$
(1)	(2)	(3)	(4)	(5)	(6)	(7)
1964	14	7.554	105.756	196	7.051	107.1
1965	15	9.101	136.515	225	7.108	128.0
1966	16	8.337	133.392	256	7.165	116.4
1967	17	7.070	120.190	289	7.222	97.9
1968	18	8.407	151.326	324	7.279	115.5
1969	19	7.807	148.333	361	7.336	106.4
1970	20	6.187	123.740	400	7.393	83.7
1971	21	8.122	170.562	441	7.450	109.0
1972	22	8.353	183.766	484	7.507	111.3
1973	23	9.079	208.817	529	7.564	120.0
1974	24	6.721	161.304	576	7.621	88.2
1975	25	6.073	151.825	625	7.678	79.1
Total	325	174.852	2,346.797	5,525		

39 Similarly,

$$\boxed{6.994 - 0.057(13.0) = 6.253} \qquad a = \overline{Y} - b\overline{X} =$$

40 Thus the equation for the trend line based on the method of least squares is

$$\boxed{6.253 + 0.057X} \qquad Y_c = a + bX =$$

41 Using this equation, determine the forecast trend value for 1976. Do not forget to substitute the appropriate coded value for 1976, by reference to columns 1 and 2 of Table 17-2.

$$\boxed{6.253 + 0.057(26) = 7.735)} \qquad Y_c \ (1976) = 6.253 + 0.057X =$$

42 Enter the value just computed and any other value from column 6 of Table 17-2 in the appropriate locations on the graph of Figure 17-2, connect the two points to form the trend line, and label this trend line *LS*. Of the freehand, semiaverage, and least-squares methods, which one resulted in the most conservative projection for 1966, in this particular case? _____

Which method resulted in the most optimistic projection? ____

_____ Which projected-trend value turned out to be closest to the actual factory car sales of domestic cars for 1976?[1] _____

43 In addition to the freehand method, we have considered three mathematical methods used in the analysis of trend: the methods of _____ , _____ , and _____ .

44 In using the methods of semiaverages and least squares for the purpose of forecasting, we have assumed that the trend line is [linear / curvilinear] .

45 If the trend component of a time series appears to be curvilinear, two kinds of approaches to its analysis are possible: (1) transforming the values in the time series into logarithms, to investigate the possibility that the logarithmic values will follow a linear trend, and (2) using the least-squares method to solve for the unknowns in equations for higher-order curves. Look at the original time-series values plotted on Figure 17-2. Does it appear that a curvilinear assumption would lead to better long-term projection of trend? [Yes / No / Uncertain]

17.3 ■ Seasonal Variation

Whereas the analysis of trend has implications for long-term managerial planning, the analysis of the seasonal component of a time series has more immediate short-term implications. Manpower and marketing plans, for example, have to take into consideration expected seasonal patterns in the employment market and in consumer purchases. The identification of the seasonal component in a time series differs from trend analysis in at least two ways. First, whereas trend is determined directly from all available data, the seasonal component is determined by eliminating the other components from the data so that only the seasonal remains. Second, whereas trend is represented by one best-fitting line, or equation, a separate seasonal

[1] Actual factory car sales for 1976 were 7.838 million units.

value has to be computed for each month (or season, etc.) of the year, usually in the form of an index number. As was true for trend analysis, several methods of measuring seasonal variation have been developed. However, because most of the seasonal index computations now used are variations of the *ratio-to-moving-average method*, we describe this method exclusively in this section.

46 The seasonal component in a time series is measured in the form of an *index number* for each segment of the year being studied. In contrast to this, the trend component of a time series is described by determining the equation for, or the location of, the _____ for the time-series data.

best-fitting line

47 The interpretation of the index number that represents the extent of seasonal influence for a particular segment of the year involves a comparison of the measured or expected values for that segment (month, quarter, etc.) with the overall average for all the segments of the year. Thus, a seasonal index of 100 for a particular month indicates that the expected time-series value for that month is exactly one-twelfth of the total for the annual period centered at that month. Similarly, a seasonal index of 110 for another month would indicate that the expected value for that month is 10 percent [greater / less] than one-twelfth of the annual total.

greater

48 A monthly index of 80 indicates that the expected level of activity that month is ____ percent [greater / less] than one-twelfth of the total activity level for the year centered at that month.

20; less

49 Thus the monthly index number indicates the expected ups and downs in monthly (or quarterly, etc.) levels of activity, with effects due to trend *T*, cyclical *C*, and irregular *I* time-series components [also included / removed].

removed

50 In Section 17.1 we used annual data as the basis for our trend analysis. As contrasted to this, why is it necessary to use monthly (or quarterly) data for the analysis of the seasonal component of the time series?_____

_____

_____ .

Because seasonal movements occur within the period of a year; seasonal variations would be lost in the process of using annual totals.

51 In our analysis of factory automobile sales we shall use the monthly data for the years 1971 through 1975 as the basis for the analysis of the seasonal component, rather than using the monthly data for the entire 1951–1975 time period. One reason for this reduction is to simplify the computations in this illustration. Another more important reason is that if there has been any significant shift in the seasonal pattern of factory car sales in recent years, using the entire 1951–1975 period for the seasonal analysis would result in [better / poorer] projections of expected seasonal patterns for 1976 than using the data for only 1971–1975.

poorer (because the influence of a previous pattern would be included in the projection)

52 Table 17-3 presents the monthly factory sales of domestic passenger cars, in thousands of units, for the period from January 1971 through December 1975. The first step in the ratio-to-moving-average method, when using monthly data, is to compute a 12-month moving average (using quarterly data, a four-quarter moving average would be computed). Because all the months of the year are included in this moving average, differential effects due to the seasonal and short-term irregular components are thus removed, leaving the effects due to longer-term _____ and _____ components in the moving averages.

trend; cyclical

Table 17-3 ■ Factory Sales of Domestic Passenger Cars from Plants in the United States: Worksheet for the Computation of Seasonal Indexes by the Ratio-to-moving-average Method

Year	Month	Sales, thousands of unit, Y	Twelve-month moving total	Two-year centered moving total of Col. (2)	Twelve-month centered moving average (Col. 3 ÷ 24)	Ratio to moving average, percent (Col. 1 ÷ Col. 4)
		(1)	(2)	(3)	(4)	(5)
1971	Jan.	678.1				
	Feb.	719.0				
	Mar.	815.9				
	Apr.	703.6				
	May	716.7				
	June	761.3	8,121.5			
	July	468.9	8,109.4	16,230.9	676.29	69.34
	Aug.	457.6	8,106.5	16,215.9	675.66	67.73

Table 17-3 ■ Factory Sales of
Domestic Passenger Cars from
Plants in the United States:
Worksheet for the Computation
of Seasonal Indexes by the
Ratio-to-moving-average Method
(*Continued*)

Year	Month	Sales, thousands of units, Y (1)	Twelve-month moving total (2)	Two-year centered moving total of Col. (2) (3)	Twelve-month centered moving average (Col. 3 ÷ 24) (4)	Ratio to moving average, percent (Col. 1 ÷ Col. 4) (5)
	Sept.	712.0		16,162.3	673.43	105.73
	Oct.	758.6	8,055.8	16,144.9	672.70	112.77
	Nov.	736.6	8,089.1	16,259.5	677.48	108.73
	Dec.	593.2	8,170.4	16,341.1	680.88	87.13
1972	Jan.	666.0	8,170.7	16,266.1	677.75	98.27
	Feb.	716.1	8,095.4	16,104.2	671.01	106.72
	Mar.	765.2	8,008.8	16,114.4	671.43	113.97
	Apr.	736.9	8,105.6	16,294.3	678.93	108.54
	May	798.0	8,188.7	16,468.2	686.17	116.30
	June	761.6	8,279.5	16,632.0	693.00	109.90
	July	393.6	8,352.5	16,898.8	704.12	55.90
	Aug.	371.0	8,546.3	17,192.0	716.33	51.80
	Sept.	808.8	8,645.7	17,409.0	725.37	111.51
	Oct.	841.7	8,763.3	17,576.3	732.35	114.94
	Nov.	827.4	8,813.0	17,708.1	737.84	112.14
	Dec.	666.2	8,895.1	17,901.9	745.91	89.32
1973	Jan.	859.8	9,006.8	18,297.5	762.40	112.78
	Feb.	815.5	9,290.7	18,626.1	776.09	105.08
	Mar.	882.8	9,335.4	18,528.1	772.00	114.36
	Apr.	786.6	9,192.7	18,430.9	767.95	102.43
	May	880.1	9,238.2	18,476.1	769.84	114.33
	June	873.3	9,237.9	18,316.7	763.20	114.43
	July	677.5	9,078.8	17,849.9	743.75	91.10
	Aug.	415.7	8,771.1	17,228.2	717.84	57.91
	Sept.	666.1	8,457.1	16,588.5	691.19	96.38
	Oct.	887.2	8,131.4	16,093.6	670.57	132.31
	Nov.	827.1	7,962.2	15,723.3	655.14	126.25
	Dec.	507.1	7,761.1	15,267.1	636.13	79.72
1974	Jan.	552.1	7,506.0	14,849.7	618.74	89.24
	Feb.	501.5	7,343.7	14,687.5	611.98	81.95
	Mar.	557.1	7,343.8	14,630.3	609.60	91.39
	Apr.	617.4	7,286.5	14,448.4	602.02	102.56
	May	679.0	7,161.9	13,996.3	583.18	116.44
	June	618.2	6,834.4	13,555.7	564.82	109.46
	July	515.2	6,721.3	13,253.3	552.22	93.30
	Aug.	415.8	6,532.0	12,919.8	538.22	77.24
	Sept.	608.8	6,387.8	12,682.3	528.43	115.21
	Oct.	762.6	6,294.5	12,501.5	520.90	146.41
			6,207.0			

Table 17-3 ■ Factory Sales of
Domestic Passenger Cars from
Plants in the United States:
Worksheet for the Computation
of Seasonal Indexes by the
Ratio-to-moving-average Method
(*Continued*)

Year	Month	Sales, thousands of units, Y	Twelve-month moving total	Two-year centered moving total of Col. (2)	Twelve-month centered moving average (Col. 3 ÷ 24)	Ratio to moving average, percent (Col. 1 ÷ Col. 4)
		(1)	(2)	(3)	(4)	(5)
	Nov.	499.6		12,290.2	512.09	97.57
	Dec.	394.0	6,083.2	12,119.5	504.98	78.03
1975	Jan.	362.8	6,036.3	12,023.9	501.00	72.42
	Feb.	357.3	5,987.6	12,007.3	500.30	71.42
	Mar.	463.8	6,019.7	12,036.3	501.51	92.49
	Apr.	529.9	6,016.6	11,944.0	497.67	106.48
	May	555.2	5,927.4	11,893.6	495.57	112.04
	June	571.3	5,966.2	12,066.6	502.77	113.63
	July	466.5	6,100.4			
	Aug.	447.9				
	Sept.	605.7				
	Oct.	673.4				
	Nov.	538.4				
	Dec.	528.2				

Source of data: U.S. Department of Commerce, *Survey of Current Business.*

January
December (*Note:* Some of the calculations in Table 17-3 appear to be slightly off, but actually reflect the fact that the computer analysis which was used carried more significant digits than reported in the table.)

53 Computation of the 12-month moving averages requires that the 12-month moving totals first be determined. Thus the first 12-month moving total listed in Table 17-3 signifies the total new-car registrations for the months _____ 1971 through _____ 1971.

February 1971
January 1972

54 Similarly, the second 12-month moving total listed in Table 17-3 is for the period _____ (month and year) through _____ (month and year).

55 Suppose each 12-month moving total were divided by 12.

For the first total, since the period included is from January 1, 1971, through December 31, 1971, what date would be at the approximate center of this 12-month period? _____ (month and day), 1971.

56 Because we want the moving average to be at the *center* of each month to correspond with the original posting of totals for each month, it is necessary to compute a two-year total to center the values before computing the averages. (Note: Some statisticians consider the uncentered averages to be close enough and do not go through this procedure of computing two-year totals.) Each two-year total is actually made up of two overlapping 12-month periods. Thus the first two-year moving total posted in column 3 of Table 17-3 is a summation of the values for the months of _____ 1971 through _____ 1971 and _____ 1971 through _____ 1972.

57 Now we are ready to compute the 12-month *centered* moving average, posted in column 4 of Table 17-3. This is accomplished by simply dividing each overlapping two-year total by _____ (number).

58 After computing the moving averages, the next step in the *ratio-to-moving-average* method is, as the name implies, to compute the ratio of each monthly value to the value of the moving average for that month. This ratio is then multiplied by 100, so that it is stated in percentage form, as posted in the final column of Table 17-3. Based on the form of the ratio, a percentage ratio of less than 100 indicates that the actual monthly value is [smaller / larger] than the moving average.

59 Before we proceed to the final step of computing the seasonal index for each month, note what the ratio to moving average represents. Since each monthly value reflects the effect of the T, S, C, and I components, and each moving average reflects the effect of the T and C components (with S and I "averaged out"), then dividing the former group of symbols by the latter yields

Ratio to moving average $= \dfrac{\text{(symbols)}}{\text{(symbols)}}$

$= $ _____ (symbols)

60 The final step in computing the seasonal index for each month is to average the percentage ratios computed in Table 17-3 according to month of the year in order to remove the irregular component and to make certain adjustments, to be described below. In order to carry out these computations, it is convenient to construct a table listing the percentage ratios according to the month of the year, as has been done in Table 17-4. Accordingly, for each of the months of the year Table 17-4 lists _____ (number) percentage ratios.

four

Table 17-4 ■ Calculation of Seasonal Indexes Using Percents of Twelve-month Moving Averages

Month	1971	1972	1973	1974	1975	Modified mean, by month	Adjusted seasonal index mean × 1.00735
Jan.		98.27	112.78	89.24	72.42	93.75	94.4
Feb.		106.72	105.08	81.95	71.42	93.52	94.2
Mar.		113.97	114.36	91.39	92.49	103.23	104.0
Apr.		108.54	102.43	102.56	106.48	104.52	105.3
May		116.30	114.33	116.44	112.04	115.31	116.2
June		109.90	114.43	109.46	113.63	111.77	112.6
July	69.34	55.90	91.10	93.30		80.22	80.8
Aug.	67.73	51.80	57.91	77.24		62.82	63.3
Sept.	105.73	111.51	96.38	115.21		108.62	109.4
Oct.	112.77	114.94	132.31	146.41		123.62	124.5
Nov.	108.73	112.14	126.25	97.57		110.44	111.3
Dec.	87.13	89.32	79.72	78.03		83.42	84.0
						1,191.24	

Source of data: Table 17-3.

61 In computing the average percentage ratio for each month, one of three methods can be used, depending on the analyst's judgment. One method is to use the median of the percentage ratios reported, another is to use the mean, and the third frequently used method, particularly when a relatively large number of ratios is available, is to compute a modified mean. The latter is the arithmetic mean of the central items in the array (i.e., after eliminating the lowest and highest ratios), thus reducing the effect of extreme and unusual observations on the mean. In Table 17-4, the average that is used is the [median / mean / modified mean].

modified mean

62 If the average seasonal index for all 12 months combined is to be equal to 100, by definition, the total of the seasonal indexes for all 12 months of the year should be equal to _____ (value).

63 Whereas the total of the monthly indexes should be equal to 1,200, the actual total of the average ratios reported in Table 17-4 is 1,191.24. Therefore the final step in the computation of the seasonal indexes is to adjust each monthly average so that the total is approximately 1,200. This is accomplished by multiplying each monthly average by the ratio

Desired total
Actual total

or, in this case, by _____ (fraction)

64 The final column of Table 17-4 lists the computed seasonal index value for each month, determined by making the adjustment described in Frame 63. In scanning these values, it is obvious that the seasonal peak in the factory automobile sales occurs in the month of _____ (at least, this was true for the years 1971–1975), and the seasonal low occurs in the month of _____ .

65 The occurrence of the seasonal peak in October is associated with the availability of new models at that time and perhaps also fleet-car purchases. What factor probably is associated with the high seasonal indexes for the spring months? _____

Summary

66 To compute seasonal indexes by the ratio-to-moving-average method, first compute the 12-month moving totals for the data, combine adjacent 12-month totals, and divide by 24 to obtain the moving averages. This combination of adjacent 12-month totals is necessitated by the desire to have the subsequent averages located at the [beginning / center / end] of each month.

67 Second, compute the ratios to moving average by dividing the actual value for each month by the _____ for each month and multiplying by 100 so that the ratio is in the form of a percentage.

68 Third, determine the average percentage ratio according to month by computing one of three kinds of averages: the

_____ , _____ , or _____ .

69 Finally, determine the seasonal indexes by multiplying each of the average ratios by a value such that the sum of all 12 monthly indexes is equal to approximately 1,200. Since this multiplier should be greater than 1 if the total of the averages before adjustment is less than 1,200, the multiplier is defined as (indicate best choice):

(a) $\dfrac{\text{Actual total}}{1,200}$

(b) $\dfrac{1,200}{\text{Actual total}}$

b

17.4 ■ Estimation of Cyclical and Irregular Variations

Whereas the analysis of trend has direct practical value for long-term forecasting, and while the analysis of the seasonal component is of direct application in forecasting for the short run, the analysis of the cyclical and irregular components, taken by itself, is of dubious forecasting value for the managers of an organization. Like the seasonal component of the time series, the cyclical component also represents wavelike movements on the time-series graph, but the cyclical movements are longer in duration and less predicatable than the seasonal movements. Economists have given extensive attention to the analysis of business cycles and their causes, but it is not our purpose here to consider the theories addressed to this analysis. For the manager who has to make operating decisions, it appears more fruitful to base cyclical expectations on the particular factors that underlie cyclical fluctuations in his industry (e.g., inventory levels), rather than to anticipate cyclical fluctuations based on the assumed mathematical characteristics of the movements themselves. Because both the cyclical and the irregular components of the time series are determined by the use of the *residual method*, described below, they are combined for discussion purposes in this section.

70 The essence of the conventional approach to identifying the cyclical and irregular components of a time series is to eliminate the effects of the trend and seasonal components from the time series, thus leaving the cyclical and irregular components. Because these components constitute that which remains after such adjustments, the method is referred to as the _____ method.

71 The specific procedure associated with the residual method depends on whether we begin the analysis with monthly or with annual time-series data; we illustrate both situations in this section. If we begin with monthly data, then the effects of both the trend and the seasonal components have to be removed so that we can identify those effects due to the cyclical and irregular components. If we begin with annual data, then the effects of the cyclical and the long-term irregular components can be identified by removing only the effects of the _____ component from the data.

72 Although the use of annual data thus results in a simpler computational procedure, it does not make possible the identification of the short-term irregular variations, but only the identification of those that are long-term and intertwined with the cyclical variations themselves. Symbolically, then, the decomposition of the time series for annual data can be represented as:

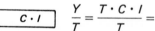

$$\frac{Y}{T} = \frac{T \cdot C \cdot I}{T} =$$

73 In dividing by trend, the first decision to be made is in regard to the basis to be used for determining trend. In our illustration we shall use the least-squares basis. Thus in Table 17-2 (page 467) the actual factory automobile sales for each year are posted in column 3, and the expected sales based on the least-squares trend line are posted in column ___ .

74 Of course, these expected values are based on the least-squares equation developed in Section 17.2. Thus, for example, the actual number of factory automobile sales for 1975 was _____ million units, and the expected number based on the least-squares trend line was _____ million units.

75 In determining the relative effect of the cyclical component on each annual value, we accept the expected value as an accurate indication of trend and treat the discrepancy (residual) as being due to the cyclical component. Thus, as indicated expected registration (Y_c)

in column 7 of Table 17-2, each cyclical relative is computed by dividing the actual registration for each year, Y, by the ____________________ and multiplying by 100 to put the ratio into percentage form.

are not

76 In order to study the cyclical movements represented in column 7 of Table 17-2 over time, it is useful to portray them graphically, as has been done in Figure 17-3. From this chart it would appear that the cyclical movements associated with new-car registrations [are / are not] of regular duration or relatively predictable.

Figure 17-3 ▪ Cycle chart for the factory sales of domestic passenger cars from plants in the United States, 1951–1975

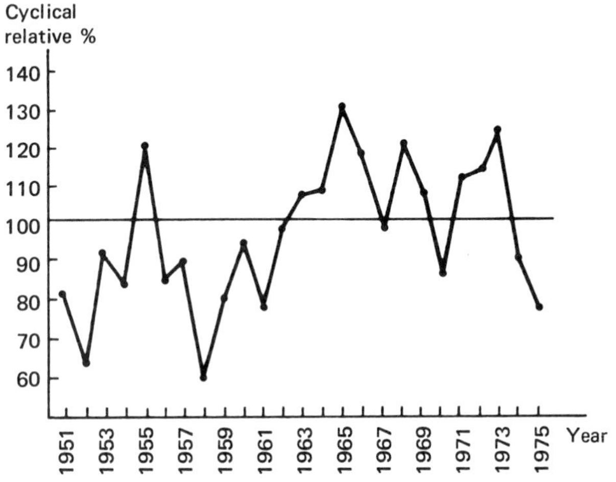

irregular

77 Of course, although Figure 17-3 is called a "cycle chart," it actually reflects the effect of two influences on the time-series values: those associated with the cyclical component and the long-term __________ component. The separation of these two influences, if it were to be attempted, could be done by calculating moving averages and considering the smoothed result as representing the cyclical component.

bottom

peak

78 To the extent that Figure 17-3 actually represents cyclical movements in factory automobile sales, the value for 1958 represents the [bottom / peak] of a cyclical movement, and the value for 1965 represents a cyclical [bottom / peak].

trend; seasonal

79 Turning now to the application of the residual method to monthly data, we illustrate the identification of the cyclical and irregular components by removing, in turn, the effect of both the ________ and the __________ components.

80 First, if the original monthly values of the time series are divided by their corresponding seasonal indexes, the resulting data are said to be "deseasonalized," or adjusted for seasonal variation. Since the resulting values still include the trend, cyclical, and irregular movements, the process of deseasonalizing data can be algebraically represented by

$T \cdot C \cdot I$

$$\frac{Y}{S} = \frac{T \cdot S \cdot C \cdot I}{S} =$$

81 Table 17-5 lists the seasonally adjusted data for new-car registrations. These values were calculated by dividing the actual monthly values of Table 17-3 by the seasonal indexes of Table 17-4 and multiplying the result by 100. Because the effect of the seasonal component has been removed from these data, notice that in this table the number of factory car sales

is not (*Note:* Some of the
figures appear to be slightly off because the computer analysis carried more significant digits than reported in Table 17-5.)

for October of each year, a high car-sales month, [is / is not] markedly higher than for August, a low car-sales month.

Month	1971	1972	1973	1974	1975
Jan.	718.0	705.2	910.4	584.6	384.1
Feb.	763.2	760.1	865.6	532.3	379.3
Mar.	784.6	735.8	848.9	535.7	446.0
Apr.	668.2	699.8	747.0	586.4	503.3
May	617.0	686.9	757.6	584.5	477.9
June	676.1	676.4	775.6	549.0	507.4
July	580.2	487.0	838.4	637.5	577.3
Aug.	723.0	586.2	656.8	657.0	707.7
Sept.	650.7	739.2	608.7	556.4	553.5
Oct.	609.1	675.9	712.4	612.4	540.7
Nov.	662.1	743.7	743.4	449.1	483.9
Dec.	705.8	792.7	603.4	468.8	628.5

Table 17-5 ■ Seasonally Adjusted Data for Factory Sales of Domestic Passenger Cars from Plants in the United States, 1971–1975 (In thousands of units)

Source of data: Tables 17-3 and 17-4.

82 Thus the data of Table 17-5 have had the effect of the seasonal component removed but still include the effects of the

trend; cyclical; irregular

the _____ , _____ , and _____ components.

83 After the data have been deseasonalized, they can be adjusted for trend, as was done with the annual data, by dividing the deseasonalized value for each month by the corresponding trend value. Note, however, that these need to be *monthly* trend values rather than the annual trend values that would be determined by use of the least-squares equation developed in Section 17.2. Suppose that for the monthly factory car sales data, the trend equation is Y_c (monthly) = 521.1 + 0.4X, with Y_c in thousands of units and $X = 1$ at January 1951. Therefore, for January 1971 the monthly trend value is:

$$Y_c = 523.3 + 0.4X$$
$$=$$

> 523.3 + 0.4(241) = 619.7
> (January 1971 is the 241st month in the time series)

84 Based on use of the monthly trend equation above, the monthly trend values posted in Table 17-6 were determined. Verify the value for December 1975, which is posted in the table:

> 523.3 + 0.4(300) = 643.3

Y_c (Dec. 1975) =

Table 17-6 ■ Monthly Trend Values: Factory Sales of Domestic Passenger Cars from Plants in the United States, 1971–1975 (In thousands of units)

Month	1971	1972	1973	1974	1975
Jan.	619.7	624.5	629.3	634.1	638.9
Feb.	620.1	624.9	629.7	634.5	639.3
Mar.	620.5	625.3	630.1	634.9	639.7
Apr.	620.9	625.7	630.5	635.3	640.1
May	621.3	626.1	630.9	635.7	640.5
June	621.7	626.5	631.3	636.1	640.9
July	622.1	626.9	631.7	636.5	641.3
Aug.	622.5	627.3	632.1	636.9	641.7
Sept.	622.9	627.7	632.5	637.3	642.1
Oct.	623.3	628.1	632.9	637.7	642.5
Nov.	623.7	628.5	633.3	638.1	642.9
Dec.	624.1	628.9	633.7	638.5	643.3

Source of data: Equation in Frame 83.

85 Now, if we divide each of the deseasonalized values of Table 17-5 by the corresponding monthly trend values of Table 17-6 and multiply by 100, the resulting percentages, reported in Table 17-7, have the effects of both the seasonal and trend components removed from them, leaving the differential influences of the _____ and _____ components of the monthly data.

> cyclical; irregular

Month	1971	1972	1973	1974	1975
Table 17-7 ■ Factory Sales of Domestic Passenger Cars by Month, 1971-1975: Seasonally Adjusted Data as Percentage of Trend (Indicating Cyclical and Irregular Effects in the Time Series)					
Jan.	115.9	112.9	144.7	92.2	60.1
Feb.	123.1	121.6	137.5	82.5	59.3
Mar.	126.4	117.7	134.7	84.4	69.7
Apr.	107.6	111.8	118.5	92.3	78.6
May	99.3	109.7	120.1	91.9	74.6
June	108.8	108.0	122.9	86.3	79.2
July	93.3	77.7	132.7	100.2	90.0
Aug.	116.1	93.4	103.9	103.2	110.3
Sept.	104.5	117.8	96.2	87.3	86.2
Oct.	97.7	107.6	112.6	96.0	84.2
Nov.	106.2	118.3	117.4	70.4	75.3
Dec.	113.1	126.0	95.2	73.4	97.7

Source of data: Tables 17-5 and 17-6.

86 When we divide the deseasonalized values in Table 17-5 by the trend values in Table 17-6, we can represent the procedure algebraically as:

$$\frac{\text{Deseasonalized values}}{\text{Trend}} = \frac{T \cdot C \cdot I}{T} =$$

$C \cdot I$

87 The general level of values in Table 17-7 for a series of months, as compared with 100, is indicative of cyclical effects in the time series. This is so because the irregular variations, by definition, are short-term effects in the context of monthly or quarterly data. By reference to Table 17-7, we can see that there were generally positive cyclical effects during the three years _____ and there were generally negative cylical effects during the two years _____ .

1971–1973
1974–1975 (which was re-flective of the oil crisis and a national recession)

88 Any sizable short-run variations from the general level of values in Table 17-7 is indicative of irregular variations in the time series, and usually are explainable in terms of knowledge of the specific events which caused the variations. For example, special discounts on new automobiles offered by the automobile manufacturers in the summer of 1974, in order to clear stocks of unpopular larger car models because of the oil crisis that year, resulted in a positive irregular variation in factory car sales during the two months of _____ and _____ of 1974, as compared with the rest of the year.

July; August

17.5 ■ The Use of Time-series Analysis in Forecasting

In this chapter we have been cautious regarding the use of time-series analysis as the basis for forecasting, particularly in regard to the use of cyclical analysis. This caution does not suggest that time-series analysis is not of practical value, for indeed it is a widely used technique in economic analysis. However, the purely mechanical forecast based on a time-series analysis alone usually represents the beginning, rather than the culmination, of the analytical efforts associated with business and economic forecasting. In addition to the time-series analysis itself, improvement in forecasts can be attained by two general approaches, both based on the analysis of information outside of the firm being studied. First, the study of general business conditions or of cyclical movements in other time series may provide clues to the timing of cyclical movements in the series being analyzed. Second, the study of relationships between specific environmental factors or managerial actions and changes in time-series values, carried out by regression and correlation analysis, may provide direct indications of the "why" of time-series changes.

trend	**89** Of the four components of the time series, the one that has primary use for long-term forecasting is the _____ component.
seasonal	**90** Similarly, the one that is useful for forecasts in the short run is the _____ component.
will will not	**91** The use of information about the trend of a time series and the seasonal variations related thereto in forecasting is predicated on the assumption that both influences [will / will not] operate in the future as they have in the past and that marked cyclical and irregular effects [will / will not] occur.
irregular	**92** Of the four classical components of the time series, the one that is of the least direct value in forecasting is the _____ component.
cyclical	**93** Finally, the component whose successful analysis would be extremely valuable in forecasting, but whose final analysis is rarely successfully achieved by the mechanical procedure of the time-series analysis alone, is the _____ component.
outside of	**94** As indicated in the introduction to this section, those concerned with business forecasting typically consider time-series analysis as the beginning, rather than the end, of forecasting efforts. As the next step, the greatest gains in forecasting effectiveness can be expected by obtaining more data from [within / outside of] the firm being studied.

95 For example, cyclical variations in the demand for a firm's products might be found to be related to general business conditions or cyclical fluctuations in other, though related, product fields. Since the classical analysis of cycles tends to be oriented toward the mathematical characteristics of the cyclical movements themselves, studies of business conditions

do

and other series [do / do not] represent a basically new direction of analysis.

96 Also, the study of specific relationships, such as that between the use of a variable price policy and its effects on seasonal levels of the time series, can add to the effectiveness of managerial forecasting. The statistical technique particularly

regression (or correlation)

useful for this purpose is that of _____ analysis.

Review
trend
seasonal; cyclical; irregular

97 (Frames 1–15) The four principal sources of influence on time-series values have been identified as the _____ , _____ , _____ , and _____ components.

98 (Frames 16–25) Where Y represents the value of a time series for some particular period in time, the conventional time-series model underlying all of the analyses in this chapter

$Y = T \cdot S \cdot C \cdot I$

can be represented by the equation _____ .

99 (Frames 26, 27) Trend analysis always involves the identification of the location or algebraic formula for the

line (not necessarily straight)
freehand

best-fitting _____ . The method of trend analysis which is mathematically least sophisticated is the _____ method.

100 (Frames 28–31) The method of semiaverages in trend analysis requires separating the data into _____ (number) parts

two

and averaging the time-series values within each of these parts, resulting in the plotting of a trend line that is always [straight /

straight

curvilinear] .

101 (Frames 32–36) The method of moving averages in trend analysis typically results in a trend line that is [straight /

curvilinear

curvilinear] .

102 (Frames 37–45) The final method of trend analysis which we discussed, and which may be used to determine the equation for the best-fitting straight line or curve, is the

least-squares

_____ method.

index	**103** (Frames 46, 47) Whereas the trend for a time series is defined in terms of a best-fitting line, or the algebraic equation representing the line, the seasonal component of the time series is represented by an _____ number computed for each month (or quarter) of the year.
ratio; moving-average	**104** (Frames 48-52) The seasonal index number is usually computed by comparing each monthly value with the moving average centered at that month, and hence the method is referred to as the _____-to-_____ method.
center	**105** (Frames 53-57) In computing the 12-month moving averages, it is necessary not only to compute 12-month moving totals but also to combine adjacent 12-month totals so that the resulting averages will be located at the [beginning / center / end] of each month.
moving average	**106** (Frames 58, 59) Next, the ratios to moving average are computed by dividing the actual value for each month by the _____ for each month and multiplying by 100 to put the ratio into percentage form.
mean; median; modified mean 1,200	**107** (Frames 60-69) Finally, the average percentage ratio by month (or quarter) is determined by using one of three types of averages: the _____ , _____ , or _____ , and these average ratios are adjusted so that the sum of all 12 monthly indexes is equal to approximately _____ (value).
residual	**108** (Frames 70-74) Because both the cyclical and the irregular components are identified by assuming that they are represented by the effects which remain after data have been adjusted for trend and seasonal factors, the general computational approach is referred to as the _____ method.
	109 (Frames 75-78) In identifying the cyclical and long-term irregular components when annual data are used, the procedure of the time-series analysis can be algebraically represented by
$C \cdot I$	$$\frac{T \cdot C \cdot I}{T} =$$
	110 (Frames 79-82) When monthly data are used in the residual method, the first step is typically that of seasonally

adjusting the data. Algebraically, this step can be represented as:

$$\frac{T \cdot S \cdot C \cdot I}{S} = T \cdot C \cdot I$$

111 (Frames 83–88) Next the deseasonalized data are adjusted for trend, which can be algebraically represented as:

$$\frac{T \cdot C \cdot I}{T} = C \cdot I$$

trend	
seasonal	
additions to	

112 (Frames 89–96) The two components of the time series that are most useful in business forecasting are the _____ and _____ components. The study of general business conditions and cyclical changes in related product fields and the correlation of specific types of events with changes in time-series values are [also part of / additions to] classical time-series analysis.

Symbols Introduced in This Chapter (with Frame Numbers)

(5) T Trend component of a time series.

(8) S Seasonal component of a time series.

(11) C Cyclical component of a time series.

(14) I Irregular component of a time series.

(24) Y A time-series value.

Formulas Introduced in This Chapter (with Frame Numbers)

(16) $Y = T \cdot S \cdot C \cdot I$

The most generally accepted model in time-series analysis, indicating the multiplicative relationship among the trend, seasonal, cyclical, and irregular components.

(59) $\dfrac{T \cdot S \cdot C \cdot I}{T \cdot C} = S \cdot I$

Algebraic representation of the first step in identifying the seasonal component by the ratio-to-moving-average method.

(72) $\dfrac{Y}{T} = \dfrac{T \cdot C \cdot I}{T} = C \cdot I$

Algebraic representation of the decomposition of annual time-series data for the purpose of identifying combined cyclical and irregular effects.

(80) $\dfrac{Y}{S} = \dfrac{T \cdot S \cdot C \cdot I}{S} = T \cdot C \cdot I$

Algebraic representation of the process of deseasonalizing monthly or quarterly time-series values.

(86) $\dfrac{T \cdot C \cdot I}{T} = C \cdot I$

Algebraic representation of the decomposition of monthly (or quarterly) time-series data for the purpose of identifying combined cyclical and short-term irregular effects.

EXERCISES

(Solutions on pages 628–634)

17.1 Indicate the component of the time series with which each of the following events would be associated by posting a T for trend, S for seasonal, C for cyclical, and I for irregular:

_____ (a) an upturn in business activity
_____ (b) inclement weather resulting in the postponement of consumer purchases
_____ (c) a fire at the subcontractor's plant resulting in a delay in parts deliveries
_____ (d) the annual January white sale in a department store
_____ (e) general increase in the demand for color television sets

17.2 The following data represent the annual sales volume, in millions of dollars, of the Acme Tool Company. Construct a line chart to portray these data graphically.

Year	Sales, millions of units
1973	$1.5
1974	1.3
1975	1.1
1976	1.7
1977	1.9
1978	2.3

17.3 (a) Determine the location of the trend line by the method of semiaverages and enter this line on the line chart constructed in Exercise 17.2, above, labeling this line *SA*.
(b) Determine the location of the trend line by computing a three-year moving average and enter this line on the chart, labeling it *3M*.

17.4 For the data of Exercise 17.2, determine the equation for the trend line by the least-squares method, coding 1975 as 0. Enter this line on the graph, labeling it *LS*. To what does the *a* in this least-squares trend equation refer?

17.5 For the annual data in Exercise 17.2:

(a) Determine the cyclical component by the residual method, using the least-squares regression line as the best estimate of the trend component of the time series.

(b) Construct a cycle chart and interpret it.

17.6 The following data represent the quarterly sales volume for the Acme Tool Company.

(a) Compute the four-quarter moving averages and moving totals for these data.

(b) Compute the four-quarter centered moving average.

Year	Quarter	Sales, thousands of units
1973	1	$500
	2	350
	3	250
	4	400
1974	1	450
	2	350
	3	200
	4	300
1975	1	350
	2	200
	3	150
	4	400
1976	1	550
	2	350
	3	250
	4	550
1977	1	550
	2	400
	3	350
	4	600
1978	1	750
	2	500
	3	400
	4	650

17.7 For the data of Exercise 17.6, above, determine the adjusted seasonal indexes by quarter, using the modified mean of the ratios representing percents of moving average.

17.8 Compute the seasonally adjusted value for each quarter for the data of Exercise 17.6 by the use of the seasonal indexes determined in Exercise 17.7.

17.9 Determine the least-squares linear trend equation for the quarterly data in Exercise 17.6, coding the first quarter of 1973 as "0."

17.10 Using the trend equation developed in Exercise 17.9, remove the effects of the trend component from the deseasonalized values in Exercise 17.8, leaving the effects of the cyclical and irregular components in the data.

17.11 Based only on the trend equation for the quarterly values which was determined in Exercise 17.9, forecast the level of quarterly sales for each quarter of 1979.

17.12 Based on both the trend and seasonal components of the time-series data in Exercise 17.6, as identified in Exercises 17.7 and 17.9, forecast the level of quarterly sales for each quarter of 1979.

ADDITIONAL EXERCISES

17.13 Indicate the component of the time series with which each of the following events would be associated by posting a *T* for trend, *S* for seasonal, *C* for cyclical, and *I* for irregular.

_____ (a) the pre-Christmas period in retail sales
_____ (b) diminished need for kerosene lanterns
_____ (c) increased demand for housing in a small community as a result of the location of a new manufacturing plant there
_____ (d) a recession
_____ (e) Father's Day and men's shaver sales

17.14 The following data represent the monthly sales volume, in thousands of dollars, of a toy-manufacturing firm incorporated July 1, 1975. Construct a line chart to portray graphically the annual sales totals, using the fiscal year of July 1 through June 30 as the basis for the totals, rather than the calendar year.

Month	1975	1976	1977	1978	1979
Jan.	...	2.7	2.9	4.3	4.8
Feb.	...	2.8	3.6	4.2	5.4
Mar.	...	3.4	4.1	4.8	6.0
Apr.	...	3.6	4.5	5.7	6.7

Month	1975	1976	1977	1978	1979
May	...	3.8	4.9	6.1	7.0
June	...	4.0	5.0	6.2	6.9
July	3.5	4.3	5.2	6.6	
Aug.	3.4	4.5	5.1	6.8	
Sept.	4.5	5.7	6.0	8.5	
Oct.	5.5	7.0	8.2	10.1	
Nov.	6.0	6.9	7.9	10.3	
Dec.	4.8	5.0	6.0	7.4	

17.15 **(a)** Using July-through-June annual totals, determine the location of the trend line by the method of semiaverages and enter this line on the chart prepared in Exercise 17.14, above, labeling this line *SA*.

(b) Determine the location of the trend line by computing a two-year moving average, and enter this line on the line chart, labeling it *2M*.

17.16 For the data of Exercise 17.14, determine the location of the trend line by using the least-squares method with the July-through-June annual totals, coding the 1975–1976 fiscal year as 0. Enter this line on the graph, labeling it *LS*. To what does the *b* in this trend equation refer?

17.17 Comment on the observed similarity or dissimilarity of the several trend lines posted on the line chart in the above exercises.

17.18 For the July-through-June annual totals in Exercise 17.14, determine the cyclical component by the residual method, using the least-squares regression line as the best indicator of the trend component of the time series. Interpret your results.

17.19 Determine the seasonal indexes for the sales values of Exercise 17.14, using the mean monthly ratios representing percents of moving average.

17.20 Deseasonalize the data presented in Exercise 17.14.

17.21 Suppose the monthly trend equation for the data in Exercise 17.14 is: $Y_c = 3.40 + 0.09X$, for $X = 0$ at July 1975. Determine the monthly trend values for the period July 1975 to June 1979.

17.22 Presuming negligible cyclical effects in these data, identify the effects due to the irregular component of the time series by using the residual method with the monthly data and using the least-squares trend values in Exercise 17.21 as the best indicators of the trend component of the time series.

17.23 Based only on the trend equation for the monthly values which is given in Exercise 17.21, forecast the level of monthly sales for the 1979–1980 fiscal year.

17.24 Based on both the trend and seasonal components of the time-series data in Exercise 17.14, as identified in Exercises 17.19 and 17.21, forecast the level of monthly sales for the 1979–1980 fiscal year.

17.25 Briefly consider the use of each of the four time-series components in business and economic forecasting. Also, what other kinds of analyses are usually performed for the purpose of forecasting?

An index number is a statistical value designed to measure changes in a variable, such as price or quantity, typically with respect to time. The study of index numbers represents the second of the two principal techniques specifically directed toward analyzing data classified over time, the other being time-series analysis, covered in Chapter 17. In this chapter we describe the basic types of index numbers used in business and economic analysis and their construction, and we consider the characteristics of three widely used index numbers published by agencies of the federal government: the Consumer Price Index, the Wholesale Price Index, and the Industrial Production Index.

18.1 ■ Introduction

An index number always indicates a comparison between a present measurement and a measurement at some previous point or interval of time that has been chosen as the base. For example, we could use 1960 as the base period for a study of unit sales of automobiles and report sales for later years as percentages of the 1960 value. Thus an index of 150 in this case would signify a sales volume 50 percent above the 1960 level. This index number would be referred to as a "simple quantity index." In this section we differentiate a simple index from a composite index and discuss the nature of price and value indexes as well as quantity indexes.

1 Suppose that a time series representing the volume of automobile sales between 1960 and 1978 is available. Could a series of quantity index numbers, with 1960 as the base, be constructed using the data in this single time series? [Yes / No]

Yes

2 The indexes computed in Frame 1 would be referred to as *simple* index numbers. Thus the essential characteristic of a simple index number is that it generally relates to [a particular commodity / a number of commodities].

a particular commodity

3 On the other hand, a *composite* index number refers to a change in quantity, price, or value for [a particular commodity / a number of commodities].

a number of commodities

4 The type of index number that could be constructed when a single time series is known is the _____ index number; the type that could be constructed when time series for several related commodities are available is the _____ index number.

simple

composite

5 The Consumer Price Index, which represents the price movement for a combination of commodities rather than for a single commodity, is an example of a [simple / composite] index number.

6 Before considering some important problems related to the construction of composite index numbers, let us briefly consider the kinds of measurements that can be represented by index numbers. In the introduction to this section, we have already indicated that index numbers can represent changes in *quantity, price,* or *value.* Thus both the Consumer Price Index and the Wholesale Price Index are examples of _____ indexes.

7 The Industrial Production Index reflects changes in physical volume of output in manufacturing, mining, and utilities. It is thus a [quantity / price / value] index.

8 Finally, an index number might relate to the total value of an output or commodity, without regard to whether the change was due to a change in price, quantity, or both. The Federal Reserve Board Index of Department Store Sales, which does not separate price and quantity as such, is thus a _____ index.

9 In this introduction we have indicated that an index number can be simple or _____ and that it can represent changes in quantity, _____ , or _____ .

10 If a composite index number is to be constructed—and all of the important indexes are of this type—then decisions have to be made regarding the particular commodities to be included in the index and the statistical weight to be used with each commodity. For example, would you expect an index of retail prices to include consideration of all commodities that could possibly be purchased? [Yes / No]

11 Thus the universe of commodities to be described by a composite index must first be identified, and then a sample of these commodities must be chosen for use in calculation of the index number. Because of the necessity of using a sample of items that is considered representative as well as comparable from period to period, the commodities to be included in the sample are chosen on the basis of their evaluated importance in the total universe of commodities. Therefore the sampling method used in the construction of a composite index number

judgment (See Chapter 8, Frames 17–27, for a review of these concepts.)

results in the collection of a [convenience / judgment / probability] sample.

12 Since the commodities to be included in a composite index are selected on the basis of judgment, the methods of statistical inference described in the previous chapters [can / cannot] be used in evaluating such index numbers.

cannot

13 Having chosen the commodities to be used as the sample items for a composite index, we then have to decide how each item should be weighted in the composite. For a composite price index, if we were to accumulate the price of one unit of each commodity to obtain the composite, the price of each item in the index would, in effect, be its weight in the composite index. Thus a truly "unweighted" composite index in fact [can / cannot] be constructed.

cannot

14 A so-called "unweighted" composite index would not be very useful because the effective weights would be arbitrary and thus would not generally reflect the importance of each item in the index. For example, if men's shoes and butter were to be included in a retail price index, including the average price of one pair of shoes and one pound of butter would have the result that greater weight in the composite index is being given to [shoes / butter / neither].

shoes (since the average price of a pair of shoes is higher than the price of a pound of butter)

15 Thus, when constructing a composite index number, we have not only a sampling problem but a weighting problem as well. If we want our retail price index to weight each commodity according to its extent of purchase, and if the average person consumes 1½ pounds of butter per month and purchases three pairs of shoes per year, then a *monthly* index would weight (or multiply) the price of butter by a factor of ____ (number) and the price of a pair of shoes by ____ (number).

1½

¼ (since, on the average, ¼ pair of shoes is purchased per month)

16 For composite index numbers to have a comparable meaning from period to period, it is desirable that the same base period be used throughout the analysis, that the same

weight

sample of commodities be included in each period, and that the _____ assigned to each commodity be identical from period to period.

17 But in constructing a retail price index, we might discover that the pattern of things being purchased is shifting over time. For example, if the selection of commodities and their relative weights were based on purchasing patterns in the year 1950, then in terms of actual purchasing patterns in 1978 home heating oil is likely to be [under- / over-] represented in the index and power tools are likely to be [under- / over-] represented.

over-

under-

18 The processes of linking and chaining, to be described in Section 18.3, make it possible to change the commodities and/or the weights used in constructing a series of composite index numbers, thus making comparison of index numbers constructed over extensive time periods [more / less] difficult.

less

18.2 ■ Construction of Index Numbers

In the preceding section we observed that index numbers can be simple or composite and that they can represent comparisons of quantity, price, or value. This section on computation is introductory in nature, and hence we describe several of the most widely used index numbers, but we do not consider the variations or combinations of the techniques that are sometimes used, even though these other techniques may be statistically interesting. Accordingly, we describe the computation of simple indexes, Laspeyres' index, Paasche's index, and the weighted average of relatives.

19 The computation of simple indexes is relatively straightforward compared with the variety of computational techniques available for constructing composite index numbers. If p_0 indicates the price of a commodity in a base period and p_1 indicates its price in a later given period, then a simple price index, or price relative, can be computed by using the formula (choose one):

(a) $\dfrac{p_0}{p_1} \times 100$

b

(b) $\dfrac{p_1}{p_0} \times 100$

20 For example, if the average price of butter was $1.10 per pound in 1970 used as the base, and its average price in 1978 was $1.50 per pound, as indicated in Table 18-1, then the simple price relative for 1978 is

$$\frac{p_1}{p_0} \times 100 =$$

$$\frac{1.50}{1.10} \times 100 = 136.4$$

(which means that the price of butter in 1978 was 36.4 percent higher than in 1970)

21 Since a simple price index is concerned only with measuring the relative change in the price of a single commodity, there is no need for weighting. Thus the weighting problems discussed at the end of Section 18.1 apply only to _____ indexes.

composite

22 Similarly, where q_0 represents the quantity of a commodity during the base period and q_1 represents the quantity during the given period, the quantity relative is designated by the formula

$$\frac{q_1}{q_0} \times 100$$

$$\frac{q_1}{q_0}$$

23 Thus, if 18 pounds of butter per person was consumed in a particular geographic area in 1970, used as the base, and 12 pounds was consumed in 1978, then the quantity relative is equal to

$$\frac{q_1}{q_0} \times 100 =$$

$$\frac{12}{18} \times 100 = 66.7$$

(which means that the per capita consumption of butter in 1978 was 66.7 percent of the consumption in 1970)

24 The third type of simple index number is the value relative. According to the data for butter price and consumption in Table 18-1, the value relative for 1978 with the 1970 base-year value being set equal to 100 is

$$\frac{p_1 q_1}{p_0 q_0} \times 100 =$$

$$\frac{18.00}{19.80} \times 100 = 90.9$$

(which means that the per capita value of the butter consumed in 1978 was 90.9 percent of the value in 1970)

		Average price		Per capita consumption	
Commodity	Unit quotation	1970, p_0	1978, p_1	1970, q_0	1978, q_1
Butter	pound	$ 1.10	$ 1.50	18	12
Coffee	pound	1.50	2.50	12	14
Shoes	pair	15.00	20.00	3	3

25 Since most of the index numbers in use are composite rather than simple, the remainder of this section is devoted to the construction of composite index numbers. Further, since composite *price* relatives are particularly important, we direct our coverage to this type of composite index. The essential difference between a simple and a composite price relative is that the prices of several commodities, rather than just one commodity, are included in the _____ price relative.

composite

26 We return now to the problem of weighting the respective prices of the commodities included in a composite price index. The general basis used for this weighting is the quantity of each item purchased during a defined period, and these quantities are applied as the weights for the accumulation of both the base-year prices and the given-year prices. Thus, if we were to use *base-year* quantities as the weighting factor, the computational formula for the composite price index would be indicated by the formula (enter missing subscripts):

$$\frac{\Sigma p_1 q_0}{\Sigma p_0 q_0} \times 100$$

Price index $= \dfrac{\Sigma p_1 q}{\Sigma p_0 q} \times 100$

27 Note that the use of the formula in Frame 26 results in the computation of a composite price index that involves a weighting factor for each commodity price. The index produced is *not* a value index, for a value index requires multiplication of unit prices during a period by quantities in the same period. Thus, for computing a composite *value* index, the formula to be used is (enter missing subscripts):

$$\frac{\Sigma p_1 q_1}{\Sigma p_0 q_0} \times 100$$

Value index $= \dfrac{\Sigma p_1 q}{\Sigma p_0 q} \times 100$

28 Getting back to the composite price indexes when both the base-year and the given-year prices are weighted by base-year quantities, the resulting index, called *Laspeyres' index*, uses the market basket of commodities of the base year for price-comparison purposes. Again, Laspeyres' index is defined by the formula (enter subscripts):

$$\boxed{\dfrac{\Sigma p_1 q_0}{\Sigma p_0 q_0} \times 100}$$

Laspeyres' index $= \dfrac{\Sigma p \; q}{\Sigma p \; q} \times 100$

29 For the data of Table 18-1, compute Laspeyres' weighted aggregate price index by first completing the table below.

Commodity	$p_0 q_0$	$p_1 q_0$
Butter	$19.80	$27.00
Coffee	18.00	30.00
Shoes		

$$\boxed{45.00 \qquad 60.00}$$

$\Sigma p_0 q_0 = \$82.80 \quad \Sigma p_1 q_0 = \$117.00$

$$\boxed{\begin{array}{l} \dfrac{117.00}{82.80} \times 100 = 141.3 \\ \text{(which means that the mar-} \\ \text{ket basket of goods using} \\ \text{base-period quantities cost} \\ \text{41.3 percent more in 1978} \\ \text{as compared with 1970)} \end{array}}$$

$$L = \dfrac{\Sigma p_1 q_0}{\Sigma p_0 q_0} \times 100 =$$

30 Based on extent of use, the Laspeyres' index is the most important of the composite price indexes. Expressed as a relative (i.e., relative to base-year prices), it can be described as being a weighted aggregate, with prices weighted by the quantities associated with the [base / given] year.

$$\boxed{\text{base}}$$

31 Instead of using the base-year quantities to define the weights to be applied in determining the composite price index, we could obviously use the given-year quantities instead, and then sum the weighted prices. The computational formula in this case would be expressed as (enter subscripts):

$$\boxed{\dfrac{\Sigma p_1 q_1}{\Sigma p_0 q_1} \times 100}$$

Price index $= \dfrac{\Sigma p \; q}{\Sigma p \; q} \times 100$

32 Such a weighted aggregate using given-year weights is referred to as Paasche's index. Compute Paasche's index for the data of Table 18-1 by first completing the table below:

Commodity	$p_0 q_1$	$p_1 q_1$
Butter	$13.20	$18.00
Coffee		
Shoes	45.00	60.00
	$\Sigma p_0 q_1 = \$79.20$	$\Sigma p_1 q_1 = \$113.00$

$$P = \frac{\Sigma p_1 q_1}{\Sigma p_0 q_1} \times 100 =$$

$\dfrac{113.00}{79.29} \times 100 = 142.7$

(which means that the market basket of goods using base-period quantities cost 42.7 percent more in 1978 as compared with 1970)

33 Although the weighted aggregate of price relatives determined by the Laspeyres and Paasche formulas may not (and should not) differ substantially from one another in a particular application, they do represent two distinct approaches to the weighting problems in constructing composite price indexes. If a large difference exists between these two indexes, it would be indicative of important changes in [prices / patterns of consumption] between the two periods.

patterns of consumption (since the difference between the indexes is in the quantity weights used)

34 Of course, the two indexes address themselves to different questions, and so we would expect their values to differ somewhat. The index which compares the total value of the package of commodities of the given period with what the same package would have cost in the base period is [Laspeyres' / Paasche's] index.

Paasche's (since the prices are weighted on the basis of given-period quantities)

35 On the other hand, Laspeyres' index uses the quantities of commodities purchased in the [base / given] period as the basis for computing the value of each package.

base

36 Thus the computational formula for Laspeyres' index is

$$L =$$

$\dfrac{\Sigma p_1 q_0}{\Sigma p_0 q_0} \times 100$

37 And the computational formula for Paasche's index is

$$P =$$

$\dfrac{\Sigma p_1 q_1}{\Sigma p_0 q_1} \times 100$

Laspeyres'

38 But which index is really the "best" index as an indicator of price levels and cost of living is a question outside the realm of statistical analysis as such. With changing consumption patterns, the use of the market basket of the base period, and thus use of [Laspeyres' / Paasche's] index, becomes less meaningful.

Paasche's

39 Yet, to the extent that a lowered price of some commodity over time has resulted in a relatively high consumption of it in the given period, the use of given-year quantities in [Laspeyres' / Paasche's] index becomes less meaningful.

Paasche (and this is one factor limiting its use)

40 As we previously indicated, in practice Laspeyres' index has been much more frequently used than Paasche's index. The index which would require an annual survey of expenditure patterns to determine the necessary weighting factors is the _____ index.

base

given

41 Both the Laspeyres and Paasche approaches to the construction of a composite price relative can be described as being *weighted-aggregate* methods, the difference being that for the Laspeyres the basis for weighting the prices is provided by the _____-period quantities, whereas for the Paasche the _____-period quantities provide this basis.

42 An alternative to the weighted-aggregate-of-prices approach is the weighted-average-of-price-relatives approach. As suggested by the name of the latter method, instead of summing weighted price figures, the computation of the weighted average of price relatives requires that the weighted values of _____ be combined.

price relatives

43 Furthermore, if the average of the weighted price relatives is to be determined, then the type of average to be used must be specified. Although geometric and harmonic means are sometimes used in this connection, the most frequently used average is the _____ itself.

(arithmetic) mean

44 Consistent with our presentation of simple price relatives at the beginning of this section, each price relative to be weighted is determined by the formula (enter subscripts):

$\dfrac{p_1}{p_0} \times 100$

$$\frac{p}{p} \times 100$$

45 The next step in the weighted-average-of-relatives method is to weight each relative by a value figure, pq, and again we have the choice of using either base-year $(p_0 q_0)$ or given-year $(p \ q \ )$ figures (enter subscripts for the latter value).

46 Since the base-year values are commonly used as the weighting factor in the weighted-average-of-price-relatives method, the price-index formula is:

$$I_p = \frac{\Sigma (p_0 q_0)(p_1 / p_0 \times 100)}{\Sigma p_0 q_0}$$

As would be true for any mean of a series of weighted values, the denominator of this fraction represents the [number of commodities / sum of the weights used].

47 The price relatives posted in Table 18-2 were computed on the basis of the data supplied in Table 18-1. Using the figures of Table 18-2, make the appropriate substitutions in the formula for the weighted average of price relatives:

$$I_p = \frac{\Sigma (p_0 q_0)(p_1 / p_0 \times 100)}{\Sigma p_0 q_0} =$$

Table 18-2 ■ Data for the Computation of the Weighted Average of Price Relatives

Commodity	Price relative, $p_1 / p_0 \times 100$	Value weight, $p_0 q_0$	Weighted relative, $p_0 q_0 (p_1 / p_0 \times 100)$
Butter	136.4	$19.80	2,700.72
Coffee	166.7	18.00	3,000.60
Shoes	133.3	45.00	5,998.50
Total		$82.80	11,699.82

48 If the value of the composite price relative in Frame 47 appears familiar to you, it is more than coincidental. The formula for the weighted average of price relatives can be algebraically simplified, so that

$$I_p = \frac{\Sigma (p_0 q_0)(p_1 / p_0 \times 100)}{\Sigma p_0 q_0} = \frac{\Sigma p_1 q_0}{\Sigma p_0 q_0} \times 100$$

Notice that this now becomes the same formula as for one of the weighted-aggregate methods, specifically, the [Laspeyres / Paasche] index.

49 Since the computational result of using the weighted average of price relatives is the same as for Laspeyres' index, it can be interpreted in the same way, i.e., as an indication of what the package of commodities associated with the base period would cost in a given period. Of these two indexes, the one that would typically be computed when we are interested in identifying the simple price relative associated with each commodity as well as in computing the composite price index is the _____

_____

_____ .

<table>
<tr><td>weighted average of price relatives (Simple price relatives are not computed when using the Laspeyres index.)</td></tr>
</table>

Summary

50 In this section it has not been our intention to consider the statistical criteria that might be used to evaluate the "goodness" of an index or to describe the indexes that are statistically interesting because of the way they are computed. Rather, we have directed our attention to the major types of indexes in actual use. Of the three types of *simple* relatives, the price relative is computed by using the formula:

$$\frac{p_1}{p_0} \times 100$$

The quantity relative is computed by the formula:

$$\frac{q_1}{q_0} \times 100$$

The value relative is computed by the formula:

$$\frac{p_1 q_1}{p_0 q_0} \times 100$$

51 In the area of composite indexes, two of the composite price indexes we have considered involve a summation, or aggregate, of the weighted prices themselves as the basis for computing the composite relative. The index in which the base- and given-year prices are weighted by the base-year quantities is _____._ index; the one in which the prices are weighted by the given-year quantities is _____ index.

<table>
<tr><td>Laspeyres'</td></tr>
<tr><td>Paasche's</td></tr>
</table>

52 Thus the appropriate formulas used in constructing Laspeyres' and Paasche's indexes are:

$$\frac{\Sigma p_1 q_0}{\Sigma p_0 q_0}$$

$$L = \frac{\qquad}{\qquad} \times 100$$

$$\frac{\Sigma p_1 q_1}{\Sigma p_0 q_1}$$

$$P = \frac{\qquad}{\qquad} \times 100$$

53 Although the computational result is the same as for Laspeyres' formula, if simple price relatives are computed first $(p_1/p_0 \times 100)$, then each of these price relatives can be weighted by the value of the commodity associated with the base year $(p_0 q_0)$, and the arithmetic mean of these weighted price relatives can then be determined. Referred to as the "weighted average of price relatives," this index is computed by using the formula

$$I_p = \frac{\Sigma(p_0 q_0)(p_1/p_0 \times 100)}{\Sigma p_0 q_0}$$

18.3 ■ Link and Chain Relatives

When a composite index number has been periodically computed over an extended period of years, it may be desirable to change the sample of commodities included in the index, or their weighting, in order to reflect current prices, quantities, or values more meaningfully. Were we not to make such changes, established commodities would have too much of a representation in the composite index and new commodities would have no representation at all. The processes of linking and chaining make it possible to make such changes while maintaining a basis for the long-run comparability of composite indexes. The use of these methods does not solve the problem generated by changes in consumption patterns, for this problem has no real solution. However, these procedures do make it computationally possible to maintain a sense of comparability in the given index over time. The actual application of linking and chaining in index-number construction can lead to considerable complexity in computations. Therefore in this section we present an example involving the use of only simple index numbers, rather than composite indexes, in order to highlight the essential characteristics of linking and chaining as such.

54 Linking involves the use of a constantly shifting base period, rather than a fixed base period. For example, the 1978 price relative would use 1977 as the base, the 1977 relative would use 1976 as the base, and so forth. Would a price relative so computed be directly comparable with, say, a price relative for a period five years earlier? [Yes / No]

No

55 Table 18-3 reports hypothetical sales data for the Acme Tool Company between 1973 and 1978. Since each link relative uses the previous year as the base, the link relative of 111.8 for 1977 indicates that the sales level for 1977 was 11.8 percent higher than the sales level reported for the year _____ .

1976

Year	Sales, millions of units	Link relative	Chain index, 1975 = 100
1973	$1.5	...	136.3
1974	1.3	86.7	118.2
1975	1.1	84.6	100.0
1976	1.7	154.5	154.5
1977	1.9	111.8	172.7
1978	2.3	121.1	209.1

56 However, direct comparisons over a number of years cannot be made by using link relatives alone. For example, the link relatives of 154.5 for 1976 and 121.1 for 1978 [do / do not] directly indicate which relative represents a higher sales volume.

> do not (In this case, the lower-valued relative represents the higher volume.)

57 In terms of the single-commodity data reported in Table 18-3, the relationship between using link relatives and changing the sample of commodities in a composite index may not be immediately obvious. Suppose we wish to add a new commodity to a composite index for 1978. We would first compute the index exactly as it had been determined in 1977, so that comparison in respect to that base year could be made. Then we would add the new item to the 1978 composite and use this revised package of commodities as the base for the _____ (year) index.

> 1979

58 Thus, even though direct comparability of indexes computed for several years is not achieved, changes in the packages of commodities used for a composite index can be made by using the process of _____ .

> linking

59 Although link relatives cannot themselves be directly compared, their conversion into chain indexes does allow this kind of comparison to be made. This suggests, then, that the conversion from link to chain relatives involves a recomputation of relatives in terms of [a single / several] base year(s).

> a single

60 For the year, or period, chosen as the base, the value of the chain index is set at 100. Thus in Table 18-3 the year that has been chosen as the base is _____ (year).

> 1975

61 The chain indexes for the years following 1975 were determined by multiplying the link relative for each year by the chain index of the preceding year. Thus, where n refers to the given year in the series,

$$C_n = \frac{L_n C_{n-1}}{100}$$

With the substitution of the appropriate values from Table 18-3 in this formula, the chain relative for 1977 is

$$\frac{111.8 \times 154.5}{100} = 172.7$$

$$C_{1977} = \frac{L_{1977} C_{1976}}{100} =$$

62 To go backward in time from a base period, the algebraic equation has to be solved for C_{n-1} instead of for C_n. Accordingly, the chain index for 1973 was computed by substituting the following values in the equation:

$$C_{n-1} = \frac{C_n}{L_n} \times 100$$

$$\frac{118.2}{86.7} \times 100 = 136.3$$

Therefore $\quad C_{1973} = \frac{C_{1974}}{L_{1974}} \times 100 =$

63 Given the chain-index values of 136.3 and 154.5 for 1973 and 1976, respectively, can we say that the second relative is indicative of a higher sales figure than the first relative? [Yes / No].

Yes

64 Thus the terms "linking" and "chaining" are aptly descriptive of what is accomplished by these processes. A change of commodity mix with direct comparison restricted to adjoining periods is made possible by the process of

linking

_____ .

65 Conversion of link relatives so that their values are all stated in respect to a common base period is accomplished by the process of _____ .

chaining

66 As indicated in the introduction to this section, however, the use of linking and chaining makes it possible to achieve numerical comparability in indexes, but it does not solve the problem of changes in consumption patterns. When outmoded commodities are continuously replaced by new ones, the meaning of the chain index becomes increasingly vague. For example, suppose that over a span of years *all* of the commodities in a price index have been changed. Would the value of the chain relative indicate the current relative cost of the original market basket? [Yes / No]

Would it indicate the comparative cost of the present market basket of goods? [Yes / No]

18.4 ■ Some Leading Published Indexes

In this section we briefly describe the characteristics of three indexes published by agencies of the federal government: the Consumer Price Index, the Wholesale Price Index, and the Industrial Production Index. Because of its widespread use as an indicator of the cost of living, the Consumer Price Index, published by the Bureau of Labor Statistics, is probably the most widely known of the indexes now being published. The Wholesale Price Index, also published by the Bureau of Labor Statistics, is somewhat misleading in its name, in that the index measures price movements in primary markets, i.e., the markets involving first commercial transactions with commodities, rather than wholesale or jobber prices as such. The Industrial Production Index is issued by the Federal Reserve Board; it reflects changes in the physical volume of activities in manufacturing, mining, and utilities and, as such, is widely used as an indicator of general business conditions.

67 In terms of the brief introduction given above, it is obvious that the Consumer Price Index, Wholesale Price Index, and Industrial Production Index are all [simple / composite] indexes.

composite

68 Furthermore, this group of three composite indexes includes _____ (number) price index(es) and _____ (number) quantity index(es).

two; one

69 The *Consumer Price Index* is the most widely known of the published indexes because of its use as an indicator of _____ .

cost of living

70 Published by the Bureau of Labor Statistics, the Consumer Price Index indicates the average change in a fixed market basket of goods and services purchased by families of urban wage earners and clerical workers. Thus the cost of

living of high-income and low-income families as such [is / is not] represented by the index.

is not (For example, changes in the price of luxury merchandise are not reflected by the index.)

71 In addition to the overall Consumer Price Index, other indexes are published both for a selected list of cities and for specific groups of commodities and services. Thus, if the overall Consumer Price Index shows a rise, the product or service groups contributing most to this rise [can / cannot] be identified by the reader.

can

72 The Consumer Price Index is of course a composite price index, as we have already indicated. In terms of its computation, it is essentially a weighted average of price relatives. According to our earlier explanation of types of indexes in this chapter, the Consumer Price Index can therefore also be described as a [Laspeyres / Paasche] type of index.

Laspeyres (See Frames 48 and 49.)

73 The index is actually a modification of Laspeyres' index in that the quantities used in weighting the prices are not base-period quantities but quantities associated with a different period. For the indexes published in April 1977, for example, the base period for price comparison (p_0) was 1967; the period whose quantities were used for the weights (q_a) was 1972–1973. If p_1 designates the prices in the given period under study, then the modified Laspeyres formula used for the Consumer Price Index (CPI) can be represented by (enter subscripts):

$$\frac{\Sigma p_1 q_a}{\Sigma p_0 q_a}$$

$$\text{CPI} = \frac{\Sigma p\, q}{\Sigma p\, q} \times 100$$

74 Although not indicated in the formula in Frame 73, over the years the particular commodities included in the Consumer Price Index and their relative weights have been modified to reflect changing patterns of consumer expenditure. These changes, then, have necessitated the application of the processes of _____ and _____ in the construction of this index.

linking; chaining

75 Although we think of many of the published indexes as being useful because they serve to summarize that which has already happened, their use can also affect future economic activity. For example, cost-of-living clauses in many wage contracts are tied to movements of the _____ _____ Index.

Consumer Price

76 Within the limits of the assumptions included in the computation of a price index, the *reciprocal* of such an index can be used as an indicator of the purchasing power of the dollar in comparison with the base period of the index. Thus, if the value of the Consumer Price Index is 120, then the current purchasing power of the dollar in comparison with the base period can be identified as:

$$\frac{1}{120} \times 100 = \$0.83$$

Purchasing power $= \dfrac{1}{CPI} \times 100 =$

77 In July 1977 the Consumer Price Index was 182.6 on the 1967 base. The purchasing power of the dollar in July 1977, in comparison with the 1967 average, was thus _____ (nearest cent), based on the market basket included in the Consumer Price Index.

$0.55

78 Or, interpreting the July 1977 Consumer Price Index in a somewhat different way, the market basket of commodities which cost $10 in 1967 cost _____ in July 1977.

$18.26

79 The *Wholesale Price Index* is also published by the Bureau of Labor Statistics. As indicated in the introduction to this section, it [is / is not] essentially a "wholesale price" index.

is not

80 Since the Wholesale Price Index reflects primary market prices of a large number of major product groups, subgroups, and product classes, it is particularly useful for the [general consumer / businessman].

businessman

81 The computation of the Wholesale Price Index is similar to that of the Consumer Price Index. Thus the Wholesale Price Index can also be described as a [Laspeyres / Paasche] index.

Laspeyres (The actual computational procedure involves the weighted average of price relatives, which simplifies the computation of additional indexes by product group.)

82 Because the pattern of commodity transactions in the primary markets has shifted over time, the Wholesale Price

linking; chaining

Index has also been updated through the application of the processes of _____ and _____ .

83 Thus the two composite price indexes of importance to the general consumer and to the businessman which we have discussed are the _____ Index and the _____ Index.

Consumer Price

Wholesale Price

84 Finally, the *Industrial Production Index*, issued by the Federal Reserve Board, reflects the amount of physical output in manufacturing, mining, and the utilities and includes indexes for major industrial groups and subgroups, as well as an overall index. In terms of this description, it is a [simple / composite] index involving the comparison of [quantity / price / value].

composite

quantity

85 Since the Industrial Production Index is a quantity index, the method by which it is calculated in not a direct modification of Laspeyres' and Paasche's indexes as such, which are composite price indexes. However, like the Consumer and Wholesale Price Indexes, the method of calculation follows the weighted _____ of relatives.

average (In this case, quantity rather than price relatives are averaged.)

86 Comparability of the Industrial Production Index over the long run has been enhanced by use of linking and chaining, and for the short run by making adjustments for seasonal variations, which thus make it useful as a continuing indicator of _____

_____ .

general business conditions (or general production level; state of the economy; etc.)

Review

87 (Frames 1-5) If an index number represents a comparison of the measurements of one commodity at two points in time, it is a _____ index. If it represents a comparison for a package of commodities, it is a _____ index.

simple

composite

88 (Frames 6-9) In terms of the kinds of measurements represented by index numbers, they are referred to as being _____ , _____ , or _____ indexes.

price; quantity; value

89 (Frames 10-12) One of the first problems encountered in the construction of a composite index number is the decision as to what commodities should be included in the index. The

judgment	sampling method generally used results in what can be described as a _____ sample.
weighted (or combined)	**90** (Frames 13-18) Once the commodities to be included in a composite index are selected, the other principal problem has to do with how these commodities should be _____ .
$\dfrac{p_1}{p_0}, \dfrac{q_1}{q_0}, \dfrac{p_1 q_1}{p_0 q_0}$	**91** (Frames 19-25) The simple price, quantity, and value relatives can be computed by the respective formulas (enter subscripts): $\dfrac{p}{p} \times 100 \qquad \dfrac{q}{q} \times 100 \qquad \dfrac{p\,q}{p\,q} \times 100$
$\dfrac{\Sigma p_1 q_0}{\Sigma p_0 q_0} \times 100$	**92** (Frames 26-30) Laspeyres' composite price index weights the prices being accumulated for comparison by the base-year quantities of the commodities; this is algebraically represented by $L =$
$\dfrac{\Sigma p_1 q_1}{\Sigma p_0 q_1} \times 100$	**93** (Frames 31, 32) On the other hand, Paasche's index applies the quantities of the given year as the weights and is therefore represented by the formula $P =$
Paasche	**94** (Frames 33-41) Whether we use the Laspeyres or Paasche approach to computing the weighted aggregate depends on whether we wish to gauge the overall impact of price movements on the basis of the purchasing pattern of the base year or on the basis of the pattern of the given year. If the current purchasing pattern is considered the most significant and meaningful factor, then the _____ index should be used.
$\dfrac{\Sigma (p_0 q_0)(p_1 / p_0 \times 100)}{\Sigma p_0 q_0}$	**95** (Frames 42-47) The computation of the weighted average of price relatives involves weighting each simple price relative $(p_1 / p_0 \times 100)$ by base-year values $(p_0 q_0)$ and then determining the arithmetic mean of the sum of these weighted values. Therefore, the computational procedure can be represented by the formula $I_p =$

96 (Frames 48-53) The weighted average of price relatives would usually be the composite index that we compute when we wish to identify the simple price relatives associated with each of the commodities that make up the composite. As a composite price index, the computational result is identical to that of [Laspeyres' / Paasche's] index.

Laspeyres'

97 (Frames 54-58) The process whereby the commodities and weights of a composite index can be changed, resulting in the construction of a series of composite indexes each of which takes the preceding period as its base, is called _____ .

linking

98 (Frames 59-65) The process by which link relatives are converted to a common base, so that long-run comparisons of index numbers can be made, is referred to as _____ .

chaining

99 (Frame 66) When the market basket of commodities has changed substantially over time, using the processes of linking and chaining [does / does not] solve the problem of making cost-of-living comparisons.

does not

100 (Frames 67-78) The weighted average of price relatives published by the Bureau of Labor Statistics and widely used as an indicator of cost of living is the _____ Index.

Consumer Price

101 (Frames 79-83) The composite index published by the Bureau of Labor Statistics to indicate changes in primary market prices of product groups, subgroups, and product classes is the _____ Index.

Wholesale Price

102 (Frames 84-86) The composite quantity index published by the Federal Reserve Board to reflect output in manufacturing, mining, and the utilities is the _____ Index.

Industrial Production

Symbols Introduced in This Chapter (with Frame Numbers)

(19) p_0 — Price of a commodity in the basic period.

(19) p_1 — Price of a commodity in the given period.

(22) q_0 — Quantity of a commodity in the base period.

(22) q_1 — Quantity of a commodity in the given period.

(61) C_n — A chain index.

(61) L_n A link relative.

(73) CPI   Consumer Price Index.

Formulas Introduced in This Chapter (with Frame Numbers)

(19) $\dfrac{p_1}{p_0} \times 100$

A simple price index, or price relative.

(22) $\dfrac{q_1}{q_0} \times 100$

A simple quantity index, or quantity relative.

(24) $\dfrac{p_1 q_1}{p_0 q_0} \times 100$

A simple value index, or value relative.

(28) $L = \dfrac{\Sigma p_1 q_0}{\Sigma p_0 q_0} \times 100$

Laspeyres' index. The composite price index in which prices are weighted by base-year quantities.

(32) $P = \dfrac{\Sigma p_1 q_1}{\Sigma p_0 q_1} \times 100$

Paasche's index. The composite price index in which prices are weighted by given-year quantities.

(46) $I_p = \dfrac{\Sigma (p_0 q_0)(p_1 / p_0 \times 100)}{\Sigma p_0 q_0}$

The weighted average of price relatives.

(61) $C_n = \dfrac{L_n C_n - 1}{100}$

The chain index for a period that follows the designated base period.

(62) $C_{n-1} = \dfrac{C_n}{L_n} \times 100$

The chain index for a period that precedes the designated base period.

(73) $\text{CPI} = \dfrac{\Sigma p_1 q_a}{\Sigma p_0 q_a} \times 100$

Algebraic representation of the basis used for calculating the Consumer Price Index. The quantities used as weights are for other than the base period.

(76) $\text{Purchasing power} = \dfrac{1}{\text{CPI}} \times 100$

Purchasing power of the dollar in the given period as compared with the base period.

EXERCISES
(Solutions on pages 634–638)

18.1 The following wholesale prices are taken from the *Survey of Current Business*, published by the U.S. Department of Commerce. **(a)** What was the percentage increase in the wholesale price of household appliances between 1971 and

1975? **(b)** What was the percentage increase in wholesale furniture prices during the same time period?

Average wholesale prices (1967 = 100)

	1971	1972	1973	1974	1975
Household appliances	107.2	107.6	108.5	117.9	132.3
Household furniture	114.8	117.3	123.0	136.6	146.3

18.2 **(a)** For the data of Exercise 18.1, if the average wholesale price of an appliance was $150 in 1971, what is the estimate of its average wholesale price in 1975?

(b) If the average wholesale price of an item of furniture was $400 in 1972, what is the estimate of its average wholesale price in 1975?

18.3 Identify two important errors in the statement: "The figures given in Exercise 18.1 indicate that in 1975 the average consumer spent 14.0 percent more of his dollar on household furniture than he did on household appliances."

18.4 The following data reporting yearly production of butter and American cheese and average wholesale prices are also taken from the *Survey of Current Business.*

(a) Compute the simple price relatives for butter for these four years, using 1972 as the base.

(b) Compute the price relatives for cheese for these four years, also using 1972 as the base.

	1972	1973	1974	1975
Factory butter production, millions of pounds	1,109.9	918.6	961.7	980.5
Wholesale price, per pound	$0.696	$0.689	$0.674	$0.818
Factory cheese production, millions of pounds	1,644.3	1,672.5	1,858.6	1,654.5
Wholesale price, per pound	$0.714	$0.843	$0.973	$1.044

18.5 **(a)** For the data of Exercise 18.4, what are the percentage changes in the wholesale prices of butter and cheese during this four-year period?

(b) Compute the quantity relatives for both butter and

cheese for 1975, using 1972 as the base, and interpret in terms of percentage change.

18.6 (a) Compute the total dollar value of butter and cheese production in 1972 and 1975, using the data in Exercise 18.4.

(b) Using the results of part (a), compute the value relatives for butter and cheese for 1975, using 1972 as the base. Interpret these indexes.

18.7 The following simplified data represent average prices and monthly quantities of some of the supplies used in a business office. (a) Compute the simple price and quantity relatives for the bond paper, using 1970 as the base. (b) Compute the simple value relatives for the bond and onionskin paper and compare them.

Item	Unit quotation	Average price		Monthly consumption	
		1970, p_0	1978, p_1	1970, q_0	1978, q_1
Paper, white bond	ream	$2.50	$4.00	2.2	2.8
Paper, onionskin	ream	2.00	4.25	5.0	2.5
Paper clips	pkg. of 100	0.15	0.20	2.0	2.0
Typewriter ribbon	each	1.00	1.50	4.0	5.0

18.8 (a) For the data of Exercise 18.7, compute Laspeyres' index and interpret its meaning.

(b) Compute Paasche's index and interpret its meaning.

(c) Compute the weighted average of price relatives and compare its value with that of the Laspeyres and Paasche indexes.

18.9 The following data are taken from the 10K Report for 1976 filed by Litton Industries, Inc., with the Securities and Exchange Commission. Compute per-share earnings indexes for the years indicated, using 1973 as the base year.

Year	Fully diluted earnings (losses) per share
1972	$0.00
1973	1.11
1974	(1.48)
1975	0.39
1976	0.64

18.10 Compute link relatives for the per-share earnings data of Exercise 18.9. What is the base year in this case?

18.11 The following indexes are taken from the *Survey of Current Business.*

(a) What kind of indexes are reported in the table?
(b) What was the percentage decline in prices between 1967 and 1976?
(c) What was the percentage increase in prices between 1972 and 1976?

Average wholesale prices (1967 = 100)

	1972	1973	1974	1975	1976
Home electronic equipment	92.7	91.9	93.1	93.5	91.2

18.12 (a) Using the data of Exercise 18.11, given a type of radio receiver whose average wholesale price during 1975 was $24, estimate its price in 1976.
(b) Given a radio receiver whose wholesale price in 1972 was $24, estimate its price in 1976.

18.13 The following data were also taken from the *Survey of Current Business.*

(a) Compute the simple price and quantity relatives for wheat for 1976, using 1972 as the base. Interpret these indexes.
(b) Compute the simple price and quantity relatives for rice for 1976, using 1972 as the base, and interpret.

	1972	1973	1974	1975	1976
Wheat production, millions of bushels	1,545	1,711	1,796	2,134	2,147
Wholesale price, per bushel	$1.87	$3.64	$5.53	$4.84	$3.87
Rice production, millions of 100-pound bags	85.4	92.8	112.4	127.6	117.0
Wholesale price, per pound	$0.098	$0.180	$0.252	$0.190	$0.140

18.14 Compute the value relative for 1976 for each commodity in Exercise 18.13, using 1972 as the base. Interpret your results.

18.15 Given the following simplified data regarding average retail price and the weekly patterns of consumption for a selected family of four, compute the simple price and quantity relatives for the two commodities, using 1970 as the base.

Commodity	Unit quotation	Average price 1970, p_0	Average price 1978, p_1	Weekly consumption 1970, q_0	Weekly consumption 1978, q_1
Bread	$1\frac{1}{2}$-pound loaf	$0.40	$0.60	4.5	4.5
Milk	$\frac{1}{2}$ gallon	0.60	0.80	4.0	6.0

18.16 **(a)** Compute Laspeyres' index for the data of Exercise 18.15.

(b) Compute Paasche's index for the data above.

(c) Compare the two composite indexes. Which do you think is more meaningful? Why?

18.17 Compute the weighted average of price relatives, using the price relatives determined in Exercise 18.15. Compare this index with the other two composite indexes you computed in Exercise 18.16.

18.18 The following data are taken from the 1976 *Annual Report* of Texaco, Inc. Compute index numbers for total net income, using 1972 as the base.

Year	Total net income, millions of dollars
1972	820.0
1973	1,243.0
1974	1,544.7
1975	830.6
1976	869.7

18.19 **(a)** Compute the link relatives for the income data in Exercise 18.18, using appropriate base years. Interpret the meanings of the link relatives in percentage terms.

(b) Convert the link relatives into chain indexes, using 1974 as the base.

18.20 The table below presents Consumer Price Indexes for the years 1967–1976, with the base year being 1967.

Determine the purchasing power of the dollar for each of these years in terms of the value of the dollar in 1967.

Year	Consumer Price Index
1967	100.0
1968	104.2
1969	109.8
1970	116.3
1971	121.3
1972	125.3
1973	133.1
1974	147.7
1975	161.2
1976	170.5

Source of data: U.S. Department of Commerce, *Survey of Current Business.*

18.21 **(a)** Referring to Exercise 18.20, determine the purchasing power of the dollar in 1976 based on 1970 dollars.

(b) Referring to Exercise 18.22, determine the purchasing power of the dollar in 1970 based on 1976 dollars.

18.22 Of the published price indexes described in this chapter, which index is generally given most public attention? Which index might be a "leading indicator" of changes in another index? Explain.

APPENDIX A ■

APPLICATION OF THE COMPUTER IN STATISTICAL ANALYSIS[1]

The development of the computer has had the effect of increasing both the number and the scope of the applications of statistical analysis in business and economics. Many analyses which formerly could not be done because of time limitations can now be obtained as a matter of routine. Further, removing the computational drudgery associated with some of the more complex techniques has made them more appealing and has freed applications-oriented analysts from being concerned about computational details. Instead, more time is available to consider the meaning of the statistical results. This appendix is not concerned with the process or techniques of computer programming as such. Rather, the information contained in the sections below is directed toward the situation in which library, or "canned," programs for statistical analysis are available for your use. First, we discuss the use of punched cards to encode data, and we describe the procedure associated with developing a computer program. Then we specify the format, or layout, requirements associated with the input of data into computer systems. Finally, we describe the typical requirements associated with using library programs for batch processing of data and using time-sharing terminals.

A.1 ■ The Punched Card

The concept underlying the punched card is that the location of punched holes in the card can be used to encode numeric and alphabetic information and can be so interpreted by machines designed for such a purpose. Although several coding systems have been devised, the predominant one in terms of the extent of use is the Hollerith system, named after the man who first conceived of the use of punched cards to encode data and who devised the system. The Hollerith system is commonly referred to as the "IBM coding system" because it is the system originally introduced for use with data processing equipment manufactured by International Business Machines. However, this encoding system is now used almost universally with electronic data processing equipment, regardless of manufacturer.

1 The type of coding system used most frequently for encoding data in punched cards is the _____ system.

Hollerith (or IBM)

---

[1] Portions of this appendix have been selected and adapted from Leonard J. Kazmier and Andreas S. Philippakis, *Fundamentals of EDP and FORTRAN*, McGraw-Hill Book Company, New York, 1970. Used with permission.

2 Figure A-1 presents the standard card with the punched codes printed along the top of the card. Each column on this card can be coded to represent a number, letter, or special character. Therefore, on any one card we can encode a maximum of ___ (no.) characters of information.

80

Figure A-1 ■ The standard punched card illustrating the Hollerith codes for numbers, letters, and special characters

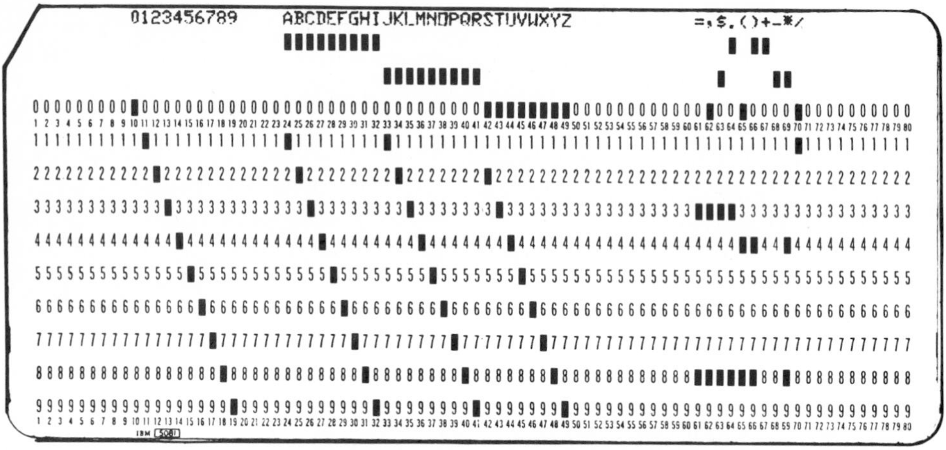

Figure A-1 ■ The standard punched card illustrating the Hollerith codes for numbers, letters, and special characters

3 A number is coded simply by punching the appropriately numbered position in the desired column. As indicated by the coding in columns 10 through 19 of Figure A-1, a given column can represent any number between the values of ___ and ___, inclusive.

0; 9

4 Thus, any given column can be only encoded with a one-digit number. However, several columns can be grouped to encode multiple-digit numbers. For example, if the number "53" is entered in columns 22–23, this would be represented by a hole in the ___ position of column ___ and the ___ position of column ___.

5; 22; 3

23

5 In addition to the 0 through 9 positions indicated in Figure A-1, so-called "11" and "12" zones are also included in each card column. The "11" zone is located just above the "0" position, while the "12" zone is located just above the "11" zone. Despite the names used for these two zones, they are never used for coding numeric symbols but are used in conjunction with coding alphabetic and special symbols. Therefore, the encoding of the number "11" or the number "12" always requires [one / two] card column(s).

two

single

0; 9

0; 3; 8

No

3

four

field

five

6 Since the information that you punch into a card is usually also printed along the top of the card, there is no reason to be concerned about interpreting the punched holes as such. The numeric codes are easily interpreted, however, because each digit is encoded by a [single / multiple] punched code.

7 On the other hand, Figure A-1 illustrates that alphabetic symbols are encoded by a combination of two punches in a given column. For example, the letter Z is represented by punches in positions ___ and ___ of a given card column.

8 Some of the special characters require as many as three punches for encoding. For example, a comma is represented by punches in positions ___, ___, and ___ of a given column.

9 When a punched card is used to input data into a computer, the exact card columns to be used for particular values must be specified and adhered to for all cards that are input. For example, suppose that it has been designated that the number of units in inventory is to be entered in columns 6–7 and that the unit cost to the nearest cent is to be entered in columns 8–12. If 112 units of a particular item are found to be in inventory, can this value be encoded on a single punched card? [Yes / No]

10 The person planning the card layout must anticipate the size of the largest value that will be input. For the inventory example above, this means that at least ___ (no.) card columns should have been provided for the number of units in inventory.

11 A *field* on a punched card is made up of one or more positions that are referenced as a unit. Examples are name, stock number, and quantity. Figure A-2 presents a punched card with the field locations identified according to card columns. In this case, ___ (no.) fields are included on the card.

12 Thus in the terminology of punched-card data processing, a group of card columns set aside for the encoding of specific information is called a ___ .

13 A field may be larger than the number of characters to be input on any given card, but it can never be smaller. Therefore, if we know that the unit costs of the items in inventory range from $1.85 to $62.50, then assuming that the decimal point is to be punched and the dollar sign is not punched, the number of card columns required for this field is ___ (no.).

PART NAME	STOCK NO.	QTY	UNIT COST	

14 Depending on the defined card specifications, the punching of a decimal point may or may not be required in conjunction with the input of data into a computer. This is discussed further in section A3 of this appendix on punched-card input. However, editing characters, such as the dollar sign and the commas, included in a number are never input. Therefore, depending on the card specifications, the value $2,375,475.25 would require either___(no.) or__(no.) card columns for encoding.

> 9; 10

15 Whenever a numeric input does not entirely fill its allotted field, it should be "justified to the right" with blanks or zeros preceding the first significant digit of the value. Thus if "9" is to be punched in the field called "QTY," which includes columns 28–30 on the card, it should be entered as (Use "b" to indicate the relative position of each blank in the field)___ .

> bb9

16 If the inventory quantity were entered as "9bb" in columns 28–30, this would be read as an input of "900" by the computer. This example indicated that a blank included with numeric input is generally interpreted as being the same as a ___.

> 0

17 Similarly, if "b9b" is entered in columns 28–30, this would be read as an input of ____ (value).

> 90

18 If columns 31–36 are defined as constituting the UNIT COST field, a unit cost of $9.00 should be entered in this field (with the decimal point punched) as _____.

> bb9.00

19 On the other hand, information in alphabetic fields is customarily justified to the left, and the unused columns to the right are left blank. Thus if columns 1-20 have been designated for the part name, we would begin punching the name "condenser" in column number ___, and the columns which would be left blank are columns ___ to ___ .

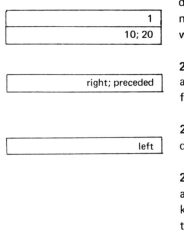

20 In summary, whenever a numeric value does not occupy an entire field, it is justified to the _____ and [preceded / followed] by blanks or zeros to fill the field.

21 Whenever information being entered in an alphabetic field does not entirely fill the field, it is justified to the _____ .

22 The device that is most frequently used to encode data in a card is the keypunch. Figure A-3 presents a close-up of the keyboard layout of the keypunch. The keyboard is similar to that of the standard typewriter except for the absence of lowercase letters and the location of the numeric keys. Because there are no separate codes for lowercase as contrasted to uppercase letters, the printing along the top of the card is all uppercase. Therefore, including lowercase letters on the keyboard of the keypunch would be [useful / unnecessary] .

Figure A-3 ▪ Close-up of the keyboard layout for the IBM 29 Keypunch
(Courtesy IBM Corporation)

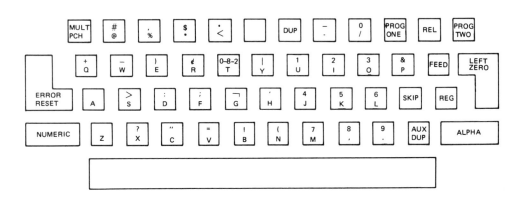

23 Keypunch machine manufacturers have taken advantage of the key spaces available as the result of the absence of lowercase letters to relocate the numeric keys. Note that there are separate "shift" keys on the keyboard in Figure A-3 for using the numeric as contrasted to the alphabetic keys. To code numeric data, the shift key located on the [right / left] is depressed.

> left

24 Still referring to Figure A-3, note that the keys clustered on the right side of the keyboard are used for various machine control purposes, while many of the keys on the left are used for special symbols. Most special symbols, such as "+," are encoded when the [alphabetic / numeric] shift key is depressed.[2]

> numeric (the upper part of each key indicates numeric shift)

25 In addition to punching the appropriate codes, a printing keypunch also prints the encoded information along the top of the card, thus making it easier for [people / machines] to identify the content of each card.

> people (of course, the machines respond only to the punched codes)

A.2 ■ The Programming Process

Even though you may not be concerned with writing computer programs as such, familiarity with the general procedure associated with writing computer programs will enhance your ability to interpret the instructions associated with the use of library programs. In this section we describe the process of developing a computer program and also describe the types of programming languages that can be used.

26 Exhibit A-1 lists the steps included in computer programming in their usual order of completion. As indicated, the first step in the programming process is "_____."

> Analyze the problem

Exhibit A-1 ■ The Basic Steps in Computer Programming

1 Analyze the problem.
2 Prepare program flowcharts.
3 Write the program.
4 Compile the program.
5 Debug the program.
6 Prepare the program for production.

27 Although analysis of the programming problem is an obvious first step, its importance is frequently overlooked, leading to errors in statistical output. For statistical programs, once the computational procedure to be programmed has been identified, it is important that the specific [data / formulas] used with that procedure be determined.

> formulas (A computer program is not concerned with specific values, but rather with specific procedures.)

[2] Detailed keypunch operating instructions are presented at the end of this appendix.

28 After analyzing the problem, the next step in computer programming is to *prepare program flowcharts*. An example of a flowchart is given in Figure A-4. In reference to this flowchart, a "trailer card" is a punched card with a designated code that follows the cards that contain the input data and that serves as a signal that all data cards have been read. In Figure A-4, after the trailer card is sensed, the value of the _____ is calculated.

| arithmetic mean |

Figure A-4 ■ **Flowchart for computing the arithmetic mean**

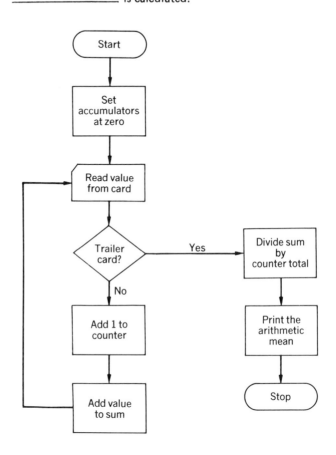

29 Thus, a "sequential analysis of the logical and computational processes to be included in the computer program" is one way of describing the program _____ .

| flowchart |

30 After the program flowchart has been prepared, we are ready to *write the program* as the third step in the computer programming process. There are three distinct types of languages, or systems of codes, that can be used for writing computer programs. These are the *machine, symbolic,* and *procedure-oriented* languages. As implied by the name, a language whose codes can be directly interpreted by the computer would be classified as a _____ language.

machine

31 For early computer applications it was necessary to write all programs in machine codes, rather than the more easily understandable symbolic or procedure-oriented languages. The symbolic languages, which use alphabetic symbols to designate computer operations, were the first improvement. Thus, a programming language in which "A" designates "add" is a _____ language.

symbolic

32 Finally, the development of procedure-oriented languages has made it possible to write programming statements whose structure is similar to general mathematical statements or to the English language. Thus, a programming language in which we can write "$A = B + C$" or "BAL = AMT − PMNT" is a _____ language.

procedure-oriented

33 In the order of their development, the three types of programming languages that can be used are the _____, _____, and _____ languages.

machine
symbolic; procedure-oriented

34 A symbolic language is just one step removed from a machine language in that only one operation, such as "add," can be specified in any one command. On the other hand, procedure-oriented languages can include more than one instruction in each command, such as in "$D = (A + B)/C$." Therefore, the type of language whose use results in the shortest computer programs is the _____ language.

procedure-oriented

35 Henceforth we will restrict our attention to procedure-oriented languages, since these are now the most frequently used languages. Examples of such languages are BASIC, FORTRAN, PL/1, ALGOL, and COBOL. In order to be able to use a programming language such as FORTRAN with a particular computer, a special program must be supplied by the manufacturer to translate the procedure-oriented language into the appropriate machine language. Thus, whereas a program written in FORTRAN would be the same no matter what computer is to be used, the translated program [is also the same / differs according to computer model].

differs according to computer model

36 The special program that performs the translation into machine-processable codes is called a *compiler*. Also, the procedure-oriented program is called the *source program* and the machine-language program is called the *object program.* Thus, a compiler is always used to translate a(n) _____ program into a(n) _____ program.

source
object

37 When you hear the expressions "source deck" and "object deck" in a computer center, this simply indicates that each of the respective programs has been punched into a deck of cards. The program that is used to produce the object deck by input of the source deck is called the _____ .

compiler

38 Note that "compile the program" is the fourth of the basic steps in computer programming, immediately following the step "write the program." We should mention, however, that a computer user typically does not see any object program as such, for this is a set of instructions that is used internally but is not usually supplied as computer output. Without the availability of a compiler, however, a _____ program could not be translated into the _____ program.

source
object

39 The fifth step in computer programming is "debug the program," which means that the program is tested and corrected where necessary. It is rare that a program runs perfectly the first time, and it is not unusual that locating and correcting program errors require as much time as writing the program in the first place. Obviously, the amount of time devoted to debugging is a function of the complexity of the program and the [skill of the programmer / reliability of the computer].

skill of the programmer (since he is the source of any program errors)

40 Thus, the process of testing and correcting the program by "trying it out" with the extreme ranges of values that can be encountered in actual data analysis is referred to as "_____ the program."

debugging

41 Following debugging, the final step in the process of computer programming is "prepare the program for production." The specific things to be accomplished in this case depend on the particular requirements of the computer center and the intended use of the program. For complex programs, instructions have to be prepared for the computer operator. These instructions and the program itself should be written so that the number of decisions and program interventions required of the operator is [minimized / maximized].

minimized

42 When a program is to be made available for general use, then instructions for other users should also be prepared. This

is referred to as *program documentation,* and includes such information as the data processing objective, the form of the required input, and the form of the output. Because future uses of a program cannot always be anticipated, it is a good practice to prepare program documentation for [all / only general purpose] programs.

all

43 Since you will probably not be involved in the actual writing of computer programs as such, your use of library, or "canned," programs is directly dependent on the program _____ supplied by your computer center.

documentation

A.3 ■ Input of Data from Punched Cards

In this section we direct our attention to punched-card input because this is the most frequent method of data input used with library programs. However, the concepts discussed apply to other forms of data entry as well, such as magnetic tape and keyboard entry. First, the difference between fixed-point and floating-point numbers is described and illustrated in this section. Afterward, the format descriptions that are often required in conjunction with the input of data are presented.

44 Computer programs generally require that a distinction be made between input data which can contain decimal (fractional) values and those which can have only integer (whole-number) values. For example, the process of counting, such as counting the number of items held in stock, results in a value that is [decimal / integer] in form.

integer

45 Different kinds of computer arithmetic are used with these two types of values, and so it is important that the kind of data be identified. The *fixed-point mode* of arithmetic is used with integers and the *floating-point mode* of arithmetic is used with _____ values.

decimal (or fractional)

46 Because of the modes of arithmetic used, the two types of data are referred to as being "fixed-point" and "floating-point" in the context of computer applications. As discussed in Chapter 1, statisticians frequently identify data as being continuous when fractional values are possible and discrete when only whole numbers are possible. Therefore, continuous data are called [fixed-point / floating-point] data in terms of computer-related terminology.

floating-point

47 Similarly, discrete data which can include only whole numbers are called _____ data.

fixed-point

48 One way to remember the distinction between fixed-point and floating-point values is that the name "fixed-point" indicates a fixed decimal location at the end of the number, which would be true for only [decimal / integer] values.

integer

49 Although fixed-point and floating-point variables are differentiated by the use of separate labels in the computer program itself, our concern in this section is restricted to the required difference in the form of the data as such. The distinction is in fact a simple one. Fixed-point values are always entered *without* any decimal point, while floating-point values include a decimal point. Thus if a count of 15 is to be punched in columns 19–22 of a card, it would appropriately be punched as _____.

bb15 (The number must be right-justified.)

50 On the other hand, if an inventory of 159 pounds, measured to the nearest pound, is to be punched in columns 25–29 of a card, it would appropriately be punched as _____.

b159. (Right-justification is not mandatory as long as the decimal is punched, but it is desirable.)

51 Therefore, a library program for which the documentation indicates that a decimal point should be included with each input value signifies that the input is to be in the _____ -point mode.

floating

52 Some library programs will define specifically the fields on the punched card that are to be used for input data. However, other library programs allow the user to identify the fields to be used in conjunction with input data. In the latter case, a *format* statement is required to specify the location of the input data on each card. Therefore, a library program which requires no format description must include specific instructions as to where_____ data are to be punched in each card.

input

53 In computer-related terminology, the statement which identifies the location of data on each punched card which is to be used as input for computer processing is called the _____ statement.

format

54 Of course, the word "format" refers directly to the idea that the format, or layout, of data fields is being described. Within a computer program, format specifications are also required to designate the form of intended output, such as on

input

a printer. Because output specifications are always already included in library programs, we are concerned only about the way that _____ specifications can be designated.

55 The documentation or instructions for a library program will always indicate where the format description should be punched, given that such a description is required. The format description is generally entered within parentheses in the designated card field. For example, the format description "(F5.2)" indicates that the variable is in the floating-point mode (F) and that the data are located in the first five columns of each card with _____ digits to the right of the decimal.

two

56 Similarly "(F3.1)" indicates that the variable is in the _____ -point mode, occupies the first _____ columns of each card, and includes _____ digit to the right of the decimal.

floating; three

one

57 For floating-point values used as computer input, the decimal point does not in fact have to be punched if the format specification is appropriate. However, it is essential that such number be right-justified, because any trailing blanks are read as zeros. If the decimal point is nevertheless punched in the input card, the punched location always supersedes the format specification if the two should differ. Therefore, given the format "(F3.1)," the punched input "b54" would be read as_____, the punched input "54b" would be read as_____, and the punched input ".54" would be read as_____.

5.4; 54.0

.54

58 If the decimal point is to be punched, then of course the designated field should include a card column for the decimal point. Therefore if the largest input value expected is 323.99 and the decimal is to be punched, then the format specification should read (_____). If the largest value to be input is 4,580.9 and the decimal point is *not* to be punched, then the format specification should read (_____).

F6.2

F5.1

59 Just as "F" is used to designate the format for a field with floating-point data, "I" is used to designate a field with integer (fixed-point) data. In the case of integer fields, however, no decimal point is involved. Thus "(I5)" indicates a fixed-point variable that is to be punched in the first five columns of a card. Similarly, a fixed-point variable that is to be entered in the first eight columns of a card is designated by "(__)".

I8

60 Of course we usually desire to input more than one value from each punched card. Suppose that three fields of five columns each (columns 1–15) are to be used for input, with one digit to the right of each decimal. This could be written as "(F5.1, F5.1, F5.1)" or as "(3F5.1)". Similarly, if we wish to enter 10 floating-point values with two digits to the right of the decimal on each card using eight-column fields, the format is most easily described as "(_____)."

10F8.2

61 If values of different variables (such as quantity and total cost) are entered on the same card, then the formats of the several fields would usually differ. For example, "(I3, F6.2)" indicates that an integer value is to be entered into the computer from the first_____ (no.) card columns and floating-point value is to be entered from columns number ___ to ___.

three
4; 9

62 Similarly, a card which includes values of integers in columns 1–3, 4–8, and 9–13 and floating-point values with two digits to the right of the decimal in columns 14–19 and 20–25 is described by the format specification "_____."

(I3, 2I5, 2F6.2) or (I3, I5, I5, F6.2, F6.2)

63, Finally, it is frequently the case that the values to be input do not begin in column 1. Further, we may also want to skip other fields in the card. Card columns can be omitted as input by using the "X" designation. For example, suppose that *Part Name* is entered in columns 1–20, *Stock Number* (an integer) in columns 21–27, *Quantity* in columns 28–30, and *Unit Cost* in columns 31–36, with two digits to the right of the decimal. Assuming that the Part Name is not to be entered as input data, the format specification should read "(20X, I7, I3, F6.2)." If neither the Part Name nor the Stock Number is to be input, the format should read "_____."

(27X, I3, F6.2)

64 As indicated by the example above, the "X" specification is not required for the columns that follow the last field to be read. To write (27X, I3, F6.2, 56X) is acceptable but unnecessary. You should now be able to infer how a field *between* two data fields can be skipped as input. Suppose that integer values are to be read from columns 6–8 and columns 20–24, but that other data included in columns 1–5 and columns 9–19 are to be skipped as input. This is designated by the format specification "_____."

(5X, I3, 11X, I5)

A.4 ■ The Use of Library Programs for Batch Processing

The term "batch processing" indicates that the data to be analyzed have already been coded on an input medium, such as punched cards or magnetic tape, and that the data are to be entered for processing at a particular point in time. This method of input contrasts with the relatively slower keyboard entry of data used in many time-sharing systems, as discussed in the next section of this appendix. Continuing with the orientation of the previous sections, we direct our attention to the use of punched cards. In general, two or three distinct types of cards are required for batch processing, and these cards are described in this section. The first group of cards identifies the user and library program to be run and describes the data to be processed. The second group of cards in the deck includes the data as such. Finally, one or more cards may be required after the data cards to signal the end of input and to request program termination.

65 Figure A-5 portrays the ordering of the input cards associated with the batch processing of data by means of library programs. The first several cards that we shall describe are those which precede the data cards. Typically, the very first card in your input deck should be a *run card* (or *job card*). The specific requirements for this card differ according to computer center, but such a card has the word "RUN" punched in a designated field followed by identification of the user, such as his name and department number. Therefore, a run card can be used to determine [if a program is available / budgetary charge for computer use] .

budgetary charge for computer use

Figure A-5 ■ Typical deck set-up for the use of a library program by batch processing

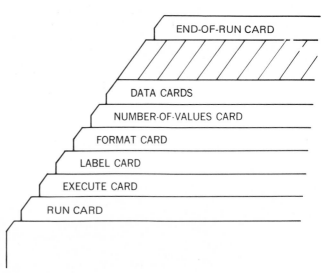

66 The first card of the input deck, which identifies the user, follows a standard format within a particular computer center. This card is called the ____ card.

run (or job)

67 Following the identification of the user, it is logical that the library program to be used should be identified. The format for this second type of card, called either the *execute card* or the *search card,* varies according to the requirements of the program library being used. The name *execute card* is used bacause the card indicates which program is to be executed. Similarly, the name *search card* is frequently used because after reading this card the computer storage will be searched for the identified program. In either case, then, the reading of this second type of card results in the retrieval of a

| library (for computer) |

_____ program from a storage location and making it available for data analysis.

68 The type of card which identifies the library program

| execute |
| search |

which is to be used is usually called the _____card or the _____ card.

69 Following the run card and the execute card in Figure A-5, a third type of card sometimes used is indicated, called the *label card* or the *header card,* and includes the user's name and a descriptive title for the analysis being performed. Because the user has already been identified on the job card, the label card is not concerned with checking user qualifications. Rather, and as the name implies, the contents of this card will be printed as the label or heading on the computer

| visual |

output, thereby facilitating [computer / visual] identification of the reports.

70 After the label card, the next type of card that may be required is the *format card.* As indicated by its name, this card indicates the format specifications of the data cards in the input deck. For example, if each input card is to contain 10 fields of eight columns each, with two digits to the right of the

| 10F8.2 |

decimal, the format specification (_____) would be punched in the designated field of the format card.

71 Some library programs do not require a format card. Since the input data must obviously conform to some designated format, the absence of a format card requirement indicates

| in the library program description |

that the format specifications are designated [in the library program description / by the user].

72 Generally, therefore, a user has the opportunity to

format

designate the layout of data on the input cards only when the library program requires the preparation of a _____ card.

73 Another card that may or may not be required is the *number-of-values* card. When such a card is not required, the computer will read the data fields until the first blank field is encountered. Therefore, the computer can "double-check" to ascertain if the number of values of some variable matches the intended input of the user only when the number-of-values card [is / is not] required.

is

74 Incidentally, some relatively sophisticated library programs may require a number-of-variables card. Note that "variables" is *not* the same thing as "values of a variable." For example, a study of the gross sales, net sales, and net profit for 50 companies involves a study of __(no.) variables each of which has___(no.) values.

3
50

75 Thus, the group of cards which precedes the data cards includes the run card, execute card, label card, and perhaps the format card and number-of-values card. As already indicated, the layout of the values punched in the data cards which follow must be consistent with the specifications included in the documentation for the library program or those defined on the_____card.

format

76 After the input data, an end-of-run card is frequently required in order to signal the end of the entire input deck. The specific layout of this card varies according to the computer center. Consider that a deck of input cards is not generally input by itself, but rather is "stacked" with other input decks. In order to assure that different input decks can be detected as being different by the computer, the _____ card may be required.

end-of-run

77 Figure A-6 illustrates an actual card deck used with a library program called "STATB," while Exhibit A-2 is the output of this program. The analysis is concerned with estimating a population mean based on sample data, as discussed in Chapter 9 on statistical estimation. Study these illustrations as an example of the use of a library program for batch processing. Note that this deck [does / does not] include a format card, [does / does not] include a number-of-values card, and [does / does not] include an end-of-run card.

does not
does
does not

Figure A-6 ■ Input deck used in conjunction with the library program named STATB

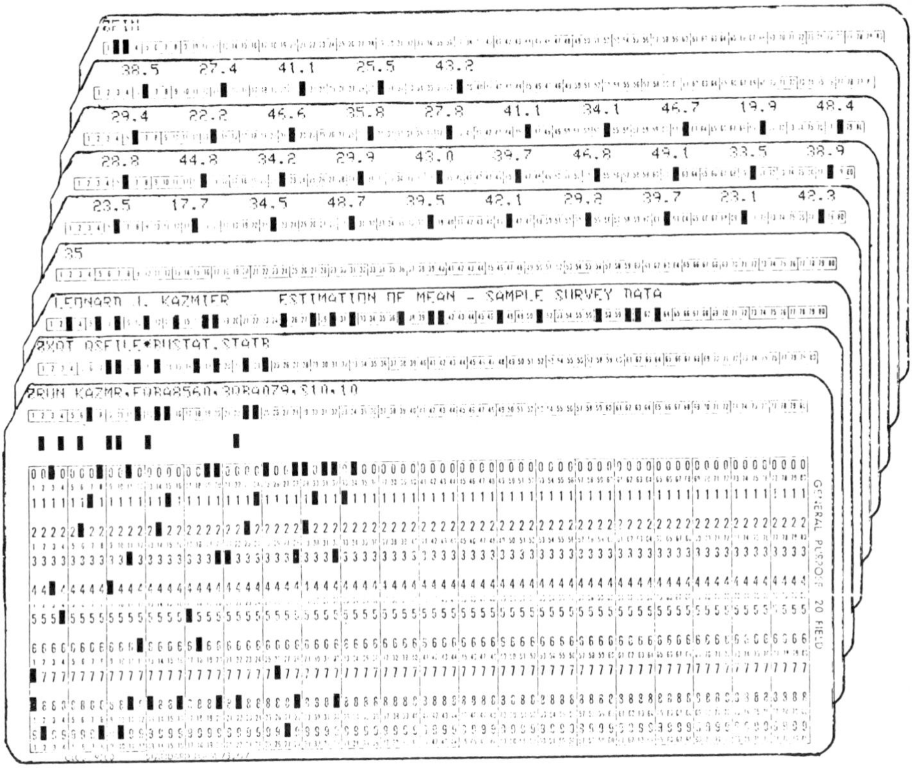

Exhibit A-2 ■ Printed Computer Output Associated with the Library Program Named STATB

```
LEONARD J. KAZMIER     ESTIMATION OF MEAN - SAMPLE SURVEY DATA

ESTIMATING THE POPULATION MEAN



   THE SAMPLE SIZE =  35
   THE SAMPLE MEAN =     35.91
   THE SAMPLE STANDARD DEVIATION =      8.98
   THE STANDARD ERROR OF THE MEAN =      1.52
```

```
THE VALUE OF THE STANDARD ERROR OF THE MEAN IS BASED UPON THE
SAMPLE STANDARD DEVIATION WITHOUT THE USE OF THE FINITE
CORRECTION FACTOR.


INTERVAL ESTIMATES
    FOR THE POPULATION MEAN
        90 PERCENT CONFIDENCE INTERVAL        33.40   TO        38.41
        95 PERCENT CONFIDENCE INTERVAL        32.93   TO        38.88
        99 PERCENT CONFIDENCE INTERVAL        31.99   TO        39.82
```

WFIN

A.5 ■ The Use of Time-sharing Terminals

As is the case for batch processing, certain general requirements are associated with the use of time-sharing terminals. Such terminals are also described as being remote-access terminals because of the fact that instructions and data are transmitted between the terminal and the processing unit of the computer by means of telephone lines. Time-sharing terminals can be used to input computer programs as such, as well as to call out library programs. As in the preceding section, our interest is directed toward the use of library programs. Typically, the input for such time-sharing systems is done through a keyboard which is much like the keyboard of a typewriter, except for the absence of uppercase letters. The messages from the computer and the results of the statistical analysis are obtained as teletype output at the same console. In this section we describe the input requirements associated with a particular library program in a typical time-sharing system. Specific requirements associated with other programs and systems can be obtained from the computer center serving the terminal.

78 Figure A-7 presents a picture of a typical input/output teletype unit used in conjunction with time sharing. Although the speed of input and output is slow relative to the speed associated with batch processing, a number of such terminals can be connected with a processor simultaneously, thus leading to the terminals being called _____ terminals.

time-sharing

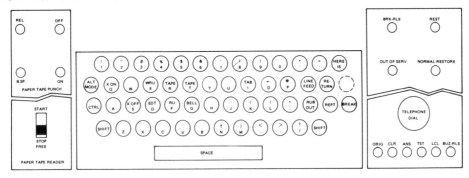

79 In this section we describe the required input and present the output for the library program called CONLIM. As was the case for the sample program in the preceding section on batch processing, the purpose of this program is to estimate a population mean based on _____ data.

sample

80 The first step in the required procedure is to establish contact between the terminal and the processing unit. This is done by pressing the ORIG button, located in the lower right corner of the keyboard in Figure A-7, after which an audible dial tone will be heard. Then the number assigned to the processor is dialed on the accompanying dial. Because the purpose of the call is to establish contact between the *terminal* and the processor, the user [is / is not] involved in picking up any telephone receiver in conjunction with this call.

is not

81 After dialing the appropriate number the user will either hear the number "ringing" at the processor or will hear a "busy signal" by means of the speaker systems. If a busy signal is heard, the attempted connection should be terminated by pressing the CLR button located adjacent to the ORIG button. Given that the connection was attempted during the hours that the system is in operation, a busy signal indicates that all available lines are being used by other _____ terminals.

time-sharing

82 When a connection is made, the teletype will identify the computer center. This initial response from the computer center is located on the first line of Exhibit A-3. In this exhibit, computer center responses begin at the margin, whereas items entered by the user always follow a "promt" signal from the computer (">" or ">>"). Thus, for this example the first input by the user is on line number ____.

2

Exhibit A-3 ■ Input and Output Associated with the Time-sharing Library Program Named CONLIM*** (Input is Underlined)

```
*UNIVAC 1100 OPERATING SYSTEM   VER. 33R1A - XA19(RSI)*
>@RUN KAZMR,FQBA8560,3QBA079
DATE: 011277        TIME: 104141
>@BASIC ASU*TSLIB.
UBASIC 7R1C RL70-1 01/12/77 10:42:21
>>OLD:CONLIM
>>RUN


THIS PROGRAM COMPUTES CONFIDENCE LIMITS FOR
AN UNKNOWN POPULATION MEAN, BASED ON RANDOM
SAMPLE DATA GIVEN.    TO USE, TYPE:

    50  DATA  (SIZE OF POPULATION)
        (OMIT THIS WHOLE LINE FOR AN INFINITE POPULATION)
    100 DATA  X(1), X(2),.....,X(N)

WHERE THE X(I) ARE THE SAMPLE OBSERVATIONS.

 TIME :    .200

>>100 DATA 23.5, 17.7, 34.5, 48.7, 39.5, 42.1, 29.2, 39.7, 23.1, 42.3
>>101 DATA 28.8, 44.8, 34.2, 29.9, 43.0, 39.7, 46.8, 49.1, 33.5, 38.9
>>102 DATA 29.4, 22.2, 46.6, 35.8, 27.8, 41.1, 34.1, 46.7, 19.9, 48.4
>>103 DATA 38.5, 27.4, 41.1, 25.5, 43.2
>>RUN


VALUES OF SAMPLE STATISTICS:

    SIZE OF SAMPLE            35
    SAMPLE MEAN VALUE         35.905711
    VARIANCE OF SAMPLE        78.406357
    SAMPLE STD DEVIATION      8.8547363
    ESTIMATED POPN STD DEV    8.9840094
    STANDARD ERROR OF MEAN    1.5185747


CONFIDENCE LIMITS ON POPULATION MEAN:

CONF LEVEL      LOWER LIM       UPPER LIM

   50           34.870392       36.941031
   75           34.128469       37.682953
   89.999999    33.337955       38.473468
```

Exhibit A-3 ■ Input and Output
Associated with the
Time-sharing Library
Program Named
CONLIM*** (Input is
Underlined) (*Continued*)

```
95              32.819685      38.991738
99              31.762873      40.04855
99.9            30.439865      41.371557
99.99           29.222483      42.58894
99.999          28.052216      43.759207


TIME :      .286


>>@FIN


UNIVAC BASIC 10:49:10    12 JAN 77
```

83 The entry on line 2 of Exhibit A-3 is essentially equivalent to a RUN card in batch processing. As such, the user and the account to be charged are identified. The next user entry, on line 4, identifies the programming language in which the library program is written and the name of the library in which the program is located. In this case, the program is written in the programming language called _____ and the name of the library of programs being referenced is _____ .

BASIC

ASU*TSLIB

84 After the next prompt signal, on line 6, the user identified the program as being an OLD program and identified the name of the program to be used in the analysis: CONLIM. Then, on the next line, the user indicated that full identification of the program to be run has been given and he is ready for further instructions from the computer by entering the word _____ .

RUN

85 The next several lines of information from the computer describe the purpose of the program called CONLIM and indicate the specific format to be followed for the input of the _____ .

data

86 The sample data are then entered in Exhibit A-3 on the next four lines. In this case, the input format includes the identification of three-digit line numbers and the separation of the input values on each line by a _____ and a _____ .

comma

space

RUN

87 After the last input value was entered in Exhibit A-3, the user pressed the RETURN key, typed in the word _____, and then again pressed the RETURN key.

@FIN

88 After a few seconds' pause, the results of the statistical analysis were output on the next several lines in Exhibit A-3. Incidentally, the results differ slightly from the output of the program used in the example on batch processing in Section A.4 because of the different number of digits included in the computations. Finally, the user signed off and terminated the connection with the central processor by entering _____ after the final prompt signal in Exhibit A-3.

Review

80

89 (Frames 1-8) The Hollerith system is the standard system used for encoding punched cards for computer input. By this system each card can be encoded with a maximum of ___ characters of information.

field

90 (Frames (9–13) A group of one or more card columns set aside for the coding of specific information is called a _____.

right

left

91 (Frames 14–21) When a numeric value does not entirely fill its allotted field, it is justified to the [right / left]. When alphabetic information does not entirely fill its allotted field, it is justified to the _____.

keypunch

92 (Frames (22–25) Punched cards are generally encoded by use of the _____ machine.

flowchart

93 (Frames 26–29) The programming process begins by analyzing the problem for which a computer program is required. The second step involves the preparation of a graphic outline of the program to be written. The chart by which this outline is presented is called a _____.

procedure-oriented

94 (Frames (30–35) Of the three types of programming languages, the type which makes it possible to write program statements which are similar in form to statements in mathematics or in the English language is the _____ language.

95 (Frames 36–38) A computer program written in a

procedure-oriented language is frequently called a "source" program. Such a program is always translated into the machine-language object program by using a special program which is called the _____ .

compiler

96 (Frames 39–43) The testing of a newly developed program with all possible extremes of data values is called program _____ . The subsequent preparation of instructions regarding the program objectives and required input is called program _____ .

debugging

documentation

97 (Frames 44–52) In the terminology of computer applications, values that can only be whole-number integers are called _____ values. Values that can contain fractional amounts are called _____ values.

fixed-point

floating-point

98 (Frames 53–58) If the largest value that can be included as input is 499.99 and the decimal point is to be punched, then the format specification should read (____).

F6.2

99 (Frames 59–64) Suppose that the five columns of the input card are to be left blank, followed by Number of Units in columns 6–8 and the Unit Price to the nearest cent in columns 9–13. The format specification for this type of input card should read "(_____)."

5X, I3, F5.2

100 (Frames 65–68) When data analysis is accomplished by batch processing, the first card of the deck of cards that is input is always the _____ card. When a library program is to be used, the next card is typically the _____ card.

run

execute (or search)

101 (Frames 69–75) Several other cards may also be required as input before the data cards as such, including the label card and number-of-values card. For library programs that allow the user to define the card-column locations of the input values on each card, a _____ card would also be required.

format

102 (Frames 76, 77) Following the data cards, at least one additional card is usually required, which is the _____ card.

end-of-job

103 (Frames 78–83) When a connection is established between a time-sharing console and a computer, the first

number	keyboard input generally requested is identification of the user by entry of the user [name / number].

104 (Frames 84–88) After the user has entered full identification of the library program to be used in a time-sharing system, he can generally obtain specific data format instructions by entering the word _____. After the desired output is obtained, the user terminates the connection with the central processor by entering @_____.

RUN	
FIN	

EXERCISES

(Solutions on pages 638–639)

A.1 Define the meaning of a "field" as used in conjunction with punched-card coding. In what sense does this concept allow flexibility in the use of punched cards and in what sense does it limit the use of punched-card columns?

A.2 What is a flowchart? Why is it considered good practice to prepare a flowchart before writing a computer program?

A.3 Describe the general characteristics of the three principal types of programming languages and indicate their relative ease of use from the standpoint of writing a computer program.

A.4 Differentiate the *source program* from the *object program*. In this context, what is the *source deck*?

A.5 The process of computer programming was described as being comprised of certain steps completed in a particular order. Suppose that one of the early steps, such as preparing program flowcharts, is omitted or given limited attention. What are likely to be the adverse effects, if any?

A.6 What is a fixed-point number, and how does it relate to the distinction between continuous and discrete numbers discussed in Chapter 1 of the text?

A.7 Suppose that the format for input data reads (10X, 2I5, F5.2). Describe the layout of the input card.

A.8 For the input card described in Exercise A.7, above, indicate the maximum possible value for each of the variables being read. In this regard, does it matter if any decimal points are punched?

A.9 Since the computer user would generally be identified on both the run card and the label card, why are *both* kinds of cards usually required in conjunction with the use of library programs by batch processing?

A.10 Time-sharing terminals are also called "remote-access" terminals in some computer installations. Why can either of these descriptions be considered correct?

ADDITIONAL EXERCISES

A.11 The examples of codified punched cards in this appendix have all included the printed (interpreted) information along the top of the card. Of what use, if any, is a card that has the codified punches but is not interpreted with the printed information?

A.12 Computer programs that are written in either a symbolic or a procedure-oriented language have to be translated into the appropriate machine language before being run on a particular computer. How, then, do the symbolic and procedure-oriented languages differ? What type of language is most frequently used for writing computer programs?

A.13 What is a *compiler* and for what purpose is it used? Is it possible that a particular computer would have more than one compiler? Explain.

A.14 What is involved in debugging a program? What kind of program testing is required by this procedure?

A.15 Although all of the steps in computer programming are necessary and important, the first concern of the user of a library program is likely to be directed toward the adequacy of program documentation. Why?

A.16 What is a floating-point number, and how does it relate to the distinction between continuous and discrete numbers discussed in Chapter 1 of the text?

A.17 Suppose that the format for input data reads (I3, 5X, I5, 2F8.1). Describe the layout of the input card.

A.18 For the input card described in Exercise A.17, above, indicate the maximum possible value for each of the variables being read.

A.19 In conjunction with the use of library programs by batch processing, the format card and the number-of-values card may or may not be required for particular programs. Discuss the implications to the user of each type of situation.

A.20 Generally, the use of time-sharing terminals results in more central-processor time being used as compared with the same program being run by batch processing. Why, then, has the use of such terminals become popular?

Keypunch Operating Instructions

1. Make sure that the power switch is on. Turn the PRINT toggle switch on; it is located just above the keyboard. Make sure that the feed hopper has an adequate number of cards.
2. Press the FEED key to feed a card from the feed hopper.
3. Press the REG (register) key to position the card under the punching station.
4. *Punch alphabetic* information by pressing appropriate keys. Keys are labeled. In order to determine the column ready to be punched next, observe the indicator inside the glass cover located to the left of the feed hopper. *Punch numeric* information by holding the NUM (numeric) key down. Keys are labeled. *Space* by means of the long space bar.
5. To remove a card from the punching station, press the REL (release) key. (In some keypunches, the label is EJECT instead of REL.) If you want to punch another card, go to reference point 2 above and repeat the cycle. If you have finished, press REL, then REG, then REL. The card will move to the output stacker in the upper left of the keypunch.
6. To duplicate a card that has just been punched, press the REL key to advance the card to the reading station. Press FEED, then REG to position a blank card under the punching station. Depress the DUP (duplicate) key. Holding the DUP key down causes duplication at the rate of 10 columns per second. Tapping the DUP key advances the card one column at a time.
7. To duplicate portions of a card and to punch corrections or additions, place the original card in the reading station. Press FEED, then REG. To duplicate a number of columns, press the DUP key. To punch in some columns, punch as usual.

8. To backspace, depress the backspace key located directly below the reading station of the punch.
9. For more efficient punching, turn AUTO FEED toggle switch on. Then depress FEED twice. After that, every time you depress REL a new card is fed and registered automatically, thus eliminating the need to depress FEED and REG every time. However, when making duplications or corrections, turn the AUTO FEED switch off.

Stat A ■ Statistical Description and Frequency Distribution

This program will accept up to 300 unsorted numbers, each with a minimum value of at least $-9,999.99$ and a maximum value no larger than $+9,999.99$. Values entered without an arithmetic sign are assumed to be positive. The initial output of the program includes the mean, median, mode, quartile values, range, average deviation, and standard deviation for the data. Following this output, the input data are sorted into a frequency distribution containing 10 classes, and a bar chart is produced which identifies the class limits and midpoint for each class and indicates the percentage of the input values that is located in each class. Finally, the values of the mean, median, mode, quartiles, range, average deviation, and standard deviation are computed and reported for the grouped data. The differences between these values and the corresponding values determined for the ungrouped data are due to the fact that computed values based on a frequency distribution of grouped data are approximations of the values that would be obtained using the original (ungrouped) data.

Required Input Deck

Card 1   Standard run card   (See your computer center for the card specifications.)

Card 2 Execute card	(See your computer center for the card specifications to call out the library program named STATA.)
Card 3 ⟋b⟋⟋⟋⟋⟋⟋⟋ . . .	Cols. 2–80 Label card—leave column 1 blank; enter user's name and program description in columns 2–80, which will be used as the label for the output.
Card 4 ⟋⟋⟋⟋	Cols. 1–3 Number of values (right-justified).
	Col. 4 Punch "0" if these are sample data or punch "1" if these are population data.

Card 5 and every card following

⟋⟋⟋⟋⟋⟋·⟋⟋⟋	Cols. 1–8 Value of variable, decimal punched as indicated.
⟋⟋⟋⟋⟋⟋·⟋⟋⟋	Cols. 9–16 Value of variable, decimal punched as indicated.
⟋⟋⟋⟋⟋⟋·⟋⟋⟋	Cols. 17–24 Value of variable, decimal punched as indicated.
⟋⟋⟋⟋⟋⟋·⟋⟋⟋	Cols. 25–32 Value of variable, decimal punched as indicated.
⟋⟋⟋⟋⟋⟋·⟋⟋⟋	Cols. 33–40 Value of variable, decimal punched as indicated.
⟋⟋⟋⟋⟋⟋·⟋⟋⟋	Cols. 41–48 Value of variable, decimal punched as indicated.
⟋⟋⟋⟋⟋⟋·⟋⟋⟋	Cols. 49–56 Value of variable, decimal punched as indicated.
⟋⟋⟋⟋⟋⟋·⟋⟋⟋	Cols. 57–64 Value of variable, decimal punched as indicated.
⟋⟋⟋⟋⟋⟋·⟋⟋⟋	Cols. 65–72 Value of variable, decimal punched as indicated.
⟋⟋⟋⟋⟋⟋·⟋⟋⟋	Cols. 73–80 Value of variable, decimal punched as indicated.

(Thus each card contains a maximum of 10 values. If the total number of values is not a multiple of 10, the last card will include some unused fields. Check to make sure that the number of values entered corresponds with the number indicated in card no. 4.)

End-of-run card   (May or may not be required; see your computer center.)

Stat B ■ Estimating the Population Mean   This program will accept a sample of up to 300 measurements with a minimum sample size of 30 when the population standard deviation (sigma) is not known. Each measurement should have a value of at least −9,999.99 and be no larger than +9,999.99. Values entered without an arithmetic sign are assumed to be positive. The initial output includes the mean, standard deviation, and standard error of the mean. The value of the standard error includes use of the finite correction factor when the population size is included in the input. The 90 percent, 95 percent, and 99 percent confidence intervals for the mean, which are then reported, are based on use of the normal probability values. Finally, the 90 percent, 95 percent, and 99 percent confidence intervals for the total quantity in the population are reported when the population size is included in the input.

Required Input Deck

Card 1   Standard run card   (See your computer center for the card specifications.)

Card 2   Execute card   (See your computer center for the card specifications to call out the library program named STATB.)

Card 3   [b/ / / / / / /] . . .   Cols. 2-80 Label card—leave column 1 blank; enter user's name and program description in columns 2-80, which will be used as the label for the output.

Card 4   [/ / /]   Cols. 1-3 Sample size (right-justified).

[/ / / / / / / /]   Cols. 4-11 Size of population, if known (right-justified).

[/ / / / / / · / /]   Cols. 12-19 Population sigma, if known, with decimal point punched as indicated.

Card 5 and every card following

[/ / / / / / · / /]   Cols. 1-8   Value of variable, decimal punched as indicated.

[/ / / / / / · / /]   Cols. 9-16 Value of variable, decimal punched as indicated.

[/ / / / / / · / /]   Cols. 17-24 Value of variable, decimal punched as indicated.

[/ / / / / / · / /]   Cols. 25-32 Value of variable, decimal punched as indicated.

[/ / / / / / · / /]   Cols. 33-40 Value of variable, decimal punched as indicated.

[/ / / / / / · / /]   Cols. 41-48 Value of variable, decimal punched as indicated.

[/ / / / / / · / /]   Cols. 49-56 Value of variable, decimal punched as indicated.

[/ / / / / / · / /]   Cols. 57-64 Value of variable, decimal punched as indicated.

[/ / / / / / · / /]   Cols. 65-72 Value of variable, decimal punched as indicated.

[/ / / / / / · / /]   Cols. 73-80 Value of variable, decimal punched as indicated.

(Thus, each card contains a maximum of 10 values. If the total number of values is not a multiple of 10, the last card will include some unused fields. Check to make sure that the number of values entered corresponds with the number indicated in card 4.)

End-of-run card   (May or may not be required; see your computer center.)

This program will accept a sample of up to 300 measurements with a minimum sample size of at least 30 when the population standard deviation (sigma) is not known. Each measurement should have a value of at least −9,999.99 and be no larger than +9,999.99. Values entered without an arithmetic sign are assumed to be positive. In addition, the hypothesized value of the population mean is input along with an indication of whether the test is one-tailed or two-tailed. For one-tailed tests the user also indicates if the desired test is lower-tail or upper-tail. The initial output includes the sample mean, standard deviation, and standard error of the mean. The value of the standard error includes use of the finite correction factor when the population size is included in the input. The z-ratio is then computed and the hypothesized mean is tested at the 0.05 and 0.01 levels of significance based on use of the normal probability distribution.

Required Input Deck

Card 1 Standard run card   (See your computer center for the card specifications.)

Card 2 Execute card   (See your computer center for the card specifications to call out the library program named STATC.)

Card 3 ⟦b/ / / / / / ⟧ . . .   Cols. 2–80 Label card—leave column 1 blank; enter user's name and program description in columns 2–80, which will be used as the label for the output.

Card 4 ⟦/ / /⟧   Cols. 1–3 Sample size (right-justified).

⟦/ / / / / / / /⟧   Cols. 4–11 Size of population, if known (right-justified).

⟦/ / / / / / · / /⟧   Cols. 12–19 Population sigma, if known, with decimal point punched as indicated.

⟦/ / / / / / · / /⟧   Cols. 20–27 Hypothesized value of the population mean, with decimal point punched as indicated.

⟦/ /⟧   Col. 28 Punch "1" for one-tailed test or punch "2" for two-tailed test.

⟦/ /⟧   Col. 29 For a one-tailed test only, punch "1" for a lower-tail test ($\mu_H \geqslant A$), or punch "2" for an upper-tail test ($\mu_H \leqslant A$).

Card 5 and every card following

⟦/ / / / / / · / /⟧   Cols. 1–8 Value of variable, decimal punched as indicated.

⟦/ / / / / / · / /⟧   Cols. 9–16 Value of variable, decimal punched as indicated.

⟦/ / / / / / · / /⟧   Cols. 17–24 Value of variable, decimal punched as indicated.

⟦/ / / / / / · / /⟧   Cols. 25–32 Value of variable, decimal punched as indicated.

⟋⟋⟋⟋⟋⟋·⟋⟋⟋	Cols. 33–40 Value of variable, decimal punched as indicated.
⟋⟋⟋⟋⟋⟋·⟋⟋⟋	Cols. 41–48 Value of variable, decimal punched as indicated.
⟋⟋⟋⟋⟋⟋·⟋⟋⟋	Cols. 49–56 Value of variable, decimal punched as indicated.
⟋⟋⟋⟋⟋⟋·⟋⟋⟋	Cols. 57–64 Value of variable, decimal punched as indicated.
⟋⟋⟋⟋⟋⟋·⟋⟋⟋	Cols. 65–72 Value of variable, decimal punched as indicated.
⟋⟋⟋⟋⟋⟋·⟋⟋⟋	Cols. 73–80 Value of variable, decimal punched as indicated.

(Thus, each card contains a maximum of 10 values. If the total number of values is not a multiple of 10, the last card will include some unused fields. Check to make sure that the number of values entered corresponds with the number indicated in card 4.)

End-of-run card   (May or may not be required; see your computer center.)

Stat D ■ Testing the Difference between Two Means

This program will accept two samples of up to 300 measurements in total, with each sample including at least 30 measurements when the population standard deviation (sigma) is not known. The samples need not be equal in size, and each measurement should have a value of at least $-9,999.99$ and be no larger than $+9,999.99$. Values entered without an arithmetic sign are assumed to be positive. The user also indicates whether the desired test is lower-tail or upper-tail. The initial output includes the mean, standard deviation, and standard error of the mean for each sample. The value of each standard error includes use of the finite correction factor when the size of the respective population is included in the input. The standard error of the difference between means is then reported, followed by the computed value of the z-ratio. Finally, the difference between means is tested at the 0.05 and 0.01 levels of significance based on use of the normal probability distribution.

Required Input Deck

Card 1 Standard run card   (See your computer center for the card specifications.)

Card 2 Execute card   (See your computer center for the card specifications to call out the library program named STATD.)

Card 3 ⟋b⟋⟋⟋⟋⟋⟋⟋⟋ . . .   Cols. 2–80 Label card—leave column 1 blank; enter user's name and program description in columns 2–80, which will be used as the label for the output.

Card 4 ⟍⟍⟍⟍ Cols. 1–3 Size of sample 1 (right-justified).

⟍⟍⟍⟍ Cols. 4–6 Size of sample 2 (right-justified).

⟍⟍⟍⟍⟍⟍⟍⟍⟍ Cols. 7–14 Size of population 1, if known (right-justified).

⟍⟍⟍⟍⟍⟍⟍⟍⟍ Cols. 15–22 Size of population 2, if known (right-justified).

⟍⟍⟍⟍⟍⟍·⟍⟍⟍ Cols. 23–30 Population 1 sigma, if known, with decimal point punched as indicated.

⟍⟍⟍⟍⟍⟍·⟍⟍⟍ Cols. 31–38 Population 2 sigma, if known, with decimal point punched as indicated.

⟍⟍ Col. 39 Punch "1" for one-tailed test, or punch "2" for two-tailed test.

⟍⟍ Col. 40 For a one-tailed test only, punch "1" for a lower-tail test $[(\mu_1 - \mu_2)_H \geq 0]$, or punch "2" for an upper-tail test $[(\mu_1 - \mu_2)_H \leq 0]$.

Card 5 and every card following

⟍⟍⟍⟍⟍⟍·⟍⟍⟍ Cols. 1–8 Value of variable, decimal punched as indicated.

⟍⟍⟍⟍⟍⟍·⟍⟍⟍ Cols. 9–16 Value of variable, decimal punched as indicated.

⟍⟍⟍⟍⟍⟍·⟍⟍⟍ Cols. 17–24 Value of variable, decimal punched as indicated.

⟍⟍⟍⟍⟍⟍·⟍⟍⟍ Cols. 25–32 Value of variable, decimal punched as indicated.

⟍⟍⟍⟍⟍⟍·⟍⟍⟍ Cols. 33–40 Value of variable, decimal punched as indicated.

⟍⟍⟍⟍⟍⟍·⟍⟍⟍ Cols. 41–48 Value of variable, decimal punched as indicated.

⟍⟍⟍⟍⟍⟍·⟍⟍⟍ Cols. 49–56 Value of variable, decimal punched as indicated.

⟍⟍⟍⟍⟍⟍·⟍⟍⟍ Cols. 57–64 Value of variable, decimal punched as indicated.

⟍⟍⟍⟍⟍⟍·⟍⟍⟍ Cols. 65–72 Value of variable, decimal punched as indicated.

⟍⟍⟍⟍⟍⟍·⟍⟍⟍ Cols. 73–80 Value of variable, decimal punched as indicated.

(First punch all the values observed in the first sample, followed by the values in the second sample. Further, begin the second sample on a new data card when the sample no. 1 data are completed.)

End-of-run card   (May or may not be required; see your computer center.)

Stat E ■ Chi-square Analysis   The input for this program can be a single row of observed frequencies for up to 10 categories of observations or a contingency table (matrix) of observed frequencies. The maximum matrix size is 10 x 10, and each observed frequency should be no larger than 9,999. The user has the option of entering the expected frequencies or allowing the computer to calculate these on the basis of proportional allocation. The maximum expected frequency for any one cell is 9,999. No observed or expected frequency can be negative. The program computes and reports the degrees of freedom (df) and the value of χ^2 (chi-square) and indicates whether or not the value is significant at the 0.05 and 0.01 levels. If Yates' correction was used (when df = 1), this is also reported in the output.

Required Input Deck

Card 1	Standard run card	(See your computer center for the card specifications.)
Card 2	Execute card	(See your computer center for the card specifications to call out the library program named STATE.)
Card 3	⫾b̶/‾/‾/‾/‾/‾/‾/‾/ . . .	Cols. 2-80 Label card—leave column 1 blank; enter user's name and program description in columns 2-80, which will be used as the label for the output.
Card 4	/‾/‾/‾/	Cols. 1-3 Number of rows of observed frequencies (right-justified—this value should be "bbl" for a goodness-of-fit test).
	/‾/‾/‾/	Cols. 4-6 Number of columns of observed frequencies (right-justified).
	/‾/	Col. 7 Punch "1" if expected frequencies are to be input and leave blank if they are to be calculated. This should always be left blank for contingency-table tests.

Card 5 and every card following

Each card is one row of the matrix of observed frequencies. The number of values in each card should correspond to the value in columns 4-6 of card 4. The number of cards should correspond to the value in columns 1-3 of card 4. Punch decimal as indicated below.

/‾/‾/‾/‾/‾/‾·/‾/‾/	Cols. 1-8 Col. 1 of observed matrix
/‾/‾/‾/‾/‾/‾·/‾/‾/	Cols. 9-16 Col. 2 of observed matrix
/‾/‾/‾/‾/‾/‾·/‾/‾/	Cols. 17-24 Col. 3 of observed matrix
/‾/‾/‾/‾/‾/‾·/‾/‾/	Cols. 25-32 Col. 4 of observed matrix
/‾/‾/‾/‾/‾/‾·/‾/‾/	Cols. 33-40 Col. 5 of observed matrix
/‾/‾/‾/‾/‾/‾·/‾/‾/	Cols. 41-48 Col. 6 of observed matrix

⟋⟋⟋⟋⟋⟋·⟋⟋⟋	Cols. 49–56 Col. 7 of observed matrix
⟋⟋⟋⟋⟋⟋·⟋⟋⟋	Cols. 57–64 Col. 8 of observed matrix
⟋⟋⟋⟋⟋⟋·⟋⟋⟋	Cols. 65–72 Col. 9 of observed matrix
⟋⟋⟋⟋⟋⟋·⟋⟋⟋	Cols. 73–80 Col. 10 of observed matrix

If *expected* frequencies are to be input, follow the same card format as for the observed frequencies and place these cards *after* the cards for the observed data. The expected frequencies can be fractional values as well as whole numbers.

End-of-run card   (May or may not be required; see your computer center.)

Stat F ■ Decision Making under Conditions of Uncertainty

This program will accept a matrix of conditional monetary values, each value being the monetary consequence associated with a particular strategy and a particular state of nature. The maximum matrix size is 10 x 10, with each conditional value being at least −99,999. and no larger than +99,999. Values entered without an arithmetic sign are assumed to be positive.

The output includes the following information:

1. The table of conditional values which was entered as the input.
2. Identification of the minimum possible outcome associated with each strategy and identification of the strategy whose minimum has the highest value. This is the best strategy from the standpoint of the "maximin" criterion.
3. Identification of the maximum possible outcome associated with each strategy and identification of the strategy whose maximum has the highest value. This is the best strategy from the standpoint of the "maximax" criterion.
4. The table of opportunity losses, or regrets, for the input table of conditional values. The maximum possible opportunity loss for each strategy is reported, and the strategy whose maximum loss has the lowest value is identified. This is the best strategy from the standpoint of the "minimax regret" criterion.
5. If the probability associated with each of the states of nature was input, the program next reports the expected monetary value (EMV) associated with each strategy and identifies the strategy whose EMV is highest. This is the best strategy from the standpoint of maximizing expected value.
6. If the probabilities are not included in the input, expected values are computed by assigning equal probabilities to each of the states of nature, and the strategy with the

highest expected value is identified. This is the best strategy from the standpoint of the "equally likely" criterion.

Required Input Deck

Card 1 Standard run card (See your computer center for the card specifications.)

Card 2 Execute card (See your computer center for the card specifications to call out the library program named STATF.)

Card 3 $\boxed{\text{/b/}\ /\ /\ /\ /\ /\ /\ /}$ . . . Cols. 2–80 Label card—leave column 1 blank; enter user's name and program description in columns 2–80, which will be used as the label for the output.

Card 4 $\boxed{/\ /}$ Cols. 1–2 Number of strategies (right-justified—the maximum number is 10).

$\boxed{/\ /}$ Cols. 3–4 Number of states (right-justified—the maximum number is 10).

$\boxed{/}$ Col. 5 Punch a "1" if probability values for each state are to be input. Otherwise, leave blank.

Card 5 and every card for the conditional values

Each card indicates all the conditional values associated with a particular strategy, and is thus one row of the matrix of conditional values. The number of values in each card should correspond to the value in Cols. 3–4 of card 4. The number of cards should correspond to the value in Cols. 1–2 of card 4.

$\boxed{/\ /\ /\ /\ /\ /\ /\ /\ /\ /}$ Cols. 1–10 Strategy name (any name designated by the user).

$\boxed{/\ /\ /\ /\ /\ /\ /\cdot/}$ Cols. 11–17 Value for State 1, decimal punched as indicated.

$\boxed{/\ /\ /\ /\ /\ /\ /\cdot/}$ Cols. 18–24 Value for State 2, decimal punched as indicated.

$\boxed{/\ /\ /\ /\ /\ /\ /\cdot/}$ Cols. 25–31 Value for State 3, decimal punched as indicated.

$\boxed{/\ /\ /\ /\ /\ /\ /\cdot/}$ Cols. 32–38 Value for State 4, decimal punched as indicated.

$\boxed{/\ /\ /\ /\ /\ /\ /\cdot/}$ Cols. 39–45 Value for State 5, decimal punched as indicated.

$\boxed{/\ /\ /\ /\ /\ /\ /\cdot/}$ Cols. 46–52 Value for State 6, decimal punched as indicated.

$\boxed{/\ /\ /\ /\ /\ /\ /\cdot/}$ Cols. 53–59 Value for State 7, decimal punched as indicated.

$\boxed{/\ /\ /\ /\ /\ /\ /\cdot/}$ Cols. 60–66 Value for State 8, decimal punched as indicated.

$\boxed{/\ /\ /\ /\ /\ /\ /\cdot/}$ Cols. 67–73 Value for State 9, decimal punched as indicated.

$\boxed{/\ /\ /\ /\ /\ /\ /\cdot/}$ Cols. 74–80 Value for State 10, decimal punched as indicated.

If probabilities are to be input, they are punched in one card and this card is placed after the cards containing the conditional values for the matrix. The following format is followed, with decimal points punched as indicated. The probability values are entered in sequential order, beginning with State 1.

1-6	7-12	13-18	19-24

25-30	31-36	37-42	43-48

49-54	55-60

End-of-run card   (May or may not be required; see your computer center.)

Stat G ▪ Linear Regression and Correlation Analysis

This program will accept up to 150 pairs of numbers, each having a minimum value of at least −9,999.99 and a maximum value no greater than +9,999.99. Values entered without an arithmetic sign are assumed to be positive. Each pair of values includes an independent variable called "X" and a dependent variable called "Y." A minimum of three pairs of values must be input.

The output includes the following information:

1. The mean and standard deviation for the independent (X) variable.
2. The mean and standard deviation for the dependent (Y) variable.
3. The values of "A" and "B" for the regression equation "$Y(c) = A + BX$," where "X" is the known value of the independent variable and "$Y(c)$" is the estimated value of the corresponding dependent variable.
4. The standard error of estimate associated with $Y(c)$.
5. The value of the Pearson coefficient of correlation and an indication as to whether the computed value is significantly different from "O" at the 0.05 and the 0.01 levels of significance.
6. The value of the coefficient of determination, which indicates the proportion of variance in the dependent variable which is "explained," or accounted for, by knowledge of the independent variable.
7. A scatter diagram for the input data, with the "X" values plotted in respect to the horizontal axis and the "Y" values plotted in respect to the vertical axis. The two end-points of the least-squares regression line are repre-

sented by "+" symbols, and the user connects these points with a straight line in order to form the regression line.

Required Input Deck

Card 1   Standard run card   (See your computer center for the card specifications.)

Card 2   Execute card   (See your computer center for the card specifications to call out the library program named STATG.)

Card 3   /b/ / / / / / /. . .   Cols. 2-80 Label card—leave column 1 blank; enter user's name and program description in columns 2-80, which will be used as the label for the output.

Card 4   / / / /   Cols. 1-3 Number of pairs of values (right-justified).

Card 5 and every card following

Independent variable	Dependent variable
"X"	"Y"
Cols. 1-8	Cols. 9-16
/ / / / / · / / /	/ / / / / · / / /

(Punch decimal points as indicated.)

End-of-run card   (May or may not be required; see your computer center.)

Stat H ■ Seasonal Analysis and Adjustment

Required inputs for this program are monthly or quarterly data for a period of at least four years. If the first input value is for the first period of the year (either "January" for monthly data or "First Quarter" for quarterly data), a maximum of eight years of data can be input. If the first input value begins within a year, then less than eight full years of data can be input as a maximum. Each input value can have a maximum value of 99,999.99. Typically, only positive values are involved in seasonal analysis, but the program will accept negative values. Values entered without an arithmetic sign are assumed to be positive. The initital output of the program is a table listing the input values. If less than eight full years of data are input, the table will include one or more values designated "0.00." These are filler values only, and are *not* included in any of the calculations. A second table of output reports the values of the percents of a 12-month centered moving average and includes the seasonal index for each period (month or quarter) in the last column of the table. The value of each index is the modified mean for each row, after the lowest and highest values in that row have been eliminated, and is arithmetically adjusted so that the sum of all index numbers is 1,200.0 (for monthly data) or 400.0 (for quarterly data). The last table of output reports the seasonally adjusted input data.

Required Input Deck

Card 1   Standard run card   (See your computer center for the card specifications.)

Card 2   Execute card   (See your computer center for the card specifications to call out the library program named STATH.)

Card 3   ⟋b⟍⟋⟋⟋⟋⟋⟋⟍ . . .   Cols. 2-80 Label card—leave column 1 blank; enter user's name and program description in columns 2-80, which will be used as the label for the output.

Card 4   ⟋⟋⟋⟋⟍   Cols. 1-4 Initial year of time series (e.g., "1965").

         ⟋⟍   Col. 5 Punch "0" for monthly data or punch "1" for quarterly data.

         ⟋⟋⟍   Col. 6-7 Beginning period of initial year. For example, if the first month reported is January, punch "01," if June, punch "06." If the first input of quarterly data is for the third quarter of the initial year, punch "03."

         ⟋⟋⟍   Cols. 8-9 Total number of data periods, which is the total number of months or quarters of input data.

Card 5 and every card following

         ⟋⟋⟋⟋⟋⟋·⟋⟋⟍   Cols. 1-8   Input value, decimal punched as indicated.
         ⟋⟋⟋⟋⟋⟋·⟋⟋⟍   Cols. 9-16 Input value, decimal punched as indicated.
         ⟋⟋⟋⟋⟋⟋·⟋⟋⟍   Cols. 17-24 Input value, decimal punched as indicated.
         ⟋⟋⟋⟋⟋⟋·⟋⟋⟍   Cols. 25-32 Input value, decimal punched as indicated.
         ⟋⟋⟋⟋⟋⟋·⟋⟋⟍   Cols. 33-40 Input value, decimal punched as indicated.
         ⟋⟋⟋⟋⟋⟋·⟋⟋⟍   Cols. 41-48 Input value, decimal punched as indicated.
         ⟋⟋⟋⟋⟋⟋·⟋⟋⟍   Cols. 49-56 Input value, decimal punched as indicated.
         ⟋⟋⟋⟋⟋⟋·⟋⟋⟍   Cols. 57-64 Input value, decimal punched as indicated.
         ⟋⟋⟋⟋⟋⟋·⟋⟋⟍   Cols. 65-72 Input value, decimal punched as indicated.
         ⟋⟋⟋⟋⟋⟋·⟋⟋⟍   Cols. 73-80 Input value, decimal punched as indicated.

         (Thus, each card contains a maximum of 10 values. If the total number of values is not a multiple of 10, the last card will include some unused fields. Check to make sure that the number of values entered corresponds with the number of data periods indicated in columns 8-9 of card 4.)

End-of-run card   (May or may not be required; see your computer center.)

APPENDIX B ■
TABLES

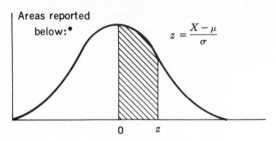

Areas reported
below:*

$$z = \frac{X - \mu}{\sigma}$$

z	.00	.01	.02	.03	.04	.05	.06	.07	.08	.09
0.0	.0000	.0040	.0080	.0120	.0160	.0199	.0239	.0279	.0319	.0359
0.1	.0398	.0438	.0478	.0517	.0557	.0596	.0636	.0675	.0714	.0753
0.2	.0793	.0832	.0871	.0910	.0948	.0987	.1026	.1064	.1103	.1141
0.3	.1179	.1217	.1255	.1293	.1331	.1368	.1406	.1443	.1480	.1517
0.4	.1554	.1591	.1628	.1664	.1700	.1736	.1772	.1808	.1844	.1879
0.5	.1915	.1950	.1985	.2019	.2054	.2088	.2123	.2157	.2190	.2224
0.6	.2257	.2291	.2324	.2357	.2389	.2422	.2454	.2486	.2518	.2549
0.7	.2580	.2612	.2642	.2673	.2704	.2734	.2764	.2794	.2823	.2852
0.8	.2881	.2910	.2939	.2967	.2995	.3023	.3051	.3078	.3106	.3133
0.9	.3159	.3186	.3212	.3238	.3264	.3289	.3315	.3340	.3365	.3389
1.0	.3413	.3438	.3461	.3485	.3508	.3531	.3554	.3577	.3599	.3621
1.1	.3643	.3665	.3686	.3708	.3729	.3749	.3770	.3790	.3810	.3830
1.2	.3849	.3869	.3888	.3907	.3925	.3944	.3962	.3980	.3997	.4014
1.3	.4032	.4049	.4066	.4082	.4099	.4115	.4131	.4147	.4162	.4177
1.4	.4192	.4207	.4222	.4236	.4251	.4265	.4279	.4292	.4306	.4319
1.5	.4332	.4345	.4357	.4370	.4382	.4394	.4406	.4418	.4429	.4441
1.6	.4452	.4463	.4474	.4484	.4495	.4505	.4515	.4525	.4535	.4545
1.7	.4554	.4564	.4573	.4582	.4591	.4599	.4608	.4616	.4625	.4633
1.8	.4641	.4649	.4656	.4664	.4671	.4678	.4686	.4693	.4699	.4706
1.9	.4713	.4719	.4726	.4732	.4738	.4744	.4750	.4756	.4761	.4767
2.0	.4772	.4778	.4783	.4788	.4793	.4798	.4803	.4808	.4812	.4817
2.1	.4821	.4826	.4830	.4834	.4838	.4842	.4846	.4850	.4854	.4857
2.2	.4861	.4864	.4868	.4871	.4875	.4878	.4881	.4884	.4887	.4890
2.3	.4893	.4896	.4898	.4901	.4904	.4906	.4909	.4911	.4913	.4916
2.4	.4918	.4920	.4922	.4925	.4927	.4929	.4931	.4932	.4934	.4936
2.5	.4938	.4940	.4941	.4943	.4945	.4946	.4948	.4949	.4951	.4952
2.6	.4953	.4955	.4956	.4957	.4959	.4960	.4961	.4962	.4963	.4964
2.7	.4965	.4966	.4967	.4968	.4969	.4970	.4971	.4972	.4973	.4974
2.8	.4974	.4975	.4976	.4977	.4977	.4978	.4979	.4979	.4980	.4981
2.9	.4981	.4982	.4983	.4983	.4984	.4984	.4985	.4985	.4986	.4986
3.0	.4987									
3.5	.4997									
4.0	.4999									

*Example: For z = 1.96, shaded area is 0.4750 out of the total area of 1.0000.

Table B-2 ■ **Coefficients of the Binomial Distribution**

For the Expansion of $(q + p)^{n}$*

Coefficient of the terms in which the exponent of p is:

n	0	1	2	3	4	5	6	7	8	9	10
1	1	1									
2	1	2	1								
3	1	3	3	1							
4	1	4	6	4	1						
5	1	5	10	10	5	1					
6	1	6	15	20	15	6	1				
7	1	7	21	35	35	21	7	1			
8	1	8	28	56	70	56	28	8	1		
9	1	9	36	84	126	126	84	36	9	1	
10	1	10	45	120	210	252	210	120	45	10	1

*Example: $(q + p)^{4} = q^{4} + 4q^{3}p + 6q^{2}p^{2} + 4qp^{3} + p^{4}$

Table B-3 ■ **Binomial Probabilities***

n	x	.01	.05	.10	.15	.20	.25	*p* .30	.35	.40	.45	.50
1	0	.9900	.9500	.9000	.8500	.8000	.7500	.7000	.6500	.6000	.5500	.5000
	1	.0100	.0500	.1000	.1500	.2000	.2500	.3000	.3500	.4000	.4500	.5000
2	0	.9801	.9025	.8100	.7225	.6400	.5625	.4900	.4225	.3600	.3025	.2500
	1	.0198	.0950	.1800	.2550	.3200	.3750	.4200	.4550	.4800	.4950	.5000
	2	.0001	.0025	.0100	.0225	.0400	.0625	.0900	.1225	.1600	.2025	.2500
3	0	.9703	.8574	.7290	.6141	.5120	.4219	.3430	.2746	.2160	.1664	.1250
	1	.0294	.1354	.2430	.3251	.3840	.4219	.4410	.4436	.4320	.4084	.3750
	2	.0003	.0071	.0270	.0574	.0960	.1406	.1890	.2389	.2880	.3341	.3750
	3	.0000	.0001	.0010	.0034	.0080	.0156	.0270	.0429	.0640	.0911	.1250
4	0	.9606	.8145	.6561	.5220	.4096	.3164	.2401	.1785	.1296	.0915	.0625
	1	.0388	.1715	.2916	.3685	.4096	.4219	.4116	.3845	.3456	.2995	.2500
	2	.0006	.0135	.0486	.0975	.1536	.2109	.2646	.3105	.3456	.3675	.3750
	3	.0000	.0005	.0036	.0115	.0256	.0469	.0756	.1115	.1536	.2005	.2500
	4	.0000	.0000	.0001	.0005	.0016	.0039	.0081	.0150	.0256	.0410	.0625
5	0	.9510	.7738	.5905	.4437	.3277	.2373	.1681	.1160	.0778	.0503	.0312
	1	.0480	.2036	.3280	.3915	.4096	.3955	.3602	.3124	.2592	.2059	.1562
	2	.0010	.0214	.0729	.1382	.2048	.2637	.3087	.3364	.3456	.3369	.3125
	3	.0000	.0011	.0081	.0244	.0512	.0879	.1323	.1811	.2304	.2757	.3125
	4	.0000	.0000	.0004	.0022	.0064	.0146	.0284	.0488	.0768	.1128	.1562
	5	.0000	.0000	.0000	.0001	.0003	.0010	.0024	.0053	.0102	.0185	.0312
6	0	.9415	.7351	.5314	.3771	.2621	.1780	.1176	.0754	.0467	.0277	.0156
	1	.0571	.2321	.3543	.3993	.3932	.3560	.3025	.2437	.1866	.1359	.0938
	2	.0014	.0305	.0984	.1762	.2458	.2966	.3241	.3280	.3110	.2780	.2344
	3	.0000	.0021	.0146	.0415	.0819	.1318	.1852	.2355	.2765	.3032	.3125
	4	.0000	.0001	.0012	.0055	.0154	.0330	.0595	.0951	.1382	.1861	.2344
	5	.0000	.0000	.0001	.0004	.0015	.0044	.0102	.0205	.0369	.0609	.0938
	6	.0000	.0000	.0000	.0000	.0001	.0002	.0007	.0018	.0041	.0083	.0156
7	0	.9321	.6983	.4783	.3206	.2097	.1335	.0824	.0490	.0280	.0152	.0078
	1	.0659	.2573	.3720	.3960	.3670	.3115	.2471	.1848	.1306	.0872	.0547
	2	.0020	.0406	.1240	.2097	.2753	.3115	.3177	.2985	.2613	.2140	.1641
	3	.0000	.0036	.0230	.0617	.1147	.1730	.2269	.2679	.2903	.2918	.2734
	4	.0000	.0002	.0026	.0109	.0287	.0577	.0972	.1442	.1935	.2388	.2734
	5	.0000	.0000	.0002	.0012	.0043	.0115	.0250	.0466	.0774	.1172	.1641
	6	.0000	.0000	.0000	.0001	.0004	.0013	.0036	.0084	.0172	.0320	.0547
	7	.0000	.0000	.0000	.0000	.0000	.0001	.0002	.0006	.0016	.0037	.0078
8	0	.9227	.6634	.4305	.2725	.1678	.1002	.0576	.0319	.0168	.0084	.0039
	1	.0746	.2793	.3826	.3847	.3355	.2670	.1977	.1373	.0896	.0548	.0312
	2	.0026	.0515	.1488	.2376	.2936	.3115	.2965	.2587	.2090	.1569	.1094
	3	.0001	.0054	.0331	.0839	.1468	.2076	.2541	.2786	.2787	.2568	.2188
	4	.0000	.0004	.0046	.0185	.0459	.0865	.1361	.1875	.2322	.2627	.2734

*Example: $P(X = 3 \mid n = 5, p = 0.30) = 0.1323$

n	x	.01	.05	.10	.15	.20	.25	p .30	.35	.40	.45	.50
8	5	.0000	.0000	.0004	.0026	.0092	.0231	.0467	.0808	.1239	.1719	.2188
	6	.0000	.0000	.0000	.0002	.0011	.0038	.0100	.0217	.0413	.0403	.1094
	7	.0000	.0000	.0000	.0000	.0001	.0004	.0012	.0033	.0079	.0164	.0312
	8	.0000	.0000	.0000	.0000	.0000	.0000	.0001	.0002	.0007	.0017	.0039
9	0	.9135	.6302	.3874	.2316	.1342	.0751	.0404	.0207	.0101	.0046	.0020
	1	.0830	.2985	.3874	.3679	.3020	.2253	.1556	.1004	.0605	.0339	.0176
	2	.0034	.0629	.1722	.2597	.3020	.3003	.2668	.2162	.1612	.1110	.0703
	3	.0001	.0077	.0446	.1069	.1762	.2336	.2668	.2716	.2508	.2119	.1641
	4	.0000	.0006	.0074	.0283	.0661	.1168	.1715	.2194	.2508	.2600	.2461
	5	.0000	.0000	.0008	.0050	.0165	.0389	.0735	.1181	.1672	.2128	.2461
	6	.0000	.0000	.0001	.0006	.0028	.0087	.0210	.0424	.0743	.1160	.1641
	7	.0000	.0000	.0000	.0000	.0003	.0012	.0039	.0098	.0212	.0407	.0703
	8	.0000	.0000	.0000	.0000	.0000	.0001	.0004	.0013	.0035	.0083	.0176
	9	.0000	.0000	.0000	.0000	.0000	.0000	.0000	.0001	.0003	.0008	.0020
10	0	.9044	.5987	.3487	.1969	.1074	.0563	.0282	.0135	.0060	.0025	.0010
	1	.0914	.3151	.3874	.3474	.2684	.1877	.1211	.0725	.0403	.0207	.0098
	2	.0042	.0746	.1937	.2759	.3020	.2816	.2335	.1757	.1209	.0763	.0439
	3	.0001	.0105	.0574	.1298	.2013	.2503	.2668	.2522	.2150	.1665	.1172
	4	.0000	.0010	.0112	.0401	.0881	.1460	.2001	.2377	.2508	.2384	.2051
	5	.0000	.0001	.0015	.0085	.0264	.0584	.1029	.1536	.2007	.2340	.2461
	6	.0000	.0000	.0001	.0012	.0055	.0162	.0368	.0689	.1115	.1596	.2051
	7	.0000	.0000	.0000	.0001	.0008	.0031	.0090	.0212	.0425	.0746	.1172
	8	.0000	.0000	.0000	.0000	.0001	.0004	.0014	.0043	.0106	.0229	.0439
	9	.0000	.0000	.0000	.0000	.0000	.0000	.0001	.0005	.0016	.0042	.0098
	10	.0000	.0000	.0000	.0000	.0000	.0000	.0000	.0000	.0001	.0003	.0010
11	0	.8953	.5688	.3138	.1673	.0859	.0422	.0198	.0088	.0036	.0014	.0005
	1	.0995	.3293	.3835	.3248	.2362	.1549	.0932	.0518	.0266	.0125	.0054
	2	.0050	.0867	.2131	.2866	.2953	.2581	.1998	.1395	.0887	.0513	.0269
	3	.0002	.0137	.0710	.1517	.2215	.2581	.2568	.2254	.1774	.1259	.0806
	4	.0000	.0014	.0158	.0536	.1107	.1721	.2201	.2428	.2365	.2060	.1611
	5	.0000	.0001	.0025	.0132	.0388	.0803	.1321	.1830	.2207	.2360	.2256
	6	.0000	.0000	.0003	.0023	.0097	.0268	.0566	.0985	.1471	.1931	.2256
	7	.0000	.0000	.0000	.0003	.0017	.0064	.0173	.0379	.0701	.1128	.1611
	8	.0000	.0000	.0000	.0000	.0002	.0011	.0037	.0102	.0234	.0462	.0806
	9	.0000	.0000	.0000	.0000	.0000	.0001	.0005	.0018	.0052	.0126	.0269
	10	.0000	.0000	.0000	.0000	.0000	.0000	.0000	.0002	.0007	.0021	.0054
	11	.0000	.0000	.0000	.0000	.0000	.0000	.0000	.0000	.0000	.0002	.0005
12	0	.8864	.5404	.2824	.1422	.0687	.0317	.0138	.0057	.0022	.0008	.0002
	1	.1074	.3413	.3766	.3012	.2062	.1267	.0712	.0368	.0174	.0075	.0029
	2	.0060	.0988	.2301	.2924	.2835	.2323	.1678	.1088	.0639	.0339	.0161
	3	.0002	.0173	.0852	.1720	.2362	.2581	.2397	.1954	.1419	.0923	.0537
	4	0000	.0021	.0213	.0683	.1329	.1936	.2311	.2367	.2128	.1700	.1208
	5	.0000	.0002	.0038	.0193	.0532	.1032	.1585	.2039	.2270	.2225	.1934
	6	.0000	.0000	.0005	.0040	.0155	.0401	.0792	.1281	.1766	.2124	.2256

Table B-3 ▪ Binomial Probabilities (*Continued*)

n	x	.01	.05	.10	.15	.20	.25	.30	.35	.40	.45	.50
12	7	.0000	.0000	.0000	.0006	.0033	.0115	.0291	.0591	.1009	.1489	.1934
	8	.0000	.0000	.0000	.0001	.0005	.0024	.0078	.0199	.0420	.0762	.1208
	9	.0000	.0000	.0000	.0000	.0001	.0004	.0015	.0048	.0125	.0277	.0537
	10	.0000	.0000	.0000	.0000	.0000	.0000	.0002	.0008	.0025	.0068	.0161
	11	.0000	.0000	.0000	.0000	.0000	.0000	.0000	.0001	.0003	.0010	.0029
	12	.0000	.0000	.0000	.0000	.0000	.0000	.0000	.0000	.0000	.0001	.0002
13	0	.8775	.5133	.2542	.1209	.0550	.0238	.0097	.0037	.0013	.0004	.0001
	1	.1152	.3512	.3672	.2774	.1787	.1029	.0540	.0259	.0113	.0045	.0016
	2	.0070	.1109	.2448	.2937	.2680	.2059	.1388	.0836	.0453	.0220	.0095
	3	.0003	.0214	.0997	.1900	.2457	.2517	.2181	.1651	.1107	.0660	.0349
	4	.0000	.0028	.0277	.0838	.1535	.2097	.2337	.2222	.1845	.1350	.0873
	5	.0000	.0003	.0055	.0266	.0691	.1258	.1803	.2154	.2214	.1989	.1571
	6	.0000	.0000	.0008	.0063	.0230	.0559	.1030	.1546	.1968	.2169	.2095
	7	.0000	.0000	.0001	.0011	.0058	.0186	.0442	.0833	.1312	.1775	.2095
	8	.0000	.0000	.0001	.0001	.0011	.0047	.0142	.0336	.0656	.1089	.1571
	9	.0000	.0000	.0000	.0000	.0001	.0009	.0034	.0101	.0243	.0495	.0873
	10	.0000	.0000	.0000	.0000	.0000	.0001	.0006	.0022	.0065	.0162	.0349
	11	.0000	.0000	.0000	.0000	.0000	.0000	.0001	.0003	.0012	.0036	.0095
	12	.0000	.0000	.0000	.0000	.0000	.0000	.0000	.0000	.0001	.0005	.0016
	13	.0000	.0000	.0000	.0000	.0000	.0000	.0000	.0000	.0000	.0000	.0001
14	0	.8687	.4877	.2288	.1028	.0440	.0178	.0068	.0024	.0008	.0002	.0001
	1	.1229	.3593	.3559	.2539	.1539	.0832	.0407	.0181	.0073	.0027	.0009
	2	.0081	.1229	.2570	.2912	.2501	.1802	.1134	.0634	.0317	.0141	.0056
	3	.0003	.0259	.1142	.2056	.2501	.2402	.1943	.1366	.0845	.0462	.0222
	4	.0000	.0037	.0349	.0998	.1720	.2202	.2290	.2022	.1549	.1040	.0611
	5	.0000	.0004	.0078	.0352	.0860	.1468	.1963	.2178	.2066	.1701	.1222
	6	.0000	.0000	.0013	.0093	.0322	.0734	.1262	.1759	.2066	.2088	.1833
	7	.0000	.0000	.0002	.0019	.0092	.0280	.0618	.1082	.1574	.1952	.2095
	8	.0000	.0000	.0000	.0003	.0020	.0082	.0232	.0510	.0918	.1398	.1833
	9	.0000	.0000	.0000	.0000	.0003	.0018	.0066	.0183	.0408	.0762	.1222
	10	.0000	.0000	.0000	.0000	.0000	.0003	.0014	.0049	.0136	.0312	.0611
	11	.0000	.0000	.0000	.0000	.0000	.0000	.0002	.0010	.0033	.0093	.0222
	12	.0000	.0000	.0000	.0000	.0000	.0000	.0000	.0001	.0005	.0019	.0056
	13	.0000	.0000	.0000	.0000	.0000	.0000	.0000	.0000	.0001	.0002	.0009
	14	.0000	.0000	.0000	.0000	.0000	.0000	.0000	.0000	.0000	.0000	.0001
15	0	.8601	.4633	.2059	.0874	.0352	.0134	.0047	.0016	.0005	.0001	.0000
	1	.1303	.3658	.3432	.2312	.1319	.0668	.0305	.0126	.0047	.0016	.0005
	2	.0092	.1348	.2669	.2856	.2309	.1559	.0916	.0476	.0219	.0090	.0032
	3	.0004	.0307	.1285	.2184	.2501	.2252	.1700	.1110	.0634	.0318	.0139
	4	.0000	.0049	.0428	.1156	.1876	.2252	.2186	.1792	.1268	.0780	.0417

n	x	.01	.05	.10	.15	.20	.25	.30	.35	.40	.45	.50
15	5	.0000	.0006	.0105	.0449	.1032	.1651	.2061	.2123	.1859	.1404	.0916
	6	.0000	.0000	.0019	.0132	.0430	.0917	.1472	.1906	.2066	.1914	.1527
	7	.0000	.0000	.0003	.0030	.0138	.0393	.0811	.1319	.1771	.2013	.1964
	8	.0000	.0000	.0000	.0005	.0035	.0131	.0348	.0710	.1181	.1647	.1964
	9	.0000	.0000	.0000	.0001	.0007	.0034	.0116	.0298	.0612	.1048	.1527
	10	.0000	.0000	.0000	.0000	.0001	.0007	.0030	.0096	.0245	.0515	.0916
	11	.0000	.0000	.0000	.0000	.0000	.0001	.0006	.0024	.0074	.0191	.0417
	12	.0000	.0000	.0000	.0000	.0000	.0000	.0001	.0004	.0016	.0052	.0139
	13	.0000	.0000	.0000	.0000	.0000	.0000	.0000	.0001	.0003	.0010	.0032
	14	.0000	.0000	.0000	.0000	.0000	.0000	.0000	.0000	.0000	.0001	.0005
	15	.0000	.0000	.0000	.0000	.0000	.0000	.0000	.0000	.0000	.0000	.0000
16	0	.8515	.4401	.1853	.0743	.0281	.0100	.0033	.0010	.0003	.0001	.0000
	1	.1376	.3706	.3294	.2097	.1126	.0535	.0228	.0087	.0030	.0009	.0002
	2	.0104	.1463	.2745	.2775	.2111	.1336	.0732	.0353	.0150	.0056	.0018
	3	.0005	.0359	.1423	.2285	.2463	.2079	.1465	.0888	.0468	.0215	.0085
	4	.0000	.0061	.0514	.1311	.2001	.2252	.2040	.1553	.1014	.0572	.0278
	5	.0000	.0008	.0137	.0555	.1201	.1802	.2099	.2008	.1623	.1123	.0667
	6	.0000	.0001	.0028	.0180	.0550	.1101	.1649	.1982	.1983	.1684	.1222
	7	.0000	.0000	.0004	.0045	.0197	.0524	.1010	.1524	.1889	.1969	.1746
	8	.0000	.0000	.0001	.0009	.0055	.0197	.0487	.0923	.1417	.1812	.1964
	9	.0000	.0000	.0000	.0001	.0012	.0058	.0185	.0442	.0840	.1318	.1746
	10	.0000	.0000	.0000	.0000	.0002	.0014	.0056	.0167	.0392	.0755	.1222
	11	.0000	.0000	.0000	.0000	.0000	.0002	.0013	.0049	.0142	.0337	.0667
	12	.0000	.0000	.0000	.0000	.0000	.0000	.0002	.0011	.0040	.0115	.0278
	13	.0000	.0000	.0000	.0000	.0000	.0000	.0000	.0002	.0008	.0029	.0085
	14	.0000	.0000	.0000	.0000	.0000	.0000	.0000	.0000	.0001	.0005	.0018
	15	.0000	.0000	.0000	.0000	.0000	.0000	.0000	.0000	.0000	.0001	.0002
	16	.0000	.0000	.0000	.0000	.0000	.0000	.0000	.0000	.0000	.0000	.0000
17	0	.8429	.4181	.1668	.0631	.0225	.0075	.0023	.0007	.0002	.0000	.0000
	1	.1447	.3741	.3150	.1893	.0957	.0426	.0169	.0060	.0019	.0005	.0001
	2	.0117	.1575	.2800	.2673	.1914	.1136	.0581	.0260	.0102	.0035	.0010
	3	.0006	.0415	.1556	.2359	.2393	.1893	.1245	.0701	.0341	.0144	.0052
	4	.0000	.0076	.0605	.1457	.2093	.2209	.1868	.1320	.0796	.0411	.0182
	5	.0000	.0010	.0175	.0668	.1361	.1914	.2081	.1849	.1379	.0875	.0472
	6	.0000	.0001	.0039	.0236	.0680	.1276	.1784	.1991	.1839	.1432	.0944
	7	.0000	.0000	.0007	.0065	.0267	.0668	.1201	.1685	.1927	.1841	.1484
	8	.0000	.0000	.0001	.0014	.0084	.0279	.0644	.1134	.1606	.1883	.1855
	9	.0000	.0000	.0000	.0003	.0021	.0093	.0276	.0611	.1070	.1540	.1855
	10	.0000	.0000	.0000	.0000	.0004	.0025	.0095	.0263	.0571	.1008	.1484
	11	.0000	.0000	.0000	.0000	.0001	.0005	.0026	.0090	.0242	.0525	.0944
	12	.0000	.0000	.0000	.0000	.0000	.0001	.0006	.0024	.0081	.0215	.0472
	13	.0000	.0000	.0000	.0000	.0000	.0000	.0001	.0005	.0021	.0068	.0182
	14	.0000	.0000	.0000	.0000	.0000	.0000	.0000	.0001	.0004	.0016	.0052

n	x	.01	.05	.10	.15	.20	.25	p .30	.35	.40	.45	.50
17	15	.0000	.0000	.0000	.0000	.0000	.0000	.0000	.0000	.0001	.0003	.0010
	16	.0000	.0000	.0000	.0000	.0000	.0000	.0000	.0000	.0000	.0000	.0001
	17	.0000	.0000	.0000	.0000	.0000	.0000	.0000	.0000	.0000	.0000	.0000
18	0	.8345	.3972	.1501	.0536	.0180	.0056	.0016	.0004	.0001	.0000	.0000
	1	.1517	.3763	.3002	.1704	.0811	.0338	.0126	.0042	.0012	.0003	.0001
	2	.0130	.1683	.2835	.2556	.1723	.0958	.0458	.0190	.0069	.0022	.0006
	3	.0007	.0473	.1680	.2406	.2297	.1704	.1046	.0547	.0246	.0095	.0031
	4	.0000	.0093	.0700	.1592	.2153	.2130	.1681	.1104	.0614	.0291	.0117
	5	.0000	.0014	.0218	.0787	.1507	.1988	.2017	.1664	.1146	.0666	.0327
	6	.0000	.0002	.0052	.0301	.0816	.1436	.1873	.1941	.1655	.1181	.0708
	7	.0000	.0000	.0010	.0091	.0350	.0820	.1376	.1792	.1892	.1657	.1214
	8	.0000	.0000	.0002	.0022	.0120	.0376	.0811	.1327	.1734	.1864	.1669
	9	.0000	.0000	.0000	.0004	.0033	.0139	.0386	.0794	.1284	.1694	.1855
	10	.0000	.0000	.0000	.0001	.0008	.0042	.0149	.0385	.0771	.1248	.1669
	11	.0000	.0000	.0000	.0000	.0001	.0010	.0046	.0151	.0374	.0742	.1214
	12	.0000	.0000	.0000	.0000	.0000	.0002	.0012	.0047	.0145	.0354	.0708
	13	.0000	.0000	.0000	.0000	.0000	.0000	.0002	.0012	.0045	.0134	.0327
	14	.0000	.0000	.0000	.0000	.0000	.0000	.0000	.0002	.0011	.0039	.0117
	15	.0000	.0000	.0000	.0000	.0000	.0000	.0000	.0000	.0002	.0009	.0031
	16	.0000	.0000	.0000	.0000	.0000	.0000	.0000	.0000	.0000	.0001	.0006
	17	.0000	.0000	.0000	.0000	.0000	.0000	.0000	.0000	.0000	.0000	.0001
	18	.0000	.0000	.0000	.0000	.0000	.0000	.0000	.0000	.0000	.0000	.0000
19	0	.8262	.3774	.1351	.0456	.0144	.0042	.0011	.0003	.0001	.0000	.0000
	1	.1586	.3774	.2852	.1529	.0685	.0268	.0093	.0029	.0008	.0002	.0000
	2	.0144	.1787	.2852	.2428	.1540	.0803	.0358	.0138	.0046	.0013	.0003
	3	.0008	.0533	.1796	.2428	.2182	.1517	.0869	.0422	.0175	.0062	.0018
	4	.0000	.0112	.0798	.1714	.2182	.2023	.1491	.0909	.0467	.0203	.0074
	5	.0000	.0018	.0266	.0907	.1636	.2023	.1916	.1468	.0933	.0497	.0222
	6	.0000	.0002	.0069	.0374	.0955	.1574	.1916	.1844	.1451	.0949	.0518
	7	.0000	.0000	.0014	.0122	.0443	.0974	.1525	.1844	.1797	.1443	.0961
	8	.0000	.0000	.0002	.0032	.0166	.0487	.0981	.1489	.1797	.1771	.1442
	9	.0000	.0000	.0000	.0007	.0051	.0198	.0514	.0980	.1464	.1771	.1762
	10	.0000	.0000	.0000	.0001	.0013	.0066	.0220	.0528	.0976	.1449	.1762
	11	.0000	.0000	.0000	.0000	.0003	.0018	.0077	.0233	.0532	.0970	.1442
	12	.0000	.0000	.0000	.0000	.0000	.0004	.0022	.0083	.0237	.0529	.0961
	13	.0000	.0000	.0000	.0000	.0000	.0001	.0005	.0024	.0085	.0233	.0518
	14	.0000	.0000	.0000	.0000	.0000	.0000	.0001	.0006	.0024	.0082	.0222
	15	.0000	.0000	.0000	.0000	.0000	.0000	.0000	.0001	.0005	.0022	.0074
	16	.0000	.0000	.0000	.0000	.0000	.0000	.0000	.0000	.0001	.0005	.0018
	17	.0000	.0000	.0000	.0000	.0000	.0000	.0000	.0000	.0000	.0001	.0003

n	x	.01	.05	.10	.15	.20	.25	p .30	.35	.40	.45	.50
	18	.0000	.0000	.0000	.0000	.0000	.0000	.0000	.0000	.0000	.0000	.0000
	19	.0000	.0000	.0000	.0000	.0000	.0000	.0000	.0000	.0000	.0000	.0000
20	0	.8179	.3585	.1216	.0388	.0115	.0032	.0008	.0002	.0000	.0000	.0000
	1	.1652	.3774	.2702	.1368	.0576	.0211	.0068	.0020	.0005	.0001	.0000
	2	.0159	.1887	.2852	.2293	.1369	.0669	.0278	.0100	.0031	.0008	.0002
	3	.0010	.0596	.1901	.2428	.2054	.1339	.0716	.0323	.0123	.0040	.0011
	4	.0000	.0133	.0898	.1821	.2182	.1897	.1304	.0738	.0350	.0139	.0046
	5	.0000	.0022	.0319	.1028	.1746	.2023	.1789	.1272	.0746	.0365	.0148
	6	.0000	.0003	.0089	.0454	.1091	.1686	.1916	.1712	.1244	.0746	.0370
	7	.0000	.0000	.0020	.0160	.0545	.1124	.1643	.1844	.1659	.1221	.0739
	8	.0000	.0000	.0004	.0046	.0222	.0609	.1144	.1614	.1797	.1623	.1201
	9	.0000	.0000	.0001	.0011	.0074	.0271	.0654	.1158	.1597	.1771	.1602
	10	.0000	.0000	.0000	.0002	.0020	.0099	.0308	.0686	.1171	.1593	.1762
	11	.0000	.0000	.0000	.0000	.0005	.0030	.0120	.0336	.0710	.1185	.1602
	12	.0000	.0000	.0000	.0000	.0001	.0008	.0039	.0136	.0355	.0727	.1201
	13	.0000	.0000	.0000	.0000	.0000	.0002	.0010	.0045	.0146	.0366	.0739
	14	.0000	.0000	.0000	.0000	.0000	.0000	.0002	.0012	.0049	.0150	.0370
	15	.0000	.0000	.0000	.0000	.0000	.0000	.0000	.0003	.0013	.0049	.0148
	16	.0000	.0000	.0000	.0000	.0000	.0000	.0000	.0000	.0003	.0013	.0046
	17	.0000	.0000	.0000	.0000	.0000	.0000	.0000	.0000	.0000	.0002	.0011
	18	.0000	.0000	.0000	.0000	.0000	.0000	.0000	.0000	.0000	.0000	.0002
	19	.0000	.0000	.0000	.0000	.0000	.0000	.0000	.0000	.0000	.0000	.0000
	20	.0000	.0000	.0000	.0000	.0000	.0000	.0000	.0000	.0000	.0000	.0000
25	0	.7778	.2774	.0718	.0172	.0038	.0008	.0001	.0000	.0000	.0000	.0000
	1	.1964	.3650	.1994	.0759	.0236	.0063	.0014	.0003	.0000	.0000	.0000
	2	.0238	.2305	.2659	.1607	.0708	.0251	.0074	.0018	.0004	.0001	.0000
	3	.0018	.0930	.2265	.2174	.1358	.0641	.0243	.0076	.0019	.0004	.0001
	4	.0001	.0269	.1384	.2110	.1867	.1175	.0572	.0224	.0071	.0018	.0004
	5	.0000	.0060	.0646	.1564	.1960	.1645	.1030	.0506	.0199	.0063	.0016
	6	.0000	.0010	.0239	.0920	.1633	.1828	.1472	.0908	.0442	.0172	.0053
	7	.0000	.0001	.0072	.0441	.1108	.1654	.1712	.1327	.0800	.0381	.0143
	8	.0000	.0000	.0018	.0175	.0623	.1241	.1651	.1607	.1200	.0701	.0322
	9	.0000	.0000	.0004	.0058	.0294	.0781	.1336	.1635	.1511	.1084	.0609
	10	.0000	.0000	.0000	.0016	.0118	.0417	.0916	.1409	.1612	.1419	.0974
	11	.0000	.0000	.0000	.0004	.0040	.0189	.0536	.1034	.1465	.1583	.1328
	12	.0000	.0000	.0000	.0000	.0012	.0074	.0268	.0650	.1140	.1511	.1550
	13	.0000	.0000	.0000	.0000	.0003	.0025	.0115	.0350	.0760	.1236	.1550
	14	.0000	.0000	.0000	.0000	.0000	.0007	.0042	.0161	.0434	.0867	.1328
	15	.0000	.0000	.0000	.0000	.0000	.0002	.0013	.0064	.0212	.0520	.0974
	16	.0000	.0000	.0000	.0000	.0000	.0000	.0004	.0021	.0088	.0266	.0609
	17	.0000	.0000	.0000	.0000	.0000	.0000	.0001	.0006	.0031	.0115	.0322
	18	.0000	.0000	.0000	.0000	.0000	.0000	.0000	.0001	.0009	.0042	.0143
	19	.0000	.0000	.0000	.0000	.0000	.0000	.0000	.0000	.0002	.0013	.0053

n	x	.01	.05	.10	.15	.20	.25	p .30	.35	.40	.45	.50
25	20	.0000	.0000	.0000	.0000	.0000	.0000	.0000	.0000	.0000	.0001	.0016
	21	.0000	.0000	.0000	.0000	.0000	.0000	.0000	.0000	.0000	.0000	.0004
	22	.0000	.0000	.0000	.0000	.0000	.0000	.0000	.0000	.0000	.0000	.0001
30	0	.7397	.2146	.0424	.0076	.0012	.0002	.0000	.0000	.0000	.0000	.0000
	1	.2242	.3389	.1413	.0404	.0093	.0018	.0003	.0000	.0000	.0000	.0000
	2	.0328	.2586	.2277	.1034	.0337	.0086	.0018	.0003	.0000	.0000	.0000
	3	.0031	.1270	.2361	.1703	.0785	.0269	.0072	.0015	.0003	.0000	.0000
	4	.0002	.0451	.1771	.2028	.1325	.0604	.0208	.0056	.0012	.0002	.0000
	5	.0000	.0124	.1023	.1861	.1723	.1047	.0464	.0157	.0041	.0008	.0001
	6	.0000	.0027	.0474	.1368	.1795	.1455	.0829	.0353	.0115	.0029	.0006
	7	.0000	.0005	.0180	.0828	.1538	.1662	.1219	.0652	.0263	.0081	.0019
	8	.0000	.0001	.0058	.0420	.1106	.1593	.1501	.1009	.0505	.0191	.0055
	9	.0000	.0000	.0016	.0181	.0676	.1298	.1573	.1328	.0823	.0382	.0133
	10	.0000	.0000	.0004	.0067	.0355	.0909	.1416	.1502	.1152	.0656	.0280
	11	.0000	.0000	.0001	.0022	.0161	.0551	.1103	.1471	.1396	.0976	.0509
	12	.0000	.0000	.0000	.0006	.0064	.0291	.0749	.1254	.1474	.1265	.0806
	13	.0000	.0000	.0000	.0001	.0022	.0134	.0444	.0935	.1360	.1433	.1115
	14	.0000	.0000	.0000	.0000	.0007	.0054	.0231	.0611	.1101	.1424	.1354
	15	.0000	.0000	.0000	.0000	.0002	.0019	.0106	.0351	.0783	.1242	.1445
	16	.0000	.0000	.0000	.0000	.0000	.0006	.0042	.0177	.0489	.0953	.1354
	17	.0000	.0000	.0000	.0000	.0000	.0002	.0015	.0079	.0269	.0642	.1115
	18	.0000	.0000	.0000	.0000	.0000	.0000	.0005	.0031	.0129	.0379	.0806
	19	.0000	.0000	.0000	.0000	.0000	.0000	.0001	.0010	.0054	.0196	.0509
	20	.0000	.0000	.0000	.0000	.0000	.0000	.0000	.0003	.0020	.0088	.0280
	21	.0000	.0000	.0000	.0000	.0000	.0000	.0000	.0001	.0006	.0034	.0133
	22	.0000	.0000	.0000	.0000	.0000	.0000	.0000	.0000	.0002	.0012	.0055
	23	.0000	.0000	.0000	.0000	.0000	.0000	.0000	.0000	.0000	.0003	.0019
	24	.0000	.0000	.0000	.0000	.0000	.0000	.0000	.0000	.0000	.0001	.0006
	25	.0000	.0000	.0000	.0000	.0000	.0000	.0000	.0000	.0000	.0000	.0001

Table B-4 ▪ Poisson Probabilities*

X	0.1	0.2	0.3	0.4	λ 0.5	0.6	0.7	0.8	0.9	1.0
0	.9048	.8187	.7408	.6703	.6065	.5488	.4966	.4493	.4066	.3679
1	.0905	.1637	.2222	.2681	.3033	.3293	.3476	.3595	.3659	.3679
2	.0045	.0164	.0333	.0536	.0758	.0988	.1217	.1438	.1647	.1839
3	.0002	.0011	.0033	.0072	.0126	.0198	.0284	.0383	.0494	.0613
4	.0000	.0001	.0002	.0007	.0016	.0030	.0050	.0077	.0111	.0153
5	.0000	.0000	.0000	.0001	.0002	.0004	.0007	.0012	.0020	.0031
6	.0000	.0000	.0000	.0000	.0000	.0000	.0001	.0002	.0003	.0005
7	.0000	.0000	.0000	.0000	.0000	.0000	.0000	.0000	.0000	.0001

X	1.1	1.2	1.3	1.4	λ 1.5	1.6	1.7	1.8	1.9	2.0
0	.3329	.3012	.2725	.2466	.2231	.2019	.1827	.1653	.1496	.1353
1	.3662	.3614	.3543	.3452	.3347	.3230	.3106	.2975	.2842	.2707
2	.2014	.2169	.2303	.2417	.2510	.2584	.2640	.2678	.2700	.2707
3	.0738	.0867	.0998	.1128	.1255	.1378	.1496	.1607	.1710	.1804
4	.0203	.0260	.0324	.0395	.0471	.0551	.0636	.0723	.0812	.0902
5	.0045	.0062	.0084	.0111	.0141	.0176	.0216	.0260	.0309	.0361
6	.0008	.0012	.0018	.0026	.0035	.0047	.0061	.0078	.0098	.0120
7	.0001	.0002	.0003	.0005	.0008	.0011	.0015	.0020	.0027	.0034
8	.0000	.0000	.0001	.0001	.0001	.0002	.0003	.0005	.0006	.0009
9	.0000	.0000	.0000	.0000	.0000	.0000	.0001	.0001	.0001	.0002

X	2.1	2.2	2.3	2.4	λ 2.5	2.6	2.7	2.8	2.9	3.0
0	.1225	.1108	.1003	.0907	.0821	.0743	.0672	.0608	.0550	.0498
1	.2572	.2438	.2306	.2177	.2052	.1931	.1815	.1703	.1396	.1494
2	.2700	.2681	.2652	.2613	.2565	.2510	.2450	.2384	.2314	.2240
3	.1890	.1966	.2033	.2090	.2138	.2176	.2205	.2225	.2237	.2240
4	.0992	.1082	.1169	.1254	.1336	.1414	.1488	.1557	.1622	.1680
5	.0417	.0476	.0538	.0602	.0668	.0735	.0804	.0872	.0940	.1008
6	.0146	.0174	.0206	.0241	.0278	.0319	.0362	.0407	.0455	.0504
7	.0044	.0055	.0068	.0083	.0099	.0118	.0139	.0163	.0188	.0216
8	.0011	.0015	.0019	.0025	.0031	.0038	.0047	.0057	.0068	.0081
9	.0003	.0004	.0005	.0007	.0009	.0011	.0014	.0018	.0022	.0027
10	.0001	.0001	.0001	.0002	.0002	.0003	.0004	.0005	.0006	.0008
11	.0000	.0000	.0000	.0000	.0000	.0001	.0001	.0001	.0002	.0002
12	.0000	.0000	.0000	.0000	.0000	.0000	.0000	.0000	.0000	.0001

*Example: $P(X = 5 \mid \lambda = 2.5) = 0.0668$
Source: R. S. Burington and D. C. May, Jr., *Handbook of Probability and Statistics with Tables,* McGraw-Hill Book Company, New York, 1970. Used with permission.

					λ					
X	3.1	3.2	3.3	3.4	3.5	3.6	3.7	3.8	3.9	4.0
0	.0450	.0408	.0369	.0334	.0302	.0273	.0247	.0224	.0202	.0183
1	.1397	.1304	.1217	.1135	.1057	.0984	.0915	.0850	.0789	.0733
2	.2165	.2087	.2008	.1929	.1850	.1771	.1692	.1615	.1539	.1465
3	.2237	.2226	.2209	.2186	.2158	.2125	.2087	.2046	.2001	.1954
4	.1734	.1781	.1823	.1858	.1888	.1912	.1931	.1944	.1951	.1954
5	.1075	.1140	.1203	.1264	.1322	.1377	.1429	.1477	.1522	.1563
6	.0555	.0608	.0662	.0716	.0771	.0826	.0881	.0936	.0989	.1042
7	.0246	.0278	.0312	.0348	.0385	.0425	.0466	.0508	.0551	.0595
8	.0095	.0111	.0129	.0148	.0169	.0191	.0215	.0241	.0269	.0298
9	.0033	.0040	.0047	.0056	.0066	.0076	.0089	.0102	.0116	.0132
10	.0010	.0013	.0016	.0019	.0023	.0028	.0033	.0039	.0045	.0053
11	.0003	.0004	.0005	.0006	.0007	.0009	.0011	.0013	.0016	.0019
12	.0001	.0001	.0001	.0002	.0002	.0003	.0003	.0004	.0005	.0006
13	.0000	.0000	.0000	.0000	.0001	.0001	.0001	.0001	.0002	.0002
14	.0000	.0000	.0000	.0000	.0000	.0000	.0000	.0000	.0000	.0001

					λ					
X	4.1	4.2	4.3	4.4	4.5	4.6	4.7	4.8	4.9	5.0
0	.0166	.0150	.0136	.0123	.0111	.0101	.0091	.0082	.0074	.0067
1	.0679	.0630	.0583	.0540	.0500	.0462	.0427	.0395	.0365	.0337
2	.1393	.1323	.1254	.1188	.1125	.1063	.1005	.0948	.0894	.0842
3	.1904	.1852	.1798	.1743	.1687	.1631	.1574	.1517	.1460	.1404
4	.1951	.1944	.1933	.1917	.1898	.1875	.1849	.1820	.1789	.1755
5	.1600	.1633	.1662	.1687	.1708	.1725	.1738	.1747	.1753	.1755
6	.1093	.1143	.1191	.1237	.1281	.1323	.1362	.1398	.1432	.1462
7	.0640	.0686	.0732	.0778	.0824	.0869	.0914	.0959	.1002	.1044
8	.0328	.0360	.0393	.0428	.0463	.0500	.0537	.0575	.0614	.0653
9	.0150	.0168	.0188	.0209	.0232	.0255	.0280	.0307	.0334	.0363
10	.0061	.0071	.0081	.0092	.0104	.0118	.0132	.0147	.0164	.0181
11	.0023	.0027	.0032	.0037	.0043	.0049	.0056	.0064	.0073	.0082
12	.0008	.0009	.0011	.0014	.0016	.0019	.0022	.0026	.0030	.0034
13	.0002	.0003	.0004	.0005	.0006	.0007	.0008	.0009	.0011	.0013
14	.0001	.0001	.0001	.0001	.0002	.0002	.0003	.0003	.0004	.0005
15	.0000	.0000	.0000	.0000	.0001	.0001	.0001	.0001	.0001	.0002

					λ					
X	5.1	5.2	5.3	5.4	5.5	5.6	5.7	5.8	5.9	6.0
0	.0061	.0055	.0050	.0045	.0041	.0037	.0033	.0030	.0027	.0025
1	.0311	.0287	.0265	.0244	.0225	.0207	.0191	.0176	.0162	.0149
2	.0793	.0746	.0701	.0659	.0618	.0580	.0544	.0509	.0477	.0446
3	.1348	.1293	.1239	.1185	.1133	.1082	.1033	.0985	.0938	.0892
4	.1719	.1681	.1641	.1600	.1558	.1515	.1472	.1428	.1383	.1339

X	5.1	5.2	5.3	5.4	λ 5.5	5.6	5.7	5.8	5.9	6.0
5	.1753	.1748	.1740	.1728	.1714	.1697	.1678	.1656	.1632	.1606
6	.1490	.1515	.1537	.1555	.1571	.1584	.1594	.1601	.1605	.1606
7	.1086	.1125	.1163	.1200	.1234	.1267	.1298	.1326	.1353	.1377
8	.0692	.0731	.0771	.0810	.0849	.0887	.0925	.0962	.0998	.1033
9	.0392	.0423	.0454	.0486	.0519	.0552	.0586	.0620	.0654	.0688
10	.0200	.0220	.0241	.0262	.0285	.0309	.0334	.0359	.0386	.0413
11	.0093	.0104	.0116	.0129	.0143	.0157	.0173	.0190	.0207	.0225
12	.0039	.0045	.0051	.0058	.0065	.0073	.0082	.0092	.0102	.0113
13	.0015	.0018	.0021	.0024	.0028	.0032	.0036	.0041	.0046	.0052
14	.0006	.0007	.0008	.0009	.0011	.0013	.0015	.0017	.0019	.0022
15	.0002	.0002	.0003	.0003	.0004	.0005	.0006	.0007	.0008	.0009
16	.0001	.0001	.0001	.0001	.0001	.0002	.0002	.0002	.0003	.0003
17	.0000	.0000	.0000	.0000	.0000	.0001	.0001	.0001	.0001	.0001

X	6.1	6.2	6.3	6.4	λ 6.5	6.6	6.7	6.8	6.9	7.0
0	.0022	.0020	.0018	.0017	.0015	.0014	.0012	.0011	.0010	.0009
1	.0137	.0126	.0116	.0106	.0098	.0090	.0082	.0076	.0070	.0064
2	.0417	.0390	.0364	.0340	.0318	.0296	.0276	.0258	.0240	.0223
3	.0848	.0806	.0765	.0726	.0688	.0652	.0617	.0584	.0552	.0521
4	.1294	.1249	.1205	.1162	.1118	.1076	.1034	.0992	.0952	.0912
5	.1579	.1549	.1519	.1487	.1454	.1420	.1385	.1349	.1314	.1277
6	.1605	.1601	.1595	.1586	.1575	.1562	.1546	.1529	.1511	.1490
7	.1399	.1418	.1435	.1450	.1462	.1472	.1480	.1486	.1489	.1490
8	.1066	.1099	.1130	.1160	.1188	.1215	.1240	.1263	.1284	.1304
9	.0723	.0757	.0791	.0825	.0858	.0891	.0923	.0954	.0985	.1014
10	.0441	.0469	.0498	.0528	.0558	.0558	.0618	.0649	.0679	.0710
11	.0245	.0265	.0285	.0307	.0330	.0353	.0377	.0401	.0426	.0452
12	.0124	.0137	.0150	.0164	.0179	.0194	.0210	.0227	.0245	.0264
13	.0058	.0065	.0073	.0081	.0089	.0098	.0108	.0119	.0130	.0142
14	.0025	.0029	.0033	.0037	.0041	.0046	.0052	.0058	.0064	.0071
15	.0010	.0012	.0014	.0016	.0018	.0020	.0023	.0026	.0029	.0033
16	.0004	.0005	.0005	.0006	.0007	.0008	.0010	.0011	.0013	.0014
17	.0001	.0002	.0002	.0002	.0003	.0003	.0004	.0004	.0005	.0006
18	.0000	.0001	.0001	.0001	.0001	.0001	.0001	.0002	.0002	.0002
19	.0000	.0000	.0000	.0000	.0000	.0000	.0000	.0001	.0001	.0001

X	7.1	7.2	7.3	7.4	λ 7.5	7.6	7.7	7.8	7.9	8.0
0	.0008	.0007	.0007	.0006	.0006	.0005	.0005	.0004	.0004	.0003
1	.0059	.0054	.0049	.0045	.0041	.0038	.0035	.0032	.0029	.0027
2	.0208	.0194	.0180	.0167	.0156	.0145	.0134	.0125	.0116	.0107
3	.0492	.0464	.0438	.0413	.0389	.0366	.0345	.0324	.0305	.0286
4	.0874	.0836	.0799	.0764	.0729	.0696	.0663	.0632	.0602	.0573

X	λ 7.1	7.2	7.3	7.4	7.5	7.6	7.7	7.8	7.9	8.0
5	.1241	.1204	.1167	.1130	.1094	.1057	.1021	.0986	.0951	.0916
6	.1468	.1445	.1420	.1394	.1367	.1339	.1311	.1282	.1252	.1221
7	.1489	.1486	.1481	.1474	.1465	.1454	.1442	.1428	.1413	.1396
8	.1321	.1337	.1351	.1363	.1373	.1382	.1388	.1392	.1395	.1396
9	.1042	.1070	.1096	.1121	.1144	.1167	.1187	.1207	.1224	.1241
10	.0740	.0770	.0800	.0829	.0858	.0887	.0914	.0941	.0967	.0993
11	.0478	.0504	.0531	.0558	.0585	.0613	.0640	.0667	.0695	.0722
12	.0283	.0303	.0323	.0344	.0366	.0388	.0411	.0434	.0457	.0481
13	.0154	.0168	.0181	.0196	.0211	.0227	.0243	.0260	.0278	.0296
14	.0078	.0086	.0095	.0104	.0113	.0123	.0134	.0145	.0157	.0169
15	.0037	.0041	.0046	.0051	.0057	.0062	.0069	.0075	.0083	.0090
16	.0016	.0019	.0021	.0024	.0026	.0030	.0033	.0037	.0041	.0045
17	.0007	.0008	.0009	.0010	.0012	.0013	.0015	.0017	.0019	.0021
18	.0003	.0003	.0004	.0004	.0005	.0006	.0006	.0007	.0008	.0009
19	.0001	.0001	.0001	.0002	.0002	.0002	.0003	.0003	.0003	.0004
20	.0000	.0000	.0001	.0001	.0001	.0001	.0001	.0001	.0001	.0002
21	.0000	.0000	.0000	.0000	.0000	.0000	.0000	.0000	.0001	.0001

X	λ 8.1	8.2	8.3	8.4	8.5	8.6	8.7	8.8	8.9	9.0
0	.0003	.0003	.0002	.0002	.0002	.0002	.0002	.0002	.0001	.0001
1	.0025	.0023	.0021	.0019	.0017	.0016	.0014	.0013	.0012	.0011
2	.0100	.0092	.0086	.0079	.0074	.0068	.0063	.0058	.0054	.0050
3	.0269	.0252	.0237	.0222	.0208	.0195	.0183	.0171	.0160	.0150
4	.0544	.0517	.0491	.0466	.0443	.0420	.0398	.0377	.0357	.0337
5	.0882	.0849	.0816	.0784	.0752	.0722	.0692	.0663	.0635	.0607
6	.1191	.1160	.1128	.1097	.1066	.1034	.1003	.0972	.0941	.0911
7	.1378	.1358	.1338	.1317	.1294	.1271	.1247	.1222	.1197	.1171
8	.1395	.1392	.1388	.1382	.1375	.1366	.1356	.1344	.1332	.1318
9	.1256	.1269	.1280	.1290	.1299	.1306	.1311	.1315	.1317	.1318
10	.1017	.1040	.1063	.1084	.1104	.1123	.1140	.1157	.1172	.1186
11	.0749	.0776	.0802	.0828	.0853	.0878	.0902	.0925	.0948	.0970
12	.0505	.0530	.0555	.0579	.0604	.0629	.0654	.0679	.0703	.0728
13	.0315	.0334	.0354	.0374	.0395	.0416	.0438	.0459	.0481	.0504
14	.0182	.0196	.0210	.0225	.0240	.0256	.0272	.0289	.0306	.0324
15	.0098	.0107	.0116	.0126	.0136	.0147	.0158	.0169	.0182	.0194
16	.0050	.0055	.0060	.0066	.0072	.0079	.0086	.0093	.0101	.0109
17	.0024	.0026	.0029	.0033	.0036	.0040	.0044	.0048	.0053	.0058
18	.0011	.0012	.0014	.0015	.0017	.0019	.0021	.0024	.0026	.0029
19	.0005	.0005	.0006	.0007	.0008	.0009	.0010	.0011	.0012	.0014
20	.0002	.0002	.0002	.0003	.0003	.0004	.0004	.0005	.0005	.0006

X	8.1	8.2	8.3	8.4	λ 8.5	8.6	8.7	8.8	8.9	9.0
21	.0001	.0001	.0001	.0001	.0001	.0002	.0002	.0002	.0002	.0003
22	.0000	.0000	.0000	.0000	.0001	.0001	.0001	.0001	.0001	.0001

X	9.1	9.2	9.3	9.4	λ 9.5	9.6	9.7	9.8	9.9	10.0
0	.0001	.0001	.0001	.0001	.0001	.0001	.0001	.0001	.0001	.0000
1	.0010	.0009	.0009	.0008	.0007	.0007	.0006	.0005	.0005	.0005
2	.0046	.0043	.0040	.0037	.0034	.0031	.0029	.0027	.0025	.0023
3	.0140	.0131	.0123	.0115	.0107	.0100	.0093	.0087	.0081	.0076
4	.0319	.0302	.0285	.0269	.0254	.0240	.0226	.0213	.0201	.0189
5	.0581	.0555	.0530	.0506	.0483	.0460	.0439	.0418	.0398	.0378
6	.0881	.0851	.0822	.0793	.0764	.0736	.0709	.0682	.0656	.0631
7	.1145	.1118	.1091	.1064	.1037	.1010	.0982	.0955	.0928	.0901
8	.1302	.1286	.1269	.1251	.1232	.1212	.1191	.1170	.1148	.1126
9	.1317	.1315	.1311	.1306	.1300	.1293	.1284	.1274	.1263	.1251
10	.1198	.1210	.1219	.1228	.1235	.1241	.1245	.1249	.1250	.1251
11	.0991	.1012	.1031	.1049	.1067	.1083	.1098	.1112	.1125	.1137
12	.0752	.0776	.0779	.0822	.0844	.0866	.0888	.0908	.0928	.0948
13	.0526	.0549	.0572	.0594	.0617	.0640	.0662	.0685	.0707	.0729
14	.0342	.0361	.0380	.0399	.0419	.0439	.0459	.0479	.0500	.0521
15	.0208	.0221	.0235	.0250	.0265	.0281	.0297	.0313	.0330	.0347
16	.0118	.0127	.0137	.0147	.0157	.0168	.0180	.0192	.0204	.0217
17	.0063	.0069	.0075	.0081	.0088	.0095	.0103	.0111	.0119	.0128
18	.0032	.0035	.0039	.0042	.0046	.0051	.0055	.0060	.0065	.0071
19	.0015	.0017	.0019	.0021	.0023	.0026	.0028	.0031	.0034	.0037
20	.0007	.0008	.0009	.0010	.0011	.0012	.0014	.0015	.0017	.0019
21	.0003	.0003	.0004	.0004	.0005	.0006	.0006	.0007	.0008	.0009
22	.0001	.0001	.0002	.0002	.0002	.0002	.0003	.0003	.0004	.0004
23	.0000	.0001	.0001	.0001	.0001	.0001	.0001	.0001	.0002	.0002
24	.0000	.0000	.0000	.0000	.0000	.0000	.0000	.0001	.0001	.0001

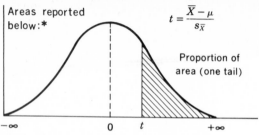

Areas reported below:*

$$t = \frac{\bar{X} - \mu}{s_{\bar{X}}}$$

Proportion of area (one tail)

$-\infty$ 0   t $+\infty$

Table B-5 ■ Areas for _t_ Distributions

df	0.10	0.05	0.025	0.01	0.005
1	3.078	6.314	12.706	31.821	63.657
2	1.886	2.920	4.303	6.965	9.925
3	1.638	2.353	3.182	4.541	5.841
4	1.533	2.132	2.776	3.747	4.604
5	1.476	2.015	2.571	3.365	4.032
6	1.440	1.943	2.447	3.143	3.707
7	1.415	1.895	2.365	2.998	3.499
8	1.397	1.860	2.306	2.896	3.355
9	1.383	1.833	2.262	2.821	3.250
10	1.372	1.812	2.228	2.764	3.169
11	1.363	1.796	2.201	2.718	3.106
12	1.356	1.782	2.179	2.681	3.055
13	1.350	1.771	2.160	2.650	3.012
14	1.345	1.761	2.145	2.624	2.977
15	1.341	1.753	2.131	2.602	2.947
16	1.337	1.746	2.120	2.583	2.921
17	1.333	1.740	2.110	2.567	2.898
18	1.330	1.734	2.101	2.552	2.878
19	1.328	1.729	2.093	2.539	2.861
20	1.325	1.725	2.086	2.528	2.845
21	1.323	1.721	2.080	2.518	2.831
22	1.321	1.717	2.074	2.508	2.819
23	1.319	1.714	2.069	2.500	2.807
24	1.318	1.711	2.064	2.492	2.797
25	1.316	1.708	2.060	2.485	2.787
26	1.315	1.706	2.056	2.479	2.779
27	1.314	1.703	2.052	2.473	2.771
28	1.313	1.701	2.048	2.467	2.763
29	1.311	1.699	2.045	2.462	2.756
30	1.310	1.697	2.042	2.457	2.750
40	1.303	1.684	2.021	2.423	2.704
60	1.296	1.671	2.000	2.390	2.660
120	1.289	1.658	1.980	2.358	2.617
∞	1.282	1.645	1.960	2.326	2.576

*Example: For shaded area to represent 0.05 of the total area of 1.0, value of _t_ with 10 degrees of freedom is 1.812.

Source: Abridged from Table IV of R. A. Fisher, _Statistical Methods for Research Workers,_ Oliver & Boyd Ltd., Edinburgh and London, 13th ed., rev., 1958, by permission of the author's literary executor and publishers.

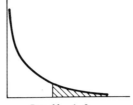

For $df = 1, 2$ For $df = 3$ or more

Areas reported below*

Table B-6 ▪ **Values of** χ^2

Degrees of freedom, df	Level of significance	
	0.05	0.01
1	3.84	6.63
2	5.99	9.21
3	7.81	11.34
4	9.49	13.28
5	11.07	15.09
6	12.59	16.81
7	14.07	18.48
8	15.51	20.09
9	16.92	21.67
10	18.31	23.21
11	19.68	24.73
12	21.03	26.22
13	22.36	27.69
14	23.68	29.14
15	25.00	30.58
16	26.30	32.00
17	27.59	33.41
18	28.87	34.80
19	30.14	36.19
20	31.41	37.57
21	32.67	38.93
22	33.92	40.29
23	35.17	41.64
24	36.41	42.98
25	37.65	44.31

*Example: For shaded area to represent 0.05 of the total area of 1.0, value of χ^2 with two degrees of freedom is 5.99.

Source: Abridged from Table III of R. A. Fisher, *Statistical Methods for Research Workers*, Oliver & Boyd Ltd., Edinburgh and London, 13th ed., rev., 1958, by permission of the author's literary executor and publishers.

Table B-7 ■ Values of the Pearson Correlation Coefficient Needed for Significance*	df, (n−2)	0.05	0.01
	1	.996917	.9998766
	2	.95000	.990000
	3	.8783	.95873
	4	.8114	.91720
	5	.7545	.8745
	6	.7067	.8343
	7	.6664	.7977
	8	.6319	.7646
	9	.6021	.7348
	10	.5760	.7079
	11	.5529	.6835
	12	.5324	.6614
	13	.5139	.6411
	14	.4973	.6226
	15	.4821	.6055
	16	.4683	.5897
	17	.4555	.5751
	18	.4438	.5614
	19	.4329	.5487
	20	.4227	.5368
	25	.3809	.4869
	30	.3494	.4487
	35	.3246	.4182
	40	.3044	.3932
	45	.2875	.3721
	50	.2732	.3541
	60	.2500	.3248
	70	.2319	.3017
	80	.2172	.2830
	90	.2050	.2673
	100	.1946	.2540

*Example: With 20 degrees of freedom, correlation coefficient of ±.4227 is needed for significance at the 0.05 level.

Source: Abridged from Table V-A of R. A. Fisher, *Statistical Methods for Research Workers,* Oliver & Boyd Ltd., Edinburgh and London, 13th ed., rev., 1958, by permission of the author's literary executor and publishers.

N	N^2	$\sqrt{N}$	$\sqrt{10N}$	N	N^2	$\sqrt{N}$	$\sqrt{10N}$
				50	2 500	7.071 068	22.36068
1	1	1.000 000	3.162 278	51	2 601	7.141 428	22.58318
2	4	1.414 214	4.472 136	52	2 704	7.211 103	22.80351
3	9	1.732 051	5.477 226	53	2 809	7.280 110	23.02173
4	16	2.000 000	6.324 555	54	2 916	7.348 469	23.23790
5	25	2.236 068	7.071 068	55	3 025	7.416 198	23.45208
6	36	2.449 490	7.745 967	56	3 136	7.483 315	23.66432
7	49	2.645 751	8.366 600	57	3 249	7.549 834	23.87467
8	64	2.828 427	8.944 272	58	3 364	7.615 773	24.08319
9	81	3.000 000	9.486 833	59	3 481	7.681 146	24.28992
10	100	3.162 278	10.00000	60	3 600	7.745 967	24.49490
11	121	3.316 625	10.48809	61	3 721	7.810 250	24.69818
12	144	3.464 102	10.95445	62	3 844	7.874 008	24.89980
13	169	3.605 551	11.40175	63	3 969	7.937 254	25.09980
14	196	3.741 657	11.83216	64	4 096	8.000 000	25.29822
15	225	3.872 983	12.24745	65	4 225	8.062 258	25.49510
16	256	4.000 000	12.64911	66	4 356	8.124 038	25.69047
17	289	4.123 106	13.03840	67	4 489	8.185 353	25.88436
18	324	4.242 641	13.41641	68	4 624	8.246 211	26.07681
19	361	4.358 899	13.78405	69	4 761	8.306 824	26.26785
20	400	4.472 136	14.14214	70	4 900	8.366 600	26.45751
21	441	4.582 576	14.49138	71	5 041	8.426 150	26.64583
22	484	4.690 416	14.83240	72	5 184	8.485 281	26.83282
23	529	4.795 832	15.16575	73	5 329	8.544 004	27.01851
24	576	4.898 979	15.49193	74	5 476	8.602 325	27.20294
25	625	5.000 000	15.81139	75	5 625	8.660 254	27.38613
26	676	5.099 020	16.12452	76	5 776	8.717 798	27.56810
27	729	5.196 152	16.43168	77	5 929	8.774 964	27.74887
28	784	5.291 503	16.73320	78	6 084	8.831 761	27.92848
29	841	5.385 165	17.02939	79	6 241	8.888 194	28.10694
30	900	5.477 226	17.32051	80	6 400	8.944 272	28.28427
31	961	5.567 764	17.60682	81	6 561	9.000 000	28.46050
32	1 024	5.656 854	17.88854	82	6 724	9.055 385	28.63564
33	1 089	5.744 563	18.16590	83	6 889	9.110 434	28.80972
34	1 156	5.830 952	18.43909	84	7 056	9.165 151	28.98275
35	1 225	5.916 080	18.70829	85	7 225	9.219 544	29.15476
36	1 296	6.000 000	18.97367	86	7 396	9.273 618	29.32576
37	1 369	6.082 763	19.23538	87	7 569	9.327 379	29.49576
38	1 444	6.164 414	19.49359	88	7 744	9.380 832	29.66479
39	1 521	6.244 998	19.74842	89	7 921	9.433 981	29.83287
40	1 600	6.324 555	20.00000	90	8 100	9.486 833	30.00000
41	1 681	6.403 124	20.24846	91	8 281	9.539 392	30.16621
42	1 764	6.480 741	20.49390	92	8 464	9.591 663	30.33150
43	1 849	6.557 439	20.73644	93	8 649	9.643 651	30.49590
44	1 936	6.633 250	20.97618	94	8 836	9.695 360	30.65942
45	2 025	6.708 204	21.21320	95	9 025	9.746 794	30.82207
46	2 116	6.782 330	21.44761	96	9 216	9.797 959	30.98387
47	2 209	6.855 655	21.67948	97	9 409	9.848 858	31.14482
48	2 304	6.928 203	21.90890	98	9 604	9.899 495	31.30495
49	2 401	7.000 000	22.13594	99	9 801	9.949 874	31.46427
50	2 500	7.071 068	22.36068	100	10 000	10.00000	31.62278

Table B-8 ■ Squares and Square Roots

N	N²	√N	√10N	N	N²	√N	√10N
100	10 000	10.00000	31.62278	150	22 500	12.24745	38.72983
101	10 201	10.04988	31.78050	151	22 801	12.28821	38.85872
102	10 404	10.09950	31.93744	152	23 104	12.32883	39.98718
103	10 609	10.14889	32.09361	153	23 409	12.36932	39.11521
104	10 816	10.19804	32.24903	154	23 716	12.40967	39.24283
105	11 025	10.24695	32.40370	155	24 025	12.44990	39.37004
106	11 236	10.29563	32.55764	156	24 336	12.40000	39.49684
107	11 449	10.34408	32.71085	157	24 649	12.52996	39.62323
108	11 664	10.39230	32.86335	158	24 964	12.56981	39.74921
109	11 881	10.44031	33.01515	159	25 281	12.60952	39.87480
110	12 100	10.48809	33.16625	160	25 600	12.64911	40.00000
111	12 321	10.53565	33.31666	161	25 921	12.68858	40.12481
112	12 544	10.58301	33.46640	162	26 244	12.72792	40.24922
113	12 769	10.63015	33.61547	163	26 569	12./6715	40.37326
114	12 996	10.67708	33.76389	164	26 896	12.80625	40.49691
115	13 225	10.72381	33.91165	165	27 225	12.84523	40.62019
116	13 456	10.77033	34.05877	166	27 556	12.88410	40.74310
117	13 689	10.81665	34.20526	167	27 889	12.92285	40.86563
118	13 924	10.86278	34.35113	168	28 224	12.96148	40.98780
119	14 161	10.90871	34.49638	169	28 561	13.00000	41.10961
120	14 400	10.95445	34.64102	170	28 900	13.03840	41.23106
121	14 641	11.00000	34.78505	171	29 241	13.07670	41.35215
122	14 884	11.04536	34.92850	172	29 584	13.11488	41.47288
123	15 129	11.09054	35.07136	173	29 929	13.15295	41.59327
124	15 376	11.13553	35.21363	174	30 276	13.19091	41.71331
125	15 625	11.18034	35.35534	175	30 625	13.22876	41.83300
126	15 876	11.22497	35.49648	176	30 976	13.26650	41.95235
127	16 129	11.26943	35.63706	177	31 329	13.30413	42.07137
128	16 384	11.31371	35.77709	178	31 684	13.34166	42.19005
129	16 641	11.35782	35.91657	179	32 041	13.37909	42.30839
130	16 900	11.40175	36.05551	180	32 400	13.41641	42.42641
131	17 161	11.44552	36.19392	181	32 761	13.45362	42.54409
132	17 424	11.48913	36.33180	182	33 124	13.49074	42.66146
133	17 689	11.53256	36.46917	183	33 489	13.52775	42.77850
134	17 956	11.57584	36.60601	184	33 856	13.56466	42.89522
135	18 225	11.61895	36.74235	185	34 225	13.60147	43.01163
136	18 496	11.66190	36.87818	186	34 596	13.63818	43.12772
137	18 769	11.70470	37.01351	187	34 969	13.67479	43.24350
138	19 044	11.74734	37.14835	188	35 344	13.71131	43.35897
139	19 321	11.78983	37.28270	189	35 721	13.74773	43.47413
140	19 600	11.83216	37.41657	190	36 100	13.78405	43.58899
141	19 881	11.87434	37.54997	191	36 481	13.82027	43.70355
142	20 164	11.91638	37.68289	192	36 864	13.85641	43.81780
143	20 449	11.95826	37.81534	193	37 249	13.89244	43.93177
144	20 736	12.00000	37.94733	194	37 636	13.92839	44.04543
145	21 025	12.04159	38.07887	195	38 025	13.96424	44.15880
146	21 316	12.08305	38.20995	196	38 416	14.00000	44.27189
147	21 609	12.12436	38.34058	197	38 809	14.03567	44.38468
148	21 904	12.16553	38.47077	198	39 204	14.07125	44.49719
149	22 201	12.20656	38.60052	199	39 601	14.10674	44.60942
150	22 500	12.24745	38.72983	200	40 000	14.14214	44.72136

N	N^2	$\sqrt{N}$	$\sqrt{10N}$	N	N^2	$\sqrt{N}$	$\sqrt{10N}$
200	40 000	14.14214	44.72136	250	62 500	15.81139	50.00000
201	40 401	14.17745	44.83302	251	63 001	15.84298	50.09990
202	40 804	14.21267	44.94441	252	63 504	15.87451	50.19960
203	41 209	14.24781	45.05552	253	64 009	15.90597	50.29911
204	41 616	14.28296	45.16636	254	64 516	15.93738	50.39841
205	42 025	14.31782	45.27693	255	65 025	15.96872	50.49752
206	42 436	14.35270	45.38722	256	65 536	16.00000	50.59644
207	42 849	14.38749	45.49725	257	66 049	16.03122	50.69517
208	43 264	14.42221	45.60702	258	66 564	16.06238	50.79370
209	43 681	14.45683	45.71652	259	67 081	16.09348	50.89204
210	44 100	14.49138	45.82576	260	67 600	16.12452	50.99020
211	44 521	14.52584	45.93474	261	68 121	16.15549	51.08816
212	44 944	14.56022	46.04346	262	68 644	16.18641	51.18594
213	45 369	14.59452	46.15192	263	69 169	16.21727	51.28353
214	45 796	14.62874	46.26013	264	69 696	16.24808	51.38093
215	46 225	14.66288	46.36809	265	70 225	16.27882	51.47815
216	46 656	14.69694	46.47580	266	70 756	16.30951	51.57519
217	47 089	14.73092	46.58326	267	71 289	16.34013	51.67204
218	47 524	14.76482	46.69047	268	71 824	16.37071	51.76872
219	47 961	14.79865	46.79744	269	72 361	16.40122	51.86521
220	48 400	14.83240	46.90415	270	72 900	16.43168	51.96152
221	48 841	14.86607	47.01064	271	73 441	16.46208	52.05766
222	49 284	14.89966	47.11688	272	73 984	16.49242	52.15362
223	49 729	14.93318	47.22288	273	74 529	16.52271	52.24940
224	50 176	14.96663	47.32864	274	75 076	16.55295	52.34501
225	50 625	15.00000	47.43416	275	75 625	16.58312	52.44044
226	51 076	15.03330	47.53946	276	76 176	16.61325	52.53570
227	51 529	15.06652	47.64452	277	76 729	16.64332	52.63079
228	51 984	15.09967	47.74935	278	77 284	16.67333	52.72571
229	52 441	15.13275	47.85394	279	77 841	16.70329	52.82045
230	52 900	15.16575	47.95832	280	78 400	16.73320	52.91503
231	53 361	15.19868	48.06246	281	78 961	16.76305	53.00943
232	53 824	15.23155	48.16638	282	79 524	16.79286	53.10367
233	54 289	15.26434	48.27007	283	80 089	16.82260	53.19774
234	54 756	15.29706	48.37355	284	80 656	16.85230	53.29165
235	55 225	15.32971	48.47680	285	81 225	16.88194	53.38539
236	55 696	15.36229	48.57983	286	81 796	16.91153	53.47897
237	56 169	15.39480	46.68265	287	82 369	16.94107	53.57238
238	56 644	15.42725	48.78524	288	82 944	16.97056	53.66563
239	57 121	15.45962	48.88763	289	83 521	17.00000	53.75872
240	57 600	15.49193	48.98979	290	84 100	17.02939	53.85165
241	58 081	15.52417	49.09175	291	84 681	17.05872	53.94442
242	58 564	15.55635	49.19350	292	85 264	17.08801	54.03702
243	59 049	15.58846	49.29503	293	85 849	17.11724	54.12947
244	59 536	15.52050	49.39636	294	86 436	17.14643	54.22177
245	60 025	15.65248	49.49747	295	87 025	17.17556	54.31390
246	60 516	15.68439	49.59839	296	87 616	17.20465	54.40588
247	61 009	15.71623	49.69909	297	88 209	17.23369	54.49771
248	61 504	15.74802	49.79960	298	88 804	17.26268	54.58938
249	62 001	15.77973	49.89990	299	89 401	17.29162	54.68089
250	62 500	15.81139	50.00000	300	90 000	17.32051	54.77226

N	N²	√N	√10N	N	N²	√N	√10N
300	90 000	17.32051	54.77226	350	122 500	18.70829	59.16080
301	90 601	17.34935	54.86347	351	123 201	18.73499	59.24525
302	91 204	17.37815	54.95453	352	123 904	18.76166	59.32959
303	91 809	17.40690	55.04544	353	124 609	18.78829	59.41380
304	92 416	17.43560	55.13620	354	125 316	18.81489	59.49790
305	93 025	17.46425	55.22681	355	126 025	18.84144	59.58188
306	93 636	17.49288	55.31727	356	126 736	18.86796	59.66574
307	94 249	17.52142	55.40758	357	127 449	18.89444	59.74948
308	94 864	17.54993	55.49775	358	128 164	18.92089	59.83310
309	95 481	17.57840	55.58777	359	128 881	18.94730	59.91661
310	96 100	17.60682	55.67764	360	129 600	18.97367	60.00000
311	96 721	17.63519	55.76737	361	130 321	19.00000	60.08328
312	97 344	17.66352	55.85696	362	131 044	19.02630	60.16644
313	97 969	17.69181	55.94640	363	131 769	19.05256	60.24948
314	98 596	17.72005	56.03670	364	132 496	19.07878	60.33241
315	99 225	17.74824	56.12486	365	133 225	19.10497	60.41523
316	99 856	17.77639	56.21388	366	133 956	19.13113	60.49793
317	100 489	17.80449	56.30275	367	134 689	19.15724	60.58052
318	101 124	17.83255	56.39149	368	135 424	19.18333	60.66300
319	101 761	17.86057	56.48008	369	136 161	19.20937	60.74537
320	102 400	17.88854	56.56854	370	136 900	19.23538	60.82763
321	103 041	17.91647	56.65686	371	137 641	19.26136	60.90977
322	103 684	17.94436	56.74504	372	138 384	19.28730	60.99180
323	104 329	17.97220	56.83309	373	139 129	19.31321	61.07373
324	104 976	18.00000	56.92100	374	139 876	19.33908	61.15554
325	105 625	18.02776	57.00877	375	140 625	19.36492	61.23724
326	106 276	18.05547	57.09641	376	141 376	19.39072	61.31884
327	106 929	18.08314	57.18391	377	142 129	19.41649	61.40033
328	107 584	18.11077	57.27128	378	142 884	19.44222	61.48170
329	108 241	18.13836	57.35852	379	143 641	19.46792	61.56298
330	108 900	18.16590	57.44563	380	144 000	19.49359	61.64414
331	109 561	18.19341	57.53260	381	145 161	19.51922	61.72520
332	110 224	18.22087	57.61944	382	145 924	19.54483	61.80615
333	110 889	18.24829	57.70615	383	146 689	19.57039	61.88699
334	111 556	18.27567	57.79273	384	147 456	19.59592	61.96773
335	112 225	18.30301	57.87918	385	148 225	19.62142	62.04837
336	112 896	18.33030	57.96551	386	148 996	19.64688	62.12890
337	113 569	18.35756	58.05170	387	149 769	19.67232	62.20932
338	114 224	18.38478	57.13777	388	150 544	19.69772	62.28965
339	114 921	18.41195	58.22371	389	151 321	19.72308	62.36986
340	115 600	18.43909	58.30952	390	152 100	19.74842	62.44998
341	116 281	18.46619	58.39521	391	152 881	19.77372	62.52999
342	116 694	18.49324	58.48077	392	153 664	19.79899	62.60990
343	117 649	18.52026	58.56620	393	154 449	19.82423	62.68971
344 345	118 336	18.54724	58.65151	394	155 236	19.84943	62.76942
345	119 025	18.57418	58.73670	395	156 025	19.87461	62.84903
346	119 716	18.60108	58.82176	396	156 816	19.89975	62.92853
347	120 409	18.62794	58.90671	397	157 609	19.92486	63.00794
348	121 104	18.65476	58.99152	398	158 404	19.94994	63.08724
349	121 801	18.68154	59.07622	399	159 201	19.97498	63.16645
350	122 500	18.70829	59.16080	400	160 000	20.00000	63.24555

N	N^2	$\sqrt{N}$	$\sqrt{10N}$	N	N^2	$\sqrt{N}$	$\sqrt{10N}$
400	160 000	20.00000	63.24555	450	202 500	21.21320	67.08204
401	160 801	20.02498	63.32456	451	203 401	21.23676	67.15653
402	161 604	20.04994	63.40347	452	204 304	21.26029	67.23095
403	162 409	20.07486	63.48228	453	205 209	21.28380	67.30527
404	163 216	20.09975	63.56099	454	206 116	21.30728	67.37952
405	164 025	20.12461	63.63961	455	207 025	21.33073	67.45369
406	164 836	20.14944	63.71813	456	207 936	21.35416	67.52777
407	165 649	20.17424	63.79655	457	208 849	21.37756	67.60178
408	166 464	20.19901	63.87488	458	209 764	21.40093	67.67570
409	167 281	20.22375	63.95311	459	210 681	21.42429	67.74954
410	168 100	20.24846	64.03124	460	211 600	21.44761	67.82330
411	168 921	20.27313	64.10928	461	212 521	21.47091	67.89698
412	169 744	20.29778	64.18723	462	213 444	21.49419	67.97058
413	170 569	20.32240	64.26508	463	214 369	21.51743	68.04410
414	171 396	20.34699	64.34283	464	215 296	21.54066	68.11755
415	172 225	20.37155	64.42049	465	216 225	21.56386	68.19091
416	173 056	20.39608	64.49806	466	217 156	21.58703	68.26419
417	173 889	20.42058	64.57554	467	218 089	21.61018	68.33740
418	174 724	20.44505	64.65292	468	219 024	21.63331	68.41053
419	175 561	20.46949	64.73021	469	219 961	21.65641	68.48357
420	176 400	20.49390	64.80741	470	220 900	21.67948	68.55655
421	177 241	20.51828	64.88451	471	221 841	21.70253	68.62944
422	178 084	20.54264	64.96153	472	222 784	21.72556	68.70226
423	178 929	20.56696	65.03845	473	223 729	21.74856	68.77500
424	179 776	20.59126	65.11528	474	224 676	21.77154	68.84706
425	180 625	20.61553	65.19202	475	225 625	21.79449	68.92024
426	181 476	20.63977	65.26808	476	226 576	21.81742	68.99275
427	182 329	20.66398	65.34524	477	227 529	21.84033	69.06519
428	183 184	20.68816	65.42171	478	228 484	21.86321	69.13754
429	184 041	20.71232	65.49809	479	229 441	21.88607	69.20983
430	184 900	20.73644	65.57439	480	230 400	21.90800	69.28203
431	185 761	20.76054	65.65059	481	231 361	21.93171	69.35416
432	186 624	20.78461	65.72671	482	232 324	21.95450	69.42622
433	187 489	20.80865	65.80274	483	233 280	21.97726	69.40820
434	188 356	20.83267	65.87868	484	234 256	22.00000	69.57011
435	189 225	20.85665	65.95453	485	235 225	22.02272	69.64194
436	190 096	20.88061	66.03030	486	236 196	22.04541	69.71370
437	190 969	20.90454	66.10598	487	237 169	22.06808	69.78530
438	191 844	20.92845	66.18157	488	238 144	22.09072	69.85700
439	192 721	20.95233	66.25708	489	239 121	22.11334	69.92853
440	193 600	20.97618	66.33250	490	240 100	22.13594	70.00000
441	194 481	21.00000	66.40783	491	241 081	22.15852	70.07139
442	195 364	21.02380	66.48308	492	242 064	22.18107	70.14271
443	196 249	21.04757	66.55825	493	243 049	22.20360	70.21396
444	197 136	21.07131	66.63332	494	244 036	22.22611	70.28513
445	198 025	21.09502	66.70832	495	245 025	22.24860	70.35624
446	198 916	21.11871	66.78323	496	246 016	22.27106	70.42727
447	199 809	21.14237	66.85806	497	247 009	22.29350	70.49823
448	200 704	21.16601	66.93280	498	248 004	22.31519	70.56912
449	201 601	21.18962	67.00746	499	249 001	22.33831	70.63993
450	202 500	21.21320	67.08204	500	250 000	22.36068	70.71068

N	N²	√N	√10N	N	N²	√N	√10N
500	250 000	22.36068	70.71068	550	302 500	23.45208	74.16198
501	251 001	22.38303	70.78135	551	303 601	23.47339	74.22937
502	252 004	22.40536	70.85196	552	304 704	23.49468	74.29670
503	253 009	22.42766	70.92249	553	305 809	23.51595	74.36397
504	254 016	22.44994	70.99296	554	306 916	23.53720	74.43118
505	255 025	22.47221	71.06335	555	308 025	23.55844	74.49832
506	256 036	22.49444	71.13368	556	309 136	23.57965	74.56541
507	257 049	22.51666	71.20393	557	310 249	23.60085	74.63243
508	258 064	22.53886	71.27412	558	311 364	23.62202	74.69940
509	259 081	22.56103	71.34424	559	312 481	23.64318	74.76630
510	260 100	22.58318	71.41428	560	313 600	23.66432	74.83315
511	261 121	22.60531	71.48426	561	314 721	23.68544	74.89993
512	262 144	22.62742	71.55418	562	315 844	23.70654	74.96666
513	263 169	22.64950	71.62402	563	316 969	23.72762	75.03333
514	264 196	22.67157	71.69379	564	318 096	23.74868	75.09993
515	265 225	22.69361	71.76350	565	319 225	23.76973	75.16648
516	266 256	22.71563	71.83314	566	320 356	23.79075	75.23297
517	267 289	22.73763	71.90271	567	321 489	23.81176	75.29940
518	268 324	22.75961	71.97222	568	322 624	23.83275	75.36577
519	269 361	22.78157	72.04165	569	323 761	23.85372	75.43209
520	270 400	22.80351	72.11103	570	324 900	23.87467	75.49834
521	271 441	22.82542	72.18033	571	326 041	23.89561	75.56454
522	272 484	22.84732	72.24957	572	327 184	23.91652	75.63068
523	273 529	22.86919	72.31874	573	328 329	23.93742	75.69676
524	274 576	22.89105	72.38784	574	329 476	23.95830	75.76279
525	275 625	22.91288	72.45688	575	330 625	23.97916	75.82875
526	276 676	22.93469	72.52586	576	331 776	24.00000	75.89466
527	277 729	22.95648	72.59477	577	332 929	24.02082	75.96052
528	278 784	22.97825	72.66361	578	334 084	24.04163	76.02631
529	279 841	23.00000	72.73239	579	335 241	24.06242	76.09205
530	280 900	23.02173	72.80110	580	336 400	24.08319	76.15773
531	281 961	23.04344	72.86975	581	337 561	24.10394	76.22336
532	283 024	23.06513	72.93833	582	338 724	24.12468	76.28892
533	284 089	23.08679	73.00685	583	339 889	24.14539	76.35444
534	285 156	23.10844	73.07530	584	341 056	24.16609	76.41989
535	286 225	23.13007	73.14369	585	342 225	24.18677	76.48529
536	287 296	23.15167	73.21202	586	343 396	24.20744	76.55064
537	288 369	23.17326	73.28028	587	344 569	24.22808	76.61593
538	289 444	23.19483	73.34848	588	345 744	24.24871	76.68116
539	290 521	23.21637	73.41662	589	346 921	24.26932	76.74634
540	291 600	23.23790	73.48469	590	348 100	24.28992	76.81146
541	292 681	23.25941	73.55270	591	349 281	24.31049	76.87652
542	293 764	23.28089	73.62065	592	350 464	24.33105	76.94154
543	294 849	23.30236	73.68853	593	351 649	24.35159	77.00649
544	295 936	23.32381	73.75636	594	352 836	24.37212	77.07140
545	297 025	23.34524	73.82412	595	354 025	24.39262	77.13624
546	298 116	23.36664	73.89181	596	355 216	24.41311	77.20104
547	299 209	23.38803	73.95945	597	356 409	24.43358	77.26578
548	300 304	23.40940	74.02702	598	357 604	24.45404	77.33046
549	301 401	23.43075	74.09453	599	358 801	24.47448	77.39509
550	302 500	23.45208	74.16198	600	360 000	24.49490	77.45967

N	N²	√N	√10N	N	N²	√N	√10N
600	360 000	24.49490	77.45967	650	422 500	25.49510	80.62258
601	361 201	24.51530	77.52419	651	423 801	25.51470	80.68457
602	362 404	24.53569	77.58868	652	425 409	25.55386	80.80842
603	363 609	24.55606	77.65307	653	426 409	25.55386	80.80842
604	364 816	24.57641	77.71744	654	427 716	25.57342	80.87027
605	366 025	24.59675	77.78175	655	429 025	25.59297	80.93207
606	367 236	24.61707	77.84600	656	430 336	25.61250	80.99383
607	368 449	24.63737	77.91020	657	431 649	25.63201	81.05554
608	369 664	24.65766	77.97435	658	432 964	25.65151	81.11720
609	370 881	24.67793	78.03845	659	434 281	25.67100	81.17881
610	372 100	24.69818	78.10250	660	435 600	25.69047	81.24038
611	373 321	24.71841	78.16649	661	436 921	25.70992	81.30191
612	374 544	24.73863	78.23043	662	438 244	25.72936	81.36338
613	375 769	24.75884	78.29432	663	439 569	25.74879	81.42481
614	376 996	24.77902	78.35815	664	440 896	25.76820	81.48620
615	378 225	24.79919	78.42194	665	442 225	25.78759	81.54753
616	379 456	24.81935	78.48567	666	443 556	25.80698	81.60882
617	380 689	24.83948	78.54935	667	444 889	25.82634	81.67007
618	381 924	24.85961	78.61298	668	446 224	25.84570	81.73127
619	383 161	24.87971	78.67655	669	447 561	25.86503	81.79242
620	384 400	24.89980	78.74008	670	448 900	25.88436	81.85353
621	385 641	24.91987	78.80355	671	450 241	25.90367	81.91459
622	386 884	24.93993	78.86698	672	451 584	25.92296	81.97561
623	288 129	24.95997	78.93035	673	452 929	25.94224	82.03658
624	389 376	24.97999	78.99367	674	454 276	25.96151	82.09750
625	390 625	25.00000	79.05694	675	455 625	25.98076	82.15838
626	391 876	25.01999	79.12016	676	456 976	26.00000	82.21922
627	393 129	25.03997	79.18333	677	458 329	26.01922	82.28001
628	394 384	25.05993	79.24645	678	459 684	26.03843	82.34076
629	395 641	25.07987	79.30952	679	461 041	26.05763	82.40146
630	396 900	25.09980	79.37254	680	462 400	26.07681	82.46211
631	398 161	25.11971	79.43551	681	463 761	26.09598	82.42272
632	399 424	25.13961	79.49843	682	465 124	26.11513	82.58329
633	400 689	25.15949	79.56130	683	466 489	26.13427	82.64381
634	401 956	25.17936	79.62412	684	467 856	26.15339	82.70429
635	403 225	25.19921	79.68689	685	469 225	26.17250	82.76473
636	404 496	25.21904	79.74961	686	470 596	26.19160	82.82512
637	405 769	25.23886	79.81228	687	471 969	26.21068	82.88546
638	407 044	25.25866	79.87490	688	473 344	26.22975	82.94577
639	408 321	25.27845	79.93748	689	474 721	26.24881	83.00602
640	409 600	25.29822	80.00000	690	476 100	26.26785	83.06624
641	410 881	25.31798	80.06248	691	477 481	26.28688	83.12641
642	412 164	25.33772	80.12490	692	478 864	26.30589	83.18654
643	413 449	25.35744	80.18728	693	480 249	26.32489	83.24662
644	414 736	25.37716	80.24961	694	481 636	26.34388	83.30666
645	416 025	25.39685	80.31189	695	483 025	26.36285	83.36666
646	417 316	25.41653	80.37413	696	484 416	26.38181	83.42661
647	418 609	25.43619	80.43631	697	485 809	26.40076	83.48653
648	419 904	25.45584	80.49845	698	487 204	26.41969	83.54639
649	421 201	25.47548	80.56054	699	488 601	26.43861	83.60622
650	422 500	25.49510	80.62258	700	490 000	26.45751	83.66600

N	N²	√N	√10N	N	N²	√N	√10N
700	490 000	26.45751	83.66600	750	562 500	27.38613	86.60254
701	491 401	26.47640	83.72574	751	564 001	27.40438	86.66026
702	492 804	26.49528	83.78544	752	565 504	27.42262	86.71793
703	494 209	26.51415	83.84510	753	567 009	27.44085	86.77557
704	495 616	26.53300	83.90471	754	568 516	27.45906	86.83317
705	497 025	26.55184	83.96428	755	570 025	27.47726	86.89074
706	498 436	26.57066	84.02381	756	571 536	27.49545	86.94826
707	499 849	26.58947	84.08329	757	573 049	27.51363	87.00575
708	501 264	26.60827	84.14274	758	574 564	27.53180	87.06320
709	502 681	26.62705	84.20214	759	576 081	27.54995	87.12061
710	504 100	26.64583	84.26150	760	577 600	27.56810	87.17798
711	505 521	26.66458	84.32082	761	579 121	27.58623	87.23531
712	506 944	26.68333	84.38009	762	580 644	27.60435	87.29261
713	508 369	26.70206	84.43933	763	582 169	27.62245	87.34987
714	509 796	26.72078	84.49852	764	583 696	27.64055	87.40709
715	511 225	26.73948	84.55767	765	585 225	27.65863	87.46428
716	512 656	26.75818	84.61578	766	586 756	27.67671	87.52143
717	514 089	26.77686	84.67585	767	588 289	27.69476	87.57854
718	515 524	26.79552	84.73488	768	589 824	27.71281	87.63561
719	516 961	26.81418	84.79387	769	591 361	27.73085	87.69265
720	518 400	26.83282	84.85281	770	592 900	27.74887	87.74964
721	519 841	26.85144	84.91172	771	594 441	27.76689	87.80661
722	521 284	26.87006	84.97058	772	595 984	27.78489	87.86353
723	522 729	26.88866	85.02941	773	597 529	27.80288	87.92042
724	524 176	26.90725	85.08819	774	599 076	27.82086	87.97727
725	525 625	26.92582	85.14693	775	600 625	27.83882	88.03408
726	527 076	26.94439	85.20563	776	602 176	27.85678	88.09086
727	528 529	26.96294	85.26429	777	603 729	27.87472	88.14760
728	529 984	26.98148	85.32292	778	605 284	27.89265	88.20431
729	531 411	27.00000	85.38150	779	606 841	27.91057	88.26098
730	532 900	27.01851	85.44004	780	608 400	27.92848	88.31761
731	534 361	27.03701	85.49854	781	609 961	27.94638	88.37420
732	535 824	27.05550	85.55700	782	611 524	27.96426	88.43076
733	537 289	27.07397	85.61542	783	613 089	27.98214	88.48729
734	538 756	27.09243	85.67380	784	614 656	28.00000	88.54377
735	540 225	27.11088	85.73214	785	616 225	28.01785	88.60023
736	541 696	27.12932	85.79044	786	617 796	28.03569	88.65664
737	543 169	27.14774	85.84870	787	619 369	28.05352	88.71302
738	544 644	27.16616	85.90693	788	620 944	28.07134	88.76936
739	546 121	27.18455	85.96511	789	622 521	28.08914	88.82567
740	547 600	27.20294	86.02325	790	624 100	28.10694	88.88194
741	549 081	27.22132	86.08136	791	625 681	28.12472	88.93818
742	550 564	27.23968	86.13942	792	627 264	28.14249	88.99438
743	552 049	27.25803	86.10745	793	628 849	28.16026	89.05055
744	553 536	27.27636	86.25543	794	630 436	28.17801	89.10668
745	555 025	27.29469	86.31338	795	632 025	28.19574	89.16277
746	556 516	27.31300	86.37129	796	633 616	28.21347	89.21883
747	558 009	27.33130	86.42916	797	635 209	28.23119	89.27486
748	559 504	27.34959	86.48609	798	636 804	28.24889	89.33085
749	561 001	27.36786	86.54479	799	638 401	28.26659	89.38680
750	562 500	27.38613	86.60254	800	640 000	28.28427	89.44272

N	N²	√N	√10N	N	N²	√N	√10N
800	640 000	28.28427	89.44272	850	722 500	29.15476	92.19544
801	641 601	28.30194	89.49860	851	724 201	29.17190	92.24966
802	643 204	28.31960	89.55445	852	725 904	29.18904	92.30385
803	644 809	28.33725	89.61027	853	727 609	29.20616	92.35800
804	646 416	28.35489	89.66605	854	729 316	29.22328	92.41212
805	648 025	28.37252	89.72179	855	731 025	29.24038	92.46621
806	649 636	28.39014	89.77750	856	732 736	29.25748	92.52027
807	651 249	28.40775	89.83318	857	734 449	29.27456	92.57429
808	652 864	28.42534	89.88882	858	736 164	29.29164	92.62829
809	654 481	28.44293	89.94443	859	737 881	29.30870	92.68225
810	656 100	28.46050	90.00000	860	739 600	29.32576	92.73618
811	657 721	28.47806	90.05554	861	741 321	29.34280	92.79009
812	659 344	28.49561	90.11104	862	743 044	29.35984	92.84396
813	660 969	28.51315	90.16651	863	744 769	29.37686	92.89779
814	662 596	28.53069	90.22195	864	746 496	29.39388	92.95160
815	664 225	28.54820	90.27735	865	748 225	29.41088	93.00538
816	665 856	28.56571	90.33272	866	749 956	29.42788	93.05912
817	667 489	28.58321	90.38805	867	751 689	29.44486	93.11283
818	669 124	28.60070	90.44335	868	753 424	29.46184	93.16652
819	670 761	28.61818	90.49862	869	755 161	29.47881	93.22017
820	672 400	28.63564	90.55385	870	756 900	29.49576	93.27379
821	674 041	28.65310	90.60905	871	758 641	29.51271	93.32738
822	675 684	28.67054	90.66422	872	760 384	29.52965	93.38094
823	677 329	28.68798	90.71935	873	762 129	29.54657	93.43447
824	678 976	28.70540	90.77445	874	763 876	29.56349	93.48797
825	680 625	28.72281	90.82951	875	765 625	29.58040	93.54143
826	682 276	28.74022	90.88454	876	767 376	29.59730	93.59487
827	683 929	28.75761	90.93954	877	769 129	29.61419	93.64828
828	685 584	28.77499	90.99451	878	770 884	29.63106	93.70165
829	687 241	28.79236	91.04944	879	772 641	29.64793	93.75500
830	688 900	28.80972	91.10434	880	774 400	29.66479	93.80832
831	690 561	28.82707	91.15920	881	776 161	29.68164	93.86160
832	692 224	28.84441	91.21403	882	777 924	29.69848	93.91486
833	693 889	28.86174	91.26883	883	779 689	29.71532	93.96808
834	695 556	28.87906	91.32360	884	781 456	29.73214	94.02027
835	697 225	28.89637	91.37833	885	783 225	29.74895	94.07444
836	698 896	28.91366	91.43304	886	784 996	29.76575	94.12757
837	700 569	28.93095	91.48770	887	786 769	29.78255	94.18068
838	702 244	28.94823	91.54234	888	788 544	29.79933	94.23375
839	703 921	28.96550	91.59694	889	790 321	29.81610	94.28680
840	705 600	28.98275	91.65151	890	792 100	29.83287	94.33981
841	707 281	29.00000	91.70605	891	793 881	29.84962	94.39280
842	708 964	29.01724	91.76056	892	795 664	29.86637	94.44575
843	710 649	29.03446	91.81503	893	797 449	29.88311	94.49868
844	712 336	29.05168	91.86947	894	799 236	29.89983	94.55157
845	714 025	29.06888	91.92388	895	801 025	29.91655	94.60444
846	715 716	29.08608	91.97826	896	802 816	29.93326	94.65728
847	717 409	29.10326	92.03260	897	804 609	29.94996	94.71008
848	719 104	29.12044	92.08692	898	806 404	29.96665	94.76286
849	720 801	29.13760	92.14120	899	808 201	29.98333	94.81561
850	722 500	29.15476	92.19544	900	810 000	30.00000	94.86833

N	N^2	$\sqrt{N}$	$\sqrt{10N}$	N	N^2	$\sqrt{N}$	$\sqrt{10N}$
900	810 000	30.00000	94.86833	950	902 500	30.82207	97.46794
901	811 801	30.01666	94.92102	951	904 401	30.83829	97.51923
902	813 604	30.03331	94.97368	952	906 304	30.85450	97.57049
903	815 409	30.04996	95.02631	953	908 209	30.87070	97.62172
904	817 216	30.06659	95.07891	954	910.116	30.88689	97.67292
905	819 025	30.08322	95.13149	955	912 025	30.90307	97.72410
906	820 836	30.09983	95.18403	956	913 936	30.91925	97.77525
907	822 649	30.11644	95.23655	957	915 849	30.93542	97.82638
908	824 464	30.13304	95.28903	958	917 764	30.95158	97.87747
909	826 281	30.14963	95.34149	959	919 681	30.96773	97.92855
910	828 100	30.16621	95.39392	960	921 600	30.98387	97.97959
911	829 921	30.18278	95.44632	961	928 521	31.00000	98.03061
912	831 744	30.19934	95.49869	962	925 444	31.01612	98.08160
913	833 569	30.21589	95.55103	963	927 369	31.03224	98.13256
914	835 396	30.23243	95.60335	964	929 296	31.04835	98.18350
915	837 225	30.24897	95.65563	965	931 225	31.06445	98.23441
916	839 056	30.26549	95.70789	966	933 156	31.08054	98.28530
917	840 889	30.28201	95.76012	967	935 089	31.09662	98.33616
918	842 724	30.29851	95.81232	968	937 024	31.11270	98.38699
919	844 561	30.31501	95.86449	969	938 961	31.12876	98.43780
920	846 400	30.33150	95.91663	970	940 900	31.14482	98.48858
921	848 241	30.34798	95.96874	971	942 841	31.16087	98.53933
922	850 084	30.36445	96.02083	972	944 784	31.17691	98.59006
923	851 929	30.38092	96.07289	973	946 729	31.19295	98.64076
924	853 776	30.39735	96.12492	974	948 676	31.20897	98.69144
925	855 625	30.41381	96.17692	975	950 625	31.22499	98.74209
926	857 476	30.43025	96.22889	976	952 576	31.24100	98.79271
927	859 329	30.44667	96.28084	977	954 529	31.25700	98.84331
928	861 184	30.46309	96.33276	978	956 484	31.27299	98.89388
929	863 041	30.47950	96.28465	979	958 441	31.28898	98.94443
930	864 900	30.49590	96.43651	980	960 400	31.30495	98.99495
931	866 761	30.51229	96.48834	981	962 361	31.32092	99.04544
932	868 624	30.52868	96.54015	982	964 324	31.33688	99.09591
933	870 489	30.54505	96.59193	983	966 144	31.43247	99.44848
934	872 356	30.56141	96.64368	984	968 256	31.36877	99.19677
935	874 225	30.57777	96.69540	985	970 225	31.38471	99.24717
936	876 096	30.59412	96.74709	986	972 196	31.40064	99.29753
937	877 969	30.61046	96.79876	987	974 169	31.41656	99.34787
938	879 844	30.62679	96.85040	988	976 144	31.43247	99.39819
939	881 721	30.64311	96.90201	989	978 121	31.44837	99.44848
940	883 600	30.65942	96.95360	990	980 100	31.46427	99.49874
941	885 481	30.67572	97.00515	991	982 081	31.48015	99.54898
942	887 364	30.69202	97.05668	992	984 064	31.49603	99.59920
943	889 249	30.70831	97.10819	993	986 049	31.51190	99.64939
944	891 136	30.72458	97.15966	994	988 036	31.52777	99.69955
945	893 025	30.74085	97.21111	995	990 025	31.54362	99.74969
946	894 916	30.75711	97.26253	996	992 016	31.55947	99.79980
947	896 809	30.77337	97.31393	997	994 009	31.57531	99.84989
948	898 704	30.78961	97.36529	998	996 004	31.59114	99.89995
949	900 601	30.80584	97.41663	999	998 001	31.60696	99.94999
950	902 500	30.82207	97.46794	1000	1 000 000	31.62278	100.00000

Table B-9 ■ An Abbreviated
Table of Random Numbers

10097	85017	84532	13618	23157	86952	02438	76520
37542	16719	82789	69041	05545	44109	05403	64894
08422	65842	27672	82186	14871	22115	86529	19645
99019	76875	20684	39187	38976	94324	43204	09376
12807	93640	39160	41453	97312	41548	93137	80157
66065	99478	70086	71265	11742	18226	29004	34072
31060	65119	26486	47353	43361	99436	42753	45571
85269	70322	21592	48233	93806	32584	21828	02051
63573	58133	41278	11697	49540	61777	67954	05325
73796	44655	81255	31133	36768	60452	38537	03529
98520	02295	13487	98662	07092	44673	61303	14905
11805	85035	54881	35587	43310	48897	48493	39808
83452	01197	86935	28021	61570	23350	65710	06288
88685	97907	19078	40646	31352	48625	44369	86507
99594	63268	96905	28797	57048	46359	74294	87517
65481	52841	59684	67411	09243	56092	84369	17468
80124	53722	71399	10916	07959	21225	13018	17727
74350	11434	51908	62171	93732	26958	02400	77402
69916	62375	99292	21177	72721	66995	07289	66252
09893	28337	20923	87929	61020	62841	31374	14225
91499	38631	79430	62421	97959	67422	69992	68479
80336	49172	16332	44670	35089	17691	89246	26940
44104	89232	57327	34679	62235	79655	81336	85157
12550	02844	15026	32439	58537	48274	81330	11100
63606	40387	65406	37920	08709	60623	2237	16505
61196	80240	44177	51171	08723	39323	05798	26457
15474	44910	99321	72173	56239	04595	10836	95270
94557	33663	86347	00926	44915	34823	51770	67897
42481	86430	19102	37420	41976	76559	24358	97344
23523	31379	68588	81675	15694	43438	36879	73208
04493	98086	32533	17767	14523	52494	24826	75246
00549	33185	04805	05431	94598	97654	16232	64051
35963	80951	68953	99634	81949	15307	00406	26898
59808	79752	02529	40200	73742	08391	49140	45427
46058	18633	99970	67348	49329	95236	32537	01390
32179	74029	74717	17674	90446	00597	45240	87379
69234	54178	10805	35635	45266	61406	41941	20117
19565	11664	77602	99817	28573	41430	96382	01758
45155	48324	32135	26803	16213	14938	71961	19476
94864	69074	45753	20505	78317	31994	98145	36168

SOLUTIONS TO EXERCISES

Chapter 1 ■ **The Use of Statistical Analysis**

1.1 **(a)** S—since it is on the basis of sample data that inferences concerning the population are made.
(b) P—by definition, this is a descriptive measurement of a population.
(c) S—used in the process of statistical inference.
(d) P—enumeration, or measurement, of an entire population.

1.2 Both statistical description and statistical inference are concerned with describing a population of values. However, in the case of statistical description all relevant values have been collected, whereas in the case of statistical inference the values for a portion of the population — i.e., a sample — have been collected. Statistical inference therefore differs from statistical description in that the reported description is not a certain one. Probability concepts and values are used to evaluate the uncertainty associated with descriptions that are based on sample information.

1.3 To the extent that scientific methods are inductive, this implies that knowledge is gained through observation. General laws are formulated on the basis of having observed a number of specific results. Of course, the observations associated with scientific disciplines are made under carefully controlled conditions and are therefore referred to as experiments.

1.4 Data whose possible values can occur at selected points along a measurement scale rather than at any fractional point. In this text the discrete numbers of particular interest are the integers (whole numbers) obtained by the process of counting.

1.5 **(a)** C; **(b)** C; **(c)** D; **(d)** D; **(e)** C; **(f)** D (Generally, only whole-number—to the penny—values are possible. However, monetary amounts typically are treated as if they were continuous data.)

1.6 **(a)** 15.5 to 16.5 ounces; **(b)** 11.95 to 12.05 ounces; **(c)** 8.445 to 8.455 centimeters; **(d)** $450 to $550; **(e)** $494.50 to $495.50; **(f)** 85.8745 to 85.8755 meters

1.7 **(a)** 5,800; **(b)** 7,000; **(c)** 131; **(d)** 28.6; **(e)** 20.0; **(f)** 32.50

1.8 When the remainder is less than --500--, simply drop the remainder. When the remainder is greater than --500--, increase the value of the last digit being reported by 1. When the remainder is exactly --500--, increase the last digit being reported by 1 only if it is an odd-numbered integer; otherwise, drop the remainder. Thus, 27.349 would be rounded as 27.3 to the first place beyond the decimal, 27.3501 would be rounded as 27.4, and 27.4500 would also be rounded as 27.4.

Chapter 2 ■ **Frequency Distributions and Graphic Description**

2.1

Class boundaries	f
2.5-5.5	1
5.5-8.5	2
8.5-11.5	2
11.5-14.5	5
14.5-17.5	4

Class interval $i = B_U - B_L = 5.5 - 2.5 = 3$

(Or any of the other methods for determining i may be used.)

2.2

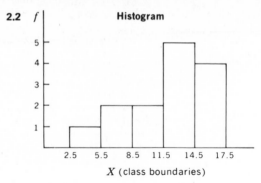

Histogram

X (class boundaries)

2.3

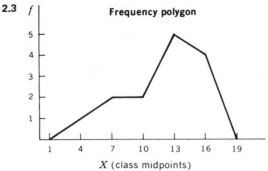

Frequency polygon

X (class midpoints)

2.4 The frequency curve for the data would be negatively skewed (skewed to the left).

2.5

Class boundaries	f	cf
2.5-5.5	1	1
5.5-8.5	2	3
8.5-11.5	2	5
11.5-14.5	5	10
14.5-17.5	4	14

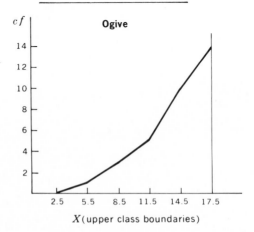

Ogive

X (upper class boundaries)

2.6 Class boundaries	f	cf	Relative frequency, percent
2.5–5.5	1	1	7.1
5.5–8.5	2	3	21.4
8.5–11.5	2	5	35.7
11.5–14.5	5	10	71.4
14.5–17.5	4	14	100.0

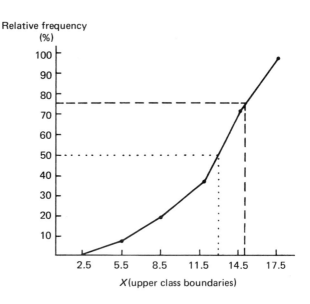

Relative frequency (%)

X (upper class boundaries)

(a) As indicated by the dashed line, the approximate percentile associated with a measured value of 15 is about 75.

(b) As indicated by the dotted line, the approximate measured value which is at the fiftieth percentile point is 13.

2.7

Bar chart for sales by region

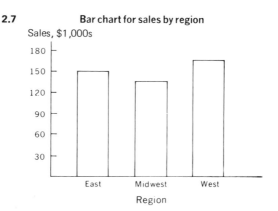

Sales, $1,000s

Region

2.8 Component bar chart for product sales by region

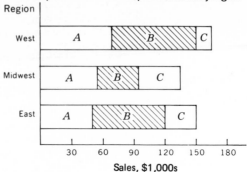

2.9 Pie chart for sales by product

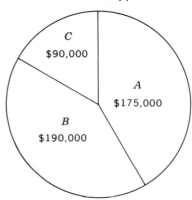

2.10 Line chart for total sales

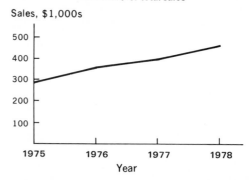

3.1 $\mu = \dfrac{\Sigma X}{N} = \dfrac{36.0}{12} = 3.0$

Array: [0.0, 1.0, 1.0, 1.5, 2.0, 2.0, 2.0, 3.0, 4.0, 5.0, 5.5, 9.0]

Med $= X_{n/2 + 1/2} = X_{6.5} = 2.0$ (which is midway between the sixth and seventh measurements in the array)

Mode $= 2.0$ (most frequent value)

3.2 Because the mean is considerably larger than the median, the distribution can be described as being positively skewed. The median and the mode happen to be equal in value (2.0), and a scanning of the values in the array identified above indicates that 2.0 may better represent what is "typical" than 3.0. Of course, the value of the mean is particularly affected by the extreme value of 9.0.

3.3 $Q_1 = X_{n/4 + 1/2} = X_{3.5} = 1.25$ (midway between the third and fourth measurements in the array listed in the answer to Exercise 3.1)

$Q_2 = X_{n/2 + 1/2} = X_{6.5} = 2.0$

$Q_3 = X_{3n/4 + 1/2} = X_{9.5} = 4.5$

Twenty-five percent of the measurements are below the point 1.25, 50 percent are below 2.0, and 75 percent are below 4.5. Of course, Q_2 is the same point as the median.

3.4 $D_7 = X_{7n/10 + 1/2} = X_{8.9} = 3.9$ (nine-tenths of the distance between the eight and ninth measurements in the array)

3.5

Number of days absent, X	$\lvert X - \mu \rvert$	$(X - \mu)^2$
5.0	2.0	4.00
0.0	3.0	9.00
1.5	1.5	2.25
3.0	0.0	0.00
1.0	2.0	4.00
2.0	1.0	1.00
9.0	6.0	36.00
5.5	2.5	6.25
1.0	2.0	4.00
4.0	1.0	1.00
2.0	1.0	1.00
2.0	1.0	1.00
$\Sigma X = 36.0$	$\Sigma \lvert X - \mu \rvert = 23.0$	$\Sigma (X - \mu)^2 = 69.50$

(a) $R = H - L = 9.0 - 0.0 = 9.0$

(b) $AD = \dfrac{\Sigma \lvert X - \mu \rvert}{N} = \dfrac{23.0}{12} = 1.92 \doteq 1.9$

3.6 Middle 90% range $= P_{95} - P_{05}$

where: $P_{95} = X_{95n/100 + 1/2} = X_{95(12)/100 + 1/2} = X_{11.9} = 8.65$

$P_{05} = X_{05n/100 + 1/2} = X_{05(12)/100 + 1/2} = X_{1.1} = 0.10$

Middle 90% range $= 8.65 - 0.10 = 8.55$

3.7 $\sigma = \sqrt{\dfrac{\Sigma(X - \mu)^2}{N}} = \sqrt{\dfrac{69.50}{12}} = \sqrt{5.7915} \doteq 2.4$

3.8

Number of days absent, X	X^2
5.0	25.00
0.0	0.00
1.5	2.25
3.0	9.00
1.0	1.00
2.0	4.00
9.0	81.00
5.5	30.25
1.0	1.00
4.0	16.00
2.0	4.00
2.0	4.00
$\Sigma X = 36.0$	$\Sigma X^2 = 177.50$

$$\sigma = \sqrt{\frac{\Sigma X^2 - N\mu^2}{N}} = \sqrt{\frac{177.50 - 12(3.0)^2}{12}} = \sqrt{5.7917} \doteq 2.4$$

3.9 $CV = \dfrac{\sigma}{\mu} = \dfrac{2.4}{3.0} = 0.8$

3.10 The median, quartiles, deciles, and percentiles are all conceptually similar in that they all divide a set of measurements into equal portions based on the frequencies of the measurements in each portion. The median is the point which divides the total set of measurements into two such portions, the quartiles divide it into four portions, the deciles divide it into 10 portions, and the percentiles divide it into 100 portions.

3.11 The median and the mode are useful statistically in order to describe a set of measurements. Specifically, the median and mode better represent the "typical" value for a nonsymmetrical set of measurements than does the arithmetic mean. The mean is the principal measure of central tendency used in conjunction with statistical inference, and thus it is used extensively in the statistical applications described in the remaining chapters of this book.

3.12 As we proceed from considering the range to considering modified ranges, the average deviation, and finally the standard deviation, we find the measures of dispersion increasingly sophisticated and useful statistically. But from a purely descriptive standpoint a measure such as the standard deviation is difficult to interpret for the nonstatistician. Therefore, what is "best" depends on the audience for whom the description is intended. For this reason, statistical analyses intended for general audiences most often report the range as an indicator of the amount of variability in a set of data. On the other hand, statistical analyses intended for quantitative specialists usually report the standard deviation.

4.1

Class boundaries	f	X	fX	cf
0.95 – 1.45	3	1.2	3.6	3
1.45 – 1.95	4	1.7	6.8	7
1.95 – 2.45	8	2.2	17.6	15
2.45 – 2.95	12	2.7	32.4	27
2.95 – 3.45	5	3.2	16.0	32
3.45 – 3.95	3	3.7	11.1	35
	$N = \Sigma f = 35$		$\Sigma fX = 87.5$	

$$\mu = \frac{\Sigma fX}{N} = \frac{87.5}{35} = 2.5$$

$$\text{Med} = B_L + \left(\frac{N/2 - cf_B}{f_c}\right) i = 2.45 + \left(\frac{17.5 - 15}{12}\right) 0.5$$

$$= 2.45 + \left(\frac{2.5}{12}\right) 0.5 = 2.45 + 0.104 = 2.554 \doteq 2.55$$

$$\text{Mode} = B_L + \left(\frac{d_1}{d_1 + d_2}\right) i = 2.45 + \left(\frac{4}{4 + 7}\right) 0.5$$

$$= 2.45 + \left(\frac{4}{11}\right) 0.5 = 2.45 + 0.18 = 2.63$$

4.2 With the mean being smaller than the median, the distribution can be described as being negatively skewed. The value of the mean is most affected by the relatively few low grade-point averages.

4.3 $Q_1 = B_L + \left(\dfrac{N/4 - cf_B}{f_c}\right) i = 1.95 + \left(\dfrac{8.75 - 7}{8}\right) 0.5$

$$= 1.95 + \left(\frac{1.75}{8}\right) 0.5 = 1.95 + 0.109 = 2.059 \doteq 2.06$$

$$Q_3 = B_L + \left(\frac{3N/4 - cf_B}{f_c}\right) i = 2.45 + \left(\frac{26.25 - 15}{12}\right) 0.5$$

$$= 2.45 + \left(\frac{11.25}{12}\right) 0.5 = 2.45 + 0.469 = 2.919 \doteq 2.92$$

Thus, 25 percent of the measurements in this distribution are below 2.06 and 75 percent of the measurements are below 2.92.

4.4 $P_{60} = B_L + \left(\dfrac{60N/100 - cf_B}{f_c}\right) i = 2.45 + \left(\dfrac{21 - 15}{12}\right) 0.5$

$$= 2.45 + \left(\frac{6}{12}\right) 0.5 = 2.45 + 0.25 = 2.70$$

Thus, 60 percent of the measurements in this distribution are below 2.70.

4.5 $R = B_U$ (highest class) $- B_L$ (lowest class) $= 3.95 - 0.95 = 3.0$

4.6 Middle 90% range $= P_{95} - P_{05}$

where:

$$P_{95} = B_L + \left(\frac{95N/100 - cf_B}{f_c} \right) i = 3.45 + \left(\frac{33.25 - 32}{3} \right) 0.5$$

$$= 3.45 + \left(\frac{1.25}{3} \right) 0.5 = 3.45 + 0.21 = 3.66$$

$$P_{05} = B_L + \left(\frac{5N/100 - cf_B}{f_c} \right) i = 0.95 + \left(\frac{1.75 - 0}{3} \right) 0.5$$

$$= 0.95 + \left(\frac{1.75}{3} \right) 0.5 = 0.95 + 0.29 = 1.24$$

Middle 90% range = 3.66 - 1.24 = 2.42

4.7

Class boundaries	f	X	$|X - \mu|$	$f|X - \mu|$	$(X - \mu)^2$	$f(X - \mu)^2$
0.95–1.45	3	1.2	1.3	3.9	1.69	5.07
1.45–1.95	4	1.7	0.8	3.2	0.64	2.56
1.95–2.45	8	2.2	0.3	2.4	0.09	0.72
2.45–2.95	12	2.7	0.2	2.4	0.04	0.48
2.95–3.45	5	3.2	0.7	3.5	0.49	2.45
3.45–3.95	3	3.7	1.2	3.6	1.44	4.32
	$N = 35$			$\Sigma f|X - \mu| = 19.0$		$\Sigma f(X - \mu)^2 = 15.60$

$$AD = \frac{\Sigma f|X - \mu|}{N} = \frac{19.0}{3.5} = 0.54$$

4.8 $\sigma = \sqrt{\dfrac{\Sigma f(X - \mu)^2}{N}} = \sqrt{\dfrac{15.60}{35}} = \sqrt{0.4457} = 0.67$

4.9

Class boundaries	f	X	X^2	fX^2
0.95–1.45	3	1.2	1.44	4.32
1.45–1.95	4	1.7	2.89	11.56
1.95–2.45	8	2.2	4.84	38.72
2.45–2.95	12	2.7	7.29	87.48
2.95–3.45	5	3.2	10.24	51.20
3.45–3.95	3	3.7	13.69	41.07
	$N = 35$			$\Sigma fX^2 = 234.35$

$$\sigma = \sqrt{\frac{\Sigma f X^2 - N\mu^2}{N}} = \sqrt{\frac{234.35 - 35(2.5)^2}{35}} = \sqrt{0.4457} = 0.67$$

4.10 Measures such as the mean, median, and standard deviation which are calculated on the basis of grouped data are considered to be approximations because the midpoint of each class is used to represent the values in the class, and this midpoint is itself an approximation of those values.

Chapter 5 ▪ Probability

5.1 $P(\text{defective}) = \frac{2}{50} = \frac{1}{25} = 0.04$. This probability value has been determined by the objective approach, using the empirical method.

5.2 $P(\text{bond price decline}) = \frac{2}{3}$. This probability value has been determined by the subjective approach, using the direct estimate method.

5.3 Amount certain = expected value of risk situation

$$60,000 = (P)(90,000) + (1 - P)(45,000)$$

$$60,000 = 90,000P + 45,000 - 45,000P$$

$$45,000P = 15,000$$

$$P = \frac{15,000}{45,000} = \frac{1}{3} \qquad \text{(based on the general assumption that he is risk-neutral)}$$

5.4 (a) The probability that the shipment will arrive on schedule is $P = 2/(2 + 1) = \frac{2}{3} = 0.67$.

    (b) The odds ratio that the component will not function properly is $P : (1 - P) = \frac{1}{5} : \frac{4}{5} = 1 : 4$.

    (c) The probability that the new product will succeed is $P = 3/(3 + 1) = \frac{3}{4} = 0.75$.

    (d) The odds ratio that the home team will win is $P : (1 - P) = \frac{1}{3} : \frac{2}{3} = 1 : 2$.

5.5 (a) $P(X < 100) = P(X < 50) + P(X \text{ between 50 and 99})$
$$= 0.20 + 0.40 = 0.60$$

    (b) $P(X \text{ between 50 and 199}) = P(X \text{ between 50 and 99})$
$$+ P(X \text{ between 100 and 149}) + P(X \text{ between 150 and 199})$$
$$= 0.40 + 0.20 + 0.10 = 0.70$$

5.6

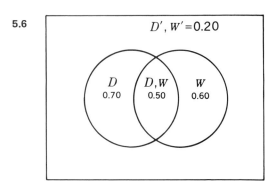

5.7 $P(D \text{ or } W) = P(D) + P(W) - (D, W)$
$= 0.70 + 0.60 - 0.50 = 0.80$
$P(D' \text{ and } W') = 1.00 - P(D \text{ or } W) = 1.00 - 0.80 = 0.20$

5.8

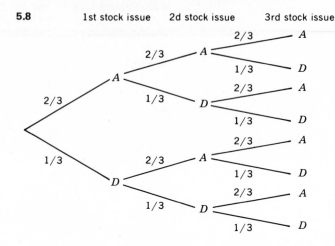

1st stock issue   2d stock issue   3rd stock issue

5.9 (a) $P(D, D, D) = P(D)P(D)P(D) = \frac{1}{3} \times \frac{1}{3} \times \frac{1}{3} = \frac{1}{27}$
(b) $P(\text{at least one } D) = 1.00 - P(A, A, A) = 1.00 - (\frac{2}{3} \times \frac{2}{3} \times \frac{2}{3})$
$= 1.00 - \frac{8}{27} = \frac{19}{27}$

5.10

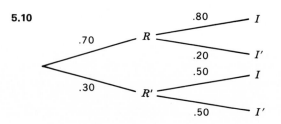

5.11 $P(R, I) = P(R)P(I|R) = (0.70)(0.80) = 0.56$

Chapter 6 ■ Discrete Probability Distributions

6.1

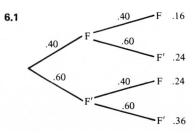

Number in favor	P
0	0.36
1	0.48
2	0.16

6.2 $(q + p)^n = (q + p)^2 = q^2 + 2qp + p^2$
$\qquad\qquad = (0.60)^2 + 2 (0.60)(0.40) + (0.40)^2$
$\qquad\qquad = 0.36 + 0.48 + 0.16$

Number in favor	P
0	0.36
1	0.48
2	0.16

6.3 $P(X = 0 | n = 2, p = 0.40) = 0.36$
$\qquad P(X = 1 | n = 2, p = 0.40) = 0.48$
$\qquad P(X = 3 | n = 2, p = 0.40) = 0.16$

6.4

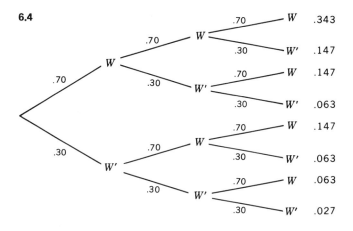

Number who watched	P
0	0.027
1	0.189
2	0.441
3	0.343

6.5 $(q + p)^n = (q + p)^3 = q^3 + 3q^2 p + 3qp^2 + p^3$
$\qquad\qquad = (0.30)^3 + 3 (0.30)^2 (0.70) + 3 (0.30)(0.70)^2 + (0.70)^3$
$\qquad\qquad = 0.027 + 0.189 + 0.441 + 0.343$

Number who watched	P
0	0.027
1	0.189
2	0.441
3	0.343

6.6 $P(X = 0 | n = 3, p = 0.70) = P(X' = 3 | n = 3, q = 0.30) = 0.0270$
$P(X = 1 | n = 3, p = 0.70) = P(X' = 2 | n = 3, q = 0.30) = 0.1890$
$P(X = 2 | n = 3, p = 0.70) = P(X' = 1 | n = 3, q = 0.30) = 0.4410$
$P(X = 3 | n = 3, p = 0.70) = P(X' = 0 | n = 3, q = 0.30) = 0.3430$

6.7 (a) $P(X = 5 | n = 10, p = 0.20) = 0.0264$
(b) $P(X \leqslant 3 | n = 15, p = 0.10) = 0.2059 + 0.3432 + 0.2669$
$$+ 0.1285 = 0.9445$$
(c) $P(X > 15 | n = 20, p = 0.30) = 0.0000$
(d) $P(X = 7 | n = 15, p = 0.70) = P(X' = 8 | n = 15, q = 0.30)$
$$= 0.0348$$
(e) $P(X \geqslant 8 | n = 10, p = 0.80) = P(X' \leqslant 2 | n = 10, q = 0.20)$
$$= 0.1074 + 0.2684 + 0.3020 = 0.6778$$

6.8 $P(X < 10 | n = 20, p = 0.60) = P(X' \geqslant 11 | n = 20, q = 0.40)$
$$= 0.0710 + 0.0355 + 0.0146 + 0.0049 + 0.0013 + 0.0003$$
$$= 0.1276$$

6.9 (a) $P(X = 5 | \lambda = 5.0) = 0.1755$
(b) $P(X \geqslant 7 | \lambda = 4.0) = 0.0595 + 0.0298 + 0.0132 + 0.0053$
$$+ 0.0019 + 0.0006 + 0.0002 + 0.0001 = 0.1106$$
(c) $P(X > 5 | \lambda = 2.5) = 0.0278 + 0.0099 + 0.0031 + 0.0009$
$$+ 0.0002 = 0.0419$$
(d) $P(X < 3 | \lambda = 3.0) = 0.0498 + 0.1494 + 0.2240 = 0.4232$
(e) $P(X \leqslant 3 | \lambda = 6.0) = 0.0025 + 0.0149 + 0.0446 = 0.0620$

6.10 (a) $P(X > 10 | \lambda = 5.0) = 0.0082 + 0.0034 + 0.0013 + 0.0005$
$$+ 0.0002 = 0.0136$$

(b) $P(X = 0 | \lambda = 5.0) = 0.0067$

Chapter 7 ■ The Normal Probability Distribution

7.1 (a) $z = \dfrac{X - \mu}{\sigma} = \dfrac{80 - 80}{20} = 0$
$P(X \leqslant 80 | \mu = 80, \sigma = 20) = P(z \leqslant 0) = 0.5000$

(b) $z = \dfrac{90 - 80}{20} = \dfrac{10}{20} = +0.50$

$z = \dfrac{100 - 80}{20} = +1.000$

$P(90 \leqslant X \leqslant 100) = P(0.50 \leqslant z \leqslant 1.00)$
$$= 0.3413 - 0.1915 = 0.1498$$

(c) $z = \dfrac{70 - 80}{20} = -0.50$

$z = \dfrac{100 - 80}{20} = +1.000$

$P(70 < X < 100) = P(-0.50 < z < 1.00)$
$$= 0.1915 + 0.3413 = 0.5328$$

(d) $z = \dfrac{70 - 80}{20} = -0.50$

$P(X < 70 | \mu = 80, \sigma = 20) = P(z < -0.50) = 0.5000$
$$- 0.1915 = 0.3085$$

(e) $z = \dfrac{60 - 80}{20} = -1.0$

$z = \dfrac{100 - 80}{20} = +1.0$

$$P(X < 60|\mu = 80, \sigma \doteq 20) = P(z < -1.00) = 0.5000$$
$$-0.3413 = 0.1587$$
$$P(X > 100|\mu = 80, \sigma \doteq 20) = P(z > +1.00) = 0.5000$$
$$-0.3413 = 0.1587$$
$$P(X < 60 \quad \text{or} \quad X > 100) = 0.1587 + 0.1587 = 0.3174$$

7.2 (a) $z = \dfrac{X - \mu}{\sigma} = \dfrac{50 - 53}{9} = \dfrac{-3}{9} = -0.33$

$$P(X < 50|\mu = 53, \sigma = 9) = P(z < -0.33)$$
$$= 0.5000 - 0.1293 = 0.3707$$

(b) $z = \dfrac{60 - 53}{9} = \dfrac{7}{9} + 0.77$

$$P(X > 60|\mu = 53, \sigma = 9) = P(z > 0.77)$$
$$= 0.5000 - 0.2794 = 0.2206$$

7.3 $P(X > 60) = 0.2206$ (from Exercise 7.2, above)
Using the rule of multiplication, $P(X_1 > 60, X_2 > 60, X_3 > 60)$
$$= 0.2206 \times 0.2206 \times 0.2206 = 0.0107$$

7.4 (a) $z = \dfrac{X - \mu}{\sigma} = \dfrac{350 - 500}{100} = -1.50$

$z = \dfrac{650 - 500}{100} = +1.50$

$P(X \geqslant 350 \quad \text{and} \quad X \leqslant 650|\mu = 500, \sigma = 100)$
$$= P(z \geqslant -1.50 \quad \text{and} \quad z \leqslant +1.50) = 0.4332 + 0.4332$$
$$= 0.8664 = 86.64\%$$

(b) $z = \dfrac{700 - 500}{100} = +2.00$

$P(X \geqslant 700|\mu = 500, \sigma = 100) = P(z \geqslant +2.00)$
$$= 0.500 - 0.4772 = 0.0228$$

Expected number $= 0.0228 \times 10,000 = 228$

7.5 For a proportion of 0.10 to be included in the upper tail of the distribution, a proportion of 0.40 has to be included in the area between μ and z. In Table B-1, the z value for which the proportion given in the body of the table is closest to 0.40 is +1.28 (proportion = 0.3997). Now algebraically solving the computational formula for z in respect to the unknown value of X:

$$z = \frac{X - \mu}{\sigma}$$
$$X - \mu = z\sigma$$
$$X = \mu + z\sigma$$

Therefore, for this problem: $X = \mu + z\sigma = 500 + 1.28(100)$
$$= 500 + 128 = 628$$

7.6 (a) $P(X = 0|n = 10, p = 0.05) = 0.5987$ (from Table B-3)
(b) $P(X \geqslant 3|n = 10, p = 0.05) = 0.0105 + 0.0010 + 0.0001$
$$= 0.0116$$

Since the probability of this sample result occurring by chance is so small, given the assumed 5 percent error rate, we would have reason to suspect that the error rate for this employee is in fact higher than 5 percent.

7.7 (a) A table of binomial probabilities for $n = 200$ is not available in this text. However, because $n \geqslant 30$, $np \geqslant 5$, and $nq \geqslant 5$, the normal approximation can be used.

$$\mu = np = (200)(0.05) = 10$$

$$\sigma = \sqrt{npq} = \sqrt{(200)(0.05)(0.95)} = \sqrt{9.5} = 3.08$$

Including the necessary correction for continuity in this approximation,

$$P(X \geqslant 10|n = 200, p = 0.05) \doteq P(X > 9.5|\mu = 10, \sigma = 3.08)$$

$$z = \frac{X - \mu}{\sigma} = \frac{9.5 - 10.0}{3.08} = \frac{-0.5}{3.08} = -0.16$$

$$P(z \geqslant -0.16) = 0.0636 + 0.5000 = 0.5636$$

(b) $P(X \geqslant 15|n = 200, p = 0.05) \doteq P(X \geqslant 14.5|\mu = 10, \sigma = 3.08)$

$$z = \frac{X - \mu}{\sigma} = \frac{14.5 - 10.0}{3.08} = \frac{4.5}{3.08} = +1.46$$

$$P(z > +1.46) = 0.5000 - 0.4279 = 0.0721$$

7.8 Since $np < 5$, the normal approximation of the binomial probability value is not appropriate. However, since $n \geqslant 30$, probability values based on the Poisson distribution can be used to approximate the binomial probabilities.

$$\lambda = np = (200)(0.01) = 2.0$$
$$P(X \geqslant 4|n = 200, p = 0.01) \doteq P(X \geqslant 4|\lambda = 2.0)$$
$$= 0.0902 + 0.0361 + 0.0120 + 0.0034 + 0.0009 + 0.0002 = 0.1428$$

7.9 $P(X \geqslant 5|\lambda = 3.0) = 0.1008 + 0.0504 + 0.0216 + 0.0081 + 0.0027$
$$+ 0.0008 + 0.0002 + 0.0001 = 0.1847$$

7.10 $\lambda = 3.0 \times 12$ five-minute intervals in an hour $= 36.0$. Because $\lambda \geqslant 10$, the normal probability curve can be used to approximate the required probability value.

$$\mu = \lambda = 36.0$$
$$\sigma = \sqrt{\lambda} = \sqrt{36.0} = 6.0$$
$$P(X < 30|\lambda = 36.0) \doteq P(X \leqslant 29.5|\mu = 36.0, \sigma = 6.0)$$
$$z = \frac{X - \mu}{\sigma} = \frac{29.5 - 36.0}{6.0} = \frac{-6.5}{6.0} = -1.08$$
$$P(z \leqslant -1.08) = 0.5000 - 0.3599 = 0.1401$$

Chapter 8 ■ Sampling Methods and Sampling Distributions

8.1 Statistical estimation is involved when we wish to estimate the value of a population parameter, such as a population mean, based on the value of a sample statistic, such as the sample mean. The estimate may be a point estimate or an interval estimate, but in either case no value of the parameter is assumed prior to obtaining the sample result. In hypothesis testing, on the other hand, the parameter has an assumed or hypothesized value prior to the sample result being known. If the sample result is considerably different from what one would expect given the hypothesized value, we would have reason to question the accuracy of the hypothesized value.

8.2 In systematic sampling the sample elements are collected at a uniform interval through time or space (for example, every tenth item), whereas in simple random sampling the choice of each element is based on a random selection. Systematic sampling is generally easier to use because it does not require the procedure associated with achieving individual random selections. For example, the use of a table of random numbers and the search for the particular elements identified by the selected numbers would be largely eliminated. Before using systematic sampling, the analyst should be satisfied that there is not some kind of repeating pattern in the listing of elements from which a sample is being taken. For example, if employees are listed by department and then according to salary level within each department, the use of systematic sampling might not be appropriate.

8.3 **(a)** For a simple random sample, the names can be chosen from the list by some random process for the purpose of individual contact. If each person's name is assigned a unique number, a table of random numbers can be used for sample selection.
(b) For a systematic sample, every nth (such as fifth) person on the list can be contacted.
(c) For a stratified sample, we might classify the population of owners according to sex or age, and then choose a simple random or systematic sample from each stratum.
(d) For a cluster sample, since we we have the addresses of the car owners, we might choose to interview all owners living on randomly selected blocks in the test area. Having a geographic basis, this type of cluster sampling can also be called "area sampling."

8.4

X	X^2
3	9
6	36
9	81
10	100
$\Sigma X = 28$	$\Sigma X^2 = 226$

(a) $\mu = \dfrac{\Sigma X}{N} = \dfrac{28}{4} = 7.0$

(b) $\sigma = \sqrt{\dfrac{\Sigma X^2 - N\mu^2}{N}} = \sqrt{\dfrac{226 - 4(7.0)^2}{4}}$

$= \sqrt{7.5} \doteq 2.74$

8.5 **(a)**

Possible samples	$\overline{X}$	$\overline{X}^2$
3, 6	4.5	20.25
3, 9	6.0	36.00
3, 10	6.5	42.25
6, 9	7.5	56.25
6, 10	8.0	64.00
9, 10	9.5	90.25
	$\Sigma\overline{X} = 42.0$	$\Sigma\overline{X}^2 = 309.00$

(b) $\mu_{\overline{X}} = \dfrac{\Sigma\overline{X}}{N_s} = \dfrac{42.0}{6} = 7.0$ [which equals μ computed in solution 8.4(a)]

8.6 **(a)** $\sigma_{\overline{X}} = \sqrt{\dfrac{\Sigma\overline{X}^2 - N_s\mu_{\overline{X}}^2}{N_s}}$ (computational formula)

$$= \sqrt{\dfrac{309.00 - 6(7.0)^2}{6}} = \sqrt{2.5} \doteq 1.58$$

(b) $\sigma_{\overline{X}} = \dfrac{\sigma}{\sqrt{n}}\sqrt{\dfrac{N-n}{N-1}}$ (formula when σ is known and population is finite)

$$= \dfrac{2.74}{\sqrt{2}}\sqrt{\dfrac{4-2}{4-1}} = \dfrac{2.74}{\sqrt{2}} \times \dfrac{\sqrt{2}}{\sqrt{3}} = \dfrac{2.74}{\sqrt{3}} =$$

$$= \dfrac{2.74}{1.73} \doteq 1.58$$

8.7 $\sigma_{\overline{X}} = \dfrac{\sigma}{\sqrt{n}} = \dfrac{300}{\sqrt{36}} = 50.0$

The standard error of 50.0 indicates that if a large number of samples of size $n = 36$ were collected, the standard deviation of the distribution of sample means in respect to the population mean would be 50.0. Accordingly, 68 percent of the sample means would be within 50 hours of the true mean of 10,000 hours (± one standard deviation unit).

8.8 Est. $\mu = \overline{X} = 9,800$

$$s_{\overline{X}} = \dfrac{s}{\sqrt{n}} = \dfrac{320}{\sqrt{36}} = \dfrac{320}{6.0} = 53.3$$

8.9 **(a)** Est. $\mu = \overline{X} = \$3.00$

(b) $s_{\overline{X}} = \dfrac{s}{\sqrt{n}}\sqrt{\dfrac{N-n}{N-1}}$ (formula when s is known and population is finite)

$$= \dfrac{0.50}{\sqrt{25}}\sqrt{\dfrac{257-25}{257-1}} = \dfrac{0.50}{5}\sqrt{\dfrac{232}{256}}$$

$$= 0.10\sqrt{0.90625} = 0.10(0.952) = 0.095$$

8.10 (a) Est. $\mu = \bar{X} = \$3.00$

(b) $s_{\bar{X}} = \dfrac{s}{\sqrt{n}} = \dfrac{0.50}{\sqrt{25}} = \dfrac{0.50}{5} = 0.10$

Therefore, the fact that the population is infinite ("very large") has no effect on the estimate of the population mean. However, the standard error of the mean is somewhat larger for the infinite population.

Chapter 9 ■ Statistical Estimation

9.1 The criterion of *unbiasedness* indicates that the expected value of the sample statistic used as an estimator should equal the value of the parameter being estimated. In general, we can represent this idea symbolically by E(estimator) = parameter. The mathematical concept of "expected value" means that the *average* value of an infinite number of estimator values would exactly equal the parameter value. The criterion of *consistency* indicates that the value of the estimator should approach the value of the parameter as sample size approaches the population size. Symbolically, we can say "estimator → parameter as $n \to N$." Thus, one of the characteristics of a good estimator is that on the average an increase in sample size results in better accuracy. An estimator which satisfies one of these criteria does not necessarily satisfy the other. For example, the sample standard deviation is a consistent estimator of the population standard deviation in that its accuracy as an estimator improves with any increase in sample size. However, as indicated in Table 9-1 in the chapter, the sample standard deviation is a biased estimator of the population standard deviation.

9.2 (a) $\hat{\mu} = \bar{X} = \$27.00$

(b) $\hat{\sigma} = s = \$8.00$

(c) $N\hat{\mu} = N\bar{X} = 500\,(\$27.00) = \$13,500.00$

(d) $N\hat{\pi} = Np = 500\,(0.70) = 350$

9.3 $s_{\bar{X}} = \dfrac{s}{\sqrt{n}} = \dfrac{14.00}{\sqrt{49}} = \dfrac{14.00}{7} = \$2.00$

(a) $\bar{X} \pm 1.65 s_{\bar{X}} = 53.00 \pm 1.65(2.00) = 53.00 \pm 3.30 = \$49.70$
to $\$56.30$

(b) $\bar{X} \pm 1.96 s_{\bar{X}} = 53.00 \pm 1.96(2.00) = 53.00 \pm 3.92 = \$49.08$
to $\$56.92$

(c) $\bar{X} \pm 2.58 s_{\bar{X}} = 53.00 \pm 2.58(2.00) = 53.00 \pm 5.16 = \$47.84$
to $\$58.16$

(d) Which of the confidence intervals is most useful depends on the objectives of the decision maker. Although the 90 percent confidence interval involves the greatest degree of risk of not including the actual mean of all accounts, it is the most precise of the three estimates. At the other extreme the 99 percent confidence interval involves least risk of an estimation error, but it is the widest of the three estimation intervals.

9.4 (a) $N(\bar{X} \pm 1.65 s_{\bar{X}}) = 3,000(\$49.70 \text{ to } \$56.30) = \$149,100$
to $\$168,900$

(b) $N(\bar{X} \pm 1.96 s_{\bar{X}}) = 3,000(\$49.08 \text{ to } \$56.92) = \$147,240$
to $\$170,760$

(c) $N(\bar{X} \pm 2.58 s_{\bar{X}}) = 3,000(\$47.84 \text{ to } \$58.16) = \$143,520$
to $\$174,480$

9.5 $s_{\overline{X}_1-\overline{X}_2} = \sqrt{s_{\overline{X}_1}^2 + s_{\overline{X}_2}^2} = \sqrt{(2.00)^2 + (3.00)^2} = \sqrt{13.00} = \$3.61$

Diff $= \overline{X}_1 - \overline{X}_2 \pm 1.96 s_{\overline{X}_1-\overline{X}_2} = 54.00 - 45.00 \pm 1.96\,(3.61)$
$= 9.00 \pm 7.08 = \$1.92$ to $\$16.08$

9.6 Mean purchase amount $= \overline{X} \pm z s_{\overline{X}}$
where $\overline{X} = \$27.00$
$s = \$8.00$
$n = 100$
$N = 500$
$z = 1.96$

and $s_{\overline{X}} = \dfrac{s}{\sqrt{n}}\sqrt{\dfrac{N-n}{N-1}} = \dfrac{8.00}{\sqrt{100}}\sqrt{\dfrac{500-100}{499}}$

$= \dfrac{8.00}{10}\sqrt{0.801603} = 0.80(0.90) = 0.72$

(Use of the finite correction factor is appropriate because $n > 5\%\,N$.)

Mean purchase amount $= \$27.00 \pm 1.96(0.72)$
$= \$27.00 \pm 1.4112 = \$25.59$ to $\$28.41$

Total purchase amount $= N(\overline{X} \pm s_{\overline{X}})$
$= 500\,(\$25.5888$ to $\$28.4112)$
$= \$12,794.40$ to $\$14,205.60$

9.7 $s_p = \sqrt{\dfrac{p(1-p)}{n-1}} = \sqrt{\dfrac{0.60(0.40)}{99}} = \sqrt{0.002424} = 0.049$

(a) $p \pm 1.65 s_p = 0.60 \pm 1.65(0.049) = 0.60 \pm 0.08 = 0.52$ to 0.68
$= 52\%$ to 68%

(b) $p \pm 1.96 s_p = 0.60 \pm 1.96(0.049) = 0.60 \pm 0.10 = 0.50$ to 0.70
$= 50\%$ to 70%

(c) $p \pm 2.58 s_p = 0.60 \pm 2.58(0.049) = 0.60 \pm 0.13$
$= 0.47$ to $0.73 = 47\%$ to 73%

9.8 $N(p \pm 1.96 s_p) = 3,000\,(0.50$ to $0.70) = 1,500$ to $2,100$

9.9 $s_{p_1} = \sqrt{\dfrac{p_1(1-p_1)}{n_1-1}} = \sqrt{\dfrac{0.60(0.40)}{49}} = \sqrt{0.004898} \doteq 0.07$

$s_{p_2} = \sqrt{\dfrac{p_2(1-p_2)}{n_2-1}} = \sqrt{\dfrac{0.50(0.50)}{49}} = \sqrt{0.005102} \doteq 0.07$

$s_{p_1-p_2} = \sqrt{s_{p_1}^2 + s_{p_2}^2} = \sqrt{0.004898 + 0.005102}$
$= \sqrt{0.0100} = 0.10$

Diff $= p_1 - p_2 \pm 1.96 s_{p_1-p_2} = (0.60 - 0.50) \pm 1.96\,(0.10)$
$= 0.10 \pm 0.20 = -0.10$ to $0.30 = -10\%$ to 30%

The -10 percent signifies that the percentage of voters in the second district who are in favor of the proposal may actually exceed the percentage in the first district by as much as 10 percent. On the other hand, the percentage in favor of the proposal in the first district may exceed the second district percentage by as much as 30 percent at the 95 percent degree of confidence.

9.10 Sample size $n = 65$

Sample proportion $p = \dfrac{38}{65} = 0.585$

$$s_p = \sqrt{\frac{p(1-p)}{n-1}} = \sqrt{\frac{0.585(0.415)}{64}} = \sqrt{\frac{0.242775}{64}}$$

$$= \frac{0.493}{8} = 0.062 \qquad \begin{array}{l} \text{(Finite correction factor not necessary} \\ \text{because } n < 5\% \ N.) \end{array}$$

(a) Ninety-five percent confidence interval for estimating the proportion of the population who will vote in favor of the bond issue:

$$p \pm zs_p = 0.585 \pm 1.96\,(0.062)$$
$$= 0.585 \pm 0.121 = 0.464 \text{ to } 0.706 \cong 0.46 \text{ to } 0.71$$

(b) Ninety-five percent confidence interval for estimating the total number in the population who will vote in favor of the bond issue:

$$N(p \pm zs_p) = 6{,}500\,(0.464 \text{ to } 0.706)$$
$$= 3{,}016 \text{ to } 4{,}589$$

Chapter 10 ▪ Hypothesis Testing

10.1 (a) In statistical estimation the confidence limits define the interval such that we can say that a certain percentage of intervals that are so defined will contain the population parameter in the long run. For example, when the 95 percent confidence interval is used as the basis for a series of interval estimates, 95 out of 100 such intervals, on the average, will include the value of the population parameter being estimated.

The point of reference for confidence intervals is of course the point estimate, for example, $\overline{X}$. In contrast, the point of reference for identifying critical limits in hypothesis testing is the hypothesized value of the population parameter rather than the point estimate of the parameter. Given that the hypothesized value is true, the percentage of sample values that will fall outside of the defined critical limit (for one-tailed tests) or limits (for two-tailed tests) is indicated by the level of significance used in defining the critical limits.

(b) Statistical estimation is used when there is no prior or established belief regarding the value of the population parameter. Neither is there some value that the parameter should equal (as in quality control or auditing situations). Rather, we simply wish to obtain an estimate of an uncertain population value. In contrast, hypothesis testing is used when there is some prior belief or standard regarding the value of the parameter. Moreover, if the prior belief is upheld (not rejected) by the sample results, then one course of action is implied; whereas if the prior belief (hypothesis) is rejected, a different course of action is implied. Thus, hypothesis testing is directly related to decision analysis techniques that are concerned with formulating decision rules that lead to the choice of different managerial actions.

10.2 **(a)** Type I error in hypothesis testing refers to the probability of incorrectly rejecting a true null hypothesis (and thereby accepting a false alternative hypothesis). The probability of this error is determined by the level of significance used in the hypothesis-testing procedure.

(b) The probability of type I error can be reduced simply by changing the level of significance that is used — for example, from the 5 percent level to the 1 percent level. Increasing the sample size does *not* reduce the probability of type I error if the same level of significance is still used, because the effect would be to change the critical limits (because of the change in the value of the standard error) rather than changing the proportion of sample results in the region(s) of rejection.

(c) Given a fixed sample size, a reduction in type I error by changing the level of significance leads to a higher probability of type II error — that of accepting a false null hypothesis (and rejecting a true alternative hypothesis). If the probability of type II error is deemed too high based on its importance, the decision maker might choose to change the decision rule (level of significance) so that the probability of type I error is increased and the probability of type II error is decreased.

10.3 $\mu_H = 2,500$
$\mu_A \neq 2,500$

Critical values of z (two-tailed, 5 percent level) $= \pm 1.96$

$$s_{\bar{X}} = \frac{s}{\sqrt{n}} = \frac{600}{\sqrt{36}} = \frac{600}{6} = 100$$

$$z = \frac{\bar{X} - \mu_H}{s_{\bar{X}}} = \frac{2,325 - 2,500}{100} = \frac{-175}{100} = -1.75$$

Since the computed z value is in the region of acceptance in respect to the null hypothesis, the manufacturer's claim cannot be rejected.

10.4 $\mu_H \geqslant 2,500$
$\mu_A < 2,500$

Critical value of z (one-tailed, 5 percent level) $= -1.65$

Computed $z = -1.75$ (from Exercise 3, above)

Since the computed z is in the region of rejection in respect to the null hypothesis, the manufacturer's claim is rejected, and the alternative hypothesis, that average bulb life is less than 2,500 hours, is accepted.

10.5 $(\mu_1 - \mu_2)_H = 0$
$(\mu_1 - \mu_2)_A \neq 0$

Critical values of z (two-tailed, 5 percent level) $= \pm 1.96$

$$s_{\overline{X}_1} = \frac{s_1}{\sqrt{n_1}} = \frac{0.02}{\sqrt{64}} = \frac{0.02}{8} = 0.0025$$

$$s_{\overline{X}_2} = \frac{s_2}{\sqrt{n_2}} = \frac{0.04}{\sqrt{64}} = \frac{0.04}{8} = 0.0050$$

$$s_{\overline{X}_1 - \overline{X}_2} = \sqrt{s_{\overline{X}_1}{}^2 + s_{\overline{X}_2}{}^2} = \sqrt{(0.0025)^2 + (0.0050)^2}$$

$$= \sqrt{0.00000625 + 0.000025} = \sqrt{0.00003125} = 0.0056$$

$$z = \frac{\overline{X}_1 - \overline{X}_2}{s_{\overline{X}_1 - \overline{X}_2}} = \frac{0.24 - 0.25}{0.0056} = \frac{-0.01}{0.0056} = -1.79$$

The computed z value is in the region of acceptance in respect to the null hypothesis. Therefore, the hypothesis that the machine is *not* out of adjustment is accepted, and no changes in adjustment would be made.

10.6 $(\mu_1 - \mu_2)_H \leqslant 0$ (Note that in this case the machine is not
$(\mu_1 - \mu_2)_A > 0$ out of adjustment if it appears that the
second mean is larger than the first mean,
by definition in the exercise.)

Critical value of z (one-tailed, 5 percent level) $= +1.65$

$z = -1.79$ (from Exercise 10.5, above)

The computed z value is in the region of acceptance, so the hypothesis that the machine is *not* out of adjustment is accepted. Because the direction of the difference *supports* the null hypothesis, we need not even compute the z value for the sample result in such a situation. Again, the exercise indicated that in order to have evidence that the machine is out of adjustment, the second sample would have to have a mean *smaller* than the first sample.

10.7 $\pi_H \geqslant 0.30$
$\pi_A < 0.30$

By reference to the table of Binomial Probabilities (Table B-3), with π = 0.30 and n = 10, the probability of zero sales is 0.0282 and the probability of one or fewer sales is 0.0282 + 0.1211 = 0.1493. Therefore, the critical number of sales for rejecting the null hypothesis at the 5 percent level is that there be *no* sales (because the probability of "one or fewer" sales is *greater* than 0.05).

Given the sample result that one sale was completed, this result is in the region of acceptance of the null hypothesis, and therefore the salesman's claim cannot be rejected.

10.8 (a) $\pi_H \geqslant 0.30$
$\pi_A < 0.30$

Critical value of z (one-tailed, 5 percent level) $= -1.65$

$$\sigma_p = \sqrt{\frac{\pi_H(1-\pi_H)}{n}} = \sqrt{\frac{0.30(0.70)}{100}} = \sqrt{\frac{0.2100}{100}}$$

$$= \sqrt{0.0021} = 0.046$$

$$z = \frac{p - \pi_H}{\sigma_p} = \frac{0.20 - 0.30}{0.046} = \frac{-0.10}{0.046} = -2.17$$

The computed z value is in the region of rejection of the null hypothesis. Therefore the salesman's claim is rejected and the alternative hypothesis that his true percentage of sales is *less* than 30 percent is accepted.

(b) Critical value of z (one-tailed, 1 percent level) $= -2.33$. Therefore we cannot reject the null hypothesis at the 1 percent level.

10.9 $\mu_H \geqslant 22.0$
$\mu_A < 22.0$

Critical value of z (one-tailed, 5 percent level) $= -1.65$

$$s_{\overline{X}} = \frac{s}{\sqrt{n}} = \frac{2.3}{\sqrt{49}} = \frac{2.3}{7} = 0.33$$

$$z = \frac{\overline{X} - \mu_H}{s_{\overline{X}}} = \frac{21.5 - 22.0}{0.33} = \frac{-0.50}{0.33} = -1.51$$

The computed z value is in the region of acceptance of the null hypothesis. Therefore the manufacturer's claim regarding overall average mileage cannot be rejected on the basis of the sample result.

10.10 $\mu_H \leqslant 22.0$
$\mu_A > 22.0$

Critical value of z (one-tailed, 5 percent level) $= +1.65$

$z = -1.51$ (from Exercise 10.9, above)

The computed z value is in the region of acceptance of the null hypothesis. In fact, the value is in the direction specified in the null hypothesis. Therefore the null hypothesis is accepted and the alternative hypothesis is rejected.

Note that the same sample data resulted in acceptance of *both* of the apparently contradictory null hypotheses included in Exercise 10.9 and in this exercise. This result illustrates the fact that the hypothesis which is designated as the null hypothesis is in effect given the "benefit of doubt." For example, the sample data did not in fact support the null hypothesis in Exercise 10.9 in a positive way; but the negative difference was not enough to lead to outright (statistical) rejection.

Chapter 11 ■ Use of Student's _t_ Distribution

11.1 Three conditions must hold for the appropriate use of the t distribution in conjunction with testing a hypothesis concerning a population mean: (a) the standard deviation of the population, σ, is unknown; (b) the sample is small, with $n < 30$; and (c) the population from which the sample has been selected is normally distributed. The last of these conditions is the most difficult to satisfy in applied studies. Of course, if $n \geqslant$ 30, then the last condition is not required because the central-limit theorem indicates that the sample means will be approximately normally distributed regardless of the form of the population. Also, with $n \geqslant 30$ the unit normal (z) distribution would generally be used as a substitute for the t distribution, because of the similarity in values between the two distributions.

11.2 The *systematic* departure from normality of the t distribution is associated with the assumption that the difference between the population mean and each of a normally distributed set of sample means is divided by a different standard error value. If the set of means is not itself normally distributed, then the effect of dividing by different standard error values would also result in a nonnormal distribution, but it would not be the systematic departure represented by the t distribution.

11.3

X	X^2
11.8	139.24
11.7	136.89
12.1	146.41
11.9	141.61
12.0	144.00
12.0	144.00
11.7	136.89
12.0	144.00
11.8	139.24
12.0	144.00
$\Sigma X = 119.0$	$\Sigma X^2 = 1{,}416.28$

(a) $\quad \bar{X} = \dfrac{\Sigma X}{n} = \dfrac{119.0}{10} = 11.90$

(b) $\quad s = \sqrt{\dfrac{\Sigma X^2 - n\bar{X}^2}{n-1}} = \sqrt{\dfrac{1{,}416.28 - 10(11.90)^2}{10-1}}$

$\quad\quad = \sqrt{\dfrac{1{,}416.28 - 1{,}416.10}{9}} = \sqrt{0.02} = 0.1414$

(c) $\quad s_{\bar{X}} = \dfrac{s}{\sqrt{n}} = \dfrac{0.1414}{\sqrt{10}} = 0.045$

(d) $\quad \bar{X} \pm ts_{\bar{X}} = 11.90 \pm 2.262(0.045) = 11.90 \pm 0.102$

$\quad\quad = 11.9 \pm 0.1 = 11.8$ to 12.0 ounces

11.4 $\mu_H \geqslant 12.0$
$\quad\quad \mu_A < 12.0$

Critical value of t (one-tailed, 5 percent level, df $= 9$) $= -1.833$

$t = \dfrac{\bar{X} - \mu_H}{s_{\bar{X}}} = \dfrac{11.9 - 12.0}{0.045} = \dfrac{-0.1}{0.045} = -2.22$

Since the computed t value is in the region of rejection in respect to the null hypothesis, the assumption that the average minimum content is being satisfied is rejected and the alternative hypothesis that the overall average weight per package is *less* than 12.0 ounces is accepted.

11.5 $s_{\overline{X}} = \dfrac{s}{\sqrt{n}} \sqrt{\dfrac{N-n}{N-1}} = \dfrac{0.25}{\sqrt{25}} \sqrt{\dfrac{100-25}{100-1}} = \dfrac{0.25}{\sqrt{25}} \sqrt{\dfrac{75}{99}}$

$= \dfrac{0.25}{5.0} \sqrt{0.757575} = 0.05(0.870) \doteq 0.044$

$\overline{X} \pm t s_{\overline{X}} = \$4.75 \pm 2.064(0.044) = \$4.75 \pm 0.09 = \$4.66$ to $\$4.84$

11.6 $\mu_H \geqslant 4.85$
$\mu_A < 4.85$

Critical value of t (one-tailed, 5 percent level, df $= 24$) $= -1.711$

$t = \dfrac{\overline{X} - \mu_H}{s_{\overline{X}}} = \dfrac{4.75 - 4.85}{0.044} = \dfrac{-0.10}{0.044} = -2.27$

Since the computed t value is in the region of rejection in respect to the null hypothesis, the null hypothesis is rejected and the alternative hypothesis that the overall average wage is less than $\$4.85$ is accepted.

11.7 $s_{\overline{X}} = \dfrac{s}{\sqrt{n}} = \dfrac{0.30}{\sqrt{10}} = \dfrac{0.30}{3.162} \doteq 0.095$

$\overline{X} \pm t s_{\overline{X}} = 11.0 \pm 2.266(0.095) = 11.0 \pm 0.2 = 10.8$ to 11.2 ounces

11.8 $\mu_H \geqslant 11.2$
$\mu_A < 11.2$

Critical value of t (one-tailed, 5 percent level, df $= 9$) $= -1.833$

$t = \dfrac{\overline{X} - \mu_H}{s_{\overline{X}}} = \dfrac{11.0 - 11.2}{0.095} = \dfrac{-0.2}{0.095} = -2.105$

Since the computed t value is in the region of rejection, the null hypothesis is rejected and the alternative hypothesis that the average weight for all cans is less than 11.2 ounces is accepted.

11.9 $n_1 = 10$
$s_1 = 0.30$ (from Exercise 11.7)
$n_2 = 10$
$s_2 = 0.20$

$\hat{\sigma} = \sqrt{\dfrac{(n_1 - 1)s_1^2 + (n_2 - 1)s_2^2}{n_1 + n_2 - 2}}$

$= \sqrt{\dfrac{(10 - 1)(0.30)^2 + (10 - 1)(0.20)^2}{10 + 10 - 2}}$

$$= \sqrt{\frac{9(0.09) + 9(0.04)}{18}} = \sqrt{\frac{1.17}{18}} = \sqrt{0.065} = 0.255$$

$$\hat{\sigma}_{\overline{X}_1 - \overline{X}_2} = \sqrt{\frac{\hat{\sigma}^2}{n_1} + \frac{\hat{\sigma}^2}{n_2}} = \sqrt{\frac{0.065}{10} + \frac{0.065}{10}} = \sqrt{\frac{0.130}{10}}$$

$$= \sqrt{0.013} \doteq 0.114$$

90% Conf. limits $= (\overline{X}_1 - \overline{X}_2) \pm t\hat{\sigma}_{\overline{X}_1 - \overline{X}_2}$
$= (11.0) - 10.8) \pm 1.734(0.114)$
$= 0.2 \pm 0.2$
$= 0$ to 0.4 ounce difference per can

11.10 $(\mu_1 - \mu_2)_H = 0$
$(\mu_1 - \mu_2)_A \neq 0$

Critical value of t (two-tailed, 5 percent level, df $= 18$) $= \pm 2.101$

$$t = \frac{\overline{X}_1 - \overline{X}_2}{\hat{\sigma}_{\overline{X}_1 - \overline{X}_2}} = \frac{11.0 - 10.8}{0.114} = \frac{0.2}{0.114} = +1.754$$

Since the computed t value of $+1.754$ is in the region of acceptance of the null hypothesis, the hypothesis that there is no difference in the overall mean weights of cans being packed in the two plants is accepted.

Chapter 12 ■ The Chi-square Test

12.1 The χ^2 (chi-square) test applied for the purpose of testing goodness of fit is concerned with determining if the pattern of categorized frequencies observed in a sample could have been selected from a population with a specified distribution of frequencies. The null hypothesis always tested is that the distribution of frequencies in the sampled population matches the distribution in the hypothesized population. The alternative hypothesis is that the two patterns are different. Of course, no one sample of observations is likely to exactly reflect the population distribution, and so the use of the χ^2 test makes it possible to determine the significance of the differences between the observed and expected frequencies for the several categories. In order to apply such a test, a necessary assumption is that the sample data are based on a probability (random) sample. In this respect, then, the χ^2 test is appropriately designated as a method of statistical inference.

12.2 (a)

	Marketing area		
	A	B	Total
Sales, prior month	120	180	300
Proportion, prior month (p)	0.40	0.60	1.00
Sales, sampled week	45	55	100
Expected sales, sampled week (np)	40	60	100

(b) Critical value of χ^2 (5 percent level, df $= 1$) $= 3.84$

$$\chi^2 = \sum \frac{(|f_o - f_e| - 0.5)^2}{f_e}$$

(Note that Yates' correction for continuity is appropriate, because df $= 1$.)

$$= \frac{(|45-40|-0.5)^2}{40} + \frac{(|55-60|-0.5)^2}{60}$$

$$= \frac{(4.5)^2}{40} + \frac{(5.5)^2}{60} = 0.506 + 0.504 = 1.01$$

Since the computed χ^2 value is in the region of acceptance in respect to the null hypothesis, the hypothesis that the sampled frequencies do not differ significantly from the expected frequencies is accepted.

(c) The result of the test means that the assumption that the proportion of sales in the two marketing areas remains the same as before the new campaign was introduced is accepted. Of course, this also means that the alternative assumption that the new promotional campaign has caused a shift in the sales pattern is not accepted. Note that the difference between obtained and expected frequencies does in fact favor the new promotional method. But the difference is not large enough to reject the null hypothesis.

12.3

	Marketing area		
	A	B	Total
Sales, sampled week	45	55	100
Expected sales, sampled week	50	50	100

Critical value of χ^2 (5 percent level, df $= 1$) $= 3.84$

$$\chi^2 = \sum \frac{(|f_o - f_e| - 0.5)^2}{f_e} = \frac{(|45-50|-0.5)^2}{50} + \frac{(|55-50|-0.5)^2}{50}$$

$$= \frac{(4.5)^2}{50} + \frac{(4.5)^2}{50} = 0.405 + 0.405 = 0.81$$

As was the case in Exercise 12.2, the computed χ^2 is in the region of acceptance in respect to the null hypothesis.

12.4 (a) Expected frequencies:

	Additional feature desired				
Respondents	Disk brakes	Collapsible steering wheel	Automatic door locks	Speed warning buzzer	Total
Men	10	20	12.5	7.5	50
Women	10	20	12.5	7.5	50
Total	20	40	25.0	15.0	100

Computiation of the above cell entries was carried out by the use of the marginal totals, as follows:

$$f_e \text{ (row 1, col. 1)} = \frac{f_r f_k}{n} = \frac{(50)(20)}{100} = \frac{1,000}{100} = 10$$

$$f_e \text{ (row 1, col. 2)} = \frac{(50)(40)}{100} = \frac{2,000}{100} = 20$$

$$f_e \text{ (row 1, col. 3)} = \frac{(50)(25)}{100} = \frac{1,250}{100} = 12.5$$

(Other values can be similarly computed or determined by subtraction from marginal totals.)

(b)

$$\chi^2 = \sum \frac{(f_o - f_e)^2}{f_e} = \frac{(5)^2}{10} + \frac{(5)^2}{20} + \frac{(-7.5)^2}{12.5} + \frac{(-2.5)^2}{7.5}$$

$$+ \frac{(-5)^2}{10} + \frac{(-5)^2}{20} + \frac{(7.5)^2}{12.5} + \frac{(2.5)^2}{7.5} = 2.50 + 1.25 + 4.50$$

$$+ 0.83 + 2.50 + 1.25 + 4.50 + 0.83 = 18.16$$

(c) With df $= (r - 1)(k - 1) = (1)(3) = 3$, the critical value of χ^2 for significance at the 1 percent level is 11.34. Since $18.16 > 11.34$, the difference is significant.

(d) A significant χ^2 value indicates that the two bases for classification are not independent. In this case it indicates that there is a relationship between the sex of the respondent and the safety feature most desired.

12.5 For this problem only the column totals are tested for goodness of fit.

Additional feature desired

	Disk brakes	Collapsible steering wheel	Automatic doorlocks	Speed warning buzzer	Total
$f_o =$	20	40	25	15	100
$f_e =$	25	25	25	25	100

$$\chi^2 = \sum \frac{(f_o - f_e)^2}{f_e} = \frac{(-5)^2}{25} + \frac{(15)^2}{25} + \frac{(0)^2}{25} + \frac{(-10)^2}{25}$$

$$= 1.0 + 9.0 + 0 + 4.0 = 14.0$$

With df $= 4 - 1 = 3$, the critical value of χ^2 for significance at the 1 percent level is 11.34. Since $14.0 > 11.34$, the difference is significant.

12.6 (a) Expected frequencies:

Present status of loan	Status at time of loan Employed	Unemployed	Total
In default	12.6	5.4	18
Not in default	57.4	24.6	82
Total	70.0	30.0	100

$$f_e \text{ (row 1, col. 1)} = \frac{f_r f_k}{n} = \frac{(18)(70)}{100} = \frac{1,260}{100} = 12.6$$

(Others are determined by subtraction from column totals.)

$$\chi^2 = \sum \frac{(|f_o - f_e| - 0.5)^2}{f_e}$$

(Note that Yates' correction for continuity is appropriate because df $= 1$.)

$$= \frac{(2.1)^2}{12.6} + \frac{(2.1)^2}{5.4} + \frac{(2.1)^2}{57.4} + \frac{(2.1)^2}{24.6}$$

$$= 0.350 + 0.817 + 0.077 + 0.179 = 1.423$$

(b) With df $= (r-1)(k-1) = (1)(1) = 1$, the critical value of χ^2 for significance at the 5 percent level is 3.82. Since $1.423 < 3.84$, the test statistic is not significant and we conclude that there is no relationship between employment status and credit status.

12.7 For this problem only the row totals are tested for goodness of fit.

	In default	Not in default	Total
$f_o =$	18	82	100
$f_e =$	10	90	100

$$\chi^2 = \sum \frac{(|f_o - f_e| - 0.5)^2}{f_e} = \frac{(7.5)^2}{10} + \frac{(7.5)^2}{90} = 5.625 + 0.625 = 6.25$$

With df $= 2 - 1 = 1$, the critical value of χ^2 for significance at the 5 percent level is 3.84. Since $6.25 > 3.84$, the difference between the expected and obtained patterns of frequencies is significant. Specifically, the sample contains a greater number of accounts in default than has been the historical experience.

12.8 **(a)** (The expected frequencies are the same as those determined in the solution to Exercise 12.6.)

(b) $\chi^2 = \sum \frac{(|f_o - f_e| - 0.5)^2}{f_e} = \frac{(7.1)^2}{12.6} + \frac{(7.1)^2}{5.4} + \frac{(7.1)^2}{57.4}$

$$+ \frac{(7.1)^2}{24.6}$$

$$= 4.001 + 9.335 + 0.878 + 2.049 = 16.263$$

(c) With df $= 1$, the critical value of χ^2 at the 5 percent level of significance is 3.84. Since $16.263 > 3.84$, the test statistic is significant, and we conclude that there is a relationship between employment status and credit status.

12.9

Sales amount	f_o	Limits in terms of z values*	Expected proportion†	f_e	x^2
Below $9.00	15	Below −1.50	0.0668	13.3	0.22
$9.00-$11.99	15	−1.50 to −1.00	0.0919	18.4	0.63
$12.00-$14.99	35	−1.00 to −0.50	0.1498	30.0	0.83
$15.00-$17.99	50	−0.50 to 0	0.1915	38.3	3.57
$18.00-$20.99	40	0 to +0.50	0.1915	38.3	0.08
$21.00-$23.99	25	0.50 to 1.00	0.1498	30.0	0.83
$24.00-$26.99	15	1.00 to 1.50	0.0919	18.4	0.63
$27.00 and above	5	1.50 to 2.00	0.0668	13.3	5.18
Total	200		1.0000	200.0	11.97

*For example, the z value for the lower boundary of the second class

$$= \frac{8.995 - 18.00}{6.00} = -1.5008 \cong -1.50$$

†For example, the proportion of area for the first class = $P(z < -1.50)$ = 0.5000 − 0.4332 = 0.0668

With df = 8 − 1 = 7, the critical value of x^2 for significance at the 5 percent level is 14.07. Since 11.97 < 14.07, the hypothesis that the distribution of sales does not differ from the historical distribution of sales cannot be rejected, and thus is accepted.

12.10

Grade	f_o	f_e
A	8	5
B	17	15
C	20	20
D	3	5
E	2	5
Total	50	50

$$x^2 = \sum \frac{(f_o - f_e)^2}{f_e} = \frac{(3)^2}{5} + \frac{(2)^2}{15} + \frac{(0)^2}{20} + \frac{(2)^2}{5} + \frac{(3)^2}{5}$$
$$= 1.80 + 0.27 + 0 + 0.80 + 1.80 = 4.67$$

With df = 5 − 1 = 4, the critical value of x^2 for significance at the 5 percent level is 9.49. Since 4.67 < 9.49, the particular distribution of grades does not differ significantly from the historical distribution of grades. Of course, an actual difference does in fact exist in this case, with there being somewhat more A's and B's and fewer D's and E's than the expected frequencies. But the point is that this amount of difference is ascribable to chance (at the 5 percent level), and we cannot reject the assumption that in the *long run* the grade distributions in this class (or in classes taught by this instructor) do conform to the historical pattern.

Chapter 13 ■ Decision Analysis

13.1 In general, a "criterion" is a standard or yardstick by which an evaluation can be made. Therefore, the term "decision criterion" refers to a standard by which decisions can be evaluated and compared. In this respect, a particular decision act may be good when evaluated from the standpoint of one criterion but poor when evaluated from the standpoint of a different criterion. The three decision criteria, or standards, by which decision acts can be evaluated when the probabilities associated with the states are not known are the maximin, maximax, and minimax regret criteria, as discussed in section 13a. For the maximin criterion the decision maker first determines the worst (minimum) conditional outcome for each decision act. The decision act for which this minimum value is the largest is the best act; in effect, this maximin value represents a minimum guarantee to the decision maker. For the maximax criterion the decision maker determines the largest (maximum) conditional outcome for each decision act and then chooses the act for which the maximum value is largest. This procedure is equivalent to the short-cut procedure of finding the largest value in the table of conditional values and designating the associated decision act as being the best act. Whereas the maximin criterion may be unduly conservative as a standard and the maximax criterion may be too cavalier in giving attention only to the best consequences, the minimax regret criterion represents something of a balance between the two approaches. A key idea associated with this criterion is the concept of opportunity loss, by which both experienced losses and missed gains are considered equally as constituting losses. Thus, the maximum regret, or opportunity loss, identified for each decision act could be based on a possible net loss, a possible missed gain, or both. A decision maker who uses the minimax regret criterion as the basis for evaluating decision acts is thus giving attention to both the "good" and the "poor" conditional consequences associated with the decision opportunities.

13.2 The table of conditional values for this decision problem is as follows:

Sets stocked	Sets demanded				Min.	Max.
	0	1	2	3		
0	$ 0	$ 0	$ 0	$ 0	$ 0	$ 0
1	−120	90	90	90	−120	90
2	−240	− 30	180	180	−240	180
3	−360	−150	60	270	−360	270

(a) The minimum values associated with the four decision acts, as indicated in the table above, are $0, $−120, $−240, and $−360, respectively. The maximum of these conditional values is "$0," and so the decision act associated with this outcome, "'stock zero sets," is the best decision from the standpoint of the maximin criterion.

(b) As indicated in the table above, the largest of the maximum conditional values is $270, which is associated with the decision act "stock three sets." This is the best decision from the standpoint of the maximax criterion.

(c) Opportunity losses:

Sets	Sets demanded				Max.
stocked	0	1	2	3	regret
0	$ 0	$ 90	$180	$270	$270
1	120	0	90	180	180
2	240	120	0	90	240
3	360	240	120	0	360

As indicated in the table above, the minimum of the maximum regret values is $180. This value is associated with the decision act "stock one set," which is the best act from the standpoint of the minimax regret criterion.

(d) The best act associated with the maximin criterion, that of ordering no sets, is unduly defensive. Use of this standard implies that the retailer wants to avoid all risk, which in turn would indicate he should not be in a risk-taking venture. Your choice here of ordering one, two, or three sets will be associated with your reaction to the possible amounts of loss associated with these "risky" decision situations. If one wants to consider the possibility of missing a profit as also being a risk, then the act "stock one set" associated with the minimax regret criterion is the best act.

13.3 Expected value for stocking one set:

Sets demanded	Conditional value, X	Probability, P(X)	XP(X)
0	$-120	0.10	$-12
1	90	0.40	36
2	90	0.30	27
3	90	0.20	18
		$EV = \Sigma XP(X) =$	$ 69

Expected value for stocking two sets:

Sets demanded	Conditional value, X	Probability, P(X)	XP(X)
0	$-240	0.10	$-24
1	-30	0.40	-12
2	180	0.30	54
3	180	0.20	36
		$EV = \Sigma XP(X) =$	$ 54

Expected value for stocking three sets:

Sets demanded	Conditional value, X	Probability, P(X)	XP(X)
0	$-360	0.10	$-36
1	-150	0.40	-60
2	60	0.30	18
3	270	0.20	54
		$EV = \Sigma XP(X) =$	$-24

Thus the decision that maximizes the expected monetary value is that of stocking one stereo set, for an expected value of $69. The expected value associated with stocking no sets is of course $0, and this decision act would be best only if the expected values for the other three decision alternatives were all negative values.

13.4

| Investment | State of economy during period | | | Min. | Max. |
	Recession	Stable	Expansion		
Savings account	$ 1,000	$ 1,000	$ 1,000	$ 1,000	$ 1,000
Common stock	−700	1,000	2,000	−700	2,000
Warrants	−10,000	−5,000	12,000	−10,000	12,000

(a) In terms of the maximin criterion, the best decision act is "the savings account," for which the minimum return possible is $1,000, as indicated in the table above.

(b) For the maximax criterion, the best act is "investment in warrants." As indicated in the table above, the maximum return of $12,000 that can occur with this act is higher than the maximum return for any other act.

(c) Table of opportunity losses:

| Investment | State of economy during period | | | Max. regret |
	Recession	Stable	Expansion	
Savings account	$ 0	$ 0	$11,000	$11,000
Common stock	1,700	0	10,000	10,000
Warrants	11,000	6,000	0	11,000

The smallest of the maximum regrets is $10,000, which is associated with the act "invest in common stocks." Therefore this is the best act from the standpoint of the minimax regret criterion.

13.5 The computational procedure is the same as illustrated in Exercise 13.3, above. The resulting expected values are listed in the table below. As indicated, the investment with the highest expected monetary value is the savings account, and therefore this is the best act from the standpoint of the expected value criterion.

Investment	EV
Savings account	$1,000
Common stock	960
Stock options	−900

13.6

| | State | | | |
Decision	Contract awarded	Contract not awarded	Min.	Max.
Bid	$500,000	−$150,000	$−150,000	$500,000
Not bid	0	0	0	0

The best act from the standpoint of the maximin criterion is "not bid," since $0 is larger than −$150,000. The best act from the standpoint of the maximax criterion is "bid," since $500,000 is larger than $0.

Opportunity losses:

| | State | | |
Decision	Contract awarded	Contract not awarded	Max. regret
Bid	$ 0	$150,000	$150,000
Not bid	500,000	0	500,000

The best decision act from the standpoint of the minimax regret criterion is "bid," since the associated maximum regret of $150,000 is less than the $500,000 maximum regret associated with the other decision alternative.

13.7   EV (Bid) = 0.40($500,000) + 0.60($−150,000) = $110,000.
EV (Don't bid) = (0.40)($0) + 0.60($0) = $0

Therefore, the best decision act from the standpoint of the expected value criterion is "bid."

13.8 The first step in decision analysis for a situation involving uncertainty is to determine the decision alternatives that are available and the states (outcomes) that can occur. The second step is to construct the decision table, or table of conditional values. (Incidentally, some texts refer to this table as the "payoff table.") If probabilities are not available, the next step is to select a decision criterion (maximin, maximax, or minimax regret) and then determine the best act based on this criterion. Generally, however, the probabilities for the various states are determined or estimated, in which case the expected value criterion is used to determine the best act. Of course, the implications of the best act in terms of the "best" and "worst" consequence that can occur in a single outcome are also considered.

Chapter 14 ■ Bayesian Inference

14.1   (a)

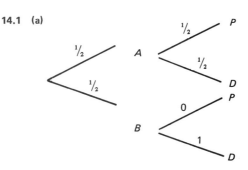

(b) $P(D|A) = \frac{1}{2} = 0.50$

(c) $P(A|D) = \dfrac{P(A \text{ and } D)}{P(D)} = \dfrac{P(A)P(D|A)}{P(A)P(D|A) + P(B)P(D|B)}$

$\qquad = \dfrac{(\frac{1}{2})(\frac{1}{2})}{(\frac{1}{2})(\frac{1}{2}) + (\frac{1}{2})(1)} = \dfrac{\frac{1}{4}}{\frac{1}{4} + \frac{1}{2}} = \dfrac{1}{3} \doteq 0.33$

(d) $P(A|P) = \dfrac{P(A \text{ and } P)}{P(P)} = \dfrac{P(A)P(P|A)}{P(A)P(P|A) + P(B)P(P|B)}$

$\qquad = \dfrac{(\frac{1}{2})(\frac{1}{2})}{(\frac{1}{2})(\frac{1}{2}) + (\frac{1}{2})(0)} = \dfrac{\frac{1}{4}}{\frac{1}{4}} = 1$

Thus, if a penny is obtained it must have come from box A.

14.2 (a)

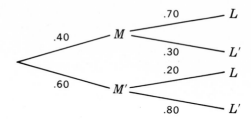

(b) $P(L'|M') = 0.80$

(c) $P(L) = P(M, L) + P(M', L)$
$\qquad = P(M)P(L|M) + P(M')P(L|M')$
$\qquad = (0.40)(0.70) + (0.60)(0.20) = 0.28 + 0.12 = 0.40$

14.3 (a) $P(M) = 0.40$

(b) $P(M|L) = \dfrac{P(M)P(L|M)}{P(M)P(L|M) + P(M')P(L|M')}$

$\qquad = \dfrac{(0.40)(0.70)}{(0.40)(0.70) + (0.60)(0.20)} = \dfrac{0.28}{0.40} = 0.70$

14.4

Fraction def.	P	Conditional costs 100% insp.	No insp.	Expected costs 100% insp.	No insp.
0.01	0.95	$400.00	$200.00	$380.00	$190.00
0.10	0.05	400.00	2000.00	20.00	100.00
				$400.00	$290.00

Because the expected cost associated with "no inspection" is less than the expected cost associated with "100% inspection," the best decision is to put the items into the assembly process without inspection.

14.5 Expected cost with perfect information:

Fraction def.	P	Best act	Conditional cost	Expected cost
0.01	0.95	No inspection	$200.00	$190.00
0.10	0.05	100% inspection	400.00	20.00
				$210.00

The $210 expected cost would be the long-run average in a series of decisions, given that the decision chosen is the right one for every individual case. The expected cost of $290 in Exercise 14.4 is the long-run average cost under uncertainty, in which case "no inspection" is the consistent decision that is made.

14.6 EVPI = expected cost of the best act under certainty — expected cost with perfect information = $290.000 − $210.00 = $80.00

This value indicates the average dollar amount by which the best act under uncertainty misses the best possible monetary result. Therefore, this is the maximum amount per decision act that any information would be worth.

14.7

Fraction def.	Prior P	Conditional probability of sample result	Joint probability	Posterior P
0.01	0.95	0.0914	0.08683	0.8176 ≐ 0.82
0.10	0.05	0.3874	0.01937	0.1824 ≐ 0.18
			0.10620	

Fraction def.	Posterior P	Conditional costs		Expected costs	
		100% insp.	No insp.	100% insp.	No insp.
0.01	0.82	$360.00	$ 180.00	$295.20	$147.60
0.10	0.18	360.00	1,800.00	64.80	324.00
				$360.00	$471.60

Based on the posterior distribution, the decision act with the lower expected cost is "100% inspection." Therefore, given no sample information (Exercise 14.5), the best consistent decision act is "no inspection." But if a sample of $n = 10$ includes one defective, the best consistent decision act for the remainder of such sets of items is "100% inspection."

14.8 For the remaining 90 items in the set, the estimated value of the sample information is the difference between the posterior expected value of the act that would have been chosen without the sample ("no inspection") and the best act based on the additional sample information:

$471.60 − $360.00 = $111.60

14.9 (a)

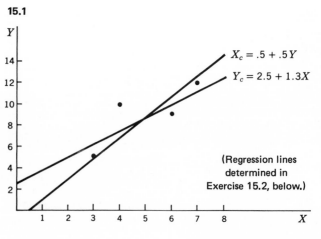

(b) $P(I) = P(E, I) + P(E', I)$
$= P(E)P(I|E) + P(E')P(I|E')$
$= (0.70)(0.80) + (0.30)(0.30) = 0.50 + 0.09 = 0.65$

14.10 $P(E|I') = \dfrac{P(E)P(I'|E)}{P(E)P(I'|E) + P(E')P(I'|E')}$

$= \dfrac{(0.70)(0.20)}{(0.70)(0.20) + (0.30)(0.70)} = \dfrac{0.14}{0.14 + 0.21} = \dfrac{0.14}{0.35} = 0.40$

14.11 The expected value of perfect information can be determined by either of two methods, given that a discrete probability distribution is associated with the uncertain states. By the first approach we can determine the expected value of the decision opportunity with perfect information and subtract from it the expected value of the best act in order to determine EVPI. The expected value with perfect information is based on the assumption that a mixed strategy is used which results in exactly the best decision act on each occasion that a decision is to be made, whereas the expected value of the best act is concerned with the risk situation wherein the same decision is made on every occasion. By the second approach we can determine the expected opportunity loss (EOL) associated with each decision alternative. The best decision act is the one with the lowest EOL, and further, this (minimum) EOL is equal to the EVPI for the decision situation. EVPI indicates the average (long-run) amount by which the expected value of the one best decision act differs from the average value that would be experienced if uncertainty were completely removed from the decision situation. Therefore, this value represents the maximum value that *any* information can have to the decision maker. To pay more than the EVPI for further information would be to pay more than the information could possibly be worth in the long run.

Chapter 15 ■ Linear Regression Analysis

15.1

Y

14

12

10

8

6

4

2

$X_c = .5 + .5Y$

$Y_c = 2.5 + 1.3X$

(Regression lines determined in Exercise 15.2, below.)

1 2 3 4 5 6 7 8 X

15.2

X	Y	XY	X²	Y²
3	5	15	9	25
4	10	40	16	100
6	9	54	36	81
7	12	84	49	144
$\Sigma X = 20$	$\Sigma Y = 36$	$\Sigma XY = 193$	$\Sigma X^2 = 110$	$\Sigma Y^2 = 350$

$$b = \frac{\Sigma XY - n\bar{X}\bar{Y}}{\Sigma X^2 - n\bar{X}^2} = \frac{193 - 4(5)(9)}{110 - 4(25)} = \frac{193 - 180}{110 - 100} = 1.3$$
$$a = \bar{Y} - b\bar{X} = 9 - 1.3(5) = 9 - 6.5 = 2.5$$

Therefore $Y_c = a + bX = 2.5 + 1.3X$.

15.3 $\quad b' = \dfrac{\Sigma XY - n\bar{X}\bar{Y}}{\Sigma Y^2 - n\bar{Y}^2} = \dfrac{193 - 4(5)(9)}{350 - 4(81)} = \dfrac{193 - 180}{350 - 324} = 0.5$

$\qquad a' = \bar{X} - b'\bar{Y} = 5 - 0.5(9) = 5 - 4.5 = 0.5$

Therefore $X_c = a' + b'Y = 0.5 + 0.5Y$.

The two regression lines both satisfy the least-squares criterion with respect to different axes, or variables. Specifically, the equation in Exercise 15.2 minimizes the sum of squares of the differences between actual and estimated values of the Y variable, whereas use of the equation developed in this exercise minimizes the sum of the squares of the differences between actual and estimated values of the X variable. The statistical assumption required in respect to the variable X is that it is a random variable whose value is not directly under the analyst's control.

15.4

X	Y	Y_c	$(Y - Y_c)$	$(Y - Y_c)^2$
3	5	6.4	−1.4	1.96
4	10	7.7	2.3	5.29
6	9	10.3	−1.3	1.69
7	12	11.6	0.4	0.16
				$\Sigma(Y - Y_c)^2 = 9.10$

$$s_{Y.X} = \sqrt{\frac{\Sigma(Y - Y_c)^2}{n - 2}} = \sqrt{\frac{9.1}{4 - 2}} = \sqrt{4.55} = 2.13$$

15.5 Point estimate:

$\qquad Y_c = a + bX = 2.5 + 1.3(6) = 2.5 + 7.8 = 10.3$

95 percent prediction interval:

$\qquad Y_c \pm t s_{Y.X} = 10.3 \pm 4.303(2.13) = 10.3 \pm 9.2 = 1.1 \text{ to } 19.5$

The relatively wide prediction interval is reflective of both the high value of t associated with the low $df = 2$ and the relatively high standard error of estimate. The statistical assumption associated with constructing this interval is that the deviations in respect to the regression line are normally distributed. Further, it should be added that the standard deviation of the Y values at any point along the X scale is assumed to be approximately the same value; otherwise, no one value of the standard error of estimate would be applicable at all points along the regression line.

15.6 The "monthly housing starts" is logically the independent variable while the "monthly dollar volume of sales six months later" is logically the dependent variable. The housing data are available first, and it is on the basis of this information that the home furnishings concern can possibly estimate the volume of business which can be anticipated in various months.

15.7

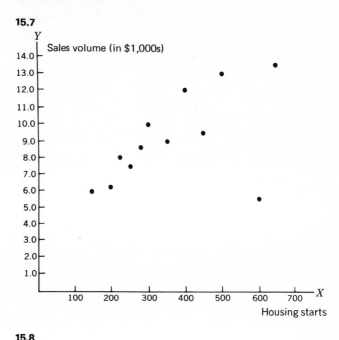

15.8

X	Y	XY	X²	Y²
450	9.5	4,275.0	202,500	90.25
150	6.0	900.0	22,500	36.00
200	6.2	1,240.0	40,000	38.44
600	5.5	3,300.0	360,000	30.25
250	7.5	1,875.0	62,500	56.25
300	10.0	3,000.0	90,000	100.00
650	13.5	8,775.0	422,500	182.25
225	8.0	1,800.0	50,625	64.00
500	13.0	6,500.0	250,000	169.00
280	8.8	2,464.0	78,400	77.44
350	9.0	3,150.0	122,500	81.00
400	12.0	4,800.0	160,000	144.00

$\Sigma X = 4,355$ $\Sigma Y = 109.0$ $\Sigma XY = 42,079.0$ $\Sigma X^2 = 1,861,525$ $\Sigma Y^2 = 1,068.88$

$$\overline{X} = \frac{\Sigma X}{n} = \frac{4,355}{12} = 362.92$$

$$\overline{Y} = \frac{\Sigma Y}{n} = \frac{109.0}{12} = 9.08$$

$$b = \frac{\Sigma XY - n\overline{X}\,\overline{Y}}{\Sigma X^2 - n\overline{X}^2} = \frac{42,079.0 - (12)(362.92)(9.08)}{1,861,525 - 12(362.92)(362.92)}$$

$$= \frac{42,079.0 - 39,543.76}{1,861,525 - 1,580,531.12} = \frac{2,535.24}{280,993.88} = 0.009$$

$$a = \overline{Y} - b\overline{X} = 9.08 - 0.009(362.92)$$
$$= 9.08 - 3.27 = 5.81$$

Therefore, $Y_c = a + bX = 5.81 + 0.009X$.

15.9

$$s_{Y.X} = \sqrt{\frac{\Sigma Y^2 - a\Sigma Y - b\Sigma XY}{n-2}}$$

$$= \sqrt{\frac{1,068.88 - (5.81)(109.0) - (0.009)(42,079.0)}{12-2}}$$

$$= \sqrt{\frac{1,068.88 - 633.29 - 378.71}{10}} = \sqrt{\frac{56.88}{10}} = \sqrt{5.688} = 2.38$$

15.10 Point estimate:

$$Y_c = a + bX = 5.81 + 0.009(550) = 5.81 + 4.95 = 10.76$$

90 percent prediction interval:

$$Y_c \pm ts_{Y.X} = 10.76 \pm 1.812(2.38) = 10.76 \pm 4.31$$
$$= 6.45 \text{ to } 15.07$$
$$\doteq \$6,400 \text{ to } \$15,100$$

Chapter 16 ■ Correlation **16.1**

X	Y	XY	X^2	Y^2
3	5	15	9	25
4	10	40	16	100
6	9	54	36	81
7	12	84	49	144
$\Sigma X = 20$	$\Sigma Y = 36$	$\Sigma XY = 193$	$\Sigma X^2 = 110$	$\Sigma Y^2 = 350$

$$r = \frac{n\Sigma XY - \Sigma X\Sigma Y}{\sqrt{n\Sigma X^2 - (\Sigma X)^2}\,\sqrt{n\Sigma Y^2 - (\Sigma Y)^2}}$$

$$= \frac{4(193) - (20)(36)}{\sqrt{4(110) - (20)^2}\,\sqrt{4(350) - (36)^2}}$$

$$= \frac{772 - 720}{\sqrt{440 - 400}\,\sqrt{1,400 - 1,296}} = \frac{52}{\sqrt{(40)(104)}}$$

$$= \frac{52}{\sqrt{4,160}} = \frac{52}{64.5} = .806 \doteq .81$$

With df $= n - 2 = 4 - 2 = 2$, a correlation value of .950 is required for significance at the 5 percent level. Since $.806 < .950$, the sample correlation value is not significantly different from 0. That is, the probability is greater than 0.05 that the sample correlation value could have been obtained given a population in which the true correlation between the variables is zero.

16.2

X (rank)	Y (rank)	D	D²
4	4	0	0
3	2	1	1
2	3	−1	1
1	1	0	0
			$\Sigma D^2 = 2$

$$r_{rank} = 1 - \frac{6\Sigma D^2}{n(n^2 - 1)} = 1 - \frac{6(2)}{4(16 - 1)}$$

$$= 1 - \frac{12}{60} = 1 - .20 = .80$$

(In this example the value of r_{rank} is unusually close to the value of r, of which it is essentially an estimate.)

16.3 $\quad Y_c = \left(Y - r\dfrac{s_Y}{s_X}\overline{X} \right) + \left(r\dfrac{s_Y}{s_X} \right) X$

where:

$$s_X = \sqrt{\frac{\Sigma X^2 - n\overline{X}^2}{n - 1}} = \sqrt{\frac{110 - 4(5)^2}{4 - 1}} = \sqrt{3.3333} \doteq 1.83$$

$$s_Y = \sqrt{\frac{\Sigma Y^2 - n\overline{Y}^2}{n - 1}} = \sqrt{\frac{350 - 4(9)^2}{4 - 1}} = \sqrt{8.6666} \doteq 2.94$$

$$Y_c = \left[9 - (.806)\left(\frac{2.94}{1.83}\right)(5) \right] + .806\left(\frac{2.94}{1.83}\right) X = (9 - 6.5) + 1.3X$$

$$= 2.5 + 1.3X$$

This regression equation is identical to the one determined in Exercise 15.2.

16.4 $\quad s_{Y.X} = s_Y \sqrt{1 - r^2} \sqrt{\dfrac{n-1}{n-2}} = 2.94\sqrt{1 - (.806)^2}\,\sqrt{\dfrac{4-1}{4-2}}$

$$= 2.94\sqrt{.350}\,\sqrt{1.500} = 2.94(0.725) = 2.13$$

This value of the standard error of estimate corresponds to the value determined in Exercise 15.4.

16.5

X	Y	XY	X^2	Y^2
450	9.5	4,275.0	202,500	90.25
150	6.0	900.0	22,500	36.00
200	6.2	1,240.0	40,000	38.44
600	5.5	3,300.0	360,000	30.25
250	7.5	1,875.0	62,500	56.25
300	10.0	3,000.0	90,000	100.00
650	13.5	8,775.0	422,500	182.25
225	8.0	1,800.0	50,625	64.00
500	13.0	6,500.0	250,000	169.00
280	8.8	2,464.0	78,400	77.44
350	9.0	3,150.0	122,500	81.00
400	12.0	4,800.0	160,000	144.00

$\Sigma X = 4{,}355 \quad \Sigma Y = 109.0 \quad \Sigma XY = 42{,}079.0 \quad \Sigma X^2 = 1{,}861{,}525 \quad \Sigma Y^2 = 1{,}068.88$

$$r = \frac{n\,\Sigma XY - \Sigma X \Sigma Y}{\sqrt{n\Sigma X^2 - (\Sigma X)^2}\,\sqrt{n\Sigma Y^2 - (\Sigma Y)^2}}$$

$$= \frac{(12)(42{,}079.0) - (4{,}355)(109.0)}{\sqrt{12(1{,}861{,}525) - (4{,}355)^2}\,\sqrt{12(1{,}068.88) - (109.0)^2}}$$

$$= \frac{504{,}948.0 - 474{,}695.0}{\sqrt{22{,}338{,}300 - 18{,}966{,}025}\,\sqrt{12{,}826.56 - 11{,}881.00}}$$

$$= \frac{30{,}253}{\sqrt{3{,}372{,}275)(945.56)}} = \frac{30{,}253}{\sqrt{3{,}188{,}688{,}349.00}} = \frac{30{,}253}{56{,}468.47}$$

$r = +.536$

With $df = n - 2 = 10$, the required correlation value for significance at the 5 percent level is $\pm.5760$. Since the sample correlation coefficient is less than this critical value, the null hypothesis that the population correlation coefficient is equal to zero is accepted.

16.6 As indicated in the introduction to Section 16.2, five assumptions are required. These are that (1) both variables are random variables; (2) both of the variables are on a continuous scale; (3) there is one independent and one dependent variable; (4) the relationship between the two variables is linear; and (5) each variable is normally distributed for any given value of the other variable. Assumptions (1), (2), and (3) above appear to be satisfied by the data. By reference to the scatter diagram prepared in Exercise 15.7, assumption (4) appears to be approximately satisfied but assumption (5) is not well supported. However, assumption (5) could not be well supported by any particular small sample, as it is concerned with the distribution of values in a large population.

16.7 $r^2 = (.536)^2 = .2879 \doteq .29$

The coefficient of determination indicates that approximately 29 percent of the sample variance in the dependent variable (home furnishings sales) is statistically accounted for by the independent variable (housing starts six months earlier).

16.8 On the face of it, it might appear that the best estimate is that 29 percent of the population variance in the dependent variable is accounted for by knowledge of the independent variable. However, given that we wish to address ourselves to the situation in the *population*, note that in Exercise 16.5, above, the correlation value of .536 was not large enough to conclude that the true correlation is different from zero at the 5 percent level of significance. Therefore, the coefficient of determination can be interpreted as being descriptive of the sample result but cannot be used to describe the proportion of explained variance in the population. Essentially, it is not appropriate to consider the *extent* of relationship when the hypothesis that there is no relationship has been accepted.

16.9 $s_{Y.X} = s_Y \sqrt{1 - r^2} \, \sqrt{\dfrac{n-1}{n-2}}$

where:

$$s_Y = \sqrt{\dfrac{\Sigma Y^2 - n\overline{Y}^2}{n-1}} = \sqrt{\dfrac{1{,}068.88 - 12(9.0833)^2}{12-1}}$$

$$= \sqrt{7.1633} \doteq 2.68$$

$$s_{Y.X} = 2.68 \sqrt{1 - (.536)^2} \, \sqrt{\dfrac{12-1}{12-2}} = 2.68(0.844)(1.049) \doteq 2.37$$

This value differs just slightly from the value of 2.38 determined in Exercise 15.9, because of the rounding of values in computations.

16.10 The Pearson correlation coefficient r expresses the extent of relationship between one independent variable and one dependent variable. On the other hand, the coefficient of multiple correlation represents an extension of the Pearson r to the case involving two or more independent variables. By this approach the statistical analyst can determine the extent of relationship between several independent variables taken as a group and a designated dependent variable.

Chapter 17 ■ Time-series Analysis

17.1 (a) *C*
(b) *I*
(c) *I*
(d) *S*
(e) *T*

17.2   Line chart

Sales, millions of dollars

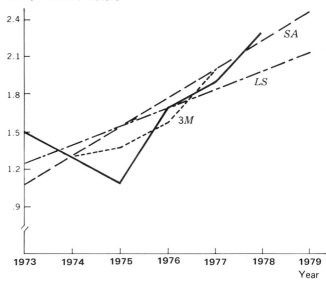

Year

17.3 **(a)** Mean for 1973–1975 = (1.5 + 1.3 + 1.1)/3 = 3.9/3 = 1.30
(entered over 1974 on the chart)
Mean for 1976–1978 = (1.7 + 1.9 + 2.3)/3 = 5.9/3 = 1.97
(entered over 1977 on the chart)

(b)

Year	Sales, millions of dollars	Three-year moving total	Three-year moving average
1973	$1.5		
1974	1.3	3.9	1.30
1975	1.1	4.1	1.37
1976	1.7	4.7	1.57
1977	1.9	5.9	1.97
1978	2.3		

17.4

Year	Year coded, X	Sales, Y, in millions	XY	X^2
1973	−2	$1.5	−3.0	4
1974	−1	1.3	−1.3	1
1975	0	1.1	0	0
1976	+1	1.7	1.7	1
1977	+2	1.9	3.8	4
1978	+3	2.3	6.9	9
	$\Sigma X = 3$	$\Sigma Y = 9.8$	$\Sigma XY = 8.1$	$\Sigma X^2 = 19$

For the equation, $Y_c = a + bX$:

$$b = \frac{\Sigma XY - n\overline{X}\,\overline{Y}}{\Sigma X^2 - n\overline{X}^2} = \frac{8.1 - 6(0.5)(1.63)}{19 - 6(0.5)^2} = \frac{8.1 - 4.89}{19 - 1.50}$$

$$= \frac{3.21}{17.5} = 0.183$$

$a = \overline{Y} - b\overline{X} = 1.633 - 0.183(0.5) = 1.633 - 0.092 = 1.541$

Thus $Y_c = 1.541 + 0.183X$.

The value of a in this equation refers to the expected dollar sales volume, in millions, for 1975. This is so since $X_{1975} = 0$.

17.5 (a)

Year	Sales, Y, in millions	Expected sales, Y_c*	Cyclical relative, $100Y/Y_c$
1973	$1.5	$1.18	127.1
1974	1.3	1.36	95.6
1975	1.1	1.54	71.4
1976	1.7	1.72	98.8
1977	1.9	1.91	99.5
1978	2.3	2.09	110.0

*For 1973: $y_c = 1.541 + 0.183X = 1.541 + 0.183(-2) = 1.541 - 0.366$
$= 1.175 \doteq 1.18$ (and similarly for the other years of this time series).

(b)   Cycle chart

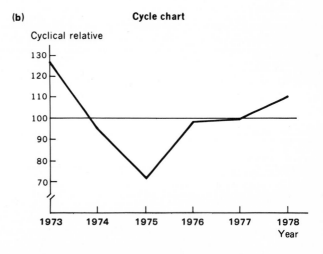

The chart indicates a cyclical dip completed in 1975 and a rise in each of the succeeding years, relative to trend. The trend line is represented at 100 on this chart.

17.6 (a) and (b)

Year	Quarter	Sales, hundreds of thousands of dollars	Four-quarter moving total	Two-year moving total	Four-quarter centered moving average	Percent of four-quarter centered moving average
1973	1	5.0				
	2	3.5				
			15.0			
	3	2.5		29.5	3.69	67.8
			14.5			
	4	4.0		29.0	3.62	110.5
			14.5			
1974	1	4.5		28.5	3.56	126.4
			14.0			
	2	3.5		27.0	3.38	103.6
			13.0			
	3	2.0		25.0	3.12	64.1
			12.0			
	4	3.0		22.5	2.81	106.8
			10.5			
1975	1	3.5		20.5	2.56	136.7
			10.0			
	2	2.0		21.0	2.62	76.3
			11.0			
	3	1.5		24.0	3.00	50.0
			13.0			
	4	4.0		27.5	3.44	116.3
			14.5			
1976	1	5.5		30.0	3.75	146.7
			15.5			
	2	3.5		32.5	4.06	86.2
			17.0			
	3	2.5		34.0	4.25	58.8
			17.0			
	4	5.5		34.5	4.31	127.6
			17.5			
1977	1	5.5		36.0	4.50	122.2
			18.5			
	2	4.0		37.5	4.69	85.3
			19.0			
	3	3.5		40.0	5.00	70.0
			21.0			
	4	6.0		43.0	5.38	111.5
			22.0			
1978	1	7.5		44.5	5.56	134.9
			22.5			
	2	5.0		45.5	5.69	87.9
			23.0			
	3	4.0				
	4	6.5				

17.7

Quarter	1973	1974	1975	1976	1977	1978	Modified mean*	Adjusted seasonal index, mean × 1.0111†
1	...	126.4	136.7	146.7	122.2	134.9	132.7	134.2
2	...	103.6	76.3	86.2	85.3	87.9	86.5	87.5
3	67.8	64.1	50.0	58.8	70.0	...	63.6	64.3
4	110.5	106.8	116.3	127.6	111.5	...	112.8	114.1
							395.6	400.1

*Highest and lowest values left out; e.g., for first quarter, modified mean = (126.4 + 136.7 + 134.9)/3 = 398.0/3 = 132.7.

†Adjustment = $\dfrac{\text{desired total}}{\text{actual total}} = \dfrac{400}{395.6} = 1.0111$.

17.8 Seasonally adjusted values:*

Quarter	1973	1974	1975	1976	1977	1978
1	3.7	3.4	2.6	4.1	4.1	5.6
2	4.0	4.0	2.3	4.0	4.6	5.7
3	3.9	3.1	2.3	3.9	5.4	6.2
4	3.5	2.6	3.5	4.8	5.3	5.7

*Determined by dividing each of the quarterly sales figures listed in Exercise 17.6 by the appropriate seasonal index and multiplying by 100. For example, the seasonally adjusted value for the first quarter of 1973 = (5.0/134.2) × 100 = 3.725 = 3.7.

17.9

Year	Quarter	Year and quarter, coded, X	Sales, Y hundreds of thousands of dollars	XY	X^2
1973	1	0	5.0	0	0
	2	1	3.5	3.5	1
	3	2	2.5	5.0	4
	4	3	4.0	12.0	9
1974	1	4	4.5	18.0	16
	2	5	3.5	17.5	25
	3	6	2.0	12.0	36
	4	7	3.0	21.0	49
1975	1	8	3.5	28.0	64
	2	9	2.0	18.0	81
	3	10	1.5	15.0	100
	4	11	4.0	44.0	121
1976	1	12	5.5	66.0	144
	2	13	3.5	45.5	169

Year	Quarter	Year and quarter, coded, X	Sales, Y hundreds of thousands of dollars	XY	X²
	3	14	2.5	35.0	196
	4	15	5.5	82.5	225
1977	1	16	5.5	88.0	256
	2	17	4.0	68.0	289
	3	18	3.5	63.0	324
	4	19	6.0	114.0	361
1978	1	20	7.5	150.0	400
	2	21	5.0	105.0	441
	3	22	4.0	88.0	484
	4	23	6.5	149.5	529
		$\Sigma X = 276$	$\Sigma Y = 98.0$	$\Sigma XY = 1,248.5$	$\Sigma X^2 = 4,324$

$$b = \frac{\Sigma XY - n\overline{XY}}{\Sigma X^2 - n\overline{X}^2} = \frac{1,248.5 - 24(11.5)(4.083)}{4,324 - 24(11.5)^2} = \frac{121.592}{1,150.000} = 0.106$$

$$a = \overline{Y} - b(\overline{X}) = 4.083 - 0.106(11.5) = 2.864$$

Therefore, $Y_c = 2.864 + 0.106X \doteq 2.86 + 0.11X$.

17.10 Quarterly trend values:

Quarter	1973	1974	1975	1976	1977	1978
1	2.86	3.30	3.74	4.18	4.62	5.06
2	2.97	3.41	3.85	4.29	4.73	5.17
3	3.08	3.52	3.96	4.40	4.84	5.28
4	3.19	3.63	4.07	4.51	4.95	5.39

Seasonally adjusted data as a percentage of trend (values in Exercise 17.8 divided by values above, × 100):

Quarter	1973	1974	1975	1976	1977	1978
1	129.4	103.0	69.5	98.1	88.7	110.7
2	134.7	117.3	59.7	93.2	97.3	110.3
3	126.6	88.1	58.1	88.6	111.6	117.4
4	109.7	71.6	86.0	106.4	107.1	105.8

17.11-17.12 Quarterly forecasts for 1979, based on the trend and seasonal components of the time series:

Quarter	Trend value[*] (1)	Seasonal index (2)	Quarterly forecast[†] for 1979 (Col. 1) × (Col. 2 ÷ 100)
1	5.50	134.2	7.53 ≐ 7.5
2	5.61	87.5	4.91 ≐ 4.9
3	5.72	64.3	3.68 ≐ 3.7
4	5.83	114.1	6.65 ≐ 6.7

[*]Forecast based only on the trend equation developed in Exercise 17.9 (in hundreds of thousands of dollars).

[†]Forecast based on both the trend and seasonal components of the time series (in hundreds of thousands of dollars).

Chapter 18 ■ Index Numbers

18.1 (a) Percentage increase $= \dfrac{132.3 - 107.2}{107.2} \times 100 = 23.4\%$

(b) Percentage increase $= \dfrac{146.3 - 114.8}{114.8} \times 100 = 27.4\%$

Note: An alternative approach by which the same answers are obtained is to shift the base for the 1975 indexes from 1967 to 1971. The value of the index then directly indicates the comparison with 1971:

(a) $\dfrac{132.3}{107.2} \times 100 = 123.4$

(b) $\dfrac{146.3}{114.8} \times 100 = 127.4$

18.2 Of course, application of the general percentage increases determined in Exercise 18.1 to specific commodities may not result in the correct values. But as the best estimates available, we have:

(a) $150 + 23.4\% ($150) = $150 + $35.10 = $185.10
(*or:* $150 × 123.4/100 = $185.10)

(b) $400 + 27.4\% ($400) = $400 + $109.60 = $509.60
(*or:* $400 × 127.4/100 = $509.60)

18.3 The price indexes reported are for wholesale prices, not retail prices as such. More importantly, the price indexes indicate nothing about value of purchases, for which quantity data would be needed. Further, the indexes indicate price changes based on earlier prices for the same items, and do not indicate any comparisons between different items (such as appliances versus furniture).

18.4 (a) $I_{1972} = \dfrac{\text{price}_{1972}}{\text{price}_{1972}} \times 100 = \dfrac{0.696}{0.696} \times 100 = 100.0$

$I_{1973} = \dfrac{\text{price}_{1973}}{\text{price}_{1972}} \times 100 = \dfrac{0.689}{0.696} \times 100 = 99.0$

$$I_{1974} = \frac{\text{price}_{1974}}{\text{price}_{1972}} \times 100 = \frac{0.674}{0.696} \times 100 = 96.8$$

$$I_{1975} = \frac{\text{price}_{1975}}{\text{price}_{1972}} \times 100 = \frac{0.818}{0.696} \times 100 = 117.5$$

(b) $I_{1972} = \dfrac{\text{price}_{1972}}{\text{price}_{1972}} \times 100 = \dfrac{0.714}{0.714} \times 100 = 100.0$

$$I_{1973} = \frac{\text{price}_{1973}}{\text{price}_{1972}} \times 100 = \frac{0.843}{0.714} \times 100 = 118.1$$

$$I_{1974} = \frac{\text{price}_{1974}}{\text{price}_{1972}} \times 100 = \frac{0.973}{0.714} \times 100 = 136.3$$

$$I_{1975} = \frac{\text{price}_{1975}}{\text{price}_{1972}} \times 100 = \frac{1.044}{0.714} \times 100 = 146.2$$

18.5 **(a)** Whereas butter increased in wholesale price by 17.5 percent (by reference to the price index for 1975), American cheese increased in wholesale price by 46.2 percent.

(b) Simple quantity relatives, 1975 (with 1972 = 100):

$$\text{Butter} = \frac{q_{1975}}{q_{1972}} \times 100 = \frac{980.5}{1,109.9} \times 100 = 88.3$$

$$\text{American cheese} = \frac{q_{1975}}{q_{1972}} \times 100 = \frac{1,654.5}{1,644.3} \times 100 = 100.6$$

Thus, production of butter in 1975 was 11.7 percent lower than in 1972, while production of American cheese was 0.6 percent higher in 1975 as compared with 1972.

18.6 **(a)** Total dollar values of production (wholesale):

Butter (1972) $= p_{1972}q_{1972} = \$0.696 \, (1,109,900,000)$
$$= \$772,490,400$$

Butter (1975) $= p_{1975}q_{1975} = \$0.818 \, (980,500,000)$
$$= \$802,049,000$$

Cheese (1972) $= p_{1972}q_{1972} = \$0.714 \, (1,644,300,000)$
$$= \$1,174,030,200$$

Cheese (1975) $= p_{1975}q_{1975} = \$1.044 \, (1,654,500,000)$
$$= \$1,727,298,000$$

(b) Value relatives:

$$\text{Butter} = \frac{p_{1975}q_{1975}}{p_{1972}q_{1972}} \times 100 = \frac{802,049,000}{772,490,400}$$
$$\times 100 = 103.8$$

$$\text{Cheese} = \frac{p_{1975}q_{1975}}{p_{1972}q_{1972}} \times 100 = \frac{1,727,298,000}{1,174,030,200}$$
$$\times 100 = 147.1$$

Thus, the wholesale value of annual butter production increased by 3.8 percent between 1972 and 1975, while the wholesale value of annual American cheese production increased by 47.1 percent. Note that the increased value of butter production is attributable entirely to the increase in price, while the increase in value of cheese production reflects primarily an increase in price but also some increase in production.

18.7 **(a)** Price and quantity relatives for bond paper:

$$I_p = \frac{p_1}{p_0} \times 100 = \frac{4.00}{2.50} \times 100 = 160.0$$

$$I_q = \frac{q_1}{q_0} \times 100 = \frac{2.8}{2.2} \times 100 = 127.3$$

(b) Value relatives:

$$\text{Bond paper} = \frac{p_1 q_1}{p_0 q_0} \times 100 = \frac{(4.00)(2.8)}{(2.50)(2.2)} \times 100 = 203.6$$

$$\text{Onionskin} = \frac{p_1 q_1}{p_0 q_0} \times 100 = \frac{(4.25)(2.5)}{(2.00)(5.0)} \times 100 = 106.2$$

Therefore, there was a 103.6 percent increase in expenditure for bond paper between 1970 and 1978 and a 6.2 percent increase in the expenditure for onionskin paper.

18.8 **(a)**

Item	$p_0 q_0$	$p_1 q_0$
Paper, white bond	$ 5.50	$ 8.80
Paper, onionskin	10.00	21.25
Paper clips	0.30	0.40
Typewriter ribbon	4.00	6.00
	$\Sigma p_0 q_0 = \$19.80$	$\Sigma p_1 q_0 = \$36.45$

$$L = \frac{\Sigma p_1 q_0}{\Sigma p_0 q_0} \times 100 = \frac{36.45}{19.80} \times 100 = 184.1$$

Thus, for the quantities (market basket) of the base period, the composite cost in 1978 was 84.1 percent higher than the cost in 1970.

(b)

Item	$p_0 q_1$	$p_1 q_1$
Paper, white bond	$ 7.00	$11.20
Paper, onionskin	5.00	10.62
Paper clips	0.30	0.40
Typewriter ribbon	5.00	7.50
	$\Sigma p_0 q_1 = \$17.30$	$\Sigma p_1 q_1 = \$29.72$

$$P = \frac{\Sigma p_1 q_1}{\Sigma p_0 q_1} \times 100 = \frac{29.72}{17.30} \times 100 = 171.8$$

This index indicates that for the market basket of items associated with the given period (1978) the cost in 1978 was 71.8 percent higher than the cost in 1970.

(c)

Item	Price relative, $p_1 / p_0 \times 100$	Value weight, $p_0 q_0$	Weighted relative, $p_0 q_0 (p_1 / p_0 \times 100)$
Paper, white bond	160.0	$ 5.50	880.00
Paper, onionskin	212.5	10.00	2,125.00
Paper clips	133.3	0.30	40.00
Typewriter ribbon	150.0	4.00	600.00
		$19.80	3,645.00

$$\text{Weighted average of price relatives} = \frac{\Sigma (p_0 q_0)(p_1 / p_0 \times 100)}{\Sigma p_0 q_0}$$

$$= \frac{3,645.00}{19.80} = 184.1$$

As expected, the index is the same as that obtained by Laspeyres' formula.

18.9	Earnings (losses) per share	Earnings index (1973 = 100)	Link relative
Year (1)	(2)	(3)	(4)
1972	$0.00	*	—
1973	1.11	100.0	*
1974	(1.48)	*	*
1975	0.39	35.1	*
1976	0.64	57.7	164.1

*Indexes cannot be computed for values of 0 or for negative values (losses).

The earnings indexes, using 1973 as the base year, are posted in column 3, above. For 1976, for example, the index is:

$$\frac{E_{1976}}{E_{1973}} \times 100 = \frac{0.64}{1.11} \times 100 = 57.7$$

18.10 The link relatives are posted in column (4) of the table in the solution to Exercise 18.9. By definition, the base year for a link relative is the preceding year in the time series. Thus, the link relative for 1976 is:

$$\frac{E_{1976}}{E_{1975}} \times 100 = \frac{0.64}{0.39} \times 100 = 164.1$$

No other link relatives can be computed in this case, because the $0.00 value for 1973 precludes determination of a link index for 1973, and the negative (loss) value for 1974 precludes determination of a link index for either 1974 or 1975.

Appendix A ▪ Application of the Computer in Statistical Analysis (Solutions to Exercises)

A.1 A *field* in punched-card input is a group of one or more columns that is treated as one unit. From the standpoint of computer programming, since any desired field can be defined, this concept provides for programming and data flexibility. Once a field has been defined, however, its specifications must be rigidly followed by the program user.

A.2 A *flowchart* is a diagram that portrays all of the logical and computational steps required in a computer program. Because the flowchart highlights the steps that need to be accomplished in their appropriate sequence, preparation of such a chart reduces the possibility that some necessary steps will be inadvertently omitted in the computer program itself.

A.3 Use of a *machine language* indicates that a program is written in a (numeric) code system that is unique to a particular computer system. *Symbolic languages* were the first user-oriented improvement that involved use of alphabetic codes as a substitute for machine-oriented codes. The *procedure-oriented languages* use systems that are similar to mathematics and/or English and are the easiest to use. Further, programs written in symbolic languages, such as BASIC, FORTRAN, and COBOL, basically are the same no matter what computer system is used.

A.4 The *source program* is the computer program which is written in a procedure-oriented language, such as FORTRAN or COBOL. The machine-language program into which this program is translated by the use of a compiler is called the *object program*. When the source program has been punched into cards, which is typical, the resulting set of program cards is called the *source deck*.

A.5 For a relatively simple programming project, a particular early step in the procedure, such as preparing a program flowchart, might be omitted without any adverse consequences. However, this type of omission increases the possibility that required computational or logical procedures will be left out of the program, resulting in more time being required for debugging. In general, any "economizing" of effort devoted to the initial steps in the programming process results in greater amounts of time being required in later steps.

A.6 A fixed-point number can have only a whole-number, or integer, value. In the terminology of statistical analysis, such numbers are called *discrete* numbers.

A.7 The first ten columns of each input card would be skipped in the reading of the card. These columns might contain information that is not relevant to the particular data processing task or they might in fact contain blanks. Following this are two fixed-point fields of five columns each. Finally, columns 21–25 have been set aside for the input of a floating-point number with two digits to the right of the decimal.

A.8 The fixed-point numbers in columns 11–15 and 16–20 can have a maximum value of 99,999 each. For the floating-point number, whether or not the decimal point is punched does make a difference. If the decimal point is punched, the maximum value that can be input in columns 21–25 is 99.99. If the decimal point is not punched, the maximum value that can be input is 999.99.

A.9 The *run card* serves to identify the user by number and is required for analysis by the computer center and possibly for budgetary charges. The *label card*, or *header card*, contains the information that is to be printed at the top of the output for general identification purposes and need not contain the user's name if he chooses not to have it included in the label.

A.10 The name "time-sharing terminals" describes the fact that several such terminals share the time available in the processor (computational unit) of the computer. The name "remote-access" describes the fact that such terminals are in a remote location relative to the location of the processor.

INDEX